THE PHILISTINES AND AEGEAN MIGRATION AT THE END OF THE LATE BRONZE AGE

In this study, Assaf Yasur-Landau examines the early history of the biblical Philistines who were among the Sea Peoples who migrated from the Aegean area to the Levant during the early twelfth century BCE. Creating an archaeological narrative of the migration of the Philistines, he combines an innovative theoretical framework on the archaeology of migration with new data from excavations in Greece, Turkey, Cyprus, Syria, Lebanon, and Israel and thereby reconstructs the social history of the Aegean migration to the southern Levant. The author follows the story of the Philistine migrants from the conditions that caused them to leave their Aegean homes to their movement eastward along the sea and land routes, to their formation of a migrant society in Philistia and their interaction with local populations in the Levant. Based on the most up-to-date evidence, this book offers a new and fresh understanding of the arrival of the Philistines in the Levant.

Assaf Yasur-Landau is Senior Researcher at the Leon Recanati Institute for Maritime Studies, University of Haifa. He has edited three volumes and published numerous articles on the archaeology of the Levant and interactions between the Aegean world and the Levant, including the Philistine migration, with an emphasis on the investigation of the personal lives of ancient people.

THE PHILISTINES AND AEGEAN MIGRATION AT THE END OF THE LATE BRONZE AGE

ASSAF YASUR-LANDAU

University of Haifa

CAMBRIDGE
UNIVERSITY PRESS

32 Avenue of the Americas, New York, NY 10013-2473, USA

Cambridge University Press is part of the University of Cambridge.

It furthers the University's mission by disseminating knowledge in the pursuit of education, learning, and research at the highest international levels of excellence.

www.cambridge.org
Information on this title: www.cambridge.org/9781107660038

© Assaf Yasur-Landau 2010

First published 2010
Reprinted 2011 (twice)
First paperback edition 2014

Printed in the United States of America

A catalog record for this publication is available from the British Library.

Library of Congress Cataloging in Publication data
Yasur-Landau, Assaf.
The Philistines and Aegean migration at the end of the Late Bronze Age / Assaf Yasur-Landau.
     p.   cm.
Includes bibliographical references and index.
ISBN 978-0-521-19162-3 (hbk.)
1. Philistines – History.   2. Philistines – Migrations.   3. Philistines – Antiquities.   4. Social archaeology – Aegean Sea Region.   5. Aegean Sea Region – Emigration and immigration – History.   6. Middle East – Emigration and immigration – History.   7. Land settlement – Middle East – History – To 1500.   8. Aegean Sea Region – Antiquities.   9. Middle East – Antiquities. 10. Bronze age.   I. Title.
DS90.Y37   2010
933 – dc22   2009028632

ISBN 978-0-521-19162-3 Hardback
ISBN 978-1-107-66003-8 Paperback

Als das Kind Kind war,
ging es mit hängenden Armen,
wollte der Bach sei ein Fluß,
der Fluß sei ein Strom,
und diese Pfütze das Meer.

from Peter Handke *Lied vom Kindsein*

When the child was a child
It walked with its arms swinging,
wanted the brook to be a river,
the river to be a torrent,
and this puddle to be the sea.

CONTENTS

Acknowledgments   *page* xi

INTRODUCTION 1

Uncharted Areas and Blind Spots in the Archaeology of the Philistines   2

The Aim of the Present Study   7

1   THE ARCHAEOLOGICAL IDENTIFICATION OF MIGRATION AND
OTHER RANGES OF INTERREGIONAL INTERACTIONS 9

Establishing the Course of Inquiry   9

Describing Interactions and the Parameters of Interaction   10

Defining *Deep Change*   13

The Archaeological Identification of Migration, When Treated
    As a Range of Interregional Interactions   14

Migration and Deep Change in Domestic Assemblages   15

Deep Change and Innovation Processes   17

Demonstrating Deep Change: Case Studies for the Influence of
    Migration on Behavioral Patterns and Material Culture   19

Causality of Migration   30

Conclusions   32

2   SETTING THE SCENE: THE MYCENAEAN PALATIAL CULTURE
AND THE OUTSIDE WORLD 34

Social Complexity in the Mycenaean Palatial System   35

Aegean Peoples and Mediterranean Geography   38

Thirteenth-Century Aegean Maritime Capabilities and Interregional
    Interactions   44

Palatial Administration and Aegean Migration and Colonization of
    the Late Thirteenth to the Early Twelfth Century BCE   54

3   THE TWELFTH-CENTURY-BCE AEGEAN: POLITICAL AND
SOCIAL BACKGROUND 58

Changing Rulership and the Decapitation Theory   58

Social Complexity in Selected Aegean Sites in LHIIIC   60
Regional Aspects of Rulership in the Twelfth Century   81
The Change in Imagery and Ideology between LHIIIB and LHIIIC   83
Conclusions   95

4   PRECONDITIONS FOR MIGRATION 97
Push and Pull Factors Affecting Migration   97
Twelfth-Century-BCE Sources of Information   102
The Maritime Option   102
The Land Option   114
Conclusions   120

5   ALONG THE ROUTES 122
Investigating Routes and New Populations   122
The Aegean Hearth   123
Cooking Activities   124
Cyprus: Interactions along the Sea Route   138
Western Anatolia: The Expansion of the East Aegean Koine   154
Cilicia and the Amuq: The Land Route from Southeastern Anatolia
    to Syria   158
The Syro-Phoenician Coast: Along the Sea and Land Routes   164
Through the Egyptian Lens   171
The Origin of the Attackers   180
Conclusions: Twelfth-Century Interactions along the Routes   186

6   STRICTLY BUSINESS? THE SOUTHERN LEVANT AND THE
AEGEAN IN THE THIRTEENTH TO THE EARLY TWELFTH
CENTURY BCE 194
Mycenaean Imports to the Southern Levant   194
Merchants and Mercenaries: Foreigners in Late Bronze Age Canaan   204
Conclusions: Strictly Business?   214

7   THE MATERIAL CULTURE CHANGE IN TWELFTH-CENTURY
PHILISTIA 216
From Canaan to Philistia   216
The End of the Bronze Age–Iron Age Transition in the Philistine Sites   220
Behavioral Patterns As Indicators of Interaction with Aegean
    Population in the Southern Levant   227
Cooking Installations: Hearths, Ovens, and *Tabuns*   234
Form, Function, and Variability in Cooking Traditions   238
Assessing the Degree of Change   240
Patterns of Use of the Pottery Assemblage: Storing and Serving Food
    and Drink in Aegean and Local Styles   241
LHIIIC-Style Pottery: Local Production of Traded Pottery or a
    Domestic Assemblage?   243
Serving and Storage Vessels in the Local, Canaanite Tradition   255

Cypriot (and Egyptian?) Shapes 262
The Nature of the Aegean-Style and Canaanite Ceramic Repertoires
    in Philistia 262
Pottery Production and Technology 264
Textile Production 267
The Organization of Domestic Space 270
Conclusions: Philistine House, Philistine Migrants 279

8 THE PHILISTINE SOCIETY AND THE SETTLEMENT PROCESS 282
Settlement Patterns in Philistia 282
Economy 295
Trade 300
Ceremonial and Cultic Activity 302
Elite in the Pentapolis 307
Literacy and Administration 308
The Role of Women in the Aegean Migration 313
Social Stratification in Twelfth-Century Philistia 315
Chronology and the Paradigm of Unified Migration 315
The Origin of the Migrants 325
Conclusions 330

9 A SHORT HISTORY OF THE AEGEAN IMMIGRATION
  TO THE LEVANT 335
A Land Much Divided: The World that Created the Aegean Migration 335
A Family Portrait with an Ox Wagon: On the Routes to the East 336
The Arrival 338
The Settlement 340
Aegean Life Abroad: The Making of Philistia 342

Bibliography 347
Index 383

ACKNOWLEDGMENTS

In my teens, I participated, for several seasons, in the Tel Miqne/Ekron excavations, directed by Trude Dothan and Seymour Gitin. Their enthusiasm for archaeology and the amazing discoveries of the early Philistine life at the tell inevitably paved my way to archaeology and sparked my long-lasting interest in the Philistines.

The initial research for this book stemmed from my Ph.D. dissertation at Tel Aviv University. I am indebted to my advisers, Israel Finkelstein, Irad Malkin, and Shlomo Bunimovitz, for their enormous help and encouragement. Generous grants from Malcolm H. Wiener and from the Greek Ministry of Education enabled my stay in Athens for two years, which changed the course of my life.

Numerous advances in the study of the Philistines and the postpalatial Aegean world occurred during the six years that have elapsed since I completed my dissertation. These include the publication of a considerable volume of new excavation data from the entire eastern Mediterranean, which essentially required that this research be rewritten before it was published. Most of the revisions were made during my stay as a postdoctoral Fellow at the Semitic Museum of Harvard University. I am most grateful to Lawrence E. Stager, the director of the museum, for his kind hospitality and for his valuable remarks on several chapters of the book. My stay at Harvard University was supported by a Fulbright Post-Doctoral Fellowship and a grant from the Rothschild Foundation.

I am indebted to the scholars, colleagues, and friends who have read and commented on the entirety or parts of different versions of this book. Among them are Daniel Master, Stephie Nikoloudis, Krzysztof Nowicki, Jeremy Rutter, and Itamar Singer. Eric H. Cline has shown true friendship by reading the manuscript twice. During the preparation of this book I have also benefited from the kind advice of many colleagues and friends, among them are David Ben-Shlomo, Yoram Cohen, Yuval Gadot, Ayelet Gilboa, Aren Maeir, Laura Mazov, Michael Press, Itzik Shai, and Alex Zukerman.

Inbal Samet has put much skill and effort into the English editing of the manuscript.

Beatrice Rehl of Cambridge University Press has walked me through the long process of preparing the manuscript for publication with admirable patience. Her comments, as well as those of two anonymous reviewers, have greatly improved this book.

This book was published with the support of the Israel Science Foundation.

Finally, I wish to thank my family for years of understanding. I am grateful to my parents, Ronit and Isaac Yasur-Landau; my brother, Daniel; my sister, Dana; my wife, Shelly; and my sons, Yonatan and Ariel, for their unconditional love and support of my archaeological dream and for putting up with piles of loose papers, dusty sherds, and excavation equipment over the years.

INTRODUCTION

The migration of the Sea Peoples, the Philistines among them, from the Aegean area to the Levant during the early twelfth century BCE is one of the most intriguing events in the history of the eastern Mediterranean. From a cultural point of view, it was a watershed process in which the movement of the populace connected East and West during the great divide between the collapse of the Late Bronze Age civilizations and the beginning of the era of nation-states in the Iron Age. As a product of the very beginning of the Dark Age of Greece, the migration illuminates the earliest efforts to reconstruct social structures in the Aegean after the fall of the Mycenaean palaces. In Cyprus, it contributed to further connect the island to the realm of Aegean culture, which would later lead to Hellenization. In the Levant, the migrants formed their own political communities, separate from both the Canaanite city-state system and the Egyptian empire. Establishing themselves along the coast, the Sea Peoples formed a long-standing cultural and political antithesis to the Israelites in the central hill country, destined to shape the history of the biblical world.

The study of the Philistine migration is also a methodological treasure trove from a point of view of both the archaeology and the anthropology of migration. During the late 1990s, the exponential rise in the theoretical examination of migration in archaeology created a plethora of methodological frameworks, as well as a need for well-documented case studies against which these frameworks could be tested. The extraordinarily rich archaeological data from twelfth-century-BCE sites in the Aegean, Anatolia, Cyprus, and the Levant, together with supporting literary evidence, make the Philistine migration one of the best-documented case studies of migration in the ancient world. The data enable us to investigate practically every aspect of the migrants' society, from political structures to perceptions of gender, and from subsistence economy to their ethnicity and intercultural relations between migrants and local populations.

UNCHARTED AREAS AND BLIND SPOTS IN THE ARCHAEOLOGY OF THE PHILISTINES

Any journey tracking the elusive Philistines should begin by becoming acquainted with and appreciating the areas that others have already explored. The infant years of the archaeology of the Philistines began in 1899, when two British archaeologists, Frederick Bliss and Robert A. S. Macalister, began digging at Tell es-Ṣafi, which they identified as biblical Gath, Goliath's hometown. They discovered a new pottery type – strainer jugs, stirrup jars, and bowls decorated with spirals and birds. F. B. Welch, a Mycenaean pottery expert who worked in the British excavations on Melos (T. Dothan 1982: 24, 94; Dothan and Dothan 1992: 32), cautiously interpreted these as suggesting "a probable northwestern origin of the Philistines." The archaeological link between the Philistine and the Mycenaean cultures was made for the first time. This discovery fit very well with the earlier interpretations of the nineteenth-century Egyptologists François Chabas and Gaston Maspero concerning the land and sea invasion of Egypt by the Sea Peoples: the *Peleset* in the inscriptions of Ramses III had been equated in 1872 with the Aegean Pelasgians and the biblical Philistines. Macalister's 1913 book, *The Philistines: Their History and Civilization* (reprinted in 1965), is a synthetic work that well represents this early phase in research. Heavily text oriented, it combines Egyptian and biblical sources with the small amount of archaeological data then available from the Aegean and Philistia. Macalister's research questions, reflected in the table of contents, and his desire to build a comprehensive history of the Philistines, are relevant to this day. Chapter 1 is devoted to the origin of the Philistines. Chapter 2 relates to their history, from Wen-Amon to the wars with the Israelites and their subsequent decline. Chapter 3 is about the land of the Philistines and is concerned mainly with problems of historical geography. Chapter 4 treats the culture of the Philistines, dealing with language; military, political, and domestic organization; religion; and the Philistines' place in history and civilization.

After a century of archaeological research, the main questions remain much unchanged, and the twenty-first century begins with archaeologists doubting previous notions of dates, material culture, and ethnicity connected to the Philistine phenomenon. In regard to the origin of the Philistines, we are more or less in the same obscure situation we were in a century ago. Even more embarrassing is that precious little has been written on the Philistines as individuals – rather than as a cultural phenomenon or historical event – and even today, Macalister's statement holds true: "On the subject of family life among the Philistines nothing is known" (1965: 90). Has indeed so little changed?

Several decades after Macalister, Albright (1932) and Alt (1944) formed the basic historical paradigm for the settlement of the Philistines, which many use to this day. Taking at face value the words of Ramses III and his successors (recorded in Medinet Habu and the Great Papyrus Harris), they argued that the Sea Peoples were defeated by the Egyptians in Year 8 of Ramses III, then settled as vassals in Egyptian strongholds (which Albright and Alt interpreted as the Egyptian centers in southern Canaan). After a short time, they assert, the Sea Peoples broke free of the Egyptian yoke and formed their own political system.

The last three decades of the twentieth century were, undoubtedly, the golden age of the archaeological investigation of the Philistines, owing much to the personal commitment and charisma of Trude Dothan. In the period between the mid-1960s and the mid-1980s, the available archaeological database grew immensely because of new excavations in Israel's coastal plain. However, the methodological scheme used during those years for the identification of migration by material culture traits was not fundamentally different from that used by Macalister: decorated fineware pottery was still the main criterion for identifying the Philistines, and changes in pottery were perceived as indicators of changes in ethnos.[1] Dothan's book *The Philistines and Their Material Culture*, published in Hebrew in 1967, was the first fully archaeological investigation of the material culture remains attributed to the Philistines. It presented a clear argument supporting the "ethnic" connotation of the Philistine Bichrome pottery assigned to the Philistines. Close parallels between the shapes and designs of this pottery and Aegean Mycenaean IIIC: 1b pottery was, to Dothan's mind, proof of Aegean migration to the Levant (1967: 71). The anthropoid coffins found at Lachish and Beth Shean were presented as another "ethnic demarcator" of the Philistines (1967: 211–46). During the same years, Moshe Dothan conducted excavations at Ashdod, the first Pentapolis site to be extensively excavated using modern methods. A new type of pottery, locally made Mycenaean IIIC: 1b with Aegean types and decoration, was found to precede the Philistine Bichrome pottery. Moshe Dothan equated these two pottery types with two different groups of people and introduced the "two waves approach": a first wave of settlement of Aegean Sea Peoples in the days of Merneptah was followed by a settlement of the Philistines in the days of Ramses III (M. Dothan 1972: 5–6). Shortly after these excavations, the renewed excavations by Amihai Mazar at Tell Qasile in 1971–4 (Mazar 1980; 1985a) uncovered a settlement, dubbed "Philistine," that was founded in the Philistine Bichrome phase. A series of overlapping temples with rich finds of cult vessels urged Mazar to formulate a detailed discussion of the Philistine cult, concentrating mainly on the origin of the "Philistine" cultic architecture – whether local or Aegean.

---

[1] Other items of Aegean derivation, or of presumed Aegean derivation, were also interpreted in these years as further evidence of Aegean migration, leading to the 1980s approach of using a checklist of traits to identify the inhabitants of a specific site as Philistines.

Nancy Sandars's 1978 book, *The Sea Peoples*, put the Philistines within a much wider spectrum of interrelated historical phenomena. It was extremely successful in providing a wide Mediterranean scope for the examination of the phenomenon of the Sea Peoples, combining literary sources and archaeological finds in a complex and colorful reconstruction of the thirteenth and twelfth centuries BCE in the eastern Mediterranean. Four years later it was followed by a revised English edition of Trude Dothan's book, in which – drawing mainly on results of the Ashdod excavations – further traits of Aegean origin were compiled, to be associated with the migration of the Philistines (1982: 40–1). Among them are the following:

* Locally made Mycenaean IIIC: 1b pottery (dubbed "Monochrome") and the later Philistine Bichrome pottery
* Seals, including one possibly with Cypro-Minoan script from Ashdod
* "Ashdoda" figurines – identified by Trude Dothan as a local version of the Mycenaean Mother Goddess figurines

Following Sandars's and Dothan's studies, the Philistine–Sea Peoples phenomenon in the southern Levantine coast was compared to other cases in the eastern Mediterranean in which "intrusive" Aegean material culture was identified as indicating migration. Mazar (1985b; 1988; 1991) compared the material culture evidence for the Philistine–Sea Peoples migration to the Levant to that of the Achaean migration to Cyprus in the twelfth century BCE. He concluded that both phenomena relate to the same migration events, and that Cyprus was a bridgehead on the route of the migrants to the Levant. Aegean migration was also identified at Ras Ibn Hani, the port of Ugarit, on the evidence of locally made Mycenaean IIIC: 1b pottery (Lagarce and Lagarce 1988).

Challenges to the existing methodology rose soon after, when the first cracks appeared in the concept of pots equal people. It was argued that the locally made Mycenaean IIIC (Monochrome) pottery was the prototype of the later Philistine Bichrome pottery rather than representing another, earlier ethnic group (Mazar 1985b: 106; Singer 1988). Further attacks were launched by Bunimovitz (1990), who questioned the value of the Philistine Bichrome pottery as an ethnic demarcator. In the same years, Singer (1992; 1993; 1994) explored aspects little tended to by most archaeologists: the political organization of the Philistines, phases in Philistine settlement as evidenced by settlement patterns, and various aspects of Philistine deities and cult.

Just as the results of the Ashdod excavations were the source of many advances in the 1970s and early 1980s, knowledge and ideas about the Philistines were heavily influenced in the late 1980s and 1990s by the excavations begun in 1984 at Tel Miqne (identified as the Pentapolis site of Ekron), directed by Trude Dothan and Seymour Gitin. The finds provided additional material culture traits for the "Aegean checklist," such as Aegean-type cooking jugs and coarseware and unique pottery kilns, as well as much data on Aegean pottery and architectural features (mainly Aegean-style hearths; Stager 1995: 347). Furthermore, the Tel Miqne/Ekron excavations opened the way for studies on behavioral aspects of the Philistine migration, such as changes in animal husbandry and economy (Hesse 1986; 1990). Other important results came from the excavation of Ashkelon by Lawrence E. Stager, begun in 1985.

The middle and late 1990s saw the appearance of new methodological approaches, putting more emphasis on aspects of human activity than on objects. The checklist approach, which focuses on material culture traits to identify migration, has been gradually modified by a focus on behavioral patterns (which reflect a change in way of life, ideology, and economy) for the same purpose. New topics investigated have included the importance of ancient foodways to the study of ancient ethnicity (Killebrew 1992; Yasur-Landau 1992), details of pottery production (Killebrew 1996; 1998b), and aspects of gender (Sweeney and Yasur-Landau 1999). An important development has been the application of archaeological, anthropological, and sociological-methodological approaches to ancient and modern migrations to understanding change in material culture assemblages in Philistia, mainly for the archaeological identification of migration and acculturation processes (Stager 1995: 333–4; Stone 1995; Bunimovitz and Yasur-Landau 1996: 89–91). Attention has been given also to other neglected aspects of migration, such as demography. The postulated number of migrants ranged from a massive migration of twenty-five thousand people (Stager 1995) to a humble movement of a few thousands (Finkelstein 1996; 1998). At the same time, more traditional topics were hotly contested, especially the chronology for the arrival of the migrants. Dothan (1989), Mazar (1985b), and Stager (1995) supported a date during the reign of Ramses III for the settlement of the Philistines in connection to his campaigns against the Sea Peoples, while Finkelstein (1995; 1998) and Ussishkin (1998) argued for a lower chronology for the beginning of the Philistine settlement, much later than the days of Ramses III, and probably after Ramses VI, postdating the end of Egyptian control in the south of Canaan.

The later 1990s were also the first time in which the paradigm of Aegean migration, which united most scholars dealing with the Philistines, was seriously challenged. Sherratt (1992; 1998; followed by Bauer 1998) suggested, for the first time, an elegant nonmigrationist explanation for the Aegean cultural traits found on Cyprus and in Philistia, preferring a process of cultural diffusion and elite emulation connected with the early post-Bronze Age trade. Another challenge to the idea of Aegean migration was raised by Killebrew (1998a: 393–7, 401–2; 2000; 2006: 231), who supports the idea of migration that originates from Cyprus and/or Cilicia rather than from the Aegean proper. Even the ethnic composition of the people of Philistia was contested: they were mostly Aegean (e.g., Stager 1995); a mixture of Canaanites, Syrians, and Aegeans (Sweeny and Yasur-Landau 1999); Canaanite (Drews 2000); or a cosmopolitan mixture of people from the eastern Mediterranean (Sherratt 1998).

It is astounding that this very active discussion of key questions relating to the Philistine migration took place in a reality in which very little published data existed on the stratigraphy, architecture, and pottery typology of the first Philistine levels. Before 2004, of the vast areas excavated at Ashdod, Ashkelon, and Tel Miqne/Ekron, only two excavation areas were published with early-twelfth-century strata: Area G in Ashdod (Dothan and Porath 1993) and Field X at Tel Miqne/Ekron (Bierling 1998). This situation has improved considerably in recent years, first with a masterly typological discussion of locally made Mycenaean IIIC pottery (Dothan and Zukerman 2004) and then with the final publication of Field INE at Tel Miqne/Ekron (Meehl, Dothan, and Gitin 2006) and Area H at Ashdod (Dothan and Ben-Shlomo 2005). At the same time, the important results of the Ashkelon excavations began to emerge (Master 2005; Cross and Stager 2006). An influx of dissertations dealing with various aspects of the Philistine and Sea Peoples problems also adds a wealth of yet unpublished material (Mazow 2005; Ben-Shlomo 2006a; Birney 2007; Press 2007).

Despite the many advances in available archaeological data and theoretical approaches made in the past years, the last attempt of a synthetic study placing the Philistine migration within a wider spectrum of interrelated historical phenomena was Nancy Sandars's 1978 book, *The Sea Peoples*, whereas the last synthesis of material from the southern Levant was the 1982 English edition of Dothan's *The Philistines and Their Material Culture*. Apart from the lack of final publication of some key sites, partially remedied only recently, the main reason for this situation may be blind spots and uncharted territories, which blur our vision and present serious difficulties to compiling such a study.

The first blind spot is the need to encompass both the Aegean and the Levant of the twelfth century BCE. With Susan Sherratt and Penelope Mountjoy being the most conspicuous exceptions, few of those who have interpreted interconnections between the Levant and the Aegean have taken the pains to examine in any depth the vast LH/LMIIIC assemblages available.

The second blind spot concerns the use of methodology for the archaeological identification of interregional interactions, including migration. Some important methodological tools have been developed in the past decade in world archaeology, yet they, as well as an overwhelmingly rich sociological and anthropological literature on migration, have usually not been used in any comprehensive manner by archaeologists dealing with the so-called Philistine problem. Every paradigm that is based on a reconstruction of Aegean migration and does not employ methodological tools to construct sound archaeological proof of migration will be vulnerable to virtually any antimigrationist challenge.

As for uncharted territories, those lie in virtually all topics connected to the migration of the Philistines. The political and economic causalities for their migration have never been thoroughly studied or examined in the context of the Aegean postpalatial society. Very little has been written on the migrants' organizational abilities and the routes they may have taken from the Aegean to the Levant. While material culture in Philistia has been amply discussed, it was usually to support chronological, typological, and technological arguments – seldom to re-create the society. There is no study dealing with questions of status and social hierarchy in the society of Philistia. Nothing has been written on its ideology and power. Very little exists on aspects of its subsistence and ancient economy, and almost nothing exists on daily life, women, and gender. The Philistines have been reduced to a list of cultural traits rather than being thought of as a living society.

THE AIM OF THE PRESENT STUDY

It may now be possible to illuminate sections of these blind spots and uncharted territories in an attempt to create an archaeological narrative of the migration of the Sea Peoples.

The vast developments in the archaeology of the Philistines in the past decade (in terms of both methodology and the availability of more databases), as well as the challenges to the paradigm of Aegean migration to the Levant, call for a reevaluation of the entire array of interregional interactions between the Aegean and the Levant in the twelfth century BCE. Similar developments in the archaeology of Cyprus and the Aegean area at the close of the Bronze Age provide not only stimulus but also much data for the conducting of such work.[2,3]

This book aims to demonstrate that the migration of groups of Aegean settlers among the Aegean areas, Anatolia, Cyprus, and the Levant was one of the most important forms of interaction in the first half of twelfth century, side by side with other forms of interaction, such as trade and raiding. The Philistines settling in the southern Levant are but the southernmost manifestation of a vast array of migration phenomena that took place through both land and sea, starting at the Aegean world during the twelfth century. Along these routes, migrants, whose number, relative power, and perhaps even origin within the Aegean differed from one place of settlement to the other, had, nevertheless, a profound effect on almost every aspect of behavioral patterns in their new homes.

Pursuing this aim leads to two interrelated foci of interest. One, with wider geographic and diachronic scope (Chapters 2–5), will follow the connection between social structures and processes in the Aegean area and changes in

---

[2] In this work, *Aegean* is defined as the area that can be considered in very general terms as the Mycenaean world of the thirteenth century BCE: mainland Greece up to Thessaly, the Cyclades, Crete, the Dodecanese, and western Anatolia.

[3] *Levant* is defined here as the area from the Syrian coast to the north and the Nile Delta to the south, including mainly the coastal zones and lower areas to the east of those zones.

interregional interaction patterns, among them migration during the thirteenth and twelfth centuries BCE. Further insights into the nature of twelfth-century interaction will be gained through the examination of sites along land and sea routes from the Aegean to the Levant. Thus, Chapter 2 deals with aspects of social complexity, rulership, and interregional interaction in the thirteenth-century Aegean. It explores the types of state-orchestrated as well as private interactions that took place and examines whether maritime migration was one of them. Chapter 3 surveys the level of social complexity and political integration after the fall of the Mycenaean palaces. Chapter 4 examines the maritime abilities achieved in the twelfth century, as well as various aspects of land and sea travel, to establish which types of interregional interaction were possible in the twelfth century. Chapter 5 follows the sea and land routes from the Aegean to the Levant in the twelfth century. A combination of archaeological evidence from sites along these routes, as well as Hittite, Ugaritic, and Egyptian literary sources, is assessed to define the nature of interaction of these areas with the Aegean world.

A second focus will be on Philistia proper (Chapters 6–8). First, the criteria of deep changes of behavioral patterns will be used for the identification of an Aegean migration in the twelfth century against the background of thirteenth-century Canaanite culture and its interaction with the Aegean world. Then, a portrait of the migrants' society will be drawn, based on various aspects of society in Philistia from the level of the individual to the level of the settlement. Thus, Chapter 6 is devoted to the situation in Canaan in the thirteenth and early twelfth centuries BCE, and to Canaan's interactions with the Aegean world prior to the fall of Ugarit and Year 8 of Ramses III. Special attention is given to the possibility of Aegean presence in Late Bronze Age Canaan. Chapter 7 examines all available material culture assemblages from Ashdod, Ashkelon, and Tel Miqne/Ekron and establishes the argument for the Aegean migration as the most plausible explanation for the changes in these assemblages. Chapter 8 deals with the various social and political aspects of the Aegean migration, including duration of contact, number of arrivals, social stratification, occupation, and questions of gender and intermarriage.

Finally, Chapter 9 presents my conclusions, an archaeological narrative reconstructing the Aegean migration to the Levant. Although this volume will not be the final word on these topics, I hope that it will serve to launch a new round of discussion, thus leading to advancement in an overall understanding of the Philistines.

1

THE ARCHAEOLOGICAL IDENTIFICATION
OF MIGRATION AND OTHER RANGES OF
INTERREGIONAL INTERACTIONS

Those who settle on foreign shores will either found their own independent settlement, or infiltrate among the local population; and they will either bring their own wives, or marry indigenous women in their new homes. Between these two pairs of alternatives there can, of course, be many intermediate situations.

– Coldstream, "Mixed Marriages at the Frontiers of the Early Greek World," 1993

ESTABLISHING THE COURSE OF INQUIRY

The great methodological advances in the archaeological identification of ancient migration conducted in the 1990s (e.g., Burmeister 2000; Anthony 1990; 1997; 2000) were achieved by implementing insights gathered from anthropological and historical case studies. The use of explicit and sound methodology to study migration effectively ended the dislike that, in the 1980s, many "new" archaeologists felt for migrationist explanations, which many archaeologists had used until then as magical, catchall explanations for material cultural change.

The theoretical advances in the study of migration have greatly benefited, and still do, from studies of historical archaeology (e.g., Cheek 1998; Deetz 1996; Diehl, Waters, and Thiel 1998). Such studies are an excellent source of specific insights and theoretical approaches for any research dealing with migration. Because this field was practically born in the New World, much of it deals with different aspects of migration and settlement in the Americas and elsewhere. It is therefore traditionally theoretically sensitive to questions of colonial interaction and migration, and it is usually supplemented by much better literary sources than are any of the cases of ancient colonization.

Although Near Eastern archaeologists are often accused of not incorporating theoretical advances into their work, many archaeologists working on the Philistine problem swiftly and amply acknowledged advances in the theory of migration (e.g., Stager 1995; Barako 2000; Gilboa 2005; Killebrew 2006; Ben-Shlomo 2006a; Mazow 2005).

Before we embark on this journey, we must put forward an explicit methodological framework that will enable us not only to identify migration but also to place it in the context of other forms or ranges of interregional interactions, such as trade and raids, all known to have co-occurred in the twelfth century BCE.

All events are unique, and irreproducible; however, all events are part of the vast continuum of interregional interaction, taken here to broadly mean any form of contact between different regions and/or cultures. This continuum may be arbitrarily divided up into three rather flexible and interconnected ranges of interactions sharing a common trait: migration, trade, and raids and conquest (Fig. 1.1).

Stein (2005: 13–14) stresses the importance of the ranges of trade and emulation in the archaeological identification of colonization: "Trade, emulation, and the presence of trade colonies should leave different archaeological signatures. If interaction is limited to trade without the presence of foreign enclave, then we would expect to see only portable trade items in the local settlement." The picture becomes more complex when, as it often happens in the Mediterranean, various ranges of interaction co-occur in the same regions, sometimes at the same location. Thus, for example, the reality of the late eighth and early seventh centuries BCE, the era of Greek colonization, included various ranges of interaction: not only settlement of Greeks in the central Mediterranean, but also trading ventures of Greeks to various parts of the Mediterranean and wars among different Greek populations. Similarly, Phoenician contacts with native populations in Spain and Sardinia were not limited to colonial domination; they included complex trade contacts and other interactions, thus resulting in a blurred distinction between locals and migrants, a practice that Dommelen (2005) terms *hybrid*.

Furthermore, when a nonmigrationist explanation for a change in material culture is promoted, such as Sherratt's (1998) trade-based explanation for the production of Aegean-style pottery in twelfth-century Cyprus and the Levant (see the Introduction to this volume), it simply cannot be properly addressed with a methodology that aims to study migration alone. The archaeological model applied to such material culture assemblages needs not only to identify migration but also to correctly differentiate it from other ranges of interaction, in which migration is seen as a mere range of events within the much broader continuum of interregional interaction. To my mind, identifying migration in archaeology by using a model that deals only with migration turns a blind eye to the complexity and variability of human interaction.

DESCRIBING INTERACTIONS AND THE PARAMETERS OF INTERACTION

As stated, every interregional interaction is unique, a composite of extraordinary and irreproducible circumstances. How, then, can we formulate a

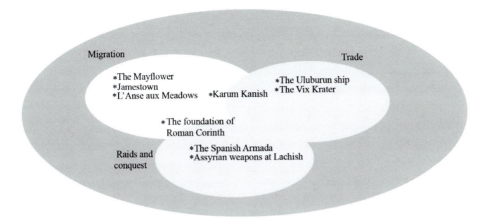

FIGURE 1.1. Interregional interaction events and interaction ranges

general methodology that will enable us to investigate the influence of specific and unique interaction phenomena on material culture assemblages? A key step toward the establishment of a workable framework for the archaeological identification of migration and other interaction ranges is to be able to describe interregional interactions.

Sociologists, anthropologists, and archaeologists have sorted out and described migration types and other interaction phenomena with generalized typologies and taxonomies.[1] However, typologies may blur the exact nature of a specific interaction: categories are deliberately set with loosely defined boundaries so that they can encompass many events. This problem was acknowledged by Lightfoot (2005: 210), who argues regarding colonization: "Given the tremendous range of variation in colonial programs . . . we do great injustice to the study of cross cultural variation by attempting to pigeonhole our case studies into few discrete colonial types." A related problem is the inherited explanatory nature of any generalization. Achieving greater accuracy in a typological description requires the use of more types; however, increasing the number of types in use necessitates naming them and defining their boundaries. In any case, a perfect typological description is achieved only when the number of types is equal to the number of possible interactions (i.e., unlimited).

The option offered here is to reduce the tension between the uniqueness of an event and a well-defined, general methodology by using a more flexible description that is based on the parameters of interactions. The values of different parameters enhance the description by adding dimensions. For example, instead of categorizing pastries by their names (e.g., Black Forest cake, napoleon), we can describe them according to their ingredients and modes of preparation. The combination of various parameters forms a rich,

---

[1] For examples of typologies of interactions or migrations consisting of two to eight types or ranges, see Willey and Latherap 1956; Peterson 1958; Adams 1968; Trigger 1968; Branigan 1981; 1984; Cadogan 1984: 13; Kilian 1990: 447; Anthony 1990; and Gosden 2004: 26.

multidimensional picture – one that is essentially different from the unidimensional typological description. The numerous combinations allowed by this categorization system result in descriptions of the nature of interactions that are more accurate than those that result from a typological approach. The use of description parameters, which are easier to define and less explanatory than types, should result in a less-biased picture of the described interaction.

Berry's (1997) study of psychological aspects of acculturation processes among migrants is especially relevant to this study, as it presents a framework for the study of migration and the acculturation processes that follow it. The framework does not use a typology of acculturation but includes parameters (which Berry [1997: 15 and fig. 2] calls variables) that influence acculturation on both group and individual levels.

For this work, I have selected several of Berry's parameters concerning migration that are expected to influence the character and extent of change caused by interaction (Fig. 1.2). The chosen parameters influence material culture directly and are, therefore, more relevant to archaeology. Furthermore, the parameters help create a framework that will describe not only cases of migration but also other cases of interregional interaction:

The number of people involved in the interaction.

The duration of the interaction. Berry's (1997: 23–4) "length of time," referring to the different phases of the immigrants' acculturation along the timeline, can be made relevant for every type of interaction affecting processes of acculturation (see Bunimovitz and Yasur-Landau 1996: 89), as well as flow of information.

The cultural distance between the cultures involved in the interaction. This parameter carries implications for practically every aspect of material culture, far beyond those of language and religion that Berry mentions. Accordingly, Triandis (1997: 56–7) suggests that the model presented here would be complete if it included most of the known dimensions of cultural variation.

The segment of population involved. Here different variables from Berry's work (e.g., sex, status, occupation) are gathered under one inclusive parameter that defines variability within the migrants' society. Similar variability within a single culture is described by Clarke (1978: 251–8) as ethnic, regional, occupational, social, and sex subcultures. Furthermore, the experience gathered in archaeological theory for the manifestations of this variability in material culture assemblages can also be used to study interactions. Several scholars (e.g., Lee 1966: 56; Burmeister 2000: 543) deal with the concept of selectivity in migration, emphasizing the influence of parameters of sex and gender, age, and class on the ability and willingness to migrate.

The balance of power between the cultures involved in the interaction. This is also considered an important factor influencing acculturation (Burmeister

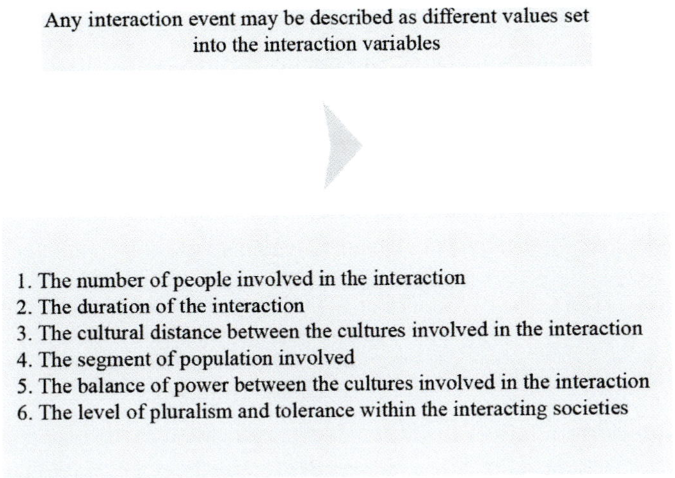

Any interaction event may be described as different values set
into the interaction variables

1. The number of people involved in the interaction
2. The duration of the interaction
3. The cultural distance between the cultures involved in the interaction
4. The segment of population involved
5. The balance of power between the cultures involved in the interaction
6. The level of pluralism and tolerance within the interacting societies

FIGURE 1.2. Interaction parameters

2000: 545–6). Berry (1997: 9) replaces the terms *mainstream* and *minority* with *dominant* and *nondominant* to describe power relations in a plural society.

The level of pluralism and tolerance within the interacting societies. Attitudes toward the migrants in the target society, prejudice and discrimination, and the migrants' social attitudes toward maintaining their cultural identity and relationship with the target society all determine the nature of the chosen acculturation strategies, which may vary from integration and segregation or separation (for groups that find it important to keep their identity and characteristics) to assimilation and marginalization (for groups that put less effort into preserving their identity; see Berry 1992; 1997: 9–11).

DEFINING *DEEP CHANGE*

To assess the influence of interregional interaction on the archaeological record, we must first differentiate material culture assemblages by the type of activity they are used for (e.g., domestic, cultic, funerary, industrial, mercantile). Even without interaction, parameters such as time, gender, occupation, and status group create variability within a material culture assemblage and among several assemblages. It is likely that, in a single interaction event, the interaction parameters influence different assemblages in different ways. To begin to formulate the relationship between interregional interaction and material culture assemblages, I suggest to examine the relation between the intensity of the interaction and its manifestation in the archaeological record. A key term in this discussion is *behavioral patterns* (Rapoport's [1990] *activity systems* or *behavioral circuits*); these are embedded with values or a lifestyle specific to a particular culture.

It is suggested, therefore, that the more intense the interactions are, and the longer the time span of the interaction is, the deeper is the change that will occur in behavioral patterns of the interacting cultures and the more numerous are the influences on material culture assemblages. In general, migration phenomena involve intense interaction,[2] and as such, they are predicted in this book to show deep changes in varied material culture assemblages.

THE ARCHAEOLOGICAL IDENTIFICATION OF MIGRATION, WHEN TREATED AS A RANGE OF INTERREGIONAL INTERACTIONS

The use of interaction parameters to describe all interactions may resolve the primary difficulty (apart from lack of archaeological data) that scholars face when dealing with migration and archaeology: distinguishing migration from other interactions (Burmeister 2000: 539–40, with further bibliography). As argued previously, a key to the solution lies in the supposition that migration is only one range of interaction events on a broader interaction continuum. Because there are no natural, clearly defined boundaries between migration and other interactions (see Fig. 1.1),[3] there can be no absolute model that will enable, in all cases, the identification of migration from archaeological evidence. However, a good approximation to identifying migration is to isolate the main difference between the migration range of interaction and others, namely high values in the duration-of-interaction parameter. People who migrate will remain in the target country for a substantial period, unlike people involved in other interaction ranges (e.g., trade), who will remain for shorter periods. This high value in the "duration of interaction" parameter has two interconnected yet distinct dimensions: one is the actual, physical length of time in which the migrants remain in the target country; the other is the personal notion or intention of the migrant to stay for a prolonged period of time (or the acceptance of the imposed reality, in the cases of forced migration and deportation). In addition, in situations of migration, phenomena of deep change in behavioral patterns occur almost instantly because of the migrants' intention to settle down.[4] This instant deep change in behavioral patterns is expected to have a simultaneous, instant, and conspicuous effect on material culture assemblages.

The foregoing two dimensions affect material culture assemblages and can therefore be used to create a workable framework for the archaeological

---

[2] The "intense interaction" label may also include interactions from other ranges.

[3] For example, when does a tourist or a traveling merchant become a migrant? Is it after one month, one year, or one decade in the target country?

[4] It should be emphasized that even low-intensity interactions may have an effect of deep change if they are conducted over an extended period and produce a gradual buildup of acculturating effects on both parties.

identification of migration. Moreover, they can be combined with deep change to formulate the core hypothesis of the present study. Deep change in behavioral patterns, resulting from enduring contacts or from an intention to engage in such contacts, is the most significant criterion for identifying migration.

MIGRATION AND DEEP CHANGE IN DOMESTIC ASSEMBLAGES

Interaction clearly has some effect on the material culture of the target society, but are all assemblages equally influenced, or are some more liable to change than others?

A starting point for this discussion is Berry's (1997: 12) observation that migrants adopt different acculturation strategies in private and public spheres:

> However, there can be a variation according to one's location: in more private spheres or domains (such as the home, the extended family, the ethnic community), more cultural maintenance may be sought than in public spheres (such as the workplace, or in politics); and there may be less intergroup contact sought in private spheres than in the more public ones.

This observation suggests a scale according to which the cultural values and lifestyles of migrants are better preserved inside their homes and less so in the public domain (i.e., outside their kinship and even cultural spheres). It follows that the material culture will reflect the migrants' chosen acculturation strategies, thus making the domestic assemblages more indicative than public ones of interactions involving migration.

The term *habitus*, coined by Bourdieu (1990), has been used in archaeological studies of migration to represent the connection between maintenance of cultural identity and socialization performed in the domestic sphere. The habitus is the core of one's identity; it comprises the "systems of durable, transportable dispositions, structured structures predisposed to function as structuring structures" (Bourdieu 1990: 53). It determines an individual's dispositions toward social constructs and practices and establishes the sense of self at an early age (Jones 1997: 88). The domestic arena, inseparable from family and kinship, is where socialization starts. Here, by participating in behavioral patterns and observing the behavior of others, one acquires some of the most important elements of identity, such as kinship (lineage) and language.[5]

Using the same term, Burmeister (2000: 542) reaches conclusions similar to those of Berry and argues for dichotomy in the migrant society: the external,

---

[5] These elements are so evidently important for establishing group identity that they appear in "old," "primordial" definitions of ethnicity noted by Jones (1997: 65–6), as well as in the latest ones (Jones 1997: 84).

public sphere, in which there is much interaction with the local population, and the internal domain. The habitus confronts change in the external sphere, inflicted by the social and economic environment of the target society; it is likely to persist in its original form in the internal domain, which is less exposed to outside conditions. Therefore, according to Burmeister (2000), the social system of the family and the household, as well as the organization of private life, is less likely to change than are behavioral patterns connected with the outside world (see also Frankel 2000). The following points may also support this suggestion:

* On a basic level, the domestic unit has a crucial role in most aspects of migration, such as the form that the migration takes. The socialization process in the family transmits cultural values, determining who migrates, the reasons for migration, and the intensity of family contact maintained across space and time. Kinship networks are essential providers of information and support for migrants. Most important for our inquiry is the fact that families are migrating units. Even if only part of the family migrates, expectations from and obligations to the family left behind keep a migrant firmly within the social and cultural systems of his or her home country (Boyd 1989: 642–3).
* The ability to choose a strategy of maintaining one's culture in a migration situation depends on the tolerance or prejudice of the dominant society (Berry 1992). The dominant society's reluctance toward or discouraging of manifestations of migrants' identity naturally have a greater effect on the public domains, controlled by the dominant society, and less on the private domains, over which the dominant society has limited control. Even in situations of cultural oppression, the home and kinship group can continue as a place for manifestation of a nondominant identity.
* Even in a situation not connected with migration, the home is where basic, slowly changing, traditional domestic activities are performed. These can include maintenance activities (Picazo 1997), such as food preparation;[6] domestic modes of production (Sahlins 1972), as with textiles;[7] and domestic cult practices. Despite the immense importance of these activities for the socialization and formation of group identity, they are usually not considered prestigious, partly because women carry out many of them

---

[6] There are many examples of food as an ethnic demarcator; some of the better known are Jewish and Muslim food taboos. However, identity in food extends beyond taboos, and different groups may eat different basic food assemblages (on the eastern Andes, see Osborne 1996: 151–2) or associate different dishes with different occasions and rituals that are special to the group – these eventually lead to the expression "ethnic cooking."

[7] For the role of homemade textiles in conveying messages of identity, see Washburn 1994; for the concept of ethnic dress as a "traditional" manifestation of identity, not related to fashion, see, e.g., Eicher and Sumberg 1995: 300–4; Walters 1995; and Renne 1995.

(Hendon 1996: 49–55; Picazo 1997). Thus, domestic activities are less susceptive to change as a whole in reaction to new fashions, new technologies, or new definitions of prestigious activity (Clark 2004).

According to the foregoing delineated points, a deep change in behavioral patterns observed in private, kinship-based assemblages is more indicative of migration than those observed in public, official ones. For example, a deep change in the behavioral patterns performed in a domestic context is most likely (though probably not exclusively) the result of an interaction along the migration range (see Anthony 2001). While domestic assemblages are the last to be thoroughly influenced by interaction ranges such as trade and emulation of elites, they are the first to be affected by the arrival of migrants, who bring with them their cultural concepts embedded in domestic behavioral patterns. In contrast, deep change in more public assemblages, such as commercial or industrial ones, is less indicative of migration, as it may result from causes not related to migration, such as the introduction of technological innovations and a change of style, for example, the appearance of French-style royal courts across Europe following the example of Versailles (Wiener 1984: 17).

DEEP CHANGE AND INNOVATION PROCESSES

Because deep change in the material culture of the target country is necessarily connected to the processes of acceptance and the implementation of innovation, it is necessary to distinguish between innovations stemming from migration and those brought about by other forms of intercultural contact. The diffusion-of-innovation theory (Rogers 1983; Shortland 2004: 4–6) defines the following five stages of the innovation process:

1. Knowledge of the existence of the innovation and understanding of its function
2. Persuasion of the merits of the innovation
3. Decision to use the innovation
4. Implementation into actual use
5. Confirmation, or reinforcement based on the positive outcomes emerging from the use

The first, crucial stages of knowledge and persuasion are intimately linked and dependent on the process of cultural transmission, the material aspects of which can be broadly defined as the transfer of knowledge regarding behavioral patterns that concern the production and use of artifacts. This transmission is carried out through teaching, imitation, and other socialization processes (Gosselain 1998: 94–7). The complexity of the teaching processes needed for the production of pottery is duly noted in Aegean archaeology. Papadopoulos (1997: 453) notes that "to see a pot, or handle it, or even discuss how it is made, is not sufficient experience to be able to reproduce it," in support of the idea that itinerant Mycenaean and Minoan potters had an important role in the production of high-quality ceramic imitations. Therefore, while the acceptance and crude reproduction of one artifact type may not need more than one foreign instructor, multiple, co-occurring, and swift cases of innovations evident in the events of deep change indicate intensive processes of teaching and learning, which cannot take place without prolonged and continuous contact between instructors and trainees.

Jeffery (1961: 1–12) raises a similar point regarding the dissemination of the Greek alphabet during the Archaic period. She argues that alphabetic literacy could not have been transferred by casual trading encounters but required that the teacher and the pupil reside in the same community until the language barrier was broken. She envisioned a mechanism by which bilingual children, born of intercultural marriages, had much to do with spreading literacy from one language to the other. To reiterate, the prolonged duration of contact is also the parameter differentiating migration from other ranges of intercultural interaction.

Schiffer and Skibo's (1987: 598) term *functional field* is useful in characterizing the barriers of the introduction and acceptance of object types as a result of interregional interaction other than migration. A functional field is "the set of techno-functions, socio-functions, and ideo-functions that the artifacts in a society have to perform" (Schiffer and Skibo 1987: 598). These barriers may be partly or entirely cultural specific; their different aspects, from production to use, represent a rich set of behavioral patterns that may not exist outside the cultural boundaries of the manufacturing society. The negotiation between behavioral patterns connected to making and use occurs within the realms of the habitus (Dietler and Herbich 1998: 247), with durable dispositions toward certain perceptions and practices (Jones 1997: 88). Hence, as argued previously, specific behavioral patterns that are closely connected to perception of group identity are less prone to changes, as the habitus of a group is likely to persist even in situations of great social stress, such as in cases of migrants in a foreign society (Burmeister 2000: 542).

Innovations that do occur in the context of ranges of interregional interaction outside migration, despite these limitations, may still be afflicted with severe problems in cultural transmission, as cultural constraints prevent the completion of the socialization process. These incomplete transmissions may, in turn, result in still more innovations, thereby creating new behavioral patterns and new types of artifacts that derive from them. Cross-cultural encounters with foreign items, such as interactions along the trade range, without proper acquaintance with the behavioral patterns connected with those items' functional field, and without a complete teaching mechanism for cultural transmission or even an encounter with objects with a modified cultural message (e.g., those made for export), may trigger a vast array of

Preparation	Consumption
hearths, ovens	vessels
other preparation installations	house layouts
tools, e.g., mortars, querns, flint and	gut contents
metal blades	coprolites
vessels; pottery, metal, basketry	cess
house layouts	human remains
food residues and remains	
butchery marks	

FIGURE 1.3. Archaeological evidence for foodways (after Samuel 1999: table 2)

innovation processes. Innovation may then be expressed in finding new uses for "foreign" pottery types by connecting them to existing behavioral patterns. Alternatively, some traits or elements of foreign object types may be adopted and incorporated into new types to fit local demands and behavioral patterns.

DEMONSTRATING DEEP CHANGE: CASE STUDIES FOR THE INFLUENCE OF MIGRATION ON BEHAVIORAL PATTERNS AND MATERIAL CULTURE

Further insights into the changes in behavioral patterns and material culture assemblages from the deep change of migration can be obtained from a survey of historical and archaeological case studies. The following case studies are connected directly or indirectly to domestic activities: foodways, subsistence patterns, architecture, gender, pottery technology, and textile production, and they have a regional emphasis on Anatolia, Cyprus, and the Levant.

It should be noted that, while all case studies have a significant role in attracting attention to and illuminating the theoretical questions posed previously about migrants' behavioral patterns, they cannot be taken as straightforward *comparanda*.

FOODWAYS

The provision of food is a complex process encompassing a variety of activities at a household level. Samuel (1999: 124, table 2; Fig. 1.3) defines five stages of food provision – procurement, storage, preparation, consumption, and disposal – all of which leave distinct material remains.

The differentiation in foodways is expected to be manifest in almost all cases of migration, even those involving a small number of migrants. First, as stated previously, foodways, as one of the most conservative aspects of culture, are a fundamental part of self-definition. However, daily cooking is generally conducted inside the house; thus, as a relatively low-prestige activity, it is expected to be influenced only slightly by outside pressures such as new fashions and styles of food preparation customs. Second, the preparation and consumption of food leaves many visible traces, such as cooking vessels, cooking implements, and food remains, making the differences between local and foreign foodways archaeologically conspicuous.

However, foodways are influenced by processes of acculturation. The possible lack of certain foodstuffs that were used in the country of origin, as well as a lack of cooking and serving utensils to fit the migrants' foodways, may result in a combination of several strategies to preserve traditional foodways. These include the import of food and utensils; the use of local ingredients and vessels, as well as the introduction of new plants and animals; and the local production of cooking and serving vessels in the migrants' tradition.

Historical archaeology provides broad evidence of the behavior of different migrant groups in North America. Chinese migrants were highly resourceful in their attempts to preserve foodways to be as similar as possible to those in their home country. Serving practices were of Chinese origin: bowls were used for serving instead of the plates used in Euro-American households, and some serving and storage vessels were imported from China (Diehl et al. 1998). A successful use of ethnographic evidence to illuminate a case of ancient migration is Branigan's (1984: 50) study of the Chinese colony in Bangkok, which he uses to support his argument for Minoan "community colonies" in the Cyclades and elsewhere. Although house design in Bangkok's Chinese quarter is similar to that in the Thai quarter, material culture within the houses clearly reflects differentiation between Thai and Chinese foodways. The Chinese kitchens include woks, wire sieves, bamboo steamers, and Mongolian hot pots; the Thai kitchens are equipped with mortars and pestles, portable stoves, and rice-boiling jars. In other regions, even slavery did not prevent the preservation of foodways. This is evident from the Colono ware – cooking and serving vessels from the eighteenth century carrying African traits, found in Virginia and South Carolina – and from the preservation of West African foodways in these regions (Deetz 1996: 242–3).

Because daily food preparation is considered a women's domestic chore in many cultures (Hendon 1996: 50), it is expected that, among migrants in a new country, women play a vital role in preserving cultural identity. The common phenomenon of intercultural marriages, either between migrants and indigenous populations or between migrants of different origins (see "Aspects of Gender") can further complicate the picture, as it may result in a combination of several traditions of foodways. An example of such a combination is in my home village of Beit Hanan, in the southern coastal plain of Israel. The village was founded mainly by immigrants from Bulgaria in 1929. The women of the village preserved the Jewish-Sephardic Balkan cooking tradition in daily dishes, and even more so in the festive ones. My late grandmother, Beracha Yesha'ayah, being of Jewish-Polish descent and married to a Jewish Bulgarian, cooked foods of both Polish and Bulgarian traditions, and passed them on to my mother.

A slightly different picture of the conservation of foodways is seen in the intermarriage of Punjabi immigrants and local Hispanic women in California at the beginning of the twentieth century. With respect to language and children's names, the domestic domain was mainly Hispanic (Leonard 1992: 131), yet cooking was both Mexican and Punjabi, as husbands or their unmarried compatriots taught Hispanic women Punjabi foodways and food taboos (Leonard 1992: 75, 129).

Other examples of the influence of intercultural marriage on foodways come from excavations conducted in St. Augustine, Florida, of eighteenth-century houses belonging to the descendants of a Native American woman who married a Spanish soldier. The finds show a mixed cultural heritage: the architecture is heavily influenced by Spanish styles, as are the prestigious majolica serving vessels, while the vessels for food preparation and cooking are entirely of Native American manufacture (Fairbanks 1976: 166).

Among the many instances of archaeological identification of so-called intrusive foodways in a Mediterranean setting, four are presented here to demonstrate the interdependency between migration and changes in foodways. It is important to note that, in all four cases, changes in foodways are not the sole criterion for the identification of migration but rather one of several deep changes in behavioral patterns that together form a pattern that can be explained only as migration.

The Early Bronze Age I Egyptian settlement in southern Palestine, of which the site of 'En Besor is representative, shows changes in foodways. The site contained a brick building (Building A, Phase III), built in the Egyptian style, which contained Egyptian sealings that indicate its function as an administrative center (Gophna and Gazit 1995: 66; Andelkovic 1995: 34). Egyptian foodways were connected to the building: beer was prepared in a large basin and bread was baked in crude, handmade, Egyptian-style baking trays (Gophna and Gazit 1995: 63, 65–6; Fig. 1.4); the cooking implements used for both differed significantly from the contemporary local Canaanite examples. Other activities, such as flint knapping (Gophna and Friedmann 1995; Fig. 1.5) and pottery manufacture, were also conducted in the Egyptian style at the site – but not inside the building. Recovered rims of Canaanite hole-mouth jars indicate some "local cooking" (Gophna 1995: 86), yet their find context is not reported, and it is unclear whether they originated from the administrative building.

The Syro-Canaanite settlement in the Nile Delta in the Middle Bronze Age ("Hyksos") was attested to not only by Syro-Canaanite burials, fineware, weapons, and architecture (Bietak 1997) but also by two distinctive Middle Bronze Age Canaanite types of cooking pots: handmade flat bottomed

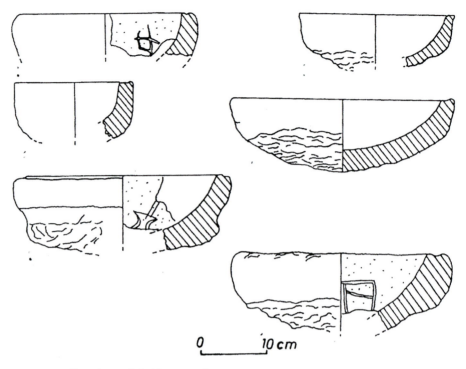

FIGURE 1.4. Egyptian-style baking trays, ʿEn Besor (after Andelkovic 1995: fig. 6: 7–12)

and hole mouth. Their appearance is especially conspicuous in Tell el-Dabʿa (Holladay 1997: 184) and in the Wadi Tumilat sites such as Tell el-Maskhuta (Holladay 1997: 195; Redmount 1995: 186; Fig. 1.6). These cooking pots are utterly different from the Egyptian ones, and they are locally made, which indicates that a change in foodways accompanied the Syro-Canaanite settlement in the Delta. Bietak (1996: 36) further argues that the lack of pig bones in the Canaanite temple of the Middle Bronze Age suggests a Canaanite food taboo.[8]

The Anatolian emigration to Cyprus in the Early Bronze Age manifests itself in changes in cooking vessels and installations alike at sites featuring Anatolian-style cooking pans and horseshoe-shaped hobs or hearth surrounds (Frankel, Webb, and Eslick 1996: 44; Frankel 2000).

These case studies demonstrate the strong relationship between migration and a change in a wide variety of behaviors relating to foodways, and they suggest that deep change in foodways may be a strong indicator of migration. Furthermore, once the case for migration is established, variability within foodways may attest to several sources for migration, including the possibility of intercultural marriages.

---

[8] On the generally slight role of domestic pigs in the Egyptian economy at that time, see Boessneck 1976: 32–3.

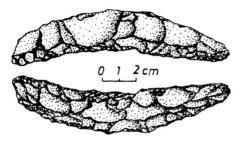

FIGURE 1.5. Egyptian-style flint blade, ʿEn Besor (after Andelkovic 1995: fig. 11: 15)

CHANGE IN SUBSISTENCE PATTERNS

Interconnected with the topic of foodways – but likely clearly visible archae-ologically only in interactions involving many participants – is change in subsistence patterns. Migrants dependent on agriculture who settle en masse in a foreign land will try to continue as much as possible their familiar patterns of subsistence, by engaging in the following:

1. Preferring a place that is physically similar to their country of origin: for example, the Greek migrants of the eighth and seventh centuries BCE chose Sybaris, Metapontum, Megara Hyblaea, and Selinus because of their agricultural land – fit for the cultivation of Mediterranean crops, mainly olive trees – despite the fact that the sites had no good natural harbors (Lombardo 1996).

2. Introducing crops familiar to them, such as the Greek colonists' introduc-tion of the olive tree to southern Italy (Lombardo 1996). The excavations in Pantanello, in the *chora* of Metapontum (Carter 1993: 354–5), have shown that there was a difference in the economy before and after the foundation of Metapontum by Greek colonists: the earlier, mixed settlements of Greeks and locals grew cereals, legumes, and vines, while olives were added only

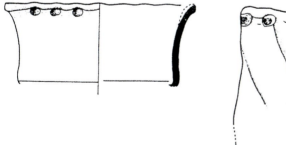
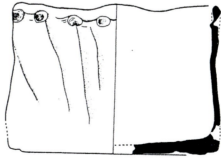

FIGURE 1.6. Typical Canaanite Middle Bronze IIA handmade cooking pot, Tell Maskhuta (after Redmount 1995: 186)

in the colonial period (ca. 600 BCE). Somewhat similarly, some Chinese immigrants introduced the ginkgo tree to North America, while others imported ginkgo nuts from China (Diehl et al. 1998: 22).

3. Introducing new animals or exploiting existing animals in a manner different from that of the local inhabitants, such as the introduction of horses, donkeys, cattle, goats, pigs, chickens, and other farm animals to North and South America, as well as to the Caribbean in the sixteenth and seventeenth centuries (Wing 1990; DeFrance 1996: 20). Such a change in animal husbandry can be demonstrated also for the *chora* of Metapontum (Carter 1993: 366): the ratios between sheep and/or goats and cattle are 1:1 in the indigenous Italian settlement of Incoronata of the seventh century BCE, while they are 2:1 in sixth-century-BCE Pantanello, after the foundation of Greek Metapontum. In the sixth century, priority was given to the breeding of horses – a phenomenon connected to the aristocratic ideal of the new settlers. Another example of change in animal husbandry patterns is the use of the pig in Toscanos, Spain (Whittaker 1974: 71). At the end of the eighth century BCE, excavations reveal that 80 percent of the bones were of pigs, but after the construction of the storage building at the site and the settlement of Phoenicians there, for whom the pig was a taboo, pig bones almost disappeared. Finally, the introduction to Cyprus of cattle and donkeys, as well as a new breed of goat, occurred at the beginning of the Early Bronze Age, simultaneous with numerous other changes in material culture that have been interpreted as emigration from Anatolia (Frankel et al. 1996: 45).

4. Introducing new agricultural implements and utensils: for example, the Egyptian-style sickle blades and knives produced locally in southern Canaan in the Early Bronze Age I period (Gophna and Friedmann 1995: 118–19; Andelkovic 1995: 34; Fig. 1.5) and the introduction of the plow and a new specialized type of sickle blade to Cyprus in the Early Bronze Age (Frankel et al. 1996: 45; Frankel 2000: 177).

5. Initiating an ecological change: mass settlement and division of land had a substantial influence on the ecology of the area settled, resulting in deforestation and pushing the local inhabitants into fringe areas. The well-organized Greek colonization in southern Italy led to the phenomena of deforestation, takeover, and redistribution of the fertile plain land by the new colonists (Lombardo 1996: 264–5). These processes pushed the autochthonous population of these areas to marginal zones while changing the patterns of their subsistence economy.

These examples illustrate that deep change in subsistence patterns may, in some cases, be the result of migrants trying to replicate subsistence patterns familiar to them from their home country. The introduction of new breeds of animals and new species of plants may accompany a migrant economy.

ARCHITECTURE

The European immigration to North America from the sixteenth to the eighteenth centuries supplies good historical case studies on the import of architectural styles and internal arrangements of houses by various migrant groups – particularly British, German, Swedes, and Finns, each of whom brought their own distinctive style. However, several architectural forms were quickly adapted by other migrant groups, as they were best fit for the climatic and economic conditions of the new land (Burmeister 2000: 541; see also Deetz 1996: 126, 134–7, 145, 215–17; Anthony 2000).

Case studies from the Mediterranean expose similar interdependence between migration and architecture, while the interaction parameter of the balance of power between the cultures involved in the interaction is related to the question of whether migrant traditions in architecture manifest only in domestic architecture or also in public and monumental architecture. In situations of conquest and colonization by an outside power of superior force, the newcomers are likely to manifest their identity not only in domestic but also in monumental architecture. Such is the case for Roman Corinth, founded as a Roman colony in 44 BCE (Alcock 2005), in which Roman-style temples to the Roman deities Apollo and Venus were built using construction techniques described as Italic. A similar situation is found in the Frankish rural settlement in the Kingdom of Jerusalem. House types were of European masonry rather than Arab (Ellenblum 1998: 90). The central planning of the villages (e.g., al-Qubaiba and Khirbet el-Burj; Boas and Arbel 1999) is manifested in their neatly organized appearance, similar to that of contemporary European villages, and by the location of central institutions and facilities, such as the church, central oven, and flour mill (Boas and Arbel 1999: 92–3). The plan of the village and its central facilities reflects the social structure and the settlers' customs, as well as their duties and their rights as landowners or leaseholders (as evidenced in contemporary documents; Boas and Arbel 1999: 69–70). In settlements for which there is documentation for a mixed Frankish and local population (as at al-Tayba, ʿAbud, and Teqoʿa), Frankish presence can be found in the evidence of Frankish-style churches and Frankish forts, or manor houses, located within or adjacent to the local Christian settlements (Ellenblum 1998: 119–41). Frankish farms and manor houses, located outside local settlements (Ellenblum 1998: 179–93), show European features in their masonry and architecture.

In Cyprus, it is only archaeological evidence that testifies to the rapid transition from the Chalcolithic single-room, circular house to the Early Bronze Age multiroom, rectilinear building. This change, as well as the introduction of mold-made mud bricks, is thought to be yet another indication of the Anatolian immigration in Cyprus (Frankel et al. 1996: 45–6; Frankel 2000: 175).

An explanation of migration should therefore be taken into account when interpreting a change in architecture, of either the interior or the exterior of structures. This is, of course, only in cases where a foreign origin of the change is demonstrated, thus eliminating the possibility of local innovation.

ASPECTS OF GENDER

A dearth of information about the destination, uncertainty concerning the manner of reception, and expectations of hardship on arrival may limit the first fleet of immigrants to unmarried young men and to husbands leaving their wives behind (Anthony 1990: 902; Leonard 1992: 23); however, there are also examples of pioneer women, the first in their family to emigrate, either single women or those who leave their husbands behind (Kadioğlu 1994: 539; Sörensen 1995: 104). These phenomena may lead to intercultural marriages between immigrant men and local women or between immigrant women and local men (Barbara 1994: 573; Stolcke 1995: 14). Such intermarriages may find their most revealing expression in domestic assemblages of material culture, as in the cases of St. Augustine, Florida, and of the Punjabi Californians, discussed previously. These interethnic unions played an important role in cultural transmission in a colonial environment; they were conduits for the introduction of cultural values and their manifestation in material culture. Furthermore, the offspring of intercultural marriages often had an important role in the creation of cultural innovation and new identities, aside from being helpful in facilitating intercultural contact as translators (Lightfoot 2005: 215).

Jeffery (1961) and Coldstream (1993) have put forward arguments for the important role of children of intercultural marriages in cultural transmission of the alphabet with respect to interaction between Greeks and other populations in the first half of the first millennium BCE.

Although immigrants bring with them to the new country their ideas about family structure and functions, as well as gender roles and labor division, these may change once they have settled, in part as a result of mixed marriages (Sakka, Dikaiou, and Kiosseoğlou 1999; Chun and Akutsu 2003: 107–9).

Textual sources relating to the era of Greek and Phoenician colonization of the first millennium BCE provide much information on the role of gender in ancient migration. However, the sources are not specific on the question of whether most of the Greek colonists were men who established families by marrying women of indigenous stock (as supported by Pomeroy 1975: 34) or whether many Greek women came with the men. The sources that mention Greek women in relation to colonization show that they were few and taken along because of their high status or their religious duties. Some were the wives of the *oikists*: the wife of Phalanthos sailed with him to Taras (Pausanias, *Description of Greece*, 10.10.6–8; Sakellariou 1990: 75). Graham (1984: 299) points out the possibility that the burial accompanying that is attributed to

Lamis, the *oikist* of Megara Hyblaea, is that of his wife. In addition, there are two cases of priestesses introducing cults of goddesses: Kleoboia at Thassos and Aristarcha at Massalia (Graham 1984: 302; see Chapter 8 in this volume). It is conceivable that these women were able to tend to the religious needs of the colony in its early days until local women or the female descendants of the colonists were trained.

There are two factors for able-bodied men being the great majority in any early stage of colonization:

1. The uncertainty of the conditions in the target country and other problems of information: in cases most typical of preindustrial colonization, preparation for settlement in a hostile environment includes securing a large proportion of potential soldiers.
2. Logistic limitations, in that most of the available space in the boats used for colonization, mostly of the oared-galley type, was filled with rowers and their equipment, with little space left for passengers. These ships simply did not have enough space to take as many women as they did male rowers (see detailed discussion in Chapter 4).

There is, however, a great deal of information on the important role of intermarriage in the shaping of the ancient Greek colonial society:

According to legendary tradition brought by Herodotus (1.146), when the Ionian settlers went to Miletus they took no wives with them, but on arrival, they killed the Carian men and married their womenfolk. This was by no means a common practice of Greek colonization, and Graham (1984: 295) suggests that the entire story is an etiological one, explaining some traditional odd practices of Milesian women in the days of Herodotus. In the historical foundation of Cyrene, all founders were men; this indicates that some intermarriages must have occurred (Herodotus 4.185; Graham 1984: 296). In addition, the fact that men and women in the North African colonies subsisted on different diets (Herodotus 4.186, mentioning women in Cyrene and Barca who observed local food taboos) suggests a situation of peaceful intermarriage between Greeks and local women, after which the women preserved their cultural origin by keeping their local foodways (Graham 1984: 297).

The quasi-historical tradition of the foundation of Phocaea combines the abduction of women and peaceful intermarriage with the local population (Sakellariou 1990: 146; Nicolaos of Damaskos no. 90 f. 51). Phocaea was settled by the illegitimate children of Phocaean fathers who took women from Orchomenos as prisoners. These children were expelled from Phokis and settled in Thorikos in Attica. Later, they participated in colonization with a band of Peloponnesians, following the Ionians. After several turns of fortune, Ouatios, the indigenous king of Kyme, granted the colonists land and the right to marry local women.

Although legendary in nature, the story of the foundation of Carthage as told by Justin (18.4–6) has three components that may reflect reality in the connection between women and migration. Both the passive and active roles of women are reflected, as is the multiethnic nature of the colonization party, even before reaching North Africa:

* The *oikist*, Elissa, is a woman, a princess.
* She is accompanied to Cyprus by the priest of Zeus, who brings along his wife and children.
* Most of the men who follow Elissa are young and unmarried. To provide them with women to marry, the fleet stops in Cyprus and abducts eighty young girls.

The archaeological evidence seems to suggest a picture as complicated as that arising from the literary sources, thereby attesting to the presence of local and Greek women in the overseas colonies. According to Morel (1984: 134–5), intermarriages were the most important form of integration of populations in the Greek colonization of southern Italy and Sicily. The name *Tataie*, inscribed on a sherd from seventh-century Cumae, has been interpreted as that of an Etruscan woman living in the Greek colony. An analysis of personal ornaments from the cemetery of Pithekoussai, which showed a clear preference for the local artistic tradition, has been interpreted as indicating that most, if not all, of the Greek colonists' women at that site were natives (Coldstream 1993: 90–4; 1994a: 145–6; Hodos 1999; for an opposing opinion, see Graham 1982: 147–8). Greek women seem to have also immigrated to Syracuse, as is evident from their names, found on stelae at Fusco, the colony's earliest cemetery (Graham 1982: 148; Holloway 1991: 51–2).

Finally, the early cemetery at Carthage, dating back to the second phase of the town's development, contains burial goods exhibiting local tradition (e.g., handmade vessels, use of ocher) that were foreign to the Phoenicians. In some tombs at the site, both Phoenician and local burial traditions are presented, indicating to Whittaker (1974: 70) a phenomenon of mixed marriages, perhaps to be connected to the account of local tribes joining the city after its foundation (Justin 18.5.16–17).

The profound and complicated effects of migration on the fabric of society, seen in the phenomena of intermarriages and migration of women, suggest that migration can explain changes in gender roles and in the division of labor observed in the archaeological record.

POTTERY TECHNOLOGY

It has been argued here that the process of pottery production is usually conservative, often preserved and taught within a kin-based group, and that innovations usually meet with considerable obstacles. Interregional interaction is a major source for the introduction of technological innovations (Frankel et al. 1996: 41). A change in pottery production necessarily means a change in behavioral patterns. As such, the criterion of instant deep change may be used to determine which changes can be suspected as results of interaction along the migration range.

Several examples of archaeological and historical cases in which such a deep change in production was recognized and associated with other changes in material culture to identify migration are mentioned here briefly. A well-documented case in literary and archaeological sources is that of the Dutch potters shipped to the Cape Colony by the Dutch East India Company to meet the demands of the local garrison and other inhabitants who did not use the local indigenous pottery (Jordan 2000: 116–17). The coarseware vases produced there were European in form and fit European foodways, yet they showed some simplifications in comparison to their European counterparts. This simplification and the lower quality of the vessels have been attributed to different causes, among them a low level of craftsmanship, lack of commercial competition, high consumer demand, and limited raw material (Jordan 2000: 135). Such a phenomenon may also have occurred in other cases of migration, thus posing difficulties for the archaeological identification of the exact origin of potters on the evidence of their products made locally in the new country.

According to Frankel and colleagues (1996: 42), "ceramics can be considered in three ways: in terms of technology, style and function." Changes detected in all three aspects of pottery are thought to document Anatolian migration to Cyprus in the Early Bronze Age (Frankel et al. 1996). Similarly, Egyptian production methods and clay recipes are among various nonlocal traits identified as Egyptian, indicating settlement in southern Canaan (Porath 1986–7).

Finally, the transition in the middle Meroitic period in Nubia from hand-made to wheel-made pottery, made of different clays, tempers, and shapes than the handmade pottery, is explained by Adams (1968: 200) as the result of the presence of foreign artisans, perhaps Egyptians. However, because a considerable portion of the decoration was of a Nubian and non-Egyptian nature, Adams supposed that local artisans were at least decorating the pots.

TEXTILE PRODUCTION

Textile production was likely the most common form of domestic product – closely associated with the work of women, and thus securely belonging in the heart of the domestic habitus. Migrant households brought spinning and weaving, essential household activities in preindustrial Europe (Hanawalt 1986: 9), to the New World. European immigrants to North America often possessed the know-how to produce household textiles. Most women immigrants knew how to spin, and this knowledge passed from mother to daughter.

Many others knew how to weave: women were taught mainly in the domestic setting, while some men came from the European weavers' guilds (Marks 1996: 3–4). The implements used were European: the horizontal frame loom, which was usually constructed in North America, sometimes incorporated parts brought from Europe. The settlers also used two types of European spinning wheels – the high or long wheel and the Saxony or flax wheel – both usually made locally (Wilson 1979: 241).

Because textile remains and looms are preserved only rarely in the archaeological record, information about changes in textile production can be retrieved only from more durable objects such as spindle whorls and loom weights. It is possible that, as in pottery production, the mechanism of accepting innovations in textile production is such that only a change in several behavioral patterns can be considered evidence for migration. Therefore, the following examples, in which changes in textile production practices have been interpreted as related to migration, cannot be considered as such without supporting evidence from other types of assemblages:

*   A soapstone spindle whorl of European shape found in L'Anse aux Meadows, the only identified Viking settlement in America, was interpreted as evidence of the presence of European women at the site (Thomas 1999: 186).
*   Two technological innovations in the textile industry are connected to the Early Bronze Age Anatolian immigration to Cyprus: the introduction of the warp-weighted loom (recovered among finds of loom weights) and the introduction of specially crafted spindle whorls with Anatolian parallels (Frankel et al. 1996: 43–4).
*   With respect to so-called Minoan colonization, Minoan-style loom weights were observed at various sites outside of Crete (Cadogan 1984: 14; Melas 1991: 180–2; Niemeier 1998: 27), indicating Minoan weaving practices.

Domestic textile production, such as the preparation of food, is among the most basic domestic behavioral patterns (discussed previously). Therefore, a deep change in domestic textile production – if it comes together with a change in other domestic behavioral patterns – may be taken as a strong indication of migration.

CAUSALITY OF MIGRATION

The possible causes of any interaction, migration included, are crucial for the reconstruction of that interaction and may, subsequently, contribute to the understanding of the complexity of the investigated phenomenon. Anthony's work (1990; 1997) on the archaeology of migration and the vast sociological and anthropological literature concerned with mechanisms of migration enables the presentation of several factors that influence the decision to migrate, the composition of the migrant population, the choice of destination, and the route taken.

The decision to migrate is often thought of as a cost-benefit process in which positive pull factors, attracting the migrant to the benefits of the new country, are joined by negative push factors that result from hardships in the society of origin (Anthony 1990: 899; 1997: 22). If the push and pull factors are strong enough, migration occurs. The following five factors are, for the most part, an elaboration of this simple concept:

1. *Motivation and personal expectation.* Most closely related to the push and pull factors, the motivation to migrate may derive from a combination of social and environmental reasons. The desire to improve one's economic and social status is prominent in many migrations, as is the desire to escape environmental pressure, such as natural catastrophe or land shortage (Anthony 1990: 900; 1997: 22–3; Burmeister 2000: 543–4). Ravenstein (1885, cited in Lee 1966: 47) supported economic motive as the most important in migration, taking push factors such as taxation, bad climate, and oppressive laws, as well as pull factors such as slavery and transportation, as other factors initiating migration.

2. *Information.* The decisions of whether and where to migrate depend heavily on the flow of information about potential destinations, their advantages, and the route to them. Information is often received through kinship networks, either through the activity of scouts sent forth to examine the possibility of settlement or through migrants who have already settled (Anthony 1990: 903; 1997: 23–4; Boyd 1989). Other informants may be members of the same kinship group who are involved in occupations that take them afar, such as soldiers, sailors, or merchants. Lee (1966: 55) highlights examples of migration streams led by reports of people of the same origin who migrated first and had information on obstacles and advantages.

3. *Obstacles en route.* Natural obstacles, such as seas, rivers, and mountains, and man-made ones (from borders to zones of war and hostility along the migration routes to residence permits), as well as the means to overcome them, add to the cost of migration (Lee 1966: 53; Anthony 1997: 24). Overcoming these factors may depend much on information and on the economic resources of the migrants.

4. *Level of technology.* The importance of technological advance as a limiting factor influencing the volume of migration was already discussed in terms of Ravenstein's laws of migration (1885: 288, cited in Lee 1966: 48).

5. *Level of social complexity.* The level of social complexity influences the ability to conduct different ranges of interaction and the degree of involvement of the rulership or government in interregional interaction. Because

it is not often discussed in the archaeological or sociological literature concerning migration, it is dealt with here in greater detail. It may be assumed that, interdependent with the technological level of the community, the greater is the social complexity, the better is the ability to conduct different ranges of interregional interaction. Complex forms of interaction, such as the establishment of large communities abroad and long-range, high-risk trade, require elaborate preparation and extensive resources. These interactions can be achieved more easily in a complex society of the level of a large chiefdom or state. In a less complex society, there are fewer ranges of interactions, and forms of interactions involving large groups of peoples are less likely to occur.

The level of power held by the rulership is tightly connected to the level of social complexity. In a centralist and complex system of government, there are greater ranges of interregional interaction that the government can manipulate and regulate to serve its own goals and benefit. In such systems, there is an emphasis on forms that bring profit to the ruler(s) or to government-related elite groups. Such forms may be interregional trade and trading posts and colonies, as well as interactions involving the maintenance and use of military might, whether domestically with the use of mercenaries or externally, as in the occupation of territories and the domination of foreign populations. The contact of the mother polity with the migrating populations is likely to remain strong and to be used to expand borders of the polity for political and economic gains. Because a centralist rulership is interested in controlling its subjects, there will be less encouragement of private migration that is not organized or supported by the government. A strong central government may have the means to prevent unwanted types of migration and interaction. The less centralist and more fragmented the type of rulership is – as when there are many groups of elites – the more likely it is that competition will lead to a greater push for migration for a part of the elite. In this way, complex forms of interactions unrelated to the mother country may be created, such as community colonies.

CONCLUSIONS

This chapter presented the methodological framework for a reconstruction of the social history of the Aegean migration to the southern Levant. It first presented a mode of description enabling the discussion of migration and other interactions without the use of typology. It then developed the criterion of an instant deep change as a tool to differentiate between changes caused by migration and those caused by other ranges of interaction. Because of the conservative nature of domestic behavioral patterns and their close connection to habitus and group identity, which is likely to persist in situations of migration, deep change in domestic assemblages is established as a strong indication of migration. A survey of historical and archaeological case studies illustrated the effects of deep change caused by migration on various behavioral patterns. Finally, the chapter presented a review of factors that affect the causality of migration, as a prelude to the discussion of causality in Chapters 3 and 4.

With these methodological tools at hand, it is now possible to set the scene for the focus of the work, and to review the social and political conditions in the thirteenth century and their effect on interregional interactions in the last phase of the Aegean palatial period.

2

SETTING THE SCENE: THE MYCENAEAN PALATIAL CULTURE AND THE OUTSIDE WORLD

Tens of thousands of Mycenaean vessels found in excavations, from Sicily in the west to Jordan in the east, are powerful attestations to various forms of inter-regional interaction involving the palatial Mycenaean civilization, the dominant power in the Aegean between the late fifteenth century and the end of the thirteenth century BCE (LHII–IIIB).[1] It is likely that for Philistine migrants reaching the southern coast of Canaan in the early twelfth century BCE, the Mycenaean palatial civilization – destroyed only one generation earlier – was fading rapidly from the realm of memory and entering the vast, vague, and perhaps mythical past. The Mycenaean palaces, each ruled by a powerful *wanax* that was supported by a literate administration and a circle of cultured elite, were a far cry from the postliterate, rough reality of the twelfth century, with its crude art and scarcity of raw material and resources.

Still, the LHIIIB Mycenaean interaction could have left a legacy of knowledge that would be highly advantageous to the Aegeans taking part in twelfth-century interactions. Thus, for example, information about foreign lands and sea and land routes used for trading in the LHIIIB period could have been used for decision making about migration destinations during the LHIIIC period. Knowledge about the organization of maritime expeditions for war and trade in the final palatial era could have been used to organize pirate raids and colonization parties during the postpalatial era.

The Linear B sources that deal with political structure and maritime activity in the thirteenth century BCE, many of which date to its very end, offer a unique and illuminating way to evaluate the scope of the palatial Mycenaean legacy compared to later interregional interaction during the twelfth century. These documents, as well as complementary archaeological evidence that has been interpreted as indicating thirteenth-century-BCE Aegean migration, allow for the reconstruction of the relationships among the Aegean social and

---

[1] The relative chronological scheme presented here follows that of Warren and Hankey (1989) and Mountjoy (1999a).

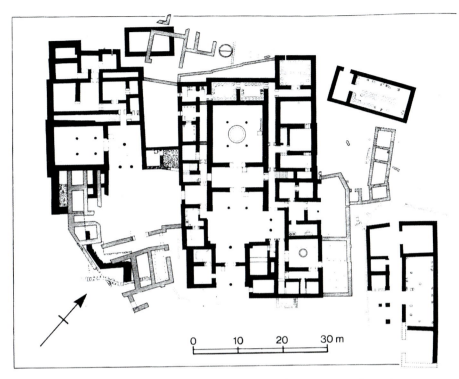

FIGURE 2.1. The LHIIIB palace at Pylos (after Blegen and Rawson 1966: fig. 417)

political structure, maritime capabilities, and possible maritime migration in the thirteenth century BCE.

SOCIAL COMPLEXITY IN THE MYCENAEAN PALATIAL SYSTEM

The Mycenaean palatial system can be defined as a set of regional polities, each centered on a large, multiroom structure, the palace, which served complex economic, religious, and political roles (Fig. 2.1). The physical remains of these palaces in sites, such as Mycenae, Pylos, Tiryns, and Thebes, and of archives of Linear B found within them allow for the reconstruction of a rich picture of the political system during the final part of the Late Bronze Age. To this study of migration and interaction, the Mycenaean data are of immeasurable value. A comparison between the power structure of the Mycenaean palatial society and the interregional interactions in which it was involved is an excellent opportunity to examine our hypothesis of the correlation between the level of social complexity and the ability to conduct different ranges of interregional interaction (Chapter 1). If this correlation indeed exists, we can expect to find variation in the more complex society of the thirteenth century than in the simpler postpalatial society. Following Clark and Parry (1990: 304–6; see also Murdock and Provost 1973), social complexity can be described as a function of social stratification and social integration (i.e., settlement hierarchy).[2] These two not only are among the most important indices in assessing the ability to conduct interregional interactions but also are most suited to the type of evidence that existed in the LHIIIB and LHIIIC Aegean.[3]

According to Linear B sources, most of which come from Pylos, the palace's complex social hierarchy was headed by the *wanax* (*wa-na-ka*). According to the tablets, this individual seems to have had both secular powers and a major role in religious activities (e.g., PY Un 2, Un 718; Palaima 1995b; 2006). Some of the workforce of the palace was under his direct command. There is no clear evidence of his military, judicial, or interstate role. It is likely that there was only one *wanax* per state (Shelmerdine 1997: 566); however, Rehak (1995) has reconstructed a model of collective rulership based on the iconography of enthroned figures and the archaeological contexts of thrones in the Aegean world. In this collective rulership, a small group of interconnected people, perhaps a family, holds positions of authority. Women who forged group unity played an important role in Mycenaean rulership. The iconography suggests that these women presided from their thrones over symposia held in the great hall of the Mycenaean palaces.

Second to the *wanax* was the *lawagetas* (*ra-wa-ke-ta*; literally, "leader of people"), who seems to have been the leader of the army or the chief minister. As in the case of the *wanax*, there was only one *lawagetas* in each polity (e.g., Un 718, Er 312; Lenz 1993: 83; Palaima 1995b: 129; 2006: 56; Shelmerdine 1997: 566–7).[4] High status was reserved for the *heqetai* (*e-qe-ta*), who were companions or followers, probably of the *wanax*. They may have constituted a chariot-borne military aristocracy or another elite group, perhaps with military as well as religious roles (Deger-Jalkotzy 1978; Aura-Jorro 1985: 230–2).

The view of the palatial system as a centralist monarchy was challenged in the late 1990s (Thomas 1995: 349; Deger-Jalkotzy 1996; Small 1998). The palace indeed had control over large estates and was involved in the allocation of land. Furthermore, it could impose obligations on individuals in the form of military or other services; however, its involvement in the economy was not absolute. It did not monopolize crafts or industries such as metallurgy. The palaces exercised direct supervision over only the most important industries that provided goods for trade (Shelmerdine 2006), and they had symbiotic relationships with a large private sector that practiced much of

[2] Because social complexity features both vertical (e.g., in general, social stratification) and horizontal (i.e., between groups of similar status) differentiation, social stratification (though a crucial element in establishing vertical complexity) cannot be used by itself to establish complexity in general. Cf. MacIntosh (1999: 9–11), who cites the Igbo (Ibo) as an example of people with a complex society, manifesting trade networks and clusters of villages with many thousands of residents, yet without centralized rulership.
[3] Other variables of social complexity, such as economic and cultural integration (Rothman 1994: 4), are also closely connected to political integration and social stratification.
[4] For different opinions of the *lawagetas* as a local official, see Thomas 1995: 351.

its economic activity outside palace control (Halstead 1992). There is also a growing conviction, based on more recent reconstructions of the formation of the Mycenaean polity (Bennet 1995; Voutsaki 1995), that local leaders, though associated with the polity headed by the *wanax*, continued to maintain considerable power within their regions (Thomas 1995: 352). These local leaders may have appeared in the Pylos tablets under the title of *basileus* (*qa-si-re-u*, pl. *qa-si-re-we*; Palaima 2006: 68). Some have suggested that this title refers to local leaders of secondary importance, vassals to the *wanax*, their territories reflecting the former polities that were incorporated into the Mycenaean state under the *wanax* (Shelmerdine 1997: 566; Palaima 1995b: 124). In their role as regional chieftains, they may have interacted with the palace in economic matters, such as supervising groups of bronze workers.

Other functionaries were probably also connected to the local leadership as well as to the palatial administration. The *koreter* (*ko-re-te*) and *prokoreter* (*po-ro-ko-re-te*) were mayors and vice mayors of the sixteen major economic districts of Pylos (PY Jn 829; Palaima 1995b: 124; Shelmerdine 1997: 566). Kilian (1988a: 293) has suggested that they were in charge of the *damoi*. The *telestai* (*te-re-ta*) were a group of officials, possibly with religious duties, or fief holders (Aura-Jorro 1993: 338; Kazanskiene 1995). The *geronsia* (*ke-ro-si-ja*) may have been a council of elders, perhaps connected to the *basileus*, or alternatively a collective of some kind, linked with plots of land and bronze working (Carlier 1995: 363). The *basileia* (*qa-si-re-wi-ja*) may have functioned in a similar role, connected with the *basileus* (Lenz 1993: 106–7).

References are also made to less powerful groups. The *damos* (*da-mo*) seems to be a lower echelon of people that held and administrated land in addition to producing food. Alternatively, it may have been a council in charge of local decision making. A possibly parallel group is the *worgioneion*, perhaps a class of outsiders (Lenz 1993: 106; Palaima 1995b: 132).

The *doeros* and *doera* (*do-e-ro*, *do-e-ra*), probably meaning "servant" or "bondsman or bondswoman," were either slaves or servants or religious titles for priests and/or priestesses, each viewed as a "servant (of the god)." Some of them are described as belonging to a god or a goddess, while others belonged to living persons (Aura-Jorro 1993: 186–7; Killen 2006).

As for settlement hierarchy – another component of social complexity – the evidence from the tablets implies three or four administrative levels above that of a local community: the local center, the inner fiscal unit within the province, the province, and the polity (Bennet 1998: 113–23). Another source of information that contributes to the investigation of political integration is analyses of site distribution and size. These studies result in the establishment of possible boundaries for polities and internal organization, and they provide clues to the hierarchies within the polities. The survey of the Pylos region again reflects a picture of a three-tier (Davis et al. 1997: 424–7, 483–4) or four-tier (Bennet 1998: 123–4) settlement hierarchy, with the palace positioned above towns and smaller communities. The settlement hierarchy for the Argolid suggested by Kilian (1988a: 297, fig. 3) and Sjöberg (2004: figs. 8–10; Fig. 2.2) shows a more complex picture. Mycenae and Tiryns present a settlement hierarchy of at least three tiers with a major center, subcenters (some fortified), villages, hamlets, and a sanctuary site. Other centers, such as Nauplion, Midea, Argos, or Asine, may have been dominated by Mycenae and Tiryns or have had only a two- to three-tiered settlement hierarchy. It is likely that other LHIIIB palaces with record-keeping capabilities (e.g., Thebes) reached a complexity similar to that of Mycenae and Tiryns.

The high level of social complexity and political integration seen in the intricate hierarchy of the Aegean polities of the thirteenth century BCE must have had a direct effect on the maritime capabilities of the polities, because, as will be argued herein, this high level of social complexity enabled, at least potentially, the launching of sophisticated and varied forms of maritime inter- action, which were impossible in a less complex system (e.g., that of LHIIIC).

AEGEAN PEOPLES AND MEDITERRANEAN GEOGRAPHY

What did the people of the Aegean know about Mediterranean geography, and was that knowledge restricted to specific sectors of society? The answer to these questions may provide us with one of the most important insights needed to determine the nature of twelfth-century migrations: the information on possible migration destinations. In this section, references to foreigners and foreign names in the Linear B tablets and evidence from Late Bronze Age maritime trade will be compared to assess the amount of relevant information available to people in the Aegean during the thirteenth century.[5]

FROM LINEAR B TO AHHIYAWA

A lack of evidence of diplomatic relations between the Aegean and the Near East in the thirteenth century BCE – save, perhaps, the contact between Hatti and the neighboring Ahhiyawa kingdom (Hawkins 1998; Mountjoy 1998; Niemeier 1998: 25–6, 41–5) – may attest to the limited involvement of the Aegean rulership in Near Eastern politics. No evidence has been found of diplomatic relations with Nineteenth Dynasty Egypt following the peak in the days of the Eighteenth Dynasty (e.g., the Aegean list of Amenhotep III and Theban tomb paintings; Wachsmann 1987; Cline 1994: 38–40). The only Aegeans depicted and mentioned in the thirteenth century BCE are not

---

[5] Other potentially valuable sources of information about interconnections, such as provenance studies of pottery and other artifacts are not discussed here because of the need to
assess and interpret trade patterns (e.g., direct and indirect trade) for each case before using
these data to study interconnections.

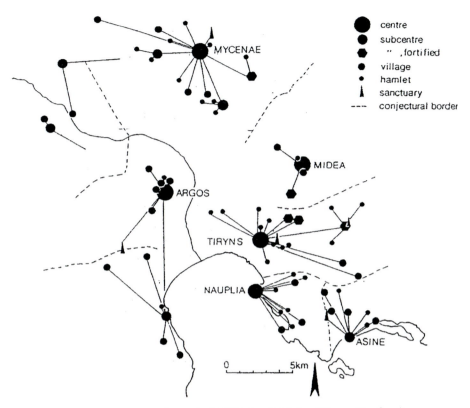

FIGURE 2.2. Settlement hierarchy in the LHIIIB Argolid (after Kilian 1988a: fig. 3)

diplomats or merchants, but Shardana mercenaries, if they were at all of Aegean origin (Sandars 1978: 106–7; Drews 1993: 152–6).

The knowledge of foreign lands available to the palatial elite and its bureaucracy is best reflected in the personal and ethnic names of foreigners, as well as in Semitic and Hittite loanwords for commodities (Shelmerdine 1998: 292; Palaima 1991: 278–9; Cline 1994: 50); however, loanwords are not decisive in terms of finding out the extent of Mycenaean geographical knowledge, as they can be transmitted through agents (e.g., traders) of a different ethnicity. A rather maximalist list of Linear B place-names outside the Mycenaean mainland and Crete includes references to people and commodities originating from western Anatolia, Egypt, and Cyprus, and possibly from Phoenicia and the Ionian Islands (Fig. 2.3, Table 2.1). Accordingly, it is possible to cautiously draw at least a rough picture of the mainland (i.e., Pylian, Theban, and Mycenaean) and Knossian spheres of interaction, at least in regard to the foreign people mentioned in the texts. These included men and women; some appear as individuals, and others – mostly women – were employed as groups in the Pylian textile industry (Chadwick 1988; Nosch 2003). The foreigners represent a plethora of status groups, from female servants and bath attendants in the Pylian palace to a Milesian man participating in a cultic event in Thebes.

TABLE 2.1. *Foreigners in the Linear B record*

Egypt	*mi-sa-ra-jo*: Egyptian man (Knossos)	KN F 841.4; Aura-Jorro 1985: 454; Cline 1994: 128
	a₃-ku-pi-ti-jo: Memphite man (Knossos)	KN Db 1105.B; Aura-Jorro 1985: 136–7; Cline 1994: 128; Shelmerdine 1998: 295
Cyprus	*ku-pi-ri-jo*: Cypriot man and Cypriot commodity (Pylos and Knossos); another option: "Gublite" (from Byblos)	Many references, among them PY Cn 719.7, Jn 320.3, Un 443.1; KN Fh347.1, Gg 995; Aura-Jorro 1985: 405; Palaima 1991: 280–1; Cline 1994: 130; Shelmerdine 1998: 295
	a-ra-si-jo: Alashiyan man (Knossos)	KN Df 1229.B, Fh 369, X 1463; Aura-Jorro 1985: 96; Cline 1994: 130
Phoenicia	*pe-ri-ta*: man from Beirut (?) (Knossos)	KN V 60.5; Aura-Jorro 1993: 112; Cline 1994: 129
	tu-ri-jo: man from Tyre (?) (Knossos and Pylos)	KN Nc 4473; PY Jn 693.8; Aura-Jorro 1993: 378; Cline 1994: 129
	po-ni-ki-jo: man (?) or spice (?) from Phoenicia (Knossos)	KN Bg 834, 992, 1021, and many other examples in Aura-Jorro 1993: 139–40
	a-ra-da-jo: man from Arad/Arvad (Knossos)	KN 1516.3; Aura-Jorro 1985: 93; Cline 1994: 124
Anatolia	*mi-ra-ti-ja*: women from Miletus (Pylos)	PY Aa 798, 1180, Ab 382.B, 573.B, Ad 380, 689; Palaima 1991: 279–80; Aura-Jorro 1993: 453–4; Cline 1994: 130; Shelmerdine 1998: 293
	mi-ra-ti-jo: man from Miletus (Thebes)	TH Fq 177, 198, 214, 244, 254 + 255, 269, 276; Shelmerdine 1998: 295; Aravantinos, Godart and Sacconi 2001: 393
	ze-pu₂-ra₃: women from Halikarnassos (Pylos)	PY Aa 61, Ad 664; Aura-Jorro 1993: 456; Cline 1994: 130
	ki-ni-di-ja: women from Knidos (Pylos)	PY Aa 792, Ab 189.B, An 292.4, Ad 683; Aura-Jorro 1985: 360; Cline 1994: 130
	ki-si-wi-ja: women from Chios (Pylos)	PY Aa 770, Ab 194.B, Ad 675; Aura-Jorro 1985: 364
	ki-si-wi-jo: man from Chios (Knossos)	KN V 60.2; Aura-Jorro 1985: 199
	ra-mi-ni-ja: women from Lemnos and *ra-mi-ni-jo*: man from Lemnos (Pylos)[a]	PY Ab 186.B, An 209.2; Aura-Jorro 1993: 218–9
	i-wa-si-jo-ta: men from Iasos (Pylos)	PY Cn 3.5; Aura-Jorro 1985: 290–1; cf. Bennet 1998: 132
	a-*64-ja: women from Asia/Lydia (Pylos)	PY Vn 1191.2, Az 701, Ab 515.B, Ad 315, 326; Aura-Jorro 1985: 125–6
	a-*64-jo: man from Asia/Lydia (Pylos and Knossos)	KN Sc 261; PY Cn 1287.1, Fn 324.3; Aura-Jorro 1985: 126
	a-si-wi-jo: man from Asia/Lydia (Mycenae, Pylos, and Knossos)	KN Df 1469.B; PY Cn 285.12, Eq 146.11; MY Au 653.5, 657.11; Aura-Jorro 1985: 100; Cline 1994: 130; Shelmerdine 1998: 295
	a-si-wi-ja; an epithet of a goddess (Pylos)	PY Fr 1206; Aura-Jorro 1985: 110
	i-ja-wo-ne: Ionian men (Knossos)[b]	KN B 164.4, Xd 146.6; Driessen and Macdonald 1984: 51; Aura-Jorro 1985: 237
Ionian Islands	*za-ku-si-jo/-ja*: Zakynthian men and type of chariot wheels (Pylos);[c] personal name (Mycenae)	PY An 610, Sa 751, 787.B; Palaima 1991: 281; MY Oe 122; Aura-Jorro 1993: 454
	ko-ro-ku-ra-i-jo: man from Corcyra (?) (Pylos)	PY An 641.4 (?), 656.7, 756.18, 661.4–6, Na 396, 405, 510; Aura-Jorro 1985: 385

[a] For archaeological aspects of the interactions between the Mycenaean world and the northeastern Aegean islands, see Guzowska and Yasur-Landau 2003.

[b] However, the location of Ionia or the Ionian tribe in the Late Bronze Age is not certain, and it is assigned here to Anatolia only because of later references.

[c] See the text of this chapter on Zakynthian men in the Rower Tablets.

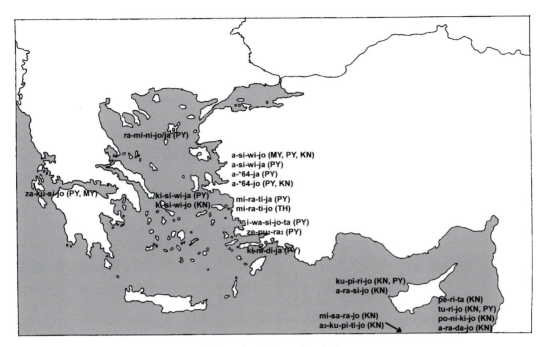

FIGURE 2.3. Foreign names in Linear B (drawn by A. Yasur-Landau)

The impact of these foreigners on their environment was probably considerable, and it was reflected in the introduction of the Anatolian deity *po-ti-ni-ja a-si-wi-ja*, "the mistress of Asia," into the Pylian pantheon (Morris 2001).

As these foreigners were apparently residing within the Aegean area for extended periods of time, they provided a source of information, accessible, perhaps, to almost all in the palatial circles. It can be tentatively suggested that such knowledge could be obtained only regarding the area between the Ionian Islands and Phoenicia. The sphere of Pylos, Thebes, and Mycenae probably did not reach Egypt at the end of the LHIIIB2 period (Shelmerdine 1998: 295) but included much of the eastern Mediterranean from Phoenicia to Lydia (including Cyprus, Crete, and the Dodecanese). The Knossian sphere of interaction, probably reflecting a reality of up to a century earlier than the Pylos tablets (Shelmerdine 1998: 294), included some mention of Egypt but did not encompass the Ionian Islands and extend to western Anatolia.

The lack of mainland references to Egypt may indicate a sharp decrease in the interaction with the Aegean during the days of the Nineteenth Dynasty, reflected also in the absence of Nineteenth Dynasty objects from Aegean LHIIIB/LMIIIB assemblages (Phillips 2005: 460). The frequent mention of commodities called Alashiyan and Phoenician is of importance in understanding the items traded with these regions and their significance to the Mycenaean economy, yet it is possible that they were named so because they were brought by Syrian or Cypriot merchants. The lack of reference to people coming from the Dodecanese and the Cyclades is remarkable but remains without a satisfactory explanation. The conspicuous absence of people from sites located on the coast of Palestine, and only very doubtful occurrences of sites along the Phoenician coast, may, however, be more easily explained than the omission of Ugarit, the most important gateway to Mycenaean pottery in the Levant. This may be another indication that trade was carried out not by Mycenaeans but by Cypriots or other intermediaries. Such a notion is also supported by the fact that while Alashiyans are frequently mentioned in the Ugarit texts (e.g., the Alashiyan ship in KTU 3.390; Hoftijzer and van Soldt 1998: 339), and Sinaranu, an Ugaritian, had a ship that sailed to Crete (Cline 1994: 120; B.3), there is no mention of Aegean traders in Ugarit. Furthermore, when men of (Ah)hiyawa are mentioned in two letters from Ugarit, they are Aegean mercenaries or traders located not in Ugarit but in the land of Lukka, in southwestern Anatolia (RS 94.2523 and RS 94.2530; Lackenbacher and Malbran-Labat 2005: 237–8; Singer 2006: 250–2).

Indeed, Hankey's 1967 idea of the instrumental role of Cypriots in the trade of Mycenaean pottery seems to gather additional support each year. Archaeological evidence for this role in the Levantine coast is discussed in Chapter 6.

The lack of any reference to the Hittites in the Linear B record is a constant source of frustration, as Ahhiyawa, mentioned several times in Hittite texts, is commonly thought to be located in the Mycenaean mainland (its center in Thebes or Mycenae) with an Anatolian bridgehead between Miletus and Bodrum (Niemeier 1998; 2005). It is apparent that many of these connections had a diplomatic nature, as Ahhiyawa was extremely active politically in western Anatolia, usually acting against the Hittite interests in the region. Some of these references are concerned with maritime activities but never with trade. The coastal location of Ahhiyawa is reflected in a letter from the Hittite king to the king of Ahhiyawa, possibly from the days of Arnuwanda I (KUB 26.91; Cline 1994: 121), which mentions islands belonging to the king of Ahhiyawa. Similarly, "The Ten Year Annals of Muršili II" (CTH 61 = KBo 3.4 + KUB 23.125) contains a fragmentary passage in which the renegade Uḫḫaziti escapes on a ship to the king of Ahhiyawa (Mineck, Van Den Hout, and Hoffner 2006: 254).

Evidence for maritime raids with Ahhiyawan participation can be seen in the "Indictment of Madduwatta" (CTH 147 = KUB 14.1 + KBo 19.38), datable to the beginning of the fourteenth century and to kings Tudhaliya I and Arnuwanda I. Madduwatta, the Hittite vassal, reported of conducting raids against Alashiya at the same time that Attarasiya of Ahhiya (the older version of Ahhiyawa) made similar raids (Güterbock 1983: 134; Cline 1994: 121; Wachsmann 1998: 128–9). Raids on Cyprus from the Anatolian coast continued later, with the Lukka as the named culprits for attacks on Cyprus during the Amarna period (EA 38: 10–12; Wachsmann 1998: 130). The "Saus-gamuwa Treaty" (StBoT 16) from the days of Tudhaliya IV – the late thirteenth century – supposedly mentions ships of Ahhiyawa that are to be prevented from unloading in the ports of Amurru (Güterbock 1983: 136; Cline 1994: 124; Mountjoy 1998: 49). However, the beginning of line 23 of the text is broken and can be reconstructed either as [ŠA KUR aḫ-ḫ]i-ia-u-wa-aš-ši GIŠ.MÁ, "ships of the land of Ahhiyawa," or, as Steiner (1989) suggests, [la-aḫ-ḫ]i-ia-u-wa-aš-ši GIŠ.MÁ, "war ships."

Further proof that the Ahhiyawan-Hittite relations were by no means commercial ones comes from the almost complete absence of Mycenaean finds in Hattusa, the capital of the Hittites. It is ironic that Hatti, the only polity that we know to have had direct diplomatic contact with Mycenaeans, is the only polity in the eastern Mediterranean that did not import massive amounts of Mycenaean pottery. With no Hittites in the Linear B archives and no Mycenaean pottery in Hattusa, the involvement of the kingdom of Ahhiyawa in trade interactions with Anatolia seems to be marginal at best, particularly when compared to its role in raids, political stirring, and active participation in the power struggle in western Anatolia.

MARINERS AND TRADERS

The existence of a flourishing thirteenth-century maritime trade in finished products and in raw material (Sherratt and Sherratt 1991: 370–3; Bass 1997a; 1998; Leonard 1998; cf. Halstead 1994: 209) indicates that knowledge of foreign lands could have been brought to the Aegean, and that the people living in the Aegean could have had some exposure to people from outside the Aegean world.

Assessing the extent and depth of knowledge of foreign lands on the part of people in the Aegean is, to a large measure, dependent on identifying the people who practiced maritime trade in the Late Bronze Age and even on estimating the volume of trade. There are only three or four extant shipwrecks dated between the end of the fourteenth and the end of the thirteenth centuries BCE; these being from Uluburun, Cape Gelidonya, and Point Iria, and perhaps another at Kibbutz Hahotrim (Bass 1997a: 168–9). The archaeological identification of the nationality of a ship may be an impossible mission, and probably also meaningless. A ship may be built in one place and used in the service of a shipowner from another port; it may carry sailors of various origins. In addition, the origins of the cargo are not necessarily related to the origins of crew members or of the ship itself (Bass 1998: 188; Vichos 1999). Identifying the origin of the ships and their crews on the basis of personal belongings presents its own complications, as those may represent a sailor's trade in small exotic objects or be souvenirs from foreign countries (Bass 1998).

The Uluburun ship presents the most compelling set of evidence in support of a reconstruction of a ship crewed by Levantines or Cypriots as well as Mycenaeans. Bass (1991: 74; 1997a: 168) first identified the ship as Syro-Palestinian. Recently, Pulak (2005) interpreted the four sets of weights in the Syro-Palestinian standard as evidence for the presence of four Canaanite or Cypriot merchants aboard the ship. Further evidence for their presence is given by cylinder seals and Syrian weapons. Two Mycenaean Type Di swords and two steatite sealstones indicated, to Pulak's (2005) mind, the presence of two Mycenaeans aboard the ship, escorting the precious cargo to the Aegean (cf. Cline 1994: 274; Bass 1998: 188). A Mycenaean drinking set, including a beaked jug, a narrow-necked jug, a cup, a dipper, and a kylix, may have been used by them. Mycenaean-style knives and razors can also be attributed to the same high-ranking individuals. A Thapsos-type sword and a stone scepter or mace, both of Balkan origin, indicated to Pulak the presence of a third foreigner on board, perhaps a Balkan mercenary in the service of the Mycenaeans.

Mariners' oral traditions may have played an important role in the conveying of knowledge from area to area and from one generation of sailors to the next. Merchants of non-Aegean origin may also have been an important source of firsthand information, available to both local merchants and ruling elite. The range of trade seems to have been extremely wide in the LHIIIA and LHIIIB (Gillis 1995; Schallin 1995: 48–9), starting with palatial and elite trade in raw materials and culminating with luxury products as well as royal gift exchanges. There was also maritime trade in more mundane objects, as demonstrated in the cargoes from Cape Gelidonya (Bass 1967; 1998: 188) and Point Iria (Lolos 1995; Vichos and Lolos 1997). Whether as a royal or a private venture, trade can be assumed to have been conducted by both Mycenaeans and people from the eastern Mediterranean alike, perhaps working in business partnerships, sharing knowledge and profit. Trade could well have been conducted alongside other interactions, which would blur the material culture evidence.

THIRTEENTH-CENTURY AEGEAN MARITIME CAPABILITIES AND INTERREGIONAL INTERACTIONS

THE ROWER TABLETS

Whether well informed about the world outside or largely oblivious to the lands beyond the Aegean proper, there is, nevertheless, ample evidence that the Mycenaean palaces had developed maritime capabilities to fit their needs. The Rower Tablets from Pylos, as well as a handful of other texts and iconographic representations, bear witness to the abilities of the LHIIIC palatial system to muster ships and crew.

Three texts from Pylos, belonging to the PY An series and mentioning *e-re-ta* (rowers), thus, coming to be known as the Rower Tablets, provide tantalizing evidence for the naval organizational capabilities of Pylos, as well as for a possible connection between settlement and land ownership and maritime activities.

The first, PY An 610, is a large tablet; its title (line 1) was damaged, but the term *e-ra-ta* indicates that it presents a list of rowers. Lines 2–15 list groups of men – two groups to a line (Ventris and Chadwick 1973: 186–7, 431; Chadwick 1987: 76; Wachsmann 1998: 123–4) – totaling 569 or 578 people. The groups are defined according to the following criteria:

⋆ Their association with the dignitaries *e-ke-ra₂-wo* (the *wanax*) and *we-da-ne-u*
⋆ Groups, connected to coastal settlements and known from other sources of names with maritime connections
⋆ Their definition as immigrants or additional people – *po-si-ke-te-re* (*ποσ–hικτήρ; Aura-Jorro 1993: 156–7)
⋆ Their definition as settlers or inhabitants – *ki-ti-ta* (κτιτᾶς or κτιστᾶς; Aura-Jorro 1985: 367–8)
⋆ Their definition as accompanying and/or new settlers – *me-ta-ki-ti-ta* (*μετα–κτιτᾶς or κτιστᾶς; Aura-Jorro 1985: 442–3)
⋆ Their definition by the attribute *po-ku-ta* (Aura-Jorro 1993: 136). While there is no agreement on the meaning of this term, Ruijgh (1992) suggests that these were individuals associated with or in charge of small animals (e.g., sheep and goats), perhaps inferior to the *ki-ti-ta*.

The second tablet, PY An 724, refers to missing or exempted rowers, possibly connected to the same event as PY An 610. It is divided into paragraphs according to place-names (Ventris and Chadwick 1973: 187–8, 431–2; Wachsmann 1998: 124–5). The numbers of people in each entry in this tablet are much smaller than in PY An 610; the largest group lists only ten men. Line 1, the title, relates to the place-name *ro-o-wa* and to the fact that this is a list of missing rowers. Lines 3–4 present the information that one of the men is a *ki-ti-ta* and is therefore obliged to row. Five other people who are also obliged to row appear in lines 5–6.

The shortest of the texts, PY An 1, is a list of thirty rowers called to crew a ship connected with Pleuron (line 1). These men come from five settlements, with a formula structure similar to that of PY An 610 (lines 2–6) (Ventris and Chadwick 1973: 185–6, 430–1; Wachsmann 1998: 126).

Judging from the Rower Tablets, it seems that the Pylos administration was able to recruit rowers according to its needs. It probably effected this through the same mechanism used for tax collection and recruitment of corvée labor (e.g., for Tiryns, Kilian 1988b: 149). The rowers were recruited from or assembled in a number of coastal settlements. Recruitment was carried out according to palace needs and the relative capacity of every settlement (Wachsmann 1998: 126), and records were kept of those rowers who reported for duty and of those who did not report or were exempted. Some of the recruits were obliged to row (*ki-ti-ta o-pe-ro-ta e-re-e*) because of their status as settlers or landholders (Palaima 1991: 286; 2000: 262).[6] The total recruitment capacity represented in these tablets is approximately six hundred men (not including the numbers of exempted men listed in PY An 724) – a large enough number to man a fleet of twenty triaconters (possibly the type of ship manned in the PY An 1 tablet), or twelve penteconters (Wachsmann 1998: 123). The title *e-re-e-u* (official in charge of rowers) that appears at Pylos and at Knossos (Palaima 1991: 286–304; Wachsmann 1998: 127) may indicate that the administration of the recruitment and training of the rowers existed at the community level. Mycenaean interest in monitoring at least some of the ships and their registration according to their place of origin and the men in charge of them is also suggested (Palaima 1991: 287–8).

The terms used in the Pylos tablets to describe recruits may offer important information not only on the administrative aspects of the recruitment procedure and the status differentiation among the recruits but also on the reason the rowers were recruited. The interpretation of these terms is, however, hampered by a lack of parallels for the texts and by their laconic, administrative nature.

Chadwick (1987: 79–82) proposed that the terms *ki-ti-ta*, *me-ta-ki-ti-ta*, *po-si-ke-te-re*, and *po-ku-ta* are connected to landholding. They refer to settlers or future settlers in places within the mainland realm of the Pylos kingdom. Such people were obliged to serve as rowers in return for their plots. However, this interpretation does not explain why these three terms do not appear in any context outside PY An 610 and 724. Moreover, had these people been allotted plots within the kingdom, one would expect the terms to appear in tablets discussing land ownership and use, such as the varied E series (Ventris and Chadwick 1973: 232–9). If indeed the semantic meaning of *ki-ti-ta* was a person who holds *ktimena*-type land (i.e., private, inhabited, or cultivated; Aura-Jorro 1985: 366–7), we would expect to find this title in records of taxation mentioning this type of land. Hence, although the words *ki-ti-me-na* and *ki-ti-ta* are connected linguistically by the root **kti-* (appearing, for example, in the words *settler* and *settled* [land]), they probably had no common ground as technical terms in the Pylian polity.

A possible solution for this problem stems from Wachsmann's suggestion that at least some of the titles were related to groups about to settle outside the boundaries of the Pylian polity, yet whom were possibly still under some sort of obligation to Pylos. Wachsmann (1998: 160) sees the *ki-ti-ta* as people previously settled in a colony founded by Pylos, and the *me-ta-ki-ti-ta* as new settlers going on a colonization expedition, perhaps to the same colony. A variation on this interpretation is the proposal that both the *ki-ti-ta* and the

---

[6] The term *o-pe-ro-* was also used in the Pylian administration to describe other obligations to the palace.

me-ta-ki-ti-ta had already settled in the colony, and the *po-si-ke-te-re* were new settlers. The fact that the terms *ki-ti-ta* and *me-ta-ki-ti-ta* appear only in a maritime context supports the identification of the recruits as a maritime colonization party. Further support is found in the presence of Zakynthian men among the rowers, perhaps indicating the direction of the fleet.

The interpretation of *me-ta-ki-ti-ta* as "fellow settler" (Ventris and Chadwick 1973: 560) hints at a difference in status by virtue of its position as a secondary group proceeding the *ki-ti-ta* in every formula, in Chadwick's reconstruction (1987) of PY An 610.

There are three possible interpretations of this differentiation according to status. The first would have far-reaching consequences for Pylos's exercise of control through a system of obligation over its newly founded settlements: The *ki-ti-ta* were still connected to the Pylos administration system, while the other groups taking part in the expedition were not obliged to row after settling, perhaps because they were not connected to the administrative system of taxation in the first place. A second possibility is that the *ki-ti-ta* were veteran settlers and that only persons of that category were obliged to row, while the *me-ta-ki-ti-ta* rowed only on their way to the destination. The third possible interpretation is the simplest and perhaps the most plausible: all categories of rowers embarked on colonization; there was an internal hierarchy headed by the main body of settlers (*ki-ti-ta*) and comprising the people accompanying them (*me-ta-ki-ti-ta*) and other smaller auxiliary groups of settlers or people with specialized duties, such as Zakynthian men.

The possible differentiation in terminology between preliminary and secondary colonists in Pylos is strikingly similar to the fifth-century-BCE terms ἄποικος and ἔποικς. The first can be translated simply as "colonist"; the other may mean "secondary settler" or "additional settler" (Figueira 1991: 14–20). Another fifth-century term is κληρούχος. (Figueira 1991: 9–10), used for the settlers of Mytilene and perhaps indicating settlers who reside in a community (κληρούχια) that is not a polis and officially belongs to the mother city. There is also evidence for a different Athenian legal status for the ἄποικος and the κληρούχος (Figueira 1991: 11, 66–72).

There is little evidence for interconnections between the Pylian polity and the island of Zakynthos, yet seven or eight Zakynthian men are listed in PY An 610 (Wachsmann 1998: 124). Other references to Zakynthos are found in the Pylos tablets that discuss chariot wheels (Palaima 1991: 281–2, 309), indicating at least a commercial connection with the island. The presence of Zakynthians may indicate a general direction for the fleet, as this is the only group outside mainland Greece mentioned in the Rower Tablets. It is unlikely that men were brought from Zakynthos to Pylos for the sole purpose of rowing to other destinations. Their small number may indicate a specialized role within the colonization party – perhaps as pilots or informants leading the expedition to Zakynthos or beyond.

Some hints to the nature of the settlement to which the expedition set off to can be obtained from the tablets. The large number of people involved implies that it was a substantial, agriculturally based colony rather than a small *emporion* or trading post. The overall lack of references to trade and traders in the Linear B tablets may further strengthen the notion of the noncommercial nature of the expedition.

The Rower Tablets should therefore be interpreted in the context of a well-coordinated mobilization mechanism, as they show a surprising amount of preparation and control:

* A mechanism for local recruitment of rowers by specially designated local officials, carried out within the framework of the existing taxation system and including the monitoring of exemptions
* A mechanism for recruitment of different types of colonists or settlers from various areas of the Pylian polity and for directing them to the port of departure (palatial and local officials were probably involved in this recruitment)
* Differentiation among types of settlers or colonists
* The participation of foreigners (eight men from Zakynthos) in the maritime efforts, possibly as guides to the destination of colonization

These efforts indicate a deep interest on the part of the *wanax* in maritime activity, perhaps even in colonization as a convenient measure of enlarging the polity. The possibility of state-orchestrated colonization in Pylos raises the additional possibility that such ventures could have been conducted by other strong Aegean polities of the LHIIIB period.

OTHER EVIDENCE FOR MYCENAEAN NAVAL CAPABILITIES

Excluding the Rower Tablets, a relatively small number of tablets deals with maritime-related matters, but they may offer evidence complementary to the PY An series tablets. The palace had skilled craftsmen, possibly from outside the palatial system, with the ability to build and maintain ships. That the palace of Pylos used expert shipbuilders is clear from two tablets: one (PY Vn 865) mentions twelve of these people and another (PY Na 568) shows them as exempted from paying taxes (Palaima 1991: 287–8). The mention of shipbuilders in the PY An series (Hiller 1988: 60) may indicate that they were granted land in return for their service.

The texts provide only two pieces of evidence about the type and size of ships, and both indicate the existence of oared galleys: The first is PY An 1, mentioned previously, which hints at the existence of a triaconter (a ship of thirty rowers). The second, PY Vn 46, lists materials for shipbuilding and may allude to the construction of a ship for fewer than thirty rowers (Palaima 1991: 296–301), which may have been slightly larger than the fifteen-meter-long

FIGURE 2.4. Ship on LHIIIB krater from Enkomi (after Wachsmann 1998: fig. 7.28)

Uluburun ship and much larger than the nine-meter-long Point Iria ship (Vichos 1999: 83).

Most iconographic depictions of Aegean ships belong to Wedde's (1991: 86–7) types V and VI – oared galleys that seem to have been popular in LHIIIB and in LHIIIC (Figs. 2.4 and 2.5). Of the varied evidence for the existence of these oared galleys, one can note the LMIIIB depiction of a ship on a larnax from Gazi (Watrous 1991: 298; Wachsmann 1998: 136, fig. 7.19, 138–9) showing a Wedde type VI ship (Wedde 1991: 86 no. 52) with twenty-eight rowing stations (i.e., slightly larger than a penteconter). Galleys could be used in various ways: type V and VI ships (Wedde 1999) had properties that enabled their use as warships for raids and naval battles, in patrol, and in trade. Among their warfare capabilities, Wedde counts rapid deployment and the ability to serve as a fighting platform.

The lack of evidence for merchant ships in the palatial period may attest to a bias toward the more prestigious and warlike galleys possibly depicted in the LHIIIC ship representations (Chapter 4). One piece of evidence for ships other than galleys may be a depiction on a Mycenaean krater from Enkomi (Vermeule and Karageorghis 1982: 202 no. V.38; Wachsmann 1998: 142) of a very round ship with a deck displaying only steering oars, entirely dissimilar from the depictions of galleys.

FIGURE 2.5. Ship on a larnax from Gazi (after Wachsmann 1998: 136, fig. 7.19)

According to Wedde (1991: 85–6), there is a possibility that large ships of type IV (similar to the type shown in the Theran frescoes) were still built and in use in the LHIIIB period. These ships were probably larger and fit for trade more than the type V and VI galleys. Among the few type IV examples that do not appear on LHIIIB seals and that have a distinctively crescent-shaped hull, a clay model from Tanagra should be noted (Basch 1987: 141, fig. 293.1; Wachsmann 1998: 148–9), as well as one of the ships in the graffiti from Dramési.[7] However, there is no evidence that these ships were larger in the LHIIIB than type V and VI galleys. The ship from Dramési seems to be about the same size as the type VI galley depicted above it.

Although there are many gaps in the evidence at hand, it may not be far from the truth to assume the existence of a variety of vessels, mostly oared galleys of different shapes and sizes, in the LHIIIB period. This versatility most probably enabled a wide range of maritime interactions in the thirteenth century BCE – from long-distance trade to maritime raids and naval fighting.

It should also be remembered that if a ship was well maintained, it might have continued to be seaworthy for decades; thus, it may be postulated that some of the ships built in the LHIIIB2 period (including merchant ships) were still in sailing condition in LHIIIC Early or LHIIIC Middle.

Finally, the LMIIIA1 ship sheds at Kommos (J. W. Shaw 1990: 426) may be the best existing example for the sophistication of Mycenaean harbor installations, suggesting that complicated harbors with well-built piers, docks, and ship sheds were available to at least some of the Mycenaean palatial polities.

AEGEANS ABROAD? COMMUNITY COLONIES AND ITINERANT ARTISANS

The apparently limited involvement of the Mycenaean polities in interregional interaction outside the Aegean during the fourteenth and thirteenth centuries, reflected in the Linear B archives, can also be seen in the absence of any substantial archaeological evidence for large-scale migration during this period, despite continuing efforts to prove the existence of such a phenomenon. Some areas outside the Aegean mainland, notably the Dodecanese and parts of western Anatolia, belonged to the sphere of Aegean culture even before the fourteenth century, when Mycenaean culture gradually replaced that of the Minoans (see Mee 1988b; 1998: 138–42). Thus, for example, Miletus IV provides a very fine archaeological record in support of a Minoan colonization, with all aspects of material culture, from cooking and textile production to art and religion, reflecting Minoan behavioral patterns (Niemeier 1998; 2005; Kaiser 2005). After the destruction of Miletus IV, Mycenaean cultural traits,

---

[7] Basch 1987: 143, 144, fig. 301 (the ship at the bottom); Wachsmann 1998: 143, fig. 7.30 (ship B), 144.

such as chamber tombs and fineware pottery, including domestic fineware pottery, began to appear (Niemeier 2005: pl. XLIXb). However, the published cooking pot fragment has Anatolian traits (horseshoe-shaped lug handle) as well as Mycenaean ones (Niemeier 1998: photo 8). Circular hearths inside the houses may conform to either Aegean or Anatolian prototypes, while one of the types of kilns found in the second building period (pre-LHIIIB) is of clear Anatolian shape (Niemeier 1998: 30–1). Evidence for a Minoan colony was also found in Trianda, in Rhodes. The nearby cemetery and settlement of Ialysos tells a tale of gradual transition to the realms of Mycenaean culture (Girella 2005; Karantzali 2005). Fineware pottery of the LHIIIA1–2 reflects Mycenaean forms, yet courseware pottery such as conical cups, cooking pots, and amphorae continues Minoan traditions. Still other forms exhibit a combination of Anatolian and Minoan traits. Burial traditions change from the Late Bronze I–II pithos and cist burials of Anatolian style to the Late Bronze III/LHIII Mycenaean-type chamber tombs, which contain Mycenaean-style fineware pottery and weapons. Without evidence for a deep change in the domestic behavioral patterns that can be ascribed to a Mycenaean migration, the appearance of elements of Mycenaean culture in Rhodes and Miletus in the fourteenth century may be ascribed to changes in the political power in LHIIIA, resulting in stylistic preferences and gradual Mycenaean acculturation.

Kilian's *Mycenaean Colonization: Norm and Variety* (1990) is perhaps the most elaborate attempt to deal with the possible Mycenaean colonization in areas outside the Aegean Sea. Kilian suggests different types of interaction between the Mycenaean world and other areas, which he sorts according to the quality and the quantity of Mycenaean material culture traits. The result of this analysis is a hierarchy of cultural radiation from Mycenaean territories and periphery, through community colonies and nucleus presence, to free exchange patterns. Kilian (1990: 465) concludes that there is no single form of Mycenaean colonization, and that contacts varied across space and time and in intensity, ranging from commercial contacts to community colonies in Cyprus, Macedonia, and Italy. Since Kilian's article, no attempt has been made to map the interaction range in the entire LHIIIA–B Mediterranean, nor has there been any other substantial claim made for the existence of Mycenaean community colonies. The case for community colonies, a term widely used in discussing Minoan colonization (Branigan 1984), has not gained support from further research. The three main cases treated by Kilian as areas where he claims there were Mycenaean community colonies – Italy (including the islands), Macedonia, and Cyprus (discussed earlier) – appear to have had no substantial Mycenaean colonization in the LHIIIB period: the Aegean colonization of Cyprus occurred only in the twelfth century BCE, not before (Chapter 5). Aegean traits in Macedonia, mainly the locally made LHIII pottery, are explained by Kiriatzi and colleagues (1997) as resulting from the

LHIIIC presence of Mycenaean potters rather than as evidence for Mycenaean community colonies. While the finds from Italy, Sicily, and Sardinia show some evidence of the presence of Aegeans abroad in the LHIIIB period, they probably do not attest the existence of community colonies.

Vagnetti and Jones (1988: 336) argue that, as yet, no Mycenaean settlement or Mycenaean quarter has been identified inside any local settlement in Italy or the islands, and that Helladic or Helladic-derived pottery constitutes only a fraction of the total amount of pottery at each site. They suggest that the local manufacture of LH pottery is a complex phenomenon that should be studied and explained case by case: for instance, the high quality of some Italian-made Aegean pottery forms (especially in Termitito near Metapontum) may indicate the presence of Mycenaean potters and possibly of other small groups of Aegeans (Vagnetti and Jones 1988: 347). Jones, Levi, and Bettelli (2005: 543) suggest that the presence of Aegean potters in southern Italy stimulated a technological transfer, with the introduction of the fast wheel, painted pottery, and kiln firing. Similarly, a combination of trade and the presence of itinerant artisans may have resulted in the phenomenon of technological transmission related to locally made bronzes in the Cypriot style (Vagnetti and Jones 1991: 140) and to faience objects (Holloway 1992: 41–2).

An explanation for a limited presence of foreigners might also solve the problem of the eastern-type architecture of rectangular warehouses found at Thapsos, in Sicily (Fig. 2.6; Holloway 1981: 85–7; 1992: 41; T. R. Smith 1987: 111), which were built on top of a local fourteenth-century-BCE settlement. The innovative plan, which was executed nonetheless in local building style, is attributed by Militello (2005: 590) to the work of an Aegean architect supervising local workers in the service of a local ruler. Although no Aegean pottery was found in these buildings (Militello 2005: 142), much LHIIIA and LHIIIB as well as Cypriot imported pottery was excavated in local Thapsos-culture tombs at the site (Militello 2005: 110–11). To Alberti and Bettelli (2005), the choice of vessel types in some of the Thapsos tomb assemblages reflects Aegean belief systems. These could have been transmitted through the presence of a number of Aegeans integrated into the local community.

Vagnetti (1999: 148–9) proposed an explanation for the movement of Mycenaean potters to Italy. The first wave of destruction that hit Mycenaean palatial sites in LHIIIB, and that at the end of LHIIIB, reduced the demand for the production of specialized pottery in Mycenaean Greece and encouraged mobility among potters, at least on a temporary basis. The presence of resident Mycenaean traders and artisans has been reconstructed at the possible emporia of Scoglio del Tonno in southern Italy and Antigori in the Gulf of Cagliari (Webster 1996: 140–1; Vagnetti 1999: 148–9). Other sites, further inland, such as Broglio and Termitito, may have supported a Mycenaean presence but were not directly involved in trade networks.

b

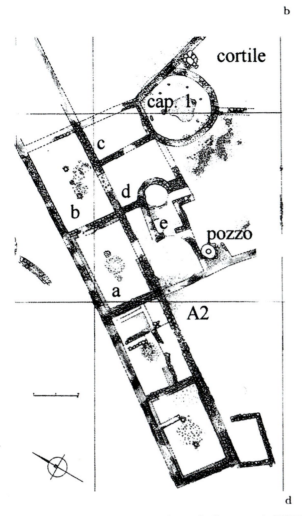

d

FIGURE 2.6. Thapsos in Sicily (after Militello 2005: pl. CXXXVI d)

In these cases, it is possible to reconstruct the temporary or permanent presence of a small number of traders and/or artisans of local and eastern origin living in and around a permanent trading station.[8] It remains to be seen whether all the activities in pottery making or other crafts were conducted in an Aegean or rather local fashion. The former (exemplified by, inter alia, Aegean-type pottery kilns and clay recipes) provides an indication of deep change following settlement or a substantial presence of Aegeans abroad. The absence of evidence for domestic Aegean behavioral patterns in Italy or the islands, expected to be reflected in objects, such as Aegean-style cooking

[8] T. R. Smith (1987: 142) uses the term *traders' enclave* to describe the site of Thapsos. Cf. the case of Imbros (Guzowska and Yasur-Landau 2003) as a possible trading stop on the route to Troy and the Black Sea.

vessels or Aegean-style loom weights,[9] rules out the possibility of a permanent settlement of Aegean kinship groups.

Whether itinerant or permanent residents, these artisans probably traveled alone or in small groups, moving on merchant ships – at times using them as a base of operations and at other times as a source of information for potential markets. Thus far, there is no clear evidence for the activity of LHIII Aegean artisans working with gold or glass, engraving seals, or painting frescoes outside the palatial context of the Greek mainland and Crete. It is plausible that more Aegean artisans were active abroad than is evident from the case studies presently available, and that their identification in Italy may provide important methodological tools for extrapolation to the thirteenth- and twelfth-century Levant (Chapter 6).

PALATIAL ADMINISTRATION AND AEGEAN MIGRATION AND COLONIZATION OF THE LATE THIRTEENTH TO THE EARLY TWELFTH CENTURY BCE

The legacy of information concerning areas outside the scope of the Aegean culture, left over from the thirteenth-century interactions to the people of the early postpalatial era, was apparently partial and sketchy. A few diplomats, commercial representatives, local and foreign merchants, and perhaps some mercenaries may have been the only populations in mainland Greece to have firsthand knowledge of the foreign countries as well as of the Levant. Only the upper echelons of the Ahhiyawan elite, engaged in Anatolian diplomacy, had accurate and updated information on non-Aegean regions. Other elite members and scribes may have heard, possibly secondhand, about foreign lands, and they may have known what commodities arrived from them. Foreign goods and loanwords may have been brought to the Aegean by Syro-Canaanite or Cypriot intermediaries (Bass 1991: 73; 1997a: 169; 1998; Holloway 1992: 41), or in ships carrying a crew of trade partners from across the eastern Mediterranean. Still, an important source of knowledge was the migrants (and perhaps traders) who reached the Mycenaean world. Those presented a widely available – yet not always reliable – picture of at least some parts of the outside world, mainly of communities in western Anatolia and the northeastern Aegean Islands.

Even this type of geographic knowledge differed from place to place in the Aegean world. The amount of information corresponded to the geographic distance from the destination, the sphere of interaction, and political and economic parameters inside each polity. From the survey of foreign ethnonyms or toponyms in Linear B, it seems likely that there was more information available about the areas closer to mainland Greece, particularly about Crete,

---

[9] I would like to thank L. Vagnetti for this information.

the Ionian Islands, and the Anatolian coast. Significantly, it seems that Pylos, Thebes, Mycenae, and Knossos hardly knew of or at least wrote very little about the Levant during the fourteenth and thirteenth centuries; they also knew nothing at all about Canaan. Similarly, knowledge about Egypt in the thirteenth century was very limited if not entirely nonexistent.

Fragmentary as it is, the evidence from Linear B sources and archaeological data provides crucial insights to the nature of Aegean maritime abilities and political power at the final days of the thirteenth-century Aegean. The evidence presented in this chapter strongly supports the hypothesis connecting the level of social complexity to the ability to conduct different ranges of interregional interaction. Indeed, the complex Mycenaean society was involved in a wide variety of interactions with various parts of the Mediterranean in the thirteenth century.

Diplomacy. If the Ahhiyawa correspondence is indeed related to mainland Greece, there was an immense diplomatic and perhaps military involvement of the Mycenaean rulership in western Anatolia during the fourteenth and thirteenth centuries BCE. This diplomatic play replaced the late-fifteenth- and early-fourteenth-century maritime raids attested in the "Indictment of Madduwatta." It is perhaps indicative of the development in the Mycenaean kingship in the fourteenth century – from piracy, reflecting the martial policy typical of the formative stages of Mycenaean rulership (cf. Acheson 1999; Davis and Bennet 1999) to power diplomacy, typical of the developed monarchies of the ancient Near East.

Trade. The flash of gold, glossy glass, and bright ivory seen in the Mycenaean palaces, as well as in the Uluburun ship, gives the impression that long-distance trade in raw materials for the palatial workshops and in finished luxury items was the most important interaction of the Aegean world with the outside. However, this picture is somewhat misleading. The lack of reference to Aegean traders in the Near Eastern sources, as well as in both the Linear B data and the Hittite references to Ahhiyawans, does not support the existence of independent, large-scale Mycenaean trade. Evidence from the cargoes of ships suggests that, although some were indeed engaged in trading expeditions, they did so in cooperation with Syro-Canaanite and Cypriot traders. The palatial involvement in trade may have been, as suggested by Pulak (2005) for the Uluburun ship, limited to the commissioning of the cargo, and providing envoys to direct and monitor the journey.

State-orchestrated maritime raids or colonization. The late LHIIIB Rower Tablets provide information on the highly developed LHIIIB recruitment mechanism related to maritime interaction and conducted as part of the enforced obligation system of the Mycenaean palaces. The ability of Pylos to recruit six hundred men from different origins for a maritime mission is an impressive military feat. However, the evidence leaves much to be desired regarding the understanding of the expedition's exact nature and its connection to settlement activities.

Maritime technology. The types of ships depicted during the LHIIIB, and Linear B data indicate the existence of vast knowledge of shipbuilding in the Aegean. Much of this activity was carried in the nonpalatial sector and therefore likely continued after the collapse of the palatial system. Ports and naval installations such as ship sheds built during the heyday of palatial power could have also served as infrastructure for postpalatial naval activities, as at least some of the ships were built during the final years of the thirteenth century.

Migration. Aegean mass migration and the permanent presence of Aegeans abroad were probably rather rare. Individual or small groups of artisans most likely lived in communities in Sardinia, southern Italy, and Sicily. Colonization carried out in the LHIIIB within the borders of the Aegean world and within the sphere of Aegean culture is not recognized in the archaeological record, as the material culture of the newcomers – not too different from that of the existing Aegean population in the area – would be interpreted as changes in settlement patterns rather than colonization. Still, the extent of the publication of excavations, the portion of the sites excavated, and archaeologists' lack of awareness about questions of interconnection limit the available archaeological data concerning material culture traits crucial for the identification of Aegean settlement.[10]

The thirteenth-century rulership enjoyed access to many resources, such as ships, human resources, information, and funds, and it was theoretically able to conduct almost any form of interregional interaction. These abilities were by no means available to all, and their application depended on factors of personal status and social complexity. Two specific ranges of interactions, the financing of long-range trade in raw materials for the production of luxury items and state-orchestrated, large-scale maritime ventures (whether for colonization or other purposes), were probably launched by only the very top echelons of the ruling elite. These interactions required an investment in resources far beyond the abilities of most individuals. In the case of international trade in raw materials, the profit may have been high, but so were the necessary funding and the danger of lost cargo. The investment and risk in a colonial venture were even greater, as they required more than great investment of resources in ships and supplies; the entire endeavor was a long-term risk, as revenues came only after an extensive period, if at all, and further investment in

---

[10] For example, cooking traditions are reflected in evidence obtained from botanical and archaeozoological evidence, as well as from analysis of coarseware pottery. See Mee 1988b: 302–3 for the lack of published kitchen kits in the eastern Aegean and western Anatolia.

human and other resources was needed even after the initial foundation. Only powerful polities, such as LHIIIA2–B Mycenae, Pylos, and Thebes, could risk commercial disasters such as the sinking of the Uluburun ship or the terrible cost in people and resources of an unsuccessful maritime raid or colonial venture. The involvement of the ruling elite in initiating these costly and dangerous interactions can be easily understood as the result of a single pull factor: they were the most ambitious yet most profitable means to strengthen the basis of power and wealth at home.

It is likely that some other members of society, such as traders, shipowners, fishermen, and artisans, had access to ships and information, yet their ability to attract human resources was naturally less than that of the palaces. The great power of the palaces may have also been used to sanction some forms of interaction, perhaps through trade monopolies and taxes (Gillis 1995: 64), as well as by keeping most of the population in its place, to ensure economic and demographic stability. Large segments of society were therefore denied resources and information and were unable to be involved in any range of interaction. Some may have been subjects of or dependents on the palaces; others may have been bound to the land. Such circumstances probably played a role in restricting mass colonization in the thirteenth century along with other forms of interaction connected with the movements of large groups of people.

The legacy left by the Mycenaean palatial culture to twelfth-century-BCE maritime interactions was therefore one of potential as well as one of praxis. It will be demonstrated (in the following two chapters) that the main differences between the thirteenth and twelfth centuries BCE are found in aspects of social complexity and rulership. Although knowledge of the outside world may have been sketchy, skills of shipbuilding, navigation, and even some aspects of organization of naval activities were ready to serve the new rulership of the twelfth century. With the collapse of the palatial civilization, a change in push and pull factors triggered new ranges of interregional interactions that had not occurred before.

3

THE TWELFTH-CENTURY-BCE AEGEAN: POLITICAL AND SOCIAL BACKGROUND

Now Mycenae may have been a small place, and many of the cities of that age may appear comparatively insignificant, but no exact observer would therefore feel justified in rejecting the estimate given by the poets and by tradition of the magnitude of the armament.   – Thucydides 1.10.1 (Strassler 1996)

CHANGING RULERSHIP AND THE DECAPITATION THEORY

The world that created the Philistine migration was not the thirteenth-century-BCE world of Mycenaean palaces with its impressive administrative abilities but rather a new Aegean social order created in the twelfth century, the LHIIIC period (Fig. 3.1), after the demise of the palatial system. With the destruction of all the Mycenaean palaces at the turn of the twelfth century, the end of the Linear B administration, and the effective loss of most forms of elite art, a new era began with new and innovative forms of social organization.

The quest for the social explanation of the Philistine migration should begin, therefore, with an understanding of the social structure of the people whose ambitions and abilities set it in motion, the rulers and elites of the Aegean area.

In recent years, it has become more widely accepted that there was significant continuity from the world of the thirteenth century BCE to that of the twelfth century. Although some sites suffered destruction and abandonment, other sites, such as Tiryns, Mycenae, and Athens, continued to be inhabited. Osborne (1996: 19–28) argues that, in the twelfth century BCE, Greece was neither cut off from the outside world nor impoverished. The process of decline seems to have been gradual, resulting in a great increase in the wealth and numbers of settlements toward the end of the LHIIIC period. However, does continuity of habitation necessarily mean continuity of rulership? Scholars differ widely in their answers to this question, which carries significant implications about the ability of the settlements to conduct various interactions.

Period	Phase in Mycenae
Transitional LHIIIB2–LHIIIC Early	? (Phase VIII, late LHIIIB2 and Transitional)
LHIIIC Early	Early (Phase IX, LHIIIC Early 1)
	Tower (Phase X, LHIIIC Early 2)
LHIIIC Middle	Developed (Phase XIA, LHIIIC Middle 1)
	Advanced (Phase XIB, LHIIIC Middle 2)
LHIIIC Late	Final (Phase XIIA)

FIGURE 3.1. LHIIIC chronological scheme (drawn by A. Yasur-Landau)

Linear B and Homeric literature attest to some continuity in the political structure from the Bronze Age to the Iron Age, manifested in the surviving rulership titles of *wanax* and *basileus*, and in attributes of kingship like the *skeptron* (scepter) and the *temenos* (Lenz 1993: 62–76; Palaima 1995b: 135–6). However, the connotation of these terms in Homeric literature seems to be different from that in the Linear B context (Lenz 1993: 56; Palaima 1995b: 122–3). Despite the apparent continuity, Lenz (1993: 108–11) suggests a dramatic change in the postpalatial rulership, dubbed "the decapitation theory" (Morris 1991: 42; Palaima 1995b: 125). It is postulated that the *wanax* fell with the palace system, and the *basileus*, a local political power during the palatial period (Palaima 2006: 68), stepped in to the vacuum and promoted himself to local ruler. Wright (1995: 75) and Thomatos (2006: 259) take a similar line of reasoning, suggesting that new local social structures emerged following the collapse of the palatial system.

Perhaps the most appealing archaeological model of LHIIIC society is that of Deger-Jalkotzy (1995), based on both archaeological data about the nature of habitation sites and a stylistic analysis of recurring themes in vase paintings of the LHIIIC Middle. The total breakdown of the Mycenaean palatial system was followed after the turbulence of LHIIIC Early by the organization of different elites in LHIIIC Middle (Deger-Jalkotzy 1995: 375–7). The Mycenaean palace system of the fourteenth and thirteenth centuries, with its overcentralized and monopolistic character, was doomed to fail. Indeed, it collapsed "like a house of cards" (Deger-Jalkotzy 1995: 375; 1996: 725–6) when the centers of all polities were dealt a fatal blow at the end of LHIIIB and local powers were able to form small polities, centered on fortresses that sometimes housed the ruler or rulers. Each fortified acropolis protected the settlement on its slopes (Deger-Jalkotzy 1991b: 148; 1995: 375–6). The polities had a limited hierarchy of power and no bureaucracy.

This plausible picture of the fragmented nature of rulership in the twelfth century provides a good starting point for a still more detailed, synthetic study of the regional and ideological aspects of the LHIIIC sociopolitical system to be presented here. First, case studies of specific sites display the variability in types of rulership in different regions of the Aegean world. Second, a detailed survey of the iconography of painted pottery is used to determine whether the change between LHIIIB and LHIIIC marked the annihilation of the former type of monarchy, and if so, what the ideological agenda of the new elite was.

SOCIAL COMPLEXITY IN SELECTED AEGEAN SITES IN LHIIIC

The key to understanding the political structure of the LHIIIC – a prerequisite for any study of migration from the Aegean during this period – lies in a detailed survey of the archaeological evidence for social change and for aspects of rulership. Following Deger-Jalkotzy's (1995) model, aspects of social complexity and rulership are extracted here through a study of both elite architecture and imagery relating to elite activity.

In contrast to the relative ease with which social complexity is extracted from literary evidence (Chapter 2), the use of material culture remains for the same purpose is an extremely complex task (e.g., Wason 1994; Dark 1995: 90–4, 99, 102–4). It seems that the most successful results have been derived from the analysis of several complementary aspects of the material culture rather than from a concentration on a single field, such as differentiation in burials or size hierarchy in domestic buildings (cf. Wason 1994: 153–79).

The criteria chosen here to represent the existence of a developed social hierarchy, and perhaps even the type of rulership, are the existence of two types of monumental architecture: rulers' dwellings (Mazarakis Ainian 1997: 271) and planned fortification systems. It is supposed that the level of social complexity stands in direct ratio to the amount of energy invested in the construction of fortifications and to the level of planning reflected in their layout (cf. Wason 1994: 146; Figs. 3.2 and 3.3). In addition, the extent of a settlement and its population size is also taken into consideration. An examination of communities in Dark Ages Greece may indicate that communities of five hundred members or more display a certain level of social hierarchy (Morris 1991: 41–3). Because architecture is an effective index of cultural complexity (Abrams 1989: 62), monumental architecture offers a correlation to types of hierarchical society (cf. Donley-Reid 1990: 125; Wason 1994: 137–45; Renfrew and Bahn 1996: 168) and certainly to those in Late Bronze Age Aegean society (Wright 1995: 73; Laffineur 1995: 82–5). One should bear in mind, however, that complex social

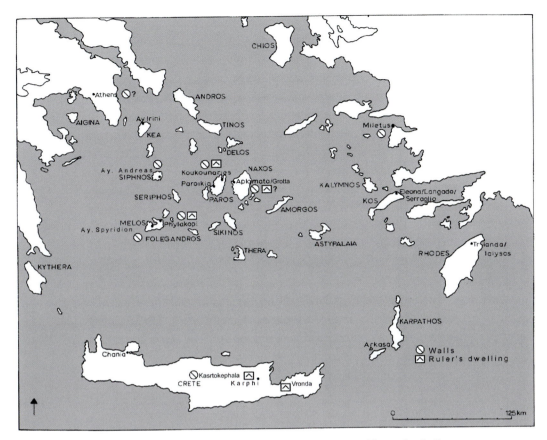

FIGURE 3.2. Manifestations of social complexity in the LHIIIC Aegean (drawn by A. Yasur-Landau)

structures may have existed at sites that display no monumental architecture, either because of limitations in the archaeological record or possibly because of a change in the pattern of rulership after LHIIIB. To deal with this problem, despite the many methodological and chronological obstacles that stem from tomb reuse, sites that display rich burials, art forms, or iconography related to elite activities have been added to the survey (Sjöberg 2004: 86–9).

The geographic scope of the site survey is within the borders of what may be generally considered the Mycenaean world of the thirteenth century BCE: mainland Greece up to Thessaly in the north, the Cyclades, Crete, the Dodecanese, and western Anatolia.

CONTINUITY OF RULERSHIP

Phylakopi and Miletus seem to be the only two centers at which monumental architecture continues with no sign of destruction; this may indicate that at these sites, there was no change in rulership between LHIIIB and LHIIIC Middle.

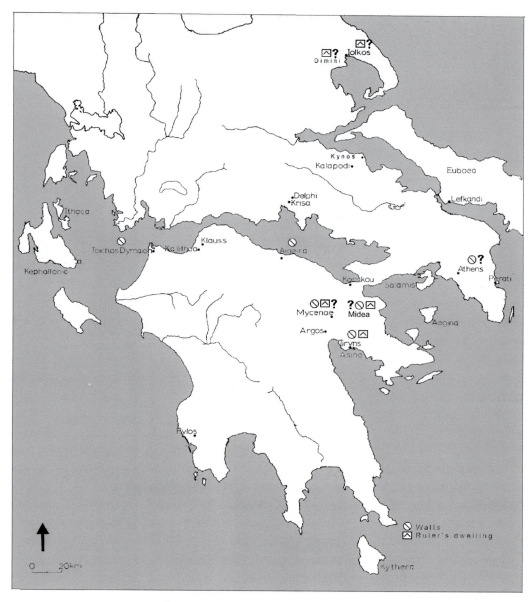

FIGURE 3.3. Manifestations of social complexity in LHIIIC mainland Greece (drawn by A. Yasur-Landau)

Phylakopi (Figs. 3.4–3.6), seems to show an uninterrupted transition from LHIIIB to LHIIIC, at least in the area of the sanctuary (Mountjoy 1999a: 888–9). According to Renfrew's stratigraphy (1978: 404), Phase F of Period IV belongs to LHIIIB/C. The site was fortified in LHIIIB1 with a wall of round boulders, added to the earlier Late Bronze Age fortifications, and more bastions were added to the west sector (Barber 1987: 234; Schallin 1993: 68; Mountjoy 1999a: 407–8). The collapse of part of this wall, possibly in an earthquake, can be

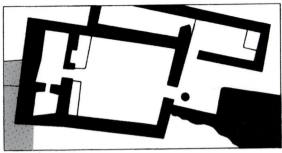

Phase 2b

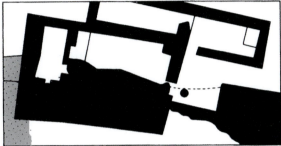

Phase 3b

FIGURES 3.4 AND 3.5. Phlylakopi temples during LHIIIC Early–Middle (Phase 2b) and Middle–Late (Phase 3b) (drawn by A. Yasur-Landau, after Renfrew 1985: fig. 3.1)

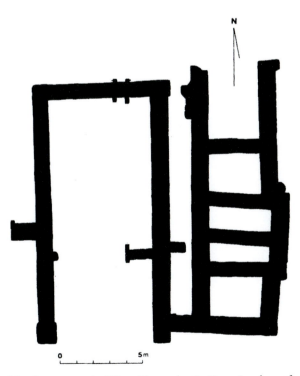

FIGURE 3.6. Phylakopi, megaron building (drawn by A. Yasur-Landau, after Schallin 1993: fig. 28)

dated to the beginning of LHIIIC Middle given ceramic assemblages from the area of the temples.

Already by LHIIIA1, a palatial structure was built on the site of an earlier mansion (see Fig. 3.6; Barber 1987: 232; Werner 1993: 115–16; Schallin 1993: 69; Mountjoy 1993: 154). This unit contains a central megaron with a hearth and an entrance unit. Because this structure was excavated and findings published early in the twentieth century, it is impossible to assess the time and circumstances of the end of its use. However, it may have been used contemporaneously with the fortifications.

Two shrines found in Phylakopi (Renfrew 1985; Whittaker 1997: 173–9; Figs. 3.4 and 3.5) were in continuous use during the end of LHIIIB and LHIIIC Early (Phase 2a) until the collapse of the fortification wall and the damage to the temples (Phase 2b: early LHIIIC Middle [LHIIIC Developed]; Mountjoy 1984: 225; 1999a: 889). The damage was repaired and a blocking wall was built along the main room of the western shrine (Phase 3a). The entire complex continued to be in use (Phases 3b, c) until it was abandoned later in LHIIIC Middle (LHIIIC Advanced) (Mountjoy 1993: 226; Thomatos 2006: 202–3).

At Miletus (Fig. 3.7), the third building period extends from LHIIIB to possibly LHIIIC (Middle), following destruction at the end of LHIIIA2 (Niemeier and Niemeier 1997: 196; Niemeier 1998: 33). A 1,100-meter fortification wall that encircled an area of five hectares was constructed during this period. The bastions set at regular intervals in the wall indicate a Hittite influence or are a combination of Hittite and Mycenaean fortification elements (Niemeier and Niemeier 1997: 196). The scant architecture preserved from this period in the area of the Athena temple includes the remains of a *Korridorhaus* of the type common in the Aegean world: it imitated palatial architecture (Werner 1993: 80; Niemeier and Niemeier 1997: 197–8; Niemeier 1998: 35). This house can be interpreted as evidence of the existence of nonruling elites. Some kind of Hittite religious influence is seen in the representation of the crown of a Hittite god on a LHIIIB–C sherd (Weickert 1959–60: 65, pl. 72: 1; Niemeier and Niemeier 1997: 205). The architecture of the third building period was destroyed violently in LHIIIC. The latest pottery is dated to LHIIIC Early by Mountjoy (2004) and to LHIIIC Late by Schachermeyer (Niemeier and Niemeier 1997: 205–6).

Evidence for elite activity continuing from LHIIIB to LHIIIC is further detected in the cemetery of Değirmentepe, 1.5 kilometers southwest of Miletus. Chamber tombs containing LHIIIB and LHIIIC pottery preserved two horse bits of a type with parallels in the Aegean world (Mee 1978: 133). Of the four swords found, one is of an Aegean form and three are non-Aegean, probably of Hittite origin (Niemeier 1998: 39).

It is important note that the sites of Phylakopi and Miletus in LHIIIB were not true palatial centers, as they do not present archives, complex administration, or palatial art. Phylakopi was the center of a small polity, isolated on an

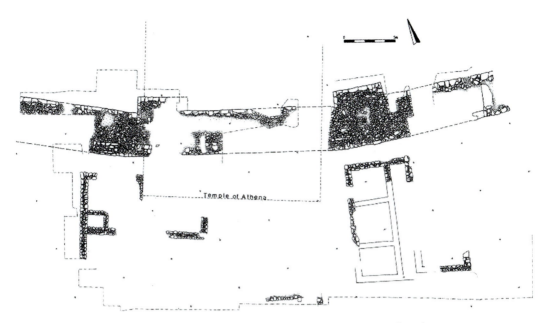

FIGURE 3.7. Miletus, remains of the third building period (after Niemeier 1998: fig. 11)

island, perhaps even a vassal of one of the palatial powers. Miletus may have been an important center in the Late Bronze Age strong entity of Ahhiyawa, mentioned in Hittite texts (Niemeier 1998: 22–5, 43–5). The decline of palatial power in the Argolid and of the Hittite kingdom at the end of LHIIIB may have resulted in an autonomous LHIIIC entity that included the Dodecanese and Miletus (cf. Deger-Jalkotzy 1994: 14). The relatively smooth transition of Miletus and Phylakopi, both probably maritime powers between LHIIIB and LHIIIC, makes them examples of polities that continued to maintain their rulership power without a break.

IMPORTED RULERSHIP?

Koukounaries on Paros (Fig. 3.8) may be an example of a settlement erected by a foreign and complex group that introduced an almost-palatial lifestyle to an area in which it had not existed before.

The rocky acropolis of Koukounaries is located at a dominating point above the bay of Naussa. The site was built and fortified in the LHIIIC Early phase (Schilardi 1984; Schallin 1993: 78–80; Mountjoy 1999a: 932; Thomatos 2006: 204–6). Remains of a cyclopean wall were found at the bottom of the hill and on terraces on the hill.

The plateau on the crest of the hill is occupied by a mansion (Fig. 3.9), sixteen meters wide and twenty-two meters long, of which the basement floor is best preserved. Two corridors forming a right angle give access to the various basement rooms. The second floor seems to have been the seat of the

FIGURE 3.8. Koukounaries on Paros (photo by A. Yasur-Landau)

ruler, as objects connected with elite activities, such as a large fragment of a decorated ivory throne and a bathtub, were found among the objects that had fallen into the storerooms (Schilardi 1984: 187–8; 1992: 627–31). The entire complex was covered with a thick ash layer, indicating violent destruction by fire. Skeletons of cattle and other domestic animals show that the defenders of the site tried to save their flocks by taking them indoors. Round stones and bent arrowheads provide evidence of a siege on the mansion. This short-lived mansion was destroyed in the later years of LHIIIC Early (Developed) (Koehl 1984; Deger-Jalkotzy 1998b: 113) or at the beginning of LHIIIC Middle (Advanced) (Mountjoy 1999a: 932).

The sudden appearance of this fortified edifice in the LHIIIC Early period strongly supports the excavator's interpretation that the site was settled by a mainland Mycenaean clan (Schilardi 1992: 633) and destroyed by a rival clan from Naxos or by pirates from Mycenaean colonies in the Aegean (Schiliardi 1992: 638–9).

CHANGES IN POWER AND/OR RULERSHIP PATTERNS

A mixture of old and new aspects of twelfth-century power and rulership can be seen at Mycenae and Tiryns, centers of palatial power in LHIIIB that suffered considerable damage from earthquake or from human agency in the LHIIIB2 and LHIIIC.

Tiryns presents a picture of fragmentation of power side by side with possible continuity in rulership and prosperity in LHIIIC Early and Middle (Mountjoy 1999a: 66; Sjöberg 2004: 57–64; Thomatos 2006: 189–96). The upper city and the LHIIIB palace were destroyed by fire at the end of LHIIIB,

FIGURE 3.9. The building at Koukounaries (drawn by A. Yasur-Landau, after Schallin 1993: fig. 36)

possibly a result of the same earthquake that struck Mycenae. The population of Tiryns apparently grew significantly in LHIIIC – perhaps as a result of the arrival of refugees from other parts of the Argolid, synoecism (Kilian 1988b: 135; Zangger 1994: 212), or the building activities of elites breaking the bonds of palatial constraints (Maran 2006: 127) – becoming the largest site in Greece (Maran 2004). Kilian reconstructs a postpalatial stratification by which a leading group resided in the smaller residence on top of the ruined megaron and other elements of society that maintained some inherited power, thus enabling control of this city of ten thousand for more than a generation. However, this picture of continuity needs to be updated with new evidence from recent excavations at the site.

A partial restoration of the rulership's power at Tiryns is found in the construction of Building T in LHIIIC, on the ruins of the LHIIIB megaron (Fig. 3.10; Maran 2000; 2001). The entire structure measures 6.9 meters by 20.9 meters. Two pillar bases of the earlier megaron are set along its axis, and there might have been an inner tripartite division similar to that of the LHIIIB megaron. Marks left by twelve pithoi between the back wall of Building T and the LHIIIB megaron, with their significant storage capacity, strengthen the notion that this was a ruler's dwelling (Mazarakis Ainian 1997: 159–61). The reuse in the new megaron structure of the throne base from the earlier structure is a clear connection to the palatial past by the constructors of Building T, and perhaps validates a claim of palatial descent. A round altar in front of the building might have been in use since the LHIIIB, thus

FIGURE 3.10. Tiryns, walls of Building T visible on top of the Mycenaean megaron (photo by A. Yasur-Landau)

marking the continuity of ritual from LHIIIB to LHIIIC (Maran 2006: 127). The Tiryns treasure, a collection of bronze vessels and implements as well as a rich array of jewelry found in 1915, supports a similar claim of palatial ancestry. Although redated to LHIIIC by Maran (2006), the treasure contained early Mycenaean (LHII) signet rings and other objects datable to both LHIIIB and LHIIIC. It may have been the heirloom collection of one of the ruling families of the twelfth century. The old heirlooms with them stories relating to the family history, thus carrying messages of the great ancestry of the family and supporting claims for palatial lineage (Maran: 131).

However, large and well-built structures were constructed outside the walls of the acropolis, suggesting the fragmentation of power in LHIIIC Tiryns. House W (Fig. 3.11), a structure 20.8 meters by 8.5 meters, stood east of the slope of the southeastern part of the acropolis. Its main feature is a large central room (11 meters by 7 meters) – larger than the central room of Building T – in which a rectangular hearth and heavy stone pillar bases were found, with smaller rooms to the south and north and remains of painted stucco (Gercke and Hiesel 1971: 11–15). The building of this structure is dated to LHIIIC (Thomatos 2006: 194), and it is interpreted as a dwelling place for a ruler and his associates (Hiesel 1990: 63–5; Werner 1993: 101–2) or an administrative building (Thomatos 2006: 211). Maran's (2004) excavations northeast of the *Unterburg* have uncovered the remains of a large structure of the LHIIIC Early, which was divided by two rows of column bases. Although not fully excavated, its overall dimensions may be similar to those of the main room in

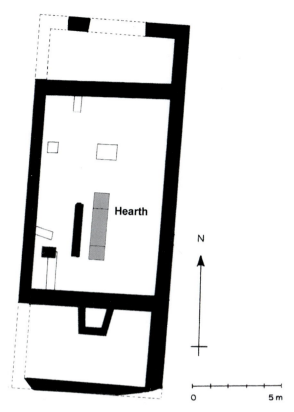

FIGURE 3.11. Tiryns, House W (drawn by A. Yasur-Landau, after Gercke and Hiesel 1971: pl. 8)

House W. Very large stones incorporated in the foundations further attest to its import.

The emergence in Tiryns of foci of power outside the upper city and the possibility of several active power bases functioning at the same time indicate a sharp break in the continuity of rulership. The use of megaronlike structures by the ruling elite, together with other features, such as painted stucco and stone pillar bases, indicates an attempt to achieve elite status by using the old language of power.

Maran (2006: 127) argues that elite families, once freed from the constrains of palatial rule, claimed areas in the surrounding of the citadel for themselves. Building T on the acropolis, despite being the seat of an individual claiming a palatial ancestry, did not rule the entire settlement.

Mycenae may provide a similar example of partial continuity in rulership, or at least of enduring power of some of the elite (Mountjoy 1999a: 60–2; Sjöberg 2004: 47–57). According to Iakovidis (1996: 1048–9), the LHIIIC period in Mycenae was "a period of retrenchment and accelerating regression, but not one of danger and distress." However, changes are seen in the differences between the symbolic languages of power in the two periods. It is impossible

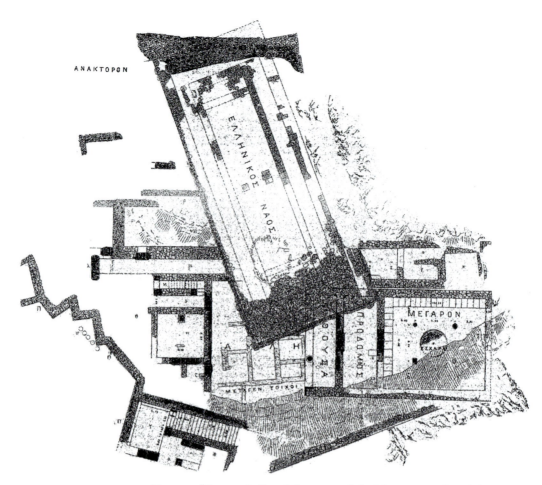

FIGURE 3.12. Mycenae, "Geometric Temple" on top of the Mycenaean palace (after French 2002: fig. 65)

to assess whether this transformation also reflects a change in lineage or shows the old, now weaker elite adjusting to a new social environment.

The citadel was probably not entirely in ruins at the end of LHIIIB or even in LHIIIC. The end of the palace may have occurred during LHIIIB2, (French 1998: 4; Thomas and Conant 1999: 9; Fig. 3.12). Fortifications continued to protect the settlement throughout LHIIIC. It seems that the fire that ravaged the Granary and the House of the Warrior Vase in LHIIIC Middle was local and did not spread beyond the immediate vicinity (Mountjoy 1993 145–6; Sjöberg 2004: 52). The other houses at Mycenae were gradually abandoned, and there is no evidence of full destruction at the end of LHIIIC. Other evidence of cultural continuity is seen in the fragments of LHIIIC frescoes found in a house in the vicinity of the Hellenistic tower in the lower acropolis – the fragments do not differ in technique and quality from those prevailing in the previous period (Lewartowski 1989: 128; Thomatos 2006: 184). If Mycenae previously had hegemony over a large part of the northeastern Peloponnese

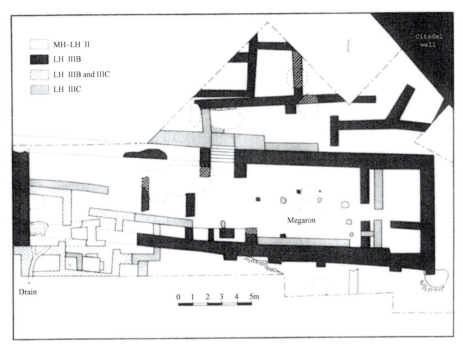

FIGURE 3.13. The megaron from Midea (after Shelmerdine 1997: fig. 3)

and perhaps even further afield (Niemeier 1998: 43–5), it is likely that much of it was lost in LHIIIC – a loss for which disintegration of the administration, resulting in a higher degree of autonomy for other powers, was symptomatic.

Continuity after destruction, similar to that seen at Tiryns, is detected clearly at Midea. The large megaron at Midea (Fig. 3.13), though located on the lower terraces, may have been the central structure of the site and the seat of its ruler or rulers (Shelmerdine 1997: 544–5; Demakopoulou et al. 1997: 24–8, 31; Mountjoy 1999a: 65; Sjöberg 2004: 69). The megaron, severely damaged by an earthquake at the end of LHIIIB, was repaired and remodeled in LHIIIC, when a row of three columns replaced the four columns that had stood around the central hearth in the LHIIIB phases. The structure suffered further damage during the LHIIIC period and was abandoned (Thomatos 2006: 188). One can certainly assume continuity in the function of the building during LHIIIC, indicating, perhaps, continuity in rulership after the natural disaster at the end of LHIIIB.

INTERNAL DEVELOPMENT

The fortified sites in Achaea offer good examples of the independent development and gradual rise in complexity that started possibly in LHIIIB (e.g., Teichos Dymaion) and continued into LHIIIC (e.g., Aigeira). Other examples include Agios Andreas on Siphnos, Grotta on Naxos, and Kastrokephala on Crete.

FIGURE 3.14. Aigeira, from the south (after http://www.oeaw.ac.at/myken/aigeira.html)

At Aigeira (Fig. 3.14; Mountjoy 1999a: 399; Alram-Stern 2003; Deger-Jalkotzy 2003), the LHIIIC Middle building phase represented a change in the plan of the site, which was encircled by a fortification wall. Little is known about the function of most of the buildings from to this phase. A main building containing three or more rooms – the large, central one measuring four meters by eight meters – was labeled the seat of a ruler (*Herrschersitz*). The disappearance of the "Barbarian" pottery after Bauphase I could indicate an acculturation of foreign elements in LHIIIC Middle (Deger-Jalkotzy 1991a: 19).

Because there were no palaces in LHIIIB Achaea, the rise of social complexity at Aigeira and other sites in Achaea in LHIIIC has been attributed to the arrival of refugees from the Argolid, given the evidence of pottery and figurines (Deger-Jalkotzy 1991a: 21–2). Mountjoy (1993: 26), however, rejects the claim of similarity between the pottery of Achaea and that of the Argolid. Deger-Jalkotzy (2003: 66) suggests that the first LHIIIC settlers originated from a nearby site but favored the strategic location of hilltop Aigeira; thus, the rise of social complexity at the site is a local phenomenon, uninfluenced by imported political structures.

Agios Andreas, on Siphnos (Figs. 3.15 and 3.16; Mountjoy 1999a: 887–8), is another example of a site that may portray internal development. The hilltop settlement was fortified with a 3.5-meter-thick wall with eight rectangular towers. At least three gateways led to the site. Recesses on the inside of the wall beside two towers contained steps. A second line of fortification, a wall 1.2-meters thick, was added later to the outer side of the existing wall. According to a reexamination of the site by Televantou (2001: 195), the initial fortifications probably had been built already in LHIIIB and the outer fortification added in

FIGURE 3.15. Agios Andreas hill (photo by A. Yasur-Landau)

LHIIIC. The settlement was abandoned before the end of LHIIIC (Televantou 2001: 202). The possibility exists, however, that the site was already abandoned in LHIIIC Early, after a destruction contemporary with that of Koukounaries (Barber 1987: 69; Deger-Jalkotzy 1998b: 113; Mountjoy 1999a: 887).

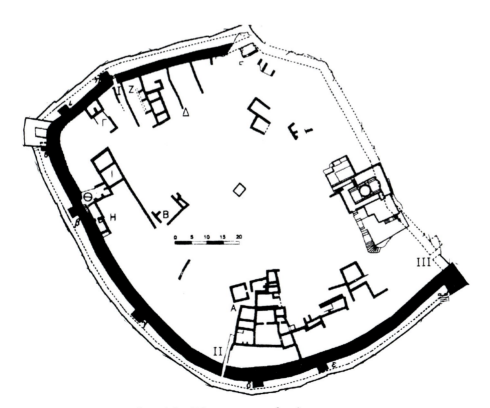

FIGURE 3.16. Agios Andreas (after Televantou 2001: fig. 2)

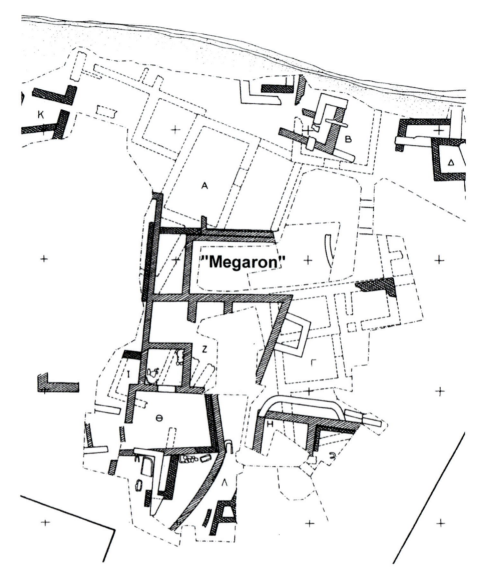

FIGURE 3.17. LHIIIC houses in Grotta, Naxos (after Vlachopoulos 1999: fig. 2)

The archaeological evidence thus shows that a rise in social complexity had occurred already in LHIIIB, as reflected in well-planned fortifications. A replanning of the fortifications in LHIIIC suggests new defensive needs (Televantou 2001: 202), which were answered by a more sophisticated system of fortification. Thus, the site is more easily interpreted as a hilltop fort of an elite group than as a place of refuge for a small community.

Grotta, on Naxos (Figs. 3.17 and 3.18; Davis 1992: 741; Mountjoy 1999a: 938; Vlachopoulos 1999: 303; Thomatos 2006: 206), portrays a phenomenon of cultural continuity from LHIIIB and a rise of complexity in LHIIIC that resulted in well-built fortifications and rich burials. The transition from LHIIIB to LHIIIC in this coastal settlement seems to have been a quiet one. Building remains dating from LHIIIA to LHIIIC Advanced were found at the western

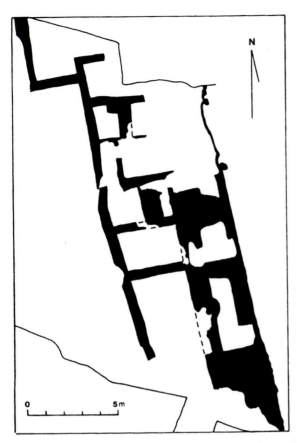

FIGURE 3.18. LHIIIC fortification wall and adjacent houses in Grotta (after Schallin 1993: fig. 35)

end of the site. In the Mitropolis area, a thick fortification wall with a foundation of well-cut stone blocks and a mud-brick superstructure was found further inland. The wall should be dated to LHIIIC Early, as it covers the remains of LHIIIB houses. West of this wall were houses of the LHIIIC period and a potter's workshop (Hadjianastasiou 1989: 207–8; Lambrinodakis and Philaniotou-Hadjianastasiou 2001: 160–1). In Grotta, north of the Mitropolis area, a large megaroid (megaron-like) structure, Building Γ, stands out in relation to other LHIIIC buildings because of its size and regular plan (Vlachopoulos 2003a: 218). The wealth of the LHIIIC settlement is reflected in the gold jewelry and fine pottery found at the Aplomata cemetery, three hundred meters northeast of Grotta, dating to LHIIIC Middle (Thomatos 2006: 160).

Agios Spyridon, on western Melos (Cherry 1982: 306 no. 94; Barber 1987: 226; Rutter 1992: 68; Mountjoy 1999a: 888), is a prominent acropolis located above the bay of Melos. Remains of an apparent Mycenaean structure built of worked stones, together with LHIIIB and LHIIIC pottery found in survey, indicate the site's importance.

The fortified site of Kastrokephala (Fig. 3.19; Platakis 1970; Kanta and Karetsou 2003) is located above the bay of Iraklion. The site belongs to LMIIIC,

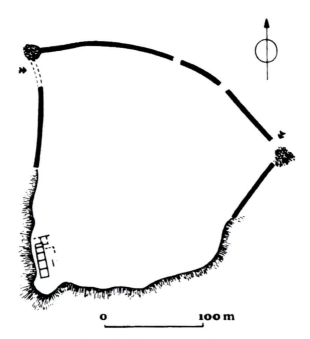

FIGURE 3.19. Kastrokephala (after Nowicki 2000: fig. 5)

yet it may have already been founded at the end of LHIIIB (Kanta 1980: 19; Hayden 1988: 3; Karageorghis 1998a: 134; Nowicki 2000: 42–4; 2001: 26). The 1.5- to 2.2-meter-thick fortification wall is built of large stone blocks (Hayden 1988: 4–5; Kanta and Karetsou 2003: 145). Two rubble piles at the east and west ends of the wall have been interpreted as buttresses. There is no indication of the construction date of this wall. At the highest point of the site, large rectangular rooms built along a single axis have been interpreted as garrisons or residences (Hayden 1988: 4; Karageorghis 1998a: 133). Nowicki views the site as resembling Mycenaean citadels more than Minoan refuge settlements (2001: 27; cf. Karageorghis 1998a: 133), while Kanta and Karetsou relate the building of the site to migrating Mycenaeans (2003: 152). At any rate, although the Kastrokephala fortifications may be compared to those of Agios Andreas on Siphnos (Hayden 1988: 19–20), the vast area enclosed within the walls (4.5 hectares; Nowicki 2000: 42) justifies the term *fortified citadel*, which Nowicki (2000: 41) uses to classify the site.

All these sites seem to have been the seat of a local ruler or rulers, but they exhibit no evidence of palatial art and almost no evidence of elite life. The rulers, probably of local origin and without connection to the palatial tradition of the Peloponnese, did not feel the need to use the Peloponnesian symbols of power or pictorial pottery showing Mycenaean elite symbols or activities. Therefore, there is no reason to assume a resemblance between the local LHIIIC sites and the type of rulership known from the LHIIIB palaces. Added to this is the "unstable" nature of the settlements (Whitley 1991a: 184): most of them changed their form or were destroyed or abandoned after a short

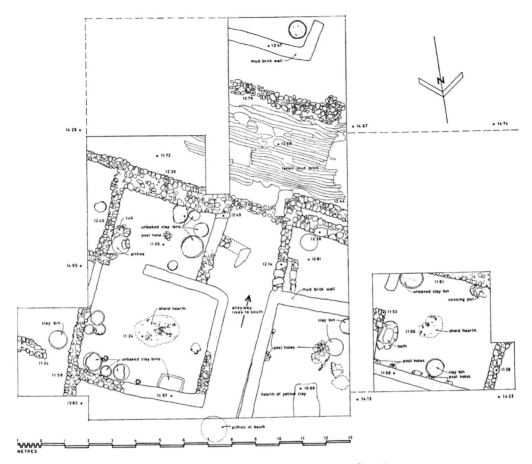

FIGURE 3.20. Lefkandi, LHIIIC Phase 1 (after Popham and Sacket 1968: fig. 14)

period. It is likely, using the terminology of Whitley (1991b: 348) and Mazarakis Ainian (1997: 375), that these sites contained a nonhereditary "big man" type of ruler or a simple hereditary system of rulership. In the case of big-man rulership in the Dark Ages, Whitley (1991b: 349–52) argues that the self-advertisement accompanied by promises of personal and economic security enabled individuals to attract followers. The rise of local powers may have filled gaps in rulership caused by the decline of the LHIIIB polities. The new powers possessed considerable recruitment abilities, enabling the building of massive fortifications. The new elites also had access to material resources, as in the example of imported luxury goods from Grotta, Aplomata, and Kamini.

THE RISE OF ELITE IN UNFORTIFIED CENTERS

The identification of twelfth-century BCE elites residing in unfortified sites may be possible given the presence of rulers' dwellings, rich cemeteries, and pictorial pottery depicting elite life; the latter is discussed here in more detail.

Lefkandi, in Euboia (Figs. 3.20 and 3.21; Popham and Sackett 1968; Popham and Milburn 1971; Hope Simpson and Dickinson 1979: 228; Mountjoy

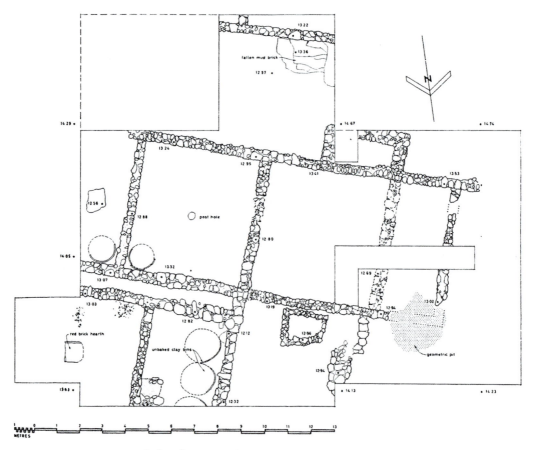

FIGURE 3.21. Lefkandi, LHIIIC Phase 2 (after Popham and Sacket 1968: fig. 21)

1999a: 694; Thomatos 2006: 201–2), was an unfortified settlement during LHIIIC Early and Middle. It yielded, however, a considerable amount of pictorial pottery depicting warriors – an important component of elite ideology during LHIII – thus indicating the presence of elites or of people assuming elite status through the use of such pottery (Vermeule and Karageorghis 1982: 128–9). Thomatos (2006: 258) attributed the flourishing of the site and the regularity in the LHIIIC Middle plan of the houses to independence from external control over Euboia following the fall of the Thebes palace. However, because of the frequent changes in the site's plan during LHIIIC and its demise in the eleventh century while nearby Toumba flourished, Whitley (1991a: 185–6) takes Lefkandi as an example of an unstable settlement, which he correlates with a big-man type of rulership.

In Karphi, on Crete, a focus of power seems to have been in the eastern quarter (Fig. 3.22; Pendlebury, Pendlebury, and Money-Coutts 1937–8: 70–2; Nowicki 2000: 157–64; Mazarakis Ainian 1997: 219–20). Three attached megaron units were found (136, 137, and 138–40), each with a hearth in the center of the room. Pendlebury and colleagues (1937–8: 137–9) attributed

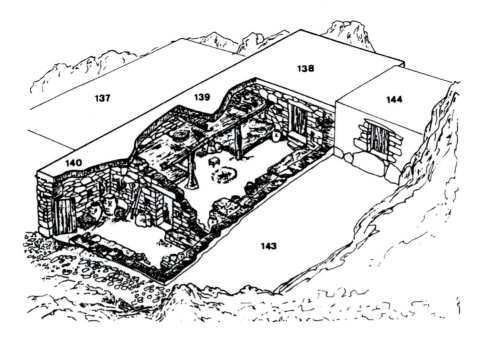

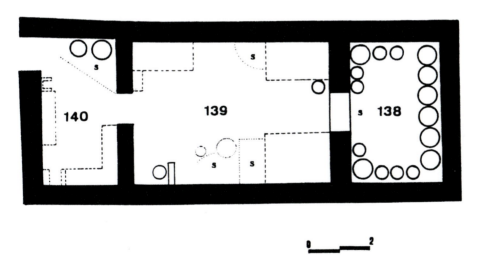

FIGURE 3.22. House 138–40 in Karphi (after Nowicki 1999: figs. 3 and 4)

these structures to the "Mycenaean Elite" that dominated the local Minoan population. The central building, House 138–40, had an impressive central room measuring 6.5 meters by 4.6 meters with a hearth in its center – a foreign element to Crete according to Nowicki (1999: 150). Mazarakis Ainian (1997: 219–20) sees the leg of a tripod found in the same megaron – a rare find in a noncultic context – as a possible prize for the winner of an elite contest. Tholos tombs with or without a dromos were found, single or in pairs, at Ta Mnimata, south of the site, and in Astiyidero, east and northeast of Megali Koprana. Some of the tombs provide evidence of multiple burials (as many as five) and preserve burial goods of pottery (stirrup jars, kraters, and cooking pots), figurines, bronze fibulae, bronze jewelry, and fragments of iron (Pendlebury et al. 1937–8: 100–12; Nowicki 1987: 246–7). If Nowicki is correct in claiming that the graves do not belong solely to the elite of Karphi, then the situation seems to reflect broad accessibility to luxury items such as bronze implements and jewelry.

Finally, one may mention a possible modest ruler's dwelling at Kavousi Vronda, Building A/B (Gesell, Day, and Coulson 1988: 282, 297; Mazarakis Ainian 1997: 208–9; Day and Snyder 2004). Whitley (1991a: 185) interprets this building, as well as other buildings from the twelfth to the tenth century BCE, as a place for symposia, aimed at creating personal bonds between the noble *basileus* and his followers.

Other settlements that may have been seats of power are, unfortunately, not as obvious. Some are burial sites that yielded rich tombs belonging to the elite, yet no walled site connected to the tombs has been located. Other elite members may have resided in unfortified sites, which, nonetheless, have yielded luxury items or painted pottery depicting elite activities. Such sites include Kalapodi (Jacob-Felsch 1987: 29–30; Felsch 1981: 86; Mountjoy 1999a: 809); Langada and Seraglio, on Kos (Macdonald 1986: 142–3; Mee 1988a: 56; Mountjoy 1999a: 1075–6; Thomatos 2006: 165–6); Kynos, in East Lokris (Dakoronia 2003); and Delos (the Artemision treasure) (Barber 1987: 239–40; cf. Mountjoy 1999a: 931). The cemetery at Perati, in Attica (Iakovidis 1969; 1970; 1979; Cavanagh and Mee 1998: 92–4; Mountjoy 1999a: 490; Thomatos 2006: 157–8; Iakovidis 2003), displayed a long sequence of burials throughout the LHIIIC. The fact that rich finds, including jewelry and Eastern imports, were not limited to one of two tombs but were found in a good number of the burials prompted Thomatos (2006: 259) to suggest that "more than a few members had the ability and need to display their wealth," indicating that access to luxury items was not very restricted. However, the LHIIIC practice of interring weapons, such as swords (sometimes of Naue II type), knives, and spears, may indicate the most prominent elite members. So-called warrior tombs found in places, such as Perati, Grotta, and Kamini, on Naxos, and Kalithea and Klauss, in Achaea, surrounded by other, elite tombs without weapons, were interpreted by Deger-Jalkotzy (2006: 176) as belonging to the people carrying the title of *basileus*.

Fragmentary and tentative as the evidence may be, it poses a strong argument for the presence of elite groups – some not connected to the old centers and settlements – that chose to live in unfortified settlements. The motives behind this phenomenon may be different from one case to the other and probably include lack of resources to build fortifications, a feeling of security, and the absence of apparent threats.

REGIONAL ASPECTS OF RULERSHIP
IN THE TWELFTH CENTURY

A region-by-region analysis of types of rulership assists in identifying areas that were likely to have participated in migration in the twelfth century BCE, discussed in Chapter 4. The type of rulership and its level of social complexity have a direct influence on a polity's ability for interregional interaction, including migration, during the twelfth century. The nature of transition from the palatial to the postpalatial period in a region may give important clues to region-specific push and pull factors affecting colonization.

Although frequently considered as part of the systemic collapse of the Mycenaean mainland (Manning 1994: 246), the picture in the Cyclades as a whole is of development rather than of continuity, at least until LHIIIC Middle. There seem to be variations in rulership within the region, and one should look at every island as a separate unit: on Melos, for example, Phylakopi maintained its power until LHIIIC Middle. If the newly founded stronghold of Agios Spyridon indeed was a dependency, Phylakopi had the ability to rule other centers, reaching at least the second level of political integration according to Clark and Parry's (1990) index (CPI), in which there is at least one administrative level above that of a single settlement. Agios Andreas, on Siphnos, and Chora, on Naxos, may be examples of local development and possibly were the main seats of power on their islands. On Paros, at the short-lived settlement at Koukounaries, there was probably a phenomenon unique in the Cyclades but not necessarily in the Aegean. All in all, for the period spanning LHIIIC Early to the beginning of LHIIIC Middle, one can reconstruct a social climax in which there was a network of interacting island polities, possibly all at some level of chiefdom. Destruction and abandonment began to take their toll as early as the end of LHIIIC Early at Koukounaries and possibly at Agios Andreas, and at the beginning of LHIIIC Middle at Phylakopi.

The Argolid and Corinthia were severely affected. The destruction of the palace at Tiryns and the partial destruction of that at Mycenae, as well as the end of literate administration, were inevitably accompanied by a decrease in levels of social hierarchy and political integration from LHIIIB. However, the continuation of elite art and possible continuity in the palace area at Mycenae, the reuse of the Midea megaron, and the claim for power exhibited by the construction of Building T at Tiryns indicate that all three sites maintained some of their past glory, and perhaps were still in the hands of LHIIIB elite groups (cf. Chadwick 1976). Pictorial pottery from the sites portrays two classes of free men – commoners and nobles – suggesting that the highest degree of social stratification was at least as high as CPI level 2, with two classes of free people (Clark and Parry 1990). The sites were still well populated during most of the LHIIIC, providing potential resources for the rulership. The rise of new elite groups, epitomized by Building W at Tiryns, for instance, doubtlessly acted as a destabilizing factor that limited the rulers' power. Consequently, some of the destruction at Tiryns and Mycenae may have been caused by humans. Political integration was apparently in constant decline throughout the beginning of the twelfth century. The destruction and abandonment of the countryside possibly left the Argolid polities with control of only the central site, thereby reducing the level of political integration (Sjöberg 2004: fig. 11).

In Attica and Euboea, there is seeming continuity and development rather than decline. Athens, while perhaps not destroyed in LHIIIB, experienced a drop in the level of political integration, as did the Argolid polities. Dependent sites such as Agios Kosmas and Brauron were abandoned very late in the LHIIIB or early in the LHIIIC (Hope Simpson and Dickinson 1979: 206, 213–14; Mountjoy 1993: 136–7; 1997: 120).

Perati and Lefkandi, coastal powers connected to trade and other maritime activities, indicate an increase in social complexity in LHIIIC Early and reached a zenith in LHIIIC Middle. Their rise probably resulted from fragmentation because of a breakdown of centralized control (Popham and Sackett 1968: 34). Pictorial pottery from Lefkandi and rich grave offerings at Perati may attest to the existence of aristocracy and a two-tiered social hierarchy.

Gradual advances occurred in Achaea between the end of LHIIIB and LHIIIC Middle, exemplified by Aigeira, where rulership developed locally. It is likely that the concepts of hereditary rulership and social boundaries among classes were much weaker at these sites than in the Argolid. A similar picture develops for the LHIIIC "warrior tombs" (Cavanagh and Mee 1998: 95), which display a wide range of weapons suited for a polity with no strong tradition of defined social stratification. Many of the fortified sites and those displaying rulers' dwellings had a low level of political integration and practiced no control beyond the site level. The existence of aristocracy suggests a social hierarchy of CPI level 2, perhaps reflecting different levels of social segmentation along the big-man continuum.

In Crete, although there is some continuity between LMIIIB and LMIIIC at sites such as Chania and Knossos, there is a major shift in the settlement pattern (Kanta 1980: 30; Andreadaki-Vlasaki 1991: 405; Rehak and Younger 1998a: 167–8), which indicates a sharp decline in the level of political integration. After the cessation of a literate administration in LMIIIB (Rehak and Younger 1998a: 166), there is little evidence for a higher level of political integration than that of the single settlement or, as argued for Karphi, perhaps two foci of power (Mazarakis Ainian 1997: 219–20). In some cases, settlements or paired villages might have cooperated for defensive or agricultural purposes (Haggis and Nowicki 1993: 334–5; Prokopiou 1997: 398–9; Rehak and Younger 1998a: 168).

Western Anatolia and the Dodecanese shared a cultural climax in LHIIIC Early and Middle. However, the political continuity at Miletus from LHIIIB to LHIIIC Middle is different from that at Kos and Rhodes, where unfortified settlements yielded rich burials and painted pottery, indicating a social hierarchy of at least CPI level 2. The latter situation may reflect the development of local power groups. The possible rejection of the yoke of Mycenae, if it indeed was the capital of the Ahhiyawan state, may have resulted in the formation of island polities or a regional polity encompassing the Dodecanese and Miletus (Chapter 5). Consequently, levels of political integration may have been as high as those in the Cyclades, thus allowing settlements to form a bloc with strong maritime elites.

THE CHANGE IN IMAGERY AND IDEOLOGY BETWEEN LHIIIB AND LHIIIC

Pictorial pottery provides an important glimpse into the ideological world of the LHIIIC elite. Almost universally, iconography plays an important role in the recognition of rank in a society, as beliefs and attitudes prevalent in a society are likely to manifest in its art (Wason 1994: 118–19). The reflection of elite ideology in art is among the most important criteria for differentiating between an egalitarian and a hierarchical society (Wason 1994: table 6.2).

With the demise of fresco art, except a few instances at Mycenae (Lewartowski 1989: 128; Tournavitou 1999: 123) and the significant decrease in seal engraving and ivory work, pictorial pottery became almost the sole medium for displaying images of elite power (Rutter 1992: 62). Thus, by default, pottery painting became the chosen elite art of the LHIIIC period, and its patterns of consumption changed dramatically: during LHIIIA and LHIIIB, pictorial pottery, such as the chariot kraters, was intended mostly for export, sending images of Mycenaean elite to Cypriots and Canaanites who aspired to belong to the "international club" of Mediterranean interconnections (Steel 1999: 808–9; Yasur-Landau 2005b; Chapter 6). However, LHIIIC pictorial pottery was created mostly for local consumption and was rarely exported. The widespread use of pictorial drinking wares, such as kraters, indicated that pictorial pottery was used in elite symposia, in which rulers forged allegiances and gained legitimacy.[1] Depictions of ship travel, hunting, dance, and combat reflected the lifestyle adopted or idealized by elite groups of that time, and they were likely used to create group identity and to differentiate one group from another (Deger-Jalkotzy 1995). In two instances, drinking is seen on pictorial pottery, which reveals the occasions in which this pottery

[1] On the important role of the feast in postpalatial societies, see, e.g., Whitley 1991b; Mazarakis Ainian 1997: 375; Borgna 2004.

FIGURE 3.23. Chariot krater from Enkomi (redrawn by A. Yasur-Landau)

was used: a man drinking from a kylix during a funeral on a krater from Agia Triada, in Elis (Fig. 3.41), and a seated person drinking during a chariot race, perhaps also in a funerary context, on a vessel from Tiryns (Fig. 3.32). In an environment poor in other forms of pictorial representations, the impact of a very large pictorial krater, such as the Mycenaean warrior vase, on the participants in a symposium must have been very striking. An analysis of LHIIIC pictorial pottery in comparison to that of LHIIIA and LHIIIB gives further answers to questions of continuity versus discontinuity in rulership after the fall of the palaces.

ARMED FIGURES

In all, there seems to be a greater number of people carrying weapons in LHIIIC painted pottery than in LHIIIB pottery; their dress also changed. Two types of people carrying weapons are depicted in the pottery of LHIIIA and LHIIIB and appear mostly on chariot kraters (Fig. 3.23). The most prominent are people carrying swords; wearing heavy, dotted clothes; and sometimes equipped with a pointed hat or helmet (Vermeule and Karageorghis 1982: 201 nos. V.17, V.19; 202 no. V.38). These people were likely aristocrats and are portrayed in nondynamic postures, mainly sitting or standing. They seem to include both men and women (cf. Younger 1995: 160 no. 24). Their status is reflected in their apparently naked attendants, who walk or run beside a chariot – sometimes armed with sticks or spears and sometimes

FIGURE 3.24. LHIIIB2 chariot and grooms from Tiryns (after Sakellarakis 1992: 122 pl. 12)

carrying chairs or a parasol (Younger 1995: 201 nos. V.17, V.19, V.28; 202 no. V.26).

In LHIIIC pottery, round shields, which appeared in late LHIIIB Tiryns (Fig. 3.24; Vermeule and Karageorghis 1982: 215 no. X.1), become common (Sakellarakis 1992: 34 no. 28) together with "hedgehog" helmets and pairs of spears (Fig. 3.25); swords became less frequent (Vermeule and Karageorghis

FIGURE 3.25. LHIIIC chariot from Tiryns (after Güntner 2000: pl. 7: 1b)

FIGURE 3.26. The Warrior Vase from Mycenae (after Sakellarakis 1992: 36–7 no. 32)

1982: 222 no. XI.39, 223 no. XI.59). The warriors are dressed in short skirts and padded armor. Rows of isocephalic warriors, without differentiation of rank, appear on warrior kraters from Mycenae (Sakellarakis 1992: 36–7 no. 32) and possibly Thermon (Wardle and Wardle 2003: fig. 3; Figs 3.26 and 3.27). Warriors are portrayed in much more dynamic postures, and in some cases are even engaged in fighting: a sherd from Seraglio, on Kos, depicts a warrior stabbing his fallen opponent with a long sword (Fig. 3.28; Karantzali 2003: fig. 8; 1, 21); a krater from Tiryns (Fig. 3.29) shows a foot soldier behind a chariot, striking an enemy; another depiction, from Grotta (Vlachopoulos 2003b: fig. 21), shows two warriors fighting with spears. Casualties are also seen in naval battles, such as the naked body floating by the rudder of a war galley from Kynos (Fig. 3.30). The sharp rise in LHIIIC in the number of armed figures and the fact that they are more heavily armed than in LHIIIB suggest a shift in the image of the aristocracy to a more bellicose one. Personal military strength and success in battle were probably essential to the acceptance of a claim for rulership and domination in LHIIIC.

CHARIOTS, SHIPS, AND HUNTING SCENES

The popular LHIIIA and LHIIIB scenes of dignitaries riding a chariot continued to be popular in LHIIIC, yet they seem to possess a different meaning (Figs. 3.25, 3.29, and 3.31). The type of chariot changed during the LHIIIB to one of lighter construction, more fit for battle (Littauer and Crouwel 1982: 186–7). The people depicted in it are mostly equipped with weapons and wear short clothes, more convenient for battle than the heavy robes of dignitaries of the former period.[2] The most remarkable scene involving chariots is the famous depiction of a chariot race from Tiryns, a scene unfamiliar in earlier

---

[2] Vermeule and Karageorghis 1982: 220 nos. XI.1B, XI.16, XI.18; 221 no. XI.28; Immerwahr 1990: 153.

FIGURE 3.27. Warrior krater from Thermon (Wardle and Wardle 2003: fig. 3)

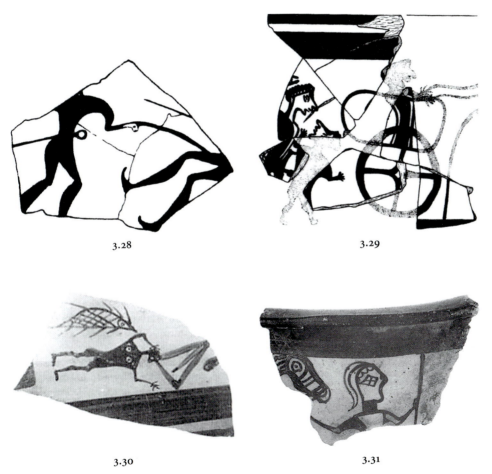

3.28

3.29

3.30

3.31

FIGURE 3.28. Fighting warriors on a sherd from Seraglio (after Karantzali 2003: fig. 8)
FIGURE 3.29. Warrior behind a chariot striking an enemy from Tiryns (after Güntner 2000: pl. 4: 1b)
FIGURE 3.30. Casualty of a maritime skirmish from Kynos (after Dakoronia and Mpougia 1999: 14)
FIGURE 3.31. LHIIIC groom before a horse from Mycenae (after Sakellarakis 1992: 35, fig. 31)

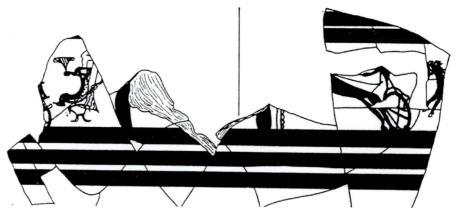

FIGURE 3.32. LHIIIC chariot race from Tiryns (after Rehak 1995: fig. 39: a)

iconography (Fig. 3.32; Vermeule and Karageorghis 1982: 127 no. XI.19, pl. 3.3: 1). These representations of fast chariots and armed charioteers may be compared with the display of military might involving chariots on the shaft grave stelae (Crouwel 1981: 120–1).

The number of ship representations (Figs. 3.33, 3.34, 3.35, and 3.36) increased significantly in LHIIIC.[3] The change is not only quantitative but also one of essence. Here, as in the chariot scenes, there is a shift from static representation of the major characters to a more dynamic one. The people carrying weapons on the Kynos ships do not sit comfortably on the deck, as they had on the LHIIIB krater from Enkomi (Vermeule and Karageorghis 1982: 202 no. V.38), but stand and wave their weapons during a fight. The larger krater from Kynos and the krater from Bademgediği Tepe (Mountjoy 2005a) show two war galleys facing each other, probably depicting a naval battle. Other fragmentary depictions are of sailors and rowers on ships (Wachsmann 1998: 140, fig. 7.26). Ships also appear without people on board and as a decorative, possibly cultic motif.[4]

In contrast to the chariot and ship scenes, hunting scenes of the LHIIIC period show a great deal of continuity. Hunting was not an uncommon theme in the LHIIIA and LHIIIB pottery (Åkerström 1987: 57) and was even more common on LMIIIA2 and LMIIIB painted larnakes (Betancourt 1985: pl. 27; Watrous 1991: 299–300) and frescoes (Immerwahr 1990: 129–30, 132). In the LHIIIA, LHIIIB, and LHIIIC periods, a similar type of hunt is depicted: on the mainland, spears and dogs were used to hunt deer or stags, as seen on

---

[3] Technological and logistic aspects of LHIIIC ships are discussed in Chapter 4.

[4] Vermeule and Karageorghis 1982: 224–5 nos. XI.92–7, 226; Wachsmann 1998: fig. 7.17, 139, figs. 7.21–7.23; Sakellarakis 1992: 115–17 no. 255–7; cf. a LMIIIB depiction of a ship on a larnax from Gazi; Watrous 1991: 298.

FIGURE 3.33. Naval battle on a krater from Bademgediği Tepe (after Mountjoy 2005a: fig. 96)

a krater from Pisaskion (Fig. 3.37). On Crete, there was a continuation in depiction of *agrimi* hunting (Betancourt 1985: 181, pl. 31E). The continuity of hunting practices may be related to the importance of the hunt in forming bonds among elite members, to the training for war it provided, and to the manifestation of control over territory it offered (Morris 1990; Hamilakis 2003; Eder 2006: 553).

Depictions of scenes of chariots and ships also show significant changes in status differentiation. On LHIIIA and LHIIIB pottery, status differentiation is indicated by the depiction of clothing. There is much contrast between naked figures carrying chairs, parasols, or spears or walking in front of chariots and

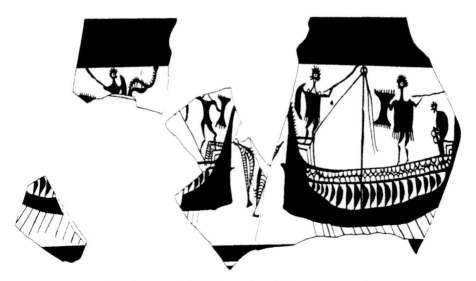

FIGURE 3.34. Naval battle, Kynos (after Dakoronia and Mpougia 1999: 23)

FIGURE 3.35. Oared galley, Kynos (after Dakoronia and Mpougia 1999: 23)

FIGURE 3.36. Sailors on a galley, Phaistos (after Wachsmann 1998: fig. 7.27)

FIGURE 3.37. Hunter and dogs, Pisaskion, Messenia (after Vermeule and Karageorghis 1982: fig. XI.80)

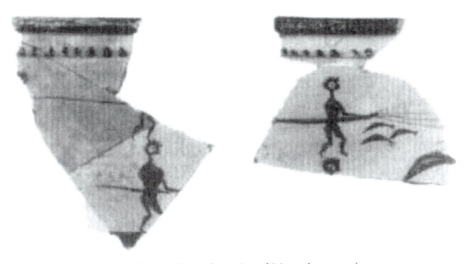

FIGURE 3.38. Fishermen, Kynos (after Dakoronia and Mpougia 1999: 23)

figures clad in spotted robes carrying swords or riding in chariots (Vermeule and Karageorghis 1982: 196 nos. III.16, III.21; 197 no. III.29). Different status is portrayed in another way in LHIIIC: there is a differentiation between large and detailed figures, such as the warriors and the helmsman on the Kynos ships, and the schematized rowers depicted on the same vessel (Dakoronia 1987: 122, fig. 3; Wachsmann 1998: 131–2; Fig. 3.34). A sherd from Phaistos (Wachsmann 1998: 141–2, fig. 7.27; Fig. 3.36) shows only two people on deck, the helmsman and another figure in the stern. The depiction of grooms who run or walk in front of the chariot changes, too: they are no longer naked and no longer carry only a stick or a spear. Already at the end of LHIIIB and into LHIIIC, grooms are dressed and are much better armed with helmets, padded armor, or shields (Figs. 3.24, 3.29, and 3.31; Vermeule and Karageorghis 1982: 215 no. X.1, 220 nos. XI.7, XI.8, 221 nos. XI.20, XI.22; Sakellarakis 1992: 26–8 no. 12, 35 no. 31, 38–9 no. 33, pl. 3.3: 2, 3). It seems that the grooms do not differ much in their appearance from the figures on the chariot (cf. Deger-Jalkotzy 1995: 377).

SYMBOLS OF RULERSHIP, LINEAGE, AND RITUALS

The general lack of kingly imagery in Mycenaean art (Davis 1995: 18) is also reflected in pottery, with the sole exception being the seated figure on the chariot-race vessel from Tiryns (Fig. 3.32). According to Rehak (1995), this is not a male ruler but an enthroned female figure, an image with a long history in the palatial period, connected with palatial functions such as presiding at symposia. If Rehak is right, this long tradition may have continued into

FIGURE 3.39. Fishermen, Aplomata (after Hadjianastasiou 1996: pl. 2a)

LHIIIC; another possible example is the enthroned figure on the painted LHIIIC stele from Mycenae (Immerwahr 1990: 151).

In line with the diminishing role of the old palatial symbols of power, a new source of power emerged in LHIIIC and was depicted on pottery: the community. Communal efforts are celebrated in the depictions of groups of fishermen from Kynos and Aplomata (Figs. 3.38 and 3.39). Men, distinguished by their feather helmets or spiky hairstyles, toil together to pull in nets full of fish. They are all depicted in the same manner, and no superior oversees them. Ceremonies also manifest the community identity, as in the group of dancers depicted on a hydria from Kamini (Fig. 3.40). The sense of community is strengthened by the image of what is perhaps a child between the dancers. A manifestation of communality, though perhaps between aristocrats, is seen also in the depiction of a funeral from Agia Triada, in Elis (Fig. 3.41; Eder 2006: 555), in which mourning women and a child are surrounding the bed of a deceased man. A dog below the bed possibly attests to his aristocratic status. A bearded man to the right drinks from what might be a kylix, while another figure, to the left, rides a horse, thus putting the event in the elite context. A sherd from Lefkandi (Fig. 3.42) shows an adult man, a child, and a vessel,

FIGURE 3.40. Dancers, Kamini (after Mastrapas 1996: fig. 2)

FIGURE 3.41. Funeral, Agia Triada in Elis (after Stoinas 1999: fig. 1)

perhaps a krater, possibly indicating a feast. The participation of both adults and children in the ceremony emphasizes elements of kinship and descent connected with the depicted aristocracy.

BEFORE AND AFTER ELITE SNAPSHOTS ON POTTERY

The LHIIIC elite ideals were considerably different from those of elites in the palatial past. The great majority of the figures are armed, many more than in LHIIIB, and the elite are portrayed as equipped and ready for battle, sometimes even engaged in it. Warrior tombs laden with weapons of the period, possibly belonging to the rulers, perhaps, as Deger-Jalkotzy (1995) argues, to *basileis* indicate the material reality behind the martial imagery. In the palatial pottery art, chariots are the center of dignified parades and a subtle display of authority rather than a combat vehicle mounted by the well-armed elite of the LHIIIC period. The violent images show one of the sources for justification of power: personal achievements and the need to ascertain the rulers' position through a personal display of might (Maran 2006: 142). This

FIGURE 3.42. Man and child at a feast (?) from Lefkandi (after Vermeule and Karageorghis 1982: fig. 11.66)

brings forth an innovative concept of LHIIIC, foreign to the LHIIIB palatial rulership: the status of the ruler can be challenged by force. Hence, the well-organized, hierarchical LHIIIB palatial system in Pylos allowed depictions of Mycenaeans fighting only foreigners, not among themselves, to be viewed by the participants in the feasts in the palace court (Davis and Bennet 1999). Groups of armed Mycenaean elite warriors facing each other or dueling, as on the warrior krater from Mycenae and examples from Grotta and Kos; naval battles between Aegean elite warriors, as on the Kynos kraters; and even chariot races like the one depicted on the Tiryns vase may have been disturbing or even subversive in the palatial reality of social stability. LHIIIC scenes of confrontation, competition, and battle between elite individuals and groups not only manifest the violent everyday reality but also demonstrate that society acknowledged the role of conflict in creating mobility within the ruling elite. Very similar images of armed rulers riding chariots and combat between members of the elite are characteristic of the shaft grave imagery, during the formative period of the creation of the Mycenaean polity in early LH (Laffineur 1995; Acheson 1999). The scenes of fights between members of the elite and the need to demonstrate personal might have been symptomatic of a formative stage in the development of rulership.

The new rulership found new venues in which to display its dominance. To the ancient status symbol of chariots, another symbol was added: the command of a light-rowing galley. More weight is given to the status of the elite warrior as a commander of a ship and to his ability to fight at sea. The domination of the ruler over his subjects or followers is no longer indicated by a host of dignitaries and servants surrounding the main figure in scenes of parades but in the image of the chariot-borne warrior surrounded by his well-armed subjects on foot, or in the image of the warrior on the deck of a ship while dozens of his followers row. To be sure, several aristocratic habits of the palatial past continued, as is evident in scenes of hunting with dogs. These scenes might have been used to connect the contemporary rulers to the relatively recent glories of the palatial past.

As pictorial pottery was often used to display elite ideology during symposia, meant to acquire allies and to strengthen social ties and group identity, the messages of military power and domination are accompanied by ones of alliance and partnership. The isocephalic rows of warriors on the warrior kraters from Mycenae, Volos, and Thermon stress the idea of at least nominal equality between members of groups of elite warriors, and the kraters were perhaps used to recruit peers into joint ventures. The cooperation among several members of the elite who stand on the deck of the Kynos and Bademgediği Tepe ships while their commoner followers row sends a message of coparticipation in a status group in the context of a maritime adventure. In contrast, the appearance of communal effort and ceremonies shows the growing power of the community of nonelite, free people. Freed from palatial constraints,

they, too, manifest their common identity on pictorial pottery, side by side
with that of the rising elites.

CONCLUSIONS

The collapse of the Mycenaean palatial system and the lifting of its bureaucratic
systems of control by taxation, drafts, and corvée duties opened the way for
accelerated processes of social mobility and to surprising variability in forms
of rulership. The fragmentation of political power allowed more people to
attempt to take part in that power. Finds from tombs indicate that, while there
might have been fewer luxury items in circulation than in previous periods,
access to them and to the elite status they showed was less restricted than it had
been in the palatial era. This was the era of social experiments in rulership side
by side with polities that remained unharmed by the turmoil on the mainland.

The justification of new rulership took two major forms: personal achievements and prowess, and claims for hereditary connection to the past palatial
rulership (Maran 2006: 143). The first found its expression in skills of command over warriors and personal combat abilities. The second is reflected
in the ability to possess and manipulate symbols of the palatial past – from
sites of palatial power to the possession of antique luxury items, which can
be connected to family history. The spirit of the LHIIIC period is reflected in
the simultaneous and innovative use of symbols of power on pictorial pottery
that are new (the ship), old (hunt scenes), and modified (chariot scenes).
The use of both old and new symbols may indicate some continuation of the
ruling elite, or lineages, side by side with the emergence of new ones. However,
the adaptation of old elite symbols by new members of the elite classes, or
even claims of descent from the former elite, was not made to reproduce the
hierarchical system of the palaces. Rather, in the context of feasts aimed to
attract allies and strengthen elite cooperation, pictorial pottery manifests the
new spirit of social mobility while supporting the ruler's claims to power by
connecting him to the powerful palatial past. Most of the experiments in rulership were impressive, yet short lived, and none continued into the eleventh
century. Nevertheless, they attest to the great ambition and resourcefulness of
the LHIIIC elite, which materialized unhindered by palatial control. A wide
array of innovative and opportunistic strategies to rise to power emerged:
some became elites close to home by taking over areas in existing settlements
and building large elite houses, as in the lower town of Tiryns, or reusing
remains of the ruined palatial structures as foundations for their new ruler's
dwelling, as in Tiryns, Midea, and perhaps Mycenae. Others traveled overseas
to build their power bases in remote areas, such as Koukounaries, on Paros,
or Kastrokephala, on Crete. These roaming adventurers, as well as pirates and
sea raiders, were among the reasons for the growth of fortified settlements and
local elites in the Mycenaean periphery, as in Grotta, on Naxos. In other areas,

such as at Miletus, rulership continued uninterrupted, perhaps strengthened by the collapse of the powerful mainland polities. With new abilities and aspirations, the willingness to use power to gain power, and without any central authority limiting their ambition, the competitive elites of the twelfth century were ready to play their role in the interregional arena of trade, piracy, and migration.

4

PRECONDITIONS FOR MIGRATION

We may take it as axiomatic that no one leaves home and embarks on colonization for fun.

— Graham 1982: 157

PUSH AND PULL FACTORS AFFECTING MIGRATION

With an almost universal consensus on the supporting paradigm of thousands of Philistines migrating mainly by boats, but also by land, during the course of a relatively short time (Chapter 1), there has been little attempt to study the migration process itself – that which occurred before the first migrant hit the shores of Philistia. It is astonishing that so little has been written on the cause for this migration, considering how important the question of causality is in any anthropological or historical study of migration. Furthermore, a rigorous debate on the number of Philistine migrants and on the power relations between the Philistine settlers and the Egyptians in Canaan (Chapter 8) has not been followed by a close scrutiny of the means that were available for migration: the organizational abilities needed to conduct mass migration as well as transport, routes, and information. Although it may be some time before these significant lacunae are filled in, it is possible to offer here some direction for the study of causality, possible sea and land routes from the Aegean to the Levant, and the logistics of migration in the twelfth century BCE. Insights into the potential to carry out different forms of migration and other interactions, as well as an understanding of which forms of migration were unlikely, may prove helpful when material culture assemblages from the vast area between the Aegean, Anatolia, Cyprus, and the Levant (Chapter 5) are analyzed for signs of interactions.

Causality for the movement of people at the end of the Late Bronze Age has been closely connected with various proposed explanations for the end of the Aegean Bronze Age civilization. Whatever the reason for the end of the palatial culture, it triggered the mass migration of refugees from the Mycenaean world. However, because the flight of refugees is but one of the causes suggested for

Greek colonization (Graham 1982: 142), case studies from Greek colonization of the first millennium and examples from anthropological literature might be relevant to twelfth-century reality in suggesting possible push and pull factors and obstacles en route.

ENVIRONMENTAL PRESSURES AND VIOLENT INVASION

Whether in the form of seasonal or acute natural disasters, environmental pressures can push the decision to migrate. Their primary effect may be an immediate loss of livelihood because of damage caused to crops, fields, plantations, water sources, and so on. The secondary effects of a catastrophe may include social instability, as in the influence of the Theran eruption on Crete (Driessen and Macdonald 1997: 90–8). This instability may, on the one hand, promote migration by breaking down the old social systems and, on the other hand, increase conditions of uncertainty and insecurity that translate into a decision to migrate. Herodotus (4.151.1; Malkin 1987: 61) gives drought as the reason for the settlement of Therans in Cyrene, Rhegium was established following a food shortage brought about by a furious god (Strabo 257; Malkin 1987: 42; Boardman 1980: 163), and the Delphic oracle was consulted before the foundation of Herakleia Pontike because of a plague (Malkin 1987: 73–4).

Drought is thought to be one of the reasons for catastrophe around the Mediterranean at the end of the Bronze Age. Some literary sources indicate famine in Hatti shortly before 1200 BCE (Drews 1993: 79; Bryce 1998: 364–5). The Karnak inscription of Merneptah, which deals with the victory over the Libyans, tells of shipments of grain to "keep alive the land of Hatti." In tablet RS 20.212, a large shipment of two thousand kor of grain, to be transferred rapidly from Mukish to Ura, is described as a matter of life or death. However, no clear signs for an early-twelfth-century-BCE drought in Greece have been found. Burned food remains from the destruction at the end of LHIIIB do not indicate any food shortage (Drews 1993: 84). Records in the Pylos tablets of the distribution of oil and the collection of food strengthen Palaima's (1995a: 626) reconstruction of "business as usual" at Pylos. Furthermore, it is unlikely that long-distance maritime migration would have been the chosen solution for hunger, as it requires a large initial investment in food and other provisions; the settlers would have had to have enough food or the means to buy it until the first harvest, as well as enough seed to sow. Earthquakes may have been another trigger for migration in LHIIIB2 and LHIIIC. A strong case is presented at Tiryns (Drews 1993: 33–47; Kilian 1996; Nur and Cline 2000: 51–3), compounded by flood damage (Zangger 1994). Evidence collected by Nur and Cline (2000: 55–6) may indicate that nearby Mycenae, Midea, and the Menelaion suffered earthquake damage in LHIIIB2, while Kynos encountered the same fate in LHIIIC Early.

Invasion and violent destruction are other explanations for the collapse of the Mycenaean world, influenced much by the myths describing the return of the Heraclides and the coming of the Dorians (Malkin 1994: 33–45) – "events" that find little support in archaeology (Drews 1993: 91–3; Hall 1997: 114–28). The adoption of these tentative mass invasions as factors influencing migration may lead to confusion between cause and result: did the destruction cause the migration, or was it migration that led to destruction? Both instances can be true at the same time. In addition, one should not rule out the possibility of chain migration (Anthony 1997: 26–7), that is, when migration is in itself the cause of other migrations (e.g., of people of the same kin group).

SOCIAL FACTORS

Political instability, personal conflict and rivalry, and social conflict between groups are commonly given as motives for Greek colonization (Chapter 1). Thus, Thucydides (1.12) mentions factions rising in the cities "after the Trojan War" as a cause for colonization. Given the turbulent political reality of the twelfth century, riddled with power struggles and rivalries among aristocrats (Chapter 3), the role of conflict in Greek colonization may be a worthwhile venue of exploration. In general, many Greek foundation stories, whether historical or legendary, depict two social components: the aristocrat who leads the expedition and the commoners who follow. The two are united in their desire to improve their social condition without changing the basis of the social order – the aristocrats still lead and the commoners still follow. The initial impetus to colonize may have come either from the aristocrat (usually acting as an individual) or from the commoners (always acting as a group). In the former case, motivating factors include fear of revenge and punishment by exile, as in the quasi-historical foundation of Rhodes or the historical tradition of the foundation of Syracuse (Dougherty 1993; Malkin 1996: 191). Aristocrats also feared their relatives, as in the quasi-historical story of Elissa of Carthage (Justin 18.4), or their townspeople, as in the case of Timesias, the founder of Abdera, who escaped from his hometown of Klazomenai having realized that he was hated there (Malkin 1987: 54). Another example is the possibly historical tradition depicting Battos, the founder of Cyrene, as a leader of an exiled political faction (Malkin 1987: 62; Dougherty 1993: 182).

Others may have joined the aristocrat for their own reasons – loyalty or personal gain. An unprivileged minority group in a community might have sought to improve its social condition. Such are the cases of the foundation of Taras by Phalanthos (most likely a historical figure), who led a group of dissatisfied people from Sparta (Boardman 1980: 163; Malkin 1987: 47; 1994: 115–22; Sakellariou 1990: 68; Dougherty 1993: 182). Another example is the quasi-historical tale of Theras leading the condemned Minyans from Sparta to Thera (Herodotus 4.146–8; Malkin 1994: 98–106). According to tradition, Phokaia was founded by the illegitimate children of Phokian fathers who took as prisoners women from Orchomenos (Sakellariou 1990: 146; cf. Herodotus 1.146, on the participation of Phokian dissidents in the Ionian colonization).

The children were expelled from Phokis, and led by Athenian aristocrats who supplied them with ships (Pausanias 7.2.4, 7.3.10), they embarked on colonization with a band of Peloponnesians, following the Ionians. Other colonists were generally unfortunate people trying to improve their position by joining an expedition, such as that described firsthand by Archilochus (Strabo 8.370; Graham 1982: 116; Forrest 1982: 256).

A chance to climb higher up the social ladder, combined with the ambition to improve one's economic status, has been postulated as the primary cause of long-distance migration for people from all social strata (Anthony 1990: 900; Chapter 1). Although there seems to have been a concern to preserve the framework of the social order of the old city in the new foundation (Forrest 1982: 257), it is likely that in this new colonial order, both the founder and the colonists gained a higher place in the social hierarchy than they had possessed in the old country. Leading a colonization party improved the status of the aristocrat to that of an *oikist*: he became more than just one of the aristocracy in his hometown. Thus, for example, Dorieus, who did not want to be ruled by his half-brother Kleomenes, the king of Sparta, requested of Sparta a group of people to lead for colonization. He had every reason to expect that, as leader and founder, his status in the colonization party and in the colony would be second to none, unlike at home (Herodotus 5.42; Malkin 1987: 78; 1994: 192–3). Miltiades the Elder, one of the most powerful people of Athens, privately gained information on a colonization site in the Chersonese through his relations of hospitality with the Dolonci (Herodotus 6.35). Unsatisfied with the supreme rule of Peisistratos in Athens, he sent a private inquiry to Delphi and later took with him the Athenians who wished to join him and sailed to the Chersonese, where his people made him their tyrant (Herodotus 6.36). This venture seems to have been entirely private (Graham 1982: 121, 143) rather than an official Athenian one, as the name of Peisistratos is not mentioned in the acts of the foundations. It is likely, however, that Peisistratos did not object to seeing his rival leaving Athens for the remote and dangerous Chersonese. That this colony was considered in Athens the hereditary domain of Miltiades is revealed by the fact that the sons of Peisistratos sent Miltiades the Younger to take over the Chersonese (Herodotus 6.38–40; Graham 1982: 122).

One can easily hypothesize similar motives for migration in the LHIIIC period – a period in which, as in the eighth century, changes and instability in the social structure, affecting both aristocracy and commoners (causing social stasis), may also have created tensions leading to colonization (Chapter 3). In LHIIIB, the strong palatial central control maintained the well-defined social boundaries, keeping peasants and aristocrats, soldiers and craft specialists, in their places, thus regulating the social balance and preventing the rise of dangerous social tensions. The disappearance of this system may have led a great number of people of all social strata to seek to improve their social position by finding a place where they were not bound to their old positions.

Such was the case for large parts of the Peloponnese and central Greece. At the other sites, rivalry between old and new aristocracies, as seen in Tiryns and possibly at other Argolid sites (Chapter 3), may have induced aristocrats and their supporters to leave.

ECONOMIC REASONS

Economic reasons to migrate are tightly connected to social reasons and affect both individuals and groups. The search for livelihood has led individuals to migrate on their own, such as Hesiod's father, leaving poverty in Aeolian Kyme and going to Askra (Hesiod *Works and Days* 699–710). The Greek colonists thought of land plots abroad as the most important means of obtaining livelihood: "Above all the colonists wanted their own plot of land" (Starr 1982: 432). Population pressure and overpopulation are among the reasons that explain the Greek colonization (see Osborne 1996: 80, 119, in response to Graham 1982: 157–8); these, however, can hardly have been the cause of migration in the twelfth century, as during this period, there was most probably a decrease in the number of settlements in mainland Greece, mainly in the Argolid, in comparison to that of LHIIIB (Chapter 3).

Indeed, economic reasons are considered by Sherratt and Sherratt (1991: 373) and Rupp (1998: 213) to be one of the major reasons for twelfth-century-BCE intercultural interactions. This may have been the case for groups of people that had no land in the palatial period and earned their living by serving the palace and receiving rations from it (Hiller 1988). In Pylos, for instance, approximately four thousand of the total population of between fifty thousand and one hundred thousand were directly connected to the palace (Hiller 1988: 63). The sudden or even gradual decline of most of the palaces must have left many of these people (mostly artisans and craftsmen) without a livelihood – their specialized skills were no longer needed. Looking for solutions, some of them may have obtained land through migration, by, for example, joining colonization parties as specialists (e.g., potters, metalworkers) whose skills would be needed in the new settlement. Others may have taken on the role of itinerant craftsmen, wandering by land or by sea (e.g., the possible tinker on the Cape Gelidonya ship: Bass 1997b: 80; Cline 1995; Bloedow 1997). These causes may have encouraged a different sort of migration – one of individuals and individual families. Such are the cases discussed in Chapter 2: the migration of Aegean potters and other artisans to Macedonia, Sicily, and elsewhere.

Desire for land may have forced mainland residents to settle other, marginal areas on the mainland in a nonmaritime migration. It is likely that the energy resources expended in this type of migration were fewer than those needed for maritime migration; therefore, such migrations were more likely practiced by people with fewer resources. Moreover, the level of organization needed for this type of settlement is of a much lesser magnitude that that needed for maritime migration. Overland migration may explain the apparent growth of settlement in Achaea (Chapter 3; Deger-Jalkotzy 1991a: 21–2; Papadopoulos 1991: 35).

TWELFTH-CENTURY-BCE SOURCES OF INFORMATION

The decline in the volume of long-distance trade between LHIIIB and LHIIIC (Cline 1994: 10–11, 16–23, 32) would have had a negative influence on the amount of information about foreign lands that found its way to the Aegean, except for that carried back by mercenaries, raiders, and settlers.

Even if one assumes a total cessation of international trade at the end of the thirteenth century BCE and a total cut in the stream of information, the Alashiyans and other foreigners (Chapter 2) familiar with destinations inside and outside the Aegean were still present in the former palatial centers. It is reasonable that some of these merchants, craftsmen, mercenaries, and others, after losing their livelihood because of the sharp decline in maritime trade, would have used their knowledge for other purposes (e.g., to assist in finding locations for migration and settlement or to guide parties to destinations they were familiar with). Some information may have passed hands in the small-scale exchange of goods in LHIIIC trade. However, the gradual decline in trade with the Orient from the twelfth century to the eleventh century led to the loss of a major source of information on migration destinations, only to reappear in the tenth century BCE, particularly in connection with Euboia (Popham and Sackett 1980; Coldstream 1994b: 47; 1998; Hoffman 1997: 247). Although the Aegean knowledge about the outside world in the thirteenth century was, in many cases, distorted by foreign intermediaries or kept in the circles of the upper elite, the collapse of the palatial system and the interaction ranges of the twelfth century opened new venues for obtaining information. Maritime raids in the Aegean and the Levant (Chapter 5), and even initial migration attempts in the twelfth century, would have provided direct, up-to-date, and more accessible sources of information about destinations, far beyond the possibilities of most of the subjects of the LHIIIB palatial system. More information reached more people of more diverse social backgrounds, thereby enabling them to make informed cost-benefit estimates, which affected the push-pull calculation – the first step in the setting for migration.

THE MARITIME OPTION

SEA ROUTES

Winds and sea currents in the eastern Mediterranean favor travel in a clockwise direction (Murray 1987). Therefore, the journey from the Aegean to the Levant

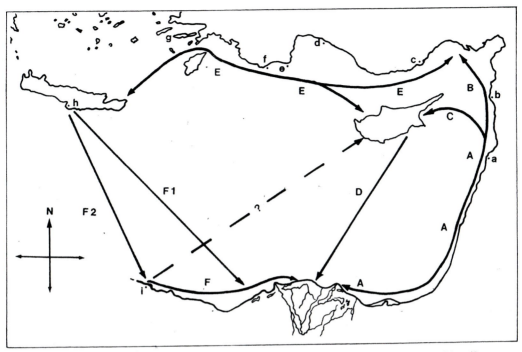

Mediterranean Bronze Age sea routes. Sites: (a) *Byblos,* (b) *Ugarit,* (c) *Ura* (?), (d) *the Side shipwreck,* (e) *Cape Gelidonya,* (f) *Uluburun,* (g) *Deveboynu Burnu,* (h) *Kommòs,* (i) *Mersa Matruh*

FIGURE 4.1. Sea routes in the eastern Mediterranean (after Wachsmann 1998: fig. 13.1)

is often much shorter than the journey in the opposite direction (Fig. 4.1). Although the counterclockwise journey is thought to have been more difficult, some Late Bronze Age ships may have sailed via Egypt, Cyprus, the southern Anatolian coast, Crete, and the Libyan landfall at Marsa Matruh (Casson 1971: 281–2, 289; Sherratt and Sherratt 1991: 357–8; Lambrou-Phillipson 1991; Watrous 1992: 183, fig. 11; Wachsmann 1998: 295–9). The cargoes on three Late Bronze Age shipwrecks discovered at Uluburun and Cape Gelidonya on the Anatolian coast and at Kibbutz Hahotrim on the Levantine coast support this route (Gillis 1995: 69–71).

Only one Late Bronze Age source appears to provide a description of a cruise within the Aegean: the Aegean toponyms carved on the famous statue base of Amenhotep III from Kom el-Hetan (Cline 1998: 238; Wachsmann 1998: 297). These were interpreted as a description of a journey in the Aegean, first circling Crete (Amnissos, Phaistos, and Kydonia) and then moving along mainland Greece (Mycenae, Tegea or Thebes, Messenia or Methana, and Nauplion). Then followed a visit to Kythera and Asia Minor (Ilios), and a return to Crete (Knossos, Amnissos, and Lyktos). This is a rather tempting idea, yet the facts that some of the sites are inland, unapproachable by a sea journey, and that the order of the sites inside mainland Greece does not correspond to their geographical position, cast some doubt on this reconstruction.

No Late Bronze Age source describes a route from the Aegean to the Levant, apart from that of Sinaranu from Ugarit to Crete. A possible solution to this problem is to use later sources on maritime travel, if only to suggest possible routes and not as proof of routes actually used. One can follow Wachsmann (1998: 296–7), who uses the route of Abbot Nicolás from the middle of the twelfth century CE as an illustration of the sea route he proposes from the Aegean to the Levant (Fig. 4.2). The abbot started at Bari and passed the Ionian Islands, the Dodecanese, the southwestern Anatolian coast, and Cyprus, landing finally in Acre. The Crusaders route to the Holy Land from Rhodes was along the coast to Cape Gelidonya, then (avoiding Cape Antalya) south to Cape Arnuati, then to Paphos on Cyprus, crossing to Beirut, and continuing along the coast to Acre or to Jaffa (Pryor 1995b: 216). Similarly, a Venetian galley fleet sailed in 1122–3 via Corfu, Methone, Rhodes, and Cyprus (Pryor 1995b). The prominence of Rhodes and Cyprus as landfalls on the way to the coast of the Levant may hint that such a route could have been used in the twelfth century by travelers between the Aegean and Philistia.

SHIPS AND THEIR CAPACITY

There is no reason to assume that the ability to build ships was curtailed by the fall of LHIIIB administration. Wedde (1998) argues for a continuation in Aegean shipbuilding from the Mycenaean period to the Late Geometric period, based on representations of ships from Proto-Geometric to Middle Geometric that bridge the gap between the twelfth and the eighth centuries BCE. He points to four factors to explain this continuity of tradition: The millennia-long tradition of shipbuilding in the Aegean, the absence of strict central control over maritime activity, locally available raw materials, and long life expectancy of ships. The decline in international trade might have restricted the vessels built to merchantmen and small-oared galleys for military purposes (Wallinga 1995: 36), but this could have been balanced by a growing demand by the private sector for fishing vessels, smaller merchantmen, and oared galleys.

The archaeological evidence for the existence of oared galleys in LHIIIC is much stronger than that for merchant ships. Almost all depictions of ships belong to Wedde's (1981: 86) types V and VI, which include galleys popular in LHIIIB. Examples of depictions of galleys on LHIIIC pottery come from Tragana (Wachsmann 1995: 28; Sakellarakis 1992: 115 no. 255), Phylakopi, Phaistos (Fig. 3.36), Skyros, and Asine. Most of them depict vessels of a similar type, propelled by oars and a sail (Wachsmann 1998: 134–41). Fragmentary depictions from Seraglio are of sailors and rowers on ships (Morricone 1972–3: 360–1, fig. 358; Wachsmann 1998: 140, fig. 7.26; fig. 5.75).

The richest and most detailed representations of LHIIIC ships come from Kynos, a site in East Lokris. Of the other two more fully preserved clay models

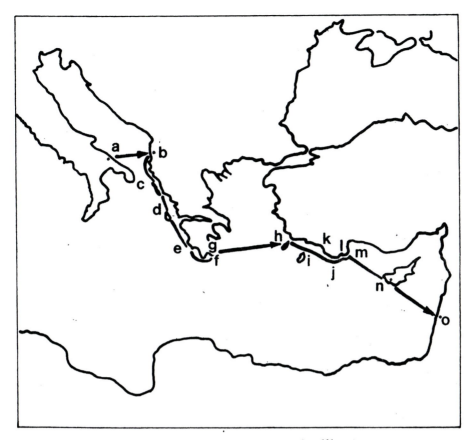

The route of Abbot Nikolás from Italy to Acco in the mid-twelfth century A.D.
included the following sites: (a) Bari, (b) Durazzo, (c) Corfu, (d) Cephalonia, (e) Sapienza,
(f) Cape Malea, (g) Martin Carabo, (h) Kos, (i) Rhodes, (j) Kastellorizon, (k) Patara, (l) Myra,
(m) Cape Gelidonya, (n) Paphos, (o) Acco

FIGURE 4.2. The sea route of Abbot Nicolás (after Wachsmann 1998: 296–7)

found at the site (Dakoronia 1996), one has a straight keel and a low hull and probably represents an oared galley. The other model has a curved keel, giving the appearance of a deeper vessel, possibly the only existing example of a LHIIIC merchantman. Depictions of oared galleys on pictorial kraters from Kynos illustrate long ships with a shallow hull (Dakoronia 1987: 118; 1996: 171, fig. 9). A fragmentary krater shows a galley with a helmsman and two warriors on board (Fig. 3.35). A more complete scene shows a naval battle between two galleys, noted before for its depiction of interelite rivalry (Chapter 3; Dakoronia and Mpougia 1999: 23; Fig. 3.34). Two warriors appear on the deck of the right-hand, more complete ship (Dakoronia 1987: 119), and a helmsman holds the steering oar at the stern. The bodies of nineteen rowers, their heads hidden by the deck, are depicted below the warriors.

The large LHIIIC Early or Transitional LHIIIB–LHIIIC krater from Bademgediği Tepe (Fig. 3.33) depicts the crew in much greater detail than the ship. On the more preserved, left-hand ship, a row of standing warriors with "hedgehog" helmets extends from bow to stern. The prow is in the shape of a bird or dragon. Below, only five rowers are depicted, yet it is likely that the detail of their depiction was at the expense of showing the accurate number of rowers. With this evidence, one cannot escape the idea that the most common – and therefore the most available – LHIIIC craft for long-range travel was the oared galley. However, it is possible that some merchantmen of the Uluburun and Kynos types, and perhaps some LHIIIA or LHIIIB Wedde type IV ships, were still seaworthy and active in LHIIIC (Wedde 1991: 85) but not depicted because of an artistic bias in favor of galleys.

THE FEASIBILITY OF MASS MARITIME MIGRATION AND EVACUATION

How many people could be carried on LHIIIC ships is a tantalizing question, because it has direct implications for the ability to execute certain types of interactions, the first of which is the mass maritime migration postulated for the Philistines. An insight into the type of maritime logic for this inquiry can be found in Thucydides (1.10.4), who explains why the Greek ships that sailed to Troy were not laden with many soldiers: first, because they were about to cross the sea with all their heavy gear, and second, because the ships were not κατάραφακα ("with deck") (Morrison 1996: 255–6). Even if these words reflect only fifth-century practice, they suggest some important variables concerning the subject of carrying capacity:

* The number of people aboard a ship was dependent on the length of the journey, the conditions of travel, and the aim of the journey.
* The presence of a deck is crucial for determining the number of passengers.

Coates (1987) gives a total of thirty-one for a triaconter. The same author gives an estimate of fifty soldiers (in addition to the fifty rowers) aboard a one-level penteconter but offers no explanation for this seemingly high number. Different numbers of people per ship are given in the catalog of ships in the *Iliad*, the only literary source that may have any bearing on this topic for the LHIIIC period. The number of 50 men given for each of the seven ships led by Philoctetes (Hom. *Il.* 2.718–19) may be more realistic than the 120 men for each Boiotian ship (Hom. *Il.* 2.509–10). Indeed, this latter number seems too high for the Bronze Age, and Morrison (1980: 12, 17) noted that "a ship of 60 oars a side on two levels is not an impossibility for the [eighth] century, but is most unlikely earlier" (cf. Meijer 1986: 14). The picture of the manning of the ships in the *Odyssey* is somewhat similar to that of the picture in the Kynos kraters and models: on each penteconter were fifty oarsmen and two officers, all of them warriors (Hom. *Od.* 8.35; Morrison 1980: 12; Porozhanov 1996: 368). A team of three officers per penteconter is reconstructed by Casson (1971: 300) from different sources belonging to the classical period. A similar picture for the crew of war penteconters is seen on an Athenian vase painting of the first half of the sixth century (Casson 1994: 68), showing three officers on board: the captain-helmsman, the rowing officer, and the bow officer. The titles held by the five trireme officers were preserved from the days when the penteconter had been the line-of-battle ship (Casson 1971: 302–3; 1994: 67, 69).

Wachsmann (1998: 159–61) uses the historical occurrences of the Phokaian escape from Ionia and the flight of Loli, the king of Sidon, and his family to Cyprus as case studies for the marine evacuation of a settlement in the face of an advancing enemy. On the basis of these examples, he re-creates a mechanism of massive marine migrations in the twelfth century, when Aegean populations such as that of Pylos chose maritime evacuation in the face of a crisis. Although it has been demonstrated here that Pylos was probably not evacuated by sea (Chapter 2), the case studies of Wachsmann require closer consideration to support the idea of mass evacuations in the early twelfth century.

In the account of the flight of Loli and his family to Cyprus, no number is given of people sailing to Cyprus, yet the relief depicting the event (Wachsmann 1998: 127, fig. 7.6, 160) shows a mixed fleet of at least twelve biremes, both war galleys and oared round merchant ships. All the rowers and most of the people aboard the ships are men; some women are also depicted, and only one child is shown, handed over by a man beside the city gates to a woman aboard one of the ships.[1] It seems that so many people were able to be taken aboard these ships because they had an additional top deck, above the two levels of rowers, which could be used in its entirety for carrying passengers (Casson 1971: 57). It is reasonable to suppose that the penteconters in Xerxes' navy were of a similar type, as Herodotus claims that they could carry a total of eighty men – thirty more than the number of rowers (Herodotus 7.184.3; Casson 1971: 305 no. 25).

The Phokaians, fleeing from the advancing Persians, placed their women, children, and possessions in their penteconters and sailed to Chios (Herodotus 1.164). No numbers are given for this evacuation, and because the duration of the enterprise is not given either, it is possible that it included several trips between Phokaia and Chios. This complicated venture was probably made possible by the relatively short distance between Phokaia and Chios. The Phokaians probably stayed on Chios for some time, as Herodotus describes several of their activities before a number of them sailed for remote Cyrnus (Corsica). During this time, they negotiated seriously, though unsuccessfully, for the purchase of the nearby Oinousses. When negotiation failed, they prepared to set out for the settlement in Cyrnus – a much more complicated

---

[1] See the flight of the eight thousand Persians from Tripoli to Cyprus, in fear of Alexander's advancing army (Arrian *Anabasis Alexandri* 2.13.2–3).

and longer-distance venture. Organizing such a venture took more time than did the fast evacuation from Phokaia. It seems that, during that phase, many people had second thoughts: a large number of the refugees were unwilling to travel that far and preferred to go back home to Phokaia. We know this because of the actions taken to prevent their desertion: a raid on the Persian garrison, which was meant to prevent refugees from returning for fear of Persian retaliation, and the oaths and curses made against anyone who was to return. These measures did not work and more than half of the population broke its oath and went back to Phokaia (Herodotus 1.165), preferring, perhaps, life on their own land under Persian occupation to the prospects of a long sea journey to an unknown land in possibly overcrowded ships.

Herodotus mentions four more cases of evacuation, and though some are described only briefly, all clearly demonstrate that maritime evacuation could be carried out only for short distances, and that evacuation did not usually lead to long-distance maritime colonization. The first case Herodotus mentions is the relatively short-distance evacuation of the Teians escaping to Thrace, where they founded Abdera (Herodotus 1.168). Because the description is so brief, however, little can be said about aspects such as duration and type of ships used. The second case is that of the ill-fortuned Phokaian colonists who, following a defeat in a naval battle, evacuated Cyrnus and traveled to Alaia, also on Corsica (Herodotus 1.167). It is likely that this evacuation was carried out in twenty warships – the remains of the Phokaian fleet; but whether these were double-decked penteconters of triremes is unknown, as is the size of the Cyrnus population. The duration of the evacuation is also not mentioned, and because the destination was close, it is possible that the ships made several trips. Another case of full evacuation (probably in a variety of vessels) is that of the Athenian population to Salamis in 480 BCE, in advance of the Persian invasion. But this evacuation was probably not only by sea; the old men, possessions, and cult objects were taken to Salamis, while the women and children were taken to Troizen (Jameson 1960: 199, 201, 210–11, 219; Herodotus 7.41). Finally, the evacuation of the Plataian population also occurred at more or less the same time as the evacuation of Athens: the Plataians did not participate in the Battle of Artemision because they were busy conveying their households to safety (Herodotus 7.44).

The evidence for the Greek and Sidonian evacuations demonstrates that oared galleys, such as penteconters, could have been used in cases of emergency to carry many more people than they were originally designed to transport. However, such irregular use would have been highly uncomfortable and efficient for only short distances, such as that between the Ionian coast and Chios, or between Athens and Salamis. It is plausible that more than one trip per ship was needed to complete the evacuations of Phokaia, Plataia, and perhaps even Sidon. Partial manning of the oars was another possible means of dealing with emergency, either to allow immediate departure or to gain more space on the ship for passengers and goods. There are examples of the partial manning of oars in triremes converted to transport men and horses (Casson 1971: 93–4). Although partial manning may have been possible on ships with two or more levels of rowers, it would have been more practical on one-row galleys employed on short journeys that did not require much maneuvering, such as approaches to a rocky port entrance; they seem to have been less common on longer expeditions. The evacuation by Loli was carried out using two-level galleys with complete decks, and this may also have been the case with the Phokaian evacuation. This type of galley, which was available to the Greek colonizers of the eighth century (Casson 1971: 53–6), was, of course, unavailable in the twelfth century BCE. If evacuation was carried out in a LHIIIC galley, where was the nonrowing population located? There was at least a partial longitudinal deck, such as that on which the Kynos warriors stood. In addition, there was a stern castle and a bow castle (Wachsmann 1995: 27; 1998: 133–4; cf. 173 for a similar reconstruction of the Sea Peoples' galleys). At maximum capacity, filling all available space in the castles, on the partial deck, and between the rowers, the number of nonrowing passengers would still have been considerably smaller than the number of rowers.

Merchantmen such as the one in the Kynos model and examples of the Homeric *eikosoros*, a twenty-oared ship (Wallinga 1995: 42–3; Casson 1995: 118), may have been in common use during LHIIIC, yet they are less documented than the more prestigious war galleys on which heroes of the past and warriors of the present could show their valor. Still, the merchantmen of the LHIIIC do not seem to have been of much use for mass migration or evacuation. Vessels the size of the Uluburun or Point Iria ships (about ten to twelve meters long) were made for transporting cargo and could not contain as many people as the longer war galleys that were built to convey maximum capacity of rowers. Merchantmen are less maneuverable and slower than war galleys and therefore much more vulnerable to attack and much harder to use as raiding vessels in colonizing missions in unfriendly environments. In addition, it is hard to believe that large merchantmen of the Uluburun size were common in the Aegean in numbers large enough to allow mass evacuation. Merchantmen could not, therefore, be a solution for mass evacuation any more than oared galleys could.

On the basis of this evidence, although the option of complete evacuation was a possibility in LHIIIC, it was practicable only for short journeys that involved more than one trip per ship. Longer sea travel demanded considerably less crowded ships; the problems of storing provisions and equipment became more severe as the number of people on board increased and the journey grew longer.

THE SIZE OF A MARITIME MIGRATION PARTY

Maritime interactions need well-trained seamen – sailors and rowers – in relatively large numbers: more than fifty for the basic crew of a penteconter and more than thirty for the basic crew of a triaconter. To assess the minimal manpower required for a migration venture at the end of the Bronze Age, one should first approximate the size of the initial migration parties – those who would form the bridgehead for settlement and would be later supplemented by additional settlers. The only probable record for the size of a fleet in the Aegean Bronze Age is that of the Pylos Rower Tablets (Chapter 2), which mention about six hundred men journeying in twelve to twenty vessels.

Evidence for maritime activity from Ugarit, discussed in Chapter 5, includes a reference to an enemy fleet of twenty ships in a letter of the chief prefect of Alashiya to the king of Ugarit (RS 20.18; Hoftijzer and van Soldt 1998: 343). However impressive the number, there is no indication of the size or capacity of the ships. Smaller fleets were also in use – seven ships of raiders later ravaged the city of Ugarit (RS 20.238; Yon 1992: 116; Hoftijzer and van Soldt 1998: 344) and during the eleventh century, eleven ships of the Tjeker (or Sikel) of Dor chased Wen-Amon to Cyprus. The nine-ship fleet assembled by Odysseus (Hom. *Od.* 14.248) in his fictitious raid on Egypt was of similar size. These numbers may be compared to the allegedly magnificently strong Ugaritic fleet – more than 150 ships, if the number in Yadinu's request to the king of Ugarit has any connection to reality (KTU 2.47; Hoftijzer and van Soldt 1998: 336–7). Allowing the modest number of twenty people for the crew of each Ugaritic ship, as reconstructed from the list of ship crews in KTU 4.40 – a text of, perhaps, some similarity to the Rower Tablets from Pylos (Hoftijzer and van Soldt 1998: 337) – Yadinu requested a minimum of three thousand seamen. This number seems exaggerated under any circumstances, constituting more than 33 percent of the urban population of the kingdom of Ugarit (Yon 1992: 113).

In the archaic period, the size of colonization parties seems to have been modest, and thus close, perhaps, to the reality of the twelfth century: one thousand at Leukas and two hundred at Apollonia in Illyria (Graham 1982: 146). Although one may question the historicity of many details in the foundation stories of Thera and Cyrene, the numbers given for the initial foundation, two penteconters (Herodotus 4.155–156) and three triaconters (Herodotus 4.148), respectively (Graham 1982: 146; Malkin 1994: 89, 98), demonstrate a plausible scale for initial settlement. Thus, it would seem that a minimum number of colonists for the initial foundation may have been about two hundred: a group that could fit inside two to three double-level penteconters of the eighth to sixth centuries, or inside three to four earlier, one-level penteconters. A smaller number of ships (fewer than two) and men seems unlikely even in situations in which no hostility was expected on arrival. The bridgeheads founded by these small expeditions were likely to be supplemented by additional migrants from the home country or from other regions, or by locals (Graham 1982: 146–7).

LHIIIC RECRUITMENT CAPABILITIES

The organization of human resources for maritime migration, even the most modest attempt, was beyond the power of a single small community. Continuation of Pylos-style corvée recruitment for state-orchestrated ventures was unlikely in LHIIIC after the end of central power and literate administration. It is possible that the recruitment of human resources was an enterprise organized by powerful individuals who assembled interested, free people in the venture. Some of the polities of the LHIIIC were probably sufficiently populous and centralized to be able to at least initiate overseas settlement on their own or to contribute substantially to a joint venture with other polities. Candidates for ventures of these sorts may have included fortified towns such as Mycenae (smaller than four hectares), Miletus (five hectares; Gates 1995: 291), and Phylakopi. In the case of the latter, an estimate can be made of the number of rowers during LHIIIC. The supportive capacity of the Phylakopi catchment area is calculated by Sanders (1984: 260) to have been of 1,400 to 2,250 people, while the entire island could easily have supported 5,000 people. If men able to row made up about 20 percent of the population, a population of this size had between five hundred (in Phylakopi) and one thousand (on the entire island) potential rowers. The potential of twenty penteconters was never fully realized for migration; it is highly improbable that the entire population of able men on the island migrated and left behind their women and children and the elders, for whom there was not room on the oared galleys. It is more likely that if a full tenth of the population wished to migrate, they would be able to crew only one or two penteconters.

Tiryns, with its twenty-five hectares and perhaps as many as ten thousand inhabitants (Kilian 1988b: 135; Shelmerdine 1997: 543), may have been one of the few polities able to start a substantial maritime migration initiative of its own.[2] The combination of powerful elites during the LHIIIC at the sites of Tiryns, Mycenae, Miletus, and Phylakopi (Chapter 3) together with strong push factors of political competition and natural disasters increases the possibility of their involvement in maritime migration. However, the scale was not of the Pylian type, as it is unlikely that the ruling elite of the four sites possessed as much recruiting power in LHIIIC as it did in LHIIIB, when one thousand people were registered on a Linear B tablet from Tiryns, perhaps for corvée labor (Kilian 1988b: 149).

Because rowing is not a pleasant work, there is a tremendous difference between the recruitment potential and the actual recruitment of needed personnel on board. Even large and strong polities (which normally did not use slaves to row; Casson 1971: 322–3, 327) such as classical Athens (Gabrielsen 1994:

---

[2] Having a potential of two thousand men able to row, or enough to crew forty penteconters in the unlikely event of a full evacuation.

105–10) and medieval Venice (Dotson 1995: 222) faced considerable difficulties in securing manpower for their fleets of oared galleys. In the complex reality of the twelfth century, persuasion, rather than force, was used to recruit rowers. The recruitment of even twenty rowers to crew a vessel the size of the Homeric *eikosoros* merchantman may have been a difficult task for an individual. This opened the arena for scenarios of business partnerships in which some of the rowers brought their merchandise on board with them (Wallinga 1995: 43). Otherwise, a core crew of a merchant or an aristocrat and his followers might have recruited people in a harbor or coastal settlement to participate in an expedition.

Cases of later Greek colonization may offer insights into ways in which an immigration party was formed and equipped in the LHIIIC. Ad hoc pacts between commoners and aristocrats can be seen, for example, in the "agreement of the founders" in which Battos is made *archegetes* and *basileus* in Cyrene (although only after the foundation; Malkin 1987: 61–2), and probably also in the case of the migration of the unwanted Partheniai from Sparta to found Taras, led by Phalanthos, who was either a Spartan or one of the Partheniai (Boardman 1980: 163; Malkin 1987: 47; 1994: 139–42; Sakellariou 1990: 68). According to a tradition reported by Pausanias (7.2.4, 7.3.10), Philogenes and Damos, sons of Euktaimon, gave the founders of Phokaia Athenian ships and led them (Sakellariou 1990: 147). These agreements allowed aristocrats the option of maritime migration with a number of supporters, and they allowed commoners without the needed resources to migrate. Pacts may have been made to recruit the necessary manpower for the migration and to gain access to leadership, resources, transportation, and information about the destination. In these instances, the size of the community of departure may have had only a secondary effect on the size of the party.

DISTANCE AND TIMING

Although space on board the ships used in the twelfth century and recruitment abilities to staff the ships seriously hindered the scale of maritime interactions, once a galley was under way with provisions for a week or so, it could have rather swiftly reached the Levantine coast from the Aegean. According to Casson (1971: 288, 291), in favorable conditions, ancient ships were able to sail at four to six knots, and at less than two or two and a half knots against the wind, depending on whether the journey was on the open sea or close to shore.[3] Eventually, the speed of a fleet was determined by its slowest ship. Casson (1971: 292–6) suggests, therefore, a speed of two to three knots with favorable winds, and one to one and a half knots with unfavorable winds.

---

[3] Speed of 1 knot = 1 nautical mile/hour; 1.85 km = 1 nautical mile.

TABLE 4.1. *An estimate of the time needed for migrants, raiders, or traders to have sailed from the Aegean to the coast of the Levant*

Voyage	Distance (nautical miles)	Length of voyage (days)	Speed (knots), condition of wind	
Rhodes–Alexandria	325	3.5	3.9, favorable wind	Casson 1971: 287
Byzantium–Rhodes	445	5	3.7, favorable wind	Casson 1971: 288
Byzantium–Gaza	855	10	3.6, favorable wind	Casson 1971: 288
Gaza–Byzantium	855	20	1.8, unfavorable wind	Casson 1971: 289
Rhodes–Gaza	410	5	3.4, favorable wind	Calculation based on the Byzantium–Rhodes and Byzantium–Gaza information
Rhodes–Gaza	410	7	2.4, unfavorable wind	Casson 1971: 289
Rhodes–Alexandria	375	4–5		Pryor 1995b: 216
Thessalonica–Ascalon	800	12	2.8, favorable wind	Casson 1971: 288
Ascalon–Thessalonica	800	13	2.6, unfavorable wind	Casson 1971: 289
Caesarea–Rhodes	400	10	1.7, unfavorable wind	Casson 1971: 289
Athens–Rhodes	275	ca. 3.5	3.4, favorable wind	Speed calculation based on the Thessalonica–Ascalon voyage; distance based on Casson 1971: 292
Eastern Crete–Nile Delta	310	4	3.2	Lambrou-Phillipson 1991: 12

There are also indications that galleys could obtain higher speeds. Malkin and Fichman (1987: 252) consider a speed of three knots likely for a ship under sail but calculate a speed of four to five knots for the legendary account of the journey of Nestor from Chios to Geraistos (Hom. *Od.* 3.153–85). The journey, of 97.5 nautical miles, started at dawn and ended that same night, probably taking about twenty hours in favorable winds. Coates (1995: 136) suggests a sustainable speed of five to five and a half knots for a one-level penteconter, yet this may be optimum for a ship with favorable winds and almost constant use of oars. A speed of 4.6 knots was achieved for thirty-one nautical miles by the crew of the reconstructed trireme *Olympias* (Shaw 1993: 42). Table 4.1, based mainly on travelers' reports collected by Casson (1971) and others, gives a rough estimate of the time needed for migrants, raiders, or traders to have sailed from the Aegean to the coast of the Levant, traveling at a speed of between two and four knots. It suggests that a convoy of ships using sails and from time to time propelled by oars (as were the twelfth-century penteconters), needed nine to eleven days to travel from the eastern Aegean mainland to Philistia, and less time if the starting point was in Rhodes or Cilicia.

THE LAND OPTION

POSSIBLE LAND ROUTES

A land route from mainland Greece to the Levantine coast is also a possibility, and it may be hinted at in the Medinet Habu reliefs, which depict Sea Peoples migrants' travel on land with ox-drawn wagons and chariots (Chapter 5; Fig. 5.68). As maritime travel was costly and had severe space limitations, most armies, as well as many travelers, preferred to travel by land, going from Europe or Anatolia to the Levant. Descriptions by early travelers and pilgrims, as well as the records of the movements of armies to the Orient, can help determine possible land routes to the Levantine coast. Mutafian (1988: 116) reconstructs the following possible routes to the Levantine coast from western Anatolia (Fig. 4.3):

1. Avoiding Cilicia: This is the longest option: from the west to Kayseri, then south to Marash, around the Taurus Mountains, and southward avoiding the Amanus.
2. Through Cilicia: This is the shortest route and goes through the Konya Plain, then across the Taurus, via the Cilician Gates to Tarsus. The route then diverges – one way goes to the south and the other to the east:
   a. The eastern way is through the Amanus Gates, near the modern village of Balçe.
   b. The southern way is across the Syrian Gates (between Alexandrette and Antiochia) of the Amanus and then along the coast to the south, continuing to the southern Levant by the main coastal highway (Aharoni 1979: 45–6; Astour 1995: 1415).

Several examples of the use of these roads between the Bronze Age and medieval times further illustrate key points along the route:

1. In his first Syrian campaign, Hattusili I (second half of the seventeenth century BCE) probably passed the Taurus Mountains through the Cilician Gates (Bryce 1998: 75–6). He then crossed the Amanus Mountains through the Syrian Gates (Beilan Pass) and entered Syria, attacking Alalakh on the northern bend of the Orontes.
2. The route taken by Alexander the Great from the Aegean to the Levantine coast (Mutafian 1988: 132–7) is somewhat similar to the one taken by the later "traveler from Bordeaux" (see section "Speed in Land Travel"). He crossed the Hellespont to Troy and then traveled to Lydia and Caria through the cities of Sardis, Ephesos, Miletus, and Halicarnassus. From there he rode to Lycia and on to central Anatolia, crossing the Pamphylian Taurus via Gordion and Angora. The road led south, crossing the Taurus Mountains through the Cilician Gates to Tarsus (Arrian *Anabasis Alexandri* 2.4.2–6).

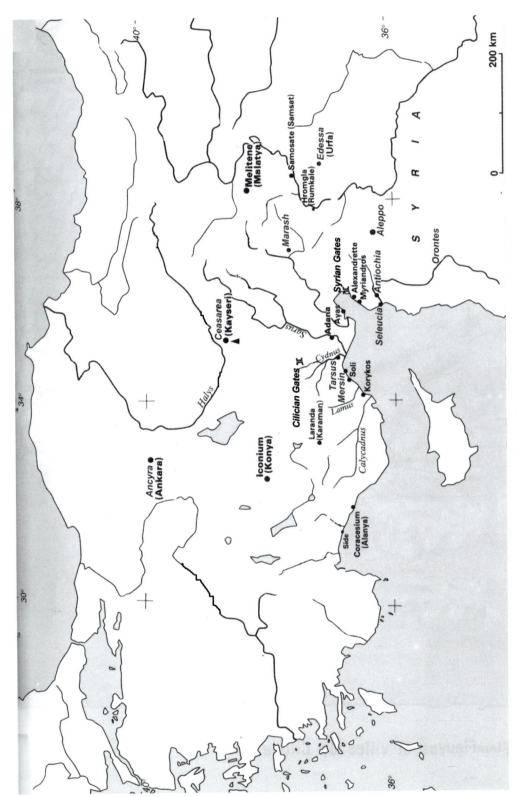

FIGURE 4.3. The land route from the Aegean to the Levant (after Mutafian 1988)

Before crossing the Amanus Mountains, Alexander fought a battle at Issos (Arrian *Anabasis Alexandri*: 2.6–11) and then continued toward the area of Antioch and down along the Phoenician coast, capturing Tyre (2.15.6–2.24.4). From Phoenicia, he continued along the coast to Gaza (2.26).

3. The Antonine route (Mutafian 1988: 116), created and used in the second to third century CE, led from Constantinople to Antioch, through Angora, Caesarea (or Iconium), the Cilician Gates, Tarsus, Adana, and Misis (or Mallos), and then – passing on the west side of the Amanus and around the Gulf of Issos – to Alexandria and Antioch, through the Syrian Gates. In a variant of this route, after the river Pyramus, one could have gone east through the Amanus Gates and then south to the Gulf of Issos.

4. The "traveler from Bordeaux" made the trip to Jerusalem from France in 333 CE (Hunt 1984: 55). His road passed through Italy, the Balkans, and Constantinople. From there, it went through Asia Minor to the Cilician Gates and Tarsus, to Antioch, and along the coast to Caesarea. A similar road from Constantinople to Jerusalem was taken by Melania the Younger (Hunt 1984: 56).

5. Finally, the First Crusade is an excellent example of the many variations of a journey that could be made taking one of the two major routes, through or around Cilicia (Mutafian 1988: 155–60, map 45). The Crusaders crossed to Asia after bypassing Constantinople, crossed Phrygia without reaching the western Anatolian coast, and split into three parties at Heraclea (Eregli). Baldwin crossed the Taurus through the pass of Aydos and reached Tarsus; from there he continued east to Edessa. Tancred crossed the Taurus at the Cilician Gates on the way to Tarsus and continued to the southeast, crossing the Amanus at the Syrian Gates and continuing toward the Holy Land through Antioch, a route similar to that taken by Alexander. Other barons continued from Heraclea to Caesarea, crossing the Anti-Taurus Mountains on the way south, flanking the Amanus along its east to reach Antioch.

Looking at these sources, one cannot avoid acknowledging the importance of Cilicia in general and Tarsus in particular for land travels from the western Anatolian coast to the Levant.

THE LAND ROUTE OPENS

Because of unusual political circumstances, the land route from western Anatolia to the Levant may have presented far fewer political obstacles for travelers at the beginning of the twelfth century than it had at any previous time. For a short period, virtually all the powers in Anatolia were overwhelmed, enabling potential migrants to use this window of opportunity and travel south and east, unhindered by the powers that controlled the area in the thirteenth

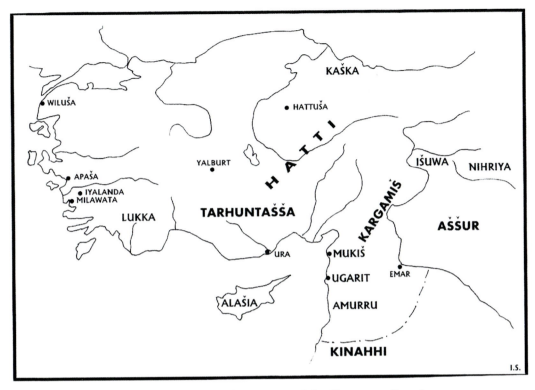

FIGURE 4.4. Anatolian powers in the thirteenth century BCE (after Singer 2000: fig. 2.1)

century (Yasur-Landau 2003d: 38; Fig. 4.4). In the northwest, the kingdom of Wilusa, with its center at Troy, had been destroyed in about 1200, as indicated by the redating of the Stratum VIIa destruction to the Transitional LHIIIB–LHIIIC by Mountjoy (1999b). Although Troy was rebuilt soon afterward, it is likely that, for a period of time, it was possible to cross the Dardanelles from Europe to Anatolia and to follow the land routes of the Troad, leading south toward Ephesos and Miletus and leading to the southeast toward Iconium. If one accepts the words of Ramses III at Medinet Habu (Chapter 5), Arzawa, located south of Wilusa, was similarly destroyed, opening the road from the Troad to the south. The road was further opened to the south and east by the destruction of Hatti proper (Hoffner 1992; Bryce 1998: 378–9) and by the considerable damage inflicted on its southern vassal kingdom Tarhuntassa (seen in the destruction of Porsuk; Yakar 1993: 12). Some of the Hittite dynasty continued to rule in Carchemish (which also suffered destruction according to Ramses III), and another branch of the family took over the kingdom of Malatya several generations later (Güterbock 1992). They were probably in no condition, however, to pose any considerable threat to land transport from the west to the south. This vacuum in central and southern Anatolia enabled free traffic from the western coast toward Cilicia. Most important, Kizzuwatna (Kode at Medinet Habu), the Cilician kingdom, which controlled the passages to Syria, was destroyed and its capital, Tarsus, burned (Yakar 1993: 14–15; Chapter 5). The destruction of Ugarit at the beginning of the twelfth century opened the coastal highway to Canaan. With the land route open, people could roam freely between Troy and the Levant. It may be that the only considerable organized military force between western Anatolia and Philistia in the twelfth century were the Egyptian garrisons in Canaan.

MEANS OF LAND TRANSPORT IN THE THIRTEENTH TO TWELFTH CENTURY

As maritime transport was certainly not the only option for migration at the close of the Late Bronze Age, a survey of the means of land transport in the thirteenth- to twelfth-century Aegean may contribute to our understanding of the possibilities for conducting an overland migration to the Levant through Anatolia. The Medinet Habu reliefs (Chapter 5) offer direct evidence that travel by foot, chariot, and ox-drawn wagons were important means of transportation used by the migrants in the twelfth century (Nelson 1930: pl. 32; for a discussion of the origin of these migrants, see Chapter 5). This comes as little surprise, because these were generally the main means of land transport, followed by pack animals or riding animals and litters, used elsewhere in the Aegean and the eastern Mediterranean during that period (Crouwel 1981: 15).

Chariots were probably too delicate for long-distance migration and were undoubtedly used only for battle (Sandars 1978: 121), after which they were dismantled and carried on journeys.

Pack animals could have been used to facilitate overland migration. The use of pack animals in the twelfth-century Aegean is manifested in a zoomorphic vessel of an equid laden with two amphorae, from LMIIIC Phaistos, and in other examples of equid-shaped vessels, some carrying pottery vessels, from LHIIIC Ialysos (Crouwel 1981: 44). Riding animals could also have been in use in the LHIIIC, continuing a somewhat unpopular tradition of Bronze Age horse riding, seen in representations such as the horse rider from Mouliana (Crouwel 1981: 46; Betancourt 1985: 181).[4] These horse riders seem to have played a limited military role rather than one of an everyday transport. Other riding animals include the LMIIIC equids carrying a sidesaddle-riding goddess in Crete (Crouwel 1981: 44, 52).

The ox-drawn wagons depicted at Medinet Habu (Nelson 1930: pl. 34; Fig. 5.68) have two disk-shaped wheels and a wicker frame, and four oxen are yoked to them abreast. This method of yoking, rather than in pairs of two, seems to Sandars (1978: 121) a solution for the hardship of the road, and to

---

[4] Figurines and vase painting show horse riders in LHIIIA2 and LHIIIB (Crouwel 1981: 45–7).

Littauer and Crouwel (1979: 74) merely a way to bring animals along on the journey.[5] The capacity of the wagons seems to have been limited to three to four people, with little space for luggage (Sandars 1978: 124). Some belongings might have been hung outside the wagon, as is one bag-shaped object in the relief (Nelson 1930: pl. 34, wagon at top, right).

In Anatolia, wagons with disk-shaped wheels drawn by zebu are still being used today (Yadin 1963: 339; Piggot 1992: 31). A fragment of a relief vase from Boğazköy from the seventeenth or sixteenth century BCE depicts a cart with solid wheels drawn by a bovid (Bittel 1976: fig. 142). The ox-drawn wagons were also used by the Hittites and their allies, and are shown as baggage wagons in the Battle of Kadesh in the thirteenth century (Naville 1930: pl. 17; Littauer and Crouwel 1979: 73–4; Spalinger 2003: 198) but have six-spoked wheels rather than solid ones. The use of ox-drawn wagons has a long history in Europe and Asia (Piggot 1992: 13–36), yet it does not find any representation in Mycenaean art, and there is only a possible reference to working oxen in the Linear B archives of Pylos and Knossos. Mycenaean terra-cotta groups of an ox and driver might show plowing by oxen (Crouwel 1981: 55–7; Piggot 1992: 28). An exceptional example is an LMIIIC or Sub-Minoan model of an ox-driven wagon or ceremonial chariot from Karphi (Pendlebury, Pendlebury, and Money-Coutts 1937–8: pl. 35: 4; Crouwel 1981: 56). Wagons drawn by oxen and mules are mentioned by Homer and Hesiod (Crouwel 1992: 77) and are documented in Greek literary sources and in iconography beginning in the eighth century. None is similar, however, to those used by the migrants depicted at Medinet Habu, as none seems to show a true full wheel and a wicker body.[6] The lack of Aegean and other contemporary parallels to the ox-drawn wagons depicted at Medinet Habu may have implications for the origin of the people depicted and the migration route that they chose.

SPEED IN LAND TRAVEL

The speed at which one completes a land journey depends on the size of the group, the condition of the road, and the means of transportation.[7] The journey from Constantinople to Jerusalem, about 1,200 miles, with fifty-eight stops, took the "traveler from Bordeaux" about eight weeks, at about twenty-one miles per day, in the summertime (leaving the Bosphorus on June 1; Hunt 1984: 56). Melania the Younger, rushing back to Jerusalem, repeated this

---

[5] See the legend told by Arrian (*Anabasis Alexandri* 2.3; Piggot 1992: 30) about the poor farmer Gordios who had two teams of oxen, one for his plow, and one for his wagon.

[6] See Crouwel 1992: pl. 18: 1, for the closest parallel in the Greek world, which is, however, Anatolian from Çesme.

[7] For example, under normal circumstances, a Roman legion covered fifteen kilometers a day at a regular pace and thirty kilometers at a quick pace (Chevallier 1976: 194). However, an army laden with booty covered only about nine miles a day (Livy 38I), and a lightly armed vanguard covered only about twenty-eight miles in two days in rough terrain (Livy 44).

journey in 437 CE, making her way in six weeks during the winter (Hunt 1984: 56). These individual travelers probably enjoyed the well-maintained imperial roads and hostels along the way, yet they were not supplied transport by the state, which made the conditions of their travel more similar to journeys of the twelfth century BCE. It is reasonable to suppose that small groups could have traveled at this speed; larger caravans would have traveled at a slower pace. The speed of a Bronze Age caravan was set by its slowest-moving vehicle, the ox-drawn wagon. An estimated progress of ten to eighteen miles per day is given by Sandars (1978: 121), based on the use of ox-drawn wagons by the settlers in Oregon and in Natal during the Zulu War; this would be a significantly slower speed than that of the pilgrims of the late Roman period. Sandars (1978: 124) also notes the great vulnerability of slow caravans composed of ox-drawn wagons and the heavy infantry escort they required. A slow caravan of this kind, similar to that shown at Medinet Habu, would need between nine and seventeen weeks to travel from the northwestern Anatolian coast to the southern Levant. This rather long journey may have been conducted more or less continuously, or it may have been broken up into several trips of varying lengths, with considerable stops between them.

CONCLUSIONS

Several causes could have led to migration in the twelfth century BCE. Case studies from the era of Greek colonization suggest the importance of push factors of political, economic, and social instability – conditions prevalent also in the twelfth century (Chapter 3). Interconnected pull factors include the desire to improve economic and social position and personal safety.

Although the amount of information on foreign destination and the types of ships available remained more or less stable between LHIIIB and LHIIIC Early, political and social changes between the thirteenth century and the twelfth century may have encouraged some forms of interaction but hindered others. The rise of new polities and the fragmentation of old ones gave more people access to power and resources and freed many others of their obligations to the palatial system, or at least meant that the elite no longer needed their services. In the absence of palace control, free enterprise was now accessible to more people. At the same time, while the elites grew in number, they had less power and fewer available resources than in the previous period. Thus, for example, instead of long-distance trade in raw material, we are likely to find more opportunistic trade in finished products conducted by rulers and private individuals.

The means of sea transport available in the Late Bronze Age enabled a rather short trip of a week and a half between the eastern coast of mainland Greece and the southern Levantine coast. However, ships could not be used as a mass-transport system in the postpalatial world. State-directed mass maritime migrations or other large-scale, state-orchestrated interactions of the type seen in the Pylos tablets, and the one sometimes envisioned for the Philistines, are unlikely to have occurred. The fragmentation of political power and the demise of palatial administration in the beginning of the twelfth century resulted in the crippling of the recruitment and financing abilities needed to support large-scale maritime enterprises. Similarly, emergency maritime evacuation and the transport of large populations of men, women, and children (i.e., of more than a few hundreds) to remote destinations is implausible, mainly because of the limited passenger capacity of the oared galleys, as well as the number of ships available.

However, a new venue for migration unexpectedly opened. Because of unusual circumstances, the land route from northwestern Anatolia to the Levant had become accessible to unhindered land travel in the early twelfth century BCE. Man-made obstacles such as political boundaries and control of the routes were probably minimal after the destruction or severe damage suffered by all Late Bronze Age polities along the land route. The three-month land journey, if it had started in northwestern Anatolia, was perhaps lengthier than the sea voyage, yet it did not require the acquisition of costly ships. Furthermore, migration by land had no restrictions of space of the sort that impeded maritime travel, and thus it enabled the participation of whole family groups rather than the mostly male population typical of maritime colonization.

Some key points along potential routes deserve special attention in the examination of material culture evidence for migration, as they are mentioned frequently as major landfalls in the maritime routes or stops along the land routes. Among these places are Rhodes, Cilicia, and Tarsus; the Cypriot littoral; and key points, such as Ugarit, the Phoenician cities, and Acco, along the Syro-Phoenician coast.

5

ALONG THE ROUTES

> The route of migration must be traced and checked for its archaeological, historical and geographical plausibility. If it was an overland route, spatial-temporal distribution of the material culture should indicate the path and direction of large scale migrations. . . . The only terrestrial evidence of . . . sea movements, if they were hostile, might be a series of coastal predation and destructions along the route and at successful beachheads.
>
>   – Stager 1995: 332–4

INVESTIGATING ROUTES AND NEW POPULATIONS

The collapse of the palatial powers in the Mycenaean heartland and the Hittite Empire in Anatolia was the perfect opportunity for the ambitious, aggressive aristocrats and their followers from other strata of the postpalatial society to engage in a variety of interregional interactions with areas outside the scope of the Aegean world. Raiding, trading, and settling – both peacefully and violently – along the land and sea routes between the Aegean and the Levant, they left behind them clear footprints in the form of Aegean-style material culture, as well as in the literary records of their Ugaritic and Egyptian adversaries.

Sites in Cyprus, Anatolia, and Syria can be used here as seismographs, recording in their strata interactions with the Aegean world that are manifest in the variability in material culture assemblages.

It was argued in Chapter 1 that everyday activities within the domestic zone are molded and organized by the habitus: a set of ideas, values, and perceptions held by members of society. Thus, embedded in the behavioral patterns within the domestic zone are social, economic, and symbolic information, indicative of the sets of beliefs and the ethnic identity of the occupants. It was also argued in Chapter 1 that, in situations of migration, the habitus of the migrants is less susceptible to change within the domestic sphere, which is less exposed than the public sphere to the influence of the culture of the target country. If so, our best chances of identifying migration are to trace a deep change in domestic assemblages. In our case, the sudden appearance of Aegean domestic behaviors during the twelfth century at sites that were outside the scope of the thirteenth-century Aegean world may be indicative of Aegean migration. From the rocky, windswept village of Karphi, high in the mountains of Crete, to the coastal, low mound of Xeropolis in Euboia, and from the huge settlement of Tiryns, sprawling beyond its Mycenaean walls, to the village of Korakou in Corinthia, Aegean domestic life during the twelfth century BCE maintained several common features. The basic activities of cooking, textile production, and food consumption in most of the Aegean world, from Crete to the mainland, created a domestic koine that can be compared to deep changes in assemblages outside the Aegean world.

THE AEGEAN HEARTH

The LH/LMIIIC domestic architecture shows great variability in size, number of rooms, and room arrangements, typical of many other cases of vernacular architecture in antiquity (Thomatos 2006: 207–18). However, a variety of hearths, mostly rectangular (or subrectangular to oval) in shape, appear at nearly all excavated LH/LMIIIC sites, indicating the important functional and symbolic role of hearths in twelfth-century Aegean architecture. This is, of course, a continuation of an earlier Mycenaean tradition. Located mostly, yet not solely, in the most important room in the building (Darcque 2006: 175), the hearth was the main source of heat, a place where cooking and eating took place, and therefore a natural focal point for gathering and feasting in the dwellings of all strata of society. Hearths occur in the centers of the throne rooms of Pylos, Mycenae, and Tiryns. The famous Pylos throne-room fresco showing a ceremony of toasting by pairs of men seated by tables is indicative of feasts perhaps held in the very room, next to its magnificent round hearth (Lang 1969: pls. 125–6; McCallum 1987: 94–7). Smaller, rectangular hearths appear in LHIIIA and B elite *Korridorhaus*-type buildings, such as Building B of the southwestern quarter and Tsountas House at Mycenae (Hiesel 1990: 113–14, 125–6), as well as in much humbler buildings, such as House M at Tiryns (Darcque 2006: pl. 61).

During the LHIIIC, hearths were usually made of clay, sometimes fully or partially covered with sherds, thus giving them an even surface. Examples of the great variability of LHIIIC house forms with hearths, most of which were located in the main room of the building, include Korakou House L and House P (Blegen 1921: 83, 85; Hiesel 1990: 49–50, 89; Figs. 5.1 and 5.2), Tiryns Building W (Chapter 3: Fig. 3.12), Tiryns *Unterburg* R 127 (Hiesel 1990: 23; Fig. 5.3), and Lefkandi Phase 1 (Popham and Sackett 1968: 12, fig. 14; Fig. 5.4). Similar LMIIIC examples include Kastelli, Chania Room M (E. Hallager 2000: 76–7, 128; Figs. 5.5 and 5.6), and Kavousi Vronda Buildings N, O, and I (Glowacki 2004: fig. 9.11).

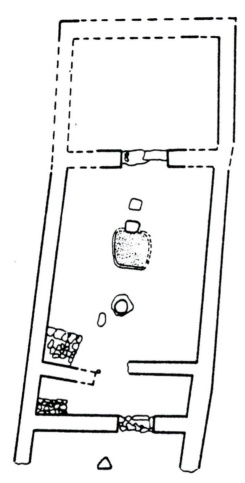

FIGURE 5.1. Korakou House L (after Hiesel 1990: 49, fig. 38)

COOKING ACTIVITIES

Cooking activities involving liquids were carried out in the Aegean in two main cooking vessels, the tripod cooking pot and the cooking jug or amphora. Tripod cooking pots vary in size, yet most LHIIIC examples from the mainland tend to have a concave base and vertical handles (Figs. 5.7 and 5.8).[1] On Crete, tripod cooking pots usually have a flat base and horizontal handles, continuing Minoan traits, although some betray Mycenaean features such as a concave base or vertical handles (Fig. 5.9).[2] The tripod

[1] E.g., Iria (Döhl 1973: fig. 14: B24); Lefkandi (Popham and Milburn 1971: 337); Athens (Rutter 2003: fig. 7: 3–4).

[2] E.g., Kastrokephala (Kanta and Karetsou 2003: fig. 9), Kavousi Vronda (Gesell et al. 1991: 166, fig. 6: 4), and in Kastelli, Chania (B. P. Hallager 2000: 158). For examples with a concave base from Karphi, see Seirdaki 1960: 7, fig. 4: 3, pl. 4b (second row, left vessel), pl. 55: d (second vessel from the right).

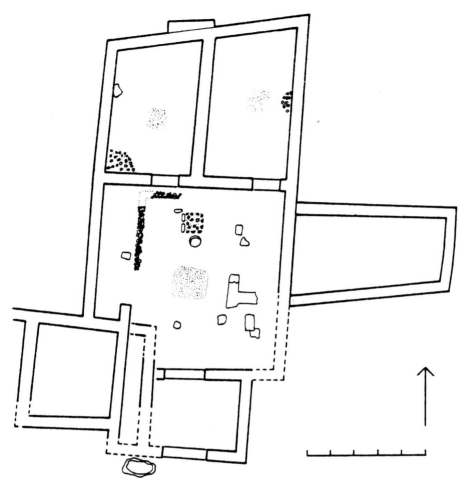

FIGURE 5.2. Korakou House P (after Hiesel 1990: 89, fig. 65)

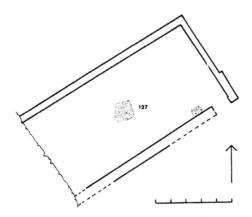

FIGURE 5.3. Tiryns *Unterburg* R 127 (after Hiesel 1990: 23, fig. 16)

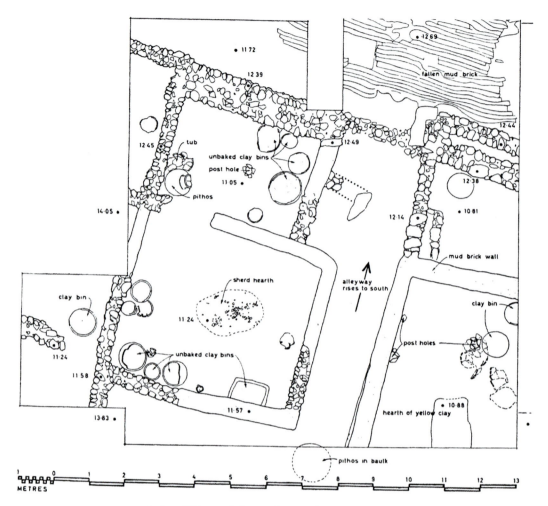

FIGURE 5.4. Lefkandi Phase 1 (after Popham and Sackett 1968: fig. 14)

configuration is an extremely stable one. Tripod cooking pots do not have to be placed on an even cooking surface and do not require any special cooking installation – any open fire will do. Indeed, the marks on the outer perimeter of the base and body of LMIIIC cooking pots indicate that they were put either over a direct fire or over smoking embers (Yasur-Landau 2003–4).

In contrast to the tripod cooking pots, the Aegean cooking jugs have a flat or ring base, one or two handles reaching the rim or below it, and a mouth narrower than the widest part of the vessel. Within this broad type, the numerous examples from the Aegean world show considerable variability in the volume of the vessel, in details of the rim and base, and in the number of handles (Figs. 5.10–5.22). The origin of this common LHIIIC shape is beyond

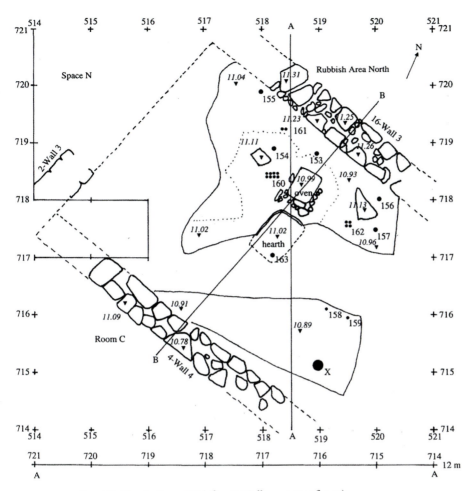

FIGURE 5.5. Kastelli, Chania Room M (after E. Hallager 2000: fig. 15)

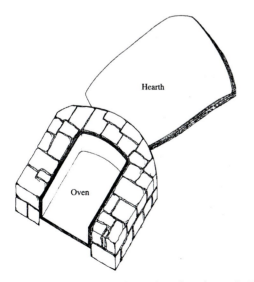

FIGURE 5.6. Kastelli, Chania, hearth and oven in Room M (after E. Hallager 2000: fig. 17)

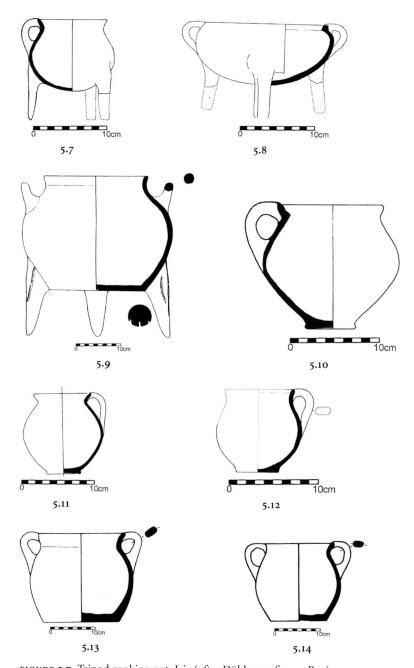

FIGURE 5.7. Tripod cooking pot, Iria (after Döhl 1973: fig. 14: B24)

FIGURE 5.8. Tripod cooking pot, Lefkandi (after Popham and Milburn 1971: 337)

FIGURE 5.9. Minoan-style tripod cooking pot, Halasmenos (after Yasur-Landau 2003–4: fig. 1.1)

FIGURE 5.10. Cooking jug/amphora, Iria (after Döhl 1973: fig. 14: B23)

FIGURE 5.11. Cooking jug/amphora, Korakou (after Rutter 1974: fig. 33: 2)

FIGURE 5.12. Cooking jug/amphora, Emporio (after Hood 1982: fig. 280: 2949)

FIGURE 5.13. Cooking jug/amphora, Halasmenos (after Yasur-Landau 2003–4: fig. 1.3)

FIGURE 5.14. Cooking jug/amphora, Halasmenos (after Yasur-Landau 2003–4: fig. 1.4)

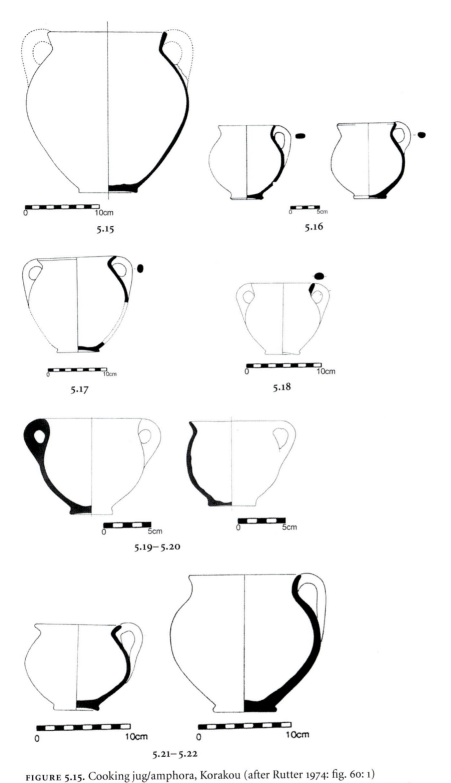

FIGURE 5.15. Cooking jug/amphora, Korakou (after Rutter 1974: fig. 60: 1)
FIGURE 5.16. Cooking jug/amphora, Athienou (after Dothan and Ben-Tor 1983: fig. 50: 7, 8)
FIGURE 5.17. Cooking jug/amphora, Midea (after Walberg 1998: pl. 91: 720)
FIGURE 5.18. Cooking jug/amphora, Phylakopi (after Mountjoy 1985; fig. 5.29: 543)
FIGURES 5.19–5.20. Cooking jugs/amphorae, Tarsus (after Goldman 1956: fig. 389: 1220, 1221)
FIGURES 5.21–5.22. Cooking jugs/amphorae, Lefkandi (after Popham and Milburn 1971: fig. 2: 5, 6)

FIGURE 5.23. Ashdod Area G, hearth (Installation 4328) (after Dothan and Porath 1993: pl. 11: 2)

doubt Aegean and stems from the cooking jug and the cooking jar or amphora of LHIIIB.[3]

The flat or ring bases of these jugs, appropriate for flat surfaces, are important for the study of Aegean domestic behavioral patterns because they were most likely intended to stand on the hearth (Fig. 5.23). A further clue to the distinctive use of the Aegean cooking jugs is presented by the blackening on the side of many of them (Figs. 5.24–5.27; Popham and Milburn 1971: 336; Mountjoy 1985: 207 no. 543; Tzedakis and Martlew 1999: 131 no. 113, 135 no. 121, possibly also 185 no. 175; Yasur-Landau 2003–4). This may mean that they were placed on the side of the hearth, perhaps on the embers, exposing one side to direct fire and higher temperatures.

Because the cooking jugs have closed shapes, with the mouths narrower than the widest part of the body, it is likely that they were designed more for liquid substances and for boiling rather than for roasting, simmering, or

---

[3] Mountjoy 1993: 117 no. 348; Tzedakis and Martlew 1999: 121 no. 100, 131 no. 112, 135 no. 120; Blegen and Rawson 1966: fig. 68 for both two-and one-handled types from Pylos; Mylonas Shear 1987: 111, nos. 138–41, pl. 32: 138–41 from the Panagia Houses at Mycenae.

5.24

5.25

5.26

5.27

FIGURE 5.24. Cooking jug blackened by fire, Ashdod Area G (after Dothan and Porath 1993: pl. 11: 1)

FIGURE 5.25. Cooking jug blackened by fire, Midea (LHIIIC) (after Tzedakis and Martlew 1999: 126, 106)

FIGURE 5.26. Cooking jug blackened by fire, Halasmenos (after Yasur-Landau 2003–4: pl. 2: 1)

FIGURE 5.27. Cooking jug blackened by fire, Mycenae (LHIIIB) (after Tzedakis and Martlew 1999: 135, 120)

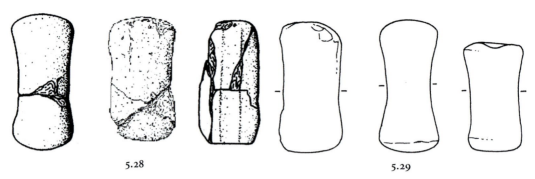

5.28   5.29

FIGURE 5.28. Spool-shaped loom weights, Tiryns (after Rahmstorf 2005: pl. 20: 5a–c)
FIGURE 5.29. Spool-shaped loom weights, Tell Afis (after Rahmstorf 2005: pl. 21: 6a–c)

frying.[4] An analysis of the contents of cooking jugs in the Aegean reveals that they were used for mixed dishes, which sometimes included wheat, pulses, meat, olive oil, wine, and beer.[5]

TEXTILE MANUFACTURE

Large numbers of unbaked or poorly fired clay spools, either cylindrical or hourglass shaped, are a common feature of LHIIIC/LMIIIC material culture assemblages. They are found in great numbers at sites from Kynos in central Greece, Lefkandi in Euboia, and Asine in the Argolid to Halasmenos and Chania in Crete[6] (Figs. 5. 28 and 5.29). The proof for their use as loom weights comes from Ashkelon (Stager 1991: 14–15), where in several instances, these objects were found in a row along walls, together with linen fibers. The use of similar objects as loom weights is seen on a painted Cypro-Geometric II bowl that depicts a loom (Fig. 5.30). Simillar spool-like objects were also found in 12th-century contexts in Cyprus, side by side with pyramidal loom weights (Figs. 5.31, 5.32, 5.33). In many cases, they were found in groups, forming distinctive sets of objects of similar size and weight (Rahmstorf 2005: 156; pl. 22: 2).

Their earliest secure find spot in the Aegean world of the thirteenth century is Kastelli, Chania, in western Crete, where the spools appear in LMIIIB2 contexts (Wiman and Bruun-Lundgren 2003: 266). In Lefkandi (Evely 2006: 296), they appear as early as LHIIIC Early; however, most mainland examples date to LHIIIC Middle and later, indicating that they were an innovative form introduced during the twelfth century. A suggested northern influence on their appearance in mainland Greece is still not supported by chronology; although

---

[4] Cf. Borgna 1997: 204, noting the appropriateness of heating and boiling liquids in a closed, globular cooking pot.

[5] Tzedakis and Martlew 1999: 126 no. 106, 131 no. 113, 135 no. 121, 186 no. 176.

[6] Kynos: Dakoronia 1998; Lefkandi: Popham and Sackett 1968: 13, fig. 16; Evely 2006: 296–8; Asine: Santillo Frizell 1986: fig. 52: 293; Halasmenos: Coulson and Tsipopoulou 1994: pl. 10: 3; Kastelli, Chania: Bruun-Lundgren and Wiman 2000: 177–8.

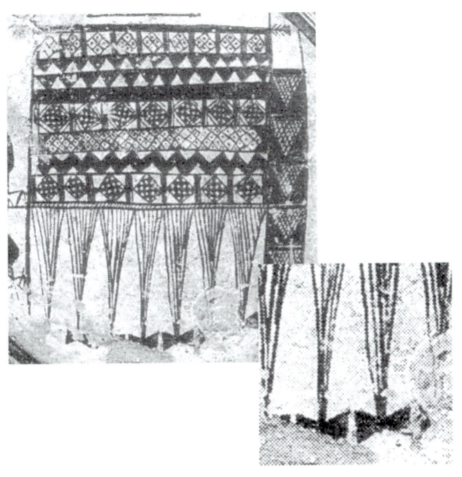

FIGURE 5.30. Loom with spool-shaped loom weights, Cypro-Geometric II bowl (after Rahmstorf 2005: pl. 22: 2)

such spools occur in Urnfield settlements of southern-middle Europe and Italy, none is certain to come from a context earlier than the twelfth century (Rahmstorf 2003; 2005). Their appearance in Troy VIIa – its demise dated to the very beginning of the twelfth century BCE – may nevertheless support the theory of a Balkan or central European origin (Becks 2003: 43; Rahmstorf 2005: 147–8). The occurrence of these objects in northwestern Anatolia during the late thirteenth century, while none of their other find spots in Anatolia can be dated to the thirteenth century or earlier, indicates a non-Anatolian origin. Another unusual appearance in Beth Shean during the thirteenth to early twelfth century BCE (James and McGovern 1993: 188) may be explained by the presence of Aegean mercenaries and their families at the site, also evident in other categories of material culture (Chapter 6). The fact that no other group of such objects has been found in any other Late Bronze Age site in the southern Levant indicates that the objects were by no means typical of the Canaanite material culture.

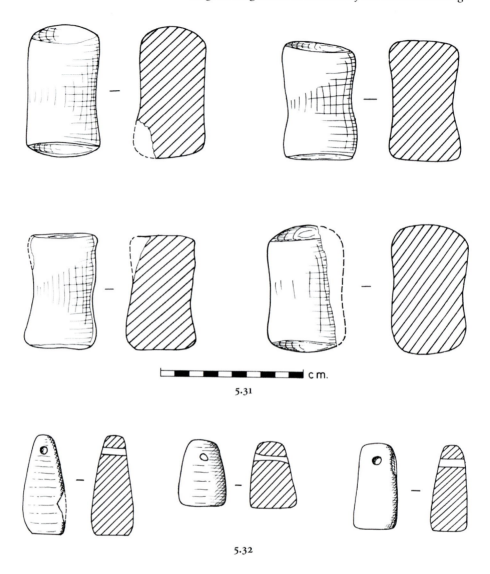

5.31

5.32

FIGURE 5.31. Spool-shaped loom weights, Kition Area II (after Karageorghis and Demas 1985b: pl. 201)

FIGURE 5.32. Pyramidal loom weights, Kition Area II (after Karageorghis and Demas 1985b: pl. 201)

AEGEAN-STYLE FIGURINES

Aegean-style figurines of the LHIIIC of the psi, tau, phi, and "mourning" types represent an important part of the Aegean belief system and continue Mycenaean cultic traditions of the palatial era. Figurines dating to LHIIIC have been found in sanctuary contexts, as in the one at Phylakopi, and at tomb assemblages, as in Perati and Ialysos.

However, although large pottery figures have been found solely in sanctuaries, smaller figurines have been found in domestic contexts, too, or within

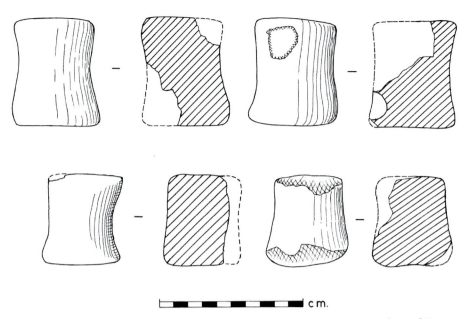

c m.

FIGURE 5.33. Spool-shaped loom weights, Maa-Palaeokastro (after Karageorghis and Demas 1988: pl. 189)

house shrines, such as House G at Asine. Others come from House P at Korakou (Thomatos 2006: 223–4), and yet more from a domestic context in Lefkandi (French 2006); fragmentary figurines come from Terraces 9 and 10 in Midea, an area that is also likely domestic in nature (Thomatos 2006: 222). These indicate that cult activities involving figurines were indeed part of the behaviors performed in a good number of twelfth-century Aegean homes. In Crete, where Minoan traditions continued into the twelfth century, figurines were rarer in domestic contexts, yet present in some, such as in Halasmenos (Coulson and Tsipopoulou 1994).

CONSUMPTION OF FOOD AND DRINK

Decorated pottery is arguably the most widely investigated aspect of LH/ LMIIIC culture, and detailed accounts of the typology exist for the period (e.g., Mountjoy 1999a; Deger-Jalkotzy and Zavadil 2003; Thomatos 2006: 6–142), yet unfortunately there is scarcely any reference to the way the vessels were used (Tournavitou 1992). Analysis of residue from Mycenaean and Minoan vessels by Tzedakis and Martlew (1999), as well as some iconographic representations, may indicate the use of the most common classes of serving vessels: bowls, kraters, cups, and kylikes.[7]

---

[7] See Mountjoy 1999a for all areas of the Aegean apart from Crete; Kanta and Karetsou 2003; D'Agata 2003a with literature on LMIIIC Crete.

The three major categories of small open vessels – cups, deep bowls, and kylikes – are not equally represented in every assemblage. Although quantitative studies are still to be conducted, it seems that on the mainland and in the Cyclades, the Dodecanese, and Crete, despite the occurrence of cups and kylikes in many assemblages, deep bowls are by far the most common open form during LH/LMIIIC (D'Agata 2003b: 23; Thomatos 2006: 98).

Judging by their open forms and two horizontal handles, it is likely that food and drink were served in deep bowls (FS 284, 285; Figs. 5.34, 5.35, and 5.36) as well as in shallow angular bowls (FS 295; Fig. 5.37), the latter, perhaps, used more for serving food (Tournavitou 1992: 199–200). A residue analysis of deep bowls and shallow angular bowls from Thebes and Mycenae supports this suggestion. Two of the bowls (Tzedakis and Martlew 1999: 122 no. 104; 133 no. 116) show traces of food, while a deep bowl from Thebes was used to serve wine and beer or a mixture of both (Tzedakis and Martlew 1999: 185 no. 174). Difference in the status and use of the bowls is also apparent in their decoration. Although the decoration on shallow angular bowls is almost always linear, that on deep bowls tends to be more elaborate and sometimes includes figurative motifs, indicating that deep bowls were considered more an item of display. Another class of common drinking vessels were the cups, existing mainly in the semiglobular (FS 211, 215) and carinated (FS 240) varieties (Figs. 5.38 and 5.39). An additional clue to the use of plainware, shallow angular bowls, and cups comes from the late LHIIIB2 deposits at the palace of Pylos. Room 21 was a pantry, used as the "bowl and cup department" of the palace (Blegen and Rawson 1966: 129–32). Of the 2,146 vessels counted, 1,099 were shallow angular bowls and 1,024 were cups. The similar number suggests sets composed of an angular bowl and a cup. If this is indeed the case, it may be safe to assume that the vessels were used for different purposes – one for food and the other for drink.

The kylix (FS 267, 274, 275; Figs. 5.40 and 5.41) is shown by LHIIIC iconography to be used on ceremonial occasions (Yasur-Landau 2005b): the kylix held in the hand of the Amyklaion terra-cotta statue(s) (Demakopoulou 1982: 54–6; Petterson 1992: 95–6; Rehak 1995: 108); the kylix held by the seated figure in the Tiryns chariot-race krater (Kilian 1980; Rehak 1995: 108; Wright 1996: fig. 18.19; 2004b: figs. 15–17; Fig. 3.32) and on the Elis Agia Triada funeral krater (Eder 2006: fig. 29.5; Fig. 3.41). The find of 608 FS kylikes (FS 267, 274) and 537 shallow angular bowls (FS 295) in Room 1 of the House of Sphinxes at Mycenae (Tournavitou 1995: 117–21, tables 7 and 8) suggests that kylikes and bowls were used in sets intended for grand feasts during the LHIIIB, similarly to the previously mentioned sets of cups and bowls from Pylos. The find of large kylikes in the "service wing" of the Big House ruler's dwelling at Building A–B in Kavousi Vronda, together with bones of cattle and pigs, further supports their use in twelfth-century elite feasts (Day, Coulson, and Gesell 1986: 371–3; Day 1997: 394; Mazarakis Ainian 1997: 208–9; Day and Snyder 2004).

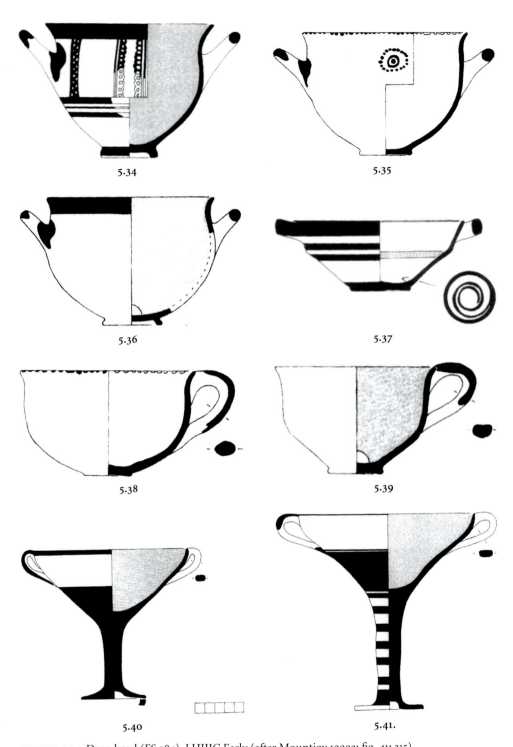

FIGURE 5.34. Deep bowl (FS 284), LHIIIC Early (after Mountjoy 1999a: fig. 41: 315)
FIGURE 5.35. Deep bowl (FS 284), LHIIIC Early (after Mountjoy 1999a: fig. 41: 316)
FIGURE 5.36. Deep bowl (FS 284), LHIIIC Early (after Mountjoy 1999a: fig. 41: 318)
FIGURE 5.37. Shallow angular bowl, LHIIIC Early (after Mountjoy 1999a: fig. 41: 320)
FIGURE 5.38. Cup (FS 215), LHIIIC Early (after Mountjoy 1999a: fig. 41: 312)
FIGURE 5.39. Carinated cup (FS 240), LHIIIC Early (after Mountjoy 1999a: fig. 74: 182)
FIGURE 5.40. Kylix (FS 275), LHIIIC Early (after Mountjoy 1999a: fig. 41: 185)
FIGURE 5.41. Kylix (FS 275), LHIIIC Early (after Mountjoy 1999a: fig. 41: 186)

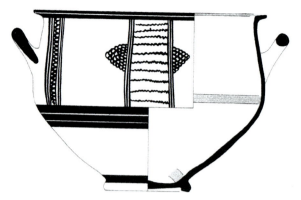

FIGURE 5.42. Krater (FS 282), LHIIIC Early (after Mountjoy 1999a: fig. 41: 314)

Kraters, mostly of the bell-shaped variety with two horizontal handles (FS 282), but also of the amphoroid variety (FS 9, 10; Fig. 5.42), were most likely used for the mixture of wine with water. Kraters (*ka-ra-te-re*) appear among the pottery vessels mentioned in MY Ue 611, an LHIIIB list of food commodities and vessels found in the House of Sphinxes at Mycenae (Ventris and Chadwick 1973: 331; Melena and Olivier 1991: 71). Nearby, Room 1 contained hundreds of vessels, including two ring-base FS 281 kraters (Tournavitou 1995: 117–21, tables 7 and 8).

During LHIIIC, kraters, in the absence of elite narrative art, became objects of display, and many of the narratives of elite life described in Chapter 3 were painted on them. Some of the kraters are of exceptionally large size, with a rim diameter sometimes exceeding fifty centimeters, and they were definitely intended to be the center of symposia. Examples of such are the Warrior Vase from Mycenae and a krater from Bademgediği Tepe (Chapter 3; Fig. 3.26), as well as the Grotta Krater decorated with a horse and rider (Vlachopoulos 2003a: fig. 10).

CYPRUS: INTERACTIONS ALONG THE SEA ROUTE

CYPRUS AND INTERNATIONAL TRADE DURING THE THIRTEENTH CENTURY BCE

Cyprus, an obvious landfall on the sea route from the Aegean to the Levant (Fig. 5.43) and with a wealth of well-published archaeological data, is a convenient place to begin an examination of the changing nature of the interregional interactions with the Aegean between the thirteenth and twelfth centuries BCE along the sea and land routes. There is greater consensus among scholars on the nature of interaction between Cyprus and the Aegean world in the thirteenth century than in the twelfth. Most of the thirteenth-century interactions can be roughly categorized within the range of international

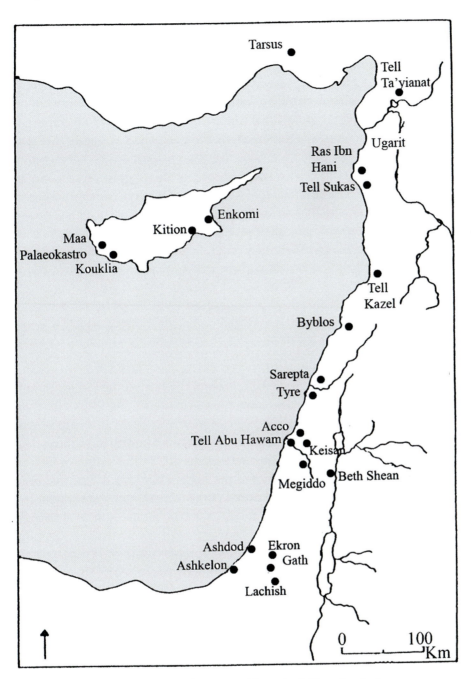

FIGURE 5.43. Map of the eastern Mediterranean (drawn by A. Yasur-Landau)

long-distance trade among the Aegean, Cyprus, and the Syro-Canaanite coast (Sherratt and Sherratt 1991: 372; Watrous 1992: 178–83; Knapp and Cherry 1994: 44–6). Cypriot commercial connections reached as far as the central and western Mediterranean. (Lo Schiavo 1995; cf. Gale 1991; Chapter 2). The Cypriots were aware of the potential of the Aegean markets, as indicated by the large amounts of Cypriot pottery found on the Uluburun ship and at mainland sites (Cline 1994: 61, 65; Cadogan 1993: 94). Reaction to the Cypriot demand for LHIII fineware was the local production of a variety of Aegean forms as early as LCIIC.[8] However, it seems that only the higher echelons of Cypriot society used Mycenaean drinking ware (Steel 1998: 296). The Cypriot copper trade, channeled through regional centers on Cyprus, played an important role in the Cypro-Aegean relationship (Gale 1991: 231–2; Karageorghis 1992: 79–80; Sherratt 1998: 297; Cline 1994: 62; Knapp 1997: 66–8). Furthermore, some Cypriots (Alashiyans) traveled abroad to the Aegean centers and are mentioned in the Linear B tablets of Knossos and Pylos (Chapter 2). All these may indicate the existence of firsthand knowledge of parts of the Aegean world among Cypriots, and most probably vice versa. This picture of close interaction in the thirteenth century stands in sharp contrast to that observed in Tarsus and Cilicia (see the subsequent section).

THE APPEARANCE OF AEGEAN BEHAVIORAL PATTERNS DURING THE TWELFTH CENTURY BCE

A major change in the contacts between the Aegean and Cyprus occurred in the transition from LCIIC to LCIIIA, around the turn of the twelfth century BCE. Mycenaean pottery was no longer imported to Cyprus (Cline 1994: 61–2). At the same time, Aegean material culture traits appear at several sites on the island (Karageorghis 1994). The accumulation of information about these changes has facilitated a lively and serious debate on the nature of interactions among Cyprus, the Levant, and the Aegean world, a debate that bears considerable similarity to the discussion of the contemporaneous situation in Philistia (Chapter 1). Two main schools exist. The first sees these changes as related to some form of immigration of Aegean populations to Cyprus. Among the many supporters of this view are Karageorghis (1994) and Deger-Jalkotzy (1994: 17; 1998a: 122). The opposing view, supported mainly by Sherratt (1992; 1998), considers the twelfth-century phenomena connected to cultural diffusion and a preference for a specific lifestyle in Cyprus and in the Levant in the twelfth century, as well as some continuation of Late Bronze Age international cultural tastes. A first step in establishing the nature of a given interaction is to examine which assemblages it affected. Even from a superficial glance, the change in many behavioral patterns in Cyprus seems to indicate interactions of rather high intensity. One can count among them the following:

* Changes in warfare customs seen in the appearance of weapons and armor of Aegean and European style, including Naue II type swords (Fig. 5.44; Karageorghis 1994: 3; 2000a: 260, 265; Pilides 1994: 99–103, 106). Another

---

[8] Kling 1989: 170–1; South and Russel 1993: 306–8.

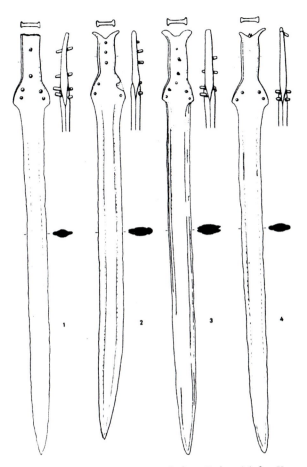

FIGURE 5.44. Naue II type swords from Enkomi (after Karageorghis 2000a: fig. 13.9)

related element is the so-called cyclopean defensive walls (Karageorghis 1994: 3).

* Possible changes in dress manifested in the appearance of violin-bow fibulae (Karageorghis 1994: 3; 2000a: 260; Pilides 1994: 103–6).
* Changes in religious patterns seen in the introduction of the Aegean "horns of consecration" and Aegean-style clay figurines (Karageorghis 1994: 3; 2000a: 258–61).
* Local, large-scale production of fineware pottery in the LHIIIC style (Mycenaean IIIC: 1b) (Kling 1989; Karageorghis 2000a: 256–7).
* Aegean cooking practices, reflected in the introduction of the Aegean-style cooking jug, appearing side by side with local types of Cypriot cooking pots (Bunimovitz 1998: 105; Bunimovitz and Yasur-Landau 2002).
* Textile production in the Aegean LHIIIC manner, evident in Aegean-style clay spools or loom weights found alongside local Cypriot pyramidal loom weights (Bunimovitz 1998: 105; Karageorghis 2000a: 263; Bunimovitz and Yasur-Landau 2002).

* The appearance of a new, handmade ceramic tradition: Handmade Burnished Ware (Fig. 5.45; Karageorghis 2000a: 257; Pilides 1994), different in all aspects of production and typology from the local ones.
* Possible Aegean social practices reflected in architectural features, including halls equipped with hearths and the Aegean wine set (Karageorghis 1994: 3; 1998b; 2000a: 266; Bunimovitz and Yasur-Landau 2002).

Not all of these changes, however, are indicative of the establishment of an instant deep change. Changes in warfare, dress, and religious architecture are less indicative of the intensity of interaction and its nature, as they are connected with elite contexts and prestigious activities – the building of monumental architecture and the possession of luxury metal items. Nevertheless, other changes connected to everyday domestic activities, such as cooking, the consumption of food and drink, weaving, and house planning, are more helpful in establishing the existence of deep change. A survey of the context of such finds at several key sites may further answer the question of which segment or segments of society were involved in the behavioral changes.

MYCENAEAN IIIC: 1B FINEWARE POTTERY AND AEGEAN-STYLE COOKING JUGS

Local production of some forms of Aegean-inspired fineware started before LCIIIA, imitating LHIIIA and LHIIIB forms. Those, however, could not have been the inspiration for the creation of the Mycenaean IIIC: 1b style of the LCIIIA, as only rude-style pottery and FS 296 shallow bowls continued from LCIIC to LCIIIA (Mountjoy 2005b: 209). Around the beginning of LCIIIA, additional shapes and decorative motifs from the Aegean tradition were introduced, contemporary with the end of LHIIIC Early (or LHIIIC Early Phase 2; Kling 1989: 170–3; Deger-Jalkotzy 1998b: 1174; Mountjoy 2005b: 165, 209). The second phase of Mycenaean IIIC: 1b pottery in level IIIB at Enkomi shows an impressive array of serving vessels that seem to compose more than a mere wine set (Figs. 5.46–5.54).[9] These include not only kraters, deep bowls, kylikes, strainer jugs, and feeding bottles, commonly associated with the consumption of drinks, but also shallow angular bowls related to the serving of food, as well as flat-based *kalathoi*. In addition, small containers, such as stirrup jars, straight-sided alabastra, and feeding bottles, complete a pottery assemblage

---

[9] Examples include: krater FS 282 (Mountjoy 2005b: figs. 4: 1, 6: 17, 8: 29), deep bowl FS 285–6 (Mountjoy 2005b: figs. 5: 1, 8: 20, 9: 36–8, 15: 66), shallow angular bowl FS 295 (Mountjoy 2005b: figs. 9: 39, 14: 62), kylix FS 267–7 (Mountjoy 2005b: fig. 14: 60), stirrup jar FS 175, 177 (Mountjoy 2005b: figs. 6: 15, 7: 18, 15: 63–4), strainer jug FS 155 (Mountjoy 2005b: figs. 8: 21, 10: 47, 14: 57), and straight-sided alabastron (Mountjoy 2005b: fig. 10: 46). Additional Aegean forms existing also earlier, in Level IIIA, are amphoriskos FS 60 (Dikaios 1971: pl. 75: 37), feeding bottle FS 162 (Dikaios 1971: 72: 16), and kalathos with flat base FS 291 (Dikaios 1971: pl. 74: 2).

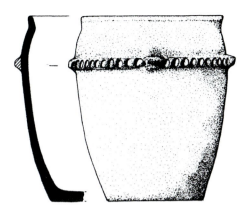

FIGURE 5.45. Handmade Burnished Ware vessel, Maa-Palaeokastro (after Karageorghis 2000a: fig. 13.3)

that represents all functional categories apart from large-scale storage and cooking, apart from large-scale storage and cooking vessels, discussed later in this section. The use of an Aegean fineware assemblage – suggesting activity that took place in the Aegean way – practically in any domestic or other assemblage excavated in Cyprus indicates a change in the twelfth century in food and drink consumption patterns.

Aegean-style cooking jugs are especially indicative of a fundamental change in behavioral patterns during LCIIIA. Wheel-made and with a flat or a ring base to stand on flat surfaces, these cooking jugs appear in Cypriot sites starting from LCIIIA side by side with Cypriot-style cooking pots. The flat or ring base is an important morphological feature significantly differentiating the Aegean-style cooking jugs from Cypriot cooking pots of LCIIC and LCIIIA, which have a concave base.[10] The jugs were found in a variety of contexts, industrial and domestic, such as at Maa-Palaeokastro, Floor II (Karageorghis and Demas 1988: 127–8 nos. 336, 374); Athienou Stratum II (Fig. 5.16; Dothan and Ben-Tor 1983: 111, 113); and Kition Area II, Floor III (Room 118, Room 120; Karageorghis 1985: 147–8; Karageorghis and Demas 1985a: 113–14; 1985b: pl. 126 nos. 5096, 5119).

HALLS AND HEARTHS

Hearths were already in use on Cyprus in the LCIIC period, such as the round one in Enkomi Area III, Room 3 (Karageorghis 1998b: 278; Dikaios 1969: 49). However, the introduction of Aegean-style cooking jugs, which carried with them a new set of behaviors connected with the use of hearths, is likely to have been responsible for the abundance of rectangular hearths in LCIIIA.

---

[10] E.g., Maa-Palaeokastro, no. 358 from Area 101A, Floor I (Karageorghis and Demas 1988: 488, pl. 245).

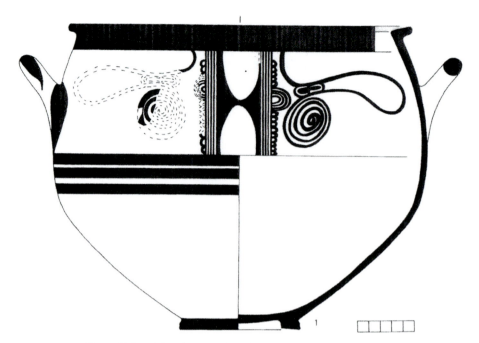

FIGURE 5.46. Krater, Enkomi Level IIIB Early (after Mountjoy 2005b: fig. 4: 1)

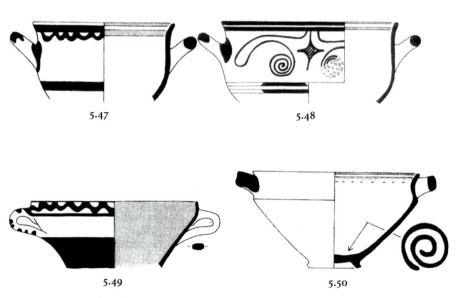

5.47   5.48

5.49   5.50

FIGURE 5.47. Deep bowl, Enkomi Level IIIB Early (after Mountjoy 2005b: fig. 14: 61)
FIGURE 5.48. Deep bowl, Enkomi Level IIIB Early (after Mountjoy 2005b: fig. 15: 66)
FIGURE 5.49. Kylix, Enkomi Level IIIB Early (after Mountjoy 2005b: fig. 14: 60)
FIGURE 5.50. Shallow angular bowl, Enkomi Level IIIB Early (after Mountjoy 2005b: fig. 14: 62)

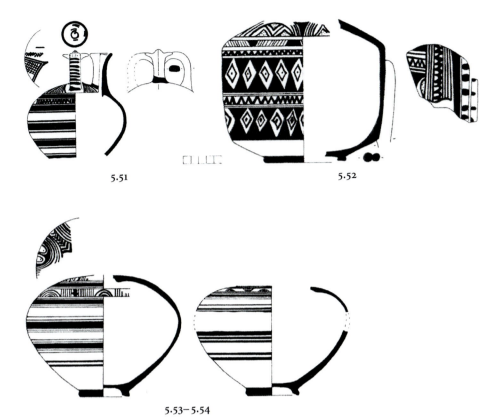

5.51

5.52

5.53–5.54

FIGURE 5.51. Stirrup jar, Enkomi Level IIIB Early (after Mountjoy 2005b: fig. 7: 18)
FIGURE 5.52. Pyxis, Enkomi Level IIIB Early (after Mountjoy 2005b: fig. 10: 46)
FIGURES 5.53–54. Stirrup jars, Enkomi Level IIIB Early (after Mountjoy 2005b: fig. 15: 63–4)

The use of rectangular hearths in the center of rooms is seen both in monumental and in more modest contexts. An example of a monumental context is the ashlar residence in Enkomi Area I, Level IIIA, where a rectangular hearth was located in the center of the megaron room (Room 14; Dikaios 1969: 174–5; Karageorghis 1998b: 277) and another in Room 45 of the same building (Dikaios 1969: 183). This may have been a continuation of a Cypriot tradition or, as Fisher (2006–7) suggests, the impact of Aegean feasting practices on local Cypriots. An additional example may be present at Alassa's Building II (Hadjisavvas 1994: 110; Hadjisavvas and Hadjisavva 1997: 145–8). Rectangular hearths also appear in monumental cultic contexts, such as inside Temple 2 at Kition (Karageorghis and Demas 1985a: 53, 28, 25), although these were present in LCIIC, as can be seen in the earlier hearth in Temple 2 and the hearth in Temple 3.

Rectangular hearths in more modest residential contexts in Enkomi are found in Rooms 77 and 89A, Area III, Level IIIA (Dikaios 1969: 106, 112; Karageorghis 1998b: 277). Both examples are located inside a rather large room, which is most probably the central room of a multiroom domestic unit.

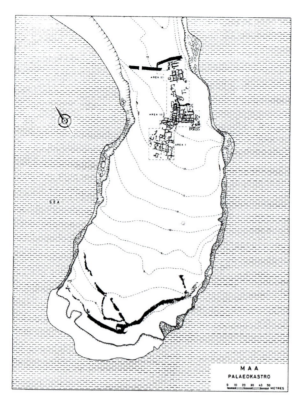

FIGURE 5.55. Maa-Palaeokastro, general plan (after Karageorghis 2000a: 267, fig. 13.13)

Such hearths existed in the smaller and more humble domestic units in Maa-Palaeokastro, Buildings II and IV (Figs. 5.55 and 5.56). A rectangular hearth and one apparently oval in shape were found in the central rooms (Rooms 61 and 75) of two simple domestic units that shared a single cooking facility (Karageorghis and Demas 1988: 19–22, 41–3; Bunimovitz and Yasur-Landau 2002).

LOOM WEIGHTS

Spools or reels appear at several sites in Cyprus side by side with the local pyramidal, perforated loom weights. Both Aegean-type reel-shaped and Cypriot pyramidal loom weights appear in Kition (Figs. 5.31 and 5.32). Examples can be found in Room 126, between Floors IIIA and III, giving further evidence of the domestic nature of activities performed in this one-room unit (Karageorghis and Demas 1985a: 78; 1985b: pl. 195; Karageorghis 1985: 125–6; Fig. 5.57). More loom weights of both types were found in the Floor III unit (Rooms 118, 121, and 121A; Fig. 5.58) that replaced Room 126 (Karageorghis and Demas 1985a: 112–13). The great majority of loom weights in Maa-Palaeokastro are of the reel type, and there are only few examples of perforated pyramidal or box-shaped weights (Fig. 5.33). The largest concentrations of loom weights come from the

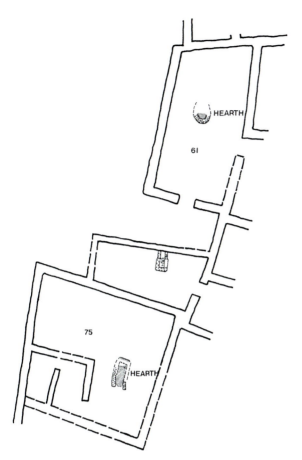

FIGURE 5.56. Maa-Palaeokastro, domestic buildings with hearths in Area III (after Karageorghis 2000a: 269, fig. 13.15)

enigmatic Building III, Floor II, mainly in the narrow Room 84, which may have been a stairwell to the upper floor (Karageorghis and Demas 1988: 34, 117–18). Others appear in the domestic units of Building II: examples can be found in Room 61 (from the hearth; Karageorghis and Demas 1988: 108).

HANDMADE BURNISHED WARE

Handmade Burnished Ware (HBW) is a group of coarse, handmade vessels that appeared in the eastern Mediterranean: Greece, Anatolia, Cyprus, and the Levant, around the end of the thirteenth and the beginning of the twelfth century BCE (Fig. 5.45).[11] The vessels are not consistent with Aegean, Anatolian, or Levantine ceramic traditions, which were at that time exclusively wheel-made, mass-produced pots fired at high temperatures. Some explanations for HBW are exogenous, connecting this type of pottery to interregional interactions

[11] Rutter 1975; 1990; Deger-Jalkotzy 1977; Catling and Catling 1981; French and Rutter 1977.

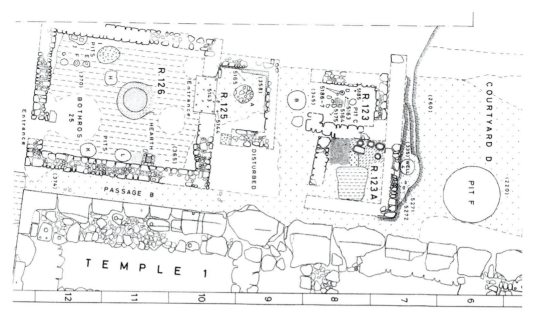

FIGURE 5.57. Kition, western workshops, Floor IIIA (after Karageorghis and Demas 1985c: pl. 32)

and to the appearance of a foreign ethnic element from the Balkans.[12] However, some scholars, such as Small (1990; 1997), perceive HBW as an endogenous phenomenon, a cultural response to the changed socioeconomic conditions and the breakdown of the Mycenaean economy at the end of the Bronze Age in Greece.

The phenomenon of HBW in Cyprus is intriguing: the crude vessels are far from elite items. The variety of shapes (in storage and serving vessels alike) seems to indicate that they are an almost complete ceramic assemblage, stemming from a non-Mycenaean European origin (Pilides 1994: 107–8). Pilides (1994) proposes that the presence of HBW documents a migration of people, perhaps of a minority in Mycenaean society, or is an ad hoc type of pottery produced by itinerant craftsmen (Pilides 1994: 110–11). These migrants, according to Pilides, were connected to the contemporary appearance of European or Aegean weapon types and ornaments in Cyprus (Pilides 1994: 99–106). This hypothesis of a relatively small-scale migration connected to HBW, whether connected to or separated from the Aegean migration, is appealing; indeed, a large measure of cultural persistence would have been needed to keep producing these forms, given their many disadvantages, their nonluxurious

---

[12] This interpretation has been used by Blegen and colleagues (1958) to explain the appearance of the coarse and knobbed wares in Troy, where the new pottery was accompanied by dramatic alteration in architecture and urban planning. Similar opinions were viewed by Bankoff and Winter (1984) and Bankoff et al. (1996).

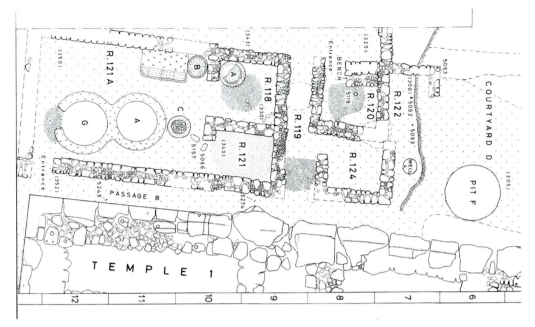

FIGURE 5.58. Kition, western workshops, Floor III (after Karageorghis and Demas 1985c: pl. 33)

appearance (to say the least), and the availability of much higher-quality wheel-made wares.

RANGES OF INTERACTION AND VARIABILITY
IN THE MIGRATION TO CYPRUS

An analysis of the technical qualities and find contexts of hearths, Aegean-style cooking jugs, and Aegean-style reel-shaped loom weights shows a deep change in the most basic domestic activities, which manifested in a similar way in all segments of society in Cyprus. Aegean-style cooking jugs and reel-shaped loom weights do not have a prestigious appearance. One may safely assume that the performance of cooking and weaving in the Aegean manner did not bear any mark of high status and, therefore, that there was no status-related motivation for the local Cypriot population to embrace them. Nor can these changes be explained by the deep influence of trade, as trade is expected to yield finished products and models for imitation in prestige items but not to influence the weaving and cooking habits and vessels of large segments of the population. The idea that the innovation was accepted because of its technical advantage also has to be rejected. The attested use of the Aegean-style cooking jug does not point to an easier or more economical mode of cooking than that using Cypriot cooking vessels. Furthermore, the crude, poorly baked clay reels seem to present many disadvantages as compared to the perforated, pyramidal loom weights. An examination of their find contexts strengthens the notion of a deep change that affected almost all assemblages and, most critically for proving migration, the domestic assemblages of the nonelite.

This deep change, which occurred within a short period during the transition from LCIIC to LCIIIA, cannot be explained in any other way other than by an actual presence of people from the Aegean in Cyprus during this period. This presence was not limited only to the higher levels of society and was best reflected in the less privileged groups. The number of migrants was probably not small, as the impression they left was substantial. Aegean migration was by no means the only interaction in twelfth-century Cyprus, but it was the most intensive. Cypriot imports to the Aegean, mainly metal objects and a few seals, indicate some form of exchange in valuable finished products (Karageorghis 1994: 1; Cline 1994: 61–2).

Voskos and Knapp (2008: 679) duly caution that a reconstruction of a massive Aegean migration to Cyprus, followed by Aegean domination "must be replaced by more nuanced considerations of the ways that migrants and local people interacted with each other." Indeed, different Cypriot polities may have had different interactions with the Aegean migrants, partly according to their relative power and partly according to political circumstances and strategies. Other factors facilitating diversity include those of power, status, and the number of migrants (Chapter 1). Three cases are presented here to illustrate the diverse types of coexistence between locals and newcomers in Cyprus during the twelfth century.

AEGEAN HOUSEHOLDS AND ASHLAR MASONRY: MAA-PALAEOKASTRO

Maa-Palaeokastro (Figs. 5.55 and 5.56), founded on a promontory in western Cyprus, was settled anew late in LCIIC (or during the transition to LCIIIA). The northern Area II was immediately south of a northern fortification wall (Karageorghis and Demas 1988: 9–17). It was probably a more elite zone, as it contains two buildings employing ashlar masonry: Building I, a massive, almost square building of two sectors, and Rooms 45 and 46, which were probably used as a fortress or tower. The situation is very different in Area III. In the more humble Buildings II and IV, fewer items of prestige and status obscure the origin of the dwellers. The use of predominantly Aegean ware, both in fineware and in cooking ware, as well as Aegean-type loom weights, suggests that Building II was a household in which all domestic activities and the organization of the domestic space – with a main room that includes a square hearth – were conducted in an Aegean manner. The same seems to be true for Building IV with respect to foodways and the organization of space; yet the use of perforated loom weights may indicate the practice of local weaving habits. These households, run in the Aegean manner, indicate the origin of the people who occupied them: most were probably family units of predominantly Aegean origin or tradition, with possibly some members of local descent, perhaps indicated by the different tradition of weaving in Building IV.

Karageorghis and Demas (1988: 26–3; Karageorghis 1998a: 132) suggest as one option for interpreting the site that Maa-Palaeokastro, situated in a remote and defensive location, was built by foreigners as a bridgehead for colonization in Cyprus. However, they prefer to explain the site as a joint enterprise of locals and foreigners (Karageorghis and Demas 1988: 264), either as a joint foundation or as a foreign foundation sanctioned by the Cypriots. According to Karageorghis and Demas (1988: 13–15), this coexistence is reflected in the Cypriot local wares and in the Cypriot ashlar masonry in Building I and in Rooms 45 and 46. Either explanation seems plausible, as the only real difference between the two is the question of who ruled the site.

ENKOMI: MORE POWER TO THE INDIVIDUAL (WITH THE FEATHERED HAT)

An example of individual migrants possibly in the service of a local lord is the famous Enkomi game board, dating from LCIIC–LCIIIA (Fig. 5.59). The main figure in this hunting scene is an archer, with scale armor or a dotted garment, riding in a chariot and accompanied by a charioteer. Assisting in the hunt are two dogs and two hunters on foot. The hunters are dressed significantly differently than the main figure, with feathered headdresses and kilts, all similar to the depiction of the Peleset/Philistines in the Medinet Habu reliefs (Sandars 1978: figs. 17 and 18). The difference in the costumes of the footmen and the main figure in the scene may pertain to their different origins. Furthermore, although hunting with a bow from a chariot was both a Near Eastern and an Aegean practice, the six-spoked wheels of the chariot indicate a Near Eastern (or Anatolian) origin of the chariot rather than an Aegean one (which almost always has four-spoked wheels; Crouwel 1981: 81). Therefore, it is possible to suggest a local Cypriot identity of the main figure in this scene. It can be safely claimed that the people with the feathered hats were not native to Cyprus, as they were not depicted there before the twelfth century. One can also cautiously suggest that the hunters in this scene are foreign mercenaries in the service of a local dignitary. The scene on this ivory luxury item was not chosen accidentally; it was a display of an image of power, indicated by the material (ivory), the topic (a hunt of wild animals), and the wealth demonstrated by the ability to own and maintain a chariot, horses, hunting dogs, and foreign mercenaries.

A greater measure of migrant independence is shown in the seal from Enkomi Level IIIB (Fig. 5.60; Karageorghis 1982: 84, fig. 68; Porada 1971: 801–2), depicting a warrior wearing a feathered hat standing behind a huge shield.

FIGURE 5.59. Warrior on a game board, Enkomi (after Dothan 1982: 277, fig. 13)

Again, we see a connection between the feathered hat and the status of a warrior. The use of this motif on a seal (a personal belonging that indicates status) may hint that the high-status owner was, or wanted to be, connected with the status group of the armed, feathered-hatted people.[13]

Further evidence for the presence of foreign – possibly Aegean – mercenaries at Enkomi comes from Tomb 18. The last phase of the rich tomb (Sjöqvist 1934: 546–58) contained the remains of seven individuals. In the center of the burial chamber lay the skeleton of a man with a large Aegean-type sword across his body. Another man had a pair of greaves (called "remains of helmet" in the report; Catling 1964: 140). According to Catling (1955: 34–5), Sandars (1978: 188), and Karageorghis (1990: 19), the greaves and the Naue type IIa sword may indicate that this was an Aegean warrior.

Further research is needed to determine whether the scarcity or absence of Aegean-type cooking jugs in Level IIIA and the absence of spool-shaped loom weights from the site are the result of preservation and excavation or publication methods, or whether they reflect the true nature of Level IIIA. If Aegean-style cooking jugs and spool weights were indeed rare or scarce in

[13] Porada, however, saw this as a depiction of an enemy (Porada 1971: 802). It is very unlikely that an enemy, heavily armed and undefeated, would be the symbol of choice for the administrative use of a local Cypriot dignitary.

FIGURE 5.60. Warrior on a seal, Enkomi (after Dothan 1982: 277, fig. 14)

Level IIIA, then the Aegean domestic activities that they represent were not performed at the site, although locally made LHIIIC pottery was used in Level IIIA, and rectangular hearths may show Aegean affinities. A cautious option is that the nature of interaction with the Aegean world was different in Enkomi from in Maa-Palaeokastro in the LCIIIA1 period.[14]

WEAVING THE SACRED AND THE PROFANE IN KITION

Area II in Kition offers an impressive example of the coexistence of cultic and industrial activities. Temples 1, 2, 4, and 5 were adjoined by the northern workshops, where metalworking was practiced, and by the western workshops, in which there is evidence for a textile industry (Figs. 5.56 and 5.57). The southern unit of the western workshops in Kition was probably an industrialized textile-producing unit. Weaving was practiced there using both perforated and spool-shaped weights.

The great majority of loom weights, both perforated and spool shaped, were found in this area, both in Floor IIIA (LCIIIA Early; pl. 5.6: 1) and in Floor III (LCIIIA Late; Karageorghis and Demas 1985a: 266, pl. 5.6: 2). In Floor IIIA, the greatest concentration of loom weights (six perforated and fifteen spool shaped) was found in Room 126, one part of a two-room unit (Karageorghis and Demas 1985a: 78; 1985b: pl. 195; Karageorghis 1985: 125–6). A round mud-brick installation and some shallow pits inside Room 126 suggest

---

[14] See Karageorghis and Demas 1988: 259, fig. 1, for the relative dating of the Enkomi levels.

activities that are not usually connected with a household. This unit was changed and enlarged during the time of Floor III (Karageorghis and Demas 1985a: 112–13), yet it still contained the largest concentration of loom weights at the site (twenty-two perforated and eight spool shaped). The circular pits with mud-brick borders in the middle of this unit further illustrate its nondomestic nature.

Why would the temple administration in Kition be interested in using two types of loom weights? One might envisage two types of looms, or at least two weaving traditions using different sets of weights and operated by weavers of different traditions – the local Cypriot tradition and the Aegean one. The commercial interest in employing weavers of different traditions becomes clear if we assume that they produced fabrics according to their own tradition. The temple economy would thereby have gained a greater variety of products to fit the tastes of both local and overseas clients. This situation brings to mind the presence of foreign women from Miletus, Chios, and Lemnos in the Pylian textile industry (Chapter 2). One can immediately see the benefit to the Pylian palace economy in the use of women who could produce fabrics that sold better overseas and sold as exotica in Greece. It is plausible, therefore, that the different weaving traditions seen in the western workshops in Kition were an adaptation of the Kition temple economy to a new ethnic reality. This new reality resulted in the opening of new markets and in the availability of weavers of both local and Aegean traditions to satisfy diverse market demands.

WESTERN ANATOLIA: THE EXPANSION OF THE EAST AEGEAN KOINE

SURVIVAL IN THE INTERFACE

During the LHIIIA and the LHIIIB, the area of the eastern Aegean–western Anatolian interface, including Miletus and the Dodecanese, was within in the realm of Aegean culture (Fig. 5.61). It had a distinctive style of Mycenaean pottery, which Mountjoy (1999a: 48) termed the *East Aegean koine*, which continued into the LHIIIC. Until the thirteenth century, these areas belonged to the kingdom of Ahhiyawa. Nearby islands, such as Chios and Lemnos, mentioned in Linear B sources, and Lesbos, mentioned in Hittite texts, were certainly familiar to the residents of Miletus and the Dodecanese during LHIIIB, yet material culture remains found in them indicate that they belonged to the realm of the western Anatolian culture (Guzowska and Yasur-Landau 2003; Privitera 2005; Cultraro 2005).

Miletus survived the turn of the twelfth century and remained a powerful fortified town, at least through some of LHIIIC Early. Unfortunately, stratified settlement remains from the Dodecanese are rare or, as in the case of

FIGURE 5.61. Map of the eastern Aegean–western Anatolian interface

Seraglio on Kos, extremely hard to decipher because of the disturbance of later, Geometric remains and the loss of the excavation notebooks during World War II (Morricone 1972–3: 147–9; Mountjoy 1998: 53; 1999a: 1075; Thomatos 2006: 207). However, tomb evidence from Rhodes may tell a tale of change. A sharp increase in the number of burials in Ialysos in LHIIIC, contemporary with a decline in the population of southern Rhodes, may indicate a synoicism toward the central site of the island (Macdonald 1986: 131–2). Still, what Rhodes, Kos, and Kalymnos lack in elite architecture is more than compensated for by the many examples of pictorial imagery previously discussed, such as images of ships with feathered-hatted rowers and plenty of armed warriors (Fig. 3.33). With the collapse of the Ahhiyawan grip on the west and the Hittite Empire in the east, the aristocracy of the Aegean interface remained the most powerful player in the region. Although Mountjoy's (1998) idea of placing the kingdom of Ahhiyawa in the interface with a capital in Rhodes may be rejected because of the lack of any evidence of a central Mycenaean administration on the island, the great cultural similarity in this region during LHIIIC may have allowed an easier cooperation between elites, perhaps even the creation of a short-lived regional alliance. Apart from the danger posed by other Aegean elites from the Cyclades and the Greek mainland, the interface elites were left to their devices. It is a small wonder, then, that the borders of the Aegean cultural sphere in the interface area expanded, apparently through peaceful migration, to areas formerly dominated by western

Anatolian material culture, while Egypt and Ugarit were plagued by maritime raids, some of which were clearly carried out by people with feathered hats of the type commonly sported in the East Aegean koine.

EMPORIO AND BADEMGEDIĞI TEPE

Two sites, Emporio on the island of Chios and Bademgediği Tepe on the western Anatolian coast, may be illuminating examples of the expansion of the East Aegean koine to nearby areas in what seem to be processes of peaceful migration of people bearing Aegean material culture.

The well-documented site of Emporio on Chios shows the most probable case of Aegean migration stemming from the East Aegean koine into its immediate vicinity. Men and women of Chios are mentioned in thirteenth-century Linear B texts from Pylos (Chapter 2), yet the island itself, as indicated by excavations at Emporio, belonged to the western Anatolian cultural tradition. A deep change in the site's material culture is indicated by two superimposed domestic levels of construction, dated to LHIIIC Middle and Late, on top of the earlier Late Bronze Age local western Anatolian settlement in Area F (Stage 7) and Area D (Stages 1 and 2; Hood 1981: 161–4, fig. 89, 147–50, figs. 79 and 81; Hood 1982: 579–622; Mountjoy 1999a: 1147–8; Fig. 5.62). As there is no evidence of violent destruction of the earlier settlement, it seems that the twelfth-century village was built on a deserted site. The nature of the entire pottery assemblage is no longer Anatolian but of the LHIIIC tradition.

The setting of the site on a rocky hill, providing natural defense and overlooking a natural harbor, is very similar to coastal acropolis sites in the Cyclades and on Crete, such as Koukounaries, Agia Spyridon, and Palaeokastro-Kastri (Chapter 3), first settled during the LHIIIC period. This choice reflects the need of a small community to be both connected to the and protected from attacks from sea and land.

A complete range of fineware is represented at the site (Mountjoy 1999a: 1149–53), showing serving vessels as well as small and medium-size storage vessels (e.g., amphorae, hydriae, stirrup jars). Even more indicative of the type of change is the change in cooking traditions. Both Aegean-style tripod cooking pots (Hood 1982: 618–19 nos. 2966–8) and cooking jugs (Hood 1982: 617–19 no. 280: 2947–52; see Fig. 5.12) appear at the site. The latter have distinctive burn marks on their sides, typical of the Aegean pattern of use (Hood 1982: pl. 127: 2947, 2948). Two *conuli* made of brown serpentine and gray chlorite schist (Hood 1982: 641, nos. 51, 56, pl. 133) and a clay spool (Hood 1982: 631, no. 25, pl. 131) suggest that textile production was probably also conducted in the Aegean manner.

Furthermore, fragments of late LHIIIB or LHIIIC clay figurines, two examples probably of the psi type and two bovine figurines, complete the typical appearance of LHIIIC material culture assemblage (Hood 1982: 628–9, nos. 16, 18, 19, 20, pls. 131–2). Because all detectable behavioral patterns at the

FIGURE 5.62. Emporio on Chios (photo by A. Yasur-Landau)

site appear to be of Aegean nature, without any substantial continuation of the local Anatolian material culture traditions, one has to accept the reconstruction of Aegean colonization of the site in the LHIIIC, as suggested by Hood (Hood 1986: 171, 180). The LHIIIC pottery and the house types similar to those at Lefkandi Phase 2 led Hood (1986: 179–80) to suggest colonization from Euboia.

The two destruction layers in Emporio, dating to LHIIIC Late, and the disastrous end of the settlement that had no continuation may indicate that Chios, just as in Koukounaries or Kastrokephala, was not a safe place for migration or settlement during the LHIIIC, and that the entire venture endured a few generations at most.

Another example of the expansion of the East Aegean koine culture is Bademgediği Tepe. Located more than thirty kilometers north of Ephesos, by the classical site of Metropolis, it was most likely the Arzawan site of Purunda, destroyed by Muršili II in the fourteenth century (Level III) (Meriç 2003). The mound was resettled in the twelfth century (Level II), and a fortification wall was built on the remains of the earlier Arzawan fortification. The material culture of this phase indicates, according to Mountjoy (2005a), the arrival of post-Hittite newcomers. Anatolian wares from this phase, such as orange-brown and grayware, manifest cultural continuity (Mountjoy (2005a: fig. 15). However, new cultural traits indicate the deep impact of Aegean culture on the site. A rich array of LHIIIC pottery, more than eight hundred sherds, was found at the site, dating from LHIIIC Early to LHIIIC Late. As the upper levels of the site are much eroded, it is difficult to assess what percentage this pottery composed of the entire twelfth-century assemblage. At any rate, it does not seem to have originated from ordinary trade in fineware pottery. Closed containers such as stirrup jars and straight-sided alabastra, which had dominated the imports of Mycenaean pottery since LHIIIA2 (Chapter 7), constitute but a small fraction of the types represented at the site. Surprisingly, the Bademgediği Tepe assemblage is dominated by serving vessels, such as kraters, deep bowls, conical bowls, and jugs (Meriç and Mountjoy 2002; Meriç 2003; Fig. 3.33). An additional novelty is a fragment of an HBW vessel (Meriç 2003: fig. 10). Most important, dozens of clay spools of at least two size categories first appear in twelfth-century Level II (Meriç 2003: fig. 11), indicating the introduction of new methods for textile production. In the absence of published domestic architecture and cooking ware from the site, it is hard to draw conclusions on the exact nature of the site. However, the existing data strongly support a case similar to that of Emporio – a settlement of people who brought traits of Aegean material culture to a deserted site, that had been settled previously by people of western Anatolian culture.

CILICIA AND THE AMUQ: THE LAND ROUTE FROM SOUTHEASTERN ANATOLIA TO SYRIA

TARSUS IN THE THIRTEENTH CENTURY

The shortest land route from western and northern Anatolia to the Levant passed through Cilicia, from there, both options leading to the south – through the Syrian Gates or the Amanian Gates – eventually traversed the Plain of Antioch, the Amuq. It is little wonder that the newly opened opportunities of land travel in the twelfth century quickly resulted in the appearance of Aegean-style material culture remains in Cilicia and in the Amuq.[15]

Tarsus in the thirteenth century (Late Bronze IIA) was an important city in the province of Kizzuwatna. Although in its heyday it was well connected to the Hittite Empire, there is almost no evidence (i.e., pottery imports) at the site of contact with the Aegean world before the LHIIIC period (French 1975: 74). Similarly, there is little evidence of Mycenaean imports to Cilicia in the LHIIIB period, apart from a few sherds from Kazanli (Mee 1978: 131–2; Sherratt and Crouwel 1987: 325–6).

The amount of Cypriot imports is also small, considering Tarsus's proximity to the island; only ten sherds and one complete vessel were found (Goldman 1956: 219–20) – none of them of a closed shape. This small amount of imports most likely indicates the real situation at the site, as almost all painted pottery found in the excavations was retained (French 1975: 55). This picture of relatively little contact with Cyprus and no contact at all with the Aegean world

---

[15] Unfortunately, none of the sites in Cilicia, except Tarsus, was published in the form of a final report, and the same situation is true for the Amuq sites, which display twelfth-century-BCE habitation.

may suggest that the land route from the Aegean to the Levant via Cilicia was not used for commerce in the thirteenth century. As for the sea route, the few imported items at Tarsus can be attributed to the presence in Ugarit of Hittite merchants from the Cilician port of Ura (Beal 1992; Cline 1994: 72). One can safely assume that the sea route between northern Syria and Cilicia was active at the time, as proposed by Wachsmann (1998: 295–7). However, the negligible amount of imported pottery probably indicates that this was not a major maritime route and that Cilicia did not fully participate in the interregional maritime trade between Syria, Cyprus, and the Aegean in the fourteenth and thirteenth centuries.

As for Aegean contacts, it may be relevant that the areas between the south-western Anatolian coast (areas further south and east than Halicarnassus) and the northern coast of Syria (north of Arados) are not mentioned in the Linear B texts. These areas probably did not belong to the interaction spheres of either Knossos or Pylos (Chapter 2). Thus, it may be cautiously suggested that little, if anything, was known in the Aegean about the main land route to the Levant at the end of the thirteenth century.

TARSUS IN THE TWELFTH CENTURY

The Late Bronze IIA level in Tarsus was destroyed in a massive fire. The site was almost immediately resettled but not to the same extent as it had previously been (Goldman 1956: 49–59). In Sector A, domestic buildings with well-laid walls were built on top of the Hittite temple (Goldman 1956: 50). Because of later disturbances, it is impossible to ascertain whether the Late Bronze IIA circuit wall continued to function in Late Bronze IIB (Goldman 1956: 49). A similar situation is also seen in Sector B, where better-preserved, if flimsy, domestic architecture covered the destruction layers of the Late Bronze IA (Goldman 1956: 58–9).

There seems to be much change in the tradition of pottery used at the site, as the LHIIIC fineware pottery in the Late Bronze IIB was, for the most part, made locally (Mee 1978: 145). The pottery is of a rather early date in the LHIIIC sequence, as only one sherd is granary style. There may have been some imports from Cyprus (from Enkomi and Paphos), and the flasks and the octopus style seem to indicate a connection to the Dodecanese (Mee 1978: 145). The decoration indicates LHIIIC Early and Middle dates but not LHIIIC Late (French 1975: 74; Mountjoy 1993: 175; 2005c). According to Sherratt and Crouwel (1987: 340), the Cilician material demonstrates a stylistic similarity with the eastern Aegean material rather than with that of the Greek mainland, which indicates less contact with the latter.

Even more helpful in defining the nature of the change in Tarsus are coarse-ware and cooking practices. Unfortunately, most of the undecorated pottery sherds were not kept (French 1975: 72), let alone the coarseware. It is there-fore possible to comment only on the local types of cooking ware and the appearance in Late Bronze II levels of a new type of cooking ware that was foreign to the Anatolian tradition. This new type is represented by wheel-made Aegean cooking jugs with one or two handles (Figs. 5.19 and 5.20) that bear traces of fire, indicating that cooking was conducted according to Aegean tradition (Goldman 1956: 217 nos. 1220, 1221). These traditions differ from the local ones evidenced by the horned hearth guard (Goldman 1956: 325 no. 31), the pan with hornlike projections (Goldman 1956: 219 nos. 1245, 1246), and the crescent-shaped handle of a cooking pot (Goldman 1956: 219, fig. 386: D;[16] cf. Goldman 1956: 198 no. 1071 for a Late Bronze I parallel). Had we expected to find additional Aegean influence in the cooking traditions, the absence of the tripod cooking pots would have been rather striking. One can only hypothesize that we observe here a process similar to that observed in Cyprus and Philistia (Chapter 7), in which the local cooking pot with concave base (Goldman 1956: 216 nos. 1212, 1213) probably replaced the Aegean tripod cooking pot and thus has been found side by side with the Aegean-style cooking jug.

LHIIIC pottery, most of it probably locally made, has been collected from various sites in Cilicia, such as Kazanli (Mee 1978: 156; Sherratt and Crouwel 1987), Soli Höyök (Yağci 2003), and Kilise Tepe (Jean 2003: 84–5). In Soli Höyök, imports of Cypriot white slip II appear together with imports of red lustrous wheel-made ware in a Hittite complex destroyed by fire. A following reoccupation level contained a small amount of LHIIIC sherds belonging to several deep bowls and a cup. At Kilise Tepe, Level III, from the thirteenth century, was violently destroyed, and the following Level II phases contained mostly local Anatolian wares with a small amount of LHIIIC Early pottery. As only preliminary publication is available without a detailed discussion of the coarseware pottery and other finds, it is hard to evaluate the evidence, apart from the fact that the use of locally made LHIIIC pottery was a common phenomenon in twelfth-century Cilicia. None of the sites, however, shows the large amounts of LHIIIC pottery found in Tarsus or published examples of Aegean-style cooking pots.

RANGES OF INTERACTION IN TARSUS AND CILICIA IN THE TWELFTH CENTURY

The transition between Levels IIa and IIb in Tarsus marks an end to the apparent isolation of Tarsus from Aegean influence during the thirteenth century. The violent destruction of the site at the end of the Bronze Age, the relatively unimpressive settlement that followed it, and the phenomenon of locally produced LHIIIC pottery have persuaded many scholars to reconstruct an event in which Aegean migrants (possibly the notorious Sea Peoples)

---

[16] Note, however, the existence of these handles in "eastern Mycenaean" contexts, such as at Miletus in the second building period (Niemeier 1998: 34).

played a major role (Sandars 1978: 153, 155; Dothan 1982: 217). Furthermore, the destruction of Kode equated with Kizzuwatna by the Sea Peoples, according to the Medinet Habu inscriptions, provides a clue for the destruction in the area of Tarsus (Desideri and Jasink 1990: 102–9). However, Sherratt and Crouwel (1987: 341–6) argue against the instinctive association of LHIIIC pottery, even if locally produced, with the arrival of Aegeans to Cilicia. Considering the scant evidence at hand, what ranges of interactions can be hypothesized for Tarsus? Large-scale trade can be dismissed, as most, if not all, the LHIIIC pottery is locally made and no other evidence for trade is found. As in the case of the Mycenaean IIIC: 1b pottery from Cyprus, the LHIIIC pottery from Tarsus encompasses an entire assemblage of both closed and open shapes (French 1975: 54, fig. 1), and thus does not represent a mere borrowing of shapes from the Mycenaean drinking kit, which, in any case, was hardly imported to Tarsus during the thirteenth century BCE. The few imported examples could not have acted as a trigger for a market demand for Aegean forms to result in consequent local production.

The existence of a rich LHIIIC repertoire of fineware and the presence of Aegean-style cooking pots in Tarsus mark the appearance of Aegean food preparation, storage, and consumption habits at the site. Therefore, even in the absence of clear proof for deep change affecting most assemblages, we may hypothesize – although will less certainty than in the case of Cyprus – the presence of some people of Aegean origin at the site. It is impossible to deduce their percentage among the population or their occupation or sex. The only claim that can be made about their social status is that they were probably not of the lowest status; otherwise, their taste would not be reflected so much in the local pottery production (Chapter 1). Therefore, it is possible that some form of immigration to the site took place in the early twelfth century and that some of it was Aegean in origin. Other documented changes, such as the change in house plans and in domestic behavioral patterns, might indicate a change in population and/or a change in social structure and economy following the fall of the province of Kizzuwatna.

THE AMUQ REGION AND NORTH-CENTRAL SYRIA

In the Amuq area, the period after the fall of the Hittite Empire in the early twelfth century and before the full bloom of the neo-Hittite entities in the middle Iron Age was characterized by the appearance of Aegean material culture traits side by side with the continuation of local traits, perhaps, as in the case of Cilicia, representing the arrival of a new population following the power vacuum in the area. However, the lack of final excavation reports hinders assessment of the number and status of the migrants. The regional survey of the Amuq (Yener et al. 2000: 188–9) suggests a picture similar to that in Cilicia concerning a wider appearance of Aegean material cultural traits during the twelfth century. Aegean imports from the fourteenth to thirteenth century were found in only five sites belonging to the Amuq M phase, almost all of which are located on trade routes. During the later Amuq N phase of the twelfth to tenth century BCE, locally made imitations of Aegean ware appeared at eighteen sites, so-called Mycenaean IIIC: 1 pottery (Janeway 2006–7: 128), indicating that locally made Aegean-style pottery had a much wider distribution than did imports and reached a wider range of communities and social classes.

Recent excavations directed by Timothy Harrison at Tell Ta'yinat have uncovered an elaborate picture of the sudden appearance of Aegean material culture traits during the Amuq N phase, including locally made LHIIIC fineware pottery (skyphoi and amphorae), spool-shaped loom weights, and Aegean-style cooking jugs (Janeway 2006–7). This is far from an isolated case in the Amuq. Similar appearance of LHIIIC-style pottery and Aegean spool-shaped loom weights is evident also at Chatal Hüyük (Haines 1971: pl. 16; Janeway 2006–7: 131). In addition to LHIIIC-style pottery (Pruss 2002: fig. 3), which includes bell-shaped bowls and an amphoroid krater, excavations at Chatal Hüyük and Tell Judeida have uncovered Aegean-style figurines, clearly stemming from a Mycenaean psi-type figurine (Pruss 2002: figs. 6a–b).

Further inland, southeast of the Amuq and at a distance from the land route going south from Cilicia, excavations at Tell Afis, located between Aleppo and Ebla, have revealed a picture of perhaps less pronounced connection to Aegean behavioral patterns. Reoccupation in the first half of the twelfth century (Levels 9a–8) included humble habitation with thin walls, equipped with *tannurs* – cooking installations reflecting local traditions – and cooking vessels of local tradition (Mazzoni 2000: 33; Ventury 2000: 507–9). LHIIIC pottery, possibly imported, appears in Levels 9a–8, mainly in the form of deep bowls (Venturi 2000: figs. 6: 2, 7: 1–4). Remains from later Levels 7–6 include amphorae and other closed vessels that bear Aegean affinities (Venturi 2000: fig. 11: 10, 15, 18). Beginning in Iron Age I, weaving was done with spool-shaped loom weights (Cecchini 2000: 217). As cooking and eating were carried out in a local manner at the site, it is possible that the introduction of spool-shaped loom weights to this site was, as Cecchini (2000: 216–17; Fig. 5.29), the result of contact with Anatolians rather than Aegean weaving practices.

PALASTIN AND HIYAWA: AEGEAN ETHNONYMS FOR IRON AGE POLITIES IN CILICIA AND SYRIA

The deep impact left by Aegean migrants on Cilicia, the Amuq area, and North-central Syria, which only begins to appear in the archaeological record, is greatly supplemented by the epigraphic evidence.

An eighth-century bilingual Luwian-Phoenician inscription from Çinköy, some thirty kilometers south of Adana (Hawkins 2005; Singer forthcoming), belongs to a monument built by Warika, who called himself "a Hiyawean king." He boasts of extending the boundaries of the Hiyawean Plain, his kingdom. The persistence of the name of the kingdom, undoubtedly derived from Ahhiyawa, the powerful Aegean polity of the Late Bronze Age, into the Iron Age is astonishing. To Singer, the case of the Iron Age kingdom of Hiyawa is of an old-country ethnonym carried into the new country by the Sea Peoples diaspora. Indeed, the most logical explanation is that the name was brought from the coast of the Aegean and inland through Anatolia by migrants, following the destruction of the Cilician province of Kizzuwatna. Furthermore, the same rulers preserved the local name for the inhabitants of the kingdom – the Adanawani/DNNYM, mentioned in the Karatepe inscriptions, a name derived from Adaniya, a town in Kizzuwatna, thus uniting both migrant and local traditions. However, according to the Çinköy and Karatepe inscriptions, the rulers traced their descent to an Aegean hero: Mukasa (Phoenician MPŠ), a name clearly connected to the legendary seer Moxos (or Mopsos) from Colophon. This hero has an important role in founding sites in classical and later sources, founding cities in Pamphylia, Cilicia, and according to Xanthus of Lydia, Ashkelon (Lemaire 2006).

Further surprising evidence for the naming of polities in the Iron Age in connection to Aegean or Sea Peoples ethnonyms comes from a Luwian hieroglyphic inscription recently discovered on the Aleppo Citadel and dated on the basis of the paleography to 1100–1000 BCE (Harrison 2006–7: 173–4). According to Hawkins's reading, it recalls the name of Taitas, the "hero and king of the land of Palastin." This name of the kingdom is clearly connected to the Peleset, a Sea People mentioned in the Medinet Habu inscriptions, and the Philistines who settled in the southern Levantine coast. The land of Palastin, literally "Philistia," just like the "Hiyawean Plain," was formed by migrants on route from the Aegean area to the south. The existence of two Philistias, one in Syria and the other in Canaan, is a clear indication of the route taken by the Sea Peoples, and especially the Philistines, and of the fact that the migration was not a sudden invasion from the Aegean to the boundaries of Egypt but a prolonged process that included settlement of migrants along the land routes in southeastern Anatolia and Syria. Furthermore, the fact that Aleppo, more than 120 kilometers from the sea, served as a center for the land of Palastin in the eleventh century BCE is, to my mind, an indication that land routes, rather than sea routes, had brought the Aegean migrants into the Amuq and into Syria on their way south to the Levant. The same is true for the kingdom of Hiyawa (Harrison 2006–7: 175), with is centers in Adana, more then forty kilometers from the sea, and Tarsus, around eighteen kilometers from the sea. These are hardly port sites, but they functioned as the head sites for a polity controlling Cilicia and were thus the land routes passing through the Taurus and Amanus Mountains.

THE SYRO-PHOENICIAN COAST: ALONG THE SEA AND LAND ROUTES

UGARIT: MARITIME AND LAND HOSTILITIES AND REOCCUPATION AT RAS IBN HANI

Further south, the land and sea routes from the Aegean to the Levant seem almost to converge along the Syro-Phoenician coast (Fig. 5.43). During the Late Bronze Age, the area was dominated by the kingdoms of Ugarit and Amurru, as well as by the independent city-states of the Phoenician coast. The transition to the twelfth century was accompanied by the destruction of the two large kingdoms, documented in dramatic literary evidence on the last days of Ugarit. Excavations of sites along the coast, from Ras Ibn Hani, the port of Ugarit, to Tyre and Acco, tell a story of destruction and reoccupation of many sites side by side with the curious, uninterrupted habitation in others. Although Aegean and Anatolian material culture traits are reported at most of the sites, the lack of final publications that include all aspects of material culture hinders the full understanding of the interaction with the Aegean in this important region.

Ugarit, a major commercial center and a gateway community with contacts in Cyprus, Crete, Egypt, and Hatti during the thirteenth century was violently destroyed in the early twelfth century. Arrowheads found in the streets testify to the last house-to-house fighting (Yon 1992). Some texts dated to the final period of existence of the city have been widely used to show the changing patterns of maritime activity in the twelfth century, that is, the attacks of the Sea Peoples on the kingdom of Ugarit and the Hittite Empire, which led to the destruction of both (e.g., Yon 1992: 115–16; Cifola 1994: 9–13; Stager 1995: 337; Singer 1999). Such texts are crucial to the understanding of interactions with the Aegean, as they represent a phase of raids and destruction preceding the appearance of Aegean material culture traits in sites along the Syro-Phoenician coast. Most substantial are the sources connected with maritime invasions and raids against the land of Ugarit. Direct evidence for maritime raids is given in three letters:[17] In RS 20.18, the chief prefect of Ugarit warns the king of Ugarit of twenty enemy ships that he has spotted. In RS L.1, the king (probably of Alashiya) urges the king of Ugarit to make preparations for a coming invasion from the sea. Finally, in RS 20.238, the king of Ugarit reports to the king of Alashiya on an attack from the sea by seven enemy ships and asks for information about the movements of other enemy ships.

The identity of the raiders is obscured in the letters, and the only apparent hint of their origin is in a fourth document, RS 34.129 (Yon 1992: 116; Hoftijzer and van Soldt 1998: 343; Singer 1999: 722), in which the Hittite king orders the

---

[17] Hoftijzer and van Soldt 1998: 343–4; Singer 1999: 719–23; cf. Beckman 1994a for a different translation.

prefect of Ugarit to hand over to him for interrogation a certain Ibnadushu who was captured by the men of Sikilaya. The object of this interrogation was to learn details of the land of the Sikilaya. Because the Shekelesh and the Tjeker (or Sikel) are mentioned in the Egyptian texts as two of the Sea Peoples attacking Egypt (Cifola 1991: 48), it is not inconceivable to connect the men of Sikilaya with the subsequent end of Ugarit, dated to some years before Year 8 of Ramses III. The Hittite king was eager to learn about the land of the Sikilaya, which may indicate its location far from Hatti (Singer 1988: 246; Stager 1995: 336). The toponym is not otherwise known from Anatolia, so it is possible that the Sikilaya people arrived from the Aegean area or even beyond.

A Hittite document of the late thirteenth or early twelfth century (KUB 12.38 [CTH 121]; Beckman 1994b: 32–3; Bryce 1998: 366; Singer 1999: 721; 2000: 27) tells of the subjection of Alashiya by King Tudhaliya IV, followed by the deeds of Suppiluliuma II: naval battles in which the Alashiyan fleet was defeated by the Hittite fleet three times and their ships were set on fire at sea. The Hittite army then landed on the shore and encountered the enemy. The events cannot be given an absolute date, although, according to Singer, they indicate that by this time Cyprus, or parts of it, had already been captured by the Sea Peoples. Even if Suppiluliuma II's Alashiyan campaign was not directly connected to the end of the Hittite Empire and to the raids on Ugarit, it may still provide a good example of the types of naval activities conducted in the days preceding the fall of Hatti.

The threat to Ugarit was by no means only from the sea. According to RS 34.143 (Singer 1999: 723–4), the best units of the Ugarit army camped in Apshuna, in the north of the kingdom of Ugarit, rather than at Mukish, as the Hittite king had ordered. The report in RS 16.402 (Singer 1999: 724–5) that the enemy was coming from Mukish in the Amuq Valley hints, according to Singer, at an enemy bridgehead there, a base for land activities against Ugarit. This combination of sea and land hostilities against the kingdom of Ugarit recalls the pattern of the later activities of the Sea Peoples against Egypt during the reign of Ramses III. A few letters concerning military defeats of Ugarit indicate that the end of the kingdom of Ugarit came soon afterward (Singer 1999: 725–7).

Although it is uncertain from the literary evidence who the enemy was that destroyed the kingdom of Ugarit, apart from a possible association with one of the Sea Peoples, archaeological data indicate that, soon after the destruction, Aegean material culture traits made their first appearance.

The royal Ugaritic palaces in the harbor site of Ras Ibn Hani were evacuated and burned at the beginning of the twelfth century (Caubet 1992: 124; Lagarce and Lagarce 1988: 140–1). A new settlement of a more humble nature, yet with a rather organized plan, was built on the ruins of the southern palace (Lagarce and Lagarce 1987: 13, fig. 14). The most notable phenomenon in this layer is the vast quantity of locally made Mycenaean IIIC: 1b pottery, comprising more than 50 percent of the total amount of painted pottery (Fig. 5.63; Lagarce and Lagarce 1988: 143; du Piêd 2006–7: 169–70). This pottery belongs to the LHIIIC tradition and consists mainly of open and small closed shapes (e.g., kraters, a deep bowl, shallow angular bowls, a cup, a spouted jug, small stirrup jars). Other painted fineware seems to represent a continuation of local styles (du Piêd 2006–7: figs. 10–11). The architecture itself does not display any features that are strikingly foreign. The continuation of local Late Bronze Age forms of burnished cooking pots into the Iron Age (du Piêd 2006–7: 165–7) and the round ovens in the second Early Iron Age phase in Square X 67 (Bounni et al. 1981: 260–1) may hint that local cooking traditions were prevalent at Ras Ibn Hani in the late twelfth century or eleventh century. Because only preliminary reports have been published (Bounni et al. 1976; 1978; 1979; 1981), it remains to be determined whether the Aegean-style cooking pots and loom weights existed at the site. Therefore, arguments for the settlement of the Sea Peoples at the site after the destruction of Ugarit (Lagarce and Lagarce 1988: 143), while certainly supported by current evidence, must await confirmation by a full publication of the site.

AFTER AMURRU: THE CASE OF TELL KAZEL

During the demise of the kingdom of Amurru and the end of its Hittite-related dynasty, Tell Kazel was violently destroyed.

Excavations at Tell Kazel, identified as Sumur of the kingdom of Amurru (Singer 1991: 138 no. 4) have demonstrated that the site enjoyed prosperity during the thirteenth century, attested to by a large number of Cypriot and Mycenaean imports; however, it was abandoned during the later part of Late Bronze II (Badre 2006: 69). The following settlement of the transitional Late Bronze Age–Iron Age period made use of the older buildings without employing significant changes to them. It contained the presently largest collection of HBW from the Levant. The vessels were found in two areas – Area II, the site of the former Late Bronze Age temple, and Area IV, a former elite domestic area. Unlike any other site in Cyprus or the Levant that yielded only a few examples of HBW, the HBW finds from Tell Kazel comprise both storage and serving vessels, forming a complete functional assemblage (Badre 2003: 95). Closed vessels include storage vessels with a burnished or partially burnished surface, a jug (Badre 2003: fig. 6: 7), and a large amphora (Badre 2003: fig. 6: 8). Open shapes are equally well represented among the HBW at Tell Kazel and include a shallow plate (Badre 2003: fig. 6: 3), a kylix (Badre 2003: fig. 7: 11), deep small goblets (Badre 2003: figs. 6: 6; 9: 1, 2), and a mug or cup (Badre 2003: fig. 9: 4). Many of these vessels have good parallels in Cyprus and the Aegean (Guzowska and Yasur-Landau 2007a), yet Neutron Activation Analysis (NAA) and petrographic analysis have established that the vessels were made in the region of Tell Kazel (Badre et al. 2005: 35).

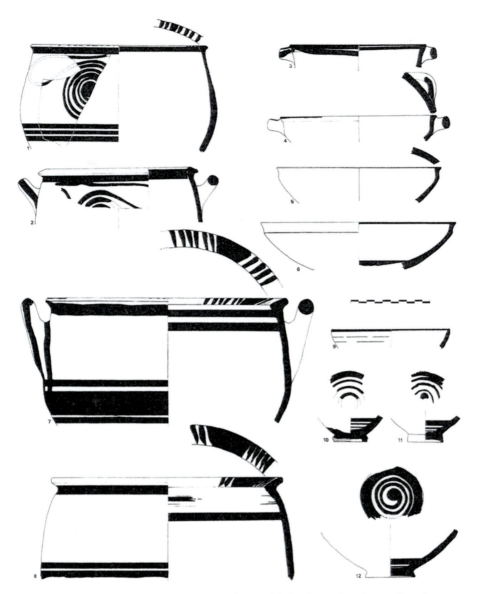

FIGURE 5.63. Aegean-style pottery from Ras Ibn Hani (after Bounni et al. 1979: fig. 25)

During this phase, two important groups of imports were also present at the site. The first is a group of Anatolian grayware containing a cup, a goblet, krater bowls, and a jug. An NAA analysis has confirmed a northwestern Anatolian provenance (Badre 2006: 87–8; Badre et al. 2005: 31–2). The second group comprises Mycenaean-style vessels, most of which are small, closed forms that were made in Cyprus and western Anatolia (Badre et al. 2005: 32–3). The transitional Late Bronze Age–Iron Age phase was short and ended in destruction by fire.

In contrast to the wealth of HBW pottery, only a small amount of LHIIIC-style pottery was found in the transitional Late Bronze Age–Iron Age I phase and in the subsequent Iron Age I phase (Jung 2007). This picture is dissimilar to that emerging from sites in which Aegean settlement has been found, as in Maa-Palaeokastro, Tarsus, or Emporio. It strongly supports the excavator's first impression of an "absence of any typical material characterizing the Sea Peoples" (Badre 2003: 92). However, the "sudden and short appearance in the Levantine pottery sequence" (Bardre 2006: 92) of large quantities of HBW at the site may be regarded as indicating a deep change. A simple look at the morphology of the HBW vessels makes it clear that its manufacturers must have mastered different skills from those of manufacturers that specialized in wheel-thrown pottery, and that the potters who produced the HBW in Tell Kazel were trained in a different pottery tradition. Producing a handmade vessel with a carefully burnished surface, complicated shape, and elaborate decoration like knobs, incisions, or burnishing requires very different mechanical skills than throwing a pot of standardized shape on a wheel. Badre (2006: 92–3) perceives the appearance of HBW at Tell Kazel as an indicator of a peaceful migration of a group of Sea Peoples, and the association of HBW with the Anatolian grayware may suggest a common origin of the migrants (Badre 2006: 87). This conclusion seems solid; the Anatolian-inspired assemblage of Tell Kazel is possibly the best evidence for a migration of a non-Aegean group into the Levant during the twelfth century.

THE NORTHERN PHOENICIAN COAST: CONTINUITY WITHOUT BREAK IN HABITATION

In Phoenicia, south of the areas affected by the violent collapse of Ugarit and Amurru, the trail of Aegean behavioral patterns gets colder. The Phoenician sites, such as Byblos, Sarepta, and Tyre, show no evidence of destruction in the transition between the Late Bronze Age and the Early Iron Age. Unlike Ugarit, whose name was forgotten, the names of the Phoenician sites are preserved to this day, showing a marked continuation in habitation. These sites yielded mainly imported pieces of LHIIIC pottery, reflecting a small-scale revival of trade with Cyprus in the middle and late twelfth century.

LHIIIC pottery has been found in Byblos in mixed deposits in Nécropole K (Salles 1980: 30–5, 66), including two bowls, six krater fragments (including ones decorated with fish and birds), and two stirrup jars (one decorated in Bichrome style). The vessels are attributed to LHIIIC Early and Middle (Warren and Hankey 1989: 163), yet their place of manufacture has not been determined. The appearance of both early and middle styles of LHIIIC at the site indicates continuation of the contacts with at least the Aegean styles through most of the LHIIIC period.

Further to the south, Sarepta, located on the Phoenician coast, about thirteen kilometers south of Sidon (Anderson 1988: 34), shows a peaceful transition between the thirteenth and twelfth centuries as well as local, Phoenician material culture. Earlier, during the Late Bronze Age, at the end of the period of Stratum J (Area II, Y), the city may have suffered a catastrophe, reflected in evidence of conflagration (Anderson 1988: 70), and was perhaps consequently abandoned, as seen in the lack of architectural remains in Stratum H. However, the renewed construction attested to in Stratum G2 had probably already been conducted in the thirteenth century (ibid.: 386), since only imported LHIIIB pottery was found, and no LHIIIC (ibid.: 606–8 pl. 26, 609–11 pl. 27). The architectural setting of G2 continued almost unaltered well into the first millennium (ibid.: 380). According to the excavator, Stratum G1 began in the thirteenth century and ended at the beginning of the twelfth. A similar picture is seen in Area II, X where Period V is dated to 1275–1150 BCE (Koehl 1985: 190, table 2). In any case, one cannot identify any Aegean material culture traits in these levels except LHIIIC Early fineware (Anderson 1988: 612–13, pl. 28: 19; Leonard 1994: 118 no. 1757), local imitations of Mycenaean pottery (Anderson 1988: pl. 28: 6). The cooking pot forms (e.g., ibid.: 612–13, pl. 28: 7–9, 11) are mostly of types typical of the local Late Bronze Age tradition (ibid.: 500–1, table 13A). The later strata – F in Area II, Y and Period VI in Area II, X – follow the same cultural pattern (ibid.: 386, 389) as Stratum G1, and LHIIIC pottery appears only as fineware (ibid.: 617–19, pl. 30: 10; Koehl 1985: 118–22). Furthermore, the U-shaped form of kilns in both Period V and IV in Area II, X reflects local patterns of pottery production (Khalifeh 1988: 27–39). This form of kiln seems to be of local origin and finds parallels at other Levantine sites (Pritchard 1975: 76–7; Wood 1990: 27–9).

Since the finds of LHIIIC pottery include only a few deep bowls and stirrup jars, one may assume that these came by trade to answer the demand (formed already in the fourteenth and thirteenth centuries) for decorated drinking ware or goods that were transported in small stirrup jars.

In Tyre, small-scale excavations (Bikai 1978: 7–8) may indicate a continuation from Stratum XV (Late Bronze Age, with Cypriot WSII imports) to XIV (Early Iron Age), and a general picture somewhat similar to Sarepta. The ceramic assemblage as a whole seems to indicate a continuation of the local pottery tradition (ibid.: pl. XXXIX). The find of a round *tannur* in Stratum XIV indicates continuation in cooking traditions, as do finds of local types of cooking pots (ibid.: pl. XXXIX: 16, 19, 22). Of the imported pottery, one can note two interesting late twelfth to eleventh century imports: one is a sherd of the Philistine Bichrome style (ibid.: pl. XLI: 19) and the other is a sherd of a rare example of a LHIIIC Late bowl (ibid.: pl. XXXIX: 20; Leonard 1994: 120 no. 1778). A possible explanation for the apparent continuity in the Phoenician coastal sites was recently put forward by Carol Bell (2006: 110). To her mind, close commercial ties between the Aegean merchants and the Phoenician sites during the thirteenth century had resulted in personal ties with the would-be Aegean raiders of the twelfth century, causing them to spare the Phoenician sites, while Ugarit and other sites that did not have direct contacts with the Aegean were destroyed.

THE SOUTHERN PHOENICIAN COAST: FAINT TRACES OF MIGRATION?

As with the northern Phoenician sites, the southern Phoenician coast between Acco and Dor shows no evidence of violent transition between the thirteenth and twelfth centuries, and the eleventh-century tale of Wen-Amon, mentioning the presence of the Tjeker/Sikel in Dor, has been used by modern scholarship to place the Sherden Shardana, appearing next to the Sikila in the late Twentieth Dynasty Onomasticon of Amenope, in Acco (Dothan and Dothan 1992: 213–14; Stager 1995: fig. 2; Gilboa 2005: 1). However, attempts to find the "northern Sea People" in the sites along the southern Phoenician coast has yielded only minute evidence of Aegean behavioral patterns, with an overall picture of material culture similar to that on the northern Phoenician coast.

The transition between the Late Bronze Age and Early Iron Age at Acco seems to have taken place without destruction. Area AB, an industrial area active from the thirteenth century to the twelfth century, contained a bilobate pottery kiln similar to those from Sarepta, much evidence of a metal industry (e.g., crucibles, tuyeres, slag, and fragments of flawed vessels), as well as evidence of a purple dye industry (Dothan 1988; 1989: 60–2; 1993b: 21; Artzy 2006: 50). Fragments of LHIIIC-style pottery, mainly deep bowls and stirrup jars (M. Dothan 1989: 61, figs. 3.1 and 3.2), were found in Area AB and in Areas K, P, and PH of the site. The NAA analysis of five of the vessels, including two deep bowls, confirmed a Cypriot rather than local origin (D'Agata et al. 2005: 375). Dothan (1986) has noted that the style of the sherds is different from the Monochrome pottery from Ashdod and bears closer resemblance to the pottery from contemporary Greece and Cyprus. Dothan (1986) attributes this pottery to the settlement of the Sherden, one of the Sea Peoples, yet final publication of the sherds, including a stylistic analysis and a larger sample for provenance studies, is necessary in order to establish an argument for local production and the source of inspiration for its creation. Another question concerning Dothan's suggestion for a settlement of Aegeans in Acco is the nature of the domestic, undecorated pottery at the site. Dothan mentions a continuation of Canaanite forms such as cooking pots and storage jars, but it is yet to be seen whether there are any Aegean-style cooking pots or other Aegean-style vessels at the site. An interesting find that may testify to maritime activities in Late Bronze Age–Iron Age I Acco is a limestone altar (Artzy 1987) from Area H, found in connection with an ash pit and pebbles on which a ship, a bird, and a dolphin were carved. One of the faces of the altar bore the images of four ships, their inwardly-curved stem finding parallels in Egyptian and Levantine vessels rather than Aegean ones or those of the Sea Peoples (Artzy 1987: 79–80). These may support a scenario in which Acco, similar to Sarepta, continued to be a Canaanite center into the twelfth century, without much of a break, while trade with Cyprus also continued but on a smaller scale than that of the Late Bronze Age.

The coastal city of Dor, in the northern Sharon Plain, is mentioned in the tale of Wen-Amon as the main city of the Tjeker/Sikel – one of the Sea Peoples mentioned by Ramses III. The nature of transition between the Late Bronze Age and the Iron Age is unclear, as the Late Bronze Age town has not been located (Gilboa 2005: 4). Excavations headed by Stern (2000: 199–200) reached two strata of the early Iron Age I, which he calls Early Sikilian (Area G, Stratum 10) and Late Sikilian (Area G, Stratum 9, and Area B1, Stratum 12). Unfortunately, little is known of the earlier stratum, exposed in only a small area (Stern 1998: 348). The later stratum, however, in Area B1, contained part of a four-meter thick mud-brick city wall that rested on cyclopean stone foundations. The wall was abutted by a sand glacis coated with plaster for protection from the rain (Stern 1998: 346). Two large rooms were built against it. In Area G, a room with a large plastered trough was found together with basalt basins and mortars; perhaps it was the kitchen of an important building. The stratum contained material culture that Stern (2000: 199–201) parallels with Philistia at the end of the twelfth and throughout the eleventh centuries (Stern 2000: 199–201): Bichrome pottery, fragments of a lion-head rhyton and an incised cow scapula, and the bone handle of an iron knife of a type found also at Tel Miqne/Ekron and Tell Qasile (Chapter 8). A small cultic area was identified by the presence of a pottery assemblage that included a chalice and a fenestrated cult stand – traits of local, Canaanite cultic practices. There is no report of other items of Aegean origin common to Philistia, such as Aegean cooking jugs and imperforated loom weights. Gilboa (2005: 17–19; 2006–7) has suggested a new interpretation of the ceramic assemblage of Dor. She argues that the presence of locally made deep bowls, the local production of "wavy band" pithoi, and the decoration of overlapping multiple diagonal strokes on kraters and strainer jugs from Iron I Dor are faint evidence of the presence of a small group of migrants originating in Cyprus and Syria. These, faced by a large, stable, local population, manifested their identity in a relatively minor way, by creating special drinking vessels fit for their feasting customs. Although there seems to be little doubt that the Tjeker/Sikel occupied Dor in the eleventh century, the Dor evidence can be interpreted at best as a small number of migrants arriving at a site inhabited by a strong coastal community.

THROUGH THE EGYPTIAN LENS

THE WIDER GEOGRAPHIC SCOPE OF THE INVASION

The Egyptians watched the turns of fortune of the Hittite and Syrian kingdoms and the arrival of invaders and migrants from a safe distance at first; but soon afterward, during the reign of Ramses III, they faced raiders and settlers at their own borders. In contrast to the Hittites and Ugaritians, the Egyptians prevailed, leaving not only a unique account of their victories over the Peleset,

Sikila (Tjeker/Sikel), Sherden, Shekelesh, Weshesh, and Denyen but also a broader geographical and temporal overview – their interpretation of the route and actions taken by the invaders before their supposedly decisive showdown with the Egyptians. As we will see, these routes, starting in the Aegean Sea, continuing through Cyprus and western and southern Anatolia, and ending in Amurru, with no mention of sites in Phoenicia, and then suddenly reappearing on the borders of Egypt itself, bear uncanny resemblance to the trails of Aegean behavioral pattern left by the twelfth-century-BCE migrants.

The events described in various sources relating to the days of Ramses III (and Ramses IV) seem to be authentic and an important historical source, within the many limitations and biases of Egyptian royal propaganda (O'Connor 2000: 86–94; Redford 2000: 11–12; Cline and O'Connor 2003: 120, 127). The need to follow patterns of narration of Pharaonic victory had dictated the display of a unified, hostile invasion culminating in two decisive battles – the sea battle and the land battle – perhaps meant to be shown as occurring simultaneously (Dothan 1982: 5–13; Redford 2000: 13). Still, even through the Egyptian schematized and formalized lens, enough evidence is left in the texts and reliefs to enable a reconstruction of a complex picture of raids and migration, made up of different processes extending across time and space.

The Medinet Habu Year 8 inscription gives a vast and unparalleled geographical background to what is known as the invasion of Egypt by the Sea Peoples. The description of the invasion in this inscription mentions the origin and route of the invaders – moving from distant to close locations and from less familiar to more familiar ones.

The origin of the invaders from unnamed islands. "The foreign lands made conspiracy in their islands" (Peden 1994: 29; Redford 2000: 12). This designation of the place of origin appears twice again in other texts from Medinet Habu: "the northern countries who were in their islands" and "the countries who came from their land in the isles in the midst of the sea" (Cline and O'Connor 2003: 137). Another relevant source is Papyrus Harris I (Cifola 1994: 5). In the scope of a wider historical account of the deeds of Ramses III, it mentions the islands of origin of the Denyen (Danuna) and records the following claim: "I slew the Danuna in their isles" (Peden 1994: 215; Cline and O'Connor 2003: 138). The isles of the Denyen may or may not be the islands mentioned in the great inscription of Year 8. It is possible to identify them with any of the Aegean islands except for Cyprus and Crete, as both islands are named elsewhere in earlier Egyptian records (Cline 1994: 34, fig. 7); furthermore, Cyprus is mentioned by the name Alashiya in the Year 8 inscription itself. The island origin of the invaders clearly points to the Aegean area, supporting the connection between the invaders and the contemporary Aegean migrants to Cyprus and Cilicia identified in the archaeological evidence.

The route of destruction. "No one could stand their arms, from Hatti, Kode, Carchemish, Arzawa, and Alashiya" (Peden 1994: 29; Cline and O'Connor 2003: 136). Although the invasion originated in the islands, its routes follow both sea and land routes. Some places, such as Carchemish and perhaps Hatti, could be reached only by land. Alashiya (Cyprus) could be reached only by sea. Arzawa and Kode (Cilicia) could be reached by sea and by land. Further evidence for the route taken is the origin of the nonfighting population depicted on the land battle relief, which is the only depiction that clearly shows migration. The wagons do not appear to have either an Aegean or Levantine origin but rather an Anatolian one (Chapter 4). Furthermore, some of the men depicted on the wagons seem to be Syro-Canaanite, and others may be Hittite men rather than women; Sweeney and Yasur-Landau 1999: 134, 138). If such is the case, the relief can be taken as additional support for an Anatolian–Syrian route of land migration, suggested by Medinet Habu Year 8 inscription.

The encampment in Amurru, just outside the scope of Egyptian political domination, before the encounter with the Egyptians. "An encampment was [estab]lished in one place in Amor and they desolated its people and its land as though they had never come into being" (Peden 1994: 29). The exact position of this camp is unknown. This encampment "in Amor (Amurru)" was most likely close to one of the inland or coastal routes connecting Anatolia and the Levant. The unusual finds in Sumur (Tell Kazel; Klengel 1992: 164–5) have brought Bader (2006) to suggest that one of the camps of the newcomers was located at the site. This encampment brings to mind the evidence from Ugarit concerning another enemy bridgehead in Mukish, north of Ugarit, in the area of the Amuq (as mentioned previously), which suggests that leapfrogging – the movement of migrants from site to site along the migration route, according to information and the presence of kin (Anthony 1990: 902) – was also implemented in this case.

There are many lacunae in the historical and geographical backgrounds of the conflict. The Egyptian sources do not mention Ugarit, although it can be assumed that Ugarit was destroyed along with the other kingdoms. The absence of Phoenician and Canaanite coastal sites may indicate that the invaders bypassed these areas on their way to the south, as seen in the apparent continuity of material culture in the sites examined, or that the land battle in Djahi – anywhere between the Phoenician and the Levantine coasts, took place in the northern Phoenician coast. Also absent is an explicit time frame for the invasion. However, the presentation of the background in discernable steps may indicate a gradual process, which Cline and O'Connor (2003: 120) estimate could have taken several years. This notion is supported by the proposed time gap of ten to fifteen years between the destruction date of Ugarit (1190–1185 BCE) and Year 5 or 8 of Ramses III (ca. 1175 BCE). The period in which there was no conflict between the Egyptians and the invaders and in which the invaders appear to have been camped in Amurru, virtually at the border of the Egyptian-controlled areas, will prove of importance in the reconstruction of the nature of interaction between the two populations.

CLOSE ENCOUNTERS: PROCESS INTO EVENT?

After the possible interval in hostilities, the invaders turned against Egypt. Taking into account the need of the Egyptians who designed the texts and reliefs at Medinet Habu to fit complex, unprecedented events and processes into the existing schemes describing Pharaonic victory, one may ask whether there were only two decisive battles, one on land and one at sea, or whether the Medinet Habu reliefs show a simplified picture that summarizes the different interactions. Two phases are mentioned in the Year 8 inscription: the Egyptian preparation for battle in Djahi and the invasion itself:

1. The building of two defense lines by the Egyptians: one against a land invasion in the Land of Djahi (roughly, Canaan) and a second against a maritime invasion in the river mouths (most probably the Nile; O'Connor 2000: 95).
2. Invasion, perhaps simultaneously, by land and by sea. Its description can be found in lines 51–9 in the Year 5 inscription (the first Libyan war), presumably connected to the events of Year 8 (Peden 1994: 7): "The northern hill countries shook in their bodies, namely the *Peleset* and the *Tjek[er]*.... [They] were *thr*-soldiers on land and another (unit) was on the sea" (Peden 1994: 17). Only the repulsion of the maritime invaders is recalled clearly in the inscription ("Those who came forward together on their sea, their seed is not").

The sites of the land and sea battles are uncertain. Although the sea battle was almost certainly at one of the mouths of the Nile, the land battle in Djahi could have occurred almost anywhere between Amurru and southern Canaan, or even at the margins of the Delta (Bietak 1993: 293; Redford 2000; O'Connor 2000: 90, 99). Cifola (1991: 54–5) offers a convincing explanation for the fact that there is no stated location or time given to the land or sea battles: the land battle was not a single event but a series of relatively small-scale hostile encounters between the Sea Peoples and Egyptian forces. One should not rule out the possibility that the sea battle, too, was not a single event of hostile maritime activity (presumably in Year 8) but the "total impression" of many similar interactions of the kind seen in Papyrus Harris I condensed into a single narrative of Pharaonic victory. Support for this interpretation comes from the inconsistencies between the names of the groups of Sea Peoples mentioned in the Egyptian Medinet Habu relief and those of Papyrus Harris I and the people

FIGURE 5.64. Sea Peoples fighting in the Lybian campaign of Ramses III (after Nelson 1930: pl. 72)

actually shown in the reliefs,[18] as well as from evidence of recurring maritime raids on Egypt during the thirteenth and twelfth centuries, thus suggesting that the battle in Year 8 may not have been an isolated event. The latter notion is further supported by the depiction of soldiers with feathered hats in the service of the Egyptians already in the campaign of Year 5 against the Libyans (Sandars 1978: 118, fig. 74; Cline and O'Connor 2003: 120; Fig. 5.64). People wearing the feathered hat had therefore reached Egypt as prisoners and/or as mercenaries before Year 5 of Ramses III. These could not have been prisoners of the Libyan campaigns of Merneptah, who were by that time too aged for battle.

THE LAND BATTLE: IMAGES OF MIGRATION

The land battle relief provides many details about the general nature of inter-actions depicted, most connected to the nonfighting population (Nelson 1930: pls. 32 and 34). Five carts carrying women, children, and noncombatant men are shown among charioteers and warriors of the Sea Peoples fighting the Egyptians (Fig. 5.65; Nelson 1930: pl. 34) – an indication of the movement of entire families within a migration rather than of a regular battle scene. The presence of ox carts with double teams may indicate the means by which animals were transported to the new agricultural settlement. Furthermore, the reliefs are the only iconographic evidence of the place of women in the migration movement in the southern Levant: even at first glance, it can be noted that there are no two identical hairstyles among the six women depicted

---

[18] For example, the Sherden are shown in the naval battle relief but are not mentioned in the inscription of Year 8, although their chief is shown elsewhere in Medinet Habu (Sandars 1978: 111, figs. 68, 69, and no. 125); they are mentioned again in Papyrus Harris I as "the *Sherden* and the *Weshesh* of the sea" (Peden 1994: 215).

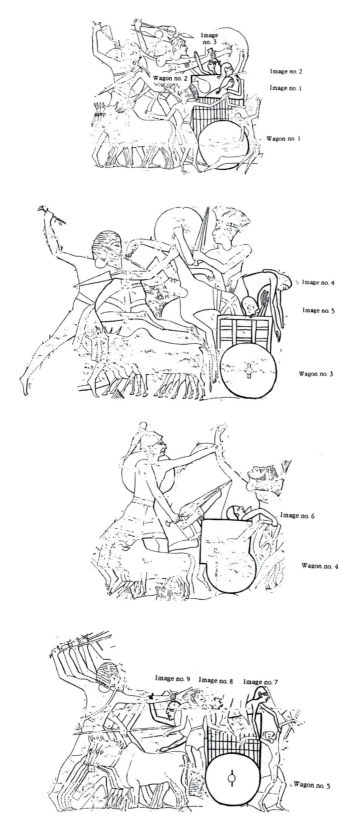

FIGURE 5.65. The land battle relief from Medinet Habu, details of ox carts. (after Sweeney and Yasur-Landau 1999: figs. 1, 2)

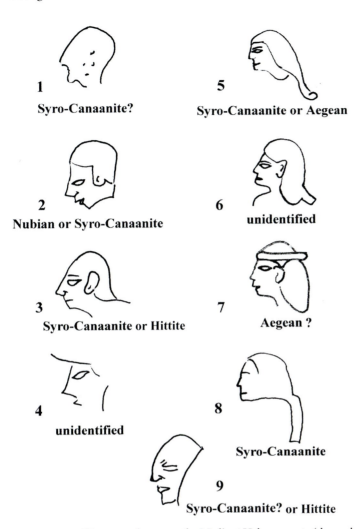

1
Syro-Canaanite?

5
Syro-Canaanite or Aegean

2
Nubian or Syro-Canaanite

6
unidentified

3
Syro-Canaanite or Hittite

7
Aegean ?

4
unidentified

8
Syro-Canaanite

9
Syro-Canaanite? or Hittite

FIGURE 5.66. Women and men on the Medinet Habu ox carts (drawn by A. Yasur-Landau)

at Medinet Habu – a hint that they were not of the same origin (Fig. 5.66). Iconographic analysis aimed to identify the origin of the women by their hairstyles was considered possible because Egyptian artists were aware of different costumes and hairstyles and used them to depict ethnic differentiation (Sweeney and Yasur-Landau 1999). A comparison of the various hairstyles was made against the corpus of female hairstyle representations of Late Kingdom Egypt, Syro-Canaan, and the Aegean, revealing that it is likely that some of the women are Syro-Canaanite, whereas at least one appears to have a hairstyle with Aegean parallels. One woman's hairstyle has no close parallel in either Egyptian or Aegean art, perhaps indicating an origin outside both Mycenaean and Egyptian cultural spheres. It is worth noting the presence of Canaanite or Hittite men on the wagons (Sweeney and Yasur-Landau 1999), adding more complexity to this picture of ethnic diversity (Fig. 5.66) and a hint concerning the route of migration.

The different origins of the women represented on the same cart may very well indicate the phenomenon of intermarriage (Sweeney and Yasur-Landau 1999); at least some of the Sea Peoples met women along their land journey through Syria. Others may have migrated together with their womenfolk or found their partners outside the areas known to the Egyptians. It seems that for mainly logistic reasons – common to modern and ancient migrations (Chapter 1) – the Aegean migration to the Levant and Cyprus consisted, most likely, of more men than women, thus leading to the phenomenon of intercultural marriages. The problem of the "shortage" of women may have been even more severe if a substantial part of the migration was carried out using oared galleys (Chapter 4), as was probably the case for Cyprus.

The age of the children portrayed may indicate a minimum time that had elapsed between the initial migration of the men (and perhaps some of the women) and the time of the depiction, in Year 8 of Ramses III. If the small children resulted from intermarriages, the minimum time would be about $8 + x$ years (as the children are lowered from the wagons, and so old enough to escape the Egyptians on their own). The appearance of youths wearing feathered hats – perhaps a sign of initiation – but unarmed is intriguing. If they are the offspring of intermarriage or were born en route to parents of the same origin, their dress should indicate a patrilineal aspect of the migrating society. Alternatively, they could have come from the original homeland of the initial migrating population, representing a long-distance migration of whole families, including women and youths too young to be first-line warriors that were therefore left with the wagons and other noncombatants.

To conclude, the iconographic evidence of what appears to be a second phase of migration matches well with the literary description of the phases on the trail of destruction left by the Sea Peoples and with the evidence for the genesis of the kingdoms of Hiyawa and Palastin in Cilicia and Syria. Furthermore, the existence of Sea Peoples at "encampment in Amurru" fills the possible chronological gap of ten to fifteen years between the destruction date of Ugarit (1190/1185 BCE) and Year 8 of Ramses III (1175) and allows for a convincing historical reconstruction for the sequence of events:

1. *Migration of men with feathered hats (and some women) to Amurru (and later to the area of the kingdom of Ugarit) by a land route and possibly by boat:* A land route through Anatolia may be suggested by the depiction of ox carts, a vehicle with clear Anatolian parallels. This migration may have originated, at least for a good number of the participants, in western Anatolia or the Aegean and may have followed or been connected in some way to the destructions of Hatti and its provinces and vassal states in Syria.

2. *Settlement at Amurru, at the borders of Egypt:* In the beginning, there might have been hostilities with the local population (as indicated in the great inscription of Year 8), but later some intermarriages with local women most

probably occurred. The beginning of the settlement at Ras Ibn Hani may tentatively be connected to this phase, which lasted for ten to fifteen years.

3. *Continued attempts to conduct migration toward the south, perhaps as secondary foundings from the initial settlement in Amurru:* These migration movements may have been directed toward the province of Canaan and possibly the Delta. The movement seems to have been that of colonizing parties of mixed origin and of entire families aiming to construct an agricultural settlement. It was composed not only of warriors of a feathered-hat origin but also of women of different origins and children. Given the time span of the migrants' stay at Amurru, it is likely that some of the youths with feathered hats were born in Syria. The long stay at Amurru may have facilitated the building of an army and of a chariot force used later for an attack on Egypt.

THE SEA BATTLE: MIGRATION OR RAID?

Crucial evidence for the aim of the attack, and for the identity of the attackers, comes from the type of ship used by the Sea Peoples (Fig. 5.67). According to Wachsmann (1998: 172), these ships find their best parallel in Mycenaean oared galleys, with the most detailed example in Kynos ship A (Wachsmann 1998: 131; Dakoronia and Mpougia 1999: 23). This ship belongs to Wedde's (1999: 466–7, pl. 87) type V of Mycenaean galleys: excellent as a fighting platform at sea (as seen on the Kynos krater), yet equipped also with the abilities to transport soldiers and plunder. It was demonstrated (Chapter 4) that, because this type of oared galley needed a full rowing crew for operation and because the ship was only partially decked, the number of passengers or amount of load that could be carried on it was rather limited – only ten or so more than the number of rowers and crew, with no extra space for provisions. This, combined with the fact that only male warriors appear in the scene, clearly indicates a different interaction than the colonization party shown in the land battle relief. The alternatives for the interpretation of this encounter (if it is a single event) are various: from colonization by an all-male party to a raiding fleet of the type that attacked in Ugarit (described earlier) or of the type Odysseus mentioned in his story about his nine-ship "raid" on Egypt (Hom. *Od.* 14: 245–9).

Piracy or raids against Egypt were not a novelty in the twelfth century. As early as the fourteenth century, the king of Egypt had probably accused people from Alashiya of participating in an activity against Egypt (el-Amarna letter 38: 7–18; Moran 1992: 111; Cifola 1994: 8). The thirteenth-century Tanis Stele of Ramses II describes the Sherden as pirates who conduct raids from ships (Cifola 1994: 2). The Ugarit example shows that sea-borne raids seem to have been of a larger scale in the twelfth century, probably employing as many as twenty ships. Such a venture would have required between four hundred and ten hundred men.[19] Sailing time would have been rather short: for example, five to seven days between the Dodecanese or southwestern Anatolia (perhaps the "islands in the midst of the sea") and the southern Levant, and ten to thirteen days back. Including raids, the entire expedition should have taken no longer than twenty days – short enough to have been worth the risk of leaving home and much easier than organizing a sea-borne colonization party – a high-risk venture for a much longer time.

THE ORIGIN OF THE ATTACKERS

HORNED HELMETS AND FEATHERED HATS

The identification of the general area of origin of the attackers is essential for the evaluation of the nature of interaction depicted in the Medinet Habu reliefs and other Egyptian sources. The proposed Aegean origin, hinted at by the reference to the islands at Medinet Habu and in Papyrus Harris I (mentioned earlier), can be cross-checked against the evidence from two other independent sources: the origin of ethnonyms mentioned in Egyptian and other sources and the iconography of the participants in the land and sea battles. The identification of the origin of the Sea Peoples' ethnonyms mentioned in Egyptian texts has occupied Egyptologists for more than 130 years. Already in 1867, Emmanuel De Rougé had suggested an identification of the foreigners mentioned in the Libyan campaign of Merneptah (Drews 1993: 54; Cifola 1994: 3–4); the Lukka, Ekwesh, Tursha, Shekelesh, and Sherden were thought to be mercenaries from Lycia, Achaea, Tyrsenia, Sicily, and Sardinia. Not long afterward, in 1872, François Chabas and Gaston Maspero (Drews 1993: 54–9) identified the Peleset in the inscriptions of Ramses III with the Aegean Pelasgoi and the biblical Philistines. In further research, the names of the different Sea Peoples that appear in Egyptian and other sources were compared with ethnic names known from later sources, to pinpoint their origins. The etymological approach to the Sea Peoples has not changed much over the past century, even since the discovery of the Ugaritic archives. It is clear that the Sea Peoples came from outside the realm of Egypt and Syro-Canaan; the connection between the Philistines and the Aegean Pelasgoi seems to be almost universally accepted (see detailed survey in Singer 1988; Niemeier 1998: 17–18, 46–7), indicating an origin somewhere in the vast area along the shores of the Aegean Sea. To this day, however, scholars differ on whether to attribute a western Anatolian (Aegean, Carian, and Lydian) or Aegean and central Mediterranean (Aegean, Italian, Sardinian, and Sicilian) origin to the other Sea Peoples (Cline and O'Connor 2003). It seems, then, that the

---

[19] The lower number is calculated for *eikosoros*, and the higher number for a force composed solely of penteconters.

FIGURE 5.67. A ship with warriors with feathered hats (after Nelson 1930: pl. 39)

etymological evidence for the origin of the Philistines and other Sea Peoples can be defined as unfocused and ambiguous at best.

The identification of the origin of the people with horned helmets (Fig. 5.68) is as complicated. They were identified in Egypt by the name Sherden and were in the service of the Pharaohs at least as early as the days of Ramses II (Drews 1993: 152–5; Cifola 1994: 2–3; Loretz 1995; Cline and O'Connor 2003: 112). They appear as foot soldiers, carrying a sword or a spear and a distinctive round shield. Sherden were also in the service of Ugarit and perhaps of other polities (Drews 1993: 154; Loretz 1995: 128–32) beginning in the fourteenth century, yet there are no depictions of them from that period. Sandars argues that all the characteristics of the Sherden – the horned helmet, a round shield, a short kilt, and greaves – can be found in North Syria, namely in Ugarit (Sandars 1978: 160–1). However, the depiction of warriors with horned helmets on the Warrior Vase from Mycenae (Fig. 3.26; Vermeule and Karageorghis 1982: 132 no. XI.42; also wearing greaves and carrying round shields) casts some doubt on the theory of a solely Levantine origin for these types of helmets. Another example of a contemporary horned helmet comes from Pisaskion (Fig. 3.37; Vermeule and Karageorghis 1982: 140–1 no. XI.80). In this case, the helmet has either two sets of horns (a large pair on its sides and a very small set on its top) or, more likely, a pair of horns and a lunate or hair decoration on top of the helmet, similar to those appearing on the Warrior Vase from Mycenae. From the point of costume alone, it is almost impossible to ascertain the origin of the Sherden warriors.

The most distinctive feature of the Peleset, Denyen, and Tjeker/Sikel is their feathered helmets or hats (Nelson 1930: pl. 44; Figs. 5.67 and 5.69), which have attracted much scholarly attention (e.g., Sandars 1978: 134; Dothan 1982: 274–5; Muhly 1984: 45). The hat consisted of a crown of feathers set in what appears to be a wide, decorated band, and is fastened under the chin by a string.

The most detailed parallels that represent feathered-hatted people are the LCIIIA depictions from Enkomi in Cyprus of bearded men wearing feathered hats (Figs. 5.59 and 5.60). The ax bearer in one hunting scene wears a feathered hat with a wide decorated headband and a distinctive kilt (Fig. 5.59). Although contemporaneous and extremely similar to the Egyptian depictions, the Enkomi depictions give little indication of the origin of these people. No previous parallels were found for them in Cyprus, yet they seem to represent a manner of dress foreign to the island. Feathered helmets, spiky headdress, and "hedgehog" helmets, all possibly relating to a single type of highly popular head attire, become extremely common among warriors during LHIIIC, many of which appear on ships. The clearest examples of feathered helmets come from Seraglio on Kos, on fragments of five different LHIIIC Middle kraters, contemporary with the hunting scene from Enkomi (Vermeule and Karageorghis 1982: 160–1 nos. 29–33; Mountjoy 1999a: 1107, fig. 452: 102–4). One of the depictions is a maritime scene showing a file of rowers (Fig 5.70,

FIGURE 5.68. A ship with Sherden warriors (after Nelson 1930: pl. 39)

FIGURE 5.69. Feathered-hatted warriors from the land battle relief, Medinet Habu

sherd in the center; Vermeule and Karageorghis 1982: 160–1 no. 33), whereas another may show a similar scene (Fig 5.70, sherd on the right; Vermeule and Karageorghis 1982: no. 31), if, in fact, the construction to the right of the person depicted is a mast and part of the rigging. Most of the Kynos representations of figures aboard ships and fishermen, as well as one from Phaistos, are depicted with particularly spiky headdress (Figs. 5.71 and 3.36; Dakoronia and Mpougia 1999: 22; Dakoronia 2006: figs. 1, 4, and 8; Wachsmann 1998: fig. 7.27). Wachsmann (1998: 177) raises the possibility that these crews also belonged to the Sea Peoples and that the headdress is a crude execution of the feathered helmet. Another peculiar headdress worn by LHIIIC mariners is the "hedgehog" helmet seen on the heads of the warriors on a krater from Bademgediği Tepe (Fig. 5.72).[20] Mountjoy (2005a: 425–6) argues that this is the same type of feathered hat worn by the Sea Peoples, composed of a leather cap into which feathers were inserted. A head of a warrior on a larnax from Mycenae provides the missing link between the Sea Peoples' feathered hats and the "hedgehog" helmet, as it shows a band at the base of the helmet, decorated with a chevron pattern, similar to the band at the base of the feathered helmets at Medinet Habu (Fig. 5.73). A closer inspection of the Bademgediği Tepe figures shows that some of them do have a similar band at the base of the helmet, one decorated with a zigzag pattern. A Bichrome krater found in Ashkelon may prove to be the missing link in Philistia between the Aegean representations and the Egyptian ones (Fig. 5.74; Stager 2006). This krater shows figures similar in style to the Kynos figures, apart from their headdress, which is too tall to be a "hedgehog" helmet and more likely to be a feathered hat. One of the figures carries a round shield, similar to that shown in the Medinet Habu reliefs. The krater is of Helladic type, although it is most probably locally made. The location of the find, in Philistia, convinced Stager (1998: 168) to view the depictions as "the first self-portraits of Philistine warriors."

[20] For distinct examples of this type of helmet see Vermeule and Karageorghis 1982: 132 no. XI.42 (the Warrior Vase from Mycenae), 134 no. XI.45 (from Mycenae), 135 no. XI.57 (the Warrior Vase from Iolkos).

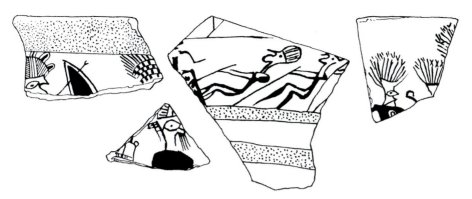

FIGURE 5.70. Warriors and sailors, Seraglio, Kos (after Sandars 1978: 155, fig. 92)

FIGURE 5.71. Naval battle, Kynos (after Dakoronia and Mpougia 1999: 23)

FIGURE 5.72. Warriors on a krater from Bademgediği Tepe (after Mountjoy 2005a: pl. 96)

FIGURE 5.73. Head on a larnax, Mycenae (after Crouwel 1991: fig. 7B)

Finally, an Egyptian-style depiction of a feathered hat found in Philistia, on a scarab seal from Tomb 936 at Tell el-Farʿah (S) Cemetery 900 depicts a person with a feathered hat in front of the Egyptian god Amon (Noort 1994: 140–1, pl. 6.2: 3).

The fact that warriors with feathered hats appear contemporaneously in the early to middle twelfth century BCE in the Aegean, Egypt, Cyprus, and the southern Levant seems to be more than mere coincidence. These represent a common LHIIIC Aegean fashion of headdress, which has a strong connotation to the status of a warrior, either on land or at sea. The distribution range of the headdress types seems to have encompassed the shores of the Aegean Sea, from the Peloponnese to the eastern coast of central Greece, and to the western Anatolian coast and the Dodecanese.

CONCLUSIONS: TWELFTH-CENTURY INTERACTIONS ALONG THE ROUTES

THE TIMING OF THE INTERACTIONS

Chronological data from Tarsus, Ugarit, and sites in Cyprus indicate that the appearance of Aegean material culture traits along the sea and land routes, as well as the destruction of the kingdom of Ugarit, occurred during the first quarter of the twelfth century, contemporary with some of the LHIIIC Early phase.

The date of the destruction of Tarsus Level IIa cannot be determined easily; it is earlier than the introduction of LHIIIC pottery to the site (Warren and Hankey 1989: 158–9), yet probably not before the last quarter of the thirteenth century. The locally made LHIIIC Early pottery from Tarsus IIb (French 1975: 74; Mountjoy 1993: 175) provides a relative date for the beginning of

FIGURE 5.74. Seated figure on a krater from Ashkelon (after Stager 2006)

substantial interactions with the Aegean world at the first quarter of the twelfth century BCE.

The destruction of Ugarit can be given a terminus post quem between 1194 and 1186 BCE, based on the letter of the Egyptian Beya to King Ammurapi, and a terminus ante quem of 1175, Year 8 of Ramses III (Singer 1999: 729). A date of 1190–1185, as suggested by Singer (1999) or 1195–1185, as suggested by Yon (1992: 119–20) is highly likely, as any later date raises more difficulties in accounting for the absence of objects of Tausert and Ramses III,[21] and of any diplomatic correspondence between Egypt and Ugarit in the critical period of the 1180s and 1170s. A higher – though still plausible – date of between 1196 and 1191 BCE is given by Warren and Hankey (1989: 159). Correlation with the Aegean sequence is given by one complete pictorial krater (the Master of the Horses krater) and two fragmentary ones (Courtois 1978: 318, 319, fig. 41: 1, 2; 346–50; Yon 2000: 8), possibly created by the same artist.[22] Warren and Hankey (1989) note the resemblance of the kraters to the LHIIIC Middle Kos/Kalymnos group; nevertheless, they date them to the LHIIIC Early. Mountjoy (2004), however, ascribes them to the transitional LHIIIB–LHIIIC phase.[23] An acute problem with the latter attribution is that

[21] Compare, e.g., the vessel with the name of Ramses III found in Byblos, or the name of Tausert found in Tell Deir Allah.

[22] Initially, the kraters were attributed by Courtois to a homogenous series of transitional Mycenaean IIIB–Mycenaean IIIC vessels from the southeastern Aegean, which includes pictorial vessels from Kos and Miletus. Partially following Courtois, Vermeule, and Karageorghis (1982: 170) attributed the vessels to their "transitional/late" stage and drew a correlation to the Koan as well as other eastern Aegean traditions of LHIIIC.

[23] Mountjoy (1999: 1080, 1126) had first attributed all the pictorial style from the East Aegean koine, which included Kos and Kalymnos, to LHIIIC Middle (see also Mountjoy 1998: 54). She argues (1998: 1180 no. 733) that the more complete amphoroid krater from Ugarit "may

the context of the vessels in Ugarit can provide only an absolute chronology, not a relative Aegean dating deriving from the stylistic analysis of the kraters and based on sequences of well-stratified pictorial pottery from the Aegean (Yasur-Landau 2003a). Mountjoy's attribution of a relative date for the vase is based on the correlation between the absolute date she ascribes to the beginning of LHIIIC (1185–1180)[24] and the date of ca. 1185 for the destruction of Ugarit.[25] There is possibly further presence of LHIIIC Early pottery in the destruction deposits of Ugarit (Monchambert 1996), although the stratigraphical connection of these few (perhaps locally made) sherds is far from clear, and they may postdate the destruction (Karageorghis 2000b: 64–5; Yon 2000: 15). Whether LHIIIC Early or transitional LHIIIB–LHIIIC, the imports found at Ugarit date to the twelfth century and provide a solid anchor for further studies of LHIIIC chronology.

At Cyprus, ^{14}C data has been used to establish the date for the end of LCIIC in 1200 BCE by +20/–10 (Manning et al. 2001: 339; Manning 2006–7). Imported LCIIIA Aegean-style pottery, mainly small stirrup jars, has been found in Strata S4 and S3 in the Egyptian garrison at Beth Shean (Yasur-Landau 2003a; D'Agata et al. 2005). The earlier stratum is dated to the days of Ramses III and the later to Ramses III and VI. Both should therefore be placed mostly within the first half of the twelfth century BCE – the earlier phase within the first third of the century, indicating that Aegean-style LCIIIA pottery was in circulation before the end of Ramses III's reign.[26] As for the correlation with the Aegean, there is a vigorous debate concerning the exact date of the beginning of LCIIIA, yet the widely used correlation between LHIIIB and LCIIC; LHIIIC Early and latest LCIIC; and the last part of LHIIIC Early as well as most of LHIIIC Middle correlated with LCIIIA seems plausible (Warren and Hankey 1989: 118; Deger-Jalkotzy 1994: 17; 1998a: 117; 1998b: 113). Even if we avoid establishing a precise date for the beginning of the Aegean settlement in Cyprus at this point (i.e., a decision between the end of LCIIC and the beginning of LCIIIA), one can conclude that the interaction most probably took place before the beginning of LHIIIC Middle. Deger-Jalkotzy's (1998b: 113) argument for a late date in LHIIIC Early for the beginning of the Aegean settlement in Cyprus, contemporaneous with the last tablets from Ugarit,

---

well be an export from Kos, Astypalaia, or Miletus." For the date of this krater, she suggests that it "seems to be in LHIIIC Early context."

[24] Based on unpublished material from Mycenae (Mountjoy 2004: 190 no. 14; Mountjoy 2005b).

[25] The same type of argument is used to ascribe the latest pictorial pottery from Miletus to transitional LHIIIB–LHIIIC rather than to LHIIIC Middle, as the previously mentioned pictorial pottery found in Ugarit resembles pottery from Miletus. Because Ugarit was destroyed circa 1185, the Milesian pottery must be attributed according to the date given to transitional LHIIIB–LHIIIC (Mountjoy 2004: 190).

[26] Mountjoy (2005b: 165) suggested a somewhat lower date, based on her renewed chronology of Mycenae, which does not include the direct correlation with the Beth Shean material.

seems convincing but awaits confirmation from more sites, such as Kition and the earliest LCIIIA phases at Enkomi.

The Cilician, Ugaritic, and Cypriot data show that in a relatively short time, within the first quarter of the twelfth century BCE, evidence for Aegean behavioral patterns appeared in vast areas of the eastern Mediterranean, sometimes but not in all cases following violent destructions. The contemporaneous clashes between the Egyptians on the one side and raiders and migrants wearing Aegean head attire and riding Anatolian-style ox carts on the other side, in Years 5 and 8 of Ramses III (ca. 1175 BC), are hardly coincidental.

RANGES OF MIGRATION ALONG THE ROUTES

In contrast to the sometimes prevalent picture of hordes of Sea Peoples storming the eastern coast of the Mediterranean, burning the cities of the local population, and settling on the still-warm ashes, the ranges of interaction seen along the land and sea routes from the Aegean to the Levant are extremely varied and complex. Migration in the twelfth century BCE was only one range of an array of intertwined interactions, each affecting the other.

Besides the many forms of migration, other interactions included raids, small-scale trade, and the presence of mercenaries in foreign armies. All of these were crucial for supplying reliable, up-to-date, firsthand information on destinations for migrations and raids, on routes, and on possible obstacles en route, thus resulting in more reliable cost-value estimates and in an increased push-pull factor toward migration, based on the available information. It has been argued that, though maritime raids were dangerous, their short-term risk and potential high yield were preferred to the long-term risk and low yield of a migration venture. The weakness displayed by Hatti and Egypt during the opening years of the twelfth century may have even decreased the perceived risks of raiding, encouraging larger-scale, coordinated activities, as the seven-ship raid on Ugarit, the twenty-ship fleet seen at Cyprus by the Alashiyans, and the possibly larger raid in Year 8 of Ramses III.

Small-scale trade in Aegean-style pottery, mostly made not in the Aegean but on Cyprus and possibly in Anatolia, is apparent from the sporadic finds of LHIIIC-style fineware pottery in communities in Phoenicia and possibly in Syria, which exhibit no sign of destruction; it is evident also from the appearance of Aegean behavioral patterns connected with food preparation and textile production.

The appearance of feathered-hatted mercenaries in the Egyptian army in the thirteenth and twelfth centuries, some before the events of Year 8 of Ramses III, sheds light on the possibility that mercenaries were informants of possible destinations for migration. It is hardly surprising that the same type of people shown as mercenaries in the Libyan service in the days of Merneptah returned to harass Egypt as invaders and colonizers in the days of Ramses III. It is extremely likely that such processes occurred either before or during the twelfth century, in locations such as Cyprus and Cilicia.

As for migration, in the case of maritime migration to Cyprus, when the number of migrants and their strength were limited by the logistics of maritime travel, a plethora of opportunistic strategies were used to avoid conflict with the local population. Individuals, as in Enkomi, or families, as in Kition, of Aegean culture joined the existing, well-established Cypriot communities, some as dependents working in the service of Cypriot aristocrats or for the temple economy. Their absorption in the Eteocypriot society while retaining their own cultural heritage reflects an acculturation strategy of integration (Chapter 1). The existence of such a strategy can indicate a considerable measure of pluralism and openness of the Cypriot society of that time. The foundation of Maa-Palaeokastro, if indeed an Aegean one, reflects structures within the migrant society larger than family units, perhaps of several households, composed of Aegean and Cypriot members, as well as the organizers of the venture – leaders of possibly Aegean origin. However, this foundation was made in a secluded place, far from Cypriot sites, and thus reflects an acculturation strategy of separation, in which a migrant population retains its identity by maintaining some form of separation from the cultural milieu of the target country (Chapter 1; Yasur-Landau 2003b). Maa-Palaeokastro's location on an easily defendable promontory reflects LHIIIC Aegean notions of founding defensible sites; these are demonstrated clearly also in Koukounaries (Chapter 3) and Emporio, where defensibility, on the one hand, and accessibility to a protected bay, on the other hand, were the most important criteria for site selection.

The material evidence for Aegean behavioral patterns indicative of a deep change in sites along the land route and relatively far from the sea, such as Cilicia and the Amuq, as well as the documentation of the land-borne migration in Medinet Habu, suggests that migrants of Aegean culture used the routes from western Anatolia to the Levant that had opened with the collapse of all Anatolian and Syrian powers. The preferred routes went through the Cilician Gates and into Cilicia, then south through the Amanian Gates to the Amuq, continuing southward along the coast up to Tell Kazel and bypassing the cities of the Phoenician coast without harming them. Those who came by land formed a migration stream (Anthony 1990: 903; Chapter 1), following routes known to them through the activities of scouts, merchants, and the presence of formerly settled kin. Many had settled in sites along the routes; others continued leapfrogging from site to site, leaving behind them a trail of sites from western Anatolia to Syria, which were filled by newcomers. In the Amuq and in Cilicia, the impact of the migrants resulted in the creation of polities with Aegean-derived names, Hiyawa and possibly Palastin, which continued into the Iron Age. One can imagine a picture of many small ox-cart caravans of whole families with all their belongings, trailing along the routes in search of a new home, either stopping when they come across communities that already contain migrants of the same area or continuing further south in search of better opportunities. The presence of a chariot force in the Medinet Habu land battle relief indicates considerable organizational abilities and the presence of elite among some of the migrants. The high value of chariots and horses and the huge investment needed for their maintenance and practice indicate a high level of social complexity and hierarchy, as well as impressive organizational abilities.[27] The large numbers of migrants along the land routes, in comparison to the limitation imposed by maritime travel, and the migrants' military power – if the Medinet Habu evidence is accepted – could have been sufficient to conquer violently some local sites. Indeed, the occupation atop the burned remains of the Late Bronze Age cities of Tarsus and Ras Ibn Hani does not hint at favorable conditions for the creation of positive relations with the local population. However, the large amounts of local pottery found in all the assemblages containing Aegean material culture remains suggest some form of coexistence. Furthermore, the choice of the easily defendable promontory of Ras Ibn Hani, rather than the large tell of Ugarit, may suggest that the migrants themselves were concerned with their safety. The power relations between them and local populations, unclear at the first stage of settlement, reflect an acculturation strategy of separation (Yasur-Landau 2003b; Chapter 1). The choice of the site may be compared to Aegean defensible settlements of that time, such as Maa-Palaeokastro.

It is noteworthy that the change in interaction patterns in the twelfth century BCE is contemporaneous with the rise of social complexity in some areas discussed in Chapter 3. This coincidence may indicate that the two processes are interrelated and that the reformation of more complex social structures in the Aegean after the collapse of the palaces enabled the practice of ranges of interaction that required a high level of organization, such as maritime migration, maritime raids, and large-scale land migration. The surveys of sites also confirm the methodology used for predicting interactions with the Aegean world posed in Chapter 4. First, in accordance with the prediction in Chapter 4, is the use of the suggested land and sea routes. Furthermore, there is a match between the interactions actually conducted in the twelfth century, as seen in the material culture evidence along the routes, and those that were predicted to be possible in the twelfth century, according to the analysis of the political and social structures, and of the logistic abilities in the Aegean. Accordingly, we have found no evidence for massive

---

[27] See Chapter 3 for chariots as status symbols in LHIIIC iconography.

long-distance trade in raw material, for state-orchestrated colonization, or for maritime mass evacuation.

ORIGINS

A combination of iconographic evidence, analysis of material culture traits, assessment of organizational abilities, and some etymological evidence points to the Aegean origin of a considerable part of the people involved in migration and in other interactions along the routes. The evidence of Aegean-style material culture along the routes definitely reflects Aegean behavioral patterns of preparation and consumption of food and textile production, as well as house architecture (mainly in Cyprus). Much additional work on regional styles in all aspects of material culture is needed to evaluate the sources of inspiration, although it is likely that more than one region of the Aegean was involved in the interactions. The great similarity between Aegean wares in Cilicia and Cyprus observed by Killebrew (1998a: 401–2; Chapter 8) probably indicates that both areas were reached by Aegean migrants of a similar origin. The migration and other interactions along the routes were certainly not a "pure Mycenaean" affair. The migrants may have come from different locations along the coast of the Aegean Sea, and people of various non-Aegean origins had joined the different ventures, as minorities, as is seen in the depiction of Syro-Canaanites and possibly Hittites in the Medinet Habu reliefs. The presence of HBW as a minor find group among Cypriot finds and the fact that it composes a good part of the assemblage in Tell Kazel show that groups comprising various numbers of people of a non-Aegean culture were involved in the interactions.

Risking some measure of speculation, one can suggest that some of the raiders (and indeed some of the colonizers) came from the area of the East Aegean koine (Mountjoy 1998) – the Dodecanese or the nearby Anatolian coast (i.e., Miletus) – an area characterized by islands, promontories, and bays, which fit well the Egyptian description of "isles in the midst of the sea." As seen in Chapter 3, this area was not affected by the collapse of either the Mycenaean palatial civilization or the Hittite Empire. Polities in this area, including the well-fortified Miletus, were powerful enough to coordinate and initiate maritime raids and to be gathering places for maritime colonization in the nearby islands and possibly in Cyprus. Nearby new foundations in Emporio and possibly in Bademgediği Tepe suggest the involvement of people from these areas in migration and trade. Raiders, settlers, and mercenaries wearing feathered hats could have come from anywhere along the coast of the Aegean, where this head attire was sported by the warrior of LHIIIC. However, the appearance of the feathered hats in the pictorial pottery of the East Aegean koine in LHIIIC (Mountjoy 1999a: 48), with examples in Seraglio and Bademgediği, further connect the area of the eastern Aegean–western Anatolian interface to maritime raiders and settlers.

There is, however, no reason to exclude the participation in the raids and maritime colonization of any maritime power surviving in the Aegean in the twelfth century, or of any coastal settlement with an Aegean cultural background. Furthermore, any group of people from virtually any community in mainland Greece or western Anatolia could have used the newly opened land routes to the Levant.

6

STRICTLY BUSINESS? THE SOUTHERN LEVANT AND THE AEGEAN IN THE THIRTEENTH TO THE EARLY TWELFTH CENTURY BCE

The situation along the land and sea routes to the southern Levant in the transition between the thirteenth and twelfth centuries showed a clear shift in the interaction patterns with the Aegean world. This chapter, by analyzing the interaction with the Aegean in this time, sets the background for the study of interactions in the southern Levant during a period of transition. First, as it was argued by Sherratt (1998) and Bauer (1998) that commercial contact in the thirteenth and twelfth centuries had inaugurated processes of elite emulation and adoption of Aegean-style wine drinking customs in the twelfth century, it will be examined whether trade interactions with the Aegean in the thirteenth century, mainly the consumption of imported Mycenaean pottery, caused a lasting change in local behavioral patterns that manifested in the twelfth century. Second, the presence of mercenaries and merchants – if that can be archaeologically established – may indicate a channel through which information about the Levant as a possible migration destination trickled into the Aegean. If such presence persisted into the twelfth century, it could have assisted potential migrants during the time of settlement.

MYCENAEAN IMPORTS TO THE SOUTHERN LEVANT

TRADE AND CONSUMPTION OF MYCENAEAN IMPORTED POTTERY

Imported Mycenaean pottery appears in the vast majority of the Late Bronze Age sites of Canaan, mainly those in the coastal plain and in the valleys (Killebrew 1998b: 160). Mycenaean pottery appears both in settlement levels and as offerings in tombs. Quantification of the spatial distribution of Mycenaean pottery in Canaan awaits future research, yet the majority of the LHIIIB imports were fineware pottery vessels, with a much smaller number of animal and human figurines, as well as other rare forms.[1] The identity of the traders who brought these vessels is important: if they were Aegeans, then they could have played an important role in the processes of cultural transmission, not only selling Aegean pottery but also disseminating the Aegean way of using it – demonstrating Aegean behavioral patterns connected with the consumption of food and drink. However, as demonstrated in Chapter 2, the southern Levant was not mentioned in the toponyms appearing in the Linear B archives; this weakens theories of direct contact. In contrast, Syro-Phoenician toponyms appear, indicating that the northern Levantine coast was within the sphere of interaction of Aegean polities. There are, however, strong indications for the important role of Cypriot, rather than Mycenaean, merchants in the import of Mycenaean pottery to the southern Levant. The volume of trade in Mycenaean pottery to Canaan was second only to the huge volume of pottery imports from Cyprus. Hankey's (1967: 146) views on the important place of Cypriots in the Mycenaean pottery trade may be strengthened by Cypro-Minoan signs that were incised after firing or painted on Mycenaean and other pottery found in the Levant. A similar phenomenon has been observed in the Aegean, where Mycenaean vessels were similarly incised with Cypro-Minoan signs. Hirschfeld (1992; 1993; 2004) considers this a clear indication that the vessel traveled through Cyprus or was handled by someone accustomed to Cypriot ways. Fifteen Mycenaean vessels incised or painted with Cypro-Minoan signs found at Tell Abu Hawam (Hirschfeld 2004), an important *emporion* to be discussed herein, point to the deep involvement of Cypriots in the trade of Mycenaean pottery. However, Cypriot signs appear also on Canaanite amphorae and other vessels from the fifteenth to thirteenth centuries, such as Ashkelon (Cross and Stager 2006: nos. 2, 4, 7, 8, 12, 18) and Aphek (Yasur-Landau and Goren 2004). As the Aphek amphora was made in the Acco Plain, it has been suggested that the vessel first traveled to Cyprus where it was incised, repurposed, and refilled, to be shipped to Aphek (Yasur-Landau and Goren 2004).

Most of the imported Mycenaean vessels were small containers, probably used for perfumed oils.[2] Luxurious dinnerware was a relatively less frequent import (Fig. 6.1). There was no import of cookware and no coarseware, which may indicate that Canaanites had no interest in Mycenaean cuisine or foodways.

---

[1] A key source for the study of Mycenaean pottery from the Levant is Leonard's (1994) *Index to the Late Bronze Age Aegean Pottery from Syria-Palestine.*

[2] Small and medium-sized closed forms, composing the majority of imports to the Levant, were, according to Leonard (1981: 91–100), containers for oils and unguents. However, work in the Aegean region on residue analysis (Tzedakis and Martlew 1999: 152, 173, 196) has demonstrated that wine was also stored in large and medium-sized stirrup jars, and was therefore a commodity potentially shipped to the Levant.

In terms of the ratio of containers[3] to open shapes,[4] the former dominate, and the small stirrup jar was the most frequent import to Canaan in LHIIIB (see further detailed discussion and statistics in Chapter 7). At Beth Shean, an Egyptian stronghold during the Late Bronze Age (Hankey 1993: 103), only 15 percent of imported Mycenaean vessels (from Strata VIII and VII) were open shapes. At Tell el-ʿAjjul (Steel 2002: 33, fig. 3), fewer than 10 percent of the imported Mycenaean pottery vessels were open forms. The Mycenaean pottery assemblage from the Aphek settlement strata represents a ratio of about 80 percent closed vessels (i.e., containers) to about 20 percent open types, including kraters and small drinking vessels (Guzowska and Yasur-Landau 2007b). A similar ratio of open to closed types is 18 percent to 82 percent of the ceramic assemblage from the Mycenaean tomb at Tel Dan (Ben-Dov 2002: 98–118), associated with an elite population of the fourteenth and thirteenth centuries BCE.

Kraters may indicate use of the imported Mycenaean drinking ware by the Canaanites; however, these vessels were not used in the Aegean way, as a complete Mycenaean drinking kit is absent. Deep bowls are almost absent, as are closed forms for decanting (e.g., jugs; Ben-Dov 2002: 39–43) or ladles and water containers for the mixing of wine in kraters. Furthermore, it seems that the Canaanites refrained from importing Mycenaean drinking ware that did not accord with their cultural preferences. Such is the case for the rare appearance of kylikes, the most common Mycenaean drinking ware, in Canaanite assemblages (Yasur-Landau 2005b). Their infrequent appearance may be explained by the profound difference between Canaanite and Aegean drinking practices that is seen in toasting customs and the way the vessels are held. Aegean toasting is characterized by the use of stemmed drinking vessels, always firmly held by their stems using the entire fist (Fig. 6.2, parts 4, 5, 6). In contrast, Canaanite depictions on the Megiddo and Tell el-Farʿah (S) ivories (Fig. 6.2, parts 1, 2, 3), show that rulers and nobles drank while nestling the round-based drinking bowl in the open palm of the hand. This was a Syrian tradition that began early in the second millennium BCE (Beck 1989: 338–40; Ziffer 1999: 195–6). The amphoroid krater, a favorite import during the fourteenth century, reflects a different phenomenon – its shape resembles the common Canaanite krater, and it could therefore have been easily used during Canaanite feasts (Fig. 6.3, parts 2, 3), as is seen in the co-occurrence of Canaanite kraters and a Mycenaean chariot krater in the elite Tomb 387 at Dan (Fig. 6.3, parts 1, 4, 5).

---

[3] Examples of some of the most common shapes are stirrup jars (Leonard 1994: 50–78), mainly small and globular-shaped pithoid and/or piriform jars (13–22), pyxides (35–9), and lentoid flasks (79–83).

[4] Open shapes were used as luxury serving vessels. Some of the most common forms are amphoroid kraters, most decorated with chariot scenes (Leonard 1994: 22–33), semiglobular cups (96–102), and shallow angular bowls (123–6).

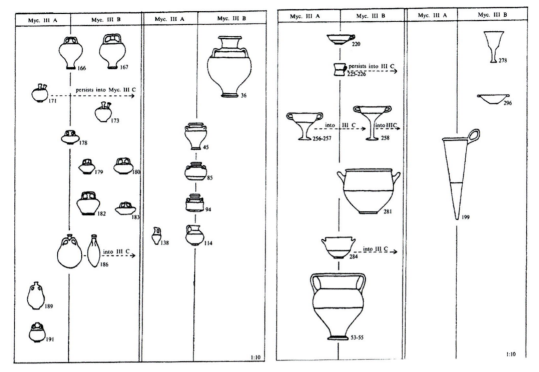

FIGURE 6.1. Common imported Mycenaean forms (after Leonard 1981: fig. 1)

At any rate, the small numbers of imported tableware may indicate that they were available only to members of the elite; thus, they could not bring about a large-scale change in behavioral patterns. They may also reflect a phenomenon similar to that in LCIIC Kalavassos-Ayios Dhimitrios on Cyprus (South and Russel 1993: 306–8), where imports of Aegean fine tableware pottery were related to high-status dwellings, while the more numerous, closed vessels were found in more varied contexts. These ratios indicate a more restricted access to high-status imported tableware than to closed forms. Steel (1998: 296) makes a similar generalization for the patterns of use of Mycenaean pottery in Cyprus:

> On the one hand, the dinner services and pictorial style were appropriated by the elite as status symbols to define their own exclusivity. On the other hand, the small, more widely available unguent containers were adopted by those members of Cypriot society who chose to emulate the elite but did not have access to the more highly valued Red Lustrous perfume bottles.

The situation in the southern Levant appears to have been very much the same. Steel (2002: 36), analyzing the distribution of imported Mycenaean pottery in Tell el-ʿAjjul, argues that, given the low number of Mycenaean pottery imports found in habitation contexts, "Mycenaean imports represent an exotic rarity

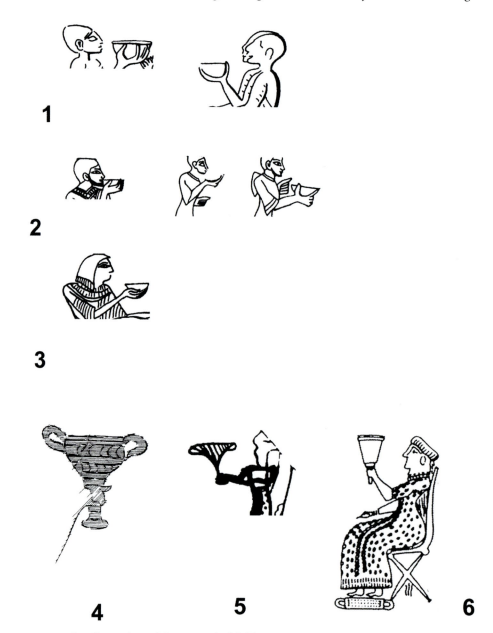

FIGURE 6.2. Canaanite and Aegean-style drinking postures
1. Detail of Megiddo Ivory no. 160 (redrawn after Loud 1939)
2. Detail of Megiddo Ivory no. 2 (redrawn after Loud 1939)
3. Detail of ivory from Tell el-Farʿah (S) (redrawn after Petrie 1930: pl. 55)
4. Detail of Campstool Fresco from Knossos (redrawn after Evans 1964: fig. 324)
5. Detail of LHIIIC krater from Tiryns (redrawn after Kilian 1980: 23, fig. 2)
6. Detail of LHII gold signet ring from Tiryns (redrawn after Sakellariou 1964: 202–3 no. 179)

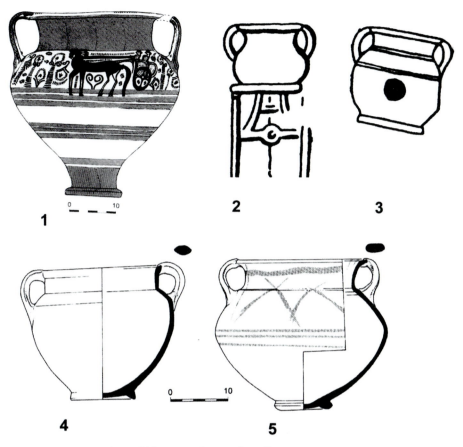

FIGURE 6.3. Canaanite and Mycenaean kraters from Dan
  1. Mycenaean krater from Tomb 387 at Dan (after Ben-Dov 2002: fig. 86)
  2. Krater used in Canaanite feast; detail of Megiddo Ivory no. 2 (redrawn after Loud 1939)
  3. Krater used in Canaanite feast; detail of Megiddo Ivory no. 160 (redrawn after Loud 1939)
  4. Local krater from Tomb 387 at Dan (after Ben-Dov 2002: fig. 2.54: 14)
  5. Local krater from Tomb 387 at Dan (after Ben-Dov 2002: fig. 2.54: 16)

that had a limited appeal or use wherein the Late Bronze Age occupation of the site."

DERIVATIVE FORMS AND CHANGE IN LOCAL CONSUMPTION PATTERNS

Further evidence that passion for Aegean tableware and drinking customs was not shared by many people in the Late Bronze Age southern Levant comes from so-called derivative forms. These were intended to answer the market demand of people with an acquired taste for Aegean pottery or for commodities shipped inside such pottery. Derivative forms are the wide range of Mycenaean-type pottery produced outside the core of the Aegean cultural sphere. Such vessels were found in Late Bronze Age Canaan (sometimes referred to as "imitations of Mycenaean pottery" or "local"; Amiran 1970: 186; Fig. 6.4) and are mostly thought to be locally made (though provenance studies have not incorporated these vessels; cf. Killebrew 1998b: 161). Examples of the most frequent local or derivative types are stirrup jars (Leonard 1994: 78–9 nos. 1171, 1177, 1178, 1192–8; Amiran 1970: pl. 57: 11), pithoid or piriform jars (Leonard 1994: 22 nos. 157–61; Amiran 1970: pl. 57: 9), and straight-sided alabastra (or pyxis; Leonard 1994: 39 nos. 474–6; Amiran 1970: pl. 57: 2–7). Derivative open shapes belonging to the LHIIIB style seem to be rarer, most likely reflecting the ratio between the closed to open shapes in the imported wares. Some examples are a stemmed cup from Hazor (Leonard 1994: 109 no. 1642) and a carinated bowl (Leonard 1994: 126 no. 1898), as well as a mug (Amiran 1970: 186 photo 204) and two kraters from Megiddo (Amiran 1970: pl. 57: 12, 13).

The fact that most imports and imitations are containers and not tableware indicates that the changes in behavioral patterns caused by Aegean imports leaned toward the consumption of exotic commodities transported in exotic containers. Exotic tableware was in less demand and less frequently imitated, indicating little, if any, change in food preparation and food consumption.

AEGEAN-STYLE CERAMIC IMPORTS IN THE TWELFTH CENTURY BCE

The nature of trade with the Levant did not remain static between the fourteenth and twelfth centuries. The quantities of LHIIIB2 imports are considerably smaller than those of the LHIIIA2 and LHIIIB1. Later, during the early to middle twelfth century, imports of Mycenaean pottery essentially stopped, as did the imports of Cypriot base-ring and white-slip wares. However, another type of import appeared, albeit in very small quantities and in a limited geographic zone: Aegean-type pottery, which, according to neutron activation analysis (NAA) analysis (D'Agata et al. 2005), was produced mostly in Cyprus. This pottery appears only in sites north of the Carmel Ridge: Tel Keisan, Acco, Beth Shean, and perhaps Dan (D'Agata et al. 2005; Figs. 6.5 and 6.6). The largest assemblage of more than twenty sherds and vessels was found at Beth Shean, in Stratum VI Lower of the University Museum excavations, Strata S4 and S3 of the Hebrew University excavations, and assigned to the early Twentieth Dynasty (Yasur-Landau 2003a) and to the reigns of Ramses III and IV.[5] At all sites, the most common type imported was the small stirrup

---

[5] Aegean stirrup jars are depicted in the tomb of Ramses III (Wachsmann 1987: pl. 59: A; Vandenabeele 1988; Hankey 1995: 123). The jars indicate that some form of trade with the Aegean world (or with Aegeanized Cyprus) still existed during the LHIIIC period, perhaps before and most probably after the troublesome events of Year 8. It is intriguing that there are no published examples of LHIIIC pottery from Egypt itself (Hankey 1993: 112). The Beth Shean evidence supports the hypothesis that while the stirrup jars were available to the Egyptian elite during the time of the Twentieth Dynasty, their rarity had rendered them fit to be portrayed in the royal tomb.

FIGURE 6.4. Derivative Mycenaean forms (after Amiran 1970: pl. 57)

 1. Pyxis from Lachish, T. 508
 2. Pyxis from Lachish, T. 4011
 3. Stirrup jar from Tell el-ʿAjjul, the governor's tomb
 4. Pyxis from Beth Shemesh, Eastern Grotto
 5. Pyxis from Megiddo, T. 989 C
 6. Piriform jar from Lachish. T. 1006
 7. Krater from Megiddo, T. 912 D

jar, similar to the pattern of LHIIIB imports. The ratios between closed and open shapes in the imported LHIIIC-style vessels (more than 70 percent are closed, and less than 30 percent are open) closely resemble the dominance of closed vessels (mainly stirrup jars) typical of the trade in Mycenaean pottery in Canaan in the fourteenth and thirteenth centuries BCE.

The small percentage of drinking wares indicates that the Canaanite population and the Egyptian officials and soldiers of twelfth-century northern sites

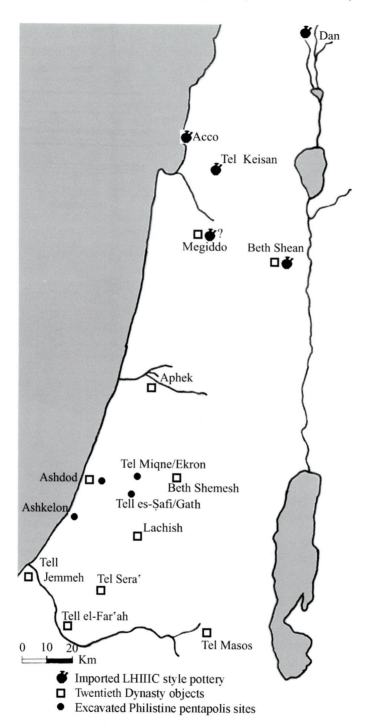

FIGURE 6.5. Distribution map of LHIIIC pottery in Canaan (drawn by A. Yasur-Landau)

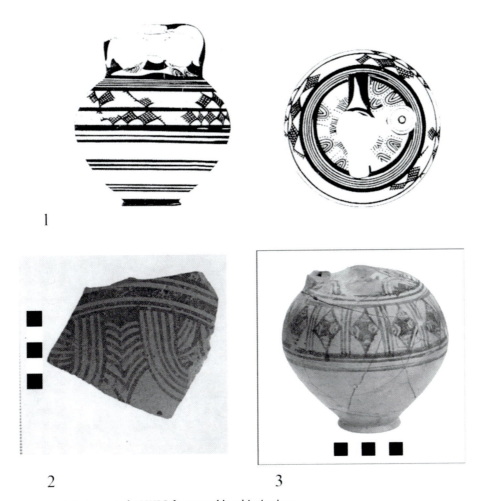

FIGURE 6.6. Imported LHIIIC forms and local imitations

   1. Cypriot-made LHIIIC-style stirrup jar from Beth Shean Stratum VI (after Warren and Hankey 1989: 165, fig. 12)

   2. Local imitation of Cypriot-made LHIIIC-style stirrup jar from Tel Keisan, surface find (photo by Pavel Shrago; cf. Yasur-Landau 2006)

   3. Local imitation of Cypriot-made LHIIIC-style stirrup jar from Megiddo (after Yasur-Landau 2006: fig. 14.1)

did not change their interest in luxurious commodities, namely those stored in small Aegean-style stirrup jars, and had not become more interested in acquiring Aegean drinking ware and drinking customs than they were in the thirteenth century.

The Cypriot origin of the vessels from Tel Keisan, Beth Shean, and Acco suggests that Cypriot products from diverse pottery workshops – from the areas of both Palaeopaphos in the west and Enkomi in the east (D'Agata et al. 2005) – replaced the Argolid-made Aegean wares after those became unavailable. It may even be hypothesized that the supposed involvement of Cypriots as intermediaries in the previously mentioned trade in LHIIIB pottery made Cypriot producers aware of the exact nature of demand for pottery in Canaan.

The distribution pattern of the imported LHIIIC pottery is intriguing; none was found south of the Carmel Ridge, and most important, none was found in Philistia. The small number of vessels found in the northern valleys of Israel came through the harbor sites in the Acco Plain, such as Acco, and possibly through anchorages connected with Tel Keisan. They were then traded to the east but not to the south. Their absence from Philistia is proof that imports of LHIIIC pottery to the north of Canaan could not have served as prototypes for the contemporary production of locally made LHIIIC-style pottery (Monochrome; Mycenaean IIIC; see Chapter 7) in Ashdod, Ashkelon, and Tel Miqne/Ekron.[6] The vessels were imitated locally, as seen in two examples of LHIIIC-style stirrup jars from Megiddo and Tel Keisan produced in the vicinity of Acco, which clearly imitate Cypriot Mycenaean IIIC prototypes (Fig. 6.6, parts 2, 3; Yasur-Landau 2006). Mazar (2002: 270) argues that "limited distribution [of LHIIIC imported pottery] to certain sites, and the fact that it does not appear at all at other sites, should not be taken decisively as a chronological factor." This argument is supported by the fact that imported LHIIIC pottery is absent from central and southern sites that were active during the Twentieth Dynasty (Fig. 6.5). Most notable is Lachish, where, similarly to Beth Shean, an Egyptian garrison existed until the days of Ramses IV (Yasur-Landau 2003a; 2005a). It seems that, for some reason, in the twelfth century BCE, Cypriot imported pottery could not pass through the ports south of the Carmel Ridge. D'Agata and colleagues (2005) have suggested that the Philistines, who settled in the southern coastal plain, may have been involved in blocking Cypriot-traded items, perhaps to prevent competition with products of the local potteries.

MERCHANTS AND MERCENARIES: FOREIGNERS IN LATE BRONZE AGE CANAAN

TELL ABU HAWAM: A GATEWAY COMMUNITY WITH FOREIGN RESIDENTS?

Cypriot, western Anatolian, and other foreigners mentioned in the Linear B archives were a possible source for information on the Orient during the late thirteenth century in the Aegean (Chapter 2). This information was most likely supplemented by the activities of Aegean and Cypriot informants, merchants, and mercenaries active in Canaan. Present in small numbers in the dominant Egyptian or Canaanite culture, and transient rather than permanent

---

[6] Contra (Sherratt 1998: 306 no. 30).

inhabitants, they carried out interactions of lesser intensity than those typical of large-scale migration and thus with less impact on the material culture of the target country. However, faint traces of changes in the domestic sphere, as well as in iconographic manifestations of group identity, enable differentiation of the archaeological record those foreigners left in trade interactions.

Tell Abu Hawam, a harbor site in the Acco Plain, was probably the most important *emporion* in northern Canaan during the fourteenth and thirteenth centuries BCE. It yielded thousands of Cypriot imports and hundreds of Mycenaean imports – far more imported Mycenaean types than in any other site in Canaan (Leonard 1994: 201–2) both in the number of vessels and in the number of forms represented (Balensi 1985: 66). The richness of imports to this site is rivaled only by that of the much larger site of Ras-Shamra/Ugarit in Syria (Leonard 1994: 208–9). Anatolian grayware and tanware (Artzy 2006: 55) complete the picture of the unique place of Tell Abu Hawam in international trade. It may thus be viewed as a gateway community: a center that controlled and channeled long-distance connections between cultural zones, and received imported goods as a first phase in a redistribution system (Branigan 1991: 103). Cline (1994: 87) has used this model to explain the concentration of LHIIIA–LHIIIB imported Orientalia at sites such as Tiryns, Kommos, Knossos, and Mycenae. If the model is appropriate for Tell Abu Hawam, it raises the question of the identity of the traders who brought the goods into the harbor.

Balensi (1985: 67) makes a compelling argument for possible Aegean presence at the site, supported by the atypical find of more than a hundred shallow cups that would have answered nonlocal needs of drinking ware. Evidence to confirm this suggestion can be found in the proportions of closed and open imported Mycenaean shapes. In contrast to the situation at most other sites in Canaan, where most of the shapes found have been closed vessels, the Tell Abu Hawam assemblage of imported wares contains closed and open shapes in similar proportions (Balensi 1985; Bell 2006: 46). Moreover, stirrup jars, otherwise the most common imported vessels, are not as common in Tell Abu Hawam as are drinking vessels. Alternatively, Balensi suggests (in Åström 1993: 312) that there was a Cypriot *emporion* at Tell Abu Hawam, which included perhaps some Aegean merchants. This is supported by the presence of Cypriot cooking vessels. Cypriot cooking bowls and a closed Cypriot cooking cauldron,[7] were found in Room 58, Stratum V (Hamilton

---

[7] Cypriot cooking bowls: Hamilton 1935: 39 no. 238; Balensi, Herrera, and Bunimovitz 1985: 106, fig. 12. Balensi (1980: 53–4 no. 238) states a Cypriot origin for this vessel (cf. examples from Enkomi: see Dikaios 1969: pl. 121 nos. 7 [2753/1], 13 [3679/5], 26 [4051/1]); additional flat baking trays and/or pans (Balensi 2004: fig. 4: 16–17) were interpreted to be of Aegean origin, yet they may also belong to a Cypriot type; and a closed cooking pot (Hamilton 1935: 39 no. 239). Balensi (1980: 55–6 no. 239) first reconstructed this vessel as a tripod cooking

1935: 37–9) together with a Canaanite cooking pot. These were certainly in use inside the site, reflecting Cypriot behavioral patterns perhaps of mariners or traders staying at Tell Abu Hawam for an unknown period. Another aspect of Cypriot influence was the local production of Cypriot-style coarseware in Tell Abu Hawam, mainly kraters and basinets, imitating in shape and technology the plain white, wheel-made pottery of Cyprus. This important discovery (Artzy 2006), which awaits final publication, indicates the rapid permeation by Cypriot-style tastes of the arena of food preparation and consumption at the site. Other cooking pots, of a Canaanite and northern Syrian variety, were found at the outskirts of the site – possibly discarded by mariners camping by the seaside (Artzy 2006: 55) – and bronze tools and figurines in Egyptian or Canaanite style were found at the site, indicating the complex ethnic mosaic of traders and mariners frequenting the site and residing there.[8]

A NOTE ON LARNAX BURIALS IN CANAAN

Larnax burials, thought to represent Aegean burial practices, are rare in Late Bronze Age Canaan (Gonen 1992: 142; Gilmour 1995: 166), with only two known examples: from Tomb I.10A in Gezer (dated to 1450–1380 BCE; Seger 1988: pl. 17: 15) and from Tomb C2 in the Persian Garden, north of Acco (dated to the fourteenth century; Ben-Arieh and Edelstein 1977: 9, pl. 15: 10). The Gezer larnax (Seger 1988: 114–15) is a rectangular clay box with a lid and multiple handles on two sides and on the lid. It was locally made and thought by the excavator to be an indicator of a Cretan colony of refugees in Gezer (Seger 1988: 52; Gonen 1992: 28). However, the lack of Minoan objects in the tomb and in settlement strata in Gezer, the absence of other larnakes at the site, and the seeming lack of close Minoan parallels to the larnax (Gilmour 1995: 166–7) leaves open the question of the nature of the interaction.

The Acco larnax is bathtub shaped, handmade, and described by Gilmour (1995: 166) as "of a type prevalent in Crete during LMII and III." Another, perhaps more plausible, option is that the larnax is a Cypriot or coastal Levantine bathtub in secondary use (Karageorghis 1983: 438). Parallels in shape, decoration, and number and position of handles can be found at Enkomi, Kalavassos-Ayios Dhimitrios, and Tell Abu Hawam (Karageorghis 1983), as well as at later, twelfth-century Maa-Palaeokastro (Karageorghis

pot and later corrected her reconstruction (Balensi 2004: fig. 6: 36). Canaanite cooking pot (Hamilton 1935: 39 no. 237). I am grateful to J. Balensi for discussing with me the material culture manifestations of the international interactions of Tell Abu Hawam (e-mail from November 3, 1999).

[8] Palmer 1979: figs. 1, 2. See especially the Egyptian knife (Palmer 1979: fig. 1 no. 374a) and the fragments of statues of armed gods (Negbi 1976: 45, 57; Palmer 1979: fig. 1: nos. 368, 376; fig. 2: no. 370).

and Demas 1988: pl. 61 no. 588, pl. 144 no. 393; Karageorghis 2000a: 266–73). It is, therefore, impossible at this point to connect the larnax burials in Canaan to the presence of Aegeans or Cypriots buried according to their native customs.

AEGEAN MERCENARIES IN THE THIRTEENTH AND EARLY TWELFTH CENTURIES BCE AND ANTHROPOID COFFINS

Beth Shean, a stronghold of the Egyptian Nineteenth and Twentieth Dynasties, with garrison buildings, a temple, and a cemetery, is located on a strategic point along the route between the coast and Transjordan, and on a north–south route leading to Syria. It is also the site from which tantalizing, yet fragmentary, evidence was yielded for the presence of Aegean or Cypriot mercenaries serving the Egyptian administration. The evidence from Beth Shean may be supplemented by finds from another Egyptian stronghold: Tell el-Farʿah (S), by Nahal Besor, in the western Negev.

Foreign mercenaries, such as Sherden and feathered-hatted people, had served in the Egyptian army before Year 8 of Ramses III (Chapter 5). Some of them, had they returned to their homelands after a period in Egyptian service, could have provided crucial information on destinations for raids and colonization, or if stationed in Canaan, they could have done the same for migrants arriving via land and sea routes in the twelfth century. Although identification of these mercenaries in the Egyptian reliefs is rather easy, their archaeological identification is less secure. Serving in the Egyptian army, they may have left fewer traces in the archaeological record than did their Egyptian masters. Some attempts have been made in previous scholarship to examine the possibility that the foreign identity of the mercenaries is in some way manifested in burial practices.

These attempts have resulted in fierce arguments pertaining to Aegean elements identified in the archaeological record, such as metal objects and anthropoid coffins. European-type metal objects – in particular swords of the Naue II family – have been viewed in several instances as an indication of the presence of Aegeans, "northerners," or Sea Peoples in Cyprus and the Levant, either as mercenaries or as groups of metalsmiths (Bouzek 1985: 210, figs. 102, 211, and 212; Mazar 1985a: 6; 1991: 101). There are, however, few metal objects of possible Aegean origin in Canaan and probably none in Transjordan. The only combat weapon of clear Aegean ancestry found in Canaan is a Naue II long dagger of Catling's type IV, found in Megiddo in Early Iron Age strata.[9] This weapon, as well as several bimetallic knives, may date to the eleventh century – too late to indicate the nature of interactions in the thirteenth and

---

[9] The type is thought by Bouzek to be later in the Naue II family than the Mycenaean weapons (i.e., Catling's type I) (Bouzek 1985: 126; Mazar 1985a: 6; Schumacher 1908: table 23: a).

early twelfth centuries.[10] All in all, these finds, though intriguing, add little to the discussion of the nature of the interactions with the Aegean world before the first quarter of the twelfth century.

More chronologically relevant evidence comes from burials in anthropoid clay coffins, a phenomenon well known from Egypt throughout the periods that appears in Canaan only in the thirteenth and perhaps early twelfth centuries BCE, in Beth Shean, Deir el-Balah, and Tell el-Far'ah (S) – sites connected to the Egyptian administration and military presence of the Nineteenth Dynasty and early Twentieth Dynasty. The initial connection between the coffin and the Philistines was made after Ranke and Pritchard (Wright 1959; Dothan 1982: 274 no. 21), who noted the resemblance between the headgear on five coffin lids from Tombs 90 and 66 from Beth Shean (Rowe 1930: 39, pls. 37–40) and the feathered hats of the Tjeker/Sikel, Denyen, and Peleset depicted at Medinet Habu. This choice of decoration is very different from the typical Egyptian headdress and Osiris beard seen on many other coffins from the southern Levant (Dothan 1982: 278, pls. 3, 22, 23). Dothan (1982: 288) pointed to the long history of use of clay anthropoid coffins, which extended from the late fourteenth and thirteenth centuries at Deir el-Balah to the thirteenth and twelfth centuries at Beth Shean and Tell el-Far'ah (S) (Fig. 6.7). The Egyptian burial practice in clay coffins, according to Dothan (1982: 288), was adopted by the Sea Peoples "who first settled as mercenaries in Egyptian strongholds in Canaan by Ramses III after he had defeated them." This wholesale attribution of the coffins to the Philistines was criticized by Brug (1985), who argued that the anthropoid coffins should be attributed to Egyptians or to Canaanites imitating Egyptians, excluding perhaps those found in Cemetery 500 at Tell el-Far'ah (S), which contain Philistine Bichrome pottery. Similarly, Stager (1995: 341–2), objecting to the existence of a settlement of Philistines by the Egyptians in Canaan, attributes all of these coffins to Egyptians. He does not, however, explain their late appearance in Tell el-Far'ah (S) Cemetery 500, some in contexts that are probably later than the end of Egyptian domination in Canaan, nor does he explain the distinctive hats on the Beth Shean anthropoid coffins.

It may be cautiously suggested here that, although most coffins followed Egyptian iconographic prototypes, and therefore cannot be connected to the Philistines, some of the people who commissioned the coffins chose to manifest their ethnic identity by placing their national headdress on the

---

[10] Bimetallic knives with a bone or ivory ring handle are known from Tell Qasile and Tel Miqne/Ekron (Mazar 1985a: 6–8; T. Dothan 1989b; cf. Brug 1985: 170) and from Beth Shean (James 1966: 342–3, fig. 114: 10). Other eleventh-century metal objects of possible Aegean origin are an adz head from Tell Qasile (Mazar 1985a: 3–4; Brug 1985: 170), a double ax from Megiddo (Negbi 1991: 226), and omega-shaped buckles from Megiddo and Tel 'Aitun (Mazar 1985a: 6). In addition, violin-bow fibulae of Aegean or European shape are also reported from Megiddo, Tell Beit Mirsim, and Tell el-Far'ah (S) (Bouzek 1985: figs. 2, 102).

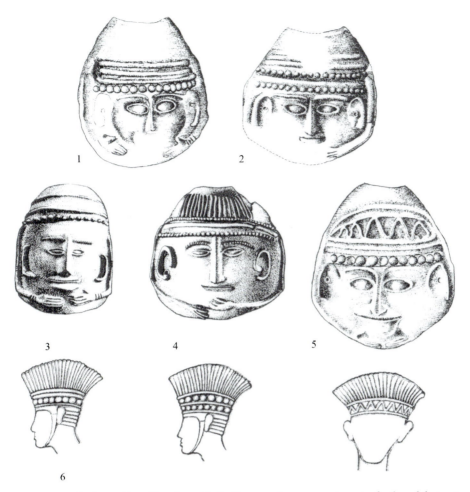

FIGURE 6.7. Anthropoid coffins from Beth Shean and a comparison to feathered hats at Medinet Habu (note: nos. 1, 3, 5 from Beth Shean Tomb 90c, no. 2 from Tomb 90, no. 4 from Tomb 66) (after Dothan 1982: figs. 11 and 12)

lid. Thus, for example, Brug (1985: 149) points to the depiction of a Libyan headdress on the lid from Tomb 562 at Tell el-Far'ah (S). This maintenance of identity in the Egyptian army manifested in traditional headdress and hairdo is well attested to in Egyptian reliefs showing Sherden, Libyans, and others serving from the days of Ramses II.

FEATHERED HATS ON SCARABS

Supporting evidence for feathered-hatted people's practice of manifesting their identity through the commissioning of Egyptian-style iconography is seen in scarabs found at Tell el-Far'ah (S) and Beth Shean, the same sites that yielded anthropoid coffins. To my mind, this phenomenon is reminiscent of the seal from Enkomi showing a feathered-hatted person, interpreted as belonging to an Aegean mercenary residing at the site (Chapter 5). According to Bietak (1993: 297, 301), the area south of Wadi Gaza, including Tell el-Farʿah (S), was still in Egyptian hands after Year 8 of Ramses III. A unique scarab seal from Tomb 936 at Cemetery 900 (Macdonald, Starkey, and Harding 1932: pl. 55: 252; Noort 1994: 140–1; Keel and Uehlinger 1998: 112; Fig. 6.8, part 3), depicts a feathered-hatted person in front of the Egyptian god Amon. The depiction conveys status: the person is an important figure and is most probably claiming a position of leadership, as Pharaoh is usually the one depicted in front of the god on scarabs; indeed, Keel and Uehlinger (1998: 110) identify this person as a prince. The cult is Egyptian, yet the figure is manifesting its ethnic background by means of the feathered hat. It may be argued that such strong influence on cult practices could have been achieved only through close and prolonged contact with Egyptian religion. This depiction of Amon is perhaps connected with the Amon temple in Gaza built by Ramses III, to which, according to Papyrus Harris I, the locals bore gifts (Singer 1994: 290). Because the tomb is dated to the first half of the twelfth century BCE (Braunstein 1998: 776–85), there is a good chance that such influence on the beliefs of at least this one individual resulted from service in Egypt or in an Egyptian-controlled area.

Further investigation of the grave goods in Tomb 936 (Braunstein 1998: 776–85) shows that the tomb did not differ significantly from the others in Cemetery 900 in the types of grave goods placed in it, though it is among the richest graves in the cemetery (Braunstein 1998: 264). It is possible, as in the case of the Beth Shean tombs, that less prestigious, daily objects of Aegean origin were not deposited in the Tell el-Farʿah (S) burials, leaving this scarab as the only object testifying to the self-identity and the high status of its owner.

Possible confirmation of the presence of foreigners at Beth Shean is provided by a unique scarab-like object (scaraboid) (Rowe 1940: pl. 39: 10; James 1966: fig. 117: 4; Fig. 6.8, parts 1, 2),[11] found in Stratum IV, yet most likely predating it. It depicts a beardless man in long robes holding a lotus flower. His hairstyle or hat is high and spiky, unlike any Egyptian or Canaanite example. The hair or headdress and the robe are comparable to those of the high-ranking prisoner depicted on a glazed tile from the palace of Ramses III (Sandars 1978: 136, fig. 90). The prisoner, who is bearded, has long and stiff hair, which Sandars compared to that of the Shekelesh prince from Medinet Habu. However, both the beardlessness and the spiky headdress or hairstyle of the figure on the Beth Shean scaraboid may be compared to those of the

---

[11] I am very grateful to Nir Lalkin for turning my attention to this scaraboid and for sharing with me his ideas about the non-Egyptian nature of its iconography and about the "Philistine" hairstyle of the figure. A second scarab with a feathered-hatted warrior figure was found in Achzib and is dated to the twelfth to eleventh centuries BCE (Giveon 1988: 28–30 no. 12; Keel 1997: 52 no. 90).

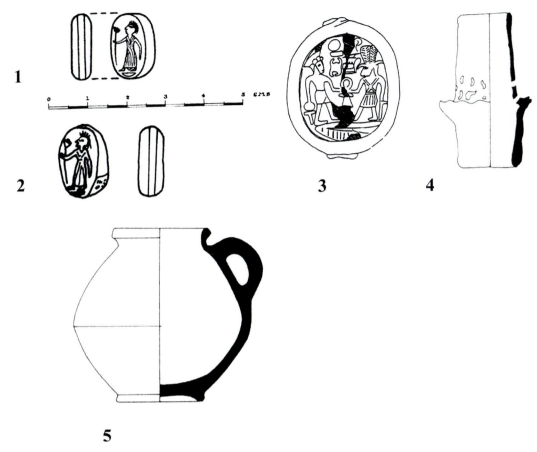

FIGURE 6.8. Objects from Beth Shean and Tell el-Farʿah (S)
1. Scaraboid from Beth Shean Stratum IV (Rowe 1940: pl. 39: 10)
2. Scaraboid from Beth Shean Stratum IV (James 1966: fig. 117: 3)
3. Scarab from Tell el-Farʿah (S) (Keel and Uehlinger 1998: 112, ill. 129, without scale)
4. Torch from Beth Shean Stratum VI (James 1966: fig. 50: 4)
5. Jug from Beth Shean Stratum VI (James 1966: fig. 56: 5)

feathered-hatted people in the Medinet Habu reliefs, and the hairstyle resembles also contemporary Aegean depictions of spiky hats (Chapter 5). His precise origin aside, the person depicted is certainly a foreigner, conspicuous by his unusual hairstyle, thus showing his ethnic identity to be different from that of the Canaanites and Egyptians at Beth Shean. His rather lofty social status is conveyed explicitly by his robes and implicitly by his ability to commission and own such a unique scaraboid. The cultural background for his appearance is heavily influenced by Egyptian cult. First, and most obvious, the object is a scaraboid. Second, and more important, the figure is depicted in an Egyptian-style posture of adoration: holding a lotus flower, probably before a god. Such Egyptian cult scenes of offering flowers to the gods, depicted on cult stelae at Beth Shean, may have been common in the Egyptian garrison at the site (Rowe 1940: figure facing the front page and pl. 49A: 1).

AEGEAN MATERIAL CULTURE AT BETH SHEAN?

Although Tombs 90 and 66 in Beth Shean, with their feathered-hat coffin lids, contained no further evidence for the ethnic identity of their owners, similarly to the case of Tomb 936 at Tell el Farʿah (S), which yielded the feathered-hat scarab, finds from the tell itself can be connected to interregional contact with Cyprus and the Aegean during Stratum VI, the latest Egyptian garrison at the site, dated to the Twentieth Dynasty. As mentioned earlier, Stratum VI was the find spot of much of the collection of imported LHIIIC-style pottery from northern Israel. One complete imported LHIIIC-style stirrup jar and fragments of others were found in this stratum, both in the old and in the renewed excavations (Fig. 6.6, part 1). Their Cypriot provenance (D'Agata et al. 2005) connects them to twelfth-century international trade rather than the presence of Aegean mercenaries. However, further evidence for the possible presence of foreigners, perhaps mercenaries, at Beth Shean is found in objects of daily use that may have nonlocal, Aegean origin, all found in Stratum VI, within the vicinity of Buildings 1500 and 1700, massive structures that were probably "headquarters for Ramses III's 'northern command' and homes for his generals and administrators" (James 1966: 13):

Aegean torch: An Aegean-style torch, with typical use marks, apparently unique in Canaan, described by James (1966: fig. 50: 4; Fig. 6.8, part 4) as a "hollow stand with a container, upper part perforated and burnt black throughout. Lower part, brown ware, blackened interior." The type is found at sites in the Aegean including Athens, Tiryns, Mycenae, the Menelaion, Knossos, and the Pylonas cemetery in Rhodes (Kilian 1986; Karageorghis 1986; 1999; Karantzali 1998: 290, fig. 18), and in Cyprus at the sites of Pyla-Kokkinokremos, Enkomi, Kition, and Palaeopaphos (Karageorghis 1986; Kilian 1986). According to Kilian (1986: 160), the only other examples known from the Levant come from Ugarit. These torches are not similar in shape to any local Canaanite or Egyptian forms. Because they appeared earlier in the Aegean than in Cyprus (where they may have appeared as early as the end of the thirteenth century), they are of Aegean origin. Karageorghis (1986: 26; 1999: 513) has suggested a military association for such objects, which may fit their find context at Beth Shean, in the Egyptian military stronghold, in Locus 1585, between Buildings 1500 and 1700.

Aegean loom weights (?): Two clay reel-shaped objects, narrower at midpoint (James 1966: fig. 105: 8, 11), were found in Locus 1343, a structure southwest of the temple. They are identical in shape and size to the reels used as loom weights at contemporary sites in the Aegean (Chapter 5). James (1966: 12) calls the objects "model bread offerings," yet she also notes the scarcity of loom weights of stone and clay in Stratum VI compared to their large numbers in Strata V and IV. In contrast to the other Aegean-style objects without predecessors in Strata VII and VIII, clay reels appear in both strata (James and McGovern 1993: 188), dated to the fourteenth to early twelfth century BCE. The fact that no other group of such objects has been found at any other Late Bronze Age site in the southern Levant indicates that the objects were not typical of Canaanite material culture. Their appearance in Stratum VIII indicates either that the objects are not Aegean loom weights or that Aegean-style weaving was practiced at the site as early as the late Eighteenth Dynasty. If the latter is true, the reels provide additional evidence for Aegean textile manufacture in the Egyptian cultural sphere, attested to elsewhere by evidence for Aegean spinning practices as early as the Middle Kingdom period (Chapter 1), yet their presence in the outpost of Beth Shean raises many difficult questions.

Aegean cooking jugs (?): A jug with a wide mouth, one handle, and clear burn marks on the sides and lower body was found in Locus 1196, in one of the houses east of the temple (James 1966: figs. 56: 5, 120: 4; Fig. 6.8, part 5). A rim fragment of a similar vessel was found in Locus 1586, the central room of Building 1500 (James 1966: fig. 49: 17). The key to interpreting the former jug lies in its burn marks, which may indicate its use for cooking or heating. Moreover, the general shape of the jug is similar to contemporary cooking jugs of the Aegean world (Chapter 5), mainly to LHIIIB examples from Midea and Mycenae (Tzedakis and Martlew 1999: 126 no. 106, 135 no. 120). If these are Aegean cooking vessels or Canaanite vessels used in an Aegean manner, their discovery at Beth Shean, side by side with Canaanite cooking pots,[12] is highly indicative of the presence of people of Aegean origin maintaining their preferred cooking habits. Overall, the number of categories of finds (up to five) is large enough to establish a firm possibility that the interactions with the Aegean and with Aegeanized Cyprus of the twelfth century extended beyond the importation of fineware pottery. Among behavioral patterns suggested by the domestic assemblages, one can count cooking, weaving, and use of perfumed oils in Aegean-style containers. The mortuary assemblages include coffins with ethnic demarcation, the religious sphere is represented by the scaraboid, and the military context is possibly represented by the torch. Such accumulation of evidence of Aegean behavioral patterns offers additional testimony to the presence of Aegeans at the site. Although the evidence presented here is still far from conclusive, it allows for the following tentative interpretation: the length of the foreigners' residence at Beth Shean or in the Egyptian cultural sphere is attested to by the adaptation of burial style and the use of Egyptian cult iconography. The length of interaction resulting in such cultural assimilation weighed against the small amount of fineware imports,

---

[12] For example, in Locus 1585 (James 1966: fig. 50: 12, 15), Locus 1224 (James 1966: fig. 50: 13), and Loci 1589 and 1590 (James 1966: fig. 50: 16).

indicating that the nature of this interaction was not primarily concerned with trade. The explicit manifestation of self-identity in relatively rich burials and in dress (as on the scaraboid) indicates the lofty status of at least some of the foreigners, as well as Egyptian tolerance for such manifestations of identity. The identity was perhaps strengthened by domestic behavioral patterns: preparation of food, consumption of luxury products in Aegean-style containers, and perhaps weaving in the Aegean style. The small number of Aegean-related objects may be the result of a relatively small number of foreigners who participated in the interaction. Alternatively (according to the possibility of equifinality; Chapter 1), their number may have been larger, and they may have had difficulties manifesting their identity because of their status or occupational group.

CONCLUSIONS: STRICTLY BUSINESS?

The survey of the nature of interactions between the Aegean and the Levant in the thirteenth to early twelfth centuries shows that most interactions can be placed somewhere along the trade range, but that the presence of Aegean mercenaries, mainly in the service of the Egyptians, is also indicated.

Aegean imported pottery and its local imitations show that interactions with the Aegean world had little effect on the behavioral patterns of the local, Canaanite society. Imported objects influenced mostly the elite's taste for Aegean luxury commodities distributed in Mycenaean containers. This preference for commodities in Aegean-style containers, rather than the adoption of Aegean drinking customs, continued in a residual form into the twelfth century, as is seen in the limited import of LHIIIC-style pottery found in the north of Israel. Other Aegean influences, in religion and foodways, for example, cannot be detected in the local Canaanite culture in the twelfth century.

The trade in Mycenaean products may have been carried out by Cypriot traders, who were present in some Levantine coastal communities, as indicated by evidence at Tell Abu Hawam. The Cypriot traders were acutely aware of the preferences of the local population and were thus able to continue the export of Cypriot-made LHIIIC-style containers during the twelfth century, after Mycenaean Argive products were no longer available. Their continuing contacts with the Levant in the twelfth century could have been another important source of information for Aegean raiders and settlers, especially those who resided in Cyprus during the early twelfth century BCE. In contrast to Sherratt (1998: 303), the Cypriot imports of the twelfth century did not inspire a taste for Aegean-style drinking ware, which would have resulted in the production of LHIIIC-style pottery in Philistia. The Cypriot traders of either the thirteenth or the twelfth century were unlikely candidates to be agents of cultural transmission and change, teaching the locals how to drink wine in the Aegean manner. Rather, they seem to have been much more interested in selling to the local population the pottery types that best fit local cultural preferences, thus continuing Late Bronze Age Canaanite consumption patterns. Furthermore, the Canaanite clientele itself was diminishing rapidly in the twelfth century. The finds of imported LHIIIC-style pottery from the northern coast of Canaan conform to the areas in which Canaanite urban centers survived at least the beginning of the twelfth century, unaffected by the turmoil and destruction following the fall of Ugarit and Amurru (Chapter 5), and by the sometimes-violent settlement of the Philistines in the southern coastal plain (Chapter 7). The end of Egyptian administration and control in the northern valleys, possibly after the days of Ramses IV, had coincided with the end of demand for LHIIIC-style imports and terminated the last remnant of Late Bronze Age trade patterns. During this time, local production of the LHIIIC style in Philistia was going strong, uninfluenced by either Cypriot or Aegean trade (Chapter 7).

The permanent presence of Aegeans in the southern Levant was minor, perhaps consisting of foreign mercenaries in Egyptian barracks with little ability to influence material culture over a wide radius. As expected, the identification of individual mercenaries in a foreign country is extremely difficult because they leave relatively little behind (see Chapter 1, for identification of individuals). The few Aegean-type weapons either are too late to be indicative or were found in unclear contexts. Better evidence for the presence of Aegeans in Canaan comes from three Twentieth Dynasty Egyptian strongholds. Most of the evidence connected with self-manifestation of identity – iconographic evidence from Beth Shean (i.e., coffins, a scaraboid, and daily objects), as well as the Tell el-Farʿah (S) scarab – suggest a close connection between Egypt and the people with the feathered hats in a context of Egyptian military presence.

The sparse evidence for the presence of Aegeans in the Levant during most of the thirteenth century does not allow for any reconstruction of an Aegean community that could have acted as a bridgehead for settlement in the twelfth century. However, Aegean mercenaries could have served as informers for later twelfth-century Aegean settlers in the southern Levant. Some indications in favor of this option come from the service of feathered-hatted soldiers in the Egyptian army during the war against the Libyans in Year 5 (Nelson 1930: pls. 17, 19). They could have easily been a source of information for would-be migrants and raiders in Cyprus, the Aegean, and Anatolia, ready and eager to take advantage of the weakness of both Egyptian overlords and Canaanite urban society to their own ends.

7

THE MATERIAL CULTURE CHANGE IN TWELFTH-CENTURY PHILISTIA

FROM CANAAN TO PHILISTIA

The southern coastal plain of Israel and the adjacent Shephela (lower foothills, two hundred meters above sea level) experienced turmoil in the transition from the thirteenth century to the twelfth century BCE, similar to many other regions of the eastern Mediterranean (Fig. 7.1). Through most of the thirteenth century, a system of Canaanite city-states controlled the area, with centers at Lachish, Tell es-Ṣafi/Gath, Ashkelon, Gezer, and Gaza or Yurza, continuing a system that had existed throughout most of the Late Bronze Age and was recorded in fourteenth-century el-Amarna Letters (Finkelstein 1996a: fig. 1). Egyptian garrisons and forts, as in Deir el-Balah south of Gaza; Tel Mor, the harbor site of Ashdod; and Tel Seraʿ in the Besor area, ensured the Nineteenth Dynasty's grip on the area, the latter continuing to the twelfth century BCE (Killebrew 2006: 60–4).

Although it endured the last decade of the thirteenth century, the system of Canaanite city-states received a considerable blow from the campaigns of Pharaoh Merneptah, who recorded in the famous Israel Stele the obliteration of two of the centers of the Canaanite polities, at Gezer and at Ashkelon: "Canaan is plundered with every evil; Ashkelon is conquered; Gezer is seized" (Stager 1985: *56; Rainey 2003: 181). The violent siege and conquest of Ashkelon, depicted also in a relief in Karnak, was possibly accompanied by the placing of an Egyptian garrison in a newly built fort (Fig. 7.2; Master 2005: 340). Although the situation at Gaza remains obscure and Tell es-Ṣafi/Gath awaits further excavation, it is possible that, by the beginning of the twelfth century BCE, only one Canaanite center survived – Lachish. However, Egyptian scarabs found in the extensive excavations at the site have shown that this city, too, was violently destroyed, either during the days of Ramses IV or shortly after, during the second half of the twelfth century (Krauss 1994). Secondary sites, such as Tel Miqne/Ekron and Tel Batash/Timnah also suffered violent destruction during the transition from the Late Bronze Age to the Early Iron Age. The

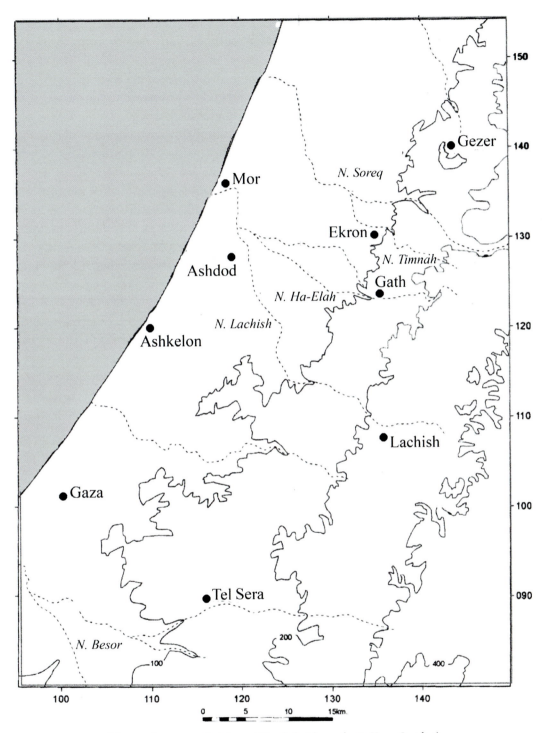

FIGURE 7.1. Map of the southern coastal plain and Shephela (drawn by A. Yasur-Landau)

destruction of the Canaanite political system was not limited to the south – it occurred throughout the late thirteenth and early twelfth centuries almost throughout the entire southern Levant, in sites such as Megiddo and Hazor, and ended in violent conflagrations. As in Greece, the end of the palatial Canaanite culture was accompanied by the loss of literate administration – in the Levantine case, of cuneiform writing. Palaces and monumental temples that were based on Syrian prototypes were no longer built in the twelfth and eleventh centuries. Monumental art, such as sculpture and reliefs, was no longer practiced.

Precisely during this time of disintegration of the former political and cultural order, the first signs of locally made, Aegean-style cultural traits appear, under similar circumstances in which they appear on the Anatolian and Syrian coasts. They possibly first appeared at Ashdod, Ashkelon, Tel Miqne/Ekron, and likely Tell es-Ṣafi/Gath, the only sites where locally made LHIIIC-style pottery (Philistine Monochrome) was found. Given the Late Bronze Age settlement patterns, these sites seem a rather random selection, though all were tell sites: Tel Ashkelon was the only port city among them and the former center of a polity. Tel Ashdod, located inland, about four and a half kilometers off the coast, was an important Canaanite town but never the center of a polity. Tel Miqne/Ekron on Nahal Timnah was a village located some twenty kilometers east of the sea, in the inner coastal plain. Tell es-Ṣafi/Gath, located some eight kilometers south of Ekron, on Nahal Ha-'Elah, was the center of a Canaanite polity. In retrospect, the four sites share an important trait: together with Gaza, they are mentioned in the Bible as the five cities of the Philistines: the Pentapolis.

As mentioned in the Introduction to this book, most facts related to the circumstances and appearance of the Aegean cultural traits are hotly debated. During the last quarter of the twentieth century, the prevailing paradigm regarding the appearance of Aegean-style material culture in the southern Levant was that it was connected to the arrival of Aegean migrants, the Philistines. The newcomers were thought to have violently conquered the southern Canaanite towns, either with the consent of the Egyptian overlords or following the demise of Twentieth Dynasty Egyptian domination in the province of Canaan (cf. Dothan 1982; 1998b; Mazar 1985b; Bietak 1993; Stager 1995; 1998; Finkelstein 1995; 1998; Barako 2000; Bunimovitz and Faust 2001). Sherratt (1992; 1998) challenges this approach (followed by Bauer 1998) and poses a nonmigrationist explanation for the Aegean cultural traits found on Cyprus and in Philistia, preferring a process of cultural diffusion and elite emulation connected with the early post-Bronze Age trade. Killebrew (1998a: 393–7, 401–2; 2000) also challenges the idea of Aegean migration, instead supporting the idea of migration that originates from Cyprus and/or Cilicia rather than from the Aegean proper. Even the ethnic composition of the people of Philistia was contested: were they mostly Aegean (e.g., Stager 1995)?

FIGURE 7.2. The conquest of Ashkelon by Merneptah (after Stager 1985: fig. 2)

A mixture of Canaanites, Syrians, and Aegeans (Sweeny and Yasur-Landau 1999)? Canaanite (Drews 2000)? Or a cosmopolitan mixture of people from the eastern Mediterranean (Sherratt 1998)?

Even among those who support a migrationist paradigm, there are serious disagreements regarding almost all aspects of migration. Although T. Dothan (1989a), Mazar (1985b), and Stager (1995) support a date for the Philistine settlement during the reign of Ramses III, in connection to his campaigns against the Sea Peoples, Finkelstein (1995; 1998) and Ussishkin (1998) argue for a later chronology for the beginning of the Philistine settlement, much later than the days of Ramses III and probably even after Ramses VI, after

Egyptian control in the south of Canaan ended. The postulated number of migrants ranges from a massive migration of twenty-five thousand (Stager 1995) to a humble movement of a few thousand (Finkelstein 1996a; 1998).

Despite the fierce academic debate, architectural sequences and pottery assemblages of the earliest Philistine levels, including locally made LHIIIC-style pottery (Mycenaean IIIC or Monochrome), were only recently made available, with the final publication of Ashdod (Dothan and Porath 1993; Dothan and Ben-Shlomo 2005) and the first volumes of final publication from Tel Miqne/Ekron (cf. Bierling 1998; Dothan 1998b; Meehl, Dothan, and Gitin 2006) and Ashkelon (Stager et al. 2008).

The first article dedicated to the systematic study of the LHIIIC-style pottery (Mycenaean IIIC) appeared only in 2004 (Dothan and Zuckerman 2004). At the same time, the understanding of the Canaanite component in the material culture was often neglected in favor of the more attractive Aegean-style pottery.

With the availability of material culture assemblages from the earliest phases of Philistine material culture from Ashdod, Ashkelon, and Tel Miqne/Ekron, three of the Pentapolis sites, it is possible to reexamine the nature of the interactions between the Aegean and the southern Levant in the twelfth century, solely on the basis of material culture assemblages.[1] Such analysis can establish the interaction range that best fits the phenomena of externally induced changes in material culture while ruling out those that could not possibly have caused the changes. Once the interaction range has been established, we can reconstruct, in the next chapter, the Philistines' society, their origin, and additional factors that contribute to the thick description of the interaction, such as the number of participants, their sex, age, social status, and occupation.

THE END OF THE BRONZE AGE–IRON AGE TRANSITION IN THE PHILISTINE SITES

ASHDOD

The paradigm of violent Philistine conquest determines that the earliest appearance of locally made, yet Aegean-style, material culture traits was predated by violent destruction of the existing Canaanite towns, followed by the foundation of large urban sites. However, a close inspection of the situation in Ashdod, Ashkelon, and Tel Miqne/Ekron suggests a more complex reality.

Excavations directed by Moshe Dothan at the tell of Ashdod have shown that some part of the prosperous Canaanite Late Bronze Age town of Stratum

---

[1] Excavations at Tell es-Ṣafi, Philistine Gath, led by Aren Maeir, have not yet reached extensive transition levels between the thirteenth and twelfth centuries. Aren Maeir (personal communication, April 17, 2007) has confirmed that, so far, locally made Mycenaean IIIC was found in Tell es-Ṣafi/Gath in a very limited amount of early Iron I and later contexts. This may hint that the find of a more extensive early Philistine settlement is imminent.

FIGURE 7.3. Tel Ashdod (after Dothan 1993a: 194)

XIV was destroyed by fire, and the city of Stratum XIII was built on it (Dothan 1993a: 96; Figs. 7.3 and 7.4; Table 7.1). The remains of the last Late Bronze Age stratum (XIV) were found in Areas A, B, H, and G (Dothan 1993a: 95–6; 1971: table of correlation of strata). The city seemed to be limited to the acropolis of the tell and the small hill to the northeast of it. The only evidence of violent destruction is a thick ash layer reported from a rather small area inside Area A (Dothan 1971: 25; 1993a: 96). No evidence of violent destruction was found in Area G (Dothan and Porath 1993: 47), the location of the thirteenth-century Canaanite or Egyptian "governor's residence." Arguments by Dothan and Porath (1993) for damage caused to the building may actually reflect radical modifications to the plan during Stratum XIIIb (see later in this section), changing it from a courtyard building to an Aegean-style structure. The size of the initial twelfth-century settlement was modest. No Strata XIII or XII architecture was found outside Areas A and G, indicating a site of about four

TABLE 7.1. *Comparative chronological table (Master 2005: 340; Dothan et al. 2006: 75)*

Tel Miqne/Ekron	Ashdod	Ashkelon	Approximate dates according to the Middle Chronology
Strata IX–VIII	Stratum XIV	Phase 21	Late Bronze IIB: end of 13th century to beginning of 12th century BCE
Strata VIIa–b	Stratum XIIIb	Phase 20a–b	Iron IA: 12th century BCE
Strata VIa–b	Strata XIIIa–XII	Phase 19a–b	Iron IA: late 12th century BCE
Strata Vc–b	Stratum XI	Phase 18	Iron IB: early 11th century BCE

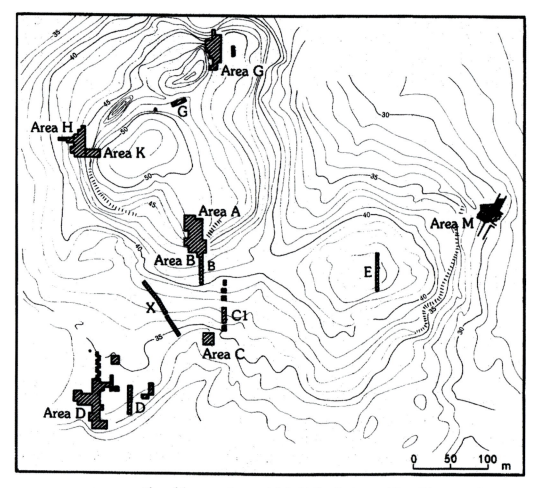

FIGURE 7.4. Plan of the excavations at Ashdod (after Dothan and Ben-Shlomo 2005)

hectares (i.e., a town rather than a city). It seems that the settlement spread outside the acropolis only in the eleventh century (Dothan 1993a: 98) and was similar in size in the twelfth century and at the end of the Late Bronze Age.

A sharp change in material culture can be detected between Strata XIV and XIII, the latter manifesting many Aegean material culture traits (Dothan and Dothan 1992: 165–6; Dothan 1993a: 96; Dothan and Porath 1993: 11–12). The final reports for Area G (Dothan and Porath 1993) and Area H (Dothan and Ben-Shlomo 2005) provide much information on the material culture assemblages of the beginning of the Iron Age. There are conflicting opinions about the nature of the building remains in Stratum XIIIb in Area G. The excavators, as well as Trude Dothan, claim that the area is an artisans' quarter in which Mycenaean IIIC: 1b pottery was manufactured and some cult activities were performed (Dothan 1982: 37; Dothan and Dothan 1992: 165–6; Dothan and Porath 1993: 12). However, the lack of evidence of pottery manufacture (e.g., kilns, pottery refuse, potters' wheels) and cultic activity (apart from

FIGURE 7.5. Tel Miqne/Ekron (after Dothan 1995: pl. 2)

hearths) suggests a domestic nature. Shlomo Bunimovitz and I (Bunimovitz and Yasur-Landau 2002; see "Ashdod Area G, Strata XIIIb and XIIIa") argue, therefore, that this area contained primarily a single, large, elite domestic unit.

Stratum XIII in Area H was most probably a domestic area. A substantial street, three and a half meters wide, ran between two building complexes (Mazar and Ben-Shlomo 2005).

TEL MIQNE/EKRON

Excavations at Tel Miqne/Ekron, directed by Trude Dothan and Seymour Gitin (T. Dothan 1989a: 2–5; 1998b: 151), have shown that violent fire destroyed the Canaanite Late Bronze Age town of Stratum IX and that a significantly larger city (Stratum VII) was built on its ruins (Figs. 7.5 and 7.6; see Table 7.1). The remains of the last Late Bronze Age town or village are limited to Field I, indicating that the area of the northeastern acropolis alone, about four hectares, was inhabited at the time (Dothan 1992: 94; Gittlen 1992; Dothan and Gitin 1993: 1051–2). The Canaanite town at Tel Miqne/Ekron was completely burned (Dothan 1998a: 150–1), yet evidence from Field I (Killebrew 1998a: 381–2) may indicate that the Canaanite settlement of Stratum VIII continued for some time after the destruction of Stratum IX and before the appearance of Aegean material culture in Stratum VII. A much larger city that included the entire lower tell was built and fortified with a mud-brick wall in Stratum VIIB, covering a total area of about twenty hectares. Remains of this stratum were found in Fields I, III, IV, and X (Killebrew 1998a). A deep change in material

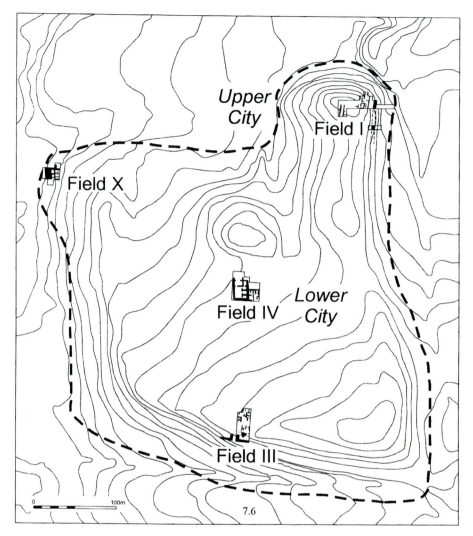

FIGURE 7.6. Plan of the excavations at Tel Miqne/Ekron (after Dothan 2003: fig. 3)

culture can be detected between Strata VIII and VII, the latter manifesting many Aegean material culture traits (ibid.: 152–7; Killebrew 1998a).

Preliminary reports of material culture assemblages have been published for Fields X and I (Killebrew 1996; 1998a; Bierling 1998), as has a final report for part of Field I (Meehl et al. 2006). Other information on these fields and on Field IV has appeared in numerous articles (for lists of these publications, see Dothan and Gitin 1993; Dothan 1998a; 2000).

The different areas of the tell provide evidence of varied functions. Field I was an industrial area in which several pottery kilns and a small shrine were discovered (Dothan and Gitin 1993: 1053; Killebrew 1998a); Field IV was an elite residential area throughout the Iron Age history of the site (Dothan and Gitin 1993: 1054–6, 1058), while Field X was a domestic area close to the town wall (Bierling 1998).

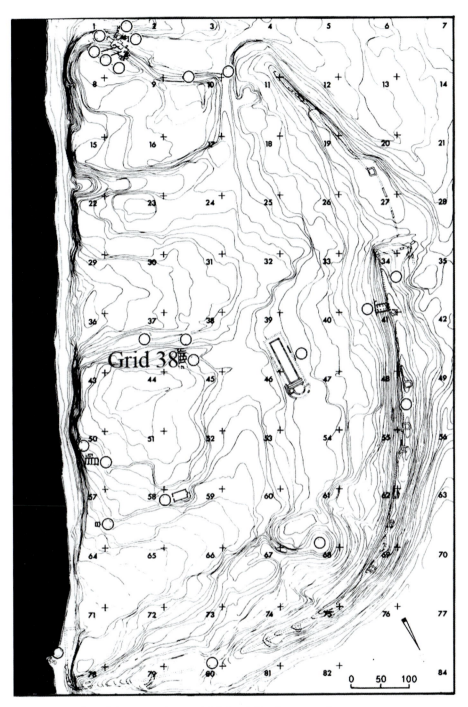

FIGURE 7.7. Plan of the excavations at Ashkelon (after Stager 1993)

ASHKELON

The evidence of the transition between the Late Bronze Age and the Early Iron Age at Ashkelon (Fig. 7.7; see Table 7.1) challenges the common view of a simultaneous, violent conquest by a large mass of migrants over a short period of time. Excavations directed by Lawrence E. Stager (1991; 1993: 107; 1995: 345–6; Stager et al. 2008) have uncovered Late Bronze Age and Early Iron Age remains in several areas, but a complete sequence exists for Grid 38. New evidence from Grid 38 indicates that, during the thirteenth century, an Egyptian-style fort was built at the site (Phase 21) (Master 2005; Cross and Stager 2006). This may have been the aftermath of the annihilation of the Canaanite city by Merneptah – possibly evident in substantial destruction found in a section excavated by Phythian-Adams (Phythian-Adams 1921; Stager 1995: 107) in Grid 57 – after which the site was abandoned. The new Iron Age settlement, Phase 20b, which included locally made Aegean-style pottery, was built not on the still-warm embers of the Canaanite town but on shifting sand. The pottery assemblage of Ashkelon is yet to be published, but a review of the Early Iron Age sequence in Grid 38 (Master 2005) and a detailed set of phase plans (Cross and Stager 2006) show the main architectural features of the humble domestic area of Phases 20 and 19, including two blocks of buildings connecting to a vast open area and a street. The size of Late Bronze Age Ashkelon is still unknown, and so far, Late Bronze Age occupation levels have been reported only for Grids 38 and 50 (Stager 1993: 107). Finkelstein (1996a) suggests that Ashkelon was of a size similar to that of Ashdod, a small, Category E settlement (5.1–10 hectares). It is likely that the Early Iron Age settlement, its remains known only from Grids 38, 50, and 57, was not larger.

TELL ES-ṢAFI/GATH

A substantial settlement existed at the site during the Late Bronze Age, with a scattering of pottery covering some thirty-four hectares, possibly originating from a somewhat smaller site (Ben-Shlomo 2006–7: 268; Wimmer and Maeir 2007: 1). A public building or a large patrician house in Area E yielded a rich local and imported pottery deposit dating to the very end of the Late Bronze Age. This building may have been destroyed as part of more general destruction of the site (Maeir 2008). However, with the current absence of excavated strata dating to the earliest Iron Age, it is difficult to estimate the exact nature of the initial Philistine settlement at Tell es-Ṣafi/Gath.

All four sites seem to exhibit evidence of violent destruction near the end of the Late Bronze Age. However, the destruction at Ashkelon, and possibly at Tel Miqne/Ekron, was followed by another Late Bronze Age phase.[2] Furthermore, it may be that Ashdod suffered only partial damage. In that case, it is even more likely that attackers intending to settle at the site would, for their own benefit, prefer to preserve it as intact as possible.[3]

---

[2] In Ashkelon it was an Egyptian-style fort in Phase 21.

[3] There is also no reason to assume that settlement immediately followed destruction at all sites. The latest material in the destruction levels should be used only as a terminus post quem.

Some differentiation in the circumstances of settlement after the destruction is seen in the variable sizes of the sites and their fortification at the beginning of the Iron Age. All three sites "reacted" differently to the transition from the Late Bronze Age to the Iron Age: Tel Miqne/Ekron grew significantly at the first Iron Age level and was fortified. Ashdod retained, more or less, its Late Bronze Age size and remained unfortified. Ashkelon was refounded in the twelfth century and remained unfortified at least until the end of the eleventh century, which suggests the arrival of opportunistic settlers rather than violent conquerors.

BEHAVIORAL PATTERNS AS INDICATORS OF INTERACTION WITH AEGEAN POPULATION IN THE SOUTHERN LEVANT

Simple household vessels of an insignificant nature, which requir[e] no special comment.   – Furumark (1941: 76), discussing coarse cylindrical jars

Over the years, a large number of Aegean cultural traits have been isolated in strata from twelfth-century Philistia. The variety of views regarding the social processes that occurred in the twelfth-century Levant (Chapter 1) shows that agreement on the nature of interaction that led to these material culture patterns is lacking. Of crucial importance to the study of the traits of Aegean origin is the fact that the items attesting to Aegean behavioral patterns were locally made, and their simple, daily nature indicates that the people who created and used them did things in the Aegean way. To estimate the range of interactions that led to the change in material culture in the twelfth-century southern coastal plain and the Shephela, one needs to estimate the quantity of change in behavioral patterns. As demonstrated in Chapter 1, the assemblages that are most indicative of deep change connected to migration are the domestic ones, those reflecting domestic behavioral patterns such as cooking and weaving. Consequently, the following overview focuses mainly on aspects of material culture and activities connected with the domestic sphere:

* Cooking
* Storage and serving of food and drink
* Pottery production
* Textile production
* Organization of domestic space

Naturally, only sites that have been extensively excavated and at least partially published can yield enough information for this overview. Tel Miqne/Ekron Strata VII and VI (mainly Areas I and X) and Ashdod Strata XIIIb and XIIIa (mainly Areas G and H) were published in the form of preliminary or final reports and in articles on pottery and other objects. These are the first strata following the destruction of the sites at the end of the Late Bronze Age, and the ones in which changes in material culture traits are most prominent. Contemporary strata at Ashkelon Phases 20 and 19, mainly from Grid 38, though awaiting further publication, are also considered here mainly for their architectural features.

COOKING AND FOOD PREPARATION

As in the analysis of the Cypriot evidence in Chapter 5, particular attention is paid here to the preparation and consumption of food, as these are activities of considerable social importance (Samuel 1999: 123, table 1), and as there is significant evidence of them in the archaeological assemblages under discussion. Procurement of food is treated in the discussion on agriculture and economy (Chapter 8), and storage is discussed later in this chapter. According to Samuel (1999), most types of evidence relevant to food preparation can be found at Tel Miqne/Ekron and Ashdod, yet the sites show only two types of evidence relevant to food consumption (vessels and house layout). As a result, the conclusions reached by examining food preparation activities at these sites may be more accurate than those reached by examining food consumption. Of the categories of evidence of food preparation, the greatest attention is given here to different cooking installations and vessels. Tools, which are not as well documented, are discussed in most publications of material culture assemblages from Philistine sites (particularly stone tools) or not dealt with at all, as their sample is extremely small and therefore less indicative of the type of interaction that occurred. Because food consumption is connected with the processes of obtaining and using fineware pottery, its discussion largely concerns serving vessels (see "Patterns of Use of the Pottery Assemblage: Storing and Serving Food and Drink in Aegean and Local Styles," this chapter).

CANAANITE COOKING POTS, AEGEAN COOKING JUGS, AND COARSEWARE BASINS

Aegean-type cooking jugs were used at Ashdod, Ashkelon, Tell es-Ṣafi/Gath, and Tel Miqne/Ekron, side by side with the local Canaanite cooking pots (Dothan and Zukerman 2004: 34; Yasur-Landau 2005b: 180–3; Ben-Shlomo et al. 2008; Tables 7.2 and 7.3; Figs. 7.8–21). Canaanite cooking pots (Figs. 7.15–.17) have a wide mouth and a concave base. Rim shapes are triangular or square and folded, which continue local traditions of the Late Bronze Age.[4] The similar appearance of Canaanite and Aegean-style cooking pots has also been reported from Ashkelon (Stager et al. 2008: fig. 15.11: 8–10). The cooking

---

[4] E.g., Ashdod Stratum XIV (Dothan and Freedman 1967: fig. 22: 9, 11; Dothan and Porath 1993: fig. 12: 10) and XIIIb (Dothan and Porath 1993: fig. 17: 6). Tel Miqne/Ekron Field I, Stratum VIII (Dothan et al. 2006: fig. 3.2.12, 13), and continue to Stratum VIIb in Field X (Dothan 1998a: pl. 1: 14).

TABLE 7.2. *Aegean-style pottery at Tel Miqne/Ekron, Ashdod, Enkomi, and Tarsus*

Type of Aegean-style pottery (FS; name according to Mountjoy 1986 or according to Dothan 1982; Killebrew 1998a; Dothan and Zukerman 2004)	Tel Miqne/Ekron[a]	Ashdod	Enkomi (Levels IIIA and IIIB Early)	Tarsus (Mountjoy 2005c)
FS 284, 285; deep bowl/bell-shaped bowl	Field I: Killebrew 1998: figs. 6: 23; 7: 8–13; 10: 6; 12: 7–8. Field X: Bierling 1998: pls. 1: 1–3 (VIIB); 3: 1–4 (VIIA); 5: 1–4 (VIB); 6: 2; 7: 1–3 (VIA).	Area G: Dothan and Porath 1993: figs. 14: 9–23; 16: 7–10, 12–13 (XIIIb); 19: 6, 11, 13 (XIIIa). Area H: Dothan 1971: fig. 84: 1–4.	Mountjoy 2005b: fig. 5: 1, 8: 20, 9: 36–8: 15: 66 (IIIB Early).	Mountjoy 2005c: fig. 8: 156–85, 9: 186–211, 10: 212–56.
FS 295 (and 296); shallow angular bowl (Type A)/carinated bowl	Field I: Killebrew 1998a: figs. 7: 4–6 (VII); 10: 3–4 (VI). (Both band decoration and plain). Field X: pl. 6: 1 (VIA).	Area G: Dothan and Porath 1993: figs. 14: 24–6; 16: 11 (XIIIb). Area H: Dothan 1971: fig. 84: 7–8.	Mountjoy 2005b: fig. 9: 39; 14: 62 (IIIB Early).	Mountjoy 2005c: fig. 15: 372–96.
FS 295; shallow angular bowl (Type B)	–	Area G: Dothan and Porath 1993: figs. 19: 10; 20: 3, 6 (XIIIa). Area H: –		
FS 282; ring-base krater/bell-shaped krater	General: – Field I: Killebrew 1998a: figs. 7: 14–15; 10: 17; 12: 13. Field X: Bierling 1998: pls. 1: 5; 2: 2 (VIIB); 3: 6–11 (VIIA).	Area G: Dothan and Porath 1993: figs. 15: 11 (XIIIb); 21: 1–6; 22: 1; 24: 1, 12 (XIIIa). Area H: Dothan 1971: fig. 84: 10, 12.	Mountjoy 2005b: fig. 4: 1; 6: 17, 8: 29 (IIIB Early).	Mountjoy 2005c: fig. 7: 131–51, 8: 152–5.
FS 289; deep bowl with vertical handles	–	–		Mountjoy 2005c: fig. 14: 368–9.
FS 294; basin/medium-sized or large round-sided bowl	Field I: Killebrew 1998a: fig. 10: 9; 12: 6 (?) (VI). Field IV (Dothan and Zukerman 2004: fig. 5: 1, 3 (VIIA, VIIIB).	–	–	Mountjoy 2005c: fig. 14: 370–1.
FS 304; spouted basin				Mountjoy 2005c: fig. 15: 397.
FS 215; cup	Field I: Killebrew 1998a: fig. 10: 7 (VI). Field X: –	Area H: Dothan and Zukerman 2004: fig. 27: 6 (XIIB).	–	Mountjoy 2005c: fig. 5: 71–2.
FS 226; mug				Mountjoy 2005c: fig. 5: 73.
FS 267–77; kylix (?)	Field I: Dothan and Zukerman 2004: fig. 27: 2 (VIIA).	Area G: Dothan and Porath 1993: fig. 17: 7 (XIIIb). Area H: Dothan and Zukerman 2004: fig. 27: 1.	FS 267–77 (Mountjoy 2005b: fig. 14: 60 (IIIB Early).	Mountjoy 2005c: fig. 17: 417

(continued)

TABLE 7.2 *(continued)*

Type of Aegean-style pottery (FS; name according to Mountjoy 1986 or according to Dothan 1982; Killebrew 1998a; Dothan and Zukerman 2004)	Tel Miqne/Ekron[a]	Ashdod	Enkomi (Levels IIIA and IIIB Early)	Tarsus (Mountjoy 2005c)
FS 242; one-handled conical bowl	–	–	–	Mountjoy 2005c: figs. 5: 74–82, 6: 83–122, 7: 123–7.
FS 322; tray	Field I: Killebrew 1998a: fig. 10: 1, 2 (?) (VI).	Area G: Dothan and Porath 1993: fig. 16: 14 (XIIIb).	–	
FS 162; feeding bottle/basket handle jug; no parallels in MP	Field I: Killebrew 1998a: figs. 6: 31 (VII); 10: 20, 22 (VI). Field X: Bierling 1998: pls. 1: 6 (?) (VIIB); 7: 8–9, 11 (VIA)	Area G: Dothan and Porath 1993: fig. 15: 4, 10 (XIIIb). Area H: –	Dikaios 1971: pl. 72: 16 (IIIA).	Mountjoy 2005c: fig. 3: 45–6.
FS 155; strainer jug/strainer spouted jug ("beer jug")	General: – Field I: – Field X: Bierling 1998: pl. 7: 7 (VIA).	Area G: Dothan and Porath 1993: fig. 17: 10 (XIIIb). Area H: –	Mountjoy 2005b: figs. 8: 21, 10: 47, 14: 57 (IIIB Early).	Mountjoy 2005c: fig. 3: 42–4.
FS 174–7; stirrup jars	General: – Field I: Killebrew 1998a: fig. 10: 21 (VI). Field X: Bierling 1998: pl. 6: 5,6 (VIA).	Area G: Dothan and Porath 1993: figs. 17: 8, 9 (XIIIb). Area H: –	Mountjoy 2005b: figs. 6: 15; 7: 18; 15: 63–4 (IIIB Early).	Mountjoy 2005c: fig. 4: 47–66.
Straight-sided alabastron/pyxis	Field I: Dothan and Zukerman 2004: fig. 30: 9.	–	Mountjoy 2005b: fig. 10: 46 (IIIB Early).	
FS 49; piriform jar				Mountjoy 2005c: fig. 1: 7.
FS 63, 64; collar-neck jar			Mountjoy 2005b: fig. 9: 32 (?) (IIIB Early).	Mountjoy 2005c: fig. 1: 12–17.
FS 115, 118; jugs	Field I:[b] Dothan and Zukerman 2004: fig. 27: 9–13, 15, 16 (VIIa). Field IV: Dothan and Zukerman 2004: fig. 27: 14.	Area G: Dothan and Porath 1993: fig. 13: 5 (XIIIB).	–	Mountjoy 2005c: figs. 1: 18; 2: 19–26; 3: 27–41.
FS 59, 60; amphoriskoi		Area G: Dothan and Porath 1993: fig. 23: 4 (XIIIa).	Dikaios 1971: pl. 75: 37 (IIIA).	Mountjoy 2005c: fig. 1: 8–11.

Type of Aegean-style pottery (FS; name according to Mountjoy 1986 or according to Dothan 1982; Killebrew 1998a; Dothan and Zukerman 2004)	Tel Miqne/Ekron[a]	Ashdod	Enkomi (Levels IIIA and IIIB Early)	Tarsus (Mountjoy 2005c)
FS 186, 191, 193, or local "Canaanite" pilgrim flask; flasks	Field I: Killebrew 1998a: fig. 7: 21 (VI). Field X: Bierling 1998: pl. 3: 20 (VIIA).	Area G: Dothan and Porath 1993: fig. 23: 8 (XIIIa). Area H: Dothan 1971: fig. 84: 17 (XIII).	–	Mountjoy 2005c: fig. 4: 67–70.
FS 291; fineware decorated kalathos	Field I: Killebrew 1998a: fig. 7: 16 (?) (VII). Dothan and Zukerman 2004: fig. 25: 5–6.	–	FS 291 Dikaios 1971: pl. 74: 2 (IIIA).	–
Coarseware kalathos/basin	Field I: Killebrew 1998a: figs. 6: 25; 7: 17, 18 (VII); 10: 11; 12: 14 (VI). Area X: Bierling 1998: pl. 3: 12, 13 (VIIA).	Area G: Dothan and Porath 1993: figs. 16: 15 (XIIIb); 24: 2 (?) (XIIIa). Area H: Dothan 1971: fig. 90: 10 (XIII)	Dikaios 1969: pl. 120: 2 (IIIB).	–
Cooking jug/amphora	Field I: Killebrew 1998a: figs. 7: 19 (VII); 10: 13, 14; 12: 15 (VI). Field X: Bierling 1998: pls. 1: 7 (VIIB); 3: 14 (VIIA); 5: 5 (VIB); 6: 7, 8 (VIA).	Area G: Dothan and Porath 1993: figs. 17: 4, 5 (XIIIb); 23: 5, 6, 7 (XIIIa).	–	Goldman 1956: 217, nos. 1220–1.

[a] For additional examples of the types from Tel Miqne/Ekron and Ashdod, see Dothan and Zukerman 2004.

[b] As the jugs from Philistia are very fragmentary, assignment to FS is tentative.

TABLE 7.3. *A comparison between functional groups of Aegean-style and Canaanite pottery*

Type	Function	Aegean-style form	Local, Canaanite form
Small, open containers (e.g., bowls, cups)	Food and drink serving	+	+
Large, open containers (kraters)	Food and drink serving; food preparation	+	+
Cooking pots	Cooking; food preparation	+	+
Small and medium-sized, closed containers (e.g., juglets, jugs)	Storage (valuable liquids); food and drink serving	+	+
Large, closed containers (jars, pithoi)	Storage (liquids and dry commodities)	–	+
Stands	Storage	+ (?)	+ (?)
Lamps	Lighting	+ (bowls used as lamps)	+

Note: + = present; − = absent

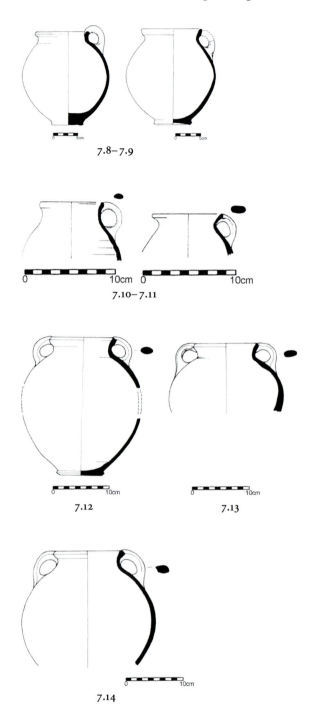

7.8–7.9

7.10–7.11

7.12   7.13

7.14

FIGURE 7.8–7.9. Tel Miqne/Ekron (Dothan 1998a: fig. 5: 16, 17)
FIGURE 7.10–7.11. Tel Miqne/Ekron Field X, Stratum VIa (Dothan 1998b: pl. 6: 7, 8)
FIGURE 7.12 Ashdod Area G, Stratum XIIIa (after Dothan and Porath 1993: fig. 23: 6)
FIGURE 7.13. Ashdod Area G, Stratum XIIIb (after Dothan and Porath 1993: fig. 17: 5)
FIGURE 7.14. Ashdod Area G, Stratum XIIIb (after Dothan and Porath 1993: fig. 17: 4)

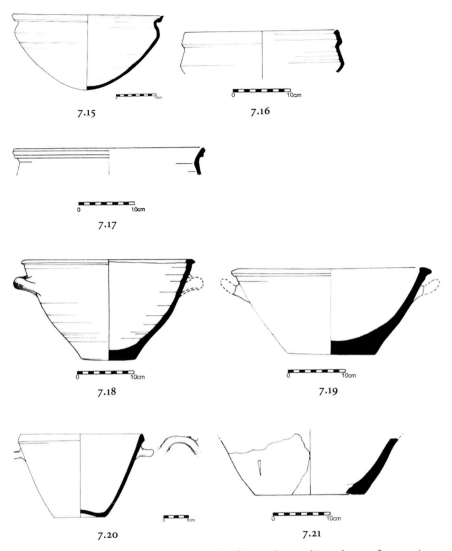

FIGURE 7.15. Ashdod Area G, Stratum XIIIb (after Dothan and Porath 1993: fig. 12: 10)
FIGURE 7.16. Ashdod Area G, Stratum XIIIb (after Dothan and Porath 1993: fig. 17: 3)
FIGURE 7.17. Tel Miqne/Ekron Field X, Stratum VIIb (after Dothan 1998b: pl. 1: 14)
FIGURE 7.18. Ashdod Area H, Stratum XII (after Dothan 1971: fig. 90: 10)
FIGURE 7.19. Tel Miqne/Ekron Field X, Stratum VIIa (after Dothan 1998b: pl. 3: 13)
FIGURE 7.20. Tel Miqne/Ekron (after Dothan 1998a: fig. 5: 15)
FIGURE 7.21. Ashdod Area G, Stratum XIIIa (after Dothan and Porath 1993: fig. 23: 13)

jugs are rather small, with one or two handles extending from shoulder to lip, and a ring or flat base. There are numerous close Aegean parallels for this form (Chapter 5; Figs. 5.10–22), yet because of the paucity of comparative studies of the typology of Aegean cooking ware, it is difficult to assess the exact origin within the Aegean world of the cooking jugs from Philistia. It can be said that they did not come from Crete, where the predominant type of closed cooking vessel was the tripod, and another common type had a flat base and no legs.[5]

As for basins, typologically, these may have been undecorated plainware versions of FS 291, a decorated fineware kalathos (see Tables 7.1–7.2; Figs. 7.18–21; Mountjoy 1986: 152, fig. 195; 179, fig. 232). However, the crudity of some of the vessels and the fact that they are not decorated caused Sherratt (1998: 305) and Killebrew (2000: 239–40) to dismiss the possibility of an Aegean origin of the vessels. It is uncertain whether the vessels were always associated with food preparation. Judging from their appearance, Dothan (1998a: 154; cf. 1998b: 23) reasonably identifies them as kitchenware. However, there is no other supportive evidence for this identification. Sherratt (1998: 303) proposes an unspecified "industrial use" for the vessels, although they do not seem to appear in a clear industrial context.

COOKING INSTALLATIONS: HEARTHS, OVENS, AND *TABUNS*

TEL MIQNE/EKRON

The use of both types of cooking pots – local and Aegean – can be understood against the background of different traditions of cooking installations: hearths, representing an Aegean tradition, and *tabun*s, representing a local, Canaanite one. The use of hearths (which probably had multiple uses: for cooking and heating and as a ceremonial center in the main room of the building; see "The Organization of Domestic Space") is a nonlocal feature that many scholars have discussed (Mazar 1986, 1988: 257–60; Stager 1995: 347; Dothan 1998a; Karageorghis 1998b).

While the hearths from Tel Miqne/Ekron await final publication, Dothan (1998a: 155–7) and Mazow (2005: 203) mention the presence of two types of hearths: freestanding, rectangular hearths and round ones paved with pebbles. Rectangular hearths (Figs. 5.1–6) made of mud or mud bricks and paved with sherds are a very common feature of LH/LMIIIC sites (Chapter 5) and LHIIIB *Korridorhaus*-type buildings, yet they are not unique to them. Rectangular hearths appear also in Tarsus in the Late Bronze IIA level, affiliated with the era of the Hittite Empire (Chapter 5), but not in the Late Bronze IIB level, where locally made LHIIIC pottery appears along with Aegean-style cooking pots. These hearths appear also on Cyprus in LCIIC and become

---

[5] These were possibly derived from a much earlier Minoan flat-based cooking pot (Borgna 1997: 207–8) or from the LHIIIB flat-based "Mycenaean" cooking pots (with handles between the body and the shoulder of the vase). See Borgna (1997: 195, fig. 4) for an example from Phaistos; Coulson and Tsipopoulou (1994: 80, fig. 15: 2) for Halasmenos; B. P. Hallager (2000: 158–9) and Tzedakis and Martlew (1999: 102, no. 72) for Kastelli, Chania; Rethimiotakis (1997: 308, fig. 8) for Kastelli Pediada.

FIGURE 7.22. Tel Miqne/Ekron Field IV, Strata VIIa–b (after Dothan 2003: fig. 4)

much more common in LCIIIA (Chapter 5). Therefore, rectangular hearths alone cannot be used to trace the origin of influence. However, the presence of Aegean-style cooking jugs at both Ashdod and Tel Miqne/Ekron, as well as the absence of local, Cypriot- or Anatolian-type cooking vessels at the sites, side by side with the appearance of rectangular hearths, points to the Aegean area as their source. Round hearths appeared in LHIIIB palatial contexts, at the center of large megaron rooms, but also in smaller structures, such as LHIIIB2 Room 123 at Tiryns (Kilian 1981: 58). Evidence of LHIIIC round hearths is scant, as most hearths are rectangular, subrectangular, or oval. However, paved bases of round ovens, of the type found at Lefkandi Phase 2 (Popham, Schofield, and Sherratt 2006: fig. 1.32), may be remains of round hearths whose superstructure had eroded. On Cyprus, round hearths appear in LCIIC (Chapter 5) and possibly continue to LCIIIA. Round hearths in Late Bronze Age structures at Beycesultan (Werner 1993: fig. 55a, b) make Anatolia another candidate for the origin of this form of hearth.

A freestanding rectangular hearth appears in the small, one-room Building 357 (Fig. 7.22), starting in Stratum VIIa or VIIb, (Dothan 2003: fig. 4; Mazow 2005: fig. 5.2). Two pillar bases flanked the hearth, and two benches running along the room's long walls allowed for seating on both its sides. Building 357 was incorporated into a larger unit in Strata VIa and VIb, but a separate entrance was maintained (Mazow 2005: fig. 5.3–4). The hearth was of built of mud bricks and paved with pebbles and sherds. Another example of a likely hearth was found in Building 353, Stratum VI, in Field IV, with a bathtub at its side and a monolith incorporated into it (Dothan 2003: fig. 14; Mazow 2005: fig. 5.3; Fig. 7.23). Round hearths seem to have been peculiar to Tel Miqne/Ekron and do not appear at other sites. With a diameter of 0.5–1.5 meters, one pebble hearth was found in Stratum VIIa and four were found in Stratum VIb, all clustered in the large front room area of Buildings 353 and 354 (Mazow 2005: 220, fig. 5.3). It is interesting to note that nowhere do pebble and rectangular hearths coappear in the same structure; this suggests that their function was similar. Both fire installations appear mostly indoors (Mazow 2005: 320).

*Tabun*s, circular ovens made of clay, exist in Field IV, but although they reflect a local, Canaanite cooking and baking tradition going back at least to the Middle Bronze Age, they first appear only in Stratum VIa (Mazow 2005: 229, fig. 5.4). One was found in an open area by Room 360 and the other inside Room 351d. *Tabun*s also appear in the more humble, domestic area of Field X, where they are reported in Stratum VII (*tabun*s 78028 and 77042; Dothan, Bierling, and Gitin 1998: 14) and Stratum VI (*tabun* 77028; Dothan, Bierling, and Gitin 1998: 15). These *tabun*s seem to be either freestanding or built against walls. Remarkably, no hearths have been reported from this field. In any case, the find of *tabun*s in Iron Age I strata is a clear indication of the concurrent use of both Aegean and local cooking installations at Tel Miqne/Ekron.

ASHDOD

In Ashdod Area G, Stratum XIIIb, there are two examples of rectangular hearths built of mud or mud bricks and plastered with *hamra* – one inside the main hall of the complex Installation 4328 (Dothan and Porath 1993: 53, 54–5; Fig. 5.23) and the other outside it (Installation 4242; Dothan and Porath 1993: 54; Fig. 7.123). Ash found on and around the two hearths indicates that they were heavily used. A photograph of Installation 4242 (Dothan and Porath 1993: pl. 14: 3) shows that it was at least partially paved with sherds. Cooking pots in Strata XIIIb and XIIIa were found nearby on the floor (Dothan and Porath 1993: figs. 17: 6 and 27: 7), perhaps indicating that the installation was used for cooking in Stratum XIII. In addition to the hearths, other types of cooking installations appear in Area G, Stratum XIIIa. The most conspicuous is a *tabun* (Installation 4113; Dothan and Porath 1993: 61, pl. 17: 3). Another probable cooking installation is Installation 4255 (Dothan and Porath 1993: 61, pl. 17: 1), which consists of two parallel rows of bricks with much ash between them. Although the authors suggest that it was used for industrial

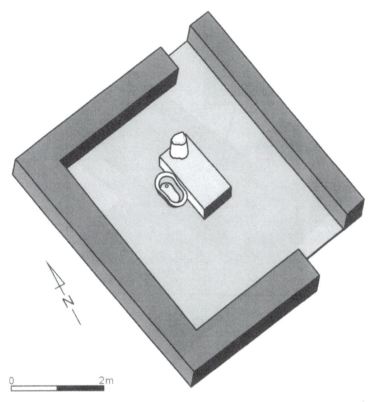

FIGURE 7.23. Tel Miqne/Ekron Field IV, Stratum VIa (after Dothan 2003: fig. 14)

purposes, no refuse or other indicator of industry was found; it may be another oven or a stand for grilling meat. Installation 4264 in Room 4262 (Dothan and Porath 1993: 61, pl. 16: 1), a flat stone enclosed on three sides by other stones, was also identified as a cooking installation by the excavators, yet they reported no ash or burn marks from it. A similar installation is known from the LHIIIC Stadt Haus D 1 in Tiryns (Hiesel 1990: 34), with numerous parallels in the Cretan pi-shaped cooking ovens or hearths frequent at LM sites such as Kommos (M. Shaw 1990: 248–54) and even more frequent in the LMIIIC period at Halasmenos, Kavousi, and Kastelli, Chania (E. Hallager 2000: 129). Its position beside a wall is similar to the position of the majority of the Cretan LMIIIC ovens. Shaw (1990) states, however, that such installations also appear at non-Cretan sites in the eastern Mediterranean, such as at Marsa Matruh.

A fine example of a rectangular hearth is in Area H, Stratum XII, where it stands between two pillar bases (Dothan 2003: fig. 10; Mazar and Ben-Shlomo 2005: plan 2.6; Fig. 7.24). The presence of hearths and a *tabun* in Ashdod at Area G indicates the contemporaneous use of both Aegean and local cooking traditions, similar to the situation at Tel Miqne/Ekron. The rather simple shape of the other cooking installations from Ashdod, and the fact that they are the only examples of these types that have been published, makes their present attribution to either local or foreign origin uncertain.

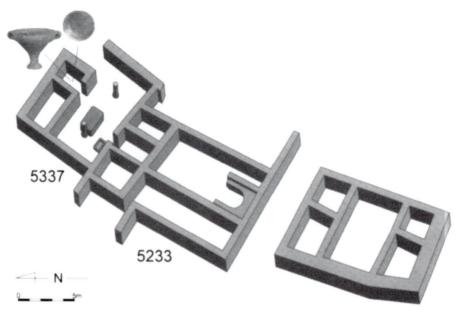

FIGURE 7.24. Ashdod Area H, Stratum XII (after Dothan 2003: fig. 10)

ASHKELON

Rectangular and subrectangular hearths first appear in Ashkelon in Grid 38, Phase 19 – the second Philistine phase at the site (Fig. 7.25). Central rectangular hearths marked the interior room of the four units excavated, in Rooms 25, 1033, 873, and 725 (Dothan 2003: fig. 15; Master 2005: 344; Stager et al. 2008: fig. 15.22). Another hearth was found attached to the north wall of Room 1023. *Tabun*s do not appear in Phase 19, and only a single *tabun* was found in Phase 20 (Stager et al. 2008: fig. 15.10). Later, in Phase 18, datable to the eleventh century BCE, additional forms of hearths appear, such as the keyhole hearth in Room 910 and the round hearth in Room 667 (Master 2005: 345; Stager et al. 2008: fig. 15.22).

TELL ES-ṢAFI/GATH

Rounded pebble hearths are reported from late Iron I strata at Tell es-Ṣafi/Gath (Ben-Shlomo et al. 2008: 236), similar to the ones found at Tel Miqne/Ekron.

FORM, FUNCTION, AND VARIABILITY IN COOKING TRADITIONS

The traditions of Aegean cooking pots and of Canaanite cooking pots display differences not only in appearance and origin but also in use (Yasur-Landau 1992; Killebrew 1992; 1998a: 397; 1999: 106–8). The concave bases of the

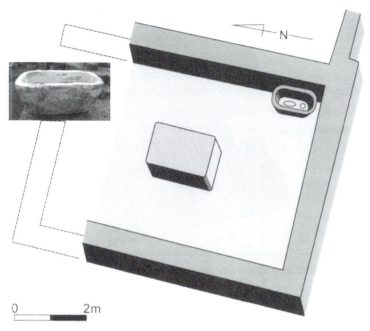

FIGURE 7.25. Ashkelon Phase 19, Room 25 (after Dothan 2003: fig. 17)

Canaanite cooking pots (Fig. 7.15) were most likely designed to rest on the uneven surface of a fire pit or even on the restricted top of a round oven (*tabun*). The wide mouth of the vessels provided easy access to the food and allowed for many methods of food preparation (e.g., boiling, simmering, frying). In contrast, the Aegean cooking jugs have a base appropriate for flat surfaces, probably intended to stand on the hearth – another Aegean feature introduced at the same time. A further clue to the distinctive use of the Aegean cooking jugs is presented by the blackening on the side of many of the jugs, both in the Levant and in the Aegean world (Chapter 5; Figs. 5.23–7). This may suggest that, similar to their use patterns in the Aegean area, they were placed on the side of the hearth, perhaps on the embers, exposing one side to direct fire and higher temperatures. Their use may have been similar to that in the Aegean (Chapter 5): multipurpose vessels used for both cooking and warming beverages.

Aegean tripod cooking pots were designed to stand on an uneven surface, perhaps above direct fire or in the central area of a hearth (Yasur-Landau 2003–4). No locally made examples of this most indicative of Aegean cooking wares are known either on Cyprus or in Philistia from sites where cooking jugs were found. The absence of tripod cooking pots, and perhaps also braziers, from the assemblages in Philistia may be because other solutions existed for cooking on direct fire and on uneven surfaces. The Canaanite wide-mouth cooking pot with convex base was fit for cooking on direct fire and highly stable, and it had considerable advantages over the tripod cooking pot: it could be placed on the top of the round cooking installation of local origin (the *tannur/tabun*), and as mentioned earlier, it allowed for frying as well as boiling and simmering.

The ratio between Aegean cooking jugs and Canaanite cooking pots changes through time at Tel Miqne/Ekron Field IV: in Stratum VIIb, 95 percent of the cooking vessels are cooking jugs and only 5 percent are Canaanite cooking pots. The ratio of the Canaanite cooking pots grows to about 10 percent in Strata VIIa and VIb and to about 20 percent in Stratum VIa (Mazow 2005: 156). Only in Stratum V do Canaanite cooking pots become the majority of the vessels.

ASSESSING THE DEGREE OF CHANGE

There was a sharp change in cooking traditions between the Late Bronze Age and the Early Iron Age at Ashdod, Ashkelon, and Tel Miqne/Ekron. The change was not merely in the typology of the cooking pots but also in their function. All cooking activities were affected with the introduction of a new cooking installation, the hearth, and the specialized cooking vessel that was used with it. The changes were accompanied by changes in the foodstuffs themselves: much more pork and beef were consumed (Chapter 8), and new types of plants may have come into intensive use. The changes in virtually every aspect of foodways occurred over a short period of time and can therefore be defined as a deep change (Chapter 1). They resulted from interaction with the Aegean world and could not have resulted from technological innovation, economic change, or fashion alone. For example, changes in the proportion of available pigs and available cattle would not have resulted in the introduction of new cookware and installations.

As demonstrated in Chapter 1, the conservative qualities of foodways, the low status connected with everyday food preparation, and the strong sense of identity and worldviews associated with food make deep change in foodways an excellent indicator of migration (Chapter 1). In the historical and archaeological case studies examined here, migrants invested considerable energy in maintaining, as much as possible, their old foodways. They cooked their familiar dishes in methods familiar to them; they imported familiar foodstuffs or grew them locally, sometimes introducing new plants; they used special cooking and serving utensils, either imported or locally made. Virtually all of these changes are seen in Philistia. The presence of people from the realm of Aegean culture is not merely the most suitable explanation for these changes, it is the only one that can account for the sudden appearance of Aegean foodways.

At the same time, the use of Canaanite cooking pots reflects an important continuity in the local cooking habits, which are seen in the use of local *tabun*s. The fact that Canaanite and Aegean-style cooking vessels always appear together indicates that Aegean and local, Canaanite behavioral patterns were conducted side by side from the very beginning of the appearance of Aegean material culture traits.

PATTERNS OF USE OF THE POTTERY ASSEMBLAGE: STORING AND SERVING FOOD AND DRINK IN AEGEAN AND LOCAL STYLES

QUESTIONS AND TERMINOLOGY

Similar to the case of the cooking vessels of both Aegean and Canaanite traditions, every Early Iron Age assemblage gleaned from Ashdod, Ashkelon, and Tel Miqne/Ekron contained a mixture of serving and storage vessels from both traditions. This co-occurrence has significant implications for understanding the social processes in twelfth-century Philistia; thus, each pottery tradition first has to be examined individually rather than in comparison with the other tradition. Although the appearance of local, Canaanite pottery forms unfortunately has been largely taken for granted and not subjected to functional or social analysis and interpretation, the local manufacture of fineware in the forms and motifs stemming from LHIIIC Aegean traditions attracted much attention, and three main approaches have dominated interpretations of this production:

1. Dothan and Zukerman (2004), Stager (1995), Bunimovitz and Yasur-Landau (1996), and others (see also Chapter 1) argue for some form of migration from the Aegean world as an explanation for the local production of both fineware and coarseware in the Aegean tradition.

2. Sherratt (1992; 1998) and others argue that demand for fineware on Cyprus and in the Levant in the twelfth century resulted from the formation of a regional traders' circle and led to the manufacture of Aegean fineware that suited the tastes of the new class. Sherratt's economically based reconstruction, focusing mainly on fineware production, seriously challenges those who favor a migrationist explanation for the phenomenon of the locally made Monochrome/Mycenaean IIIC: 1b pottery in the Levant.

3. Killebrew (1998a) brings another proposal challenging the idea of migration from the Aegean, arguing for migration from Cyprus and/or Cilicia. Killebrew (2000: 243) asserts that the Mycenaean IIIC: 1b made in Canaan is almost identical to that of Cyprus and differs significantly from the pottery made in the Aegean proper with respect to the variety of shapes, decorative motifs, and associated cookware. Killebrew (1998a: 397) views the locally made Mycenaean IIIC: 1b as representing "only a select and limited repertoire of Aegean Mycenaean IIIB and IIIC shapes known from the Aegean. The repertoire is based on Late Helladic and Late Minoan IIIA and IIIB drinking sets and does not include the complete corpus known from the Aegean." This approach was somewhat modified later to suggest that the migration was of Aegean people who had already spent several generations on Cyprus (Killebrew 2006: 231).

One way to test Sherratt's reconstruction is to pay attention to more indicative behavioral patterns, such as cooking and weaving, which she treats minimally in her analysis. Another way is to reexamine the form or forms of interaction that may have led to the local production of Aegean forms. Here, the published ceramic assemblages of Tel Miqne/Ekron and Ashdod are analyzed according to functional categories of the vessels and according to their affiliation with local or Aegean forms. To test Killebrew's conclusion that the locally made LHIIIC forms are mainly drinking sets,[6] the variety of locally made forms (Tables 7.2 and 7.3) is compared to the variety of imported forms in LHIIIB and to the LHIIIC assemblages at three Aegean sites: domestic assemblages at Lefkandi and Emporio, and the shrine and street assemblages at Phylakopi.[7]

As for terminology, I prefer here the term *LHIIIC-style* (Yasur-Landau 2006) for pottery made in Aegean forms mainly during the twelfth century BCE, outside the Aegean world, to the terms *Mycenaean IIIC: 1b* or *Mycenaean IIIC: 1*, which are often used to describe this pottery on Cyprus (Kling 1989) and in Philistia (Dothan and Zukerman 2004). The term *Mycenaean IIIC: 1b* indicates an affinity with Aegean mainland production, which is not necessarily the case for pottery made on Cyprus, in Cilicia, or in the southern Levant; the term also preserves Furumark's antiquated division of the Aegean pottery sequence, which has been completely replaced by divisions of LHIIIC into three to five parts (e.g., Mountjoy 1999a: 38–41). A similarly thorny problem is embedded in the ethnically laden terms *Philistine Monochrome* (the same ceramic ware as *Mycenaean IIIC: 1*) and *Philistine Bichrome* (cf. Dothan and Zukerman 2004: 2). The same terms were replaced by *Philistine 1* and *Philistine 2* by Dothan and colleagues (2006). Killebrew (2000) steered clear of the "ethnically charged" term *Mycenaean IIIC: 1b* by renaming the Mycenaean IIIC: 1b forms from Canaan *AS* (for "Aegean style"). However, to avoid further confusion, I use the term *LHIIIC-style pottery* together with the more familiar terms *(Philistine) Monochrome* and *(Philistine) Bichrome*.

Much research has been dedicated to the comparison between Aegean pottery and Philistine Bichrome and Monochrome. The most comprehensive work is that of Dothan (1982), which now serves as the cornerstone for such study. Dothan's work includes a set of typological terms, and later studies have contributed additional names to describe locally made, Aegean-inspired pottery. Here, for convenience of comparing the Aegean material and the locally made LHIIIC forms, I use primarily Furumark's shapes (FS) and Mountjoy's (1986; 1993) terminology to describe the forms of Aegean

---

[6] The production of these drinking sets was perhaps encouraged by the sharp decline in the importation of Mycenaean pottery after the end of the LHIIIB.

[7] The argument for a Cypriot/Cilician origin of the assemblage is addressed in a general discussion on the origin of the migration in Chapter 8.

descent.[8] However, to allow for comparisons to works by Dothan (1982) and Killebrew (1998a), I also use their terminology to refer to the locally produced shapes. Pottery of local (Canaanite) shapes is described in the terminology used by the excavators of the sites.

LHIIIC-STYLE POTTERY: LOCAL PRODUCTION OF TRADED POTTERY OR A DOMESTIC ASSEMBLAGE?

STIRRUP JARS AND STRAIGHT-SIDED ALABASTRA

In comparing the entirety of types of LHIIIC-style pottery at Tel Miqne/Ekron and the Ashdod assemblages and a sample of the Aegean-style pottery from Ashkelon (Tables 7.2 and 7.3) with the types of the Aegean pottery imports to the southern Levant in LHIIIB, one can see many pronounced differences in nature and quantity.[9] In contrast, there is a similarity between the assemblages of Philistia and contemporary LHIIIC ones. Aegean material from Tel Miqne/Ekron and Ashdod represents more or less complete LHIIIC assemblages rather than local imitations of foreign traded items.

By far, the most common types of LHIIIB imports to the southern Levant are small stirrup jars (Leonard 1994: 50–66). These types continued to dominate the trade in Cypriot LHIIIC-style pottery in the early Iron Age I (Chapter 6), though on a more limited scale. Contrary to what might be expected had local production replaced imported items, stirrup jars appear in rather small quantities in twelfth-century Ashdod and Tel Miqne/Ekron (Killebrew 1998a: 397; Dothan and Zukerman 2004: fig. 31; Ben-Shlomo 2006a: 42; Table 7.2; Figs. 7.26–.28). This fits well with the fewer stirrup jars found in domestic LHIIIC assemblages at Emporio (Hood 1982: 606–7 nos. 2845–51, fig. 273 [Stage 7, II. Rare]) and Lefkandi.[10] A low percentage of stirrup jars in the assemblage is also seen in Phases 2b–3c of the shrine and adjacent street at Phylakopi (mainly LHIIIC Middle), where only 14 sherds of a total 321 diagnostic, decorated sherds were of stirrup jars (about 4 percent) (Mountjoy 1985: 187, table 5.5).

A similar case is presented by FS 94–95 and 96 – the straight-sided alabastra. This type was a rather common import to the southern Levant, with nineteen

---

[8] In reference to the Aegean pottery from Cyprus, on the danger of introducing new pottery terms and the resulting terminological confusion and overlap in wares, see Cadogan 1993: 96.

[9] Initial publication of a sample of pottery from Ashkelon Phases 20 and 19 (Stager et al. 2008: figs. 15.11–13, 15.23) may indicate that the variety of forms in Ashkelon is similar to that of Ekron and Ashdod. Further observations await a more detailed publication of these important assemblages.

[10] E.g., Popham and colleagues (2006: 147), referring to stirrup jars in the destruction level of Phase 1b, have observed that "the small number of sherds in the deposits demonstrates that this shape was not at all common." Their number increases in Phase 2a, but they still are uncommon (Popham et al. 2006: 165).

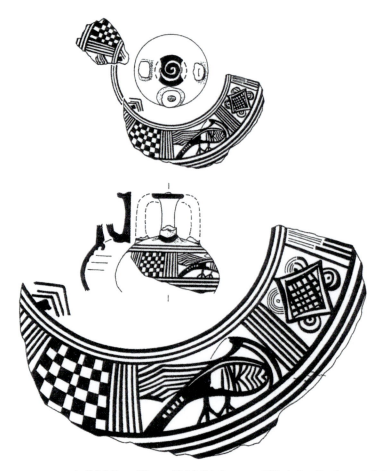

FIGURE 7.26. Tel Miqne/Ekron Field IV, Stratum VIb (after Dothan and Zukerman 2004: fig. 31: 3)

examples dated to the LHIIIA–LHIIIB or LHIIIB, eight of them found at Tell Abu Hawam (Leonard 1994: 36–9). The vessels are absent from Emporio, rather rare in Lefkandi,[11] and extremely rare in Phylakopi (less than 1 percent). They are almost entirely absent from Ashdod and Tel Miqne/Ekron, with one unstratified example from Tel Miqne/Ekron Field I (Dothan and Zukerman 2004: fig. 30: 9) and another round-sided variant of FS 96 (or rather FS 59; amphoriskos/pyxis; Table 7.2; Figs. 7.29 and 7.30) – the prototype of the later Bichrome pyxis (Dothan 1982: 125–31). Notably, this type of alabastron was locally produced at Ashdod as early as Late Bronze II (Area H, local Stratum XIV; Dothan 1971: fig. 81: 12).

---

[11] They are nearly absent from the Phase 1b destruction, with only two examples uncovered (Popham et al. 2006: 147), and they remain uncommon in Phase 2a (Popham et al. 2006: 164–5).

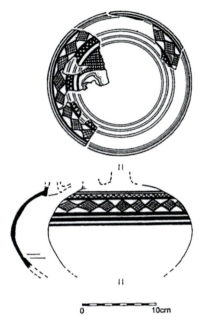

FIGURE 7.27. Tel Miqne/Ekron Field IV, Stratum VIb (after Dothan and Zukerman 2004: fig. 31: 4)

SPOUTED AND STRAINER JUGS

Spouted jug or feeding bottle FS 162 and strainer jug FS 155 appear in the LHIIIC-style repertoire at Ashdod and Tel Miqne/Ekron (Dothan and Zukerman 2004: 24–6; Ben-Shlomo 2006a: 42; Figs. 7.31–7; Table 7.2). Although they are thought to constitute an integral part of the wine-drinking sets of the LHIIIC-style pottery (Stager 1995: 345), they are totally absent from the LHIIIB and LHIIIC imports to the southern Levant (Leonard 1994: 44–5). Although spouted jugs were part of the LH tradition from at least LHIIIA1 (Mountjoy 1986: 61), strainer jugs are very rare in the Aegean repertoire before LHIIIC (Mountjoy 1986: table 3; see Mountjoy 1999a: 138 no. 246, for LHIIIB1 Prosymna); therefore, their frequent appearance in the locally

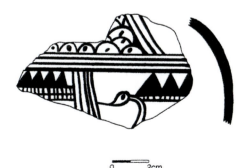

FIGURE 7.28. Tel Miqne/Ekron Field IV, Stratum VIb (after Dothan and Zukerman 2004: fig. 31: 5)

made LHIIIC assemblage of Philistia cannot be attributed to the influence of LHIIIB trade.

The complete examples from Philistia suggest that spouted jugs were furnished with a basket handle, while strainer jugs were equipped with a vertical handle running from below the rim to the shoulder (Dothan and Zukerman 2004: fig. 30). The decoration on the feeding bottles appears to have always been linear, while strainer jugs were decorated with a more varied array of motifs, from streamers to birds. This differentiation may indicate a different function for each vessel – the more elaborate strainer jugs perhaps were connected to more prestigious wine sets.

JUGS

Lip-handled jugs with both trefoil mouths and rounded mouths (FS 115, 118, 137?) (Dothan and Zukerman 2004: fig. 27: 8–16; Figs. 7.38–42; Table 7.2) were the only medium-sized containers made in the Aegean tradition in Philistia. No complete examples have been found, yet they appear to be considerably larger than the strainer and feeding jugs. As with their Aegean prototypes, their decoration is mostly linear.

DEEP (BELL-SHAPED) BOWLS

Deep bowls FS 284, 285 are the most common decorated fineware form in LHIIIC-style pottery from Philistia (Dothan and Zukerman 2004: figs. 8 and 9; Ben-Shlomo 2006a: 30; Table 7.2; Figs. 7.43–.55). This probably reflects an LHIIIC trend prevailing in the Aegean area: it seems that on the mainland, in the Cyclades, in the Dodecanese, and on Crete, despite the occurrence of cups and kylikes in many assemblages, deep bowls were by far the most common open form during LH/LMIIIC (Chapter 5; Thomatos 2006: 98). For example, they constitute 48.9 percent of the indicative sherds at Phylakopi (Mountjoy 1985: 185, table 5.5) and are overwhelmingly the most common pottery type in Lefkandi Phase 2 (Popham et al. 2006: 155). A similar phenomenon is seen in the LHIIIC assemblage from Tarsus, in which deep bowls are the dominant group (Mountjoy 2005c).

Typologically, the body of deep bowls is tall and bell shaped, with a delicate, everted rim. Most bell-shaped bowls have a linear decoration on their interior and exterior, and frequently have a spiral drawn at the bottom of their interior. Their horizontal handles are often decorated with several strokes or dots of color. The color of decoration is dark brown or black, sometimes on a white or other light-colored slip. A good number of bowls, however, are decorated with more elaborate geometric patterns, such as triglyphs, tongues/streamers, or spirals, and only rarely with figurative patterns such as birds or fish.

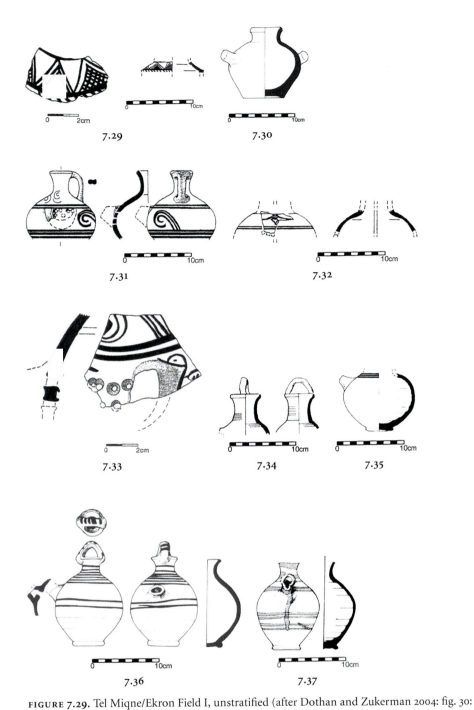

7.29

7.30

7.31

7.32

7.33

7.34

7.35

7.36

7.37

FIGURE 7.29. Tel Miqne/Ekron Field I, unstratified (after Dothan and Zukerman 2004: fig. 30: 9)

FIGURE 7.30. Ashdod Area G, Stratum XIIIa (after Dothan and Porath 1993: fig. 23: 4)

FIGURE 7.31. Tel Miqne/Ekron Field IV, Stratum VIb (after Dothan and Zukerman 2004: fig. 30: 1)

FIGURE 7.32. Tel Miqne/Ekron Field I, Stratum VIIa (after Dothan and Zukerman 2004: fig. 30: 2)

FIGURE 7.33. Ashdod Area G, Stratum XIIIb (after Dothan and Porath 1993: fig. 17: 10)

FIGURE 7.34. Tel Miqne/Ekron Field I (after Killebrew 1998a: fig. 6: 31)

FIGURE 7.35. Tel Miqne/Ekron. Field I (after Killebrew 1998a: fig. 10: 22)

FIGURE 7.36. Ashdod Area G, Stratum XIIIb (after Dothan and Porath 1993: fig. 15: 10)

FIGURE 7.37. Ashdod Area G, Stratum XIIIb (after Dothan and Porath 1993: fig. 15: 4)

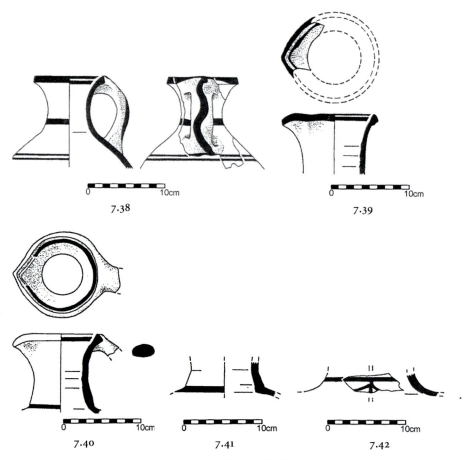

7.38   7.39

7.40   7.41   7.42

FIGURE 7.38 Ashdod Area G, Stratum XIIIb (after Dothan and Porath 1993: fig. 13: 5)

FIGURE 7.39 Tel Miqne/Ekron Field I, Stratum VIIa (after Dothan and Zukerman 2004: fig. 27: 10)

FIGURE 7.40 Tel Miqne/Ekron Field I, Stratum VIIa (after Dothan and Zukerman 2004: fig. 27: 11)

FIGURE 7.41 Tel Miqne/Ekron Field IV, Stratum VIIa (after Dothan and Zukerman 2004: fig. 27: 14)

FIGURE 7.42 Tel Miqne/Ekron Field IV, Stratum VIIa (after Dothan and Zukerman 2004: fig. 27: 15)

Deep bowls appear in different size categories, ranging from small (with a rim diameter of about eleven centimeters) to medium (about sixteen centimeters) to large (about twenty centimeters). Examples of this phenomenon have been found at Ashdod Area G, Stratum XIIIb, Locus 4106 (cf. Figs. 7.46 and 7.55, for the smaller examples).[12] The variability in size may reflect different uses, such as the type of beverage served or the disparity in status among participants in a feast. There are few examples of bell-shaped bowls with a solid painted monochrome interior – a feature common in the LHIIIC Aegean

[12] Small: Dothan and Porath 1993: fig. 14: 9, 17, 18; large: Dothan and Porath 1993: fig. 14: 21–3.

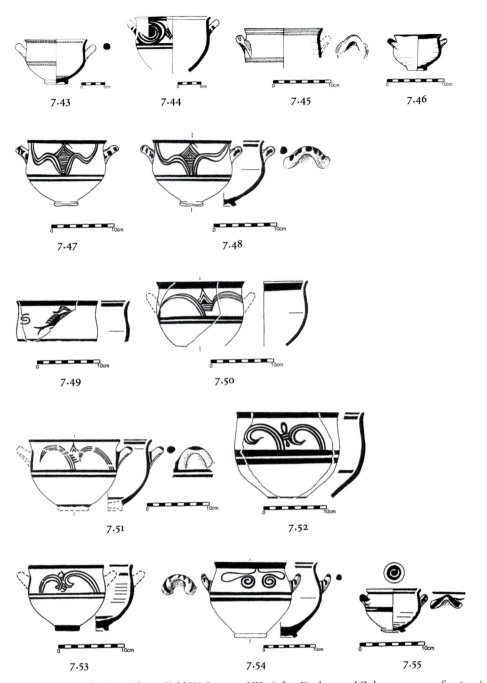

7·43   7·44   7·45   7·46

7·47   7·48

7·49   7·50

7·51   7·52

7·53   7·54   7·55

FIGURE 7.43 Tel Miqne/Ekron Field IV, Stratum VIIa (after Dothan and Zukerman 2004: fig. 6: 14)
FIGURE 7.44 Tel Miqne/Ekron Field I, Stratum VI (after Dothan and Zukerman 2004: fig. 6: 16)
FIGURE 7.45 Ashdod Area G, Stratum XIIIb (after Dothan and Porath 1993: fig. 14: 19)
FIGURE 7.46 Ashdod Area G, Stratum XIIIb (after Dothan and Porath 1993: fig. 14: 20)
FIGURE 7.47 Tel Miqne/Ekron Field IV, Stratum VIIa (after Dothan and Zukerman 2004: fig. 8: 7)
FIGURE 7.48 Tel Miqne/Ekron Field IV, Stratum VIIa (after Dothan and Zukerman 2004: fig. 8: 7)
FIGURE 7.49 Tel Miqne/Ekron Field I, Stratum VIIa (after Dothan and Zukerman 2004: fig. 8: 14)
FIGURE 7.50 Tel Miqne/Ekron Field I, Stratum VIIa (after Dothan and Zukerman 2004: fig. 8: 10)
FIGURE 7.51 Tel Miqne/Ekron Field IV, Stratum VIIa (after Dothan and Zukerman 2004: fig. 8: 11)
FIGURE 7.52 Tel Miqne/Ekron Field I, Stratum VI (after Dothan and Zukerman 2004: fig. 8: 12)
FIGURE 7.53 Tel Miqne/Ekron Field IV, Stratum VI (after Dothan and Zukerman 2004: fig. 8: 13)
FIGURE 7.54 Tel Miqne/Ekron Field IV, Stratum VIIb (after Dothan and Zukerman 2004: fig. 6: 19)
FIGURE 7.55 Ashdod Area G, Stratum XIIIb (after Dothan and Porath 1993: fig. 14: 17)

(e.g., Mountjoy 1999a: fig. 77: 194–9), yet rarely attested to in Philistia (e.g., an example from Tel Miqne/Ekron; Dothan and Zukerman 2004: fig. 7.8).

Despite its popularity in the LHIIIC Aegean and in Early Iron Age Philistia, the deep bowl is somewhat rare among LHIIIB imports, with only five known examples, excluding the thirteen found at Tell Abu Hawam (Leonard 1994: 117–21). It is therefore unlikely that trade contributed to the conspicuous presence of the bowls in twelfth-century Philistia.

SHALLOW ANGULAR BOWLS

Shallow angular bowls FS 295 are less frequent than bell-shaped bowls, yet still one of the most common types of LHIIIC-style fineware in Philistia (Figs. 7.56–61; Table 7.2; Dothan and Zukerman 2004: figs. 5: 10–11, 6: 1–5). Their relatively frequent occurrence corresponds to their popularity in the Aegean, where there are many undecorated LHIIIC examples (for Phylakopi, see Mountjoy 1985: 189, table 5.6, 192). Typologically, the examples from Philistia have a ring base and strap handles; many of the bowls are undecorated, and the painted examples always have linear decoration, often with a spiral on the bottom of the interior – a phenomenon known from the Argolid during LHIIIC Early and Middle (Mountjoy 1986: figs. 197: 1 and 233: 1–3). The decoration was applied in dark brown or black paint, sometimes on a light-colored or white slip. None of the vessels is decorated with more elaborate designs, reflecting a similar trend to that in other Philistine sites and in the Aegean (Mountjoy 1986: 13–154), as well as on Cyprus (e.g., Tomb 9 Upper Burial in Area I at Kition; Karageorghis 1974: pls. 74–89).

The simplicity of decoration on the vessels can be attributed to their use as eating bowls (Chapter 5), while the bell-shaped bowls, used for drinking (perhaps wine), were ampler media for the display of symbols and individuality in the context of symposia. As do bell-shaped bowls, shallow angular bowls appear in several size categories. Very small bowls were found at Ashdod Stratum XIIIa, Locus 4106 (Dothan and Porath 1993: fig. 14: 24; Figs. 7.59 and 7.60) and at Tel Miqne/Ekron Stratum VIIa (Dothan and Zukerman 2004: fig. 6: 5). Large shallow angular bowls, greater than twenty centimeters in diameter, have been published from Tel Miqne/Ekron Stratum VIb (Dothan and Zukerman 2004: fig. 5:10–11).

On Cyprus, a very similar bowl comes from Tomb 9 Upper Burial at Kition (Karageorghis 1974: pl. 69: 80), yet its spiral-decorated base is also found somewhat later, in Level IIIB Early at Enkomi (Mountjoy 2005b: fig. 14: 62).

Shallow angular bowls are more frequent than deep bowls among the LHIIIB imports into the Levant, with eleven examples, not including the twenty examples from Tell Abu Hawam (Leonard 1994: 123–6), yet their occurrence as imports is far from abundant, and they could hardly have sparked a massive wave of local imitations.

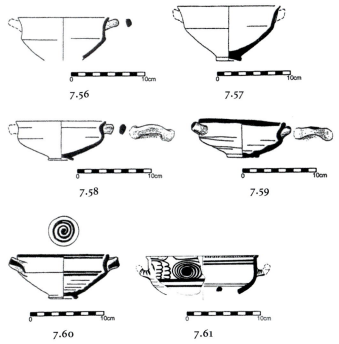

FIGURE 7.56 Tel Miqne/Ekron Field I, Strata VII–VI (after Dothan and Zukerman 2004: fig. 6: 1)

FIGURE 7.57 Tel Miqne/Ekron Field IV, Stratum VIIa (after Dothan and Zukerman 2004: fig. 6: 2)

FIGURE 7.58 Tel Miqne/Ekron Field I, Stratum Vc (after Dothan and Zukerman 2004: fig. 6: 3)

FIGURE 7.59 Ashdod Area G, Stratum XIIIb (after Dothan and Porath 1993: fig. 14: 25)

FIGURE 7.60 Ashdod Area G, Stratum XIIIb (after Dothan and Porath 1993: fig. 14: 24)

FIGURE 7.61 Ashdod Area G, Stratum XIIIb (after Dothan and Porath 1993: fig. 19: 10)

RING-BASE KRATERS

Ring-base kraters FS 282, are frequent at Ashdod and Tel Miqne/Ekron (Dothan and Zukerman 2004: figs. 16–9; Ben-Shlomo 2006a: 30; Figs. 7.62–67; Table 7.2). The body is bell shaped and there is some variability in rim shapes, most with variants of the T- and L-shaped rims. There may be more than a single size category, with rims ranging from eighteen centimeters in diameter to as wide as twenty-eight centimeters. The decoration is in brown or black, sometimes on a white or light-colored slip. No two kraters are decorated in the same manner, and they reflect less standardization than any other Philistine Monochrome type. Motifs are linear, geometric (e.g., spirals, panels, checkered), floral (tongues), and figurative (birds, fish). This variability indicates the important display role of kraters in symposia. As the centerpiece of wine-serving kits, and laden with Aegean symbolism, they were used by hosts wishing to convey messages of ethnicity and common ancestry. However, the lack of uniformity in the krater assemblage also suggests a clear message of the independence and individuality of the host.

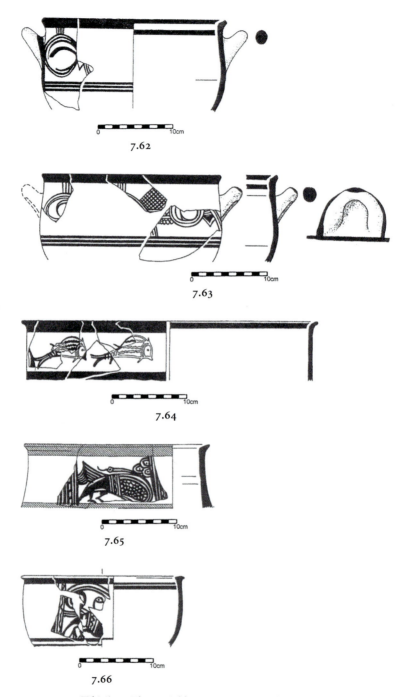

7.62

7.63

7.64

7.65

7.66

FIGURE 7.62 Tel Miqne/Ekron Field I, Stratum VIIa (after Dothan and Zukerman 2004: fig. 16: 7)

FIGURE 7.63 Tel Miqne/Ekron Field I, Stratum VIIa (after Dothan and Zukerman 2004: fig. 16: 6)

FIGURE 7.64 Ashdod Area H, Stratum XII (after Dothan and Zukerman 2004: fig. 19: 4)

FIGURE 7.65 Tel Miqne/Ekron Field I, Stratum VI (after Dothan and Zukerman 2004: fig. 19: 2)

FIGURE 7.66 Ashdod Area H, Stratum XIII (after Dothan and Zukerman 2004: fig. 19: 3)

FIGURE 7.67. Tel Miqne/Ekron Field X, Stratum VIIb (after Dothan and Zukerman 2004: fig. 16: 1)

In contrast to their steady occurrence in every assemblage in Philistia and in the LHIIIC Aegean, as in the settlement assemblages of Lefkandi,[13] Emporio (Hood 1982: 590–2 nos. 2742–52, fig. 265 [Stage 7, I]), and Phylakopi, ring-base kraters are rather rare LHIIIB imports to the southern Levant. Only five examples have been mentioned in Leonard's (1994: 114–17) catalog, excluding the nine additional examples uncovered at Tell Abu Hawam.

KYLIKES AND CUPS

It is interesting that kylikes, which are conspicuous LHIIIC Aegean drinking forms, are rather rare LHIIIB imports and are extremely rare among the locally produced LHIIIC fineware (Dothan and Zukerman 2004: fig. 27: 1–3; Ben-Shlomo 2006a: 31; Table 7.2; Figs. 7.68–70). Their rarity as imports in the thirteenth century can be explained as a result of Canaanite drinking preferences (Chapter 6), but their rarity as a local product during the twelfth century may reflect either a local preference or a regional tradition brought along by Aegean migrants in which bowls were more popular than kylikes as drinking vessels. The infrequency of kylikes in the LHIIIC-style pottery of Enkomi and Tarsus (Table 7.2) supports the second idea.

Cups similar to FS 215 are also infrequent LHIIIC-style pottery in Philistia (Dothan and Zukerman 2004: fig. 27: 6, 7; Figs. 7.71 and 7.72; Table 7.2). They are equipped with a vertical handle with a rounded section rather than with strap handles, typical of many examples of cups in the Aegean. Their decoration is linear. Similar to the kylikes, cups are infrequent in the LHIIIC-style pottery of Enkomi and Tarsus.

---

[13] Kraters are not common in Phase 1b but become more numerous in Phase 2a, with the onset of the nonlinear decoration (Popham et al. 2006: 157).

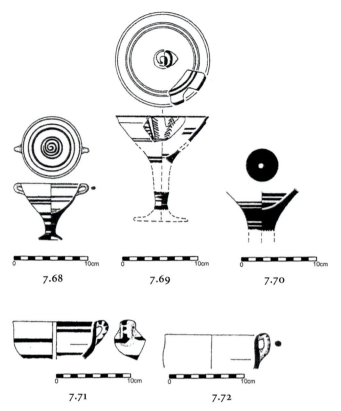

7.68   7.69   7.70

7.71   7.72

FIGURE 7.68. Tel Miqne/Ekron Field III, Stratum VIa (after Dothan and Zukerman 2004: fig. 27: 3)

FIGURE 7.69. Ashdod Area H, Stratum XII (after Dothan and Zukerman 2004: fig. 27: 6)

FIGURE 7.70. Tel Miqne/Ekron Field I, Stratum VI (after Dothan and Zukerman 2004: fig. 27: 7)

FIGURE 7.71. Tel Miqne/Ekron Field I, Stratum VIIa (after Dothan and Zukerman 2004: fig. 27: 4)

FIGURE 7.72. Tel Miqne/Ekron Field I, Stratum VI (after Dothan 1998a: fig. 5: 9)

TRAYS, ROUND-SIDED BOWLS, AND FINEWARE DECORATED KALATHOI

Trays FS 322 (Dothan and Zukerman 2004: fig. 27: 4; Fig. 7.73) are rare LHIIIC-style vessels, yet have been found at both Tel Miqne/Ekron and Ashdod. It is of interest that they have not been reported from either twelfth-century Enkomi or Tarsus. Round-sided bowls with horizontal handles attached to the lip are a type found only at Tel Miqne/Ekron (Dothan and Zukerman 2004: 7; Figs. 7.74 and 7.75). With a profile varying from hemispherical to shallow, they may have stemmed from either FS 296 or FS 294. Finally, fineware decorated kalathos FS 291 (Dothan and Zukerman 2004: fig. 25: 6) may also be present in the local repertoire.

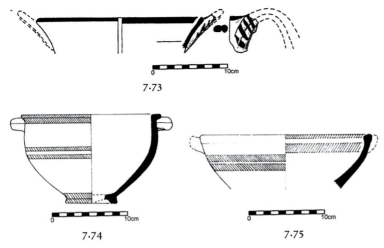

7.73

7.74   7.75

FIGURE 7.73. Tel Miqne/Ekron Field I, Stratum VI (after Dothan 1998a: fig. 5: 10)
FIGURE 7.74. Ashdod Area H, Stratum XIIa (after Dothan and Zukerman 2004: fig. 27: 1)
FIGURE 7.75. Tel Miqne/Ekron Field I, Stratum VIIa (after Dothan and Zukerman 2004: fig. 27: 2)

SERVING AND STORAGE VESSELS IN THE LOCAL, CANAANITE TRADITION

HEMISPHERICAL BOWL

In contrast to the LHIIIC-style pottery from Philistia, no study has yet been devoted to the local, Canaanite pottery tradition. The final publication of Ashdod and the first volume of final publication from Tel Miqne/Ekron allow for a preliminary assessment of the most common types of pottery, which, in turn, enables a comparison between the different pottery traditions. It must, however, be emphasized that a comprehensive typological study is still required.

The Canaanite pottery, just like the Aegean-style pottery, was dominated by bowls. A very common type is the hemispherical bowl (Figs. 7.76–80) with curved sides, a sharp or rounded simple rim, and a concave disk or ring base. These simple bowls, often undecorated, are a continuation of the hemispherical bowls of the late-thirteenth- and early-twelfth-century Canaanite pottery tradition, with many minute variants in the shape of the base and rim and in the aperture of the rim.[14]

In addition to the majority of these bowls, which are undecorated, there is a smaller number of shallow and hemispherical bowls made in the reddish fabric typical of the Monochrome pottery, decorated with bands, and sometimes

[14] Examples for this type come from Tel Miqne/Ekron Field X, Stratum VIIb (Dothan 1998a: pl. 1: 8–10); Ashdod Area A, Stratum XIV (Dothan 1971: fig. 1: 2); Area G, Strata XV–XIV (Dothan and Porath 1993: fig. 11: 7–9, 11–12); Stratum XIIIb (Dothan and Porath 1993: figs. 14: 1–4, 16: 4, 6); Area H, Stratum XIII (Ben-Shlomo 2005: fig. 3.5: 1).

even with a spiral on the bottom of the interior, typical of Monochrome shallow angular bowls and bell-shaped bowls. Examples of these come from Tel Miqne/Ekron Stratum VIb (Dothan 1998b: pl. 5: 8) and Ashdod Stratum XIIIb (Dothan and Porath 1993: figs. 14: 1–7 and 16: 4). This phenomenon may have stemmed from the existence of an Aegean or Cypriot prototype of the form that existed side by side with the Canaanite one. Such a prototype may have been the small bowl with hemispherical body and linear decoration of the LHIIIB2 (Mountjoy 1986: fig. 164: 1). These types also exist on Cyprus, such as at Tomb 9 Upper Burial at Kition, which includes several hemispherical bowls with linear decoration and a spiral drawn on the bottom of the interior (Karageorghis 1974: pl. 69: 327, 175, 260, 99, 316; Sherratt 2006: 365).

OTHER TYPES OF BOWLS, CHALICES, AND GOBLETS

Shallow bowls form a large group of mostly undecorated bowls with a shallow body and walls that are neither curved nor carinated (Figs. 7.81–3). Many examples come from Tel Miqne/Ekron and Ashdod.[15] As is evident from the parallels from the thirteenth-century strata in the Philistine sites and from Lachish Levels VII and VI, these bowls all have ancestry in thirteenth-century Canaanite tradition.

Other bowl types include carinated (Figs. 7.84–6) and shallow bowls with an upturned rim,[16] open bowls with a hammer or in-turned rim,[17] and bowls with a cyma profile (both decorated and undecorated).[18]

The few examples of chalices and goblets (Figs. 7.87–9) indicate that local forms of stemmed drinking vessels were never very popular among the Canaanites.[19]

CANAANITE KRATERS

Canaanite kraters are characterized by carinated or rounded bodies and two vertical handles (Figs. 7.90–2). This is a prevalent type that continued from the Late Bronze Age (see Chapter 6, Fig. 6.3, parts 4–5, for examples from Dan). Surface treatment varies greatly from undecorated to burnished and

---

[15] Tel Miqne/Ekron: Stratum VIIb (Dothan 1998b: pl. 1: 11); Ashdod Area A, Stratum XIV (Dothan 1971: fig. 1: 1); Area H, Strata XIV (Dothan 1971: fig. 81: 3); and XIII (Ben-Shlomo 2005: 3, 6); Area G, Strata XV–XIV (Dothan and Porath 1993: fig. 11: 1–5); yet probably less common in Stratum XIIIb (Dothan and Porath 1993: fig. 16: 1).

[16] Examples: Tel Miqne/Ekron Stratum VIb (Dothan 1998b: pl. 5: 8); Ashdod Area H, Stratum XIV (Dothan 1971: fig. 81: 1) with flat base; Area G, Stratum XIIIb with low ring base (Dothan and Porath 1993: fig. 16: 2).

[17] For examples, see Ashdod Area H, Stratum XIII (Ben-Shlomo 2005: fig. 3.5: 9).

[18] At Ashdod, they appear in Stratum XIII (Ben-Shlomo 2005: fig. 3.5: 8, 10) but exist well into Stratum XI (Dothan 1971: fig. 85: 2).

[19] Chalices: Tel Miqne/Ekron Field X (Dothan 1998b: pl. 8: 16); Ashdod Area G (Dothan and Porath 1993: fig. 19: 12). Goblet: Ashdod Area G (Dothan and Porath 1993: fig. 16: 16).

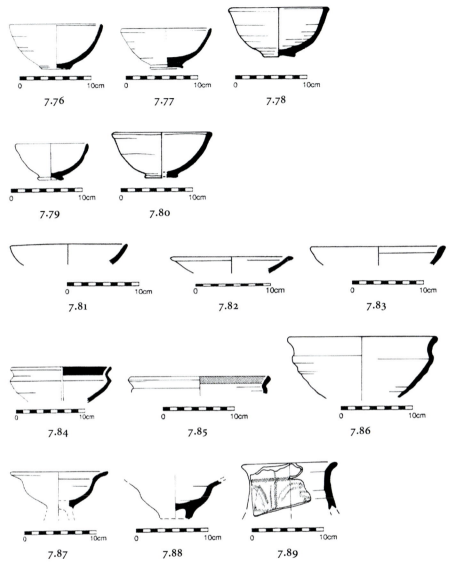

FIGURE 7.76. Tel Miqne/Ekron Field X, Stratum VIIb (after Dothan 1998b: pl. 1: 8)

FIGURE 7.77. Tel Miqne/Ekron Field X, Stratum VIIb (after Dothan 1998b: pl. 1: 9)

FIGURE 7.78. Ashdod Area G, Stratum XIIIb (after Dothan and Porath 1993: fig. 16: 3)

FIGURE 7.79. Tel Miqne/Ekron Field I, Stratum VIa (after Killebrew 1998a: fig. 6: 1)

FIGURE 7.80. Ashdod Area G, Stratum XIIIb (after Dothan and Porath 1993: fig. 16: 6)

FIGURE 7.81. Tel Miqne/Ekron Field X, Stratum VIIa (after Dothan 1998b: pl. 3: 16)

FIGURE 7.82. Tel Miqne/Ekron Field I, Stratum VIIb (after Killebrew 1998a: fig. 6: 10)

FIGURE 7.83. Ashdod Area G, Stratum XIIIb (after Dothan and Porath 1993: fig. 16: 5)

FIGURE 7.84. Tel Miqne/Ekron Field I, Stratum VIIb (after Dothan et al. 2006: fig. 3.6)

FIGURE 7.85. Tel Miqne/Ekron Field I, Stratum VIIb (after Dothan et al. 2006: fig. 3.8)

FIGURE 7.86. Tel Miqne/Ekron Field I, Stratum VIIb (after Dothan et al. 2006: fig. 3.8)

FIGURE 7.87. Tel Miqne/Ekron Field X, Stratum VIa (after Dothan 1998b: pl. 8: 16)

FIGURE 7.88. Ashdod Area G, Stratum XIIIb (after Dothan and Porath 1993: fig. 19: 12)

FIGURE 7.89. Ashdod Area G, Stratum XIIIa (after Dothan and Porath 1993: fig. 16: 16)

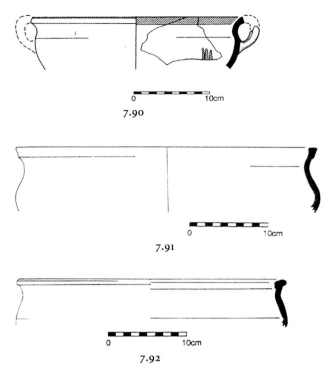

7.90

7.91

7.92

FIGURE 7.90 Ashdod Area G, Stratum XIIIb (after Dothan and Porath 1993: fig. 15: 7)
FIGURE 7.91 Ashdod Area G, Strata XIIIb and XIIIa (after Dothan and Porath 1993: fig. 17: 2)
FIGURE 7.92 Ashdod Area G, Strata XIIIb and XIIIa (after Dothan and Porath 1993: fig. 23: 3)

painted. It may be significant that there is much similarity between the Aegean and Canaanite krater rim form, including L- and T-shaped rims. Rim forms show much variety and include several types, reflecting continuity of the Late Bronze Age tradition.[20] The appearance may indicate that drinking traditions in the Canaanite manner continued unhindered into the twelfth century in Philistia.

PILGRIM FLASKS

The pilgrim flask (Figs. 7.93–5) has been found in the Canaanite assemblage of the thirteenth century (Amiran 1969: 166–7, pl. 51). Its earlier, fourteenth-century Aegean imitations, FS 188, 189, the vertical flask, were no longer in circulation by LHIIIB1 (Mountjoy 1986: 108); hence, their presence in twelfth-century Philistia can be attributed to either local or foreign traditions.

---

[20] Some examples of rim types include the L-shaped rim: Ashdod Stratum XV (Dothan and Freedman 1967: fig. 19: 6); Stratum XIII (Ben-Shlomo 2005: fig. 3.14); out-turned rim with thickened inner protrusion or rim slightly folded to the inside: Ashdod Stratum XV (Dothan and Freedman 1967: fig. 19: 7); Stratum XIV (Dothan and Freedman 1967: fig. 22: 8); Tel Miqne/Ekron Stratum VIIIb (Dothan 1998: pl. 1: 12); club–shaped rim with no inner gutter: Ashdod Stratum XIV (Dothan 1971: fig. 36: 1; Dothan and Freedman 1967: fig. 23: 7).

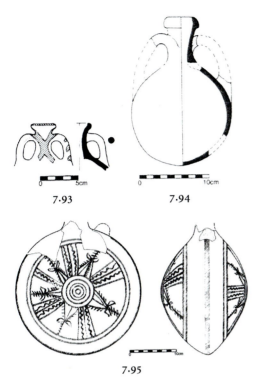

7·93   7·94

7·95

FIGURE 7.93 Ashdod Area G, Stratum XIIIa (after Dothan and Porath 1993: fig. 20: 2)
FIGURE 7.94 Ashdod Area G, Stratum XIIIa (after Dothan and Porath 1993: fig. 20: 5)
FIGURE 7.95 Tel Miqne/Ekron Field I, Stratum VIa (after Killebrew 1998a: fig. 12: 12)

Pilgrim flasks have been found at Ashdod Area H, Stratum XIII (Ben-Shlomo 2005: fig. 3.7: 3, 4), continuing a Late Bronze II tradition at the site (Dothan 1971: fig. 82: 1; Dothan and Porath 1993: figs. 23: 8 and 32: 13). A similar case is seen at Tel Miqne/Ekron Strata VIII and VII (Dothan et al. 2006: figs. 3.2: 22 and 3.11: 20). All the examples from Philistia display bodies decorated with concentric circles.

JUGS, STORAGE JARS, AND DIPPER JUGLETS: An array of rim forms can be assigned either to storage jars or to jugs (Fig. 7.96–101). Complete examples of Canaanite-style jugs are absent, apart from a very large jug from Ashdod Stratum XIIIb (Dothan and Porath 1993: fig. 15: 1; Fig. 7.102). A complete storage jar, or Canaanite amphora with an ovoid body, short neck, and two handles, was found at Ashdod Stratum XIIIb (Dothan and Porath 1993: fig. 15: 7–9; Fig. 7.103), its shape showing a clear continuation of Late Bronze Age traditions.

Connected to the storage jars, yet surprisingly uncommon, is another local type of serving vessel, the dipper juglet (Figs. 7.104 and 7.105),[21] with

---

[21] Examples of dipper juglets come from Ashdod Area G: Dothan and Porath 1993: figs. 17: 2 (XIIIb); 23: 3 (XIIIa), with earlier, Late Bronze Age examples of the same site: Area G: Dothan and Porath 1993: fig. 10: 9 (XV); Area B: Dothan 1971: fig. 34: 8.

published examples only from Ashdod. Ladling in the Aegean was commonly performed with a long-handled ladle or scoop (Mountjoy 1993: 118), but the dipper juglet was probably used only for ladling from open shapes such as cooking pots and kraters (Mountjoy 1993: 122, table 3). Such ladles would probably have fit into the wide mouth of the collar-neck jar and the pithos but not into the narrower neck of the Canaanite amphora. An array of small jugs or large juglets (Figs. 7.106–9) may belong either to Aegean or to Canaanite forms.

Killebrew (1998a: 397) rightly notes the absence of medium-sized and large Aegean storage vessels from the locally produced LHIIIC repertoire in Philistia. She attributes this absence to the continued use of the Canaanite amphorae (Fig. 7.103). Killebrew (1998a: 397) further argues that the LHIIIC-style assemblage at Tel Miqne/Ekron and Ashdod is "not complete," pointing to the absence of Aegean collared-rim and piriform jars. These vessels, however, are also absent from the published material from Lefkandi and Emporio, though they are present in Phylakopi (e.g., Mountjoy 1985: 171, fig. 5.10: 81, 86) and in Enkomi and Tarsus (Table 7.2). Their presence, therefore (and that of straight-sided alabastra), may not have been essential to LHIIIC domestic life. The absence in Philistia of large, Aegean storage vessels such as the pithos and large domestic stirrup jars (Mountjoy 1993: fig. 18, 122, table 4) can be explained by the fact that the large, domestic stirrup jars declined in popularity in LHIIIC, and there is an almost complete absence of any type of pithoi from the Philistia sites. The shape of the Canaanite amphora, an item imported into the Aegean and Cyprus during the thirteenth century, was perhaps familiar to some Aegean migrants, while its shape and capacity may have been adequate for the regular activities in an Aegean household.

STANDS AND LAMPS

Plain jar stands (Fig. 7.110) found at Ashdod Stratum XIII (Area G: Dothan and Porath 1993: fig. 23: 1 [Stratum XIIIa]; Area H: Dothan 1971: fig. 84: 16) seem to be a continuation of a local Late Bronze Age tradition, seen also at sites such as Lachish and Hazor.[22] Plain stands (and decorated cultic stands) also appear in Crete and the eastern Aegean.[23] Another, possibly slightly later example of a plain, undecorated stand was found in the sanctuary of the "ingot god" in Enkomi (Courtois 1971: 263, fig. 100).

Ceramic oil lamps (Figs. 7.111 and 7.112) of local tradition continue into the Early Iron Age at Tel Miqne/Ekron.[24] No Aegean or other foreign vessel seems

---

[22] Lachish, Fosse Temples II and III (Tufnell, Inge, and Harding 1940: pl. 53A: 325–6, 329, 330–2). Hazor, Late Bronze II, Area F, Stratum I (Yadin et al. 1960: pl. 147: 1, 2).

[23] For example, at Halasmenos (Coulson and Tsipopoulou 1994: pl. 9: 4), Miletus (Mountjoy 1998: 44, fig. 3.4), Armenochori on Astypalaia and Pilona on Rhodes (Mountjoy 1998: 57, fig. 12: 2, 3).

[24] Some examples are from Tel Miqne/Ekron Field I (Killebrew 1998a: fig. 12: 18) (Stratum VI), and Field X (Bierling 1998: pl. 2: 1) (Stratum VIIb).

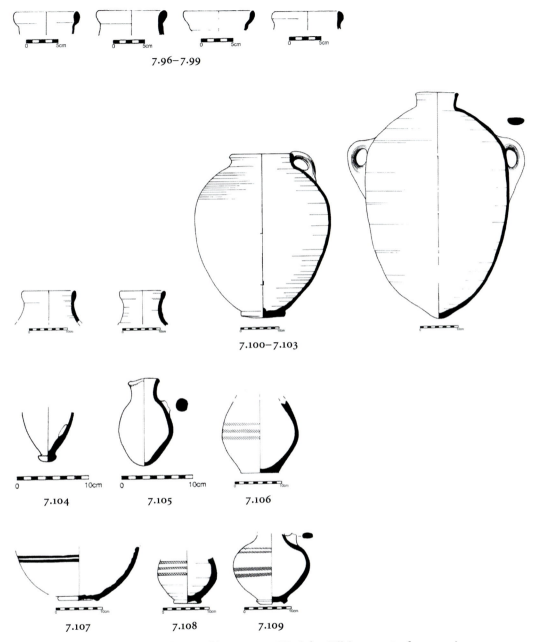

7.96–7.99

7.100–7.103

7.104   7.105   7.106

7.107   7.108   7.109

FIGURES 7.96–7.99 Tel Miqne/Ekron Field I, Stratum VIIa (after Killebrew 1998a: fig. 7: 22–5)
FIGURES 7.100–7.103 Ashdod Area G, Stratum XIIIb (after Dothan and Porath 1993: fig. 15: 7–9)
FIGURE 7.104 Tel Miqne/Ekron Field I, Stratum VIIa (after Killebrew 1998a: fig. 7: 21)
FIGURE 7.105 Tel Miqne/Ekron Field X, Stratum VIIa (after Dothan 1998b: pl. 3: 20)
FIGURE 7.106 Ashdod Area G, Stratum XIIIa (after Dothan and Porath 1993: fig. 20: 4)
FIGURE 7.107 Ashdod Area G, Stratum XIIIa (after Dothan and Porath 1993: fig. 23: 1)
FIGURE 7.108 Tel Miqne/Ekron Field I, Stratum VIa (after Killebrew 1998a: fig. 12: 18)
FIGURE 7.109 Tel Miqne/Ekron Field X, Stratum VIIb (after Dothan 1998b: pl. 2: 1)

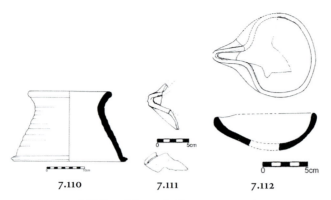

7.110   7.111   7.112

FIGURE 7.110 Tel Miqne/Ekron Field I, Stratum VIIb (after Dothan et al. 2006: fig. 3.7: 16)
FIGURE 7.111 Tel Miqne/Ekron Field X, Stratum VIb (after Dothan 1998b: pl. 5: 10)
FIGURE 7.112 Tel Miqne/Ekron Field X, Stratum VIIb (after Dothan 1998b: pl. 1: 13)

to have been used for this function at the two sites. However, the Aegean-type lamp FS 321a was not a must in an Aegean household. This is evident from its single appearance at Emporio and from the fact that it is not among the published material from Lefkandi or Phylakopi. It may be that the stands and lamps are simply less common local forms, added to the LHIIIC repertoire, either replacing rare parallel forms or, more likely, filling a functional gap in this assemblage.

CYPRIOT (AND EGYPTIAN?) SHAPES

During the late twelfth century BCE and in the beginning of the eleventh century, later than the first appearance of LHIIIC-style pottery in Philistia, Cypriot forms, such as the cylindrical bottle and the horn-shaped vessel, entered the early Philistine Bichrome repertoire (Stager 1995: 338–9, fig. 3). One example of a cylindrical bottle, painted in bichrome, appears in Ashdod Stratum XIIIa (Dothan and Porath 1993: fig. 20: 9; Fig. 7.113). There are no published examples from Tel Miqne/Ekron Strata VI or VII.

Another single vessel from Ashdod Area G, Stratum XIIIa, is a bichrome-painted jug with an everted rim (Dothan and Porath 1993: fig. 20: 7; Fig. 7.114). Dothan (1982: 172–85) identified this type as Egyptian in origin. As in the case of the cylindrical bottle, the bichrome decoration on this jug excludes it from the earliest phase of intense interaction with the Aegean world. Further examples of this type are needed to establish the date of its appearance and the mechanism of its introduction into Philistia.

THE NATURE OF THE AEGEAN-STYLE AND CANAANITE CERAMIC REPERTOIRES IN PHILISTIA

The assemblages of LHIIIC-style serving vessels and small and medium-sized containers from Tel Miqne/Ekron and Ashdod give the overall impression of

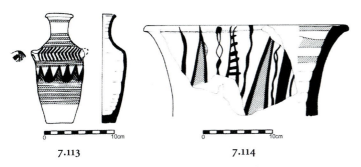

7.113   7.114

FIGURE 7.113 Ashdod Area G, Stratum XIIIa (after Dothan and Porath 1993: fig. 20: 9)
FIGURE 7.114 Ashdod Area G, Stratum XIIIa (after Dothan and Porath 1993: fig. 20: 7)

full assemblages in their own right. Considering the wide variability among the types of serving vessels in the other LHIIIC Aegean assemblages, claims of the meaningful absence of some LHIIIC types from the Levantine assemblage should be dismissed. The strong emphasis evident in the assemblage on vessels used to serve food (mainly deep bowls) and on food preparation vessels (mainly cooking jugs) is similar to that seen in settlement sites in the LHIIIC Aegean. The Levantine repertoire may contain fewer types than those at Aegean sites as Tiryns, Lefkandi, or Emporio, yet it contains examples of almost all essential groups of Aegean serving vessels in the LHIIIC tradition: small, probably personal vessels for food and drink (deep and shallow angular bowls); larger open containers for drink and food (kraters); and small and medium-sized pouring vessels (spouted, strainer, and other jugs). Most important, the variety of forms in Philistia compares remarkably with the types of LHIIIC-style pottery found at Enkomi and Tarsus (Table 7.2) – other sites that were affected by Aegean migration in the twelfth century BCE, although each site displays its own idiosyncrasies regarding the presence and absence of some forms. The notion that LHIIIC-style pottery was produced in Philistia as a substitute for previously traded items (Sherratt 1998; Bauer 1998) should be entirely rejected. The appearance of cooking pots, an item never imported to the Levant during LHIIIB; the prevalence of deep bowls, almost never traded during LHIIIB; and the relative rarity of the small stirrup jar, by far the most common imported type, make a "trade substitution" theory impossible (Barako 2000: 514–15; Dothan and Zukerman 2004: 45). When LHIIIC-style pottery was imported in small quantities to the southern Levant (Chapter 6), it was not imported to the area that, according to the trade substitution theory, was supposed to have imitated it – Philistia – but it was imported as a response to the small-scale demand from Egyptian garrisons and some Canaanite merchants in the north. The latter had indeed created their own trade substitution – albeit not in the form of mass production of kitchenware, but in a limited number of local imitations in the form of stirrup jars, imitating the Cypriot-made, LHIIIC-style traded ones (Fig. 6.6, part 2–3).

TABLE 7.4. *A comparison between functional categories (excluding storage jars) in Tel Miqne/Ekron*

	VIIb	VIIa
Eating and drinking (mainly bowls)	LHIIIC-style, 71% Canaanite, 53%	LHIIIC-style, 79% Canaanite, 60%
Cooking (cooking pots, cooking jugs, basins)	LHIIIC-style, 24% Canaanite, 15%	LHIIIC-style, 16% Canaanite, 8%
Serving (kraters)	LHIIIC-style, 2% Canaanite, 1%	LHIIIC-style, 2% Canaanite, 3%
Pouring and specialized containers (e.g., jugs, juglets, stirrup jars, bottles, flasks)	LHIIIC-style, 3% Canaanite, 31%	LHIIIC-style, 3% Canaanite, 28%

A comparison between the functional categories of the Aegean-style and Canaanite pottery at Ashdod and Tel Miqne/Ekron (Table 7.3) points to the coexistence of two complete functional repertoires in the same assemblage. The most common household activities of preparing food, serving food and drink, and storing food and drink in small and medium-sized containers could have been practiced in either Aegean-style or Canaanite vessels.

Mazow's (2005: 164–71; see also Table 7.4) pioneering quantitative study of pottery in Tel Miqne/Ekron Field IV lends further support to this notion. Both ceramic repertoires are dominated by serving vessels, mainly bowls, while the similar low percentage of both Canaanite and Aegean-style kraters shows that wine drinking, while practiced in both traditions, was probably a more ceremonial, restricted activity. Mazow explains the relatively small number of Canaanite cooking pots as a result of their larger size, compared with that of the smaller Aegean-style cooking jugs. Another important difference between the repertoires is the considerably more frequent occurrence of jugs in the Canaanite one. It is possible that the general shape of the Canaanite jugs, not significantly different from that of the Aegean ones, enabled their inclusion in Aegean-style behavioral patterns.

Despite the existence of two distinct repertoires – the Aegean and the Canaanite – their co-occurrence in the same assemblages indicates that they were used at the same time by the same groups of people. Canaanite cooking and food consumption patterns were carried out alongside Aegean ones. This observation has important implications for the manner in which the Aegean migration process and early Philistine society are reconstructed.

POTTERY PRODUCTION AND TECHNOLOGY

Closely related to the changes in the pottery types are some innovations related to pottery technology. A group of kilns found at Tel Miqne/Ekron in Field I may mark an industrial quarter built at the edge of the early Philistine town. Work carried out by Killebrew (1996: 148; 1998a: 401) shows that the kilns

FIGURE 7.115. Kiln from Tel Miqne/Ekron Field I, Stratum VIIb (after Killebrew 1996: fig. 15)

found in Strata VII and VI resemble no known Levantine kiln type. Although no vitrified wasters or pottery-making implements have been reported from the site, Killebrew (1998a: 391–7) argues that the kilns were used to produce a variety of locally made LHIIIC forms, both fineware and coarseware, including cooking jugs and basins. At least two types of nonlocal kilns were found in Strata VII and VI. The earlier of them has a square firing chamber and a bilobate combustion chamber (Figs. 7.115 and 7.116). Possibly two kilns belong to this type: Kiln 4104 of Stratum VII (Killebrew 1996: 146; 1998a: 392–3, figs. 8, 9) and Kiln 36069 of Stratum VI (Killebrew 1996: 148), which has the same bilobate combustion chamber. There are no known parallels for these kilns in the Aegean world.[25] The second type (Fig. 7.117), built probably only slightly later, has an oval combustion chamber with parallel flutes designed to support the floor of the firing chamber. It is represented by one clear example, Kiln 36024 in Stratum VI (Killebrew 1996: 148, 149, fig. 18), and perhaps Kiln 37015 (Killebrew 1996: 151, fig. 20). Parallels for this type are found in the kilns of Type 3c from Miletus (Niemeier 1997: 350; 1998: 31–2). These kilns appear in Miletus in both the second and the third building periods (LHIIIA2 and LHIIIB–LHIIIC) and probably stem from a Minoan prototype. Despite the lack of clear Aegean parallels for the Tel Miqne/Ekron kilns, some of the kilns also lack clear Levantine parallels (Ben-Shlomo 2006a: 96–112, 116–17). The mixture of continuity and change in kiln forms at Tel Miqne/Ekron may be

[25] I thank E. Hasaki for discussing with me possible Aegean parallels to the Tel Miqne/Ekron kilns.

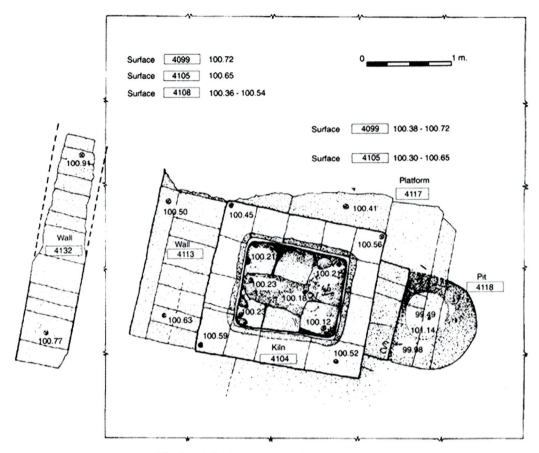

FIGURE 7.116. Kiln from Tel Miqne/Ekron Field I, Stratum VIIb (after Killebrew 1998a: fig. 13)

indicative, at the very least, of the employment of potters trained in different potting traditions in the same industrial quarter in the twelfth and early eleventh centuries BCE.

The Tel Miqne/Ekron pottery industry also differs from the Late Bronze II Canaanite tradition in clay sources, construction techniques, and firing temperature, which seems to have been relatively low at about six hundred degrees Celsius (Killebrew 1998a: 400–1). Lighter, calcareous clay sources were chosen by the Tel Miqne/Ekron pottery makers to imitate the fine and light appearance of Aegean wares, and they created some high-quality examples (Killebrew 1998a: 400). Ben-Shlomo (2006a: 205–6) has shown that Ashdod and Ashkelon had also produced Aegean-type pottery, but in the coastal areas, fine, calcareous clays were not available, and clay recipes used for the production of LHIIIC-style pottery were similar to those used to produce Canaanite pottery. Because of the fine quality of some of the Tel Miqne/Ekron Monochrome wares, they were eventually imported to Ashdod and Ashkelon, and they amount to as much as 18 percent of the samples from both sites (Ben-Shlomo 2006a: fig. 5.2).

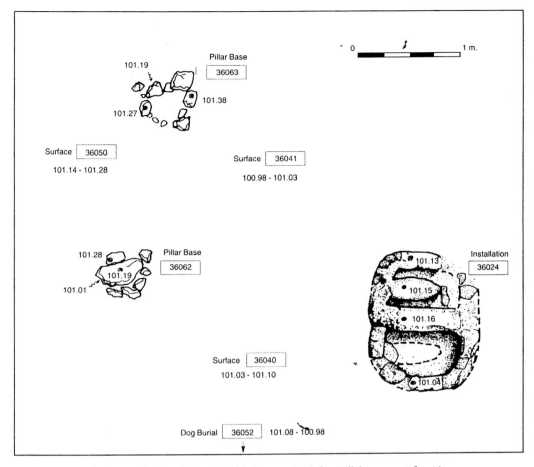

FIGURE 7.117. Kiln from Tel Miqne/Ekron Field I, Stratum VI (after Killebrew 1996: fig. 18)

TEXTILE PRODUCTION

IMPERFORATED SPOOL-SHAPED LOOM WEIGHTS

During the Late Bronze Age, the prevalent loom type did not require loom weights. A similar picture emerges from several Late Bronze II sites in Canaan; for example, no Late Bronze II loom weights have been published from Hazor, Megiddo, or Lachish. This perhaps is because of the introduction of the Egyptian vertical loom there (Yasur-Landau 2007a). A marked change has been noticed in the sites of Philistia – Tel Miqne/Ekron, Ashkelon, and Ashdod – with the introduction of the imperforated reel- or spool-shaped objects, shown to be loom weights of Aegean origin (Chapter 5; Fig. 7.118). At Ashdod, the monumental domestic complex in Area G Stratum XIIIa produced a few weights of the same type (Dothan and Porath 1993: fig. 24: 3–5). In Tel Miqne/Ekron, these weights first appear in Field X, Stratum VIIb, in Room F, a possible cultic room (Bierling 1998: pl. 7b). Other examples come from Field

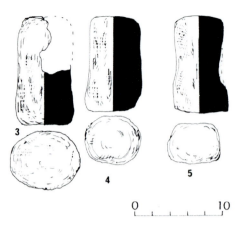

FIGURE 7.118. Loom weights from Ashdod Area G (after Dothan and Porath 1993: fig. 24: 3–5)

IV, Strata VIb and VIa (Mazow 2005: 167; Shamir 2007). In Ashkelon Phase 20, two large concentrations of these loom weights have been found, seventy-one on one floor and fifty-two on another (Master 2005: 342). Another large concentration was found in the large northern complex of Phases 19 and 18, which yielded more than 150 of the weights dated to the two phases of its existence. The latter examples from Ashkelon (Stager 1991: 14–15), which had been, in several instances, found in a row along a wall together with linen fibers, established the identification of these objects as loom weights of a type previously unknown in Canaan and on Cyprus.

The use of spool-shaped loom weights does not seem to have any technical advantage over the use of perforated ones. In fact, the opposite may be true: the spool-shaped weight is a crude object, and tying thread to it is a more complicated procedure than tying thread to the perforated weight. Moreover, its unbaked and muddy composition obviously would not have contributed to the final product.

SPINDLE WHORLS

The typology of spindle whorls does not show conclusive evidence for either change or continuity in textile production. The spindle whorls from Ashdod Area G, Strata XIIIb and XIIIa, and Area H, Stratum XIII, are predominantly domed on one side and flat on the other (Fig. 7.119; Dothan and Porath 1993: fig. 13: 14, 15, 17, 18, fig. 18: 3, 5, 6, 7, fig. 25: 10; Ben-Shlomo 2005: fig. 3.37: 15–17). They are made mainly of stone but also of bone and clay. Their shape is similar to Eighteenth Dynasty spindle whorls (Barber 1991: 46, fig. 2.7) and to Late Bronze Age and Early Iron Age examples from southern Levantine sites including Gezer, Lachish, Beth Shean, and Megiddo.[26]

---

[26] For examples, see Gezer (Field IV: Dever 1986: pl. 54: 3 [Stratum 7], pl. 55: 5 [Stratum 6c]); Lachish (the Fosse Temple: Tufnell et al. 1940: pl. 29: 29, 30–3); Beth Shean (Stratum VI:

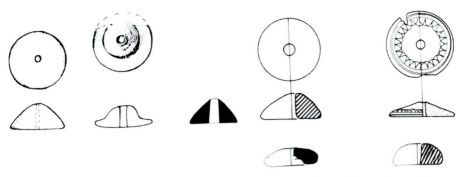

FIGURE 7.119. Spindle whorls from Ashdod Area G (after Dothan and Porath 1993: figs. 13: 14–17; 18: 3, 5–7)

Parallels for these forms are also found in the Aegean world. The best parallels come from the LHIIIC cemetery at Perati (Iakovidis 1980: 78, pl. 7.3: 8), which provides examples of both the domed type (Iakovidis 1980: 79, fig. 92: 2, 3) and the hatlike type (Iakovidis 1980: 79, fig. 92: 8).

SPINNING BOWLS

Spinning bowls, designed for wetting linen fibers, were used both in Crete and in Egypt starting in the Middle Bronze Age (Dothan 1963; Barber 1991: 70–6) and continuing into the Late Bronze Age in the Aegean and across the Levantine coast, and into the Early Iron Age in the Levant (cf. Carington Smith 1992: 686–7, for a LHIIA example from Nichoria). At Tel Miqne/Ekron, spinning bowls appear from Stratum VI on (Mazow 2005: 389 no. 299), and three of the four examples from Stratum VI were discovered in Building 353. Examples of spinning bowls from Ashdod have been found in the slightly later Stratum XII (Dothan and Porath 1993: 79). As is true of the spindle whorls, the use of spinning bowls is documented on both the Aegean and the Levantine sides of the Mediterranean in the Late Bronze Age; therefore, it is impossible to decide whether it reveals newly arrived Aegean practices, the continuation of local practices, or more plausibly, both.

INNOVATION AND CONTINUITY IN TEXTILE PRODUCTION

Two contemporary trends in textile production are detectable in the transition from the Bronze Age to the Early Iron Age. The first phenomenon is a clear and rather sudden change in weaving practices: a change in the types of weights used, indicating the introduction of a new type of loom in which

James 1966: fig. 101: 25; Strata VIII and VII: James and McGovern 1993: 181–2); Megiddo (Barber 1991: 62); and Ashdod Area G (Middle Bronze II: Dothan and Porath 1993: fig. 3: 16, 17).

different fabrics were most likely produced rather than the traditional ones of the Late Bronze Age. Because the spool-shaped weights were not traded items, it is likely that this radical deep change in loom weights was triggered by direct and enduring contact with a population that used spool-shaped weights. Moreover, the change in technology seen in the change to spool-shaped weights strongly resembles the changes resulting from migration that have been seen in the historical and archaeological case studies in which a deep change in textile production accompanied migration (Chapter 1).

Side by side with this change, there is an apparent continuation of spinning techniques: the spindle whorls and, probably, the spinning bowls used in the Late Bronze Age Aegean and Levant are virtually indistinguishable from those used in the Early Iron Age. This may indicate that in Philistia, as in Kition (Chapter 5), two textile production traditions, an Aegean one and a local one, existed side by side.

THE CHIPPED-STONE INDUSTRY

The site of Ashdod has produced two publications of chipped-stone tools (Rosen 1993; Matskevitz 2005). The great majority of the tools from Strata XIII and XII, consists of large, geometric sickle segments. These are typical of the local flint industry from the Middle Bronze Age onward (Rosen 1997: 60; Matskevitz 2005), and thus their production indicates a continuation of local tradition. Rosen (1993: 117–18) has suggested that some differences between the dimensions of the sickle segments from Stratum XIII and those from Stratum XII are the result of the "Philistine settlement." However, the changes in the ratio of the length to the width of the segments do not indicate a radical change in typology or in manufacturing technique.

THE ORGANIZATION OF DOMESTIC SPACE

The Aegean domestic behavioral patterns, which re-created and reenacted long-familiar patterns from the Aegean, were encompassed by house architecture that also reflected the migrants' habitus.

The earliest architecture in Philistia inspired by Aegean prototypes is of a strictly vernacular nature. Unlike the palaces and the patrician houses of the Aegean in the thirteenth century BCE, none is masterfully designed or bears ornamentation that can be assigned to a specific style. Yet even with the irregular appearance of the agglomerated and seemingly chaotic plans of the Early Iron Age structures, at Tel Miqne/Ekron, Ashdod, and Ashkelon patterns emerge, which indicate that the Aegean migrants had a clear mental image of how a house should be built and organized. They reconstructed and negotiated an Aegean habitus by re-creating an Aegean domestic space in a land in which it was not previously familiar. Although a considerable number

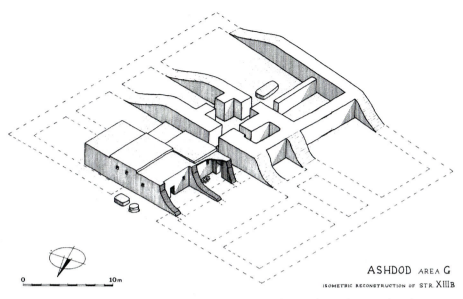

FIGURE 7.120. Ashdod Area G, Stratum XIIIb (after Dothan and Porath 1993: plan 9)

of the houses excavated in Philistia have been published so far, at least in the form of plans, three examples, one from each of the excavated sites, best illustrate this point. Two, from Tel Miqne/Ekron and Ashkelon, comprise a structure built *ex novo*, according to an Aegean ideal. The third, perhaps more striking, example is an Egyptian-style patrician house at Ashdod, refitted to resemble an Aegean house.[27]

ASHDOD AREA G, STRATA XIIIB AND XIIIA

The structure in Area G in Ashdod Stratum XIIIb (Figs. 7.120 and 7.121) is one large domestic complex in which some walls were reused from the Late Bronze Age Strata XV–XIV "residency" (Dothan and Porath 1993: 52, plan 9, 53–5; Bunimovitz and Yasur-Landau 2002). However, the Late Bronze Age local model of a courtyard house or an Egyptian residency, a building centered on an inner court, apparently did not fit the needs of the new inhabitants (cf. Oren 1992: 115–20; Ben-Dov 1992: 103; Herzog 1997: 180, fig. 4.30, 186, fig. 4.34).

An analysis of the contents of this complex (Bunimovitz and Yasur-Landau 2002: 214) has shown that it was divided into two functional units separated by a corridor: a northern one, in which domestic activities such as food preparation, spinning, and weaving took place, and a southern one, more monumental in structure and probably more ceremonial in nature.

---

[27] Later buildings, however important (e.g., the temple or palace from Tel Miqne/Ekron Stratum V and the massive fortification of Ashdod Area G, Stratum XII), are not examined here because their plans and arrangements may reflect independent development and thus may not indicate earlier foreign influence.

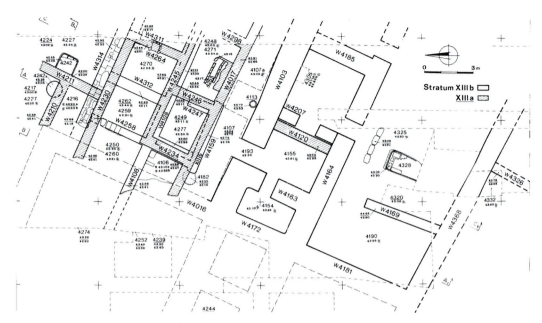

FIGURE 7.121. Ashdod Area G, Strata XIIIb and XIIIa (after Dothan and Porath 1993: plan 8)

The southern unit was probably similar to the plan of the former Strata XV–XIV "residency" (Dothan and Porath 1993: 42, plan 7) and incorporated most of its southern walls. It included three rather small rooms with a thick wall in the north of the unit and a larger hall to the south of the rooms. The main changes made to the unit in Stratum XIIIb were the building of Curtain Wall W.4169 and Installation 4328 ("altar"). The main entrance to the southern unit may have been on the north side, through an opening in Wall 4103. It is also possible that another opening to Locus 4325 existed at the northeast.

The northern part of the complex was entirely different from that of the "residency" of Stratum XV and contained five newly built, small rooms (4277, 4160, 4260, 4259, and 4270). The only identifiable entrance to this complex is from the south, into Room 4106 – a storage room for serving vessels containing mainly deep bowls and carinated bowls of several sizes.[28] It is possible to reconstruct another entrance into Room 4260, via its western wall, which was not preserved. North of the northern unit was a court containing Installation 4242 ("altar") and a pillar base, apparently in secondary use.

The concept of the building plan of Stratum XIIIb is radically different from that of the "residency" of Stratum XV (Dothan and Porath 1993: 42, plan 7, 41), which had a monumental entrance in its south (Dothan and Porath 1993: 41) leading to the large rooms in its north. Because this change in plan was

---

[28] The lack of wasters, potter's wheels, and kilns does not support Dothan and Porath's (1993: 5) initial notion that the large quantity of the pottery belongs to a potter's shop.

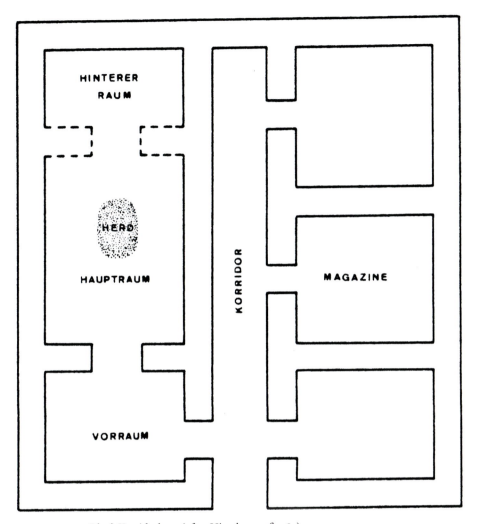

FIGURE 7.122. Ideal *Korridorhaus* (after Hiesel 1990: fig. 85)

accompanied by the building of two hearths of distinctively nonlocal character and by the introduction of other material culture traits indicating Aegean behavioral patterns, it may have been constructed to accommodate foreign cultural preferences. Other excavated examples of a service unit separated by a corridor from a more ceremonial unit suggest an Aegean origin of the plan.

The origin of such a separation can be found in the LHIII period *Korridorhaus* (Hiesel 1990: 111). An "ideal" version of this elite-type house (Fig. 7.122) is composed of two units separated by a corridor. One unit is a service unit, while the other is a ceremonial unit containing a main room with a hearth, a front room leading to it, and in some cases, a back room. Hiesel (1990: 111–45) counts fourteen examples of such houses from LHIIIB, eight of which are from Mycenae. This plan existed into the LHIIIC period, as is evident from

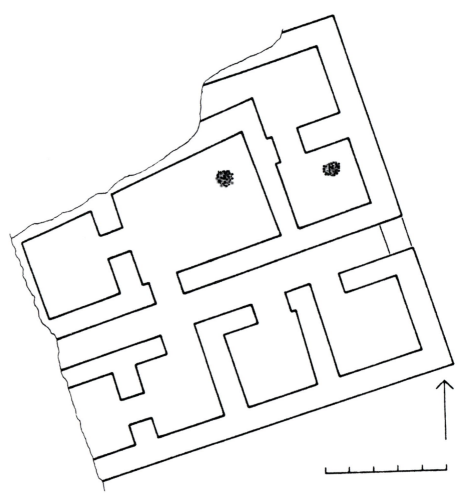

FIGURE 7.123. Menelaion, Mansion 3 (after Hiesel 1990: fig. 99)

the example from the third building period in Miletus (Niemeier 1998: 35).
Variation among the examples in the size and number of rooms reflects different statuses of the owners. This includes elaborate buildings such as Mansion
3 in the Menelaion (Fig. 7.123; Hiesel 1990: 131–2), the Tsountas House and the
House of the Columns at Mycenae (Hiesel 1990: 115–19), and Building B in the
South Quarter (Fig. 7.124), as well as more humble examples such as the Panagia House I at Mycenae (Hiesel 1990: 121–3) and the house at Miletus. One can
cautiously state that the alteration in the plan of the Ashdod Area G structure
was carried out to make the building function like an Aegean *Korridorhaus*.
The division into two units separated by a corridor, the different functions of
the units, and most significant, the division of the main room with the hearth
in the south wing into two by means of a curtain wall – resulting in a main
room and a front or back room – all point in this direction. Some parallels
for the remodeled Ashdod structure are South Quarter Building B and the
Tsountas House at Mycenae (Fig. 7.125).

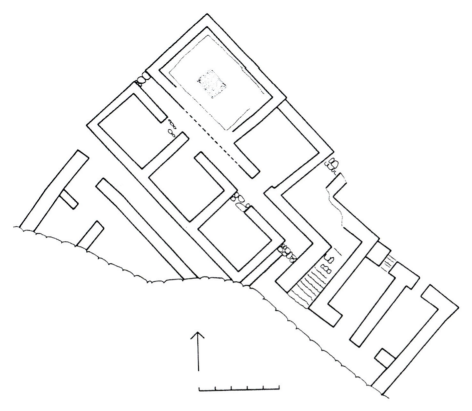

FIGURE 7.124. Mycenae, South Quarter, Building B (after Hiesel 1990: fig. 84)

Area G at Ashdod, then, contains what appears to be an example of an elite building of the Late Bronze Age local tradition, altered to fit the needs of an elite with an Aegean notion of an elite house.

ASHKELON GRID 38, PHASE 19, AND TEL MIQNE/EKRON FIELD IV

The initial Aegean settlement at Phase 20, which did not yield full house plans, was soon replaced by Phase 19, still containing LHIIIC-style pottery, alongside the first appearance of Philistine Bichrome pottery (Fig. 7.126). The entire area was rebuilt with a new ground plan during this phase; several domestic units seem to be crowded together, their natural growth hindered by the nearby sprawling units, or more regularly, by a north–south street (Master 2005: fig. 20.7; Cross and Stager 2006: plan 3).

The northern unit was centered on Room 25, in the middle of which was a large rectangular hearth. A short bench was attached to the southern wall of the room – so short, in fact, that it may have served as a seat for one person. A large, finely carved limestone bath was located in the southeastern corner of the room. The co-occurrence of hearths or raised platforms also has been recognized elsewhere in Philistia. Dothan (2003: figs. 10–14) brings examples

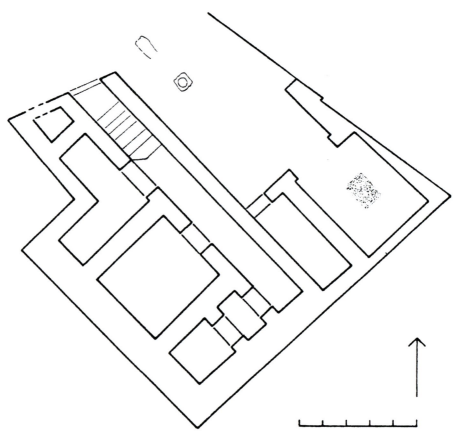

FIGURE 7.125. Mycenae, Tsountas House (after Hiesel 1990: fig. 95)

from Ashdod Areas H and G, Stratum XII, and Tel Miqne/Ekron Field I, Stratum VII, and Field IV, Building 353, Stratum VI. She suggests an Aegean ancestry to this arrangement of the inner space, supporting a cultic association with it, and points to the Cypriot occurrences of bathtubs in LCIIC, though none is in connection to a hearth.

The use of bathtubs in the Aegean persisted into LHIIIC, as is evident by the bathtubs found in the ruins of Koukounaries (Schilardi 1984: 187–8; 1992: 627–31). Even in the humble context of Lefkandi Phase 1b, Room 11, a ceramic bathtub was found by the wall, near a central hearth (Popham et al. 2006: fig. 1.8). The southern unit was composed of a jagged chain of four rooms, built toward the southeast, doubtlessly because of constraints of similar units north and south of it. An L-shaped vestibule (Room 5170/1023), which included a hearth attached to the wall, led to three more rooms: 873 and 725, with central hearths, and the tiny 858. The largest and most furnished room was 725, possibly the center of the house, dominated by the center rectangular hearth; a clay bin was found by its western wall, and a round, cobble surface, another installation, was located by its northeastern corner. Although the plan of this complex was entirely irregular, its interior furnishing reflects an attempt to

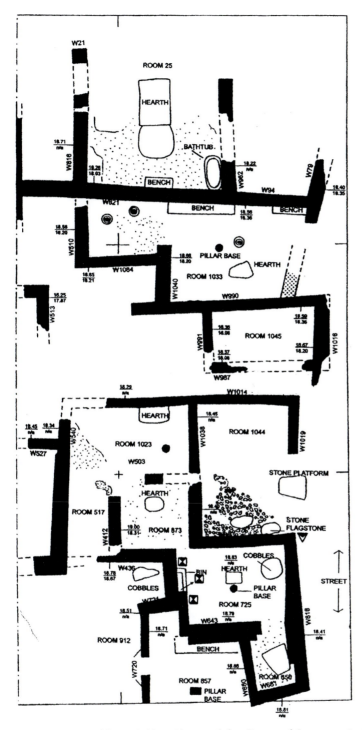

FIGURE 7.126. Ashkeon Grid 38, Phase 19 (after Cross and Stager 2006: plan 3)

create a series of living rooms, each accommodated with a hearth – perhaps a structure similar to Korakou House P. The co-occurrence of a rectangular clay bin and a central hearth is found also in Lefkandi Phase 1b, Room 3.

The earliest Iron Age building in Tel Miqne/Ekron Field IV was Room 357 in Stratum VIIb: a one-room structure built in the middle of a vast, open area that contained several outdoor installations (Mazow 2005: fig. 5.1). Shortly after, in Stratum VIIa, another one-room structure was built to the south of Room 357, aimed to cover a round silo (Fig. 7.127; Mazow 2005: fig. 5.2; Dothan 2003: fig. 4). Room 357 was furnished with a central rectangular hearth on a raised platform built between the two central pillars of the room. Two benches were attached to the long walls of the structure, which maximized the seating around the hearth. A small bin in the southwestern corner of the room gives a final touch to a room that would not seem out of place on the Greek mainland,[29] or on LMIIIC Crete.[30] This small unit, to which both Dothan (2003) and Mazow (2005) ascribed a ceremonial function, continued to serve as a one-room unit into Stratum VIa.

A CONTINUATION OF LOCAL BUILDING TRADITIONS?

Aegean-inspired domestic furnishings were not found in every single building, and there is reason to believe that some structures continued traditions of local, Canaanite vernacular architecture or mixed Aegean and local traditions. Differences were manifested in the earliest phases of house construction by the placing of foundation deposits. Canaanite rituals relating to house building – the foundation deposit documented already in the thirteenth century (Bunimovitz and Zimhoni 1993), usually comprising a lamp sandwiched between two bowls – are not rare finds in Early Iron Age Philistia. At Tel Miqne/Ekron, for example, the earliest deposit in Field VI was linked to the construction of Building 351 in Stratum VIb (Mazow 2005: 436); it contained a lamp placed between two Canaanite bowls. A foreign style of foundation deposit is evident in Ashkelon Phase 19, where equid skulls placed in cairns mark the position of the new centers of buildings (Master 2005: 344). An intriguing example is the deposit from Tel Miqne/Ekron Field X, Stratum VIIb (Bierling 1998: 15), arguably the earliest deposit from the area and indicative of the first phase of Iron Age settlement. The deposit found under a corner of one of the rooms was a mixture of Canaanite and Aegean traditions: it contained a Canaanite-style lamp that was handmade, unlike the vast majority of Iron Age lamps, placed in an Aegean-style krater.

---

[29] Examples of a hearth between two pillars exist in LHIIIC Building W at Tiryns (Hiesel 1990: 63–4), Unit IV 4 from Nichoria (LHIIIA2; Hiesel 1990: 80–1), and Panagia House II at Mycenae (LHIIIB2; Hiesel 1990: 149–53).

[30] See also the very large hearth in Building 1 at Sybrita (Thronos Kephala), central Crete, dating to LHIIIC or slightly later (D'Agata 2001: 48, 57).

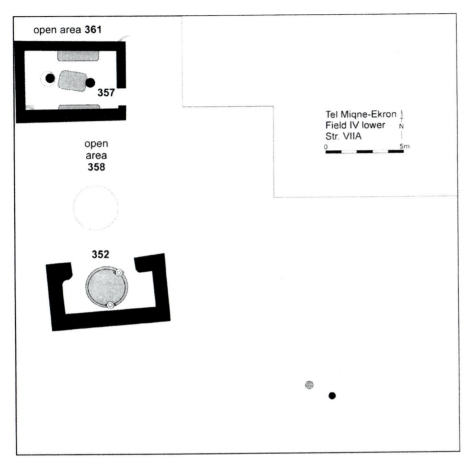

FIGURE 7.127. Tel Miqne/Ekron Field IV, Stratum VIIa (after Mazow 2005: fig. 5.2)

Indeed, Field X yielded domestic structures from Strata VII and VI (Fig. 7.128; Dothan et al. 1998: 14–16) that do not exhibit clearly Aegean furnishing. The structures are mainly small rooms (9–7, varying between the strata) adjacent to Fortification Wall 90006 and extending into the earlier Middle Bronze Age II rampart (Dothan et al. 1998: 13). Room F had, in Strata VIIb and VIIa, plastered walls and floor as well as a plastered *bamah*. Still only partially excavated, the complex has not yet provided a clear plan, but the configuration of small rooms adjacent to a wall brings to mind the later complex from Area G, Stratum XII, at Ashdod (Dothan and Porath 1993: 70–2, plans 10, 11). The use of *tabuns* in Complex 200 and the absence of hearths may hint at a local rather than an Aegean method of organizing domestic space.

CONCLUSIONS: PHILISTINE HOUSE, PHILISTINE MIGRANTS

The infrequent Mycenaean mercenary passing through the streets of Ashdod or stopping in the remote village of Ekron in the thirteenth century would not find any resemblance in the local Canaanite houses, garments, and dishes to those familiar in his faraway home. However, most people from the LHIIIC world would have felt almost at home sitting on benches by the rectangular hearths of Philistia, surrounded by the irresistible smell of food slowly cooked in Aegean cooking jugs and the repetitive sound of the loom, its warp weighed down by spool-shaped imperforated reels. The house is a microcosm, its arrangement reflecting social structures and cultural conventions that appear in the outside world (Chapter 1). During the twelfth century, it is evident that a new habitus was reshaping both house architecture and the activities performed inside the house. A deep change in the plan of a house and its interior arrangements reflects a conscious effort to replicate, in some cases, Aegean house forms and indicates a change in the cultural notion of what a house should look like. Inside the house, virtually every aspect of everyday domestic life at the sites mirrors behavioral patterns of Aegean origin previously unattested to in the Late Bronze Age local, Canaanite tradition. A deep change in the activities carried out in the house, such as the appearance of Aegean-style cooking and weaving, indicates that the most basic practices were carried out in a nonlocal manner. The phenomenon of a sudden rather than a gradual change, in which people began to do things in the Aegean way, cannot be explained as a result of trade and close economic connections with Cyprus, as Sherratt (1998) argues. It has been demonstrated here (Chapter 6) that the small amount of LHIIIC-style imports that arrived during the twelfth century was limited to the north, never arriving in Philistia, and thus could not be imitated there. Furthermore, Sherratt (1998: 303) attributes the important processes of cultural transmission reflected in the appearance of Aegean-style cooking pots to the "spread of some Cypriot practices and equipment as a result of close economic and cultural interactions with the Island." Indeed, a model of an eastern Mediterranean, coastal, economic community is appealing, until the practical mechanism of cultural transmission is considered. It is especially imperative to point out the agents of change and the exact process of interaction between them and the local population. If a model of economic contact alone is to be adopted, without migration, resulting in the introduction and implementation of cultural innovations (Chapter 1), one would expect to see prolonged commercial contact followed by gradual adoption of several foreign traits. To make the commercial-cultural model work, one needs to assume the presence in Philistia of a good number of agents of change – Cypriot men and women busily teaching the locals how to weave, cook, build their houses, eat, and drink, all with an impressive success rate, during an extremely short period of time, yet without the prospect of selling any significant amount of Cypriot goods.

Rather, the deep change in the behavioral patterns in Philistia can be interpreted only by the arrival of people from within the sphere of the expanding Aegean and Aegeanized world of the twelfth century – a process very similar to that witnessed in Emporio, Maa-Palaeokastro, and Tarsus. As seen in the

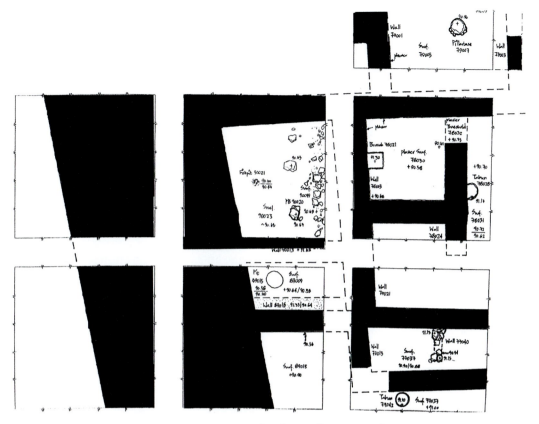

FIGURE 7.128. Tel Miqne/Ekron Field X, Stratum VIb (after Bierling 1998: 308)

great variability in settlement circumstances in Anatolia, Syria, and Cyprus, the interaction with the local population was probably only seldom violent. A pragmatic and opportunistic settlement strategy in sites as Ashkelon and perhaps Ashdod resulted in the significant continuation of the old Canaanite tradition, which appears side by side with the new intrusive assemblage. Houses, whether built with or without Aegean-style installations, contain assemblages indicative of activities carried out in both the Canaanite and the Aegean manner, which hints at the birth of a multicultural society.

8

THE PHILISTINE SOCIETY AND THE
SETTLEMENT PROCESS

The archaeological evidence supporting an Aegean migration to the southern Levant in the twelfth century enables us to address the conflicting views (see Chapter 7) concerning the nature of this migration, from the origin and number of migrants to their social and political structure, and the absolute chronology of the settlement. The different circumstances of settlement at each site demonstrated in Chapter 7 are a strong indication that, rather than a simple, unified event of migration and violent conquest, suggested by Ramses III's Year 8 inscription and the Ugarit letters, the Aegean settlement should be seen as complex, co-occurring migration processes, with great variability between the different sites in Philistia. Hence, rather than reconstructing the settlement process from preexisting historical dogma, this chapter attempts to answer questions relating to the migration by first examining the society created by the earliest migrants, from general settlement patterns to economy, and to the makeup of the Philistine population in the twelfth century BCE. This reconstruction lays the foundations needed to address the thorny questions of the sequence of events of the settlement and its chronology: was the settlement process a long or short one? Was it contemporaneous in all Philistia or was it gradual? Did it take place during the Egyptian domination of Canaan? Was it perhaps controlled by the Egyptians? Or did it mark the end of Egyptian domination?

SETTLEMENT PATTERNS IN PHILISTIA

THE PENTAPOLIS AND THE TWELFTH-CENTURY SETTLEMENT CRISIS

The concept of the Pentapolis, the five city-states of the Philistines and the base for a pan-Philistine confederation, is based on biblical references, the most prominent of which is Judges 16. Ashdod, Ashkelon, Ekron, Gaza, and Gath were each ruled by one of the five *seranim* of the Philistines (the term is discussed herein). Even without arguing for the early date of the biblical tradition, it is universally accepted that the Pentapolis system existed not only in Iron II but also as early as Iron I (Dothan 1982: 16–18; Singer 1993; Finkelstein 1996a; 2002), possibly even starting with the earliest Aegean settlement. Although it is impossible to show that the institution of the *seranim* and their council was active in the twelfth century, two pieces of evidence attest to a territorial division into five city-states as early as the twelfth-century Aegean migration. The first is the rank-size data of sites in Philistia. The five largest sites in twelfth- and eleventh-century Philistia were Ashdod, Ashkelon, Tel Miqne/Ekron, Gaza, and Tell es-Ṣafi/Gath, those mentioned as the Pentapolis sites, whose locations are positively and independently identified.[1] Three of the sites, Ashkelon, Tell es-Ṣafi/Gath, and Gaza, were already heads of territorial units in the Late Bronze Age (Finkelstein 1996a: 229, fig. 1). This hardly seems a coincidence, but rather a good indication that the sites were the heads of their surrounding territories in the twelfth century. A second piece of evidence comes from the Onomasticon of Amenope, compiled around 1100 BCE, which reflects a reality of the late twelfth century. In this list of names (Gardiner 1947: 190–1; Dothan 1982: 3–4; Singer 1993: 296), three of the Pentapolis sites are mentioned – Ashkelon, Ashdod, and Gaza (nos. 262–4) – followed by names of three groups of the Sea Peoples (after *Asher*, no. 265): the Sherden, the Tjeker/Sikel, and the Peleset (Gardiner 1947: 194–204, nos. 268–70). The connection of the three coastal Pentapolis sites (Tell es-Ṣafi/Gath and Tel Miqne/Ekron are not mentioned, as they are inland) with the Sea Peoples shows their central place in the territorial settlement of the Aegean groups, thus further supporting the existence of the Pentapolis – the division of Philistia into five territorial units – at the end of the twelfth century at the latest.

The division into polities whose centers were in Ashdod, Ashkelon, Tel Miqne/Ekron, Tell es-Ṣafi/Gath, and possibly Gaza was accompanied by a sharp change in the settlement patterns in the transition from the Bronze Age to the Early Iron Age (Figs. 8.1 and 8.2). The number of Iron I (twelfth and eleventh centuries BCE) settlements was reduced by half (49 compared to 102 in the Late Bronze Age; Finkelstein 1996a: 231), yet there was a lesser drop in the total built-up area of the Iron Age I (155 hectares compared to 173 hectares in the Late Bronze Age). This near equality of the built-up area occurred because most of the Late Bronze Age sites that were destroyed or abandoned were of a small or medium size, while there was an increase in the size of some, yet probably not all, large Early Iron Age sites. Finkelstein (1996a: 232) pointed out two phenomena: the near abandonment of the countryside

---

[1] The identification of Ashdod, Ashkelon, and Gaza poses little problem because their ancient names were preserved in the sites' names to modern times. Ekron is identified by a royal inscription of Achish, son of Padi, ruler of Ekron (Gitin, Dothan, and Naveh 1997). Gath is convincingly identified by historical and geographical considerations with Tell es-Ṣafi (Rainey 1975).

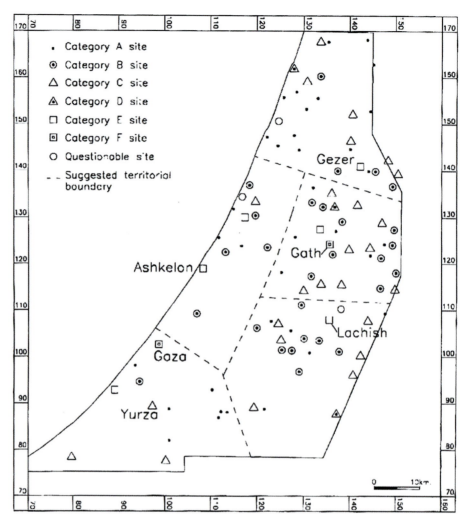

FIGURE 8.1. Late Bronze Age settlements in the southern coastal plain and the Shephela (after Finkelstein 1996a: fig. 1)

and an expansion in urban life. This, however, is a picture that includes the considerable recovery of the settlement in Philistia during the late twelfth or eleventh century. A good number of sites, such as Tell Qasile, Tell Jerisheh, Azor, Beit Dagan, Tel Ma'aravim (Oren and Mazar 1993: 920–1), and most likely Gezer (Dever 1993: 540) and Tell Beit Mirsim (Greenberg 1993: 180), were either founded or resettled in this period, as they exhibit only Philistine Bichrome pottery, first appearing in the late twelfth century, and no LHIIIC-style Philistine Monochrome (Greenberg 1993: 230, fig. 2). Admittedly, the lack of such pottery at some of the sites may indicate cultural preferences of the local population (Bunimovitz and Faust 2001) rather than a break in occupation. However, further confirmation of the settlement crisis in the twelfth century comes from the larger sites. In fact, the only site that exhibited growth in

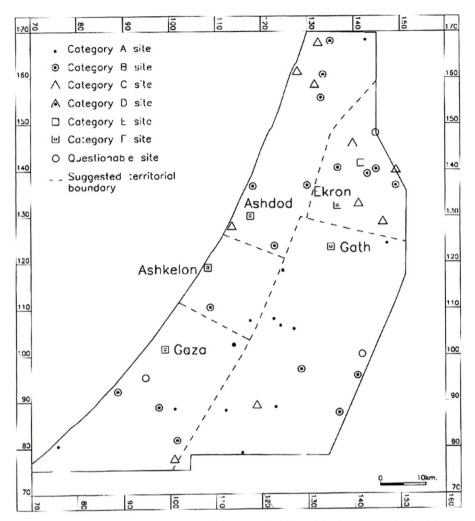

FIGURE 8.2. Iron I settlements in the southern coastal plain and the Shephela (after Finkelstein 1996a: fig. 2)

the twelfth century was Tel Miqne/Ekron, reaching an area of about twenty hectares. The urban growth observed by Finkelstein occurred at Ashdod and Ashkelon only in the late eleventh century, when Ashkelon was fortified for the first time, and Ashdod grew to include Areas D and M. Prior to that, both sites maintained their Late Bronze Age areas, of about six to eight hectares each. Similarly, while the Late Bronze Age settlement at Tell es-Ṣafi/Gath covered a vast area of twenty-seven to thirty-four hectares (Wimmer and Maeir 2007), the twelfth-century site may have been limited to the upper tell only, with an area of about seven hectares (Barako 2001: 87). Later, during the late eleventh century, the site of Tell es-Ṣafi/Gath substantially grew to cover an area of twenty-three hectares (Ben-Shlomo 2006–7: 268). In fact, the settlement crisis during the transition from the thirteenth century to the twelfth century may have been considerably more acute, with a sharp decline not only in the number of sites but also in the settled area.

THE FORMATION OF DIFFERENTIATION: REGIONAL VARIABILITY IN POLITICAL INTEGRATION AT PENTAPOLIS SITES

Using Clark and Parry's index of political integration again (see Chapter 2) on the data in Finkelstein's study (Figs. 8.1 and 8.2), it becomes evident that the settlement patterns in Philistia reflect a low level of political integration. At the same time, there are differences in settlement hierarchy among the Pentapolis territories. Eleventh-century Ekron seems to have exhibited the highest level, with at least a three-tiered settlement hierarchy (small village, large village and/or towns, and the city) equivalent to a CPI level 2 or 3 – two or possibly even three administrative levels above that of a local community. The situation in the twelfth century was less complex, with a settlement hierarchy of only two tiers. Tell es-Ṣafi/Gath basically exhibits a two-tiered settlement hierarchy in the eleventh century with much dichotomy: between the small rural settlements and the city. The territory of Tell es-Ṣafi/Gath shows a CPI level 1 (or level 2 at most), with one administrative level above that of a local community, probably without local centers. It should also be noted that, in general, the size of settlements in the Tell es-Ṣafi/Gath territory appears to be much smaller than that of settlements in the other territories (mainly that of Tel Miqne/Ekron). There are probably no Category C sites, and most sites are of the smallest, Category A. The settlements in the Tell es-Ṣafi/Gath territory are also much more sparsely distributed than those in the Tel Miqne/Ekron territory, most likely because of the available area.

Ashdod probably portrays a two-tiered settlement hierarchy (showing political integration of CPI level 1), yet its territory is much smaller than that of Tell es-Ṣafi/Gath, and it contains far fewer settlements.

Last is Ashkelon, which had almost no settlement hierarchy at all, showing a CPI level 0 (or level 1 at most) of political integration.

The situation in the area of Gaza in the twelfth century remains perplexing. Any attempt to find settlement hierarchy must begin with an a priori decision regarding the chronological relations between the Aegean settlement in Gaza and the end of Egyptian presence at sites such as Tell el-Farʿah (S), Deir el-Balah, and Tell Jemmeh, as well as with an estimate of the size of these settlements in the years immediately following the end of Egyptian rule. Because such constructs can be no more than the result of an educated guess, given the current state of knowledge, the question of political integration in the twelfth-century territory of Gaza is left for future research.

An overall pattern emerges in which the inland territories (Tell es-Ṣafi/Gath and Tel Miqne/Ekron) show a higher level of political integration than do the coastal territories (Ashkelon and Ashdod). Tel Miqne/Ekron shows the highest level of political integration, probably consistent with the fact that it is the only large site that experienced significant growth in the transition to the twelfth century. These phenomena, which cannot be explained independently, are nevertheless to be accounted for in the presentation of regional variability in social complexity and power in Philistia.

INTERACTION WITH THE LOCAL POPULATION AND THE CHOICE OF SITE FOR SETTLEMENT

The strategy for contact with indigenous populations has direct bearing on the nature of the site chosen for settlement. Uncertainty about the reaction of the local population had led colonists, at times, to choose a site for initial settlement primarily according to its defensibility rather than other properties, such as the availability of large areas of arable land. Thus, settlers often selected small islands or peninsulas in larger bays: during the eighth century BCE, Euboians chose to settle in Pithekoussai, on the island of Ischia, in the bay of Naples (Graham 1982: 97–9); Therans settled on the island of Platea, off the coast of Libya (Herodotus 4.157); and the Mayflower pilgrims first settled in Provincetown at Cape Cod. In some cases, when interaction with the indigenous population was regulated, or at least the power relations between migrants and locals became favorable for the migrants, some of the settlements moved to better locations in terms of agricultural and economic needs. Thus, the Theran settlers first moved to the site Aziris opposite the island (Herodotus 4.157–8), and the seventeenth-century-CE Puritans moved on to build Plymouth. Such settlement patterns are seen also in the Phoenician settlement on the island of Motya, Sicily (De Angelo 2003: 116–19). It is noteworthy that Thucydides (4.2.6) saw the Phoenicians' settling in promontories and islands around Sicily as a settlement pattern aimed for trade with the Sikels, while the site at Motya was actually a response to the external threat of the growing number of Greek colonists.

Returning to the twelfth century BCE, it has been suggested here that the choice of site at Ras Ibn Hani and Maa-Palaeokastro on defensible promontories reflects similar considerations, as well as separation as an acculturation strategy (Chapter 5). The choice of sites for settlement in Philistia does not show similar concern for security. Small, easily defensible coastal tells that were settled during the Late Bronze Age but experienced a hiatus in the twelfth century, such as the summit of the tell of Jaffa or Tel Mor at the outlet of Nahal (*Wadi*) Lachish, would have been perfect for building an Emporio-style, defensive coastal settlement. They were, however, left uninhabited by the Aegean migrants. Similarly, other coastal natural hills by outlets of wadis, such as the hill on which Tell Qasile was set in the late twelfth century, were readily available but not used by the migrants. Furthermore, although Ashkelon is coastal and Ashdod only a few kilometers from the coast, the lack of twelfth-century imports of any significant scale and the lack of any other signs of maritime activity preclude sea access as being a significant factor in the choice of sites. Bearing in mind the commonly accepted notion of the Philistines' aggressive, maritime nature, it may be surprising that fear of outside attack, by either Egyptians or others, and the need for access to sheltered harbors were not obvious considerations in choosing sites for settlement. Rather, the common factor of Tel Miqne/Ekron, Ashdod, Ashkelon, and Tell es-Ṣafi/Gath is their position in the midst of considerable areas of arable land. Land, rather than sea, was the main resource that the Philistine migrants sought.

What were the reasons for this distinctively non-Aegean choice of sites? It has been demonstrated here (Chapter 7) that there is no direct connection between the possibly violent destruction of Tel Miqne/Ekron and the Aegean settlement that followed it, while Ashkelon shows no destruction, and Tell es-Ṣafi/Gath and Ashdod show only ambiguous evidence. A unified event of a hostile Aegean takeover is highly improbable. However, the destruction of Ugarit and Ras Ibn Hani, and the description of the destruction inflicted by the settlers in the "camp in the land of Amurru" described by Ramses III (Chapter 5) may be an indication that the choice between an aggressive policy and a peaceful one depended on the parameter of power relations rather than on permanent policy. Despite the variability in the circumstances of settlement (Chapter 7) and, apparently, the organizational abilities of the first settlers at each site, the acculturation strategy (Chapter 1) that the Philistines chose was never separation from the local, Canaanite culture, as would have been expected in the case of violent conquerors. Instead, as is evident from the nature of combined Aegean and local behavioral patterns reflected in each domestic assemblage that has been excavated (Chapter 7), the Aegean migrants chose from the onset a strategy of integration with the local population. They may have already adopted this strategy of acculturation during their move through Syria, as seen in the multiethnic Philistine camp on the land battle relief at Medinet Habu (Chapter 5), which includes not only women but also men of non-Aegean descent. Although not precluding the option of a violent solution when one seemed necessary, it is likely that the integration strategy at least enabled peaceful interactions, and thus facilitated what appears to be the nonviolent, opportunistic nature of Philistine settlement. It is proposed here, therefore, that the foundation of Philistine sites was a cooperative effort of both migrants and local Canaanite populations who allied themselves with the newcomers, perhaps as a buffer against the unstable security and economic conditions that accompanied the end of Canaanite urban culture. We can further speculate on the role of local guides in pointing the migrants to unoccupied sites with plenty of arable land and no threatening neighbors. Examples of such relations are found in two cases of Greek foundation stories. After living six years in Aziris, a location better than the island of Platea but apparently still unfavorable for the growth of the colony, local Libyans showed the Theran settlers to a better place, where they finally built Cyrene (Herodotus 4.158). Another case is that of the unfortunate Megarian settlers in eastern Sicily. After many turns of fortune, the local king Hyblon directed the Megarians to a good place to settle, possibly in his own kingdom, and the city was named Megara Hyblaea after him (Malkin 1985: 117–18; Thucydides 6.4.1). As the site is completely flat, defense and fear of local attack were not considerations in the foundation. Furthermore, archaeological explorations at the site have shown that it was not settled before the arrival of the Greeks, which further supports the nonviolent foundation story (De Angelis 2003: 13–14).

Final proof for the important role of the Canaanite population in the foundation of the Philistine sites comes from the continued use of Semitic toponyms: Gath, Ashkelon, and Ekron. These names show a clear continuity from the Bronze Age to the Iron Age.[2]

AN URBAN FOUNDATION?

Mazar (1990: 313), Stager (1995), and Killebrew (2006) stress the urban component in the foundation of the Philistine sites; Stager coined the phrase "urban imposition" regarding the process of settlement. According to him, the migrants carried with them Aegean urban traditions and replicated them immediately on arrival. Singer (1993) has suggested a contrary opinion, arguing that the migrants came without an urban tradition of their own and adopted the Canaanite system of city-states. The expectation of the Philistines as an urban population was without doubt influenced by the biblical traditions on the mighty cities of the Philistines, on the one hand, and by images of the fortified centers of the Mycenaean palatial era, such as Mycenae or Tiryns, on the other hand. However, the postpalatial era from which the Aegean migrants had emerged was also a posturban one. It was a world in which the pinnacle of complexity were the small, fortified towns of Grotta and Phylakopi, and a variety of fortified acropolises and rulers' dwellings (Chapter 3). With the exception of Miletus, nothing in the Aegean world of the twelfth century was even remotely urban.

It should be no surprise, then, that a closer scrutiny of site planning in twelfth-century Philistia shows no patterns that can be attributed solely to Canaanite or Aegean urban traditions. Furthermore, such scrutiny calls into question the assignment of the term *urban* to any Philistine site of the twelfth century, except for Tel Miqne/Ekron. In other words, common eastern Mediterranean features of urban settings, such as large temples, palaces, storage and redistribution facilities, and evidence of any form of administration,

---

[2] A similar situation of population continuation is seen in the preservation of Late Bronze Age toponyms in the kingdom of Ugarit until present times (Caubet 1992: 126).

are altogether missing from twelfth-century Philistia, just as they are nonexistent in the twelfth-century Aegean.

Tel Miqne/Ekron (Figs. 7.5, 7.6, and 7.129) is the only site that can be properly called a town rather than a village, and it is the only site that was fortified from its beginning. It seems to be the best evidence of the foundation of a site by Aegean migrants and their Canaanite allies: the twenty-hectare town of Stratum VII rested on deposits from the much smaller, four-hectare Canaanite settlement of Stratum VIII. The Stratum VII town underwent profound changes in regard to layout and land use compared to its rural predecessor. Most important, the area of the settlement was defined and protected by a solid wall, 3.25 meters thick (Killebrew 1998a: 383; Dothan, Gitin, and Bierling 1998: 13–15), which encircled the entire site from its beginning. The outline of the walls reflected a pragmatic consideration, as it followed delineation of the tell already from the Middle Bronze Age. Still, the wall is an unusual structure in twelfth-century Canaan and reflects a level of planning and control. Few fortifications, if any, were built in the southern Levant during the Late Bronze II and III (Herzog 1997: 164) that could have provided inspiration for the Tel Miqne/Ekron walls. In addition, the Tel Miqne/Ekron wall is unique in its construction method: in Field X, it was composed not of bricks but of "poured mud" (Dothan et al. 1998: 13–14). Brick fortifications are not abundant, but they do exist in the Aegean, with the example of the LHIIIC mud-brick wall in Grotta, Naxos (Chapter 3). The low availability of building stones in the immediate vicinity of Tel Miqne/Ekron, in addition to defense needs, probably contributed to the building of this simple but robust wall, which displays no refinements such as towers or bastions. The area within the walls was allotted for specific functions. Field I, the site of the former Canaanite town, became mainly an industrial zone. Field X, near the wall, contains ordinary dwellings and was densely built from its beginning. However, Field IV, at the center of the tell, appears to have been more sparsely settled, as indicated by the open areas excavated in Stratum VIIb with one-room structures. This area would become later, in Stratum VI, a center of elite dwelling.

Ashdod, unlike Tel Miqne/Ekron, was not fortified at the first stage of the Aegean settlement, only in Stratum XIIb (early eleventh century). A wide, mud-brick casemate wall was built on top of the earlier "residency" in Area G (Dothan and Porath 1993: 70–3). In other areas (D, M), fortifications were built following the enlargement of the site in later phases of the eleventh and tenth centuries, consisting of a solid mud-brick wall about five meters wide (Herzog 1997: 202). The only evidence for planning in the twelfth century (Stratum XIII) was the division of land in Area H into private plots in which houses were constructed (Dothan 1982: 37, 41; Mazar and Ben-Shlomo 2005: plan 2.2; Chapter 7; Figs. 7.3, 7.4, and Fig. 8.3). The area was divided into two building complexes, separated by a street almost four meters wide. The width

FIGURE 8.3. Ashdod Area H plan (after Ben-Shlomo 2005: plan 2.2)

of the street, its partial paving, and its continuation in Stratum XII suggest that the boundaries of private building were determined by a deliberate act of plot division at the very beginning of the Aegean settlement. Area G continued to be used as a locus for elite dwelling. The "governor's residence" of Stratum XIV was renovated in Stratum XIIIb to fit an Aegean ideal of elite house (Chapter 7). This continuity and the scanty evidence for destruction of the Canaanite town bring into question the notion that Ashdod was an entirely new foundation.

The evidence from Ashkelon, in contrast, supports a hypothesis of a new foundation by Aegean migrants (Chapter 7). The site was not fortified from its onset, and architectural remains from Grid 38, Phase 20 (Fig. 8.4) appear to belong to ordinary domestic structures. The site was fortified in the late eleventh century, when mud-brick fortifications were added atop the earlier, massive Middle Bronze Age rampart. Distinct refinements of this fortification system included an impressive mud-brick tower (5.5 meters by 10.5 meters) and a glacis lined with mud bricks (Stager 1993: 107).

It seems that a complete, planned layout of the town, including symmetrical, parallel insulae (a Hippodamian plan) was not used in twelfth-century Philistia. The first example of town planning is the regular plan of parallel streets and insulae at Tell Qasile, which dates either to the very late twelfth century or to the early eleventh century or was given its semiorthogonal plan of Stratum X after it was founded (Fritz 1995: 47–9; Herzog 1997: 201–2).

The villagelike features of the first phase of Philistine settling and the allotment of different areas at the site for specialized use are reminiscent of acts in the foundation of new sites by Greek colonists. The organization of the area intended to be settled is a necessary component of any act of foundation. Thus, the early phase of the Greek colonization to southern Italy and Sicily (Fischer-Hansen 1996: 319) included complex acts of the division of land for private and public uses. It included allotment of agricultural land around the area of the town (*Kleroi*) and division of land inside the town into areas intended for houses and gardens (*oikopeda, gepeda*). Public domains included large areas inside the town that were allotted for the common cults or for the cult of the *oikist*.

In some cases, as in Megara Hyblaea (Fischer-Hansen 1996: 345), the allotment of land inside the settlement resulted in a quasi-orthogonal plan (Di Vita 1990: 349). Yet, despite their organized beginnings, the settlements resembled in the eighth century more of a village than a city, with houses set far apart. The first houses of the settlers in Megara Hyblaea and Syracuse were small and simple one-room structures (Graham 1982: 106; De Angelis 2003: 21).

Only in the early seventh century BCE, a generation or two after the foundation, did two- and three-room houses begin to appear and the settlement density begin to rise in Megara Hyblaea (De Angelis 2003: 24). This situation resembles closely that in Tel Miqne/Ekron Field IV, where the one-room

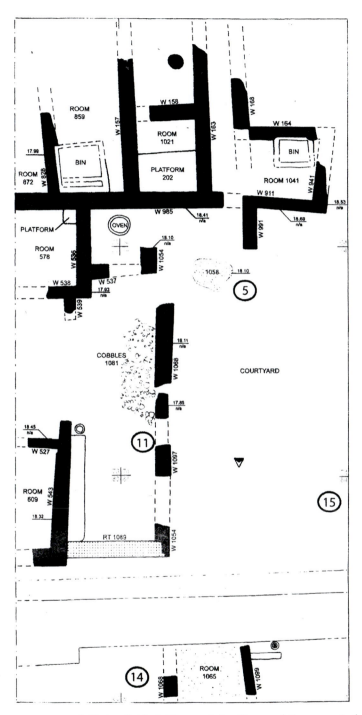

FIGURE 8.4. Ashkelon Grid 38, Phase 20 (after Cross and Stager 2006: plan 2)

structures of Stratum VII were gradually replaced by the multiroom structures of Stratum VII (Chapter 7). Similarly, the rise in settlement density and the filling of the large open spaces between the houses is reminiscent of the situation in Ashkelon Grid 38, where large open areas of Phase 20 were filled with Phase 19 structures a generation later. Very similar to Philistia, fortifications are rare at the first stage of Greek colonization in the west (Di Vita 1990: 319–20, 349) and appear, along with more advanced orthogonal town planning only in the seventh- and sixth-century colonies founded by earlier-stage colonies (e.g., Kyme, Kaulonia, Taras) or in the reorganization and fortification of existing colonies (e.g., Naxos [Di Vita 1990: 357–9] or Megara Hyblaea [Holloway 1991: 53–4]). Similarly, monumental buildings and more urban features made their first appearance only a century after the initial settlement (De Angelo 2003: 33–5).

Although not urban and not founded by migrants from an urban society, the Philistine settlements were artifacts of a new social order, reflected in the act of foundation. The allotment of land inside the town, seen in the Pentapolis sites, and possibly also of agricultural land outside it, can be reconstructed as one of the most important events in the life of any Aegean settlement in Philistia. Concluding a period of long and dangerous migration, allotment is an act of regulating life in the new location, where several demands and needs have to be met. The mass of migrants, mostly farmers, may have joined the venture in return for a promise of a plot (Chapter 4) and needed agricultural land and a place of residence. Some areas were needed for cult practices, while much land was required for the aristocrats' and rulers' dwellings and agricultural plots.

THE NUMBER OF MIGRANTS

Without additional data from further excavations in the three Pentapolis sites and in the surrounding sites, calculating the number of Aegean migrants that came during the twelfth century is highly speculative. The inability to clearly differentiate between migrants and local households at the same settlement makes the calculation according to site size useful only in assessing the highest possible number of migrants (i.e., if none of the local population remained at the site). Furthermore, because it is impossible to differentiate archaeologically between deposits of the first years of the Aegean settlement and those of twenty to thirty years later, the number calculated for the inhabited area includes not only migrants but also the second (if not the third) generation, born in Philistia, many of whom were likely offspring of intercultural marriages.

Based on evidence of the size of the inhabited area in Philistia, the route of migration, the duration of the process, and the nature of interaction with the local population, a rough estimate of the number of migrants can be made.

The population of Philistia at the end of the Iron Age I, two centuries or so after the beginning of the Philistine migration, numbered around thirty thousand people (Finkelstein 1996a: 236). To reach the population of the twelfth century, one needs to subtract sites first built in the eleventh century and the areas added to Ashdod and Ashkelon during the same period, to reach a considerably lower number of about twenty thousand people. However, material culture remains indicate that the Aegean migrants of the twelfth century concentrated in the head settlements of each polity rather than spreading throughout the countryside. The entire area of these settlements most likely did not exceed fifty hectares: Tell es-Ṣafi/Gath, with seven hectares, Ashdod and Ashkelon with six to eight hectares each, and Tel Miqne/Ekron with twenty hectares give a total of about forty hectares, to which 25 percent should be added to account for Gaza. A population of 12,500 for the Pentapolis sites is reached using a coefficient of 250 people per hectare, used by Finkelstein (1996a) and Barako (2001: 99). However, only part of these people were migrants, given the strong evidence for the survival of a significant local population at the Pentapolis sites. Considering the modest evidence at hand, the range of possibilities for the number of migrants can be anything between Finkelstein's (1996a) minimalist suggestion of a "few thousands" and ten thousand migrants suggested by Barako (2001: 123); the latter assuming that nearly half of the population were migrants. Naturally, a lower estimate of the number of migrants would make maritime migration logistically more feasible, while larger numbers of colonists could have reached the southern Levant by a combination of land transportation and crossing waters in boats. Evidence along the land route from Cilicia to the Levant suggests that this was indeed the case.

ECONOMY

CHANGES IN ANIMAL HUSBANDRY

The arrival of migrants in Ashdod, Ashkelon, and Tel Miqne/Ekron was accompanied by a radical change in animal husbandry to subsistence patterns that were probably familiar to the migrants from their homelands. Because migrants try to shape their new environment according to patterns familiar to them from their old environment (Chapter 1), mass migration results in the changing of subsistence patterns. The change in animal husbandry seen in the Philistine settlements may have been partly caused by migrants bringing with them the economy of their point of origin. However, the changes may also be attributed to the change in settlement patterns between the Canaanite Late Bronze Age system and the new, sparsely settled Early Iron Age Philistia. Studies by Hesse and Wapnish (Hesse 1986, 1990; Hesse and Wapnish 1997) of the faunal remains from Ashkelon and Tel Miqne/Ekron show changes in the

TABLE 8.1. *Pig:sheep/goat:cattle ratio in Philistia (after Maher 2005; Hesse 1990)*

	Late Bronze Age	Early Iron Age	Pig percentage: LBA/IA
Ashkelon	(thirteenth–twelfth century) 1:15:10	(twelfth century) 1:2:2	4%/19%
Tel Miqne/Ekron	(Late Bronze Age–Iron I) 1:9:3	(Iron I) 1:2.5:2	8%/18%
Ashdod	N.A.	1:5:0.5	N.A./14.7%
Batash	(Late Bronze Age) 1:13:5	(Iron I) 1:8:4	5%/8%

ratios of swine, cattle, and sheep and goats between the beginning of the Late Bronze Age and the Early Iron Age (see Table 8.1). This change is characterized by two phenomena:

1. A massive increase of swine remains found mainly in the two Pentapolis sites. The percentage of swine in Ashkelon rises from 4 percent of the faunal assemblage from the thirteenth and twelfth centuries to 19 percent in the twelfth century, and at Tel Miqne/Ekron from 8 percent in Late Bronze Age/Iron I to 18 percent in Iron I.

2. An increase in cattle in comparison to a decrease in sheep and goat bones. The ratio of sheep and/or goats to cattle changes in Ashkelon from 3:2 from the thirteenth and twelfth centuries to 1:1 in the twelfth century and at Tel Miqne/Ekron from 3:1 in Late Bronze Age/Iron I to 5:4 in Iron I.

The small faunal assemblage from Area H, Stratum XII, in Ashdod, indicative of the earlier stratum of Philistine settlement, shows a somewhat different picture with a stronger pastoral component but still a high swine ratio (Maher 2005).[3]

The cultural significance of the use of pigs in the ancient Near East is not discussed here, although much attention has been ascribed to the aspects of ethnicity that were or were not manifested in the exploitation of swine in the "Philistine" and "Proto-Israelite" societies (Hesse and Wapnish 1997; Finkelstein 1997). Hesse and Wapnish (1997: 240–53) suggest eight dimensions to the raising of pigs, based on ethnographic, historical, and archaeological case studies. Four of these are of special interest for the reconstruction of the economic structure in Early Iron Age Philistia:

1. Pigs are found in higher numbers in societies displaying domestic agropastoralism than in those with intensive agriculture, which is usually marked by a rise in cattle (Hesse and Wapnish 1997: 242–6).

2. Pigs are more closely related to the independent, rural subsistence economy than to the urban, elite-controlled markets. Accordingly, swine husbandry

---

[3] Of the entire assemblage, ovicaprines were 58.8%: sheep, 10.3%; goats, 5.9%; pigs, 14.7%; and cattle, 7.3%.

may be used as an indicator of the level of regional integration inside the political economy (Hesse and Wapnish 1997: 246–7).

3. Raising pigs is an initial strategy that new arrivals use to obtain rapid protein yields. Cattle and sheep are used in the next phase, when the economy "matures" (Hesse and Wapnish 1997: 247–8).

4. Pigs are associated with the low strata of societies, and pork is not considered a luxury meat (Hesse and Wapnish 1997: 252–3).

The change in animal husbandry patterns may, therefore, be a result of a combination of factors: the arrival of new people who needed fast protein; the enlargement of the urban population (seen in Tel Miqne/Ekron and perhaps in Ashkelon); and possibly a decline in the level of political integration, with less control by the elite on markets and meat products. A break in the connection with the highland pastoral systems brought about by migration may have caused the inhabitants of Philistia to turn to more independent meat production, focusing on the raising of cattle and swine, animals that are best adapted to the plains (Hesse 1990: 219).

Although Hesse and Wapnish (1997) view pigs as demarcators of less centralized agricultural systems, the contemporaneous rise in the ratios of cattle may suggest that there was some intensification in land tenure around the large sites. The sample from Tel Miqne/Ekron (Hesse 1986: 22) also seems to support this notion, as most animals are more than four years old. It also includes finds for pathologies in cattle toe bones (Lev-Tov 2006: 211–12) from Iron I, resulting from strenuous labor. Similarly, cattle remains from Ashdod show pathologies that "resulted from a lifelong of pulling and hauling heavy loads" (Maher 2005: 284).

AN AEGEAN ORIGIN FOR THE CHANGE?

Further information on the nature of change in animal husbandry at the beginning of the Early Iron Age can be obtained from comparing the ratios of swine, sheep and/or goats, and cattle in Philistia with those from earlier and contemporary Aegean and Cypriot sites (Tables 8.1 and 8.2). Theoretically, two main phenomena lead to the creation of a similar ratio (1:2:2) in Aegean, Cypriot, and Philistine assemblages:

1. According to the diffusionist explanation, if the Aegean migrants indeed brought from their homeland a distinctive type of subsistence economy and animal husbandry, some sites in the Aegean should portray similar ratios (i.e., 1:2:2 between swine, sheep and/or goats, and cattle).

2. According to the evolutionist explanation, similar social and economic structures, not necessarily connected to any origin or tradition, may also lead to the same ratio; that is, although the Aegean immigrants to the Levant did not come directly from the sites that portray similar ratios

TABLE 8.2. *Pig, sheep/goat, and cattle in the Aegean and Cyprus*

	Pig	Sheep/goat	Cattle	Ratio pig:sheep/goat:cattle	Source
The Aegean					
Nichoria LHIIIB2*[a]	23.5	46.9	10.9	2.2:4.3:1	Sloan and Duncan 1978: 62–3
Nichoria Dark Age I*	23.7	25.4	28.8	1:1.1:1.2	Sloan and Duncan 1978: 62–3
Vronda LMIIIC*	15.9	70	5	3.1:14:1	Klippel and Snyder 1991: 180
Phylakopi LHIII#[b] (phase IV)	19.6	46.1	20.5	1:2.3:1	Gamble 1982: 168
Tiryns LHIIB2*	21.0	40.8	35	1:2:1.7	von den Driesch and Boessneck 1990: 93
Tiryns LHIIIC Early*	19.7	46.1	31.3	1:2.3:1.6	von den Driesch and Boessneck 1990: 93
Tiryns LHIIIC Adv.*	21.5	37.2	38.8	1:1.7:1.8	von den Driesch and Boessneck 1990: 93
Tiryns LHIIIC Late*	19.4	26.2	41.2	1:1.4:2.1	von den Driesch and Boessneck 1990: 93
Pylos Late Bronze Age#	32	47	21	1.5:2.2:1	Halstead 1996: 29
Kommos Late Bronze Age #	22	74	4	5.5:18.5:1	Halstead 1996: 29
Knossos Late Bronze Age #	25	63	12	2:5.2:1	Halstead 1996: 29
Kastanas Late Bronze Age (11–19) #	40	37	22	1.8:1.7:1	Halstead 1996: 29
Pevkakia Late Bronze Age #	30	37	33	1:1.2:1.1	Halstead 1996: 29

[a] * = Percentage of the entire collection of bone remains.
[b] # = Percentage of the total of only sheep/goat, cattle, and pig.

of animals, the settlement conditions and the sociopolitical structure of Philistia created an economic structure similar to that of some Aegean sites.

From the data exhibited in Table 8.2, pigs appear very frequently in all types of settlements in the Aegean: palatial and nonpalatial sites, from the time before or after the fall of the palaces. Pigs (e.g., *si-a$_2$-ro*, SUS+SI, SUS+KA, SUS) are mentioned in the Linear B tablets but less frequently than sheep and goats – the main components of the palatial economy (Ventris and Chadwick 1973: 131, 198). The nature of raising pigs is revealed in a reference to "fat pigs" (*si-a$_2$-ro*; PY Cn 608; Ventris and Chadwick 1973: 205–6; Aura-Jorro 1993: 290), which towns had to fatten as a tribute to the Pylian palace. The breeding of pigs was thus in the hands of the locals for the purpose of the palace. This abundance of swine does not occur in Cyprus, where pigs were considerably less frequent: pigs do not appear in Kouklia, and they appear in Kition only in LCIIIA, and even then in very small numbers. The only exception is the site of Maa-Palaeokastro, a site of LCIIIA Aegean settlers (Chapter 5). It seems, therefore, that massive exploitation of pigs was not characteristic of the autochthonous Cypriot economy.

The Cretan sites of Knossos and Kommos are the furthest from the Philistia ratio. Their large proportion of sheep and/or goats seems to settle well with the importance known to be attributed to flocks in the Cretan-Mycenaean palatial economy (Halstead 1992: 60, 67–8). In Vronda, a postpalatial site, there is an evident emphasis on sheep and/or goats that may result from adaptation to the environs of eastern Crete.

Most of the Aegean mainland sites exhibit a more balanced ratio between sheep and other animals than do the Cretan sites. This phenomenon in the palatial centers of Pylos and in Tiryns may be related to what Halstead (1992: 64) termed *non-palatial production* and can be explained in two ways. The first is that the palaces imported large amounts of cattle and swine and/or exported large numbers of sheep. The second, perhaps more likely for Tiryns, is that most faunal remains found in the town represent not the palatial economy but rather nonpalatial production and consumption in an urban context.

The site that portrays an almost identical ratio to the Philistia ratio of 1:2:2 is Tiryns of LHIIIB2–LHIIIC/Developed. A comparison of the nature of settlement in Tiryns with that in Philistia demonstrates that the similarity in the economic patterns is hardly a coincidence. Tiryns was a very large settlement in LHIIIB2 and in LHIIIC, with a massive *Unterburg* and a total population of as many as ten thousand people (Chapter 3). It had, however, limited agricultural hinterland, sharing the Argolid with the powerful – most likely rival – polities of Mycenae and Midea (both of which were still strong in the LHIIIC period), as well as with smaller towns like Argos and Nauplion. Agricultural intensification was needed to feed everybody. The solution was to raise large amounts of swine and cattle – better suited for urban environments and for plains – with less emphasis placed on sheep (more identified with palatial economy) and goats than had been in the Knossos and even the Pylos palaces. This situation did not change much in the LHIIIC period: the population was still large; the other Argolid polities were still around – their elite perhaps broken down or changed – but so was Tiryns. It is impossible, at this stage of research, to ascertain whether this similarity results only from similar political, socioeconomic, and ecological circumstances. Other options remain open: the migrants of Philistia may have come from an Aegean polity or polities similar in situation to Tiryns, or even from the same region of the Aegean world.

A second settlement that exhibits a similarity to the Philistia ratio is Maa-Palaeokastro. At first sight, the ratio of 1:4:4 for swine, sheep and/or goats, and cattle shows a lower percentage of swine, yet it should be remembered that deer bones account for 26 percent of the total animal remains. Deer provided much of the meat and perhaps lessened the need to raise pigs. In any case, the pig ratios at Maa-Palaeokastro were much higher than in contemporary Kition and Kouklia, indicating that the raising of pigs, and similar proportions of cattle and sheep and/or goats, are traits of the LHIIIC Aegean settlement in both Cyprus and Philistia.

CHANGES IN CROPS?

It is possible that the Aegean migrants indeed introduced new plants, as did other migrants (Chapter 1), or placed a different emphasis on the cultivation of plants that were previously known in Canaan. A type of vetch, *Lathyrus sativus*, was probably introduced into significant cultivation during the Iron I period in Philistia and has been found in Ashkelon, Tel Miqne Ekron, and Tel Qasile (Kislev and Hopf 1985: 140; Mahler-Slasky 2004: 96, 176–7). The finding of large amounts of this vetch is curious because the unprocessed beans are poisonous and require specific knowledge of preparation for consumption (Kislev and Hopf 1985: 143). Remains of *Lathyrus sativus* from Late Bronze Age contexts in Israel or Cyprus have not been published, yet they are well known from the Aegean world and Europe in the Bronze and Iron Ages (Ventris and Chadwick 1973: 129; Kislev 1989: 264–5). Is it possible that the cultivation of these types of vetch is of Aegean origin, and that they were introduced by the Aegean migrants?

TRADE

INTERNATIONAL TRADE AND CHANGES IN INTERACTIONS WITH CYPRUS THROUGHOUT THE TWELFTH CENTURY

The lack of imported twelfth-century objects in Philistia and the relatively meager evidence for connections with Cyprus in the first phase of the Aegean settlement are rather surprising. Both Philistia and Cyprus were settled by Aegean migrants at approximately the same time and perhaps even by people of similar origins, given the similarity between the material cultures of both regions. However, from the Cypriot side, different Orientalia found in LCIIIA contexts include Levantine objects such as a bronze drinking set (Sherratt 1998: 304–5) and, more important, "Canaanite amphorae" (Åström 1993; Gilboa 1998: 423). Most of the amphorae from Maa-Palaeokastro examined by Jones and Vaughan (1988) were shown by petrography and chemical analysis to be made in either the central or the southern Levant (i.e., the Carmel Coast and perhaps even Philistia). Sherratt's (1998) argument that these amphorae and other Orientalia reached Cyprus via the Levantine coast seems correct. Imported amphorae appear in Maa-Palaeokastro in Floors I and II (Hadjicosti 1988: 363–81), indicating that the contact with the Levant occurred through most of the twelfth century, the LCIIIA period. The apparent paradox of Levantine finds in Cyprus compared with the lack of Cypriot objects in Philistia until the end of the twelfth century can easily be settled through a model of indirect trade through one of the ports to the north of modern-day Israel, such as Dor or Acco, which maintained contacts with Cyprus in the beginning of the Iron Age, as evident by the finds of imported Cypriot LHIIIC-style pottery in the Acco Plain. Some amphorae from Philistia may have reached the northern ports through regional trade and later have been shipped to Cyprus, most likely together with other Levantine goods obtained elsewhere. Support for this model comes from a petrographic study of twelfth-century-BCE Canaanite amphorae from Ashkelon, showing that their vast majority originated from Ashkelon itself, southern Canaan, and the Shephela; about a quarter of the sample, from the central coast, Dor, and the Acco Plain; and few from southern Lebanon and northern Syria. None originated in Egypt or in Cyprus (Master 2009).

This picture had probably changed by the late twelfth century and early eleventh century, when different elements of Cypriot material culture appeared in Philistia, the vast majority of which were locally made. First to enter the Bichrome repertoire were Cypriot pottery types, perhaps as early as Ashdod Stratum XIIIa (Chapter 7) and the contemporary incised scapulae from Tel Miqne/Ekron. Slightly later, in the "middle" phase of Bichrome pottery, iron knives from Tel Miqne/Ekron (Stratum V) and Tell Qasile (Stratum XII; T. Dothan 1989b; Sherratt 1998: 304) made their appearance, as did the incised scapula from Dor (Stern 1997: 132), the seals from Ashdod (Strata XII and X), and possibly the Cypro-Minoan script on them and on the contemporary Aphek tablet (see "Literacy and Administration").

How can we interpret these connections? Although Sherratt (1998: 304–5) interprets them as trade, almost no traded items manufactured in Cyprus are to be found (as opposed to the Cypriot traits seen on items made locally in Philistia), save perhaps the few iron knives. The case of the Philistine Bichrome pottery with Cypriot prototypes is exceptionally intriguing, as there are virtually no such Cypriot imports into the Levant until the late eleventh or the tenth century (Gilboa 1998: 432), almost a century after the appearance of the bottle and the horn-shaped vessels in the "Philistine" repertoire. How could these items have been imitated in Philistia without first having been brought there as imports? As trade is ruled out, a possible solution is a limited Cypriot component in the Aegean migration during the late twelfth and early eleventh centuries (as has already been discussed).

REGIONAL TRADE

Regional trade (within the boundaries of Philistia) has been detected by a few finds of fineware pottery that were manufactured away from their site of find. Most of the LHIIIC pottery from Tel Miqne/Ekron was manufactured at the site (Gunneweg et al. 1986: 10, 15), yet a figurine from Stratum VI (Gunneweg et al. 1986: 14) – as well as an Aegean-type cooking pot (Gunneweg et al. 1986: 8, table 1, no. 41) and possibly other vessels belonging to the early phases of the Aegean settlement at the site – was made in Ashdod. In Ashdod itself, most of the LHIIIC pottery was locally made (Asaro, Perlman, and Dothan 1971), although a few pieces may have originated in Tel Miqne/Ekron (Gunneweg et al. 1986: 15). According to Ben-Shlomo (2006a: fig. 5.2), imports of Tel Miqne/Ekron Monochrome wares to Ashdod and Ashkelon amounted to as much as 18 percent of the sample from both sites.

The phenomenon of trade in pottery, decorated (Bichrome) and undecorated, became even more frequent by the end of the twelfth century and during the eleventh century, as seen in the mixed origin of the assemblages from Tel Miqne/Ekron (Ben-Shlomo 2006a: 11), Ashdod, Tel ʿAitun, Tell Qasile (Yellin and Gunneweg 1985), and Tell en-Naṣbeh (Gunneweg et al. 1994).

An assessment of the exact nature and scale of this trade in pottery awaits additional data from provenance studies on vessels from Tel Miqne/Ekron.

PHILISTIA'S ECONOMY

The twelfth-century economy of Philistia seems to have been based on high-intensity agriculture, while regional and interregional trade probably played only a minor role. The basis of the system was mostly farmers living in the cities rather than in smaller settlements, which were almost nonexistent in the period. They focused on raising pigs as a convenient source of protein. Cattle were raised extensively, for intensive exploitation of available land outside the city and as a source of protein and fat through dairy products. It is also possible that new types of legumes, introduced by the migrants, enriched the diet. The economic systems may have been primarily limited to the boundaries of the polities. Limited contact with agropastoral groups of the highlands and the fringe resulted in less sheep and/or goat products. There was little long-distance or international commerce. There is also no evidence for the involvement of rulership in the economy: no storage rooms and no accumulation of social surplus in the form of elite goods. However, it is likely that, as in other cases of colonization, the aristocrats received a fair proportion of the best lands, or perhaps even a *temenos* in the Mycenaean sense (i.e., a plot of land allotted to the leader) (Halstead 1992: 66).

CEREMONIAL AND CULTIC ACTIVITY

CULT ROOMS, FIGURINES, ZOOMORPHIC VESSELS, AND BOVID SCAPULAE

The number of published cult-related objects from the first phase of Philistine settlement is negligible compared with their significantly greater number in eleventh-century Strata XII and XI at Ashdod, in Stratum V at Tel Miqne/Ekron, and among the wealth of evidence from contemporary Tell Qasile.[4]

---

[4] See most recently Mazar 2000, for a thorough presentation of the cult finds from eleventh-century Philistia.

The discussion here attempts to establish the origin of all published objects from the relevant strata that may be connected with cultic or ceremonial activity.

The only certain cult place reported from the sites of either Ashdod or Tel Miqne/Ekron is a cult room at Tel Miqne/Ekron Field I, Stratum VI (T. Dothan 1989a: 9; Dothan and Gitin 1993: 1053) containing a stone pillar base and a pit with a kalathos and an incised scapula. This shrine was further modified late in Stratum V, when its floor was plastered and a platform and benches were added (T. Dothan 1989a; Dothan and Dothan 1992: 242; Dothan 2003: fig. 17). A possible cult room is Room F in Field X (Dothan et al. 1998: 14; Dothan 2003: fig. 16). This small and nearly square room has a plastered threshold, plastered surface, and a small plastered platform that the excavators called a bamah. Finds from this room make its association to cult activity uncertain: an imperforated loom weight and pottery (assigned to Area XNW78) of the types found elsewhere in Fields X and I.

Cult objects are also not numerous in the first phase of Philistine settlement. There are no human figurines in the Pentapolis before the very end of the twelfth century (Press 2007: 269; Ben-Shlomo and Press 2009: fig. 9), and only few bovine figurines of Aegean style may have some cultic significance.

Later, in Ashkelon Phase 19, Tel Miqne/Ekron Stratum VI, and Ashdod Stratum XII, female figurines of the "mourning" or Mycenaean-type psi-figurines make their first appearance (Ben-Shlomo and Press 2009: figs. 1: 1, 1: 5, 1: 7, 1: 9). These are also a rather rare type, with only a dozen examples found. They are small female figurines, crudely made, often painted, their hands raised upward. The LHIIIC find context of such figurines is often in tombs, such as in the Perati, Ialysos, and Kamini cemeteries (Dothan 1982: 242). At Ashkelon, one such figurine was found in Phase 19 (the late twelfth century BCE), while three others were found in Phase 18 (Press 2007: 271). The earliest example from Tel Miqne/Ekron (Ben-Shlomo and Press 2009: fig. 1: 1) comes from Stratum VIb, while the earliest example from Ashdod comes from Stratum XII (Ben-Shlomo and Press 2009: fig. 1: 5). According to Press (2007: 272), the evidence from Tel Miqne/Ekron and Ashkelon indicates that "mourning" or Mycenaean psi-type figurines in Philistia preceded the appearance of the "Ashdoda" figurines in the eleventh century BCE.

Some ceremonial use can be elucidated for zoomorphic vessels. A drinking vase in the shape of a lion's head is reported from the vicinity of the cult room in Field I (T. Dothan 1998a: 155; Dothan and Gitin 1993: 1053). This type of vase is of Canaanite rather than Aegean origin (Dothan 1982: 229–34). Another type of zoomorphic vase, in shape of a hedgehog – an Aegean form – was found in Field X and in Field IV, Stratum VII but not in a clear cultic context.

Bovid scapulae, with incisions on their edges, make their first appearance early in the eleventh century in the cult room at Tel Miqne/Ekron in Field I,

FIGURE 8.5. Bovid scapulae from the Ekron Field I shrine (after Dothan and Dothan 1992: 242)

Stratum VI, as well as in Stratum V (Dothan and Gitin 1993: 1053; Hesse 1986: 25 fig. 4; Fig. 8.5). These scapulae were compared by the excavators to incised scapulae from Cyprus, mainly Kition and Enkomi (Webb 1985: 317, 321; T. Dothan 1998a: 155). The earliest appearance of incised scapulae in Cyprus is at the Myrtou-Pigadhes sanctuary, in a context together with Base Ring bowls (ibid.: 320); this indicates that incised scapulae were used in Cyprus at least as early as the thirteenth century. Their earliest use at Kition and Enkomi was later, in LCIIIA. These scapulae could have been used either for divination or as musical instruments (ibid.: 326–7; T. Dothan 1998a: 155). Tel Miqne/Ekron is not the only find spot of bovid scapulae in Israel. An example is also reported from the Iron IIA stratum from Tell es-Safi/Gath (Zukerman, Lev-Tov, and Maier 2007) as well as from the eleventh-century stratum in Dor (Stern 1997: 132), both definitely of a later date than the Tel Miqne/Ekron finds (Chapter 5).

However faint, some change in cultic activity is seen between the Late Bronze Age and the Early Iron Age at Ashdod and Tel Miqne/Ekron, both in the vanishing of an old tradition and the arrival of a new one. It is extremely telling that the Late Bronze Age tradition of depicting naked female goddesses does not continue into Early Iron Age strata at either site (Dothan and Friedman 1967: 162–3, fig. 35: 4; Dothan 1971: 80–1, fig. 35: 9), but rather they are replaced by crude, *polos*-wearing figurines. Other new elements that appear are the incised scapulae, mentioned previously, and the Aegean hedgehog rhyton.

At both sites, the origin of the change is suggested by two indicative elements: the scapula and the figurine, which indicate, respectively, Cypriot and Aegean cultic practices or ceremonial behavior. Both types of objects are functional, and their extreme simplicity opposes their interpretation as imported objects or imitations of luxury items. However, the late appearance of the scapulae and the rarity of the figurines in the earliest Iron Age strata at Ashdod and Tel Miqne/Ekron make them of little value in the initial identification of the existence of migration.

THE ELEVENTH-CENTURY ICONOGRAPHIC EXPLOSION

The absence of clay figurines from Ashdod Strata XIIIb and XIIIa and the extremely small number of religious architecture and cult objects from Tel

FIGURE 8.6. "Ashdoda" figurine (Dothan 1971: fig. 91: 1)

Miqne/Ekron Strata VII and VI stand in great contrast to the explosion of cult imagery in the late twelfth century or beginning of the eleventh century, when we find the sanctuaries and cult objects of Tell Qasile (Mazar 1985a; 2000), and the cult room in the monumental structure in Field IV in Tel Miqne/Ekron Stratum V (T. Dothan 1998a: 155). Typical are the many female figurines (Dothan 1982: 234–49), most of which are the "Ashdoda" figurines (Fig. 8.6). First brought to light by Moshe Dothan's excavations at Ashdod, these figurines were found later at sites such as Aphek, Tell Qasile, and Tel Batash/Timnah, as well as at Gezer, Tel Miqne/Ekron, and Ashkelon (Yasur-Landau 2001; Press 2007: 85–91) The "Ashdoda" figurines, unparalleled in the coroplastic art of the Levant, were interpreted by Dothan as "a variant of the Mycenaean female figurine seated on a throne, and sometimes holding a child" (Press 2007: 234). Other figurines of the late twelfth and eleventh centuries, the "mourning" figurines, were also identified by Dothan as stemming directly from Aegean tradition (Press 2007: 237). A detailed iconographic and contextual analysis of the origin, the function, and the identity of the goddess depicted in the "Ashdoda" figurines (Yasur-Landau 2001) strongly supports Dothan's notion that the prototype for the "Ashdoda" figurines was an Aegean earth goddess. A comparison of the iconographic elements of the figurines with the array of Aegean, Canaanite, and Cypriot figurines of the Late Bronze Age has shown that the composition of iconographic elements on the "Ashdoda" painted figurine from Ashdod finds its best parallel in LHI-IIC ceramic figures from Tiryns (Kilian 1978; Fig. 8.7). The occurrence of at least five distinct, well-defined elements–a *polos* hat; applied nose and ears; many necklaces on a very long neck; exposed breasts emphasized by circles of paint; and a triangular pendant on the chest – form strong evidence for the continuation of twelfth-century Aegean cultic iconography in the late twelfth century iconography of the "Ashdoda." The clear eleventh-century date for the first appearance of the "Ashdoda" figurines strongly suggests that these figurines did not belong to the cultural baggage of the first Aegean migrants but were added later, perhaps as part of the Cypriot cultural influence of the early eleventh century, seen also in the incised scapulae and in some seal imagery.

A final piece of evidence of the elite's association with the worship of an Aegean earth goddess in Philistia comes from the excavation of a seventh-century temple/palace complex at Tel Miqne/Ekron Field IV (Dothan and Gitin 1993: 1058; Gitin 1993: 250–1; 1998: 175). This temple yielded a monumental inscription, in Phoenician script, which states both the name of the king who built the temple and the deity to which it is dedicated: "The temple which (he) built, 'kyš, son of Padi, son of Ysd, son of Ada, son of Yaʿar, ruler of Ekron, for Ptgyh his lady, may she bless him, and prote[ct] him, and prolong his days, and bless his [l]and" (Gitin et al. 1997; Gitin 1998: 173, 178). Achish, the ruler of Ekron, is Ikausu, mentioned in an Assyrian inscription. His non-Semitic name is derived from *Ik(h)ayus/š=* ᾿Αχαιϝός or* ᾿Αχαιός – meaning "the Achaean" (Naveh 1998). The goddess's name, Ptgyh, is also non-Semitic (Gitin et al. 1997: 11–12). The name was interpreted by Schäfer-Lichtenberger (1998: 72–3; 2000: 89–91) as deriving from Πύθω – Γαῖα, or "Gaia from Pytho." Another possibility is a derivation from Πότ[ν]ια Γαῖα =, or "the Lady Gaia."[5] In any case, the component of Gaia in both proposals is indeed a pleasant surprise, establishing an Aegean earth goddess as the protector of the well-being of the dynasty in the Philistine city of Ekron. Gitin and colleagues (1997: 12) suggest, without relating to the name Gaia (yet obviously relating to the name of Asherah found near the temple), the possibility that Ptgyh was "identified with the local Semitic deity of Asherah." To my mind, this not only is the case but also hints at the identity of the earth goddess Ashdoda. The cult of the Aegean great mother-goddess Gaia, a ruling earth goddess and "the mother of all," gods, plants, and animals, seems to have been preserved in Philistia from the time of the Aegean migration between the twelfth century and the seventh century.

---

[5] Cf. Homeric Epigrams VII (Πότνια Γῆ). Gaia/Ge is not mentioned in Linear B sources, and indeed not until the eighth century. The combination is rare even later, with few examples: Athenagoras *Legatio* 18.6.6; Hesichius Πότνια Γῆ Fragmenta Orphica frag. 13: 41; *Vita Homeri* 249.

FIGURE 8.7. LHIIIC figure from Tiryns (after Demakopoulou 1988: pl. 25)

ELITE IN THE PENTAPOLIS

EVIDENCE FOR THE EXISTENCE OF ELITE

Coming from the rather humble architectural tradition of the LHIIIC world, it is little wonder that the architecture at the initial phase of Philistine settlement seems vernacular, domestic, and not monumental. Even the Ashdod Area G structure, which may be the only twelfth-century building that can qualify as a ruler's dwelling, was a reused Canaanite/Egyptian "residency." However, it was modified (Chapter 7) to create a building that resembles an Aegean *Korridorhaus*, an elite building, which has yielded a number of elite objects.[6]

As families settled down and expanded in the twelfth and eleventh centuries, some gradually became elite. The first fifty years or so in the settlement of the Philistines were apparently a quiet time in which many families grew in power and economic abilities, obtaining some access to luxury items. Such, for example, is the case of Structure 5337 in Ashdod Stratum XII, which developed from an earlier, Stratum XIII domestic structure (Mazar and

---

[6] These included a gold sword pommel (Dothan and Porath 1993: pl. 9), a dagger (Dothan and Porath 1993: fig. 17: 17), a bronze uraeus (Dothan and Porath 1993: fig. 17: 11), a faience bead (Dothan and Porath 1993: fig. 24: 7), an amber bead (Dothan and Porath 1993: fig. 24: 8), a gold and jasper scarab (Dothan and Porath 1993: fig. 24: 10), and a faience figurine (Dothan and Porath 1993: fig. 24: 11).

Ben-Shlomo 2005: plan 2.7). Finds within it include two gold disks, ivory and bone objects, four necklaces of faience beads, a glazed terra-cotta pendant, a scarab, and a miniature kylix.

A similar process can be seen in Ashkelon, where the two rather humble houses of Stratum 20b, separated at first by an open area, grow in size considerably in Stratum 19, the northern one equipped with a large hearth room and a massive limestone bathtub, which must have been quarried in the Judean foothills and shipped from a distance of twenty kilometers or more to the coast.

The same gradual rise of power can be seen at Tel Miqne/Ekron Field IV. The humble, yet symbolically laden, single-room, Hearth Building 357 of Stratum VII was incorporated into the more monumental Building 351 of Stratum VI. During the eleventh century, parts of the latter were incorporated into the monumental building 350 of Stratum V (Dothan 2003: fig. 4; Mazow 2005: 85, 391). It was a true ruler's dwelling, with a central pebble-paved hearth, which has yielded elite objects such as parts of a bronze cultic stand, an iron knife with an ivory handle, and a bronze chariot linchpin. After the destruction of this house in the tenth century, the importance of the area as the seat of the ruler was not forgotten, and the seventh-century temple and palace of Achish, son of Padi, were built at exactly the same place (Gitin 1998).

Further evidence for the existence of elite comes from evidence for chariots and horses in the Pentapolis. Chariot bronze linchpins and other fittings found at Tel Miqne/Ekron and Ashkelon (Stager 2006), as well as horse bones from Tel Miqne/Ekron Stratum VII (Lev-Tov 2006: 221), indicate that a few elite members still had access to the Aegean and Canaanite costly symbols of power.

Although it is likely that both buildings at Ashdod Area G and Tel Miqne/Ekron Field IV were important buildings at the sites in the early stages of migration, it is unlikely that they were the only important buildings. The example of Tiryns, with its two megara, and even that of Karphi, are reminders of the possibility that some LHIIIC settlements may have had more than one focus of power.

LITERACY AND ADMINISTRATION

The twelfth-century Aegean world from which the Philistines emerged was a postliterate society; its Linear B script and administrative system quickly disappeared with the fall of the palatial system. There is little wonder, therefore, that no Linear B texts have been found in Philistia. In contrast, with the Aegean migration to Cyprus, the last bastion of linear scripts in the twelfth century had exposed the Philistines to the Cypro-Minoan script. Similarly, an encounter with the Cypriot and Levantine traditions of cylinder and stamp seals introduced them to the administrative technique of sealing. However,

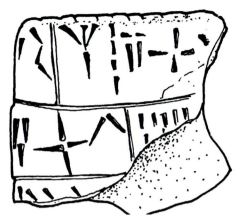

FIGURE 8.8. Linear script tablet from Aphek (after Kochavi and Beck 1990: 24)

all evidence for administration and scripts is later than the first arrival of the Philistine migrants, and it begins to appear only with the rise of the social complexity after a generation or so in Philistia.

LINEAR INSCRIPTIONS

Only two linear inscriptions containing more than one or two signs were found in Philistia, both originating in eleventh-century-BCE contexts. The identification of both as Cypro-Minoan is not without doubt. The first comes from Phase 17 in Ashkelon, datable to the later eleventh century (Cross and Stager 2006: 131–4). It is a *dipinto* in red paint on a body sherd of a storage jar. A petrographic analysis of this sherd concluded that the vessel was made in the area of Ashkelon. The inscription comprises nine characters written from right to left. Seven of the characters find parallels in the Cypro-Minoan script. However, both writing direction and the use of paint are unusual in the Cypro-Minoan tradition, in which inscriptions are usually written from left to right, with a stylus on wet clay or incised with a sharp object on pottery, stone, or metal.

Further intriguing evidence for administration in Philistia comes from Aphek (Kochavi 1989; Beck and Kochavi 1993: 68–9; Singer 1994: 334; Fig. 8.8), where a small clay tablet inscribed in a linear script was found in an eleventh-century context (see the line drawing in Kochavi and Beck 1990). The same stratum, which included mainly pits, also yielded heads of "Ashdoda" figurines and Philistine Bichrome pottery. This unique tablet is yet to be fully published, but its line drawing shows possible numerals, indicating that it may be an economic tablet. Some signs appear to be similar to the Cypro-Minoan syllabary but certainly not all (Singer 2009). A petrographic examination of the tablet showed that it is composed of clay typical of the Tell es-Ṣafi/Gath

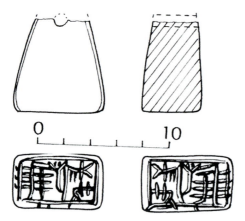

FIGURE 8.9. Seal from Ashdod Area G, Stratum XII (after Dothan and Porath 1993: 217, fig. 36: 9)

region, while a southern, coastal provenance was found for the "Ashdoda figurines" (Goren, Yasar-Landau, and Buzaglo, 2009).[7]

Some of the signs incised also on "Canaanite amphorae" and other vessels from Ashkelon have been interpreted as belonging to the Cypro-Minoan repertoire (Cross and Stager 2006; Chapter 6). Some come from Late Bronze Age levels (nos. 2, 4, 7, 8, 12, 18), and others from Iron I levels, but those have plain signs that may or may not belong to the Cypro-Minoan corpus (simple cross nos. 13, 14; two horizontal bars nos. 15, 16, 17). Few seem to have good parallels in the Cypro-Minoan syllabary (nos. 1 and 10, Phases 19 and 18) yet some of these may be residual from Late Bronze Age levels.

SEALS AND SEALINGS

The seals and sealings from Philistia do not seem to continue any trend of Aegean Bronze Age administration. Although remains from Ashkelon await publication, at Tel Miqne/Ekron only four sealings and one seal come from Strata VII and VI (Ben-Shlomo 2006b: 150). The seal is an Egyptianizing handled faience seal. Three of the sealings are string and finger impressions, whereas the only seal impression from Stratum VII is the sealing of a scarab, which depicts an Egyptian king between two pillars (Ben-Shlomo 2006b: 141, fig. 8). Later, in the Iron Age, sealings became more common, with eleven additional examples from eleventh-century contexts. Most motifs on the later sealings appear to be either Canaanite or Egyptian (Ben-Shlomo 2006b: 148).

Similarly, at Ashdod, no sealings or seals are known from the first stage of Philistine settlement, while evidence from later Strata XII and XI point to Cypriot and local inspiration rather than an Aegean one.

---

[7] I am grateful to the late M. Kochavi and the late P. Beck for allowing me to examine the Aphek material.

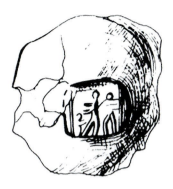

FIGURE 8.10. Bulla from Ashdod Area G, Stratum XII (after Dothan and Porath 1993: 221, fig. 38: 2)

Thus, for example, a pyramidal seal from Area H, Stratum XII, at Ashdod (Ben-Shlomo 2005: 130–1) shows a motif common to Cypriot seals of two men and a bucranium. In Area G, an additional seal and a bulla were found on the floors of Stratum XII rooms south of the city wall. The stamp seal from Stratum XII (Dothan and Porath 1993: 81, fig. 36: 9; Keel 1994: 22–3; 1997: 672–3 no. 27; Fig. 8.9) bears what was first interpreted as a Linear or Cypro-Minoan script inscription, yet it may be a figurative motif of horned animals. The stamped bulla from Stratum XII (Dothan and Porath 1993: 82, fig. 38: 2; Fig. 8.10) has an impression of two back-to-back figures with outstretched arms. String impressions on the back of the bulla indicate that it was indeed used for sealing.

Later examples come from the late-eleventh-century Stratum XI. Another example of a possibly inscribed seal comes from Area H, Stratum XI (Dothan 1982: 41, pl. 6; Dothan and Dothan 1992: 167, pl. 11; Ben-Shlomo 2005: 165–6). It depicts in a crude, linear style three seated figures, each raising one hand in what is possibly a blessing gesture. The figures are separated from one another by a linear or Cypro-Minoan inscription. The central figure seems more prominent than the other figures: it is clearly enthroned and wearing some type of headdress or crown. Although other attributes are not depicted, this figure may be associated with the Aegean enthroned *polos*-wearing goddess, later to be represented by the "Ashdoda" figurines (see "The Eleventh-Century Iconographic Explosion"). However, the general theme of the seal and the gesture of the figures suggest much Near Eastern and/or Cypriot iconographic influence (Collon 1987: figs. 304, 312, 316; Amiet 1992: 60 no. 107; Webb 1999: 257, fig. 89).

In summary, the evidence for administration in Philistia is extremely sketchy in the first phase of the Philistine settlement and is composed mainly of a few sealings, none in Aegean style. Sealing activity as well as Cypriot stylistic influence appears only in the second half of the Iron I, during the eleventh century. This is also true for the possibly inscribed cylinder seal from Ashdod, which may relate to a common Cypriot phenomenon of the LCIIC and LCIII periods (Masson 1957; Smith 1994: 142–62; Hirschfeld 1996: 21, 36, 47, 61, 76). The two possible linear texts from Ashkelon and Aphek belong to the eleventh century. Thus, there is no evidence implying that the Philistines were literate on arrival but rather that the gradual rise in social complexity in Philistia during the eleventh century resulted in borrowing administrative traditions from both Canaanites and Cypriots.

RULERSHIP IN THE PENTAPOLIS ACCORDING TO LATER (IRON II AND III) LITERARY SOURCES

In the story of the ark in Philistia (1 Sam. 5–6) the *seranim* (סרנים) are mentioned as leaders of the Pentapolis. This story, which mentions the pivotal role of Gath, which was destroyed in the ninth century BCE, is one of the few instances in which biblical traditions regarding the Philistines can be traced back to the Iron I (Finkelstein 2002: 140–1). The *seranim* are assembled twice (1 Sam. 5:8, 11), in Ashdod and in Ekron, working as a council to deal with the ark crisis. It is noted later that there are five *seranim* (1 Sam. 6:4). The term *seren* has long been considered an Indo-European term, parallel to the Luwian *tarwanis*, a title of neo-Hittite rulers, or the Greek τύρραννος (Macalister 1965: 79; Singer 1993: 132; 1994: 336). How useful is the use of this term in a possibly seventh-century literary source – mainly the books of Judges and 1 Samuel – to our study of twelfth-century rulership? Such a characteristic non-Semitic term could be introduced and accepted, in my opinion, only in a period when the rulers themselves were of nonlocal origin or had embraced a nonlocal cultural background. This was precisely the situation in the twelfth century, when new Aegean rulership arrived in Canaan (contra Finkelstein 2002: 137). Arguing that *seren* is a seventh-century term would demand proof that approximately at this time a new, foreign leadership came to Philistia, an event unaccounted for anywhere. However, the Ekron inscription indicates that the rulership that arrived in southern Canaan in the twelfth century maintained a good part of its Aegean traditions, including Aegean names and "Mycenaean" cult, until the seventh century, thus supporting the plausibility that the term *seren* could have been preserved for five centuries.

As for the origin of the term, Singer (1993; 1994) argues that it came from Asia Minor, in support of his views that the Philistines were of Anatolian descent. At any rate, this term and similar ones do not appear in Linear B.[8] If this is not a coincidence, and if one accepts that the term *seren* was brought with the Aegean migrants, it can be argued that the early Aegean government system in the Pentapolis was not imported from any of the known palatial centers in Crete or the Argolid.

In addition to the *seranim* (סרנים), two more terms are used for the rulership in the Pentapolis in biblical terminology: *sarim* (שרים) and *melek* (מלך) (Singer 1993: 133; Machinist 2000: 58). The possibly Indo-European term *seren* was probably interchangeable with the Semitic terms *sar* and *melek*. A clear example for the perplexing use of terms is the story of the preparation for the Battle of Gilboa (1 Sam. 29), when the rulers of Philistia withheld David from joining the forces that were to fight Saul. The biblical author uses the term "the *sarim* of the Philistines" (שרי פלשתים; Machinist 2000: 3–4) to refer to the leaders who refused to let David join the army, while Achish, the ruler of Gath, refers to the same rulers as both "*seranim*" (Machinist 2000: 6) and "the *sarim* of the Philistines" (Machinist 2000: 9). Finally, to add to the confusion, David refers to Achish, who has the same rank as the other *sarim* or *seranim*, as "my lord the *melek*" (אדני המלך; Machinist 2000: 8; cf. 1 Sam. 21:11).[9] The use of these interchangeable terms is perhaps a question not only of Semitic/non-Semitic titles but also of chronology: *seranim* being an earlier term and *sarim* a later one. Although the term *seren* is not mentioned outside the Bible, Achish, son of Padi, the ruler of Ekron in the seventh century, calls himself "*sar Ekron*" in his dedicatory inscription (Gitin et al. 1997). The use of the Semitic term *sar* for later kings of Philistia corresponds to the fact that all eighth- and seventh-century Philistine kings known from Assyrian inscriptions have Semitic names (Tadmor 1966: 101), except for Ikausu/Achish (Naveh 1998).

THE ROLE OF WOMEN IN THE AEGEAN MIGRATION

In addition to the Medinet Habu reliefs, which show women of both Aegean and Syro-Canaanite origin on their way to settlement (Chapter 5), there are several pieces of evidence supporting the actual settlement of Aegean women in Philistia and their important role in the maintenance of group identity and

---

[8] However, the Mycenaean terms for rulership, *lawagetas* and *wanax*, have also been detected in Anatolia, in the grave inscription of Midas (ca. 600 BCE) from Gordion (Lenz 1993: 85): "Μιδαι λαϝαγαται ϝαναϰατει."

[9] Singer (1993: 133) argues that Achish may have been, in his title of "king" (*melek*), the *primus inter pares* of the other Philistine rulers. However, there is little in the text to support a more elevated status for Achish.

Aegean habitus (Chapter 7) through the preservation of Aegean-style domestic behavioral patterns. First, and most convincingly, weaving was practiced in the Pentapolis sites exclusively in an Aegean manner and in domestic contexts. Textile production was, to use Barber's words (1994: 29–33), mainly "women's work." Evidence supporting this is not restricted to the Bronze Age Aegean (Ventris and Chadwick 1973: 123; Barber 1997; Nordquist 1997: 535–6) or to ancient Mesopotamia and Egypt (Pinch 1995: 375; Greengus 1995: 492; and esp. Barber, 1994: 164–206) but has been found even in the modern-day Argolid (Koster 1976). Other household activities conducted in an Aegean manner, such as cooking with Aegean-style cooking pots on hearths (Chapter 7), are, of course, not as indicative as weaving. Although wheat grinding in the Bronze Age Aegean and in the ancient Near East seems to have been done almost exclusively by women (Ventris and Chadwick 1973: 123; Imparati 1995: 583; Greengus 1995: 495; Gruber 1995: 644), it seems that both men and women baked and cooked, at least in a specialized and/or palatial context. Bearing in mind the examples of women as maintainers of culinary practices in situations of migration and intercultural marriages (Chapter 1), one should not rule out the possibility that the finds of Aegean cookware and cooking installations at Area G at Ashdod were also used by women, preserving their cultural identity by practicing Aegean cooking traditions.

Intermarriage between Aegean migrants and Syro-Canaanite women is seen in the presence of such women in the Medinet Habu land battle relief. If such intermarriages were conducted prior to the settlement in Philistia, it is even more plausible to assume that this practice continued after the initial settlement as well.[10]

It is also possible that Aegean women took part in the introduction of the cult of the Aegean goddess(es) seen in the "Ashdoda" and other female figurines. Women with such roles are referred to in the traditions of the Greek colonization, where there are several examples of priestesses involved in the introduction of cults of female deities to the newly founded colonies (Graham 1982: 148). A Greek woman named Cleoboea (Pausanias 10.28.3) brought the cult of Demeter to Thassos from Paros, and Aristarcha (Strabo 4.1.4) not only was appointed by Artemis of Ephesos to guide the Phokaians to Massalia but also founded the cult of the goddess and became her priestess. The founding of a cult is accomplished through the transfer of an *aphidruma*, a statue or another sacred object. In the case of Massalia, the *aphidruma* was a cult statue (Malkin 1991: 78–9). The participation of a priestess in this, as in other cases of a cult of female deities being transferred, was essential: only women could wash and adorn a female cult image (Malkin 1991: 84–5).

---

[10] Domestic activities conducted in the local Canaanite manner, such as cooking using local cooking pots and *tabun*s (e.g., in Tel Miqne/Ekron Field X; Chapter 7) are almost impossible to engender. Even if they are attributed to local women, it is still impossible to determine a mixed household, as the entire household may be of local origin.

SOCIAL STRATIFICATION IN TWELFTH-CENTURY PHILISTIA

Demarcators of social hierarchy in twelfth-century Philistia are surprisingly sparse. Although the existence of emerging power foci in the form of ruler's dwellings and the apparent evidence of horses and chariots shows the existence of elite, there is little evidence of established government that used administration of any sort. No central storage, literacy, consistent sealing practices, or any other sign of accounting and redistribution has appeared. The level of craft specialization is low, and there is scarce evidence for full-time artisans other than potters. The absence of elite art and monumental architecture of any sort, either palaces or temples, apart from the Tel Miqne/Ekron fortification, attests to extremely modest economic abilities of the coetaneous elite and rulership. Social stratification can be estimated at CPI level 2, demonstrating two classes of free men: commoners and nobles. Most of the population, either Canaanite or Aegean, seems to have enjoyed basically the same level of prosperity throughout the twelfth century. The unhindered organic development and growth of houses from the twelfth century into the eleventh century seen at Ashkelon, in Area H at Ashdod, and in Field IV at Tel Miqne/Ekron strongly suggests that a great deal of power was in the hands of heads of kinship groups, enough, at least, to preserve the prosperity and development of their kinship group through most of the Iron Age I. It is likely that some of them bore foreign titles of rulership, like *seren*, from the onset of settlement. In the struggling subsistence economy of the first decades of settlement, such titles were not necessarily reflected in conspicuous architecture and luxurious items. Later, with the renewal of trade in the eleventh century and the territorial expansion of Philistia into the north, all the way to the Yarkon River line (Gadot 2006), social complexity increased and has been manifested in more evidence of administration: fortifications at Ashdod and Ashkelon, the appearance of residential monumental architecture at Tel Miqne/ Ekron, and the building of temples and shrines at Tel Miqne/Ekron and Tell Qasile.

CHRONOLOGY AND THE PARADIGM OF UNIFIED MIGRATION

WHY DO WE NEED AN ABSOLUTE CHRONOLOGY?

The fierce, decades-old battle between High, Middle, and Low Chronologies for the exact date of the end of the Late Bronze Age is closely connected to questions of the beginnings of "Philistine" and "Israelite" settlement (e.g., Ussishkin 1985; Finkelstein 1988: 315–23; T. Dothan 1989a; Bietak 1993). With respect to the date of the initial Philistine settlement, two main views exist.

The first, represented by scholars such as Mazar (1997: 155–7), Bietak (1993), T. Dothan (1989a: 8), and Stager (1995: 335), places the events around Year 8 of Ramses III, about 1175 BCE, also as the beginning of Philistine settlement. The second alternative, of a considerably lower chronology, was put forward by Finkelstein (1995a; 1996b; 1998), presented first in the mid-1990s. To Finkelstein's mind, and later to Ussishkin's (1998), the Philistine migration took part only after the final collapse of the Egyptian administration in Canaan, which left evidence from as late as Ramses IV's time at Beth Shean and Lachish and from as late as the days of Ramses III and perhaps Ramses VI at Megiddo. Thus, the Philistines' first arrival is dated fifty years or so later.

The reason for the conflicting opinions is the absence of any direct dating tool for the first phase of Aegean settlement in Philistia (i.e., datable Egyptian objects) from any of the three Pentapolis sites that have been extensively excavated. All Egyptian inscribed objects from Philistia are scarabs, easily transferred from one stratum to the other and providing only a terminus post quem to the stratum in which they have been found. Unfortunately, for those who favor the Middle Chronology, scarabs of Ramses III, even when found, as in Ashkelon (Master 2005), have never been followed by scarabs of Ramses IV in later strata to create a necessary chronological "sandwich." Scarabs of Ramses III and VI have been found in Ashdod Stratum XII (Brandl 1993: 138–9; Keel and Münger 2005: 276). Although this proves that Stratum XII is from later than the beginning of Ramses IV's reign, there is no way of saying how much later it is. The scarab could have even arrived from Stratum XIV, the last "Canaanite" stratum, just like another scarab from Stratum XII with the name of Ramses II that is attributed to Stratum XIV by Brandl (1993: 134–5). This unfortunate situation is by no means unique in the rather grim chronological landscape of the transition between the Bronze and Iron Ages in Canaan (Bietak 1993; Singer 1994; Finkelstein 1995; 1998). Lacking direct evidence, various indirect chronological leads are heavily relied on to reconstruct the date of the beginning of the Aegean settlement and its historical circumstances.

However, even if a conclusion is reached, what is its meaning to our understanding of the Philistine settlement process? Was the start date of the Aegean settlement the time when the first scout reached his destination, the arrival of the first small pioneer group by land or by sea, or the settlement of large family groups of migrants following the pioneer settlers? Is the start date marked by the building of the first house or by the beginning of Aegean-style pottery manufacture? What lies behind the quest for an absolute date (Yasur-Landau 2007b) can be named the "paradigm of unified migration," which most researchers follow implicitly or explicitly. The Philistine settlement at different sites is considered a set of chronologically unified events with a clear beginning and end rather than as a complex of migration processes, each with

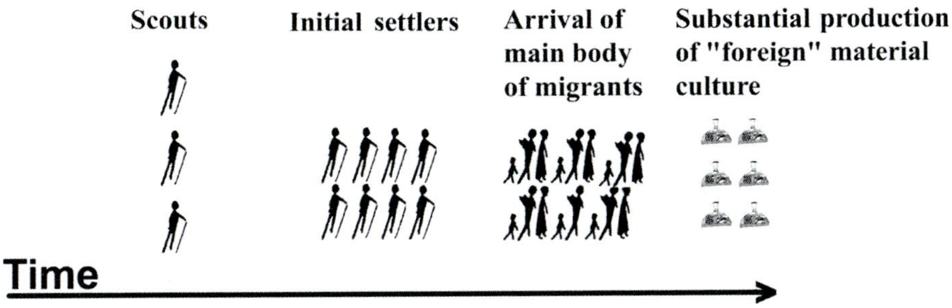

Scouts	Initial settlers	Arrival of main body of migrants	Substantial production of "foreign" material culture

Time →

FIGURE 8.11. Model of a migration and settlement process of a single group (after Yasur-Landau 2007b: fig. 1)

its own rhythm. However, current understanding of migration processes in archaeology, presented in Chapter 1, does not perceive migration as a sudden, single event of migrants flowing from their home countries to the new land. It is a prolonged process, in which information is gathered, sometimes from the services of scouts, guides, or informants. Then the initial migrants arrive, usually young men (Leonard 1992: 23), who prepare the ground for the arrival of the rest of the family or larger kinship group (Boyd 1989). These events may ignite different processes such as chain migration (Lee 1966: 55), in which groups follow one another, and leapfrogging. Viewing migration as a complex process composed of different phases, each with its own temporal aspects, stresses the importance of precisely defining the starting point of migration, which is crucial to the question of Philistine chronology: would all these phases in migration processes be archaeologically visible, or can we detect only the phase in which the settlers have already been established and began to produce conspicuous amounts of their material culture (Fig. 8.11)?

Furthermore, it is implicitly assumed in the study of the Philistines that the three major excavated sites of Philistia – Ashdod, Ashkelon, and Tel Miqne/Ekron – were simultaneously settled by the same groups of people. This is, of course, the easiest solution, but it is hardly the rule. Frequently, groups of similar or different origins that settle in one geographical area do not colonize simultaneously; rather, each settlement is founded on a different date. Can we, using only archaeological data, correctly solve the complex equation of a migration process, which includes more than one group in more than one site (Fig. 8.12)?

To answer this question, let us first examine several examples of similar situations. The early-seventeenth-century English settlement on the northeastern coast of North America included eight settlements, the earliest of which, Plymouth, was founded in 1620, and the latest, Newport, in 1639 (Gilbert 2003: 10; Fig. 8.13).

A most illuminating example of the problem of temporal variation in migration is the complex migration events known as the Greek colonization

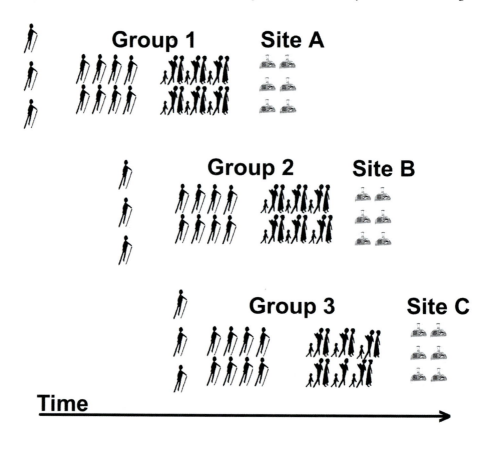

FIGURE 8.12. Model of a migration and settlement process of several groups (after Yasur-Landau 2007b: fig. 2)

to southern Italy and Sicily (Fig. 8.14). We know from literary sources that each of the foundations at the last third of the eighth century BCE was conducted by colonists originating in different city-states, and that each settlement was established on a different date, from Naxos, settled by the Chalkidians in 734, according to tradition (Graham 1982: 161; Malkin 1987: 175), to Taras, settled by Spartans in 706 BCE (Graham 1982: 162). Is it possible to determine such accurate data on the chronology and origin of the migrants solely on the basis of archaeological evidence? The answer is probably no. Even in the cases where the literary date agrees with the date of the earliest Greek pottery at the site,[11] it may prove impossible to differentiate between pottery made in Greece in 734 BCE, the date of the foundation of Naxos, and that made in 716 BCE, the date of

---

[11] Thus, for example, is the opposite case of Metapontum, with a Eusebian foundation date of 773–2 and an archaeological date of about 650 or even later (Malkin 1987: 181; Carter 1993: 354–5).

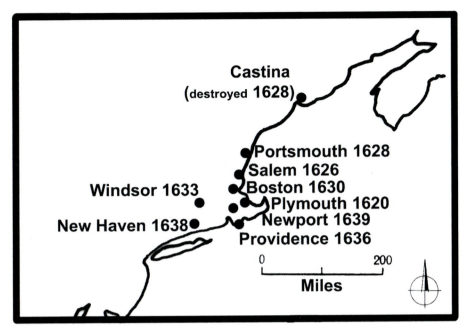

FIGURE 8.13. Settlement dates in seventeenth-century CE New England (after Yasur-Landau 2007b: fig. 3)

the foundation of Mylai. Furthermore, the identification of the origin of the settlers in Greece according to pottery found in the earliest levels of the sites is also incredibly shaky. Is it fair to assume that, without literary evidence, some scholars interpret all foundations of the late eighth century as the outcome of contemporary mass migration from Greece, similar to that conjectured of the Philistines in the early twelfth century?

We have encountered, in Chapter 5, the historical depth given in the Medinet Habu inscriptions to the activities of the Sea Peoples before their defeat in the supposedly decisive battles of Year 8 of Ramses III. The enemies had made plans on their islands, most likely in the eastern Aegean, and then had invaded Anatolia and Cyprus. Their invasion was followed by an encampment in Amurru, north of the Egyptian-controlled area. Finally, they moved against Egypt by land and by sea, yet, as argued previously, an unknown number of hostile encounters occurred in two decisive battles. How long did this process, so laconically described by Ramses III, continue? If Ugarit and Hatti were both destroyed between 1195 and 1185, it is not inconceivable to speak of a migration stream that comprises different groups of people of various origins and lasting a decade or two before 1175. It must be emphasized that 1175 is only the date in which the Egyptians stopped the migrants at the Delta. But how long before this date had they already been in Canaan, and how long after this date did they continue to arrive? The Egyptian sources have little to say, perhaps because Egypt was probably rapidly losing its grip on Canaan after the days of Ramses

III. Much clearer evidence comes from the Onomasticon of Amenope, not meant for regal propaganda, which mentions the Philistines, the Sikel, and the Sherden, as well as Gaza, Ashkelon, and Ashdod, thus giving a terminus post quem of about 1100 for the Aegean settlement, at least in the coastal parts of Philistia. The entire duration of the events connected with the settlement of the Philistines is at least several decades: between ten and twenty years before 1175 for the beginning of the movement of the first groups of migrants from their homes, and any amount of time between the latter date and 1100 for the arrival of the last groups in Philistia. Supporting evidence comes from the types of Aegean pottery that the migrants produced, which include types influenced by LHIIIC Early and Middle traditions, but LHIIIC Late types and decoration are absent from the Pentapolis fineware pottery. This fits well with the LHIIIC Late decline in the political power and organizational abilities of the major LHIIIC Aegean polities noted in Chapter 3. Thus, a time frame of fifty to seventy-five years for the majority of the immigration to Philistia may be not far from reality. This is a considerably long time that would allow for multiple migration and other interaction phenomena to take place – not a swift, uniform event of mass invasion.

THE END OF EGYPTIAN DOMINATION IN CANAAN AND DATA FROM LACHISH AND BETH SHEAN

The Philistine settlement paradigm of Alt and Albright (Finkelstein 1998), relying heavily on Ramses III's Medinet Habu reliefs and Papyrus Harris I, has cast a long shadow on the history of research. Ramses III claims in Papyrus Harris I that he had destroyed and captured the Denyen, Tjeker/Sikel, Philistines, Sherden, and the Weshesh; brought them as captives to Egypt; settled them in strongholds; and gave them clothing and food (Stager 1995: 341). Alt and Albright had interpreted these passages as evidence that the Philistines were first subdued by the Egyptians and then settled in Egyptian forts in Canaan. Later, they managed to break free of the Egyptian yoke, ending Egyptian domination in Canaan. Other reconstructions, each with its own chronology, have been suggested as an elaboration or an antithesis of this paradigm. All scholars maintained that the mass settlement of the Philistines could not have gone unnoticed by the Egyptians. As a result, two schools were formed: one argued for a peaceful or, at the most, tense coexistence at least for some time; the other argued for a Philistine settlement that superseded the Egyptian administration after its collapse. The supporters of the Middle Chronology claim contemporaneity of the latest phase of Egyptian domination in southern Canaan (starting from the days of Ramses III) and the settlement of the Pentapolis (T. Dothan 1989a: 8, fig. 1.6; Dothan 1992: 97; Bietak 1993: 295; Singer 1994: 342; Stager 1998: 152–4). This concurrence is interpreted as the result of a wide range of possible interactions between the Aegeans

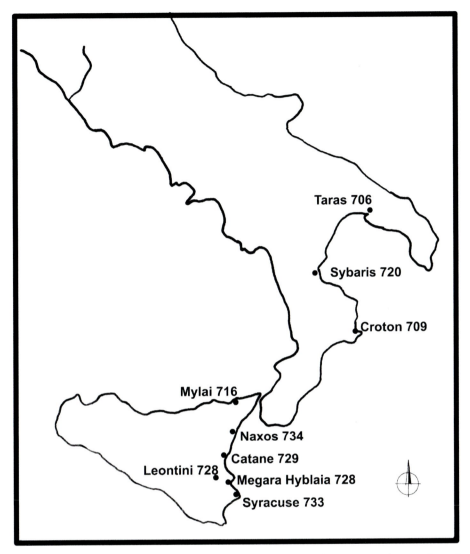

FIGURE 8.14. Settlement dates of eighth-century-BCE Greek colonies in southern Italy and Sicily

and the Egyptians: from the settling of Philistines by the Egyptians (Singer) to tense coexistence (Dothan) and the conquest of part of a former Egyptian domain by a well-coordinated invasion (Stager). Finkelstein (1995; 1998), supporting the Low Chronology, points to the fact that locally made LHIIIC pottery (Monochrome) does not appear in Egyptian strongholds such as Lachish, Tel Seraʿ, and Tell el-Farʿah (S), which remained under Egyptian control at least until late in the reign of Ramses III, if not later. According to Finkelstein, finds of Monochrome pottery (at sites such as Tel Haror, Tell Jerisheh, and perhaps Tel Seraʿ, all of which are yet to be published) outside the Pentapolis negate the possibility of an Aegean cultural enclave and a limited distribution of the Monochrome pottery only in the Pentapolis. In contrast, no locally made Egyptian pottery, common in the Egyptian strongholds in the south, has been found in the early Aegean levels in Philistia. Thus, he argues that the Aegean settlement in the Pentapolis began later than the days of Ramses III, perhaps not until the days of Ramses VI.

Unfortunately, there is no evidence from Ashdod, Ashkelon, or Tel Miqne/Ekron either of Philistines settled by the Egyptians or of Philistines who terminated Egyptian presence. Philistine material culture has not been accompanied by evidence for Egyptian administration. Nor is there evidence for Egyptian strongholds destroyed by the Philistines. Even at Ashkelon, the Egyptian fort seems to have been abandoned before the first Philistine had set foot at the site.

With the lack of evidence from the Pentapolis sites themselves, arguments have been made based on continuity exhibited in sites controlled by the Egyptians into the twelfth century, mainly Beth Shean, Megiddo, and Lachish. Ussishkin (1998: 216) argues, relating to the land movements of the Sea Peoples, that "such hordes must have come from the north by using a cardinal land route, and therefore had to pass Megiddo and the Nahal ʿIron gorge before heading south." If so, a strong force based in Megiddo could have held back the Sea Peoples to the days of Ramses VI, whose statue base (found in a less-than-reliable context; Breasted 1948: 135 no. 1; Weinstein 1992: 147) is presumed to date the end of Stratum VII and to give a terminus post quem for the Philistine incursion (Finkelstein 1996b; Ussishkin 1998; but see Mazar 1997; Yasur-Landau 2003a). Nevertheless, small and even large groups of migrants could have bypassed Megiddo altogether by using two major alternative roads that avoid the center of the Jezreel Valley and later crossing the Carmel Ridge: a northern road ending by Yokneʿam and a southern one ending by Jenin, and then going west through the Dothan Valley and Nahal (*Wadi*) Hadera (Dorsey 1991: 79, map 3; Ussishkin 1998: 215–16). A third possible route, less convenient for travel but entirely unguarded, was along the coast.

Beth Shean, though strategically located on the route to the Jordan Valley, is not a necessary passing point for travelers coming into Canaan from the north, and its role in holding back land movements of the Sea Peoples is therefore minimal. Consequently, the vast body of datable Egyptiaca and accompanying LHIIIC (or rather Cypriot-made Mycenaean IIIC: 1b) pottery (James 1966: fig. 94: 4; Hankey 1966; 1967: 127–8; Warren and Hankey 1989: 164–5; Mazar 1993: 216; 2007; Yasur-Landau 2003a; D'Agata et al. 2005) is of no direct chronological value for the settlement of the Philistines, although it is of great importance for the dating of the LHIIIC style, at least in Cyprus.

Finally, the lack of locally made, Monochrome LHIIIC pottery at Lachish, which has yielded datable Egyptian material, is another cornerstone in the chronology of the beginning of Philistine settlement presented by Ussishkin (1998: 217) and Finkelstein (1995: 230–1). The lack of such pottery is taken as positive evidence that the Philistine settlement did not occur in nearby Philistia before the reign of Ramses III or even Ramses IV, whose scarab (Krauss 1994) was found in the lower city of Lachish (and, indeed, not before Ramses VI, according to the Megiddo evidence). However, the lack of imported LHIIIC-style pottery from Lachish has no chronological implications. Such pottery, mostly Cypriot made (D'Agata et al. 2005), has never been found south of the Jezreel Valley, and its presence in the northern valleys reflects no more than the continuation of trading networks with Cyprus in the north and their severance in the south. The lack of locally made, LHIIIC-style pottery from Lachish is explained by Bunimovitz and Faust (2001), who show cases in the anthropological record in which certain items do not cross "ethnic" boundaries, despite close interactions, thus leading to a difference in material culture even between two neighboring settlements. They argue, therefore, that the Aegean-style serving vessels and cookware produced in Philistia, often unattractive in appearance and fired at low temperatures, were of no interest to the Egyptian garrisons who maintained their own foodways and cultural preferences. This theory is extremely convincing for two additional reasons: First, locally made (Monochrome) LHIIIC pottery has not been found at Beth Shemesh, much closer to Tel Miqne/Ekron then Lachish. Because there seems to be continued habitation at the site from the Late Bronze Age to the Early Iron Age, the reason for the absence cannot be temporal. Second, as argued earlier, Canaanite drinking and eating habits were not changed by Mycenaean imports, which were mostly of containers – predominantly small stirrup jars. The Canaanites and the remaining Egyptian soldiers would not have needed the Aegean cooking pots and bowls, yet, whenever available, they continued to consume products stored within Aegean-style containers, such as the small stirrup jars from Beth Shean or even the local imitations of stirrup jars in Cemetery 900 at Tell el-Farʿah (S) (Braunstein 1998: 262).

Would the connection between the migration of the Aegeans/Philistines and the end of the Egyptian administration hold water if we put aside the preconception of mass, simultaneous migration in favor of more complex processes, involving different groups settling over an extended period of time? For those in favor of the Low Chronology, the immediate, inconvenient outcome is that without a fast, well-coordinated attack by the migrants, there is no possibility of reconstructing a swift end for the Egyptian administration, which can be used, via evidence in Egyptian centers in Canaan, to date absolutely the Philistine settlement. For those who argue for the contemporaneity of the beginning of Philistine settlement with the last days of the Egyptian administration, or at least overlap between them, the result is an inability to fix a clear date for the beginning of the Philistine settlement.

TOWARD A NONUNIFIED PARADIGM OF MIGRATION

An overview of the circumstances of settlement in Ashdod, Ashkelon, and Tel Miqne/Ekron (Chapter 7) all but excludes the possibility of a unified, violent conquest by a large mass of migrants over a short time. The migrants had minimized the need for violence by choosing sites that were either small or already deserted. The coappearance of Canaanite and Aegean-style pottery in every household in Philistia does not attest to any animosity between newcomers and the local population. Furthermore, the image of the mighty Philistine conquerors is somewhat weakened by the fact that their total number was not greater than several thousands. Their level of social complexity was likely less than that of the Canaanites of the Late Bronze Age. They were not an urban society, did not use administration, and did not build any public buildings.

Just as the circumstances of settlement were different at each Pentapolis site, it is possible to see differentiated aspects of material culture among sites in Philistia. The differences, though minute, may be significant, having survived the powerful assimilation mechanisms of migrant societies.[12]

First is the differentiation in pottery iconography (Yasur-Landau 2003a; 2007b). Human figures, which have not been found at Ashdod or Tel Miqne/Ekron, appear in the pictorial repertoire of Ashkelon both in Monochrome and Bichrome styles (Figs. 5.74 and 8.15; Stager 2006; Wachsmann 2000: 134, fig. 6.29). The pictorial LHIIIC-style pottery from Tel Miqne/Ekron and Ashdod contains fish and bird images.[13] Most important, both sites include images of the "Philistine bird," depicted with a rounded breast, a curved body divided by a triglyph, a tapering tail, and a chevron-shaped wing (Figs. 8.16–24). This motif continued into the Philistine Bichrome style and became the emblem of Philistine iconography (Dothan 1982: 198–200). Such bird figures are conspicuously absent from the earliest Philistine levels at Ashkelon. A bird that does appear on a Phase 18 krater from Ashkelon, very different from the Ashdod and Tel Miqne/Ekron birds, has a body rendered as one field and filled with dots (Fig. 8.24).

The settlements differ also in aspects of ritual activity: although wide-shouldered, long-necked "Ashdoda" figurines are quite common at Ashdod (Yasur-Landau 2001) and have been found at Ashkelon, they are absent from

---

[12] One such mechanism is the principle of first effective settlement, according to which new arrivals try to assimilate to the first founders, who have already adapted to the social, economic, and environmental conditions in the new land and have managed to consolidate their community (Cheek 1998: 153; Anthony 2000).

[13] E.g., Ashdod: Dothan and Porath 1993: fig. 15: 11, fig. 16: 19, fig. 17: 10. Other examples of pictorial pottery: Stager 1995: fig. 3: 30, 31. Tel Miqne/Ekron Stratum VII (Phase 9a, but note that there are none from Phases 9c and 9b: Killebrew 1998a: fig. 7: 15 and probably 13. Other examples of pictorial pottery: Stager 1995: fig. 3: 22, 23; Dothan 2000: 154, fig. 7.7: 8.

FIGURE 8.15. Ship from Ashkelon (after Wachsmann 2000: 134, fig. 6.29)

Tel Miqne/Ekron, which produced other types of figurines, more similar to the "mourning" figurines (Gunneweg et al. 1986: 5, fig. 1: 14; Dothan and Gitin 1993: 1053; Dothan 1995: 48, 50, fig. 3.12). In contrast, incised cow scapulae have been found at Tel Miqne/Ekron (Hesse 1986: 25; Dothan and Gitin 1993: 1053) and Tell es-Ṣafi/Gath but have not yet been reported from Ashdod or Ashkelon.

Recent advances in the relative and absolute chronology of LHIIIC pottery (e.g., Deger-Jalkotzy 2003) encourage optimism that, once the material from Philistia is fully accessible, it will provide additional important chronological data.

However, the archaeological picture from Philistia demonstrates not only variability in the circumstances of settlement but also regional differentiation among the sites in Philistia in pictorial iconography and ritual customs, which are closely connected to notions of ideology and self-identity. This variability brings forth the possibility that we witness here a model of colonization similar to that seen in southern Italy and Sicily: not a single event of settlement but separate processes of settlement for each site; Ashdod, Ashkelon, and Tel Miqne/Ekron would have been settled in different circumstances, by Aegean migrants arriving perhaps from close but different places of origin.

THE ORIGIN OF THE MIGRANTS

WHY NOT (MAINLY) CYPRUS AND CILICIA?

The most basic question concerning the origin of the Aegean migration (i.e., the existence of migration from the Aegean cultural area), has been answered in Chapter 7, which proved that the change in almost all domestic behavioral patterns found in the transition between the Bronze Age and the Iron Age in Philistia can have been caused only by a massive migration from areas of Aegean culture.

Killebrew (1998a: 401–2) argues for a migration from Cilicia and Aegeanized Cyprus rather than from the Aegean world per se. The Aegean influence manifested in the material culture of the Philistines is removed several generations from its Aegean origin (Killebrew 2006: 231). Killebrew (2006: 393–7, 401–2; following works by Kling 1989; Sherratt and Crouwel 1987) claims that there is a great similarity between Mycenaean IIIC: 1b wares from Philistia and white-painted, wheel-made III wares from Cyprus and Cilicia. She assumes that the similarity in ware, shape, and decoration indicates the origin of the migration from Cyprus and/or Cilicia to Canaan. Killebrew (2000: 243) has argued that locally made Aegean pottery in Philistia is "nearly identical" to the Mycenaean IIIC: 1b of Cyprus and "differs significantly from Mycenaean IIIC: 1b from the Aegean proper" in three main features:

1. Variety of shapes
2. Decorative motifs
3. Associated cooking wares

As for variety of shapes, Chapter 7 demonstrated that all the shapes from Philistia have proper Aegean parallels and furthermore form a distinctive Aegean ceramic assemblage. Types that appear only in the pottery of Cyprus (and not in the Aegean world), such as the wishbone-handled wheel-made bowl (belonging to the Cypriot Mycenaean IIIC: 1b repertoire; Kling 2000: 283, fig. 14.1: f), do not appear in Philistia, as would be expected if there has been a migration from Cyprus. Furthermore, no non-Aegean, LCIIIA Cypriot pottery, such as Cypriot-style cooking pots or cooking trays (Chapter 7), pithoi (with or without relief decoration; Porada 1988: 301–4), wall brackets (e.g., Karageorghis and Demas 1985b: pl. 104: 5009, 5234), bowls with wishbone handles or Bucchero-style pottery (Karageorghis and Demas 1985b: pl. 113: 4207, 4263) have been found in twelfth-century Philistia. It is hardly likely that potters who knew how to make only "pure" Aegean forms migrated from Cyprus while more talented potters, who could make both Aegean and Cypriot forms, were left behind.

Distinctive Cypriot pottery types, such as the bottle and the horn-shaped vessel, appear only in late-twelfth- or early-eleventh-century contexts and are unconnected to the first phase of migration. The same is true for the bovine scapula – a Cypriot element found at Tel Miqne/Ekron only as early as Stratum VI, and to the Cypro-Minoan (?) seal from Ashdod and inscription from Ashkelon, further decreasing the plausibility of a Cypriot element having dominated the migration from its beginning. A final piece of evidence is the rapid increase in the use of pigs following the migration (see "Changes in Animal Husbandry"). Similarly, no Cypriot architectural features, such as ashlar masonry, are found in twelfth-century Ashdod, Ashkelon, or Tel

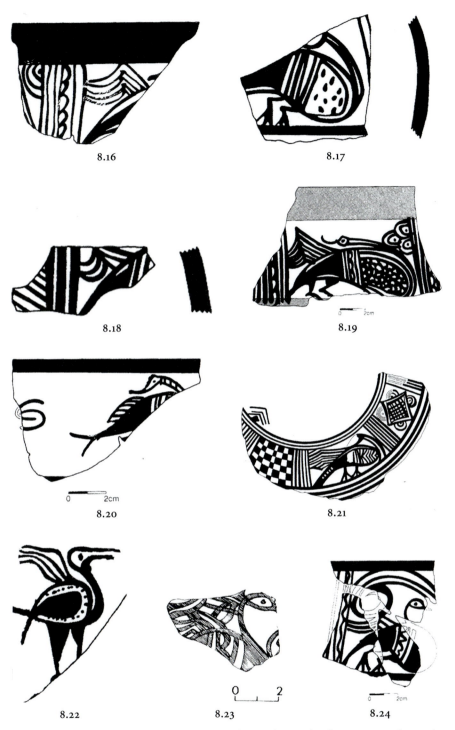

8.16

8.17

8.18

8.19

8.20

8.21

8.22

8.23

8.24

FIGURE 8.16. Tel Miqne/Ekron Stratum VIIa (after Dothan and Zukerman 2004: fig. 19: 1)
FIGURE 8.17. Tel Miqne/Ekron Stratum VII (VI?) (after Dothan and Zukerman 2004: fig. 35: 8)
FIGURE 8.18. Tel Miqne/Ekron Stratum VII (VI?) (after Dothan and Zukerman 2004: fig. 35: 9)
FIGURE 8.19. Tel Miqne/Ekron Stratum VI (after Dothan and Zukerman 2004: fig. 19: 2)
FIGURE 8.20. Tel Miqne/Ekron Stratum VIIa (after Dothan and Zukerman 2004: fig. 8: 14)
FIGURE 8.21. Tel Miqne/Ekron Stratum VI (after Dothan and Zukerman 2004: fig. 31: 3)
FIGURE 8.22. Ashkelon Phase 18 (after Stager 2006: fig. 5)
FIGURE 8.23. Ashdod Stratum XIIIb (after Dothan and Porath 1993: fig. 15: 11)
FIGURE 8.24. Ashdod Stratum XIII (after Dothan and Zukerman 2004: fig. 19: 3)

Miqne/Ekron. Pig farming was not an important element in the Cypriot economy in the Late Bronze Age, and the rise in pig breeding is seen in Cyprus, as in the southern Levant, as a result of Aegean migration.

The motifs on the LHIIIC-style vases and their origin deserve special attention, beyond the limits of this work. There are many similarities among Cypriot, Cilician, and Levantine wares. A possible direction for future research on the origin of motifs might concentrate on region-specific motifs or compositions. For example, motifs found only in Cyprus and Philistia but not in the Aegean proper may support a special connection with Cyprus. In contrast, LHIIIC motifs that appear in the southern Levant and in the Aegean but not in Cyprus may show the opposite tendency.

Furthermore, to allow for even the possibility of migration from Cyprus and Cilicia, one must prove first that the Aegean migration to Cyprus and Cilicia (or other phenomena of LCIIIA interactions) occurred earlier than the migration to Philistia. This is a rather difficult task. It is impossible to show, in terms of either absolute or relative chronology, the date of the Aegean settlement in either Cyprus or Cilicia, although it probably postdates the destruction of Ugarit, as indicated by the correspondence between the local king of Alashiya and the last king of Ugarit. However, French (2007: fig. 3) has suggested that the earliest locally made LHIIIC assemblages from Philistia – from Ashdod Stratum XIIb and Tel Miqne/Ekron Stratum VIIb – belong stylistically to the LHIIIC Early 1 phase, earlier than the earliest well-defined Mycenaean IIIC deposits from Cyprus, Enkomi Level IIIA, and Kition Tomb 9 Upper Burial.

Alternatively, I suggest that the similarity of the locally made LHIIIC wares (and other aspects of Aegean material culture) among Philistia, Cyprus, and Cilicia results from similar phenomena of migration and similar origin of migrants. It was demonstrated that the land and sea routes from the Aegean to the Levant passed through Cyprus and Cilicia. In the same migration streams, some migrants may have remained along the routes while others ventured further east, leaving a picture of cultural similarity between the areas.

The bulk of the twelfth-century immigration to Philistia did not come from the autochthonous dwellers of Cyprus and Cilicia but from beyond, from areas of the Aegean cultural sphere. This does not mean, however, that a good number of Aegeanized or local Cypriots or Cilicians did not join the migrants on their way or join them half a century or more later, once the settlement had been established, perhaps as indicated by the Tel Miqne/Ekron scapulae or by the seals and inscriptions from Ashdod and Ashkelon.

MATERIAL CULTURE AND SIMULTANEOUS MIGRATION FROM MULTIPLE SOURCES

An analysis of the iconography of the feathered hats (Chapter 5) suggests a larger area from which migrants originated than the etymological survey:

from Kynos in northern central Greece to Phaistos in southern Crete, and from Mycenae in the Argolid to the island of Kos and the western Anatolian coast. Similarly, an analysis of the LHIIIC powers that were able to organize maritime immigration to Cyprus (and possibly to the Levant) proposes Mycenae, Phylakopi, Tiryns, and Miletus, as well as the Dodecanese, as candidates for the origins of migration. It seems, therefore, that the Aegean migrants could have originated in virtually anywhere in the central and eastern Aegean world.

It may be possible to narrow this area down somewhat by excluding Crete, as Cretan-style cooking pots (tripod or flat-based) have not been found in Philistia, nor have other types of distinctively Cretan vessels, such as pithoi with decorated lids and large, straight-sided alabastra.

Some difficulties in establishing the origin of the Aegean migration may be caused by the likelihood that it was a phenomenon of mixed migration from different parts of the Aegean world (Yasur-Landau 2003c; 2007b), joined by individuals and families from Anatolia, the northern Levant, and perhaps Cyprus. Direct evidence for the mixed nature of this migration can be found in Egyptian texts. Even without trying to pinpoint ethnic names of the different Sea Peoples mentioned by Ramses III, one cannot escape the obvious observation that the invaders were not a single group, but five groups: Philistines (*prst*), Tjeker (or Sikel), Shekelesh, Denyen, and Weshesh. This diversity existed for at least several decades after the actual settlement: three of the Sea Peoples groups are mentioned at the turn of the eleventh century in the Onomasticon of Amenope: Sherden, Tjeker/Sikel, and the Philistines (*prst*), as well as the cities of Ashkelon, Ashdod, and Gaza (Dothan 1982: 3–4; Stager 1995: 336). Other evidence for diversity, thus reducing the possibility of finding a single origin, is seen in the phenomenon of mixed marriages and in the Hittite or Canaanite men who were part of the migrants' caravan in the land battle relief at Medinet Habu.

The result of this mixed migration is the "Philistine" material culture, decisively Aegean in nature but without distinctive resemblance to any known regional LHIIIC culture. A situation of mixed immigration into Philistia may hinder attempts to identify the origin of the newcomers through decorated pottery; a complex picture of potters coming from different workshops in the Aegean world, possibly cooperating with active Canaanite potters (Chapter 7), is easily imaginable. Such potters produced vessels for a varied population of Aegeans, Canaanites, Syrians, and others. To satisfy the demands and cultural preferences of the diverse market, they produced, even at the beginning of settlement, a pottery assemblage that seems to have been a compromise between the abilities and traditions of the potters and the tastes and demands of the customers. The origins of some of the migrants who came later could be obscured by the principle of first effective settlement (Chapter 1), in which the latecomers would have imitated some aspects of the material culture of the first migrants to settle the area. Such phenomena may explain the locally made Cypriot scapulae, linear inscriptions, and fineware pottery forms, which appear at the end of the twelfth century and at the beginning of the eleventh century. These were the result of the arrival of people from Cyprus following the initial arrival of the Aegean migrants. Their small number and the previously mentioned principle would have caused them to use Aegean architectural forms and the locally made LHIII pottery and Aegean cooking jugs rather than Cypriot ones.

CONCLUSIONS

FORMING A SOCIETY: FROM THE REGIONAL LEVEL TO THE SITE AND POLITY LEVELS – SETTLEMENT PATTERNS, POLITICAL STRUCTURES, POLITICAL INTEGRATION, AND SUBSISTENCE ECONOMY

Regardless of the chronology of their arrival, the Aegeans and other settlers in the Pentapolis had a tremendous effect on settlement patterns in Philistia. In contrast to the pyramidal settlement hierarchy in the thirteenth century, the transition to the twelfth century was accompanied by the disappearance of most small and medium-sized settlements.

From these changes, a political division of Philistia emerged in the late twelfth century and remained stable for the next two centuries or so: the Pentapolis – five polities, each well centered on a site that is larger than the other settlements in the territory.

As has already been noted, not all the local inhabitants were expelled, as evidenced by strong local material culture traits that exist at the excavated Pentapolis sites. Furthermore, there is no indication that the local population was driven en masse from the countryside into the principal sites, or that the Pentapolis had an urban nature from its beginning.

The settlement of the Pentapolis sites, though not urban, was followed by what seems to be a replanning of settlement space and an allotment of land for different purposes. Tel Miqne/Ekron is the most elaborate example: the entire area was redefined and enlarged by a wall, an industrial area was located where the Canaanite acropolis once was, an elite area was set in the middle of the lower tell (Field IV), and a domestic area was built in another area (Field X). Some evidence for changes in the allotment of land for different uses inside the settlement exists also for Ashdod and Ashkelon. However, the reuse of the Ashdod "governor's residence" in the twelfth century probably conveyed a message reflecting a different political agenda than that prevalent at Tel Miqne/Ekron. At Ashdod, the old ruler's possessions were apprehended and altered to meet the needs of the new rulers, whereas at Tel Miqne/Ekron, a center of power was established anew. Still, none of the twelfth-century settlements can safely be called cities, as they all lack features common to urban settings in both the Aegean and the Levant, such as large temples, palaces, storage and redistribution facilities, and evidence of any form of administration.

The allotment of land to the settlers in the countryside (a phenomenon discussed for its parallels in Greek colonization) occurred at a later stage in the Aegean migration and is perhaps indicated by the establishment of several small settlements in the late twelfth and early eleventh centuries, such as Tel Haror, Tel ʿAitun, and later Tell Qasile and Aphek.

The change in settlement patterns was accompanied by a change in the subsistence economy. The sharp rise in the percentage of pig and cattle bones as opposed to the decrease in those of sheep and goats seen at Ashkelon and Tel Miqne/Ekron reflects an economy in which most meat products were manufactured relatively close to the town, or even inside it, thus requiring little contact with specialized pastoralists in the highlands. This pattern fits well with the settlement patterns of the twelfth century: a principle settlement surrounded by a few smaller sites, probably unable to produce enough surplus to meet the demands of the city dwellers. The migrants themselves did not tend to fill this need during the first stage of settlement by establishing small farming communities away from the city.

In general, the economy of Philistia seems to have been based almost exclusively on high-intensity farming, and most farmers seem to have lived within the safety of the large cities. Some regional trade in Philistia must have taken place, visible at some sites in the small amounts of decorated pottery made at other centers of production. It is also reasonable that agricultural products were transported across the borders of the polities. As for direct international trade, there seems to have been virtually none. The few imported luxury goods in Philistia may be heirlooms brought by the migrants or items taken from the local population. Amphorae filled with agricultural products found in Cyprus may have originated in Philistia, yet probably reached Cyprus through a port in northern Canaan, as there are no Cypriot finds that can be interpreted as the return for such export.

RULERSHIP, OCCUPATION AND TRADE GROUPS, DAILY LIFE, SOCIAL HIERARCHY, AND SOCIAL COMPLEXITY

The Aegean migrants and the local Canaanite population in Philistia did not reproduce the power structure of either the palatial Aegean culture or the Canaanite Late Bronze Age city-states. Rather, the sparse evidence of rulership shows strong affinity to Aegean postpalatial patterns. One may assume that the rulership in the Pentapolis sites was most likely of Aegean origin, as is evident in the Aegean-style ruler's dwelling found in Ashdod Area G, Tel Miqne/Ekron Field IV, and perhaps at Ashkelon. The rulers used Aegean symbols of rulership, mainly the central hearth, to consolidate their power by ritual feasting and drinking in the Aegean manner. During this feasting, various prestigious types of meat were probably consumed, as indicated by the animal bone finds from Field IV at Tel Miqne/Ekron. *Seren*, a title of Aegean/Anatolian origin designating a leader, was most likely preserved from the time of migration and recorded several times as the standard term for the ruler of a Philistine city. It is unknown if the governing system of one *seren* per city and a council of *seranim* was prevalent in the twelfth century or, more likely, developed after a significant period. It seems probable that the twelfth century was a formative period for the development of rulership in Philistia, and indeed there is some evidence that there was a difference between the power and abilities of the rulership at the various sites. The rulership at Tel Miqne/Ekron displays power and stability from its beginning; this is exhibited in the building of a city wall and the laying of a new town plan, both attesting to organizational abilities exceeding those of twelfth-century Ashdod and Ashkelon. Even more telling is the location of the ruler's dwelling, which did not change until the tenth century (and returned to the same spot in the seventh century) and suffered no damages throughout this time but was rather enlarged. This may indicate the continuation of a single dynastic line throughout the period. The Achish inscription provides further evidence of the continuation of rulership of Aegean nature at Tel Miqne/Ekron: Achish was an Aegean name that can be traced back to the fifteenth century BCE, and the ruler bearing the name worshipped a goddess of Aegean descent. This situation stands in contrast to that in Ashdod, where the ruler's dwelling in Area G was short lived and damaged by fire even in the twelfth century. The twelfth-century elite of Ashdod and Ashkelon did not have the organizational powers to build walls. Fortifications were erected only in the late eleventh century; the rise of organizational powers that enabled this are easily explained by a contemporary consolidation of rulers' power, almost a century later than at Tel Miqne/Ekron, after which both Ashdod and Ashkelon became urban centers. This rise in power seems to have been accompanied by limited use of literate or semiliterate administration, evidenced by the economic document from Aphek, sent from Ashkelon, and the seals and bullae from Ashdod. The practice of literate administration was restricted to the modest needs of the elite or rulership, which engaged in practically no international trade and maintained no central storage of provisions and supplies large enough to require monitoring by scribes. Central storage, or the lack of it, in either the twelfth or the eleventh century, is another indication of the rulership's modest abilities. The rulership's power was not sufficient for collecting substantial taxes and tributes, and it owned no private estates with surpluses large enough to justify central storage.

The nonelites are archaeologically conspicuous in Philistia by their products. These were farmers, potters, flint knappers (in the local "Canaanite" tradition), and perhaps a few artisans who made luxury goods like seals. The houses of the commoners were excavated in only one place: Field X at Tel

Miqne/Ekron. At least some of them were of local origin, judging by the local cooking habits in *tabun*s and the lack of Aegean hearths.

Of much interest is the role of women in the Aegean migration. Analyses of the Medinet Habu land battle reliefs and of finds in the Pentapolis sites suggest that some Aegean women arrived with the first immigrants to Canaan, although phenomena of intercultural marriages were common even before the arrival in Canaan, as the land battle reliefs indicate. The activity of Aegean women in elite contexts is attested to by the Aegean weaving practices in Area G at Ashdod and Field IV at Tel Miqne/Ekron, which show that at least some of the rulers or elite had migrated as family units (a phenomenon seen also in Maa-Palaeokastro). It has also been proposed that women of Aegean origin played an important role in the introduction of the cult of the Aegean mother (earth) goddess into Philistia and in maintaining it as a household cult.

ARRIVING IN CANAAN: TIMING, NUMBERS, ROUTE, AND ORIGIN

The chronological debate on the commencement of the Aegean settlement in Philistia can be approached differently if, as suggested here, the settlement is envisaged as a long and complicated series of processes rather than as an event or a single migration wave. The continuous nature of the settlement process in Philistia, not connected to a single event, finds support from different sources.

First, a comparison of the inscription of Year 8 of Ramses III and the pictorial description of the land battle may suggest that what the Egyptians presented as an event of a specific year (war with the Sea Peoples) was actually a longer and continuous process of land migration to the south and subsequent settlement, which they had tried to stop. It is unclear how successful this attempt was. Ramses III repelled some of the raids on Egypt itself, yet it is not likely that the garrisons in Canaan could have intercepted and eliminated all the groups of migrants.

A second reason for ruling out a single starting date and a reconstruction of a single event is apparent from the examination of the Pentapolis sites as independent entities, each with its own history. Such analyses have shown the difference among the polities in Philistia in terms of regionalism in material culture and variation among polities in terms of power, organizational skills, and settlement hierarchy. This variability opens the door to the rejection of existing schemes of Aegean settlement and to a reconstruction of different circumstances for the foundation of each polity, each built in a different settlement event by different people, perhaps also of different origins.

What was the volume of this migration? Finkelstein suggests that the Iron I population in Philistia was approximately thirty thousand. It seems that the number for the twelfth century was lower, perhaps twenty-five thousand, bringing into account the settlements that were founded in the early eleventh century and the increase in the size of sites like Ashdod at that time. This number could not have been composed of migrants alone (as Stager has suggested), as a substantial part of the local population remained in Philistia, as is seen in the continuation of some local "Canaanite" material culture traits and the preservation of the Semitic site names of all five Pentapolis sites. In contrast, reliance on land transport (probably with the addition of ships) would mean that there were several logistic limitations to the number of migrants that could come to Philistia. As a hypothesis, I would suggest a range between Finkelstein's "few thousands" and ten thousand to twelve thousand – approximately half of Stager's proposal and half of the population of Philistia following the migration – with a personal preference for the lower estimate.

As in the case of chronology, the question of origin does not have a single answer. It has been argued, on the basis of the lack of common local Cypriot or southern Anatolian derived elements in the material culture of the earliest phases of Aegean settlement, that the migration came from the Aegean cultural sphere via Cilicia and Cyprus rather than from those places. Furthermore, the Aegean settlements of Cilicia, Cyprus, and Philistia seem to be almost contemporaneous, with the possibility that the settlement of the Pentapolis came approximately a decade after that of Cyprus. The origin of the migrants cannot be pinpointed by the iconography of the feathered hats or elucidated through an analysis of the source of different toponyms, ethnonyms, personal names, and terms connected to the Sea Peoples or the Philistines. Both iconographic and linguistic evidence, however, point generally to the area of the Aegean Sea and its shores, between the Greek mainland and the western Anatolian coast. It has also been suggested that the exact origin of the migrants may never be determined, as they may have come from different places in the Aegean world. The mixture of traditions, perhaps amplified by the phenomenon of mixed marriages, may have resulted in a material culture assemblage that is wholly within the LHIIIC tradition (as are the twelfth-century Pentapolis assemblages) but does not correlate precisely with any of the known regional LHIIIC styles. A few elements of Cypriot origin: the use of incised bovid scapulae; the use of linear script; and Cypriot forms in the Bichrome repertoire may be interpreted as a presence of Cypriots, including some high-ranking ones, among the later immigrants to Philistia. Another possibility is that some of these traits may be ascribed to Aegeans that spent time in Cyprus (as mercenaries?) and picked up a few practices, without significantly changing other aspects of their behavioral patterns.

9

A SHORT HISTORY OF THE AEGEAN IMMIGRATION TO THE LEVANT

A LAND MUCH DIVIDED: THE WORLD THAT CREATED THE AEGEAN MIGRATION

The butterfly that launched a chain of events effecting the massive Aegean immigration to the Levant must have fluttered its wings in the thirteenth-century Mycenaean heartland.

The palatial civilization of the thirteenth century had all the necessary means to initiate virtually any form of interregional interaction (Chapter 2). The evidence from the Linear B tablets suggests that ships, human resources, knowledge about destinations, and funds were available, at least to the largest palaces, thus enabling them to engage in the most expensive and risky enterprises: international trade in raw materials and state-orchestrated migration.

The destination of this early colonization is still obscure. There is still no evidence of thirteenth-century settlement in the Levant or Cyprus, and while the evidence from western regions (e.g., Sicily, peninsular Italy, and Sardinia) may indicate some Aegean presence (e.g., artisans, traders), it hints at nothing nearing the scale suggested by the Pylos tablets. It may be, therefore, that this settlement was confined to the boundaries of the Aegean cultural sphere, somewhere in the vast area between the Ionian Islands and the western Anatolian coast.

The thirteenth-century geographical knowledge of destinations, technical skills for ship construction, and organizational abilities necessary to conduct maritime migration were probably not entirely lost after the changes in the political systems and patterns of rulership at the beginning of the twelfth century (Chapter 3). Moreover, the changing political climate of the LHIIIC period provided favorable conditions for migration. In the Argolid and elsewhere on the Greek mainland, the breaking of the palatial yoke enabled more freedom of action for elites eager to win power and domination through interregional trade and raids, and even through settlement abroad. In contrast, competition and rivalry between elites over domination may have been a trigger for the migration of dissatisfied or overwhelmed aristocrats and their followers. Off-core polities, such as Phylakopi and Miletus, unhurt by the mainland turmoil (Chapter 3), could have even used the vacuum of power to increase their international activities. The rise and fall of small, fortified coastal settlements, like Koukounaries, may indicate the movements of elites with their followers within the scope of the Aegean world in search of rulership.

The sources concerning the Late Geometric and Archaic Greek colonization are a key to further understanding of the motives for LHIIIC migration as well as its logistic aspects. Much like in the LHIIIC, these colonization events were borne of a similar situation of competition among elites during times of political change and the redefinition of society (Chapter 4).

The answers to questions of where to go and how to get there were within the scope of information, technical abilities, and material means available to different communities. Traders, mercenaries returning home from service in Egypt and on the Levantine coast, and foreigners still living in the Aegean world were sources of knowledge about possible destinations in the east, at least at the beginning of the twelfth century. In addition, twelfth-century raids supplied not only exotic booty but also fresh information about specific destinations for further raids and settlement. Considering the available means of transport, both maritime and land migrations were possible. However, not all forms of maritime migration were possible in the twelfth century. First, the high cost of ships limited the number of available sea vessels. Second, on the oared galley (the predominant type of ship in the twelfth century), there was not room for many passengers other than rowers and a few officers, which makes it highly unlikely that many complete households migrated by boat. Consequently, maritime evacuation of an entire community, followed by setting out for maritime migration to the east, was simply impossible in the twelfth-century nautical reality. Migration may have been carried out in many different forms; individuals, as well as small and large kinship groups, leapfrogged with their belongings by foot and wagon from one town to another, eastward, following other members of their community, paid guides, or information about the great opportunities abroad. At the same time, small fleets of war galleys, gathered in such Aegean coastal centers as Phylakopi or the Rhodian and Koan harbors, may have aimed to colonize rather than to raid.

A FAMILY PORTRAIT WITH AN OX WAGON: ON THE ROUTES TO THE EAST

The sea and land routes of migration leading from the Aegean world to Cyprus, southern Anatolia, and further to the Levant are clearly marked by a trail of material culture finds (Chapter 5). The sudden appearance of various Aegean behavioral patterns indicates an Aegean presence.

A careful examination of the contexts of these finds reveals the varied and complex nature of the Aegean migration and settlement along the routes. Such complexity may be best seen in Cyprus, where Aegean migrants interacted in different ways with the local population. Individuals served as mercenaries for Cypriot elites at sites, such as Enkomi, perhaps paving the road for the later, more extensive Aegean settlement at the site. In Kition, Aegean weavers, most probably women, were integrated into the temple economy at the sacred precinct, which suggests that there was settlement of complete Aegean household units within the local Cypriot population. Maa-Palaeokastro was a fortified settlement founded by Aegean settlers in a remote location; its architecture, pottery, and almost all material culture remains indicate that it was meant to be an Aegean home away from home. A similar tale is told by the more fragmentary evidence from several sites along the land route between Cilicia and the Levantine coast – evidence of Aegean settlement differs in nature from site to site. The information given by Ramses III about the "camp in the land of Amurru," together with the depiction of probable intermarriages with Syrian women, strongly suggests that a substantial number of the migrants stayed in Syria for some years after the destruction of Ugarit, before continuing south into Canaan. Therefore, although the Aegean migration eastward can be described as a migration stream, it was far from homogeneous. Rather, it comprised many different events, each unique in its circumstances, history, and pace. It is possible that various groups and individuals used both land and sea routes. Moreover, some migrants may have made stops for periods of time or even stayed in one site along the route while others continued on. Some were joined by other groups of migrants of different origin and by people of non-Aegean origin, partly via intermarriages, mostly between migrating men and local women.

The time span in which Aegeans migrated eastward can be roughly estimated as the major part of the twelfth century (i.e., three to four generations); locally made LHIIIC Early pottery found in Tarsus indicates a rather early beginning, soon after the fall of the palatial culture on the mainland. Imported LHIIIC pottery found at Ugarit indicates that the city still existed during this phase, thereby dating the Aegean movement to before 1185 BCE. Because much of the locally made Aegean decorated pottery found on Cyprus and in the Levant was attributed to LHIIIC Middle styles, it is reasonable to assume that migration and settlement were conducted during that phase, datable to the days of Ramses III and Ramses IV (and possibly even later) by the Beth Shean finds. Aegean settlement was also carried out elsewhere in the same phase, for example, the foundation of Emporio on Chios. Interactions between the Aegean world and the Levant, including migration, ceased after LHIIIC Middle, with no locally made pottery in the LHIIIC Late style and almost no found imported examples of this ware.

This picture of complex events of migration that occurred over the course of two or three generations greatly hinders the possibility of answering two of the most crucial questions in the study of migration: "What was the number of migrants?" and "What was their exact origin?" An unknown, yet probably substantial, number of migrants that reached Philistia was born not in the Aegean world but in Aegean households along the routes, in places like Cilicia, Cyprus, and Syria, second and even third generations to the original Aegean migrants of LHIIIC Early. Consequently, it is nearly impossible to estimate how many people left the core of the Aegean world for the east or to try to calculate the number of newcomers from the numbers of people who left and who settled along the routes.

Similarly, although the material culture and the behavioral patterns at the sites in which Aegeans had settled can be identified clearly as distinctively Aegean in the LHIIIC tradition, they are not exact copies of either regional Aegean styles of the period and thus hinder pinpointing the exact origin of the migrants.

There are, however, still other pieces of evidence relevant to the study of origin: the type of Aegean cooking jugs used by the migrants in Cilicia, Cyprus, and Philistia is common on the mainland and in some of the Cyclades but not on Crete. The suggestion that Cretans did not play an important role in the migration to the east can be supported by the study of other traits of material culture, mainly the style of decorated pottery. Some of the pottery kilns found in Field I at Tel Miqne/Ekron are of a type found in Miletus (which, in turn, probably has a Cretan prototype) but not on the Greek mainland, where other types of kilns were used. Another important clue is the similarity of the feathered hats of the Sea Peoples in the Medinet Habu reliefs and on the seal and the game board from Enkomi to those of the contemporary sailors and warriors on the LHIIIC, and mainly Koan, pottery. The Ashkelon krater showing a warrior with a feathered hat and/or hedgehog helmet seems to bridge the gap between the Koan and other Aegean depictions and the Egyptian ones. Finally, the ethnonym *Philistines*, Philistine words and names in the Bible, and the goddess name PTGYH (Chapter 7) point to the general area of the Aegean Sea. We should look therefore for the tentative place of origin of at least some of the migrants in an area where people with feathered hats, Aegean cooking jugs, or Milesian-style kilns appear. The Dodecanese and the western Anatolian coast seem to be the best candidates, yet it is also likely that others came from the vast area between the eastern coast of mainland Greece and the Cyclades.

THE ARRIVAL

Canaan was not a priority target for Aegeans before the twelfth century BCE (Chapter 6). The interactions between the Aegean world and the southern Levant were restricted almost only to the trade range. Aegean pottery – stirrup jars, piriform jars, and flasks – was imported mainly to serve as containers for precious liquids or unguents. Serving vessels, such as kraters, cups, and kylikes, were imported in smaller numbers and not usually used by the local "Canaanites." Other objects, such as figurines, were imported in very small quantities, probably bought as exotic curiosities rather than used as cultic objects. No evidence was found for the residences of Aegean merchants in Canaan. Moreover, finds of Cypriot domestic pottery at Tell Abu Hawam – probably the entry point of much of the Mycenaean pottery to Canaan – suggest the residence at the site of Cypriots, who may have been intermediaries in the trade in Aegean goods. Some mercenaries of Aegean origin who served in the Egyptian army starting in the el-Amarna period (and possibly before) probably passed through or were stationed in Canaan, yet they left no visible mark on the local material culture. Consequently, because the personal contact with Aegean people was limited, the local "Canaanite" behavioral patterns were not influenced in any significant way by the Aegean world. In the thirteenth century, wine (or beer) drinking, for example, was practiced in a local form, influenced only by Egyptian manners: depictions on ivories show that the beverage was drawn from a bottle or a krater and served in a shallow drinking bowl.

This nature of connection with the Aegean world changed dramatically at the beginning of the twelfth century. The destruction of the Hittite kingdom, Ugarit, and Amurru opened the land routes to the Levant. Aegean settlements in Cilicia, Cyprus, and most probably Syria could be used as stepping-stones to pave the road for settlement in Canaan proper. The time frame for the beginning of the movement toward Canaan can be no earlier than 1190–1185 (the date of the destruction of Ugarit) and no later than 1175 (Year 8 of Ramses III).

Most of the Aegean migrants entered Canaan by land, leapfrogging between sites in Syria, such as Ras Ibn Hani. Such a reconstruction is strongly supported by the Egyptian sources, which depict not a maritime migration but a land migration of family groups. The very few finds in Philistia that have any connection to sea activity (e.g., anchors, ship depictions, imported goods) suggest that seafaring was not an important component of the migrants' life before or after their settlement in Philistia. The sea battle relief, thought by some to be directly connected to a migration event, actually portrays what was typical maritime activity of that period: a raid, the type of which Ugarit suffered a decade or more earlier. The assembling of a fleet for a raid was beyond the abilities of most single polities; in light of this, we can understand the words of Ramses III regarding the enemies who made conspiracy in their islands and the depictions of ships of different polities or groups that raided the Nile Delta. The migrants' arrival and settlement should not be understood as a single event or an organized invasion that ran like clockwork. Rather, as in the case of the migration to Cyprus and Cilicia, it was a recurrent process, conducted in small or large groups. Considering the chariots portrayed in the land battle relief, it is likely that some of the groups were fairly well organized and contained a good number of aristocrats.

The presence of Egyptian garrisons in various places in Canaan evidently did not seriously limit the migration. Although some groups (perhaps only those who ventured to penetrate into the Delta) were intercepted by Egyptian forces, as seen in the Medinet Habu reliefs, most groups probably reached their destination unharmed, having evaded encounter with the Egyptian garrison or having been organized in large enough numbers for the small garrison troops to deliberately avoid them.

THE SETTLEMENT

On arrival, the choice of site for settlement was an opportunistic one. It seems that only in the case of Tel Miqne/Ekron was local opposition faced with force, leading to the destruction of the small Canaanite village (Chapter 8). In Ashkelon, settlement was conducted on the abandoned remains of an Egyptian fort, and in Ashdod, there is no real evidence for destruction. A local Canaanite population was an integral part of every Philistine settlement from its emergence. Every Philistine household displayed evidence of behavioral patterns that reflected both Aegean and local practices. This is not to say that the interaction with the local population around the sites was harmonious: it is possible that villages and small towns were destroyed during the migrants' struggle to gain possession of agricultural land and to consolidate their polity. An unknown number of the locals doubtlessly fled, yet many remained in the area that now predominately boasted Aegean settlements. Following the parallels of the Greek colonization and other migrations, it is highly probable that the attainment of control over land was immediately followed by its redistribution and actual settlement. The settlers were allotted plots of land for agriculture and for building their houses. In the towns, special areas were dedicated to the residences of the elite and to cult places. Each of the major settlements built by the migrants – though mere villages in terms of quality (discussed later in this chapter) – immediately became the most prominent in its area, unrivaled by any of the local settlements and challenged only by other Aegean settlements. The local elites understood this situation well: by default, each settlement had the power to become the center of a new polity.

The challenge faced by the scribes of Ramses III – trying to fit complex social processes into a historical narrative – also has been encountered by modern-day archaeologists. Thus, as the attack of the Sea Peoples was condensed into a single, massive event of Year 8 in Medinet Hebu, the Philistine migration was often seen as a unified conquest of the southern coastal plain and Shephela, a single historical event that can be given a single date. Rather, as the archaeological evidence suggests (discussed later in this chapter), it was a complex process in which various sites were settled by different groups of migrants over a period that may have lasted as long as several decades (Chapter 8). Compelling examples in other contexts for such processes are those of British settlement in New England in the sixteenth century CE and Greek settlement in Sicily in the eighth century BCE – each a prolonged process of colonists arriving from various places within a single cultural zone and creating a network of new sites over a period shorter than half a century. As in Philistia, the settlement sites were not formed by a single, unified invasion that can be given a single date.

Although there are many similarities between the settlements built by the Aegean migrants, and it is generally accepted that the migrants' society in the different sites exhibited a similar nature, the settlement of Philistia was far from uniform (Chapter 8). In fact, the opposite may be true; the following are indications (perhaps somewhat similar to those of the Greek colonization of the eighth century) of the unique nature of every settlement event, leading to varying characters of the Pentapolis sites:

* Divergence in the interrelations between the migrants and the local population and the circumstances of foundation is seen in evidence of the presence or absence and the nature of the destruction horizon separating the last Canaanite town from the Aegean settlement.
* Dissimilarity between sites in regard to the origin of the settlers or the composition of the settling party is suggested by variability in several traits of Aegean material culture, such as some styles of Aegean pictorial pottery and of Aegean cooking jugs.
* Differences in the level of organization, the power held by the Aegean rulership, and perhaps the scale of the colonizing body can be deduced from changes in the plan and the size of the site immediately following the transition to the Iron Age.

The first phase of Aegean settlement was of nonurban nature. It is perhaps not surprising that, arriving from the mostly posturban society of the twelfth-century Aegean, the Aegean migrants did not build urban sites. None of the first phases of Philistine settlement at Ashdod, Tel Miqne/Ekron, or Ashkelon portrays any sign of urbanism, such as large public buildings, temples, and palaces; the production of elite art; administration; or even well-planned fortification. With two exceptions – the Tel Miqne/Ekron mud-brick wall, only three meters wide and lacking any refinements as towers or gates, and the reused Egyptian-style "residency" at Ashdod – all architecture remaining from the first phase of migrants is of thin-walled, mud-brick domestic buildings. The vast open areas between the houses seen in Ashkelon Grid 38, Phase 20, and between those in Tel Miqne/Ekron Field IV, Stratum VII, support the notion of a sparsely settled, villagelike form of the initial stage of the

Philistine sites. This stands in striking contrast to the rich temples and palaces of Megiddo and Lachish, Canaanite cities that continued to exist until the middle of the twelfth century, during the first phase of Philistines settlement. It appears that neither the Aegean migrants nor their Canaanite allies wanted or were able to re-create any form of a city, whether Aegean or Canaanite. Only in the eleventh century, with the renewal of trade with Cyprus and Egypt, and the expansion of Philistia north of the Yarkon River line, did Ashdod and Ashkelon become fortified centers, and a massive ruler's dwelling was built at Tel Miqne/Ekron. The appearance of first, scant remains of linear writing at both sites, as well as that of luxury items such as carved ivory pieces in the Philistine sites, may be an indication that only at that stage did the villages of Philistia become urban centers – the Pentapolis.

AEGEAN LIFE ABROAD: THE MAKING OF PHILISTIA

The number of migrants that reached Philistia in the twelfth century cannot be established, yet something can be said about the scale of migration (Chapter 8). According to calculations of the inhabited area, the population of Philistia after the arrival of the migrants numbered about twenty-five thousand in the twelfth century (reaching a peak of thirty thousand in the eleventh century). The continuation of local Canaanite material culture and toponyms indicates that a good part of the population was local. The number of migrants amounted, at most, to half of the population, and perhaps much less. Even the migrant population probably accumulated over at least two generations, the minimum estimated time for the continuous process of migration.

The migrants who reached Philistia were of various social strata and personal status. Most of the volume of the migration was probably of commoners; of these, most were farmers – the backbone of every preindustrial migration. They came as individuals or as family groups, some containing non-Aegean members. Others were professional potters, skilled in the Aegean tradition. Few, if any, were artisans capable of producing elite art. It is plausible that people with clerical duties came, too, and were responsible for the introduction of the Aegean cult. Because the cults were of a female goddess or goddesses, it is reasonable to assume that a good number of these people were female priestesses, though there is no direct evidence for full-time priesthood in Philistia.

It is likely that, in some cases, perhaps as in the case of Tel Miqne/Ekron, which shows significant continuity in the location of the ruler's dwelling in Field IV, Aegean aristocratic lineages continued for centuries after the migration. It is still to be found whether there was a hierarchy among the aristocrats themselves, a situation that cannot be ascertained from the data currently at hand.

Being an Aegean settler abroad meant employing one's cultural values, concepts, and worldview in a new country. Although it was not the old home, it would become a new one. In a way, looking at the Canaanite landscape through Aegean eyes inaugurated a process that resulted in southern Canaan becoming a new entity: Philistia, the land of the Philistines. Philistia came into being because the settlers were doing things the Aegean way in the microcosm of their domestic sphere and in their macrocosm of the community, the site, and society (Chapters 7 and 8).

Outside the domestic arena, the area of the site and even the agricultural landscape were shaped to a large extent by the combination of Aegean rulership, industry, and subsistence economy. In the household – the most elementary unit of society, and the most indicative for identifying migration – behavioral patterns were dramatically different from those in the Late Bronze Age Canaanite culture. The domestic space was fashioned to accommodate Aegean lifestyle: the preparation and consumption of food and drink, as well as the cottage textile industry. Hearths were used not only for cooking but also as ceremonial and utilitarian focal points. Of special interest is the elite building in Area G at Ashdod, whose plan was converted from the Canaanite/Egyptian type to resemble an Aegean elite, *Korridorhaus*-type building. An analysis of the fineware pottery from habitation levels shows the existence of complete Aegean wine-drinking sets, composed of kraters, spouted or strainer jugs, and deep bowls. Such sets were previously not in any significant use in Canaan and indicate Aegean wine-drinking practices. Aegean cooking practices were at least as common in Philistia as the local Canaanite ones. Aegean cooking jugs and kalathoi and the cooking on hearths (and perhaps Aegean ovens) were in widespread use side by side with *tabun*s and Canaanite cooking pots. Aegean-style imperforated loom weights show that domestic textile production was practiced according to an Aegean tradition. The strongest socialization of the younger generation into the Aegean traditions happened, without doubt, at home. The families, most of which had intermarried with locals or other non-Aegeans, kept their Aegean tradition of the domestic cult of an Aegean goddess, which seems to appear everywhere in Philistia. The women – Aegean, local, or offspring of intercultural marriages – not only preserved in their homes the traditions of Aegean and Canaanite foodways and textile production but also, doubtless, passed these on to their children.

From our sparse knowledge of twelfth-century rulership, it seems that rulers or elites did not have similar power in all the Pentapolis sites. Stronger rulers or elites, as in Tel Miqne/Ekron, had presided over the changing of the site layout and conducting of public projects. Others, like those from Ashdod, were weaker and did not possess the power to carry out such deeds. However, the general social landscape was fashioned by the rulers and by elites, who created a type of rulership similar in some respects to its LHIIIC origins. As in the Aegean, the Philistine rulership of the twelfth century did not employ written administration or implement a redistributive economy of any visible scale. With the exception of the Tel Miqne/Ekron fortifications, the rulers did not engage in any public projects, build large temples, or support elite art. Still, as in the Aegean, the rather modest rulers' houses were the foci of power in the settlement, and having been executed in Aegean plan, they gave a clear message of identity. The rulers in Philistia used hearth rooms and communal dining and drinking to consolidate their power and the status of the elite, much in the way it had been done in the contemporary Aegean. In addition, the use of the traditional title *seren* later in the Iron Age may indicate that the migrants imported at least some of the Aegean or Anatolian lexicon of power. Religion outside the domestic sphere may have not resided in conspicuous buildings like the Late Bronze Age temples, yet the small shrines were indeed landmarks inside the towns and provided additional bonding for the migrants' community by alluding to familiar ceremonies or rituals.

Similarly, the pottery industry had an important effect on both society and the face of the settlements. Practically every major settlement had one or more workshop. The kiln area at Tel Miqne/Ekron, with its prominent position on the northeastern acropolis, shows the important position of the Aegean ceramic industry in the site's life, not only as the birthplace of material culture but also in the creation of the Aegeanized settlement landscape. The potters, most probably migrants themselves, needed to satisfy the needs of both migrating households and some local residents. As a result, they created a repertoire of pottery that was virtually dominated by Aegean forms but contained some Canaanite forms. Both were made locally, in kilns of non-Canaanite forms, using clay recipes different from the ones used by the local potters of the Late Bronze Age.

A comparison of the Aegean domestic pottery forms in Philistia with LHIIIC assemblages from Lefkandi, Phylakopi, and Emporio not only strongly supports an explanation of Aegean settlement (rather than of local imitation of LHIIIB trade forms) but also shows that the vessels from Philistia form a complete LHIIIC domestic assemblage.

Finally, the Aegean nature of subsistence economy affected all landscapes. It dictated the agricultural timetable and thus paced the rhythm of the settlement, from the schedule of individual farmers to the timing of public labors. The old Late Bronze Age system of animal husbandry could no longer continue: there was almost an absence of agricultural hinterland settlements, as most migrants settled in towns, having felt insecure outside the large concentration of migrants. Perhaps familiar with a similar situation from their countries of origin, the migrants turned to a process of agricultural intensification in a close range around the major settlements. Large numbers of pigs, providing much protein, and cattle, providing milk and traction power, were probably raised proximate to the town or even inside it. Sheep and goats, less available from the seminomads of the hill country or impossible to herd on a large scale in the insecure conditions of the twelfth century, became less important in this new economy.

The Canaanite elders at the end of the twelfth century saw their country changing before their eyes: their old rulers were gone and their small-town palaces replaced by fast-growing cities of foreigners, smoky from pottery kilns and filled with pigs and cows. Many of their old villages were gone, and fewer people could be seen between the new cities. What had been Canaan was made into Philistia.

THE JOURNEY BEGINS HERE

Woven into a crude tapestry of sherds and mud-brick walls, the story of the Aegean migration to the Levant is first of all a human one. It is the sum of the aspirations, fears, and hopes of a great number of real people – Aegean, Levantine, and others – who went through intense experiences of travel and settlement. Accordingly, the goal set here was to analyze the phenomena of the Philistines and Sea Peoples as events of human migration so as to open new portals and to offer a fresh view toward new, possibly more successful, manners of reconstructing past Mediterranean societies.

This work has suggested an outline rather than a complete narrative of the Aegean migration to the Levant. Filled with lacunae and masked or exposed by the whims of the depositional processes, excavated areas, and published data, the story here is destined to be retold and rewritten following new discoveries or theoretical constructs.

BIBLIOGRAPHY

Abrams, E. M. 1989. Architecture and Energy: An Evolutionary Perspective. In: Schiffer, M. B. (ed.) *Archaeological Method and Theory*. Vol. 1. Tucson, AZ: 47–87.

Acheson, P. E. 1999. The Role of Force in the Development of Early Mycenaean Polities. In: Laffineur, R. (ed.) *Polemos: Le contexte guerrier en Égée à l'âge du Bronze* (Aegaeum 19). Liège: 97–104.

Adams, W. Y. 1968. Invasion, Diffusion, Evolution? *Antiquity* 42: 194–215.

Aharoni, Y. 1979. *The Land of the Bible: A Historical Geography*. London.

Åkerström, A. 1987. *Berbati 2: The Pictorial Pottery*. Stockholm.

Alberti, L. and Bettelli, M. 2005. Contextual Problems of Mycenaean Pottery in Italy. In: Laffineur, R. and Greco, E. (eds.) *Emporia: Aegeans in the Central and Eastern Mediterranean: Proceedings of the 10th International Aegean Conference. Athens, Italian School of Archaeology, 14–18 April 2004*. Liège: 547–9.

Albright, W. F. 1932. The Excavation at Tell Beit Mirsim I: The Pottery of the First Three Campaigns *AASOR* 12: 1–89.

Alcock, S. E. 2005. Roman Colonies in the Eastern Empire: A Tale of Four Cities. In: Stein, G. J. (ed.) *The Archaeology of Colonial Encounters: Comparative Perspectives*. Santa Fe, NM: 297–329.

Alram-Stern, E. 2003. Aigeira-Acropolis: The Stratigraphy. In: Deger-Jalkotzy, S. and Zavadil, M. (eds.) *LHIIIC Chronology and Synchronisms: Proceedings of the International Workshop Held at the Austrian Academy of Sciences at Vienna, May 7th and 8th, 2001*. Vienna: 15–21.

Alt, A. 1944. Ägyptiche Tempel in Palästina und die Landnahme der Philister. *ZDPV* 67: 1–20.

Amiet, P. 1992. *Corpus des cylindres de Ras Shamra-Ougarit II: Sceaux-cylindres en hèmatite et pierres diverses*. Paris.

Amiran, R. 1970. *Ancient Pottery of the Holy Land from Its Beginnings in the Neolithic Period to the End in the Iron Age*. New Haven, CT.

Andelkovic, B. 1995. *The Relations between Early Bronze Age I Canaanites and Upper Egyptians*. Belgrade.

Anderson, W. P. 1988. *Sarepta I: The Late Bronze and Iron Age Strata of Area II,Y. The University Museum of the University of Pennsylvania Excavations at Sarafand, Lebanon*. Beirut.

Andreadaki-Vlasaki, M. 1991. The Khania Area, ca 1200–700 B.C. In: Musti, D., Sacconi, A., Rocchetti, L., Rocchi, M., Scafa, E., Sportiello, L., and Giannotta, M. E. (eds.) *Transizione dal Miceneo all'Alto Archaismo: dal palazzo alla città. Atti del Convegno Internazionale, Roma, 14–19 marzo 1988*. Rome: 403–23.

Anthony, D. W. 1990. Migration in Archaeology: The Baby and the Bathwater. *American Anthropologist* 92: 895–914.

Anthony, D. W. 1997. Prehistoric Migrations As a Social Process. In: Chapman, J. and Hamerow, H. *Migrations and Invasions in Archaeological Explanation* (BAR International Series 664). Oxford: 21–32.

Anthony, D. W. 2000. Comment to S. Burmeister. In: Burmeister, S. *Archaeology and Migration: Approaches to an Archaeological Proof of Migration. CurrAnthr* 41, no. 4: 554–5.

Aravantinos, V. L., Godart, L., and Sacconi, A. 2001. *Thèbes: Fouilles de la Cadmée I. Les tablettes en linéaire B de la Odos Pelopidou. Édition et commentaire.* Pisa and Rome.

Artzy, M. 1987. On Boats and Sea Peoples. *BASOR* 266: 75–84.

Artzy, M. 2006. The Carmel Coast during the Second Part of the Late Bronze Age: A Center for Eastern Mediterranean Transshipping. *BASOR* 343: 45–64.

Asaro, F., Perlman, I., and Dothan, M. 1971. An Introductory Study of Mycenaean IIIC: 1 Ware from Tel Ashdod. *Archaeometry* 13: 169–75.

Astour, M. C. 1995. Overland Trade Routes in Ancient Western Asia. In: Sasson, J. M. (ed.) *Civilizations of the Near East.* Vol. 3. New York: 1401–20.

Åström, P. 1993. Late Cypriot Bronze Age Pottery in Palestine. In: Biran, A. and Aviram, J. (eds.) *Biblical Archaeology Today, 1990: Proceedings of the Second International Congress on Biblical Archaeology. Jerusalem, June–July 1990.* Jerusalem: 307–13.

Aura-Jorro, F. 1985. *Diccionario Griego-español, Anejo I: Diccionario micénico, 1* (Consejo Superior de Investigaciones Científicas). Madrid.

Aura-Jorro, F. (ed.) 1993. *Diccionario micénico: Diccionario Griego-español, Anejo, 2* (Consejo Superior de Investigaciones Científicas). Madrid.

Badre, L. 2003. Handmade Burnished Ware and Contemporary Imported Pottery from Tell Kazel. In: Stampolidis, C. and Karageorghis, V. *Ploes... Sea Routes... Interconnections in the Mediterranean 16th–6th C. BC: Proceedings of the International Symposium Held at Rethymnon, Crete, September 29th–October 2nd 2002.* Athens: 83–99.

Badre, L. 2006. Tell Kazel-Simyra: A Contribution to a Relative Chronological History in the Eastern Mediterranean during the Late Bronze Age. *BASOR* 343: 65–95.

Badre, L., Boileau, M.-C., Jung, R., and Mommsen, H. 2005. The Provenance of Aegean and Syrian Type Pottery Found at Tell Kazel (Syria). *Egypt and the Levant* 15: 15–47.

Balensi, J. 1980. *Les fouilles R.W. Hamilton a Tell Abu Hawam: Niveaux IV et V.* 3 vols. Thèse soutenue publiement le 21 mai 1980 au Palais Universitaire de Strasbourg. Strasbourg.

Balensi, J. 1985. Revising Tell Abu Hawam. *BASOR* 257: 65–74.

Balensi, J. 2004. Relativité du phénomène mycénien à Tell Abou Hawam: Un «proto-marketing»? In: Balensi, J., Monchambert, J.-Y., and Müller Celka, S. (eds.) *La céramique mycénienne de l'Égée au Levant, Hommage à Vronwy Hankey.* Lyon: 141–82.

Balensi, J., Herrera, M. D., and Bunimovitz, S. 1985. Tel Abou Hawam 1983–1984, rapport préliminaire. *RBibl* 92: 82–128.

Bankoff, H. A. and Winter, F. A. 1984. Northern Intruders in LHIIIC Greece: A View from the North. *JIES* 12: 1–30.

Bankoff, H. A., Meyer, N., and Stefanovich, M. 1996. Handmade Burnished Ware and the Late Bronze Age of the Balkans. *JMA* 9, no. 2: 193–209.

Barako, T. J. 2000. The Philistine Settlement As Mercantile Phenomenon? *AJA* 104: 513–30.

Barako, T. J. 2001. "The Seaborne Migration of the Philistines." Ph.D. dissertation, Harvard University.

Barbara, A. 1994. Mixed Marriages: Some Key Questions. *International Migration* 32: 571–85.

Barber, E. J. W. 1991. *Prehistoric Textiles: The Development of Cloth in the Neolithic and Bronze Age, with Special Reference to the Aegean.* Princeton, NJ.

Barber, E. J. W. 1994. *Women's Work: The First 20,000 Years: Women, Cloth and Society in Early Times.* London.

Barber, E. J. W. 1997. Minoan Women and the Challenges of Weaving for Home, Trade and Shrine. In: Laffineur, R. and Betancourt, P. P. (eds.) *TEXNH: Craftsmen, Craftswomen and Craftsmanship in the Aegean Bronze Age* (Aegaeum 16, 2). Liège: 516–19.

Barber, R. L. N. 1987. *The Cyclades in the Bronze Age.* Iowa City, IA.

Basch, L. 1987. *Le musee imaginaire de la marine antique.* Athens.

Bass, G. F. 1967. *Cape Gelidonya: A Bronze Age Shipwreck Transactions of the American Philosophical Society* 57, no. 8.

Bass, G. F. 1991. Evidence of Trade from Bronze Age Shipwrecks. In: Gale, N. H. (ed.) *Bronze Age Trade in the Mediterranean: Papers Presented at the Conference Held at Rewley House, Oxford, in December 1989* (SIMA 90). Jonsered: 69–82.

Bass, G. F. 1997a. Prolegomena to a Study of Maritime Traffic in Raw Materials to the Aegean during the Fourteenth and Thirteenth Centuries B.C. In: Laffineur, R. and Betancourt, P. P. (eds.) *TEXNH: Craftsmen, Craftswomen and Craftsmanship in the Aegean Bronze Age* (Aegaeum 16, 1). Liège: 153–70.

Bass, G. F. 1997b. Beneath the Wine Dark Sea: Nautical Archaeology and the Phoenicians of the Odyssey. In: Coleman, J. E. and Walz, C. A. *Greeks and Barbarians: Essays on the Interactions between Greeks and Non-Greeks in Antiquity and the Consequences for Eurocentrism.* Bethesda, MD: 71–101.

Bass, G. F. 1998. Sailing between the Aegean and the Orient in the Second Millennium B.C. In: Cline, E. and Harris-Cline, D. (eds.) *The Aegean and the Orient in the Second Millennium* (Aegaeum 18). Liège: 183–9.

Bauer, A. A. 1998. Cities of the Sea: Maritime Trade and the Origin of Philistine Settlement in the Early Iron Age Southern Levant. *OJA* 17: 149–68.

Beal, R. H. 1992. The Location of Cilician Ura. *AnatSt* 42: 65–73.

Beck, P. 1989. Stone Ritual Artifacts and Statues from Area A and H at Hazor. In: Ben-Tor, A. (ed.) *Hazor III–IV, Text: An Account of the Third and Fourth Seasons of Excavations, 1957–1958.* Jerusalem: 322–38.

Beck, P. and Kochavi, M. 1993. Aphek (in Sharon). In: Stern, E. (ed.) *The New Encyclopedia of Archaeological Excavations in the Holy Land.* Vol. 1. Jerusalem: 64–72.

Beckman, G. 1994a. Akkadian Documents from Ugarit. In: Knapp, A. B. (ed.) *Sources for the History of Cyprus.* Vol. 2. *Near Eastern and Aegean Texts from the Third to the First Millennia BC.* Altmont, NY: 26–8.

Beckman, G. 1994b. Hittite Documents from Hattusa. In: Knapp, A. B. (ed.) *Sources for the History of Cyprus.* Vol. 2. *Near Eastern and Aegean Texts from the Third to the First Millennia BC.* Altmont, NY: 31–5.

Becks, R. 2003. Troia VII: The Transition from the Late Bronze Age to the Early Iron Age. In: Fischer, B., Genz, H., Jean, É., and Köroğlu, K. (eds.) *Identifying Changes: The Transitions from Bronze to Iron Ages in Anatolia and Its Neighbouring Regions: Proceedings of the International Workshop Istanbul, November 8–9, 2002.* Istanbul: 41–53.

Bell, C. 2006. *The Evolution of Long Distance Trading Relationships across the LBA/Iron Age Transition on the Northern Levantine Coast* (BAR International Series 1574). Oxford.

Ben-Arieh, S. and Edelstein, G. 1977. *Akko: Tombs near the Persian Garden* (ʿAtiqot 12). Jerusalem.

Ben-Dov, M. 1992. Middle and Late Bronze Age Dwellings. In: Kempinski, A. and Reich, R. (eds.) *The Architecture of Ancient Israel: From the Prehistoric to the Persian Periods.* Jerusalem: 99–104.

Ben-Dov, R. 2002. The Late Bronze Age "Mycenaean" Tomb. In: Biran, A. and Ben-Dov, R. *Dan II: A Chronicle of the Excavations and the Late Bronze Age "Mycenaean" Tomb.* Jerusalem: 33–248.

Bennet, J. 1995. Space through Time: Diachronic Perspectives on the Special Organization of the Pylian State. In: Laffineur, R. and Niemeier, W.-D. (eds.) *Politeia: Society and State in the Aegean Bronze Age* (Aegaeum 12, 2). Liège: 587–602.

Bennet, J. 1998. The Linear B Archives and the Kingdom of Nestor. In: Davis, J. L. (ed.) *Sandy Pylos: An Archaeological History from Nestor to Navarino.* Austin, TX: 111–33.

Ben-Shlomo, D. 2005. Material Culture. In: Dothan, M. and Ben-Shlomo, D. *Ashdod VI: Excavations of Areas H–K* (IAA Reports 24). Jerusalem: 63–246.

Ben-Shlomo, D. 2006a. *Decorated Philistine Pottery: An Archaeological and Archaeometric Study* (BAR International Series 1541). Oxford.

Ben-Shlomo, D. 2006b. New Evidence on Seals and Sealings from Philistia. *Tel Aviv* 33: 134–62.

Ben-Shlomo, D. 2006–7. Cultural Diversity, Ethnicity and Power Imbalance in Early Iron Age Philistia. *Scripta Mediterranea* 27–8: 267–90.

Ben-Shlomo, D. and Press, M. D. 2009. A Reexamination of Aegean-Style Figurines in Light of New Evidence from Ashdod, Ashkelon, and Ekron. *BASOR* 353: 39–74.

Ben-Shlomo, D., Shai, I., Zukerman, A., and Maeir, A. 2008. Cooking Identities: Aegean-Style and Philistine Cooking Jugs and Cultural Interaction in the Southern Levant during the Iron Age. *AJA* 112, no. 2: 225–46.

Berry, J. W. 1992. Acculturation and Adaptation in a New Society. *International Migration* 30: 69–85.

Berry, J. W. 1997. Immigration, Acculturation, and Adaptation. *Applied Psychology: An International Review* 46, no. 1: 5–34.

Betancourt, P. P. 1985. *The History of Minoan Pottery*. Princeton, NJ.

Bierling, N. 1998. *Report on the 1995–1996 Excavations in Field XNW: Areas 77, 78, 79, 89, 101, 102. Iron Age I. Text and Data Base (Plates, Sections, Plans)* (Tel Miqne–Ekron Limited Edition Series, No. 7). Jerusalem.

Bietak, M. 1993. The Sea Peoples and the End of the Egyptian Administration in Canaan. In: Biran, A. and Aviram, J. (eds.) *Biblical Archaeology Today, 1990: Proceedings of the Second International Congress on Biblical Archaeology. Jerusalem, June–July 1990*. Jerusalem: 292–306.

Bietak, M. 1996. *Avaris: The Capital of the Hyksos: Recent Excavations at Tell el-Dabʻa*. London.

Bietak, M. 1997. The Center of Hyksos Rule: Avaris (Tell el-Dabʻa). In: Oren, E. D. (ed.) *The Hyksos: New Historical and Archaeological Perspectives* (University Museum Monograph 96). Philadelphia: 87–139.

Bikai, P. M. 1978. *The Pottery of Tyre*. Warminster, UK.

Birney, K. J. 2007. "Sea People or Syrian Peddlers? The Late Bronze Age–Iron I Aegean Presence in Syrian and Cilicia." Ph.D. dissertation, Harvard University.

Bittel, K. 1976. *Die Hethiter*. Munich.

Blegen, C. W. 1921. *Korakou: A Prehistoric Settlement near Corinth*. Boston.

Blegen, C. W., Boulter, C. G., Caskey, J. L., and Rawson, M. 1958. *Troy IV: Settlements VIIa, VIIb and VIII*. Princeton. NJ.

Blegen, C. W. and Rawson, M. 1966. *The Palace of Nestor at Pylos in Western Messenia*. Vol. 1. *The Buildings and Their Contents. Part 1 Text. Part 2 Illustrations*. Princeton, NJ.

Bloedow, E. F. 1997. Itinerant Craftsmen and Women and Trade in the Aegean Bronze Age. In: Laffineur, R. and Betancourt, P. P. (eds.) *TEXNH: Craftsmen, Craftswomen and Craftsmanship in the Aegean Bronze Age* (Aegaeum 16, 1). Liège: 439–47.

Boardman, J. 1980. *The Greek Overseas*. London.

Boas, A. and Arbel, Y. 1999. Jerusalem, Khirbet el-Burj. *Hadashot Arkheologiyot* 109: 73.

Boessneck, J. 1976. *Tell el-Dabʻa III: Die Tierknochenfunde 1966–1969*. Vienna.

Borgna, E. 1997. Kitchen-Ware from LMIIIC Phaistos. *SMEA* 39: 189–217.

Borgna, E. 2004. Aegean Feasting: A Minoan Perspective. *Hesperia* 73, no. 2: 247–79.

Bounni, A., Lagarce, E., and Saliby, N. 1976. Rapport préliminaire sur la première campagne de fouilles (1975) à Ibn Hani (Syrie). *Syria* 53: 233–79.

Bounni, A., Lagarce, E., and Saliby, N. 1978. Rapport préliminaire sur la deuxième campagne de fouilles (1976) à Ibn Hani (Syrie). *Syria* 55: 233–301.

Bounni, A., Lagarce, E., and Saliby, N. 1979. Rapport préliminaire sur la troisième campagne de fouilles (1977) à Ibn Hani (Syrie). *Syria* 56: 217–91.

Bounni, A., Lagarce, E., Saliby, N., Badre, L., Leriche, P., and Touma, M. 1981. Rapport préliminaire sur la quatrième campagne de fouilles (1978) à Ibn Hani (Syrie). *Syria* 58: 215–99.

Bourdieu, P. 1990. *The Logic of Practice*. Stanford, CA.

Bouzek, J. 1985. *The Aegean, Anatolia and Europe: Cultural Interrelations in the Second Millennium B.C.* (SIMA 29). Gothenburg.

Boyd, M. 1989. Family and Personal Networks in International Migration: Recent Developments and New Agendas. *International Migration* 23: 638–70.

Brandl, B. 1993. Appendix 6: Scarabs, a Scaraboid and a Scarab Impression from Area G (1968–1970). In: Dothan, M. and Porath, Y. *Ashdod V: Excavations of Area G: The Fourth–Sixth Seasons of Excavations 1968–1970*. ('Atiqot 23). Jerusalem: 129–42.

Branigan, K. 1981. Minoan Colonization. *BSA* 76: 23–33.

Branigan, K. 1984. Minoan Community Colonies in the Aegean? In: Hagg, R. and Marinatos, N. (eds.) *The Minoan Thalassocracy: Myth and Reality (Proceedings of the Third International Symposium of the Swedish Institute at Athens, 31 May–5 June, 1982)*. Stockholm: 49–52.

Branigan, K. 1991. Mochlos – An Early Aegean "Gateway Community"? In: Laffineur, R. (ed.) *Thalassa: L' Égée prehistorique et la mer* (Aegaeum 7). Liège: 97–106.

Braunstein, S. L. 1998. "The Dynamics of Power in an Age of Transition: An Analysis of the Mortuary Remains of Tell el Far'ah (South) in the Late Bronze and Early Iron Age." Ph.D. dissertation, Columbia University, New York.

Breasted, J. H. 1948. Bronze Base of a Statue of Ramses VI Discovered at Megiddo. In: Loud, G. (ed.) *Megiddo II: Seasons of 1935–39. Text*. Chicago: 135–6.

Brug, J. F. 1985. *A Literary and Archaeological Study of the Philistines* (BAR International Series 265). Oxford.

Bruun-Lundgren, M. and Wiman, I. 2000. Industrial Activities and Personal Adornments. In: Hallager, E. and Hallager, B. P. (eds.) *The Greek-Swedish Excavations at the Agia Aikaterini Square, Kastelli, Khania 1970–1987*. Vol. 2. *Text and Plates: The Late Minoan IIIC Settlement*. Stockholm: 175–82.

Bryce, T. 1998. *The Kingdom of the Hittites*. Oxford.

Bryce, T. 2002. *Life and Society in the Hittite World*. Oxford.

Bunimovitz, S. 1990. Problems in the "Ethnic" Identification of the Philistine Material Culture. *Tel Aviv* 17: 210–22.

Bunimovitz, S. 1998. Sea Peoples in Cyprus and Israel: A Comparative Study of Immigration Processes. In: Gitin, S., Mazar, A., and Stern, E. (eds.) *Mediterranean Peoples in Transition: Thirteenth to Early Tenth Centuries BCE*. Jerusalem: 103–13.

Bunimovitz, S. and Faust, A. 2001. Chronological Separation, Geographical Segregation, or Ethnic Demarcation? Ethnography and the Iron Age Low Chronology. *BASOR* 322: 1–10.

Bunimovitz, S. and Yasur-Landau, A. 1996. Philistine and Israelite Pottery: A Comparative Approach to the Question of Pots and People. *Tel Aviv* 23: 88–101.

Bunimovitz, S. and Yasur-Landau, A. 2002. Women and Aegean Immigration to Cyprus in the 12th Century BCE. In: Bolger, D. and Serwint, N. (eds.) *Engendering Aphrodite: Women and Society in Ancient Cyprus* (CAARI Monograph 3). Boston: 211–22.

Bunimovitz, S. and Zimhoni, O. 1993. "Lamp-and-Bowl" Foundation Deposits in Canaan. *IEJ* 43, nos. 2–3: 99–125.

Burmeister, S. 2000. Archaeology and Migration: Approaches to an Archaeological Proof of Migration. *CurrAnthr* 41, no. 4: 539–67.

Cadogan, G. 1984. A Minoan Thalassocracy? In: Hägg, R. and Marinatos, N. (eds.) *The Minoan Thalassocracy: Myth and Reality. Proceedings of the Third International Symposium at the Swedish Institute in Athens, 31 May–5 June, 1982*. Stockholm: 13–15.

Cadogan, G. 1993. Cyprus, Mycenaean Pottery, Trade and Colonization. In: Zerner, C., Zerner, P., and Winder, J. (eds.) *Proceedings of the International Conference "Wace and Blegen: Pottery As Evidence for Trade in the Aegean Bronze Age 1939–1989," Held at the American School of Classical Studies at Athens, December 2–3, 1989*. Amsterdam: 91–9.

Carington Smith, J. 1992. Spinning and Weaving Equipment. In: McDonald, W. A. and Wilkie, N. C. (eds.) *Excavation at Nichoria in Southwest Greece*. Vol. 2. *The Bronze Age Occupation*. Minneapolis: 674–711.

Carlier, P. 1995. QA-SI-RE-U et QA-SI-RE-WI-JA. In: Laffineur, R. and Niemeier, W.-D. (eds.) *Politeia: Society and State in the Aegean Bronze Age* (Aegaeum 12, 2). Liège: 355–64.

Carter, J. C. 1993. Taking Possession of the Land: Early Colonization in Southern Italy. In: Scott, R. T. and Scott, A. R. (eds.) *Eius Virtutis Studiosi: Classical and Postclassical Studies in Memory of Frank Edward Brown (1908–88)*. Washington, DC: 342–76.

Casson, L. 1971. *Ships and Seamanship in the Ancient World*. Princeton, NJ.

Casson, L. 1994. *Ships and Seafaring in Ancient Times.* London.

Casson, L. 1995. Merchant Galleys. In: Gardiner, R. and Morrison, J. (eds.) *The Age of the Galley: Mediterranean Oared Vessels since Pre-Classical Times.* Brasseys: 117–26.

Catling, H. W. 1955. A Bronze Greave from a 13th Century B.C. Tomb at Enkomi. *OpAth* 2: 21–36.

Catling, H. W. 1964. *Cypriot Bronzes in the Mycenaean World.* Oxford.

Catling, H. W. and Catling, E. 1981. "Barbarian" Pottery from the Mycenaean Settlement at the Menelaion, Sparta. *BSA* 76: 71–82.

Caubet, A. 1992. Reoccupation of the Syrian Coast after the "Crisis Years." In: Ward, W. A. and Joukowski, M. S. (eds.) *The Crisis Years: The 12th Century B.C. from beyond the Danube to the Tigris.* Dubuque, IA: 123–31.

Cavanagh, W. and Mee, C. 1998. *A Private Place: Death in Prehistoric Greece.* Jonsered.

Cecchini, S. M. 2000. Textile Industry in Northern Syria during the Iron Age according to the Evidence of the Tell Afis Excavations. In: Bunnenes, G. (ed.) *Essays on Syria in the Iron Age* (Ancient Near Eastern Studies Supplement 7). Louvain: 211–33.

Chadwick, J. 1976. Who Were the Dorians? *PdP* 31: 103–17.

Chadwick, J. 1987. The Muster of the Pylian Fleet. In: Ilievsky, P. H. and Crepajac, L. (eds.) *Tractata Mycenaea: Proceedings of the Eighth International Colloquium on Mycenaean Studies, Ohrid, September 15–20, 1985.* Skopje: 75–84.

Chadwick, J. 1988: The Women of Pylos. In: Olivier, J.-P. and Palaima, T. G. (eds.) *Texts, Tablets and Scribes: Studies in Mycenaean Epigraphy and Economy Offered to Emmett L. Bennett, Jr., Salamanca* (Minos Supplement 10): 43–95.

Chapman, J. 2000. Comment to S. Burmeister. In: Burmeister, S. *Archaeology and Migration: Approaches to an Archaeological Proof of Migration. CurrAnthr* 41, no. 4: 556–7.

Cheek, C. D. 1998. Massachusetts Bay Foodways: Regional and Class Influence. *Historical Archaeology* 32, no. 3: 152–72.

Cherry, J. F. 1982. Appendix A: Register of Archaeological Sites on Melos. In: Renfrew, C. and Wagstaff, M. *An Island Polity: The Archaeology of Exploitation in Melos.* Cambridge, UK: 291–309.

Chevallier, R. 1976. *Roman Roads.* Berkeley, CA.

Chun, K. M. and Akutsu, P. D. 2003. Acculturation among Ethnic Minority Families. In: Chun, K. M., Organista, P. B., and Marín, G. (eds.) *Acculturation: Advances in Theory, Measurement and Applied Research.* Washington, DC: 95–119.

Cifola, B. 1991. The Terminology of Ramses III's Historical Records with a Formal Analysis of the War Scenes. *Orientalia* 60: 9–57.

Cifola, B. 1994. The Role of the Sea Peoples at the End of the Late Bronze Age: A Reassessment of Textual and Archaeological Evidence. *Oriens Antiqvi Miscellanea* 1: 1–57.

Clark, J. E. and Parry, W. J. 1990. Craft Specialization and Cultural Complexity. *Research in Economic Anthropology* 12: 289–346.

Clark, J. J. 2004 Tracking Cultural Affiliation: Enculturation and Ethnicity. In: Mills, B. J. (ed.) *Identity, Feasting, and the Archaeology of the Greater Southwest.* Boulder, CO: 42–73.

Clarke, D. L. 1978. *Analytical Archaeology.* London.

Cline, E. H. 1993. Contact and Trade or Colonization? Egypt and the Aegean in the 14th–13th Centuries B.C. *Minos* 25–6: 7–36.

Cline, E. H. 1994. *Sailing the Wine-Dark Sea: International Trade and the Late Bronze Age Aegean.* Oxford.

Cline, E. H. 1995. Tinker, Tailor, Soldier, Sailor: Minoans and Mycenaeans Abroad. In: Laffineur, R. and Niemeier, W.-D. (eds.) *Politeia: Society and State in the Aegean Bronze Age* (Aegaeum 12, 1). Liège: 265–87.

Cline, E. H. 1998. Amenhotep III, the Aegean, and Anatolia. In: O'Connor, D. and Cline, E. H. (eds.) *Amenhotep III: Perspectives on His Reign.* Ann Arbor, MI: 236–50.

Cline, E. H. and O'Connor, D. 2003. The Mystery of the "Sea Peoples." In: O'Connor, D. and Quirke, S. (eds.) *Mysterious Lands.* London: 107–38.

Coates, J. E. 1987. Pentakonters and Trieres Compared. In: Tzalas, H. E. (ed.) *TROPIS II: 2nd International Symposium on Ship Construction in Antiquity*. Athens: 111–16.

Coates, J. E. 1995. The Naval Architecture and Oar Systems of Ancient Galleys. In: Gardiner, R. and Morrison, J. (eds.) *The Age of the Galley: Mediterranean Oared Vessels since Pre-Classical Times.* London 125–41.

Coldstream, J. N. 1993. Mixed Marriages at the Frontiers of the Early Greek World. *OJA* 12, no. 1: 89–108.

Coldstream, J. N. 1994a. *What Sort of Aegean Migration?* In: Karageorghis, V. (ed.) *Proceedings of the International Symposium Cyprus in the 11th Century B.C.* Nicosia: 143–6.

Coldstream, J. N. 1994b. Prospectors and Pioneers: Pithekoussai, Kyme and Central Italy. In: Tsetskhladze, G. R. and De Angelis, F. *The Archaeology of Greek Colonization: Essays Dedicated to Sir John Boardman.* Oxford: 47–59.

Coldstream, J. N. 1998. The First Exchanges between Euboeans and Phoenicians: Who Took the Initiative? In: Gitin, S., Mazar, A., and Stern, E. (eds.) *Mediterranean Peoples in Transition: Thirteenth to Early Tenth Centuries BCE.* Jerusalem: 353–60.

Collon, D. 1987. *First Impressions: Cylinder Seals in the Ancient Near East.* London.

Coulson, W. and Tsipopoulou, M. 1994. *Preliminary Investigations at Halasmenos, Crete, 1992–1993. Aegean Archaeology* 1: 65–86.

Courtois, J.-C. 1971. Le sanctuaire du dieu au lingot d'Enkomi-Alasia. In: Schaeffer, C. F.-A. *Mission Archéologique d'Alasia.* Vol. 4 (Alasia première série). Paris: 151–362.

Courtois, J.-C. 1978. Corpus céramique de Ras Shamra-Ugarit, niveaux historique: Bronze Moyen et Bronze Récent. In: Schaeffer, C. F.-A. (ed.) *Ugaritica* 7: 131–370.

Cross, F. M. and Stager, L. E. 2006. Cypro-Minoan Inscriptions Found in Ashkelon. *IEJ* 56: 129–59.

Crouwel, J. H. 1981. *Chariots and Other Means of Transport in Bronze Age Greece* (Allard Pierson Series 3). Amsterdam.

Crouwel, J. H. 1991. *Mycenaean Pictorial Pottery.* (Well Built Mycenae 21). Oxford.

Crouwel, J. H. 1992. *Chariots and Other Means of Transport in Iron Age Greece* (Allard Pierson Series 9). Amsterdam.

Cultraro, M. 2005. Aegeans on Smoke Shrouded Lemnos: A Re-assessment of the Mycenaean Evidence from Poliochni and Other Sites. In: Laffineur, R. and Greco, E. (eds.) *Emporia: Aegeans in the Central and Eastern Mediterranean: Proceedings of the 10th International Aegean Conference. Athens, Italian School of Archaeology, 14–18 April 2004.* Liège: 237–46.

D'Agata, A.-L. 2001. Ritual and Rubbish in Dark Age Crete: The Settlement of Thronos/Kephala (Ancient Sybrita) and the Pre-Classical Roots of a Greek City. *Aegean Archaeology* 4: 45–59.

D'Agata, A.-L. 2003a. Late Minoan IIIC–Subminoan Pottery Sequence at Thronos/Kephala and Its Connections with the Greek Mainland. In: Deger-Jalkotzy, S. and Zavadil, M. (eds.) *LHIIIC Chronology and Synchronisms: Proceedings of the International Workshop Held at the Austrian Academy of Sciences at Vienna, May 7th and 8th, 2001.* Vienna: 23–35.

D'Agata, A.-L. 2003b. Crete at Transition from Late Bronze to Iron Age. In: Fischer, B., Genz, H., Jean, É., and Köroğlu, K. (eds.) *Identifying Changes: The Transition from Bronze to Iron Ages in Anatolia and Its Neighbouring Regions. Proceedings of the International Workshop Istanbul, November 8–9, 2002.* Istanbul: 21–8.

D'Agata, A.-L., Goren, Y., Mommsen, H., Schwadt, A., and Yasur-Landau, A. 2005. Imported Pottery of LH IIIC Style from Israel: Style, Provenance, and Chronology. In: Laffineur, R. and Greco, E. (eds.) *Emporia: Aegeans in the Central and Eastern Mediterranean: Proceedings of the 10th International Aegean Conference. Athens, Italian School of Archaeology, 14–18 April 2004.* Liège: 371–9.

Dakoronia, P. 1987. War-Ships on Sherds of LHIIIC Kraters from Kynos. In: Tzalas, H. E. (ed.) *TROPIS II: 2nd International Symposium on Ship Construction in Antiquity.* Athens: 117–22.

Dakoronia, P. 1996. Kynos . . . Fleet. In: Tzalas, H. E. (ed.) *TROPIS IV: 4th International Symposium on Ship Construction in Antiquity.* Athens: 159–71.

Dakoronia, P. 1998. Kynos. *Arheologikon Deltion 44 (1989) Chronika*: 171–2.

Dakoronia, F. 2003. The Transition from Late Helladic III C to the Early Iron Age at Kynos. In: Deger-Jalkotzy, S. and Zavadil, M. (eds.) *LHIIIC Chronology and Synchronisms: Proceedings of the International Workshop Held at the Austrian Academy of Sciences at Vienna, May 7th and 8th, 2001.* Vienna: 37–51.

Dakoronia, F. 2006. Bronze Age Pictorial Tradition on Geometric Pottery. In: Rystedt, E. and Wells, B. (eds.) *Pictorial Pursuits: Figurative Painting on Mycenaean and Geometric Pottery. Papers from Two Seminars at the Swedish Institute at Athens in 1999 and 2001.* Stockholm: 171–5.

Dakoronia, P. and Mpougia, P. 1999. *Ton kairon tov Mykenaion sti Fthiotida.* Lamia.

Darcque, P. 2006. *L'habitat mycénien: Formes et functions de l'espace bâti en Grèce continentale à la fin du IIe millénaire avant J.-C.* Athens.

Dark, K. R. 1995. *Theoretical Archaeology.* New York.

Davis, E. N. 1995. Art and Politics in the Aegeans: The Missing Ruler. In: Laffineur, R. and Niemeier, W.-D. (eds.) *Politeia: Society and State in the Aegean Bronze Age* (Aegaeum 12, 1). Liège: 11–20.

Davis, J. L. 1992. Review of Aegean Prehistory I: The Islands of the Aegean. *AJA* 96: 699–756.

Davis, J. L. and Bennet, J. 1999. Making Mycenaeans: Warfare, Territorial Expansion, and Representations of the Other in the Pylian Kingdom. In: Laffineur, R. (ed.) *Polemos: Le contexte guerrier en Égée à l'âge du Bronze* (Aegaeum 19): Liège: 105–20.

Davis, J. L., Alcock, S. E., Bennet, J., Lolos, Y. G., and Shelmerdine, C. W. 1997. The Pylos Regional Archaeological Project. Pt. 1, Overview and the Archaeological Survey. *Hesperia* 66: 391–494.

Day, L. P. 1997. The Late Minoan IIIC Period at Vronda, Kavousi. In: Driessen, J. and Farnoux, A. (eds.) *La Crète mycénienne* (BCH Supplement 30). Paris: 391–406.

Day, L. P. and Snyder, L. M. 2004. The "Big House" at Vronda and the "Great House" at Karphi: Evidence for Social Structure in LMIIIC Crete. In: Day, L. P., Mook, M. S., and Muhly, J. D. (eds.) *Crete beyond the Palaces: Proceedings of the Crete 2000 Conference. Philadelphia 2004.* Philadelphia: 63–79.

Day, L. P., Coulson, W. D. E., and Gesell, G. 1986. Kavousi, 1983–1984: The Settlement at Vronda. *Hesperia* 55: 355–87.

De Angelis, F. 2003. *Megara Hyblaia and Selinous: The Development of Two Greek City-States in Archaic Sicily* (Oxford University School of Archaeology Monograph No. 57). Oxford.

Deetz, J. 1996. *In Small Things Forgotten: An Archaeology of Early American Life.* New York.

DeFrance, S. D. 1996. Iberian Foodways in the Moquegue and Torata Valleys of Southern Peru. *Historical Archaeology* 30, no. 3: 20–48.

Deger-Jalkotzy, S. 1977. *Fremde Zuwanderer im spätmykenischen Griechenland* (Österreichische Akademie der Wissenschaften 326). Vienna.

Deger-Jalkotzy, S. 1978. *E-qe-ta: Zur Rolle des Gefolgschaftswesens in der Sozialstruktur mykenischer Reiche.* Vienna.

Deger-Jalkotzy, S. 1991a. Zum Verlauf der Periode SH III C in Achaia. In: Rizakis, A. D. (ed.) *Achaia und Elis in der Antike. Akten des 1. Internationalen Symposiums Athen, 19–21 Mai 1989.* Athens: 19–29.

Deger-Jalkotzy, S. 1991b. Die Erforschung des Zusammenbruchs der sogenannten mykenischen Kultur und der sogenannten dunklen Jahrhunderte. In: Latacz, J. (ed.) *Zweihundert Jahre Homer-Forschung. Rückblick und Ausblick* (Colloquium Rauricum Band 2). Stuttgart: 127–54.

Deger-Jalkotzy, S. 1994. The Post Palatial Period of Greece: An Aegean Prelude to the 11th Century b.c. in Cyprus. In: Karageorghis, V. (ed.) *Proceedings of the International Symposium Cyprus in the 11th Century b.c.* Nicosia: 11–29.

Deger-Jalkotzy, S. 1995. Mykenische Herrschaftsformen ohne Paläste und die griechische Polis. In: Laffineur, R. and Niemeier, W.-D. (eds.) *Politeia: Society and State in the Aegean Bronze Age* (Aegaeum 12, 2). Liège: 367–77.

Deger-Jalkotzy, S. 1996. On the Negative Aspects of the Mycenaean Palatial System. In: De Miro, E., Godart, L., and Sacconi, A. (eds.) *Atti e memorie del secondo congresso internazionale di micenologia.* Vol. 2. *Storia.* Rome: 715–28.

Deger-Jalkotzy, S. 1998a. The Last Mycenaeans and Their Successors Updated. In: Gitin, S., Mazar, A., and Stern, E. (eds.) *Mediterranean Peoples in Transition: Thirteenth to Early Tenth Centuries BCE.* Jerusalem: 114–28.

Deger-Jalkotzy, S. 1998b. The Aegean Islands and the Breakdown of the Mycenaean Palaces around 1200 B.C. In: Karageorghis, V. and Stampolidis, N. (eds.) *Proceedings of the International Symposium Eastern Mediterranean: Cyprus-Dodecanese-Crete 16th–6th Cent. B.C.* Athens: 105–19.

Deger-Jalkotzy, S. 2003. Stratified Pottery Deposits from the Late Helladic IIIC Settlement at Aigeira/Achaia. In: Deger-Jalkotzy, S. and Zavadil, M. (eds.) *LHIIIC Chronology and Synchronisms: Proceedings of the International Workshop Held at the Austrian Academy of Sciences at Vienna, May 7th and 8th, 2001.* Vienna: 53–75.

Deger-Jalkotzy, S. 2006. Late Mycenaean Warrior Tombs. In: Deger-Jalkotzy, S. and Lemos, I. S. (eds.) *Ancient Greece: From the Mycenaean Palaces to the Age of Homer.* Edinburgh: 151–79.

Deger-Jalkotzy, S. and Zavadil, M. (eds.) 2003. *LHIIIC Chronology and Synchronisms: Proceedings of the International Workshop Held at the Austrian Academy of Sciences at Vienna, May 7th and 8th, 2001.* Vienna.

Demakopoulou, K. 1982. *To mykeniako iero sto Ammyklaio ke i IEIIIC sti Lakonia.* Athens.

Demakopoulou, K. (ed.) 1988. *The Mycenaean World: Five Centuries of Early Greek Culture 1600–1100 BC.* Athens.

Demakopoulou, K., Divari-Valakou, N., Åртsöm, P., and Walberg, G. 1997. Excavations in Midea 1994. *OpAth* 21: 13–32.

Desideri, P. and Jasink, A. M. 1990. *Cilicia: Dall'età di Kizzuwatna alla conquista macedone.* Turin.

Dever, W. G. 1986. *Gezer IV: The 1969–71 Seasons in Field VI, the "Acropolis."* Pt. 2, *Plates, Plans.* Jerusalem.

Dever, W. G. 1993. Gezer. In: Stern, E. (ed.) *The New Encyclopedia of Archaeological Excavations in the Holy Land.* Vol. 1. Jerusalem: 496–506.

Di Vita, A. 1990. Town Planning in the Greek Colonies of Sicily from the Time of Their Foundation to the Punic Wars. In: Descoeudres, J.-P. (ed.) *Greek Colonists and Native Populations: Proceedings of the First Australian Congress of Classical Archaeology.* Oxford: 343–63.

Diehl, M., Waters, J. A., and Thiel, H. 1998. Acculturation and the Composition of the Diet of Tucson's Overseas Chinese Gardeners at the Turn of the Century. *Historical Archaeology* 32, no. 4: 19–33.

Dietler, M. and Herbich, I. 1998. Habitus, Techniques, Style: An Integrated Approach to the Social Understanding of Material Culture and Boundaries. In: Stark, M. T. (ed.) *The Archaeology of Social Boundaries.* Washington, DC: 232–63.

Dikaios, P. 1969. *Enkomi: Excavations 1948–1958.* Vol. 1. *The Architectural Remains: The Tombs.* Mainz am Rhein.

Dikaios, P. 1971. *Enkomi: Excavations 1948–1958.* Vol. 3a. Mainz am Rhein.

Döhl, H. 1973. *Iria: Die Ergebnisse der Ausgrabungen 1939* (Tiryns, Forschungen und Berichte 6). Mainz am Rhein: 127–94.

Dommelen, P. van. 2005. Colonial Encounters and Hybrid Practices: Phoenicians and Carthaginian Settlement in the Ancient Mediterranean. In: Stein, G. J. (ed.) *The Archaeology of Colonial Encounters: Comparative Perspectives.* Santa Fe, NM: 109–41.

Donley-Reid, L. W. 1990. A Structured Structure: The Swahili House. In: Kent, S. (ed.) *Domestic Architecture and the Use of Space.* Cambridge: 114–26.

Dorsey, D. A. 1991. *The Roads and Highways of Ancient Israel.* Baltimore.

Dothan, M. 1971. *Ashdod II–III: The Second and Third Season of Excavations 1963, 1965, Sounding in 1967. Text and Plates* ('Atiqot 9–10). Jerusalem.

Dothan, M. 1972. Ashdod: Seven Seasons of Excavation. *Qadmoniot* 17: 2–13 (in Hebrew).

Dothan, M. 1986. Šardina at Akko? In: Balmuth, M. S. (ed.) *Studies in Sardinian Archaeology.* Vol. 2. *Sardinia and the Mediterranean.* Ann Arbor, MI: 105–15.

Dothan, M. 1988. The Significance of Some Artisans' Workshops along the Canaanite Coast. In: Heltzer, M. and Lipinski, E. (eds.) *Society and Economy in the Eastern Mediterranean (c. 1550–100 B.C.).* Louvain: 295–303.

Dothan, M. 1989. Archaeological Evidence for Movements of Early "Sea Peoples" in Canaan. *AASOR* 49: 59–70.

Dothan, M. 1993a. Ashdod. In: Stern, E. (ed.) *The New Encyclopedia of Archaeological Excavations in the Holy Land.* Vol. 1. Jerusalem: 93–102.

Dothan, M. 1993b. Acco. In: Stern, E. (ed.) *The New Encyclopedia of Archaeological Excavations in the Holy Land.* Vol. 1. Jerusalem: 16–24.

Dothan, M. and Ben-Shlomo, D. 2005. *Ashdod VI: Excavations of Areas H–K* (IAA Reports 24). Jerusalem.

Dothan, M. and Friedman, D. N. 1967. *Ashdod I: The First Season of Excavations* ('Atiqot 7). Jerusalem.

Dothan, M. and Porath, Y. 1993. *Ashdod V: Excavations of Area G: The Fourth–Sixth Seasons of Excavations 1968–1970* ('Atiqot 23). Jerusalem.

Dothan, T. 1963. Spinning Bowls. *IEJ* 13: 97–113.

Dothan, T. 1967. *The Philistines and Their Material Culture.* Jerusalem (in Hebrew).

Dothan, T. 1982. *The Philistines and Their Material Culture.* Jerusalem.

Dothan, T. 1989a. The Arrival of the Sea Peoples: Cultural Diversity in Early Iron Age Canaan. *AASOR* 49: 1–22.

Dothan, T. 1989b. Iron Knives from Tel Miqne-Ekron. *ErIsr* 20: 154–63 (in Hebrew).

Dothan, T. 1992. Social Dislocation and Cultural Change in the 12th Century B.C.E. In: Ward, W. A. and Joukowski, M. S. (eds.) *The Crisis Years: The 12th Century B.C. from beyond the Danube to the Tigris.* Dubuque, IA: 93–8.

Dothan, T. 1995. Tel Miqne-Ekron: The Aegean Affinities of the Sea Peoples' (Philistines') Settlement in Canaan in Iron Age I. In: Gitin, S. (ed.) *Recent Excavations in Israel: A View to the West: Reports on Kabri, Nami, Miqne-Ekron, Dor, and Ashkelon.* Dubuque, IA: 41–56.

Dothan, T. 1998a. Initial Philistine Settlement: From Migration to Coexistence. In: Gitin, S., Mazar, A., and Stern, E. (eds.) *Mediterranean Peoples in Transition: Thirteenth to Early Tenth Centuries BCE.* Jerusalem: 148–61.

Dothan, T. 1998b. The Pottery. In: Bierling, N. *Report on the 1995–1996 Excavations in Field XNW: Areas 77, 78, 79, 89, 101, 102. Iron Age I. Text and Data Base (Plates, Sections, Plans)* (The Tel Miqne-Ekron Limited Edition Series No. 7). Jerusalem: 20–48.

Dothan, T. 2000. Reflections on the Initial Phase of Philistine Settlement. In: Oren, E. D. (ed.) *The Sea Peoples and Their World: A Reassessment* (University Museum Monograph 108). Philadelphia: 145–58.

Dothan, T. 2003. The Aegean and the Orient: Cultic Interactions. In: Dever, W. G. and Gitin, S. (eds.) *Symbiosis, Symbolism and the Power of the Past: Canaan, Ancient Israel and Their Neighbors from Late Bronze Age through Roman Palaestina: Proceedings of the Centennial Symposium W. F. Albright Institute of Archaeological Research and American School of Oriental Research, Jerusalem, May 29–31, 2000.* Winona Lake, IN: 189–213.

Dothan, T. and Ben-Tor, A. 1983. *Excavations at Athienou, Cyprus 1971–1972* (Qedem 16). Jerusalem.

Dothan, T. and Dothan, M. 1992. *People of the Sea: The Search for the Philistines.* New York.

Dothan, T. and Gitin, S. 1993. Miqne, Tel (Ekron). In: Stern, E. (ed.) *The New Encyclopedia of Archaeological Excavations in the Holy Land.* Vol. 3. Jerusalem: 1051–9.

Dothan, T. and Zukerman, A. 2004. A Preliminary Study of the Mycenaean IIIC:1 Pottery Assemblages from Tel Miqne-Ekron and Ashdod. *BASOR* 333: 1–54.

Dothan, T., Gitin, S., and Bierling, N. 1998. Summary of Results. In: Bierling, N. *Report on the 1995–1996 Excavations in Field XNW: Areas 77, 78, 79, 89, 101, 102. Iron Age I. Text and Data Base (Plates, Sections, Plans)* (The Tel Miqne-Ekron Limited Edition Series No. 7). Jerusalem: 12–18.

Dothan, T., Gitin, S., and Zukerman, A. 2006. The Pottery: Canaanite and Philistine Traditions and Cypriote and Aegean Imports. In: Meehl, M. W., Dothan, T., and Gitin, S. (eds.) *Tel*

Miqne-Ekron Excavations 1995–1996: Field INE East Slope – Iron Age I (Early Philistine Period) (Tel Miqne Ekron Final Field Report Series No. 8). Jerusalem: 71–179.

Dotson, J. E. 1995. Economics and Logistics of Galley Warfare. In: Gardiner, R. and Morrison, J. (eds.) *The Age of the Galley: Mediterranean Oared Vessels since Pre-Classical Times.* London: 217–23.

Dougherty, C. 1993. It's Murder to Found a Colony. In: Dougherty, C. and Kurke, L. (eds.) *Cultural Poetics in Archaic Greece, Cult, Performance, Politics.* Cambridge, UK: 178–98.

Drews, R. 1993. *The End of the Bronze Age: Changes in Warfare and the Catastrophe ca. 1200 B.C.* Princeton, NJ.

Drews, R. 2000. Medinet Habu: Oxcarts, Ships, and Migration Theories. *JNES* 59: 161–90.

Driessen, J. and MacDonald, C. 1984. Some Military Aspects of the Aegean in the Late Fifteenth and Early Fourteenth Centuries B.C. *BSA* 79: 49–74.

Driessen, J. and Macdonald, C. F. 1997. *The Troubled Island: Minoan Crete before and after the Santorini Eruption* (Aegaeum 17). Liège.

du Piêd, L. 2006–7. The Early Iron Age in the Northern Levant: Continuity and Change in the Pottery Assemblages from Ras El-Baasit and Ras Ibn Hani. *Scripta Mediterranea* 27–8: 161–85.

Eder, B. 2006. The World of Telemachus: Western Greece 1200–700 BC. In: Deger-Jalkotzy, S. and Lemos, I. S. (eds.) *Ancient Greece: From the Mycenaean Palaces to the Age of Homer.* Edinburgh: 549–80.

Eicher, J. B. and Sumberg, B. 1995. World Fashion, Ethnic and National Dress. In: Eicher, J. B. (ed.) *Dress and Ethnicity: Changes across Space and Time.* Oxford: 295–306.

Ellenblum, R. 1998. *Frankish Settlement in the Latin Kingdom of Jerusalem.* Cambridge, UK.

Evans, A. 1964. *The Palace of Minos at Knossos.* Vol. 5, 2 pts. New York.

Evely, D. 2006. The Small Finds. In: Evely, D. (ed.) 2006. *Lefkandi IV: The Bronze Age: The Late Helladic IIIC Settlement at Xeropolis.* Athens: 265–302.

Fairbanks, C. H. 1976. Spaniards, Planters, Ships and Slaves. *Archaeology* 29: 164–72.

Felsch, R.C.S. 1981. Mykenischer Kult im Heiligtum bei Kalapodi? In: Hägg, R. and Marinatos, N. (eds.) *Sanctuaries and Cults in the Aegean Bronze Age: Proceedings of the First International Symposium at the Swedish Institute in Athens, 12–13 May 1980.* (SkrAth, 4°, 27. Svenska Institutet i Athen). Stockholm: 81–9.

Figueira, T. J. 1991. *Athens and Aigina in the Age of Imperial Colonization.* Baltimore.

Finkelstein, I. 1988. *The Archaeology of the Israelite Settlement.* Jerusalem.

Finkelstein, I. 1995. The Philistines in Canaan. *Tel Aviv* 22: 213–39.

Finkelstein, I. 1996a. The Philistine Countryside. *IEJ* 46: 225–42.

Finkelstein, I. 1996b. The Stratigraphy and Chronology of Megiddo and Beth-Shan in the 12th–11th Centuries B.C.E. *Tel Aviv* 23: 170–84.

Finkelstein, I. 1997. Pots and People Revisited: Ethnic Boundaries in the Iron Age. In: Silberman, N. A. and Small, D. (eds.) *The Archaeology of Israel: Constructing the Past, Interpreting the Present* (JSOT Supplement 237). Sheffield: 216–37.

Finkelstein, I. 1998. Philistine Chronology: High, Middle or Low? In: Gitin, S., Mazar, A., and Stern, E. (eds.) *Mediterranean Peoples in Transition: Thirteenth to Early Tenth Centuries BCE.* Jerusalem: 140–7.

Finkelstein, I. 2002. The Philistines in the Bible: A Late-Monarchic Perspective. *JSOT* 27: 131–67.

Fischer-Hansen, T. 1996. The Earliest Town-Planning of the Western Greek Colonies, with Special Regard to Sicily. In: Hansen, M. H. (ed.) *Introduction to an Inventory of Poleis: Symposium August, 23–26, 1995* (Acts of the Copenhagen Polis Centre Vol. 3). Copenhagen: 317–73.

Fisher, K. D. 2006–7. The "Aegeanization" of Cyprus at the End of the Bronze Age: An Architectural Perspective. *Scripta Mediterranea* 27–8: 81–103.

Forrest, W. G. G. 1982. Euboea and the Islands. In: Boardman, J. and Hammond, N. G. L. (eds.) *The Cambridge Ancient History,* 2nd ed., vol. 3, pt. 3. London: 249–60.

Frankel, D. 2000. Migration and Ethnicity in Prehistoric Cyprus: Technology as Habitus. *European Journal of Archaeology* 3, no. 2: 167–87.

Frankel, D., Webb, J. M., and Eslick, C. 1996. Anatolia and Cyprus in the Third Millennium B.C.E.: A Speculative Model of Interaction. In: Bunnens, G. (ed.) *Cultural Interaction in the Ancient Near East* (Abr-Nahrain Supplement Series 5). Louvain: 37–50.

French, E. 1975. A Reassessment of the Mycenaean Pottery at Tarsus. *AnatSt* 25: 53–75.

French, E. 1998. The Ups and Downs of Mycenae: 1250–1150 BCE. In: Gitin, S., Mazar, A., and Stern, E. (eds.) *Mediterranean Peoples in Transition: Thirteenth to Early Tenth Centuries BCE.* Jerusalem: 2–5.

French, E. 2002. *Mycenae, Agamemnon's Capital: The Site in Its Setting.* Charleston, SC.

French, E. 2006. The Terracotta Figurines. In: Evely, D. (ed.) *Lefkandi IV: The Bronze Age: The Late Helladic IIIC Settlement at Xeropolis.* Athens: 257–63.

French, E. 2007. The Impact on Correlations to the Levant of the Recent Stratigraphic Evidence from the Argolid. In: Bietak, M. and Czerny, E. (eds.) *The Synchronisation of Civilizations in the Eastern Mediterranean in the Second Millennium B.C. III. Proceedings of the SCIEM 2000 – 2nd EuroConference Vienna, 28th of May–1st of June 2003.* Vienna: 525–36.

French, E. and Rutter, J. 1977. The Handmade Burnished Ware of the Late Helladic IIIC Period: Its Modern Historical Context. *AJA* 81: 111–12.

Fritz, V. 1995. *The City in Ancient Israel.* Sheffield.

Furumark, A. 1941. *The Mycenaean Pottery: Analysis and Classification.* Stockholm.

Gabrielsen, V. 1994. *Financing the Athenian Fleet.* Baltimore.

Gale, N. H. 1991. Copper Oxhide Ingots: Their Origin and Their Place in the Bronze Age Metals Trade in the Mediterranean. In: Gale, N. H. (ed.) *Bronze Age Trade in the Mediterranean: Papers Presented at the Conference Held at Rewley House, Oxford, in December 1989* (SIMA 90). Jonsered: 197–239.

Gardiner, A. H. 1947. *Ancient Egyptian Onomastica.* Vol. 1. Oxford.

Gates, C. 1995. Defining Boundaries of a State: The Mycenaeans and Their Anatolian Frontier. In: Laffineur, R. and Niemeier, W.-D. (eds.) *Politeia: Society and State in the Aegean Bronze Age* (Aegaeum 12, 2). Liège: 289–97.

Gercke, P. and Hiesel, G. 1971. *Grabungen in der Unterstadt von Tiryns von 1889 bis 1929* (Tiryns, Forschungen und Berichte 5). Mainz am Rhein: 1–19.

Gesell, G. C., Coulson, W. D. E., and Day, L. P. 1991. Excavations in Kavousi, Crete, 1988. *Hesperia* 60: 145–77.

Gesell, G. C., Day, L. P., and Coulson, W. D. E. 1988. Excavations at Kavousi, Crete 1987. *Hesperia* 57: 279–301.

Gilboa, A. 1998. Iron I–IIA Pottery Evolution at Dor: Regional Contexts and the Cypriot Connection. In: Gitin, S., Mazar, A., and Stern, E. (eds.) *Mediterranean Peoples in Transition: Thirteenth to Early Tenth Centuries BCE.* Jerusalem: 413–25.

Gilboa, A. 2005. Sea Peoples and Phoenicians along the Southern Phoenician Coast – A Reconciliation: An Interpretation of Šikila (SKL) Material Culture. *BASOR* 337: 1–32.

Gilboa, A. 2006–7. Fragmenting the Sea Peoples, with an Emphasis on Cyprus, Syria and Egypt: A Tel Dor Perspective. *Scripta Mediterranea* 27–8: 209–44.

Gillis, C. 1995. Trade in the Late Bronze Age. In: Gillis, C., Risberg, C., and Sjöberg, B. (eds.) *Trade and Production in Premonetary Greece: Proceedings of the Third International Workshop, Athens 1993* (SIMA Pocketbook 134). Jonsered: 61–86.

Gilmour, G. 1995. Aegean Influence in Late Bronze Age Funerary Practices in the Southern Levant. In: Campbell, S. and Green, A. (eds.) *The Archaeology of Death in the Ancient Near East* (Oxbow Monograph 51). Exeter: 155–70.

Girella, L. 2005. Ialysos: Foreign Relations in the Late Bronze Age: A Funerary Perspective. In: Laffineur, R., and Greco, E. (eds.) *Emporia: Aegeans in the Central and Eastern Mediterranean: Proceedings of the 10th International Aegean Conference. Athens, Italian School of Archaeology, 14–18 April 2004.* Liège: 129–39.

Gitin, S. 1993. Seventh Century B.C.E. Cultic Elements in Ekron. In: Biran, A. and Aviram, J. (eds.) *Biblical Archaeology Today, 1990: Proceedings of the Second International Congress on Biblical Archaeology. Jerusalem, June–July 1990.* Jerusalem: 248–58.

Gitin, S. 1998. Philistia in Transition: The Tenth Century BCE and Beyond. In: Gitin, S., Mazar, A. and Stern, E. (eds.) *Mediterranean Peoples in Transition. Thirteenth to Early Tenth Centuries. BCE.* Jerusalem: 162–83.

Gitin, S., Dothan, T., and Naveh, J. 1997. A Royal Dedicatory Inscription from Ekron. *IEJ* 47: 1–16.

Gittlen, B. M. 1992. The Late Bronze Age "City" at Tel Miqne/Ekron. *ErIsr* 23: 50*–53*.

Glowacki, K. T. 2004. Household Analysis in Dark Age Crete. In: Day, L. P., Mook, M. S., and Muhly, J. D. (eds.) *Crete beyond the Palaces: Proceedings of the Crete 2000 Conference.* Philadelphia 2004: 125–36.

Goldman, H. 1956. *Excavations at Gözlü Kule, Tarsus.* Vol. 2. *Text and Plates: From the Neolithic through the Bronze Age.* Princeton, NJ.

Gonen, R. 1992. *Burial Patterns and Cultural Diversity in Late Bronze Age Canaan* (ASOR Dissertation Series Vol. 7). Winona Lake, IN.

Gophna, R. 1995. The Egyptian Pottery of ʿEn Besor. In: Gophna, R. (ed.) *Excavations at ʿEn Besor.* Tel Aviv: 71–93.

Gophna, R. and Friedmann, E. 1995. The Flint Implements from Tel ʿEn Besor. In: Gophna, R. (ed.) *Excavations at ʿEn Besor.* Tel Aviv: 105–22.

Gophna, R. and Gazit, D. 1995. The First Dynasty Egyptian Residency at ʿEn Besor. In: Gophna, R. (ed.) *Excavations at ʿEn Besor.* Tel Aviv: 61–70.

Goren, Y., Yasur-Landau, A., and Buzaglo, E. 2009. Petrographic Analyses of a Fragmentary Tablet and "Philistine Associated" Pottery Objects from Tel Aphek. In: Gadot, Y., and Yadin, E. (eds.) *Aphek II: The Remains on The Acropolis. The Moshe Kochavi and Pirhiya Beck Excavations.* Tel Aviv: 487–8.

Gosden, C. 2004. *Archaeology and Colonialism: Cultural Contact from 5000 BC to the Present.* Cambridge, UK.

Gosselain, O. P. 1998. Social and Technical Identity in Clay Crystal Ball. In: Stark, M. T. (ed.) *The Archaeology of Social Boundaries.* Washington, DC: 78–106.

Graham, A. J. 1982. The Colonial Expansion of Greece. In: Boardman, J. and Hammond, N. G. L. (eds.) *The Cambridge Ancient History,* 2nd ed., vol. 3, pt. 3. London: 83–162.

Graham, A. J. 1984. Religion, Women and Greek Colonization. *ATTI* 11: 293–314.

Greenberg, R. 1993. Beit Mirsim, Tell. In: Stern, E. (ed.) *The New Encyclopedia of Archaeological Excavations in the Holy Land.* Vol. 1. Jerusalem: 180.

Greengus, S. 1995. Private Life in Ancient Mesopotamia. In: Sasson, J. M. (ed.) *Civilizations of the Near East.* New York: 485–501.

Gruber, M. I. 1995. Private Life in Ancient Israel. In: Sasson, J. M. (ed.) *Civilizations of the Near East.* New York: 633–48.

Gunneweg, J., Asaro, F., Michel, H. V., and Perlman, I. 1994. Interregional Contacts between Tell En-Nasbeh and Littoral Philistine Centers in Canaan during Early Iron Age I. *Archaeometry* 36, no. 2: 227–39.

Gunneweg, J., Dothan, T., Perlman, I., and Gitin, S. 1986. On the Origin of Pottery from Tel Miqne-Ekron. *BASOR* 264: 3–16.

Güntner, W. 2000. *Figürlich bemalte mykenische Keramik aus Tiryns* (Tiryns, Forschungen und Berichte 12). Mainz am Rhein.

Güterbock, H. G. 1983. The Hittites and the Aegean World. Pt. 1, The Ahhiyawa Problem Reconsidered. *AJA* 87: 133–8.

Güterbock, H. G. 1992. Survival of the Hittite Dynasty. In: Ward, W. A. and Joukowski, M. S. (eds.) *The Crisis Years: The 12th Century B.C. from beyond the Danube to the Tigris.* Dubuque, IA: 53–5.

Guzowska, M. and Yasur-Landau, A. 2003. Before the Aeolians: Prolegomena to the Study of Interactions with the North-East Aegean Islands in the 13th and 12th Centuries BC. In: Kyparissi-Apostolika, N. and Papakonstantinou, M., (eds.) *The 2nd International Interdisciplinary Colloquium: The Periphery of the Mycenaean World. 26–30 September, Lamia 1999.* Athens: 471–86.

Guzowska, M. and Yasur-Landau, A. 2007a. Handmade Burnished Ware in the Levant. In: Galanaki, I., Tomas, H., Galanakis, Y., and Laffineur, R. (eds.) *Between the Aegean and Baltic Seas: Prehistory across Borders. Proceedings of the International Conference Bronze and Early Iron Age Interconnections and Contemporary Developments between the Aegean and Regions of the Balkan Peninsula, Central and Northern Europe. University of Zagreb, 11–14 April 2005* (Aegaeum 27). Liège: 471–80.

Guzowska, M. and Yasur-Landau, A. 2007b. The Mycenaean Pottery from Tel Aphek: Chronology and Patterns of Trade. In: Bietak, M. and Czerny, E. (eds.) *The Synchronization of Civilisations in the Eastern Mediterranean in the Second Millennium B.C. III. Proceedings of the SCIEM 2000 – 2nd EuroConference Vienna, 28th of May–1st of June 2003.* Vienna: 537–45.

Hadjianastasiou, O. 1989. Some Hints of Naxian External Connections in the Earlier Late Bronze Age. *BSA* 84: 205–15.

Hadjianastasiou, O. 1996. A Mycenaean Pictorial Vase from Naxos. In: De Miro, E., Godart, L., and Sacconi, A. *Atti e memorie del secondo congresso internazionale di micenologia.* Vol. 3. *Archeologia.* Rome: 1433–41.

Hadjicosti, M. 1988. Appendix IV: Pt. 1: "Canaanite" Jars from Maa-Palaeokastro. In: Karageorghis, V. and Demas, M. (eds.) *Excavations at Maa-Palaeokastro 1979–1986.* Nicosia: 340–81.

Hadjisavvas, S. 1994. Alassa Archaeological Project 1991–1993. *RDAC:* 107–28.

Hadjisavvas, S. and Hadjisavva, I. 1997. Aegean Influence at Alassa. In: Hadjisavvas, Y. (ed.) *Proceedings of the International Archaeological Conference Cyprus and the Aegean in Antiquity: From the Prehistoric Period to the 7th Century A.D. Nicosia, 8–10 December 1995.* Nicosia: 143–8.

Haggis, D. C. and Nowicki, K. 1993. Khalasmeno and Katalimata: Two Early Iron Age Settlements in Monastiraki, East Crete. *AJA* 62: 303–37.

Haines, C. R. 1971. *Excavations at the Plain of Antioch II: The Structural Remains of the Later Phases, Chatal Hüyük, Tell Al-Judaidah, and Tell Ta'yinat.* Chicago.

Haldane, C. 1993. Direct Evidence for Organic Cargos in the Late Bronze Age. *WorldArch* 24, no. 3: 348–60.

Hall, J. M. 1997. *Ethnic Identity in Greek Antiquity.* Cambridge, UK.

Hallager, B. P. 2000. The Late Minoan IIIC Pottery. In: Hallager, E. and Hallager, B. P. (eds.) *The Greek-Swedish Excavations at the Agia Aikaterini Square, Kastelli, Khania 1970–1987.* Vol. 2. *Text and Plates: The Late Minoan IIIC Settlement.* Stockholm: 135–74.

Hallager, E. 2000. The Architecture. In: Hallager, E. and Hallager, B. P. (eds.) *The Greek-Swedish Excavations at the Agia Aikaterini Square, Kastelli, Khania 1970–1987.* Vol. 2. *Text and Plates: The Late Minoan IIIC Settlement.* Stockholm: 127–34.

Halstead, P. 1992. The Mycenaean Palatial Economy: Making the Most of the Gaps in the Evidence. *PCPS* 38: 57–86.

Halstead, P. 1994. The North-South Divide: Regional Paths to Complexity in Prehistoric Greece. In: Mathers, C. and Stoddart, S. *Development and Decline in the Mediterranean Bronze Age* (Sheffield Archaeological Monographs 8). Sheffield: 195–219.

Hamilakis, Y. 2003. The Sacred Geography of Hunting: Wild Animals, Social Power and Gender in Early Farming Societies. In: Kotjabopoulou, E., Hamilakis, Y., Halstead, P., Gamble, C., and Elefanti, P. (eds.) *Zooarchaeology in Greece: Recent Advances* (British School at Athens Studies 9). London: 239–47.

Hamilton, R. W. 1935. Excavations at Tell Abu Hawam. *QDAP* 4: 1–69.

Hanawalt, B. A. 1986. Peasant Women's Contribution to the Home Economy in Late Medieval England. In: Hanawalt, B. A. (ed.) *Women and Work in Preindustrial Europe.* Bloomington, IN: 3–19.

Hankey, V. 1966. Late Mycenaean Pottery at Beth-Shan. *AJA* 70: 169–71.

Hankey, V. 1967. Mycenaean Pottery in the Middle East: Notes on Finds since 1951. *BSA* 62: 107–47.

Hankey, V. 1993. The Mycenaean Pottery. In: James, F. W. and McGovern, P. E. (eds.) *The Late Bronze Egyptian Garrison at Beth Shan: A Study of Levels VII and VIII* (University Museum Monograph 85). Philadelphia: 103–10.

Hankey, V. 1995. Stirrup Jars at el-Amarna. In: Davis, W. V. and Schofield, L. (eds.) *Egypt, the Aegean and the Levant: Interconnections in the Second Millennium* BC. London: 116–24.

Harrison, T. P. 2006–7. Lifting the Veil on a "Dark Age": Ta'yinat and the North Orontes Valley during the Early Iron Age. *Scripta Mediterranea* 27–8: 171–84.

Hawkins, J. D. 1998. Tarkasnawa King of Mira, "Tarkondemos," Bogazköy Sealings and Karabel. *AnatSt* 48: 1–31.

Hawkins, J. D. 2005. Die Inschrift des Warikas von Hiyawa aus Çineköy. In: Janowski, B. and Wilhelm, G. (eds.) *Texte aus der Umwelt des Alten Testaments. Neue Folge. Band 2. Staatsverträge, Herrscherinschriften und andere Dokumente zur politischen Geschichte.* Gütersloh, Germany: 155–6.

Hayden, B. J. 1988. Fortifications of Postpalatial and Early Iron Age Crete. *AA* 1988: 1–21.

Hendon, J. A. 1996. Archeological Approaches to the Organization of Domestic Labor: Household Practice and Household Relation. *Annual Review of Anthropology* 25: 45–61.

Herzog, Z. 1997. *Archaeology of the City: Urban Planning in Ancient Israel and Its Social Implications.* Tel Aviv.

Hesse, B. 1986. Animal Use at Tel Miqne-Ekron in the Bronze Age and Iron Age. *BASOR* 264: 17–27.

Hesse, B. 1990. Pig Lovers and Pig Haters: Patterns of Palestinian Pork Production. *Journal of Ethnobiology* 10, no. 2: 195–225.

Hesse, B. and Wapnish, P. 1997. Can Pig Remains Be Used for Ethnic Diagnosis in the Ancient Near East? In: Silberman, N. A. and Small, D. (eds.) *The Archaeology of Israel: Constructing the Past, Interpreting the Present* (JSOT Supplement 237). Sheffield: 238–70.

Hiesel, G. 1990. *Späthelladische Hausarchitektur.* Mainz am Rhein.

Hiller, S. 1988. Dependent Personnel in Mycenaean Texts. In: Heltzer, M. and Lipinski, E. (eds.) *Society and Economy in the Eastern Mediterranean (c. 1550–100 B.C.).* Louvain: 53–68.

Hirschfeld, N. 1992. Cypriot Marks on Mycenaean Pottery. In: Olivier, J.-P. (ed.) *Mykenaïka* (BCH Supplement 25). Paris: 315–19.

Hirschfeld, N. 1993. Incised Marks (Post-Firing) on Aegean Wares. In: Zerner, C., Zerner, P., and Winder, J. (eds.) *Proceedings of the International Conference "Wace and Blegen: Pottery As Evidence for Trade in the Aegean Bronze Age 1939–1989," Held at the American School of Classical Studies at Athens, December 2–3, 1989.* Amsterdam: 311–18.

Hirschfeld, N. 1996. *The PASP Data Base for the Use of Scripts on Cyprus* (Minos Supplement 13). Salamanca.

Hirschfeld, N. 2004. Eastwards via Cyprus? The Marked Mycenaean Pottery of Enkomi, Ugarit and Tell Abu Hawam. In: Belensi, J., Monchambert, J.-Y., and Müller Celka, S. (eds.) *La céramique mycénienne de l'Egée au Levant: hommage à Vronwy Hankey.* Lyon: 97–104.

Hodos, T. 1999. Intermarriage in the Western Greek Colonies. *OJA* 18, no. 1: 61–78.

Hoffman, G. L. 1997. *Imports and Immigrants: Near Eastern Contacts with Iron Age Crete.* Ann Arbor, MI.

Hoffner, H. A., Jr. 1992. The Last Days of Khatusha. In: Ward, W. A. and Joukowski, M. S. (eds.) *The Crisis Years: The 12th Century B.C. from beyond the Danube to the Tigris.* Dubuque, IA: 46–52.

Hoftijzer, J. and van Soldt, W. H. 1998. Appendix: Text from Ugarit Pertaining to Seafaring. In: Wachsmann, S. (ed.) *Seagoing Ships and Seamanship in the Bronze Age Levant.* London: 333–44.

Holladay, J. S., Jr. 1997. The Eastern Nile Delta during the Hyksos and Pre-Hyksos Periods: Towards a Systematic/Socioeconomic Understanding. In: Oren, E. D. (ed.) *The Hyksos: New Historical and Archaeological Perspectives* (University Museum Monograph 96). Philadelphia: 183–252.

Holloway, R. R. 1981. *Italy and the Aegean: 3000–700 B.C.* Louvain-la-Neuve.

Holloway, R. R. 1991. *The Archaeology of Ancient Sicily.* London.

Holloway, R. R. 1992. Italy and the Central Mediterranean in the Crisis Years. In: Ward, W. A. and Joukowski, M. S. (eds.) *The Crisis Years: The 12th Century B.C. from beyond the Danube to the Tigris.* Dubuque, IA: 40–5.

Hood, S. 1981. *Excavations in Chios 1938–1955: Prehistoric Emporio and Ayio Gala.* Vol. 1 (BSA Supplement 15). Oxford.

Hood, S. 1982. *Excavations in Chios 1938–1955: Prehistoric Emporio and Ayio Gala.* Vol. 2 (BSA Supplement 16). Oxford.

Hood, S. 1986. Mycenaeans in Chios. In: Boardman, J. and Richardson, C. (eds.) *A Conference at the Homereion in Chios 1984.* Oxford: 169–80.

Hope Simpson, R. and Dickinson, O. T. P. K. 1979. *A Gazetteer of Aegean Civilization in the Bronze Age.* Vol. 1. *The Mainland and Islands* (SIMA 52). Gothenburg.

Hunt, E. D. 1984. *Holy Land Pilgrimage in the Later Roman Empire AD 312–460.* Oxford.

Iakovidis, S. E. 1969. *Perati: To nekrotafion A.* Athens.

Iakovidis, S. E. 1970. *Perati: To nekrotafion. B. Yenikes Paratirisis.* Athens.

Iakovidis, S. E. 1979. *Perati: To nekrotafion. C. Pinakes.* Athens.

Iakovidis, S. E. 1980. *Excavations of the Necropolis at Perati* (Occasional Paper 8, Institute of Archaeology, University of California). Los Angeles.

Iakovidis, S. E. 1996. Mycenae in the Light of Recent Discoveries. In: De Miro, E., Godart, L., and Sacconi, A. (eds.) *Atti e memorie del secondo congresso internazionale di micenologia.* Vol. 3. *Archeologia.* Rome: 1039–49.

Iakovidis, S. 2003. Late Helladic III C at Perati. In: Deger-Jalkotzy, S. and Zavadil, M. (eds.) *LHIIIC Chronology and Synchronisms: Proceedings of the International Workshop Held at the Austrian Academy of Sciences at Vienna, May 7th and 8th, 2001.* Vienna: 125–30.

Immerwahr, S. A. 1990. *Aegean Painting in the Bronze Age.* University Park, PA.

Imparati, F. 1995. Private Life amongst the Hittites. In Sasson, J. M. (ed.) *Civilizations of the Near East.* Vol. 1. New York: 571–86.

Jacob-Felsch, M. 1987. Bericht zur spätmykenischen und submykenischen Keramik. In: Felsch, R. C. S. (ed.) *Kalapodi: Bericht über die Grabungen im Heiligtum der Artemis Elaphebolos und des Apollon von Hyampolis 1978–1982. AA* 1987: 29–35.

James, F. 1966. *The Iron Age at Beit Shan: A Study of Levels VI–IV.* Philadelphia.

James, F. W. and McGovern, P. E. 1993. *The Late Bronze Egyptian Garrison at Beth Shan: A Study of Levels VII and VIII* (University Museum Monograph 85). Philadelphia.

Jameson, M. H. 1960. A Decree of Themistokles from Troizen. *Hesperia* 29: 198–223.

Janeway, B. 2006–7. The Nature and Extent of Aegean Contact at Tell Ta'yinat and Vicinity in the Early Iron Age: Evidence of the Sea Peoples? *Scripta Mediterranea* 27–8: 123–46.

Jean, É. 2003. From Bronze to Iron Ages in Cilicia: The Pottery in Its Stratigraphic Context. In: Fischer, B., Genz, H., Jean, É., and Köroğlu, K. (eds.) *Identifying Changes: The Transition from Bronze to Iron Ages in Anatolia and Its Neighbouring Regions: Proceedings of the International Workshop Istanbul, November 8–9, 2002.* Istanbul: 79–91.

Jeffery, L. H. 1961. *The Local Scripts of Archaic Greece.* Oxford.

Jones, A. H. 1972. The Philistines and the Hearth: Their Journey to the Levant. *JNES* 31: 343–50.

Jones, R. E. and Vaughan, S. J. 1988. Appendix IV: Pt. 2: A Study of Some "Canaanite" Jar Fragments from Maa-Palaeokastro by Petrographic and Chemical Analysis. In: Karageorghis, V. and Demas, M. *Excavations at Maa-Palaeokastro 1979–1986.* Nicosia: 386–96.

Jones, R. E., Levi, S. T., and Bettelli, M. 2005. Mycenaean Pottery in the Central Mediterranean: Imports, Imitations and Derivatives. In: Laffineur, R. and Greco, E. (eds.) *Emporia: Aegeans in the Central and Eastern Mediterranean: Proceedings of the 10th International Aegean Conference. Athens, Italian School of Archaeology, 14–18 April 2004.* Liège: 539–45.

Jones, S. 1997. *The Archaeology of Ethnicity: Constructing Identities in the Past and Present.* London.

Jordan, S. C. 2000. Coarse Earthernware at the Dutch Colonial Cape of Good Hope, South Africa: A History of Local Production and Typology of Products. *Historical Archaeology* 4, no. 2: 113–43.

Jung, R. 2007. Tel Kazel and the Mycenaean Contacts with Amurru (Syria). In: Bietak, M. and Czerny, E. (eds.) *The Synchronisation of Civilizations in the Eastern Mediterranean in the Second Millennium B.C. III. Proceedings of the SCIEM 2000 – 2nd EuroConference Vienna, 28th of May–1st of June 2003.* Vienna: 551–70.

Kadioğlu, A. 1994. The Impact of Migration on Gender Roles: Findings of Field Research in Turkey. *International Migration* 32: 533–60.

Kaiser, I. 2005. Minoan Miletus: A View from the Kitchen. In: Laffineur, R. and Greco, E. (eds.) *Emporia: Aegeans in the Central and Eastern Mediterranean: Proceedings of the 10th International Aegean Conference. Athens, Italian School of Archaeology, 14–18 April 2004.* Liège: 193–7.

Kanta, A. 1980. *The Late Minoan III Period in Crete: A Survey of Sites, Pottery and Their Distribution* (SIMA 58). Gothenburg.

Kanta, A. and Karetsou, A. 2003. The Acropolis of Kastrokephala and Its Pottery. In: Deger-Jalkotzy, S. and Zavadil, M. (eds.) *LHIIIC Chronology and Synchronisms: Proceedings of the International Workshop Held at the Austrian Academy of Sciences at Vienna, May 7th and 8th, 2001.* Vienna: 145–65.

Karageorghis, V. 1974. *Excavations at Kition. I: The Tombs (Plates).* Nicosia.

Karageorghis, V. 1982. *Cyprus from the Stone Age to the Romans.* London.

Karageorghis, V. 1983. Appendix XI: An 11th-Century B.C. Bathtub from Paleopaphos-Skales, T. 49: 198. In: Karageorghis, V. *Paleopaphos-Skales: An Iron Age Cemetery on Cyprus.* Text. Nicosia: 435–8.

Karageorghis, V. 1985. *Excavation at Kition V: The Pre Phoenician Levels.* Pt. 2. Nicosia.

Karageorghis, V. 1986. Torch-Holders or Bellows? In: *Filia epi is Georgion E. Mylonan* Vol. 2. Athens: 22–6.

Karageorghis, V. 1990. *The End of the Late Bronze Age in Cyprus.* Nicosia.

Karageorghis, V. 1992. The Crisis Years: Cyprus. In: Ward, W. A. and Joukowski, M. S. (eds.) *The Crisis Years: The 12th Century B.C. from beyond the Danube to the Tigris.* Dubuque, IA: 79–86.

Karageorghis, V. 1994. The Prehistory of Ethnogenesis. In: Karageorghis, V. (ed.) *Proceedings of the International Symposium Cyprus in the 11th Century B.C.* Nicosia: 1–9.

Karageorghis, V. 1998a. Mycenaean "Acropoleis" in the Aegean and Cyprus: Some Comparisons. In: Cline, E. and Harris-Cline, D. (eds.) *The Aegean and the Orient in the Second Millennium* (Aegaeum 18). Liège: 127–34.

Karageorghis, V. 1998b. Hearths and Bathtubs in Cyprus: A "Sea Peoples" Innovation? In: Gitin, S., Mazar, A., and Stern, E. (eds.) *Mediterranean Peoples in Transition: Thirteenth to Early Tenth Centuries BCE.* Jerusalem: 276–82.

Karageorghis, V. 1999. Notes on Some "Enigmatic" Objects from the Prehistoric Aegean and Other East Mediterranean Regions. *AA*: 501–14.

Karageorghis, V. 2000a. Cultural Innovations in Cyprus Relating to the Sea Peoples. In: Oren, E. D. (ed.) *The Sea Peoples and Their World: A Reassessment* (University Museum Monograph 108). Philadelphia: 255–79.

Karageorghis, V. 2000b. Mycenaean and Other Sherds in the Louvre. In: Yon, M., Karageorghis, V., and Hirschfeld, N. *Céramique mycénienne d'Ougarit* (Ras Shamra-Ougarit 13). Paris: 37–65.

Karageorghis, V. and Demas, M. 1985a. *Excavations at Kition V: The Pre-Phoenician Levels.* Pt. 1. Nicosia.

Karageorghis, V. and Demas, M. 1985b. *Excavations at Kition V: The Pre-Phoenician Levels.* Plates. Nicosia.

Karageorghis, V. and Demas, M. 1985c. *Excavations at Kition V: The Pre-Phoenician Levels.* Plans and Sections Area I and II. Nicosia.

Karageorghis, V. and Demas, M. 1988. *Excavations at Maa-Paleokastro 1979–1986.* Nicosia.

Karantzali, E. 1998. Neoi mykinaikoi tafoi Rodou. In: Froussou, E. (ed.) *I Perifereia tou Mykinaikou Kosmou: A' Diethnes Diepistimoniko Symposio, Lamia, 25–29 Septemvriou 1994.* Lamia: 285–300.

Karantzali, E. 2003. I mymenaiki enkatastasi sta Dodekanisa: I priptosi tin Rodou. In: Kyparissi-Apostolika, N. and Papakonstantinou, M. (eds.) *The 2nd International Interdisciplinary Colloquium: The Periphery of the Mycenaean World. 26–30 September, Lamia 1999.* Athens: 513–34.

Karantzali, E. 2005. The Mycenaeans at Ialysos: Trading Station or Colony? In: Laffineur, R. and Greco, E. (eds.) *Emporia: Aegeans in the Central and Eastern Mediterranean: Proceedings of the 10th International Aegean Conference. Athens, Italian School of Archaeology, 14–18 April 2004.* Liège: 141–51.

Kazanskiene, V. P. 1995. Land Tenure and Social Position in Mycenaean Greece. In: Laffineur, R. and Niemeier, W.-D. (eds.) *Politeia: Society and State in the Aegean Bronze Age* (Aegaeum 12, 2). Liège: 603–11.

Keel, O. 1994. Philistine "Anchor Seals." *IEJ* 44: 21–35.

Keel, O. 1997. *Corpus der Stempelsiegel-Amulette aus Palästina/Israel.* Katalog Band I. *Von Tell Abu Farag bis 'Atlit* (Orbis Biblicus et Orientalis 83). Göttingen.

Keel, O. and Münger, S. 2005. The Stamp Seal Amulets. In: Dothan, M. and Ben-Shlomo, D. *Ashdod VI: Excavations of Areas H–K* (IAA Reports 24). Jerusalem: 273–9.

Keel, O. and Uehlinger, C. 1998. *Gods, Goddesses and Images of God in Ancient Israel.* Edinburgh.

Khalifeh, I. 1988. *Sarepta II: The Late Bronze and Iron Age Strata of Area II, X* (University Museum of the University of Pennsylvania Excavations at Sarafand, Lebanon). Beirut.

Kilian, K. 1978. Ausgrabungen in Tiryns 1976. *Archäologische Anzeiger*: 449–70.

Kilian, K. 1980. Zur Darstellung eines Wagenrennens aus spätmykenischer Zeit. *AM* 95: 21–31.

Kilian, K. 1981. Zeugnisse mykenischer Kultausübung in Tiryns. In: Hägg, R. and Marinatos, N. (eds.) *Sanctuaries and Cults in the Aegean Bronze Age: Proceedings of the First International Symposium at the Swedish Institute in Athens, 12–13 May 1980.* Stockholm: 49–58.

Kilian, K. 1986. Ein mykenische Beleuchtungsgerät. In: *Filia epi is Georgion E. Mylonan.* Vol. 2. Athens: 152–66.

Kilian, K. 1988a. The Emergence of Wanax Ideology in the Mycenaean Palaces. *OJA* 7: 291–302.

Kilian, K. 1988b. Mycenaeans Up to Date: Trends and Changes in Recent Research. In: French, E. B. and Wardle, K. A. (eds.) *Problems in Greek Prehistory.* Bristol: 115–52.

Kilian, K. 1990. Mycenaean Colonization: Norm and Variety in: Descoeudres, J. P. (ed.) *Greek Colonists and Native Populations: Proceedings of the First Australian Congress of Classical Archaeology, Sydney, 9–14 July 1985.* Oxford: 445–67.

Kilian, K. 1996. Earthquakes and Archaeological Context at 13th Century BC Tiryns. In: Stiros, S. and Jones, R. E. (eds.) *Archaeoseismology* (British School at Athens). Athens: 63–8.

Killebrew, A. 1992. *Functional Analysis of Thirteenth and Twelfth Century BCE Cooking Pots.* Lecture at the ASOR/SBL Annual Meeting. San Francisco.

Killebrew, A. 1996. Pottery Kilns from Deir el-Balah and Tel Miqne-Ekron. In: Seger, J. D. (ed.) *Retrieving the Past: Essays on Archaeological Research and Methodology in Honor of Gus W. Van Beek.* Winona Lake, IN: 131–59.

Killebrew, A. 1998a. Ceramic Typology and Technology of Late Bronze II and Iron I Assemblages from Tel Miqne-Ekron: The Transition from Canaanite to Philistine Culture. In: Gitin, S., Mazar, A., and Stern, E. (eds.) *Mediterranean Peoples in Transition: Thirteenth to Early Tenth Centuries BCE.* Jerusalem: 379–405.

Killebrew, A. 1998b. Mycenaean and Aegean-Style Pottery in Canaan during the 14th–12th Centuries BC. In: Cline, E. and Harris-Cline, D. (eds.) *The Aegean and the Orient in the Second Millennium* (Aegaeum 18). Liège: 158–66.

Killebrew, A. 1999. Late Bronze and Iron I Cooking Pots in Canaan: A Typological, Technological and Functional Study. In: Kapitan, T. (ed.) *Archaeology, History and Culture in Palestine and the Near East: Essays in Memory of Albert E. Glock.* Atlanta: 83–126.

Killebrew, A. 2000. Aegean-Style Early Philistine Pottery in Canaan during the Iron I Age: A Stylistic Analysis of Mycenaean IIIC:1b Pottery and Its Associated Wares. In: Oren, E. D. (ed.) *The Sea Peoples and Their World: A Reassessment* (University Museum Monograph 108). Philadelphia: 233–53.

Killebrew, A. E. 2006. *Biblical People and Ethnicity: An Archaeological Study of Egyptians, Canaanites, Philistines, and Early Israel, 1300–1100 B.C.E.* Leiden.

Killen, J. T. 2006. The Subjects of the Wanax: Aspects of Mycenaean Social Structure. In: Deger-Jalkotzy, S. and Lemos, I. S. (eds.) *Ancient Greece: From the Mycenaean Palaces to the Age of Homer.* Edinburgh: 87–99.

Kiriatzi, E., Andreou, S., Dimitrias, S., and Kostakis, K. 1997. Co-existing Traditions: Hand-made and Wheelmade Pottery in Late Bronze Age Central Macedonia. In: Laffineur, R. and Betancourt, P. P. (eds.) *TEXNH: Craftsmen, Craftswomen and Craftsmanship in the Aegean Bronze Age* (Aegaeum 16, 2). Liège: 361–7.

Kislev, M. E. 1989. Origins of the Cultivation of *Lathyrus sativus* and *L. cicera* (Fabaceae). *Economic Botany* 43, no. 2: 262–70.

Kislev, M. E. and Hopf, M. 1985. Food Remains from Tell Qasile. In: Mazar, A. *Excavations at Tell Qasile.* Pt. 2. *The Philistine Sanctuary: Various Finds, The Pottery, Conclusions, Appendixes* (Qedem 20). Jerusalem: 140–7.

Klengel, H. 1992. *Syria 3000–300 B.C.: A Handbook of Political History.* Berlin.

Kling, B. 1989. *Mycenaean IIIC: 1b and Related Pottery in Cyprus* (SIMA 87). Gothenburg.

Kling, B. 2000. Mycenaean IIIC: 1b and Related Pottery in Cyprus: Comments on the Current State of Research. In: Oren, E. D. (ed.) *The Sea Peoples and Their World: A Reassessment* (University Museum Monograph 108). Philadelphia: 281–95.

Knapp, A. B. 1997. *The Archaeology of Late Bronze Age Cypriot Society: A Study of Settlement, Survey and Landscape.* Glasgow.

Knapp, A. B. and Cherry, J. F. 1994. *Provenience Studies and Bronze Age Cyprus: Production, Exchange and Politico-Economic Change* (Monographs in World Archaeology No. 21). Madison, WI.

Kochavi, M. 1989. *Aphek-Antipatris: Five Thousand Years of History.* Tel Aviv (in Hebrew).

Kochavi, M. and Beck, P. 1990. *The Egyptian Governor's Residence and Its Finds* (Israel Museum Catalogue 312). Jerusalem.

Koehl, R. B. 1984. Observations on a Deposit of LC IIIC Pottery from the Koukounaries Acropolis on Paros. In: MacGillivray, J. A. and Barber, R. L. N. (eds.) *The Prehistoric Cyclades: Contributions to a Workshop on Cycladic Chronology (In Memoriam: John Langdon Caskey, 1908–1981).* Edinburgh: 207–24.

Koehl, R. B. 1985. *Sarepta III: The Imported Bronze and Iron Age Wares from Area II, X* (University Museum of the University of Pennsylvania Excavations at Sarafand, Lebanon). Beirut.

Koster, J. B. 1976. From Spindle to Loom: Weaving in the Southern Argolid. *Expedition* 19, no. 1: 29–39.

Krauss, R. 1994. Ein wahrscheinlicher Terminus post quem für das Ende Lachisch VI. *MDOG* 126: 123–30.

Lackenbacher, S. and Malbran-Labat, F. 2005. Ugarit et les Hittites dans les archives de la "Maison d'Urtenu." *SMEA* 47: 227–40.

Laffineur, R. 1995. Aspects of Rulership at Mycenae in the Shaft Grave Period. In: Rehak, P. (ed.) *The Role of the Ruler in the Prehistoric Aegean* (Aegaeum 11). Liège: 82–93.

Lagarce, J. and Lagarce F. 1987. *Ras Ibn Hani: Archéologie et histoire.* Damascus.

Lagarce, J. and Lagarce, E. 1988. The Intrusion of the Sea Peoples and Their Acculturation: A Parallel between Palestinian and Ras Ibn Hani Data. In: *Studies in the History and Archaeology of Palestine III: Proceedings of the First International Symposium on Palestine Antiquities.* Aleppo: 137–69.

Lambrinodakis, V. and Philaniotou-Hadjianastasiou, O. 2001. The Town of Naxos at the End of the Late Bronze Age: The Mycenaean Fortification Wall. In: Karageorghis, V. and Morris, C. E. (eds.) *Defensive Settlements of the Aegean and the Eastern Mediterranean after c. 1200 B.C.* Nicosia: 157–67.

Lambrou-Phillipson, C. 1991. Seafaring in the Bronze Age Mediterranean: The Parameters Involved in Maritime Travel. In: Laffineur, R. (ed.) *Thalassa: L'Égée préhistorique et la mer* (Aegaeum 7). Liège: 11–20.

Lang, M. L. 1969. *The Palace of Nestor in Western Messenia.* Vol. 2. *The Frescoes.* Princeton, NJ.

Lee, E. S. 1966. A Theory of Migration. *Demography* 3, no. 1: 47–57.

Lemaire, A. 2006. La maison de Mopsos en Cilicie et en Pamphylie à l'époque du Fer (XIIe–VIe s. Av. J.-C.). *Res Antiquae* 3: 99–107.

Lenz, J. R. 1993. "Kings and the Ideology of Kingship in Early Greece (c.1200–700 B.C.): Epic, Archaeology and History." Ph.D. dissertation, Columbia University, New York.

Leonard, A., Jr. 1981. Consideration of Morphological Variations in the Mycenaean Pottery from the Southeastern Mediterranean. *BASOR* 241: 87–101.

Leonard, A., Jr. 1994. *An Index to the Late Bronze Age Aegean Pottery from Syria Palestine.* Jonsered.

Leonard, A., Jr. 1998. Trade during the Late Helladic III Period. In: Cline, E. and Harris-Cline, D. (eds.) *The Aegean and the Orient in the Second Millennium* (Aegaeum 18). Liège: 99–104.

Leonard, K. I. 1992. *Making Ethnic Choices: California's Punjubi Mexican Americans.* Philadelphia.

Lev-Tov, J. 2006. The Faunal Remains: Animal Economy in Iron Age I. In: Meehl, M. W., Dothan, T., and Gitin, S. (eds.) *Tel Miqne-Ekron Excavations 1995–1996: Field INE East Slope Iron Age I (Early Philistine Period)* (Tel Miqne Ekron Final Field Report Series No. 8). Jerusalem: 207–33.

Lewartowski, K. 1989. *The Decline of the Mycenaean Civilization: An Archaeological Study on Events in the Greek Mainland.* Wroclaw.

Lightfoot, K. G. 2005. The Archaeology of Colonization: California in Cross-Cultural Perspective. In: Stein, G. J. (ed.) *The Archaeology of Colonial Encounters: Comparative Perspectives.* Santa Fe, NM: 207–35.

Littauer, M. A. and Crouwel, J. H. 1979. *Wheeled Vehicles and Ridden Animals in the Ancient Near East.* Leiden.

Littauer, M. A. and Crouwel, J. H. 1982. Chariots and Harness in Mycenaean Vase Painting. In: Vermeule, E. and Karageorghis, V. *Mycenaean Pictorial Vase Painting.* Cambridge, MA: 181–91.

Lo Schiavo, F. 1995. Cyprus and Sardinia in the Mediterranean Trade Routes towards the West. In: Karageorghis, V. and Michaelides, D. (eds.) *Proceedings of the International Symposium Cyprus and the Sea: Organized by the Archaeological Research Unit of the University of Cyprus and the Cyprus Port Authority. Nicosia 25–26 September 1993.* Nicosia: 45–60.

Lolos, Y. G. 1995. Late Cypro-Mycenaean Seafaring: New Evidence from Sites in the Saronic and the Argolid Gulfs. In: Karageorghis, V. and Michaelides, D. (eds.) *Proceedings of the International Symposium Cyprus and the Sea: Organized by the Archaeological Research Unit of the University of Cyprus and the Cyprus Port Authority. Nicosia 25–26 September 1993.* Nicosia: 65–87.

Lombardo, M. 1996. Food and "Frontier" in the Greek Colonies of South Italy. In: Wilkins, J., Horver, D., and Dobson, M. (eds.) *Food in Antiquity.* Exeter: 256–72.

Loretz, O. 1995. Les Šerdanu et la fin d'Ougarit: Á propos des documents d'Égypte, de Byblos et d'Ougarit relatifs aux Shardana. In: Yon, M., Szycer, M., and Bordreuil, P. (eds.) *La pais d'Ougarit: Autour de 1200 av. J.-C. Histoire et archéologie. Acts du colloque international. Paris, 28 juin–1er juillet 1993* (Ras Shamra-Ougarit 11). Paris: 125–40.

Loud, G. 1939. *The Megiddo Ivories.* Chicago.

Macalister, R. A. S. 1965. *The Philistines: Their History and Civilization* (Schwiech Lectures 1911, 2nd ed.). Chicago.

Macdonald, C. 1986. Problems of the Twelfth Century BC in the Dodecanese. *BSA* 81: 125–51.

Macdonald, E., Starkey, J., and Harding, L. 1932. *Beth-Pelet II.* London.

Machinist, P. 2000. Biblical Traditions: The Philistines and Israelite History. In: Oren, E. D. (ed.) *The Sea Peoples and Their World: A Reassessment* (University Museum Monograph 108). Philadelphia: 53–83.

MacIntosh, S. K. 1999. Pathways to Complexity: An African Perspective. In: MacIntosh, S. K. (ed.) *Beyond Chiefdoms: Pathways to Complexity in Africa.* Cambridge, UK: 1–30.

Maeir, A. M. 2008. Zafit, Tel. In: Stern, E. (ed.) *The New Encyclopedia of Archaeological Excavations in the Holy Land.* Vol. 5. Jerusalem: 2079–81.

Maher, E. F. 2005. Chapter 8: The Faunal Remains. In: Dothan, M. and Ben-Shlomo, D. (eds.) *Ashdod VI: Excavations of Areas H–K* (IAA Reports 24). Jerusalem: 283–90.

Mahler-Slasky, Y. 2004. "Philistine Material Culture As Reflected by the Archaeological Remnants from Ashkelon, Ekron, Gath and Aphek." Ph.D. dissertation, Bar-Ilan University. Ramat-Gan (Hebrew with English abstract).

Malkin, I. 1985. What's in a Name? The Eponymous Founders of Greek Colonies. *Athenaeum* 63: 114–30.

Malkin, I. 1987. *Religion and Colonization in Ancient Greece* (Studies in Greek and Roman Religion 3). Leiden.

Malkin, I. 1991. What Is an Aphidruma? *ClAnt* 10: 77–96.

Malkin, I. 1994. *Myth and Territory in the Spartan Mediterranean*. Cambridge, UK.

Malkin, I. 1996. Rhodes and Sicily: Dorian Colonization in Two Islands. In: Gizelis, G. (ed.) *Proceedings of the International Scientific Symposium Rhodes: 24 Centuries. October 1–5, 1992*. Athens: 188–98.

Malkin, I. and Fichman, A. 1987. Odyssey 3.153–85: A Maritime Commentary. *Mediterranean Historical Review* 2: 250–8.

Manning, S. W. 1994. The Emergence of Divergence: Development and Decline on Bronze Age Crete and the Cyclades. In: Mathers, C. and Stoddart, S. (eds.) *Development and Decline in the Mediterranean Bronze Age* (Sheffield Archaeological Monographs 8). Sheffield: 221–70.

Manning, S. W. 2006–7. Why Radiocarbon Dating 1200 BCE Is Difficult: A Sidelight on Dating the End of the Late Bronze Age and the Contrarian Contibution. *Scripta Mediterranea* 27–8: 53–80.

Manning, S. W., Weninger, B., South, A. K., Kling, B., Kuniholm, P. I., Muhly, J. D., Hadjisavvas, S., Sewell, D. A., and Cadogan, G. 2001. Absolute Age Range of the Late Cypriot IIC Period on Cyprus. *Antiquity* 75: 328–40.

Maran, J. 2000. Das Megaron im Megaron: Zur Datierung und Funktion des Antenbaus im mykenischen Palast von Tiryns. *AA* 2000, no. 1: 1–16.

Maran, J. 2001. Political and Religious Aspects of Architectural Change on the Upper Citadel of Tiryns: The Case of Building T. In: Laffineur, R. and Hägg, R. (eds.) *Potnia: Deities and Religion in the Aegean Bronze Age* (Aegaeum 22). Liège: 113–22.

Maran, J. 2004. Architektonische Innovation im spätmykenischen Tiryns – Lokale Bauprogramme und Fremde Kultureinflüsse. In: *Tagungsband Althellenische Technologie und Technik. 21–23.03.2003. in Ohlstadt/Odd. Deutschland*. Weilheim: 261–86.

Maran, J. 2006. Coming to Terms with the Past: Ideology and Power in Late Helladic IIIC. In: Deger-Jalkotzy, S. and Lemos, I. S. (eds.) *Ancient Greece: From the Mycenaean Palaces to the Age of Homer*. Edinburgh: 123–50.

Marks, P. M. 1996. *Hands to the Spindle: Texas Women and Home Textile Production, 1822–1880*. Collage Station, TX.

Masson, A. 1957. Cylindres et cachets chypriotes portant des caractères chypro-minoens. *BCH* 81: 6–37.

Master, D. M. 2005. Iron I Chronology at Ashkelon: Preliminary Results of the Leon Levy Expedition. In: Levy, T. E. and Higham, T. (eds.) *The Bible and Radiocarbon Dating*. London: 337–48.

Master, D. M. 2009. The Renewal of Trade at Iron Age I Ashkelon. *ErIsr* 29 (Ephraim Stern Volume). Jerusalem: 111*–22*.

Mastrapas, A. M. 1996. Idría me ithmoto kiathio apo to IK/IE III C nekrotafío Kaminíou Naxou. In: De Miro, E., Gobart, L., and Sacconi, A. (eds.) *Atti e memorie del secondo congresso internazionale di micenologia*. Vol. 2. *Storia*. Rome: 797–803.

Matskevitz, Z. 2005. The Flint Assemblage from Area H at Tel Ashdod. In: Dothan, M. and Ben-Shlomo, D. *Ashdod VI: Excavations of Areas H–K* (IAA Reports 24). Jerusalem: 265–71.

Mazar, A. 1980. *Excavations at Tell Qasile*. Pt. 1. *The Philistine Sanctuary* (Qedem 12). Jerusalem.

Mazar, A. 1985a. *Excavations at Tell Qasile*. Pt. 2. *The Philistine Sanctuary: Various Finds, The Pottery, Conclusions, Appendixes* (Qedem 20). Jerusalem.

Mazar, A. 1985b. The Emergence of the Philistine Material Culture. *IEJ* 35: 95–107.

Mazar, A. 1986. Excavations at Tell Qasile 1982–1984. *IEJ* 36: 1–15.

Mazar, A. 1988. Some Aspects of the "Sea Peoples" Settlement. In: Heltzer, M. and Lipinski, E. (eds.) *Society and Economy in the Eastern Mediterranean (c. 1500–1000 B.C.)*. Louvain: 251–60.

Mazar, A. 1990. *The Archaeology of the Land of the Bible (10,000–586 B.C.E.)*. New York.

Mazar, A. 1991. Comment on the Nature of the Relations between Cyprus and Palestine during the 12th–11th Centuries B.C. In: Karageorghis, V. (ed.) *Proceedings of an International Symposium: The Civilizations of the Aegean and Their Diffusion in Cyprus and the Eastern Mediterranean, 2000–600 B.C.* Larnaca: 94–104.

Mazar, A. 1993. Beth Shean in the Iron Age: Preliminary Report and Conclusions of the 1990–1991 Excavations. *IEJ* 43: 201–29.

Mazar, A. 1997. Iron Age Chronology: A Reply to I. Finkelstein. *Levant* 29: 157–67.

Mazar. A. 2000. The Temples and Cult of the Philistines. In: Oren, E. D. (ed.) *The Sea Peoples and Their World: A Reassessment* (University Museum Monograph 108). Philadelphia: 213–32.

Mazar, A. 2002. Megiddo in the Thirteenth–Eleventh Centuries BCE: A Review of Some Recent Studies. In: Oren, E. D. and Ahituv, S. (eds.) *Aharon Kempinski Memorial Volume: Studies in Archaeology and Related Disciplines* (Beer Sheva 15): 264–82.

Mazar, A. 2007. Myc IIIC in the Land of Israel: Its Distribution, Date and Significance. In: Beitak, M. and Czerny, E. (eds.) *The Synchronisation of Civilizations in the Eastern Mediterranean in the Second Millennium B.C. III. Proceedings of the SCIEM 2000 – 2nd EuroConference Vienna, 28th of May–1st of June 2003*. Vienna: 571–82.

Mazar, A. and Ben-Shlomo, D. 2005. Stratigraphy and Building Remains. In: Dothan, M. and Ben-Shlomo, D. *Ashdod VI: Excavations of Areas H–K* (IAA Reports 24). Jerusalem: 11–61.

Mazarakis Ainian, A. 1997. *From Rulers' Dwellings to Temples: Architecture, Religion and Society in Early Iron Age Greece (1100–700 B.C.)* (SIMA 121). Jonsered.

Mazow, L. B. 2005. "Competing Material Culture: Philistine Settlement at Tel Miqne-Ekron in the Early Iron Age." Ph.D. dissertation, University of Arizona, Tucson.

Mazzoni, S. 2000. Syria and the Periodization of the Iron Age: A Cross Cultural Perspective. In: Bunnenes, G. (ed.) *Essays on Syria in the Iron Age* (Ancient Near Eastern Studies Supplement 7). Louvain: 31–59.

McCallum, L. R. 1987. "Decorative Program in the Mycenaean Palace of Pylos: The Megaron Frescoes." Ph.D. dissertation, University of Pennsylvania.

Mee, C. 1978. Aegean Trade and Settlement in Anatolia in the Second Millennium B.C. *AnatSt* 28: 121–56.

Mee, C. 1988a. The LH IIIB Period in the Dodecanese. In: Dietz, S. and Papachristodoulou, I. (eds.) *Archaeology in the Dodecanese*. Copenhagen: 56–8.

Mee, C. 1988b. A Mycenaean Thalassocracy in the Eastern Aegean? In: French, E. B. and Wardle, K. A. (eds.) *Problems in Greek Prehistory*. Bristol: 301–6.

Mee, C. 1998. Anatolia and the Aegean in the Late Bronze Age. In: Cline, E. and Harris-Cline, D. (eds.) *The Aegean and the Orient in the Second Millennium* (Aegaeum 18). Liège: 137–45.

Meehl, M. W., Dothan, T., and Gitin, S. (eds.) 2006. *Tel Miqne-Ekron Excavations 1995–1996: Field INE East Slope Iron Age I (Early Philistine Period). Tel Miqne Ekron Final Field Report Series No. 8*. Jerusalem.

Meijer, F. 1986. *A History of Seafaring in the Classical World*. London.

Melas, M. 1991. Acculturation and Social Mobility in the Minoan World. In: Laffineur, R. (ed.) *Thalassa: L'Égée préhistorique et la mer* (Aegaeum 7). Liège: 169–88.

Melena, J. L. and Olivier, J.-P. 1991. *Tithemy: The Tablets and Nodules in Linear B from Tiryns, Thebes and Mycenae: A Revised Transliteration*. Salamanca.

Meriç, R. 2003. Excavations at Bademgediği Tepe (Purunda) 1999–2002: A Preliminary Report. *IstMitt* 53: 79–98.

Meriç, R. and Mountjoy, P. A. 2002. Mycenaean Pottery from Bademgediği Tepe (Purunda) in Ionia: A Preliminary Report. *IstMitt* 52: 79–98.

Militello, P. 2005. Mycenaean Palaces and Western Trade: A Problematic Relationship. In: Laffineur, R. and Greco, E. (eds.) *Emporia: Aegeans in the Central and Eastern Mediterranean:*

Proceedings of the 10th International Aegean Conference. Athens, Italian School of Archaeology, 14–18 April 2004. Liège: 585–97.

Mineck, K. R., Van Den Hout, T., and Hoffner, H. A. 2006. *Hittite Historical Texts II.* In: Chavalas, M. W. (ed.) *The Ancient Near East: Historical Sources in Translation.* Malden, MA: 253–79.

Monchambert, J.-Y. 1996. Du Mycénien III C à Ougarit. *Orient Express* 1996, no. 2: 45–6.

Moran, W. L. 1992. *The Amarna Letters.* Baltimore.

Morel, J. P. 1984. Greek Colonisation in Italy and the West (Problems of Evidence and Interpretations). In: Hackens, T., Holloday, N. D., and Holloday, R. R. (eds.) *Crossroads in the Mediterranean* (Archaeologia Transatlantica 2). Providence, RI: 123–61.

Morgan, L. 1990. Island Iconography: Thera, Kea, Milos. In: Hardy, D. A. (ed.) *Thera and the Aegean World III.* Vol. 1. *Archaeology: Proceedings of the Third International Congress. Santorini, Greece, 3–9 September 1989.* London: 252–66.

Morricone, L. 1972–3. Coo-scavi e scoperte nel "Serraglio" e in località minori (1935–1943). *Annuario* 50–1: 139–396.

Morris, C. H. 1990. In Pursuit of the White Tusked Boar. In: Hägg, R. and Nordquist, G. C. (eds.) *Celebrations of Death and Divinity in the Bronze Age Argolid.* Stockholm: 149–55.

Morris, I. 1991. The Early Polis As City and State. In: Rich, J. and Wallace-Hadrill, A. (eds.) *City and Country in the Ancient World.* London: 25–58.

Morris, S. P. 2001. Potnia Aswiya: Anatolian Contributions to Greek Religion. In: Laffineur, R. and Hägg, R. (eds.) *Potnia: Deities and Religion in the Aegean Bronze Age: Proceedings of the 8th International Aegean Conference/8e rencontre égéenne internationale. Göteborg, Göteborg University, 12–15 April 2000* (Aegaeum 22). Liège: 423–34.

Morrison, J. S. 1980. *The Ship: Long Ships and Round Ships: Warfare and Trade in the Mediterranean 3000 BC–500 AD.* London.

Morrison, J. S. 1996. *Greek and Roman Oared Warships.* Oxford.

Mountjoy, P. A. 1984. The Mycenaean IIIC Pottery from Phylakopi. In: MacGillivray, J. A. and Barber, R. L. N. (eds.) *The Prehistoric Cyclades: Contributions to a Workshop on Cycladic Chronology (In Memoriam: John Langdon Caskey, 1908–1981).* Edinburgh: 225–39.

Mountjoy, P. A. 1985. The Pottery. In: Renfrew, C. *The Archaeology of Cult: The Sanctuary at Phylakopi.* London: 151–208.

Mountjoy, P. A. 1986. *Mycenaean Decorated Pottery: A Guide to Identification* (SIMA 73). Gothenburg.

Mountjoy, P. A. 1993. *Mycenaean Pottery: An Introduction* (Oxford University Committee for Archaeology Monograph No. 36). Oxford.

Mountjoy, P. A. 1997. The Destruction of the Palace at Pylos Reconsidered. *BSA* 92: 109–37.

Mountjoy, P. A. 1998. The East Aegean–West Anatolian Interface in the Late Bronze Age: Mycenaeans and the Kingdom of Ahhiyawa. *AnatSt* 48: 33–67.

Mountjoy, P. A. 1999a. *Regional Mycenaean Decorated Pottery.* Rahden, Westphalia.

Mountjoy, P. A. 1999b. Troia VII Reconsidered. *Studia Troica* 9: 295–346.

Mountjoy, P. A. 2004. Miletos: A Note. *BSA* 99: 190–200.

Mountjoy, P. A. 2005a. Mycenaean Connections with the Near East in LH IIIC: Ships and Sea Peoples. In: Laffineur, R. and Greco, E. (eds.) *Emporia: Aegeans in the Central and Eastern Mediterranean: Proceedings of the 10th International Aegean Conference. Athens, Italian School of Archaeology, 14–18 April 2004.* Liège: 423–7.

Mountjoy, P. A. 2005b. The End of the Bronze Age at Enkomi, Cyprus: The Problem of Level III B. *BSA* 100: 125–214.

Mountjoy, P.A. 2005c. Mycenaean Pottery from the 1934–1939 Excavations at Tarsus. In: Özyar, A. (ed.) *Field Seasons 2001–2003 of the Tarsus-Gözlükule Interdisciplinary Research Project.* Istanbul: 83–134.

Muhly, J. D. 1984. The Role of the Sea Peoples in Cyprus during the LCIII Period: In: Karageorghis, V. and Muhly, J. D. (eds.) *Cyprus at the Close of the Late Bronze Age.* Nicosia: 39–56.

Murdock, G. P. and Provost, C. 1973. Measurement of Cultural Complexity. *Ethnology* 12: 379–92.

Murray, W. M. 1987. Do Modern Winds Equal Ancient Winds? *Mediterranean Historical Review* 2: 139–67.

Mutafian, C. 1988. *La Cilicie au carrefour des empires.* Paris.

Mylonas, G. E. 1959. *Agios Kosmas: An Early Bronze Age Settlement and Cemetery in Attica.* Princeton, NJ.

Mylonas Shear, I. 1987. *The Panagia Houses at Mycenae* (University Museum Monograph 68). Philadelphia.

Naveh, J. 1998. Achish-Ikausu in the Light of the Ekron Dedication. *BASOR* 310: 35–7.

Naville, E. 1930. *Détails relevées dans les ruines de quelques temples égyptiens.* Paris.

Negbi, O. 1976. *Canaanite Gods in Metal: An Archaeological Study of Ancient Syro-Palestinian Figurines.* Tel Aviv.

Negbi, O. 1991. Were There Sea Peoples in the Central Jordan Valley at the Transition from the Bronze to the Iron Age? *Tel Aviv* 18: 206–43.

Nelson, H. H. 1930. *Medinet Habu I: Earlier Historical Records of Ramses III.* Chicago.

Niemeier, B. and Niemeier, W.-D. 1997. Milet 1994–5: Projekt "Minoisch-mykenisches bis protogeometrisches Milet": Zielsetzung und Grabungen auf dem Stadionhügel und am Athenatempel. *AA* 1997: 189–248.

Niemeier, W.-D. 1997. The Mycenaean Potter's Quarter at Miletus. In: Laffineur, R. and Betancourt, P. P. (eds.) *TEXNH: Craftsmen, Craftswomen and Craftsmanship in the Aegean Bronze Age* (Aegaeum 16). Liège: 347–52.

Niemeier, W.-D. 1998. The Mycenaeans in Western Anatolia and the Problem of the Origin of the Sea Peoples. In: Gitin, S., Mazar, A., and Stern, E. (eds.) *Mediterranean Peoples in Transition: Thirteenth to Early Tenth Centuries BCE.* Jerusalem: 17–65.

Niemeier, W.-D. 2005. The Minoans and Mycenaeans in Western Asia Minor: Settlement, Emporia or Acculturation? In: Laffineur, R. and Greco, E. (eds.) *Emporia: Aegeans in the Central and Eastern Mediterranean: Proceedings of the 10th International Aegean Conference. Athens, Italian School of Archaeology, 14–18 April 2004.* Liège: 200–4.

Noort, E. 1994. *Die Seevölker in Palästina.* Kampen, Netherlands.

Nordquist, G. 1997. Male Craft and Female Industry: Two Types of Production in the Aegean Bronze Age. In: Laffineur, R. and Betancourt, P. P. (eds.) *TEXNH: Craftsmen, Craftswomen and Craftsmanship in the Aegean Bronze Age* (Aegaeum 16). Liège: 533–7.

Nosch, M.-L. B. 2003. Center and Periphery in the Linear B Archives. In: Kyparissi-Apostolika, N. and Papakonstantinou, M. (eds.) *The 2nd International Interdisciplinary Colloquium: The Periphery of the Mycenaean World. 26–30 September, Lamia 1999.* Athens: 63–70.

Nowicki, K. 1987. The History and Setting of the Town at Karphi. *SMEA* 26: 235–58.

Nowicki, K. 1999. Economy of Refugees: Life in the Cretan Mountains at the Turn of the Bronze and Iron Ages. In: Chaniotis, A. (ed.) *From Minoan Farmers to Roman Traders: Sidelights on the Economy of Ancient Crete.* Stuttgart: 145–71.

Nowicki, K. 2000. *Defensible Sites in Crete c. 1200–800 B.C. (LMIIIB/IIIC through Early Geometric)* (Aegaeum 21). Liège.

Nowicki, K. 2001. Sea-Raiders and Refugees: Problems of Defensible Sites in Crete c. 1200 B.C. In: Karageorghis, V. and Morris, C. E. (eds.) *Defensive Settlements of the Aegean and the Eastern Mediterranean after c. 1200 B.C.* Nicosia: 23–40.

Nur, A. and Cline, E. H. 2000. Poseidon's Horses: Plate Tectonics and Earthquake Storms in the Late Bronze Age Aegean and Eastern Mediterranean. *JAS* 27: 43–63.

O'Connor, D. 2000. The Sea Peoples and the Egyptian Sources. In: Oren, E. D. (ed.) *The Sea Peoples and Their World: A Reassessment* (University Museum Monograph 108). Philadelphia: 85–101.

Oren, E. D. 1992. Palaces and Patrician Houses in the Middle and Late Bronze Ages. In: Kempinski, A. and Reich, R. (eds.) *The Architecture of Ancient Israel: From the Prehistoric to the Persian Periods.* Jerusalem: 105–20.

Oren, E. D. and Mazar, A. 1993. Ma'aravim, Tel. In: Stern, E. (ed.) *The New Encyclopedia of Archaeological Excavations in the Holy Land.* Vol. 3. Jerusalem: 920–1.

Osborne, R. 1996. *Greece in the Making, 1200–479 B.C.* London.

Palaima, T. G. 1991. Maritime Matters in the Linear B Tablets. In: Laffineur, R. (ed.) *Thalassa: L'Égée préhistorique et la mer* (Aegaeum 7). Liège: 273–310.

Palaima, T. G. 1995a. The Last Days of the Pylos Polity. In: Laffineur, R. and Niemeier, W.-D. (eds.) *Politeia: Society and State in the Aegean Bronze Age* (Aegaeum 12, 2). Liège: 623–32.

Palaima, T. G. 1995b. The Nature of the Mycenaean Wanax: Non-Indo-European Origins and Priestly Functions. In: Rehak, P. (ed.) *The Role of the Ruler in the Prehistoric Aegean* (Aegaeum 11). Liège: 119–42.

Palaima, T. G. 2000. The Transactional Vocabulary of Mycenaean Sealings and the Mycenaean Administrative Process. In: Perna, M. (ed.) *Administrative Documents in the Aegean and Their Near Eastern Counterparts: Proceedings of the International Colloquium Naples, February 29–March 2, 1996.* Turin: 261–73.

Palaima, T. G. 2006. Wanax and Related Power Terms in Mycenaean and Later Greek. In: Deger-Jalkotzy, S. and Lemos, I. S. (eds.) *Ancient Greece: From the Mycenaean Palaces to the Age of Homer.* Edinburgh: 53–71.

Palmer, R. L. 1979. "Archaeological Analysis of LHIIIB Bronzes at Tell Abu Hawam." Master's thesis, California State University, Fullerton.

Papadopoulos, J. K. 1997. Innovations, Imitations and Ceramic Style: Modes of Production and Modes of Dissemination. In: Laffineur, R. and Betancourt, P. P. (eds.) *TEXNH: Craftsmen, Craftswomen and Craftsmanship in the Aegean Bronze Age* (Aegaeum 16, 2). Liège: 449–62.

Papadopoulos, T. J. 1991. Achaea's Role in the Mycenaean World. In: Rizakis, A. D. (ed.) *Achaia und Elis in der Antike: Akten des 1: Internationalen Symposiums Athen, 19–21 Mai 1989.* Athens: 31–7.

Peden, A. J. 1994. *Egyptian Historical Inscriptions of the Twentieth Dynasty* (Documenta Mundi Aegyptiaca 3). Jonsered.

Pendlebury, H. W., Pendlebury, J. D. S., and Money-Coutts, M. B. 1937–8. Excavations in the Plain of Lasithi. III. Karphi: A City of Refuge of the Early Iron Age in Crete. *BSA* 38: 57–148.

Peterson, W. 1958. A General Typology of Migration. *American Sociological Review* 23: 256–66.

Petrie, W. F. 1930. *Beth Pelet I.* London.

Petterson, M. 1992. *Cults of Apollo at Sparta.* Stockholm.

Phillips, J. 2005. The Last Pharaohs on Crete: Old Contexts and Old Readings Reconsidered. In: Laffineur, R. and Greco, E. (eds.) *Emporia: Aegeans in the Central and Eastern Mediterranean: Proceedings of the 10th International Aegean Conference. Athens, Italian School of Archaeology, 14–18 April 2004.* Liège: 455–61.

Phythian-Adams, W. J. 1921. Askalon Reports: Stratigraphical Sections. *PEQ*: 163–9.

Picazo, M. 1997. Hearth and Home: The Timing of Maintenance Activities. In: Moore, J. and Scott, E. (eds.) *Invisible People and Processes: Writing Gender and Childhood into European Archaeology.* London: 59–67.

Piggot, S. 1992. *Wagon, Chariot and Carriage: Symbol and Status in the History of Transport.* London.

Pilides, D. 1994. *Handmade Burnished Wares of the Late Bronze Age in Cyprus* (SIMA 105). Jonsered.

Pinch, G. 1995. Private Life in Ancient Egypt. In: Sasson, J. M. (ed.) *Civilizations of the Near East.* Vol. 1. New York: 363–81.

Platakis E. 1970. Isterominoika-Ipominoika ktismata is Kastrokefalan Almiru Irakliu. *CretChron* 22: 511–44.

Pomeroy, S. B. 1975. *Goddesses, Whores, Wives and Slaves.* New York.

Popham, M. R. and Milburn, E. 1971. The Late Helladic IIIC Pottery of Xeropolis (Lefkandi): A Summary. *BSA* 66: 333–53.

Popham, M. R. and Sackett, L. H. 1968. *Excavations at Lefkandi, Euboea, 1964/1966: A Preliminary Report.* London.

Popham, M. R. and Sackett, L. H. 1980. *Historical Conclusions.* In: Popham, M. R., Sackett, L. H., and Themelis, P. G. (eds.) *Lefkandi I: The Iron Age. The Settlement. The Cemeteries. Text.* London: 355–69.

Popham, M., Schofield, E., and Sherratt, S. 2006. *The Pottery.* In: Evely, D. (ed.) *Lefkandi IV: The Bronze Age. The Late Helladic IIIC Settlement at Xeropolis.* Athens: 137–231.

Porada, E. 1971. Appendix I: Seals. In: Dikaios, P. *Enkomi: Excavations 1948–1958.* Vol. 2. *Chronology, Summary and Conclusions, Catalogue, Appendices.* Mainz am Rhein: 783–817.

Porada, E. 1988. *Appendix I: Relief Friezes and Seals from Maa-Palaeokastro.* In: Karageorghis, V. and Demas, M. *Excavations at Maa-Paleokastro 1979–1986.* Nicosia: 301–13.

Porath, N. 1986–7. Local Industry of Egyptian Pottery in Southern Palestine during the Early Bronze I Period. *Bulletin of the Egyptological Seminar* 8: 109–29.

Porozhanov, K. 1996. Ships in Homer's Epic Work. In: Tzalas, H. (ed.) *TROPIS IV: 4th International Symposium on Ship Construction in Antiquity.* Athens: 367–74.

Press, M. D. 2007. "Philistine Figurines and Figurines in Philistia in the Iron Age." Ph.D. dissertation, Harvard University.

Pritchard, J. B. 1975. *Sarepta: A Preliminary Report on the Iron Age: Excavations of the University Museum of the University of Pennsylvania, 1970–72.* Philadelphia.

Privitera, S. 2005. Hephaestia on Lemnos and the Mycenaean Presence in the Islands of the Northeastern Aegean. In: Laffineur, R. and Greco, E. (eds.) *Emporia: Aegeans in the Central and Eastern Mediterranean: Proceedings of the 10th International Aegean Conference. Athens, Italian School of Archaeology, 14–18 April 2004.* Liège: 227–35.

Prokopiou, N. 1997. *LMIII Pottery from the Greek-Italian Excavations at Sybritos Amariou.* In: Hallager, E. and Hallager, B. P. (eds.) *Late Minoan III Pottery: Chronology and Terminology: Acts of a Meeting Held at the Danish Institute at Athens, August 12–14, 1994* (Monographs of the Danish Institute at Athens, Vol. 1). Athens: 371–94.

Pruss, A. 2002. Ein Licht in der Nacht? Die Amuq-Ebene während der Dark Ages. In: Braun-Holzinger, E. A. and Matthäus, H. (eds.) *Die nahöstlichen Kulturen und Griechenland an der Wende vom 2. zum 1. Jahrtausend v. Chr.: Kontinuität und Wandel von Strukturen und Mechanismen kultureller Interaktion. Kolloquium des Sonderforschungsbereiches 295 "Kulturelle und sprachliche Kontakte" der Johannes Gutenberg-Universität Mainz, 11–12. Dezember 1998.* Möhnesee: 161–76.

Pryor, J. H. 1995b. The Geographical Conditions of Galley Navigation in the Mediterranean. In: Gardiner, R. and Morrison, J. (eds.) *The Age of the Galley: Mediterranean Oared Vessels since Pre-Classical Times.* London: 206–16.

Pulak, C. 2005. Who Were the Mycenaeans Aboard the Uluburun Ship? In: Laffineur, R. and Greco, E. (eds.) *Emporia: Aegeans in the Central and Eastern Mediterranean: Proceedings of the 10th International Aegean Conference. Athens, Italian School of Archaeology, 14–18 April 2004.* Liège: 295–310.

Rahmstorf, L. 2003. Clay Spools from Tiryns and Other Contemporary Sites: An Indication of Foreign Influence in LHIIIC? In: Kyparissi-Apostolika, N. and Papakonstantinou, M. (eds.) *The 2nd International Interdisciplinary Colloquium: The Periphery of the Mycenaean World. 26–30 September, Lamia 1999.* Athens: 397–415.

Rahmstorf, L. 2005. Ethnicity and Changes in Weaving Technology in Cyprus and the Eastern Mediterranean in the 12th Century BC. In: *Cyprus: Religion and Society: From the Late Bronze Age to the End of the Archaic Period: Proceedings of an International Symposium on Cypriote Archaeology, Erlangen, 23–24 July 2004.* Münster: 143–69.

Rainey, A. F. 1975. The Identification of Philistine Gath. *ErIsr* 12: 63*–76*.

Rainey, A. F. 2003. Amarna and Later: Aspects of Social History. In: Dever, W. G. and Gitin, S. (eds.) *Symbiosis, Symbolism and the Power of the Past: Canaan, Ancient Israel and Their Neighbors from Late Bronze Age through Roman Palaestina: Proceedings of the Centennial Symposium W. F. Albright Institute of Archaeological Research and American School of Oriental Research, Jerusalem, May 29–31, 2000.* Winona Lake, IN: 169–87.

Rapoport, A. 1990. Systems of Activities and Systems of Settings. In: Kent, S. (ed.) *Domestic Architecture and the Use of Space.* Cambridge, UK: 9–20.

Redford, D. B. 2000. Egypt and Western Asia in the Late New Kingdom: An Overview. In: Oren, E. D. (ed.) *The Sea Peoples and Their World: A Reassessment* (University Museum Monograph 108). Philadelphia: 1–20.

Redmount, C. A. 1995. Ethnicity, Pottery and the Hyksos at Tell El-Maskhuta in the Egyptian Delta. *BA* 58, no. 4: 182–90.

Rehak, P. 1995. Enthroned Figures in Aegean Art and the Function of the Mycenaean Megaron. In: Rehak, P. (ed.) *The Role of the Ruler in the Prehistoric Aegean* (Aegaeum 11). Liège: 95–127.

Rehak, P. and Younger, J. G. 1998a. Neopalatial, Final Palatial, and Postpalatial Crete. *AJA* 102: 91–173.

Renfrew, C. 1978. Phylakopi and the Late Bronze Age I in the Cyclades. In: Doumas, C. and Puchelt, H. C. (eds.) *Thera and the Aegean World I*. London: 403–21.

Renfrew, C. 1985. *The Archaeology of Cult: The Sanctuary at Phylakopi*. Oxford.

Renfrew, C. and Bahn, P. 1996. *Archaeology: Theories, Methods and Practice*, 2nd ed. London.

Renne, E. P. 1995. Becoming a Bunu Bride: Bunu Ethnic Identity and Traditional Marriage Dress. In: Eicher, J. B. (ed.) *Dress and Ethnicity: Changes across Space and Time*. Oxford: 117–37.

Rethimiotakis, G. 1997. Late Minoan III Pottery from Kastelli Pediada. In: Hallager, E. and Hallager, B. P. (eds.) *Late Minoan III Pottery: Chronology and Terminology: Acts of a Meeting Held at the Danish Institute at Athens, August 12–14, 1994* (Monographs of the Danish Institute at Athens, Vol. 1). Athens: 305–26.

Rogers, E. M. 1983. *Diffusion of Innovations*. New York.

Rosen, S. A. 1993. A Note on the Flint Assemblage (from Ashdod Area G). In: Dothan, M. and Porath, Y. *Ashdod V: Excavations of Area G: The Fourth–Sixth Seasons of Excavations 1968–1970* (ʿAtiqot 23). Jerusalem: 117–21.

Rosen, S. A. 1997. *Lithics after the Stone Age*. Walnut Creek, CA.

Rothman, M. S. 1994. Evolutionary Typologies and Cultural Complexity. In: Stein, G. and Rothman, M. S. (eds.) *Chiefdoms and Early States in the Near East: The Organizational Dynamics of Complexity*. Madison, WI: 1–10.

Rowe, A. 1930. *The Topography and History of Beth-Shan*. Philadelphia.

Rowe, A. 1940. *The Four Canaanite Temples of Beth-Shan*. Philadelphia.

Ruijgh, C. J. 1992. Po-ku-ta et po-ku-te-ro, dérivés de *póku. In: Olivier, J.-P. (ed.) *Mykenaïka* (BCH Supplement 25). Paris: 543–62.

Rupp, D. W. 1998. The Seven Kings of the Land of Iaʾ, a District on the Ia-ad-na-na: Achaean Bluebloods, Cypriot Parvenus or Both? In: Hartwick, K. J. and Sturgeon, M. C. (eds.) *STHEFANOS: Studies in Honor of Brunilde Sismondo Ridgeway*. Philadelphia: 209–21.

Rutter, J. 1974. "The Late Helladic IIIB and IIIC Periods at Korakou and Gonia in the Corinthia." Ph.D. dissertation, University of Pennsylvania (University Microfilms, Ann Arbor 1975).

Rutter, J. 1975. Ceramic Evidence for Northern Intruders in Southern Greece at the Beginning of the Late Helladic IIIC Period. *AJA* 79: 17–32.

Rutter, J. 1990. Some Comments on Interpreting the Dark-Surfaced Handmade Burnished Pottery of the 13th and 12th Century B.C. Aegean. *JMA* 3: 29–49.

Rutter, J. 1992. Cultural Novelties in the Post-Palatial Aegean World: Indices of Vitality or Decline? In: Ward, W. A. and Joukowski, M. S. (eds.) *The Crisis Years: The 12th Century B.C. from beyond the Danube to the Tigris*. Dubuque, IA: 61–78.

Rutter, J. B. 2003. The Nature and Potential Significance of Minoan Features in the Earliest Late Helladic III C Ceramic Assemblages on the Central and Southern Greek Mainland. In: Deger-Jalkotzy, S. and Zavadil, M. (eds.) *LHIIIC Chronology and Synchronisms: Proceedings of the International Workshop Held at the Austrian Academy of Sciences at Vienna, May 7th and 8th, 2001*. Vienna: 193–216.

Sahlins, M. 1972. *Stone Age Economics*. Chicago.

Sakellarakis, J. A. 1992. *The Mycenaean Pictorial Pottery in the National Archaeological Museum of Athens*. Athens.

Sakellariou, A. 1964. *Die Minoischen und Mykenischen Siegel des Nationalmuseums in Athen* (Corpus der Minoischen und Mykenischen Siegel, Band I). Berlin.

Sakellariou, M. B. 1990. *Between Memory and Oblivion: The Transmission of Early Greek Historical Traditions*. Athens.

Sakka, D., Dikaiou, M., and Kiosseoğlou, G. 1999. Return Migration: Changing Roles of Men and Women. *International Migration* 37, no. 4: 741–64.

Salles, J.-F. 1980. *La Nécropole "K" de Byblos* (Recherche sur les grandes civilisations, Mémoir No. 2). Paris.

Samuel, D. 1999. Bread Making and Social Interactions at the Amarna Workmen's Village, Egypt. *WorldArch* 31, no. 1: 121–44.

Sandars, N. K. 1978. *The Sea Peoples*. London.

Sanders, G. D. R. 1984. Reassessing Ancient Populations. *BSA* 79: 251–62.

Santillo Frizell, B. 1986. *Asine II: The Late and Final Mycenaean Periods*. Stockholm.

Schäfer-Lichtenberger, C. 1998. PTGJH – Göttin und Herrin von Ekron. *BN* 91: 64–76.

Schäfer-Lichtenberger, C. 2000. The Goddess of Ekron and the Religious-Cultural Background of the Philistines. *IEJ* 50: 82–91.

Schallin, A.-L. 1993. *Islands under Influence: The Cyclades in the Late Bronze Age and the Nature of Mycenaean Presence* (SIMA 111). Jonsered.

Schallin, A.-L. 1995. Trade in the Late Bronze Age. In: Gillis, C., Risberg, C., and Sjöberg, B. (eds.) *Trade and Production in Premonetary Greece: Proceedings of the Third International Workshop, Athens 1993* (SIMA Pocketbook 134). Jonsered: 43–53.

Schiffer, M. B. and Skibo, J. M. 1987. Theory and Experiment in the Study of Technological Change. *CurrAnthr* 25, no. 5: 595–622.

Schilardi, D. U. 1984. The LH III C Period at the Koukounaries Acropolis, Paros. In: MacGillivray, J. A. and Barber, R. L. N. (eds.) *The Prehistoric Cyclades: Contributions to a Workshop on Cycladic Chronology (In Memoriam: John Langdon Caskey, 1908–1981)*. Edinburgh: 184–206.

Schilardi, D. U. 1992. Paros and the Cyclades after the Fall of the Mycenaean Palaces. In: Olivier, J.-P. (ed.) *Mykenaïka* (BCH Supplement 25). Paris: 621–39.

Schumacher, G. 1908. *Tell el-Mutesellim. I Band Fundbericht*. Leipzig.

Seger, J. D. 1988. *Gezer V: The Field I Caves*. Jerusalem.

Seirdaki, M. 1960. Pottery from Karphi. *BSA* 55: 1–37.

Shamir, O. 2007. Loomweights and Textile Production at Tel Miqne-Ekron: A Preliminary Report. In: Ben-Tor, A., Dessel, J. P., Dever, W. G., Mazar, A., and Aviram, J. (eds.) *"Up to the Gates of Ekron": Essays on the Archaeology and History of the Eastern Mediterranean in Honor of Seymour Gitin*. Jerusalem: 43–9.

Shaw, J. T. 1993. The Voyage and Speed Trials of Olympias in 1990. In: Shaw, T. (ed.) *The Trireme Project: Operational Experience 1987–90: Lessons Learnt* (Oxbow Monograph 31). Exeter: 39–44.

Shaw, J. W. 1990. Bronze Age Aegean Harboursides. In: Hardy, D.A. (ed.) *Thera and the Aegean World III*. Vol. 1. *Archaeology: Proceedings of the Third International Congress. Santorini, Greece, 3–9 September 1989*. London: 420–36.

Shaw, M. 1990. Late Minoan Hearths and Ovens at Kommos, Crete. In: Darcque, P. and Treuil, R. (eds.) *L'habitat égéen préhistorique* (BCH Supplement 19). Paris: 231–54.

Shelmerdine, C. W. 1997. Review of Aegean Prehistory VI: The Palatial Bronze Age of the Southern and Central Greek Mainland. *AJA* 101: 537–85.

Shelmerdine, C. W. 1998. Where Do We Go from Here? And How Can the Linear B Tablets Help Us Get There? In: Cline, E. and Harris-Cline, D. (eds.) *The Aegean and the Orient in the Second Millennium* (Aegaeum 18). Liège: 292–8.

Shelmerdine, C. W. 2006. Mycenaean Palatial Administration. In: Deger-Jalkotzy, S. and Lemos, I. S. (eds.) *Ancient Greece: From the Mycenaean Palaces to the Age of Homer*. Edinburgh: 73–86.

Sherratt, A. and Sherratt, S. 1991. From Luxuries to Commodities: The Nature of Mediterranean Bronze Age Trading System. In: Gale, N. H. (ed.) *Bronze Age Trade in the Mediterranean: Papers Presented at the Conference Held at Rewley House, Oxford, in December 1989* (SIMA 90). Jonsered: 351–86.

Sherratt, S. 1992. Immigration and Archaeology: Some Indirect Reflections. In: Åström, P. (ed.) *Acta Cypria: Acts of an International Congress on Cypriote Archaeology Held in Göteborg on 22–24 August 1991*. Pt. 2 (SIMA Pocketbook 117). Jonsered: 316–47.

Sherratt, S. 1998. "Sea Peoples" and the Economic Structure of the Late Second Millennium in the Eastern Mediterranean. In: Gitin, S., Mazar, A., and Stern, E. (eds.) *Mediterranean Peoples in Transition: Thirteenth to Early Tenth Centuries BCE.* Jerusalem: 292–313.

Sherratt, S. 2006. In: Maeir, A. M. and de Miroschedji, P. (eds.) *"I Will Speak the Riddles of Ancient Times": Archaeological and Historical Studies in Honor of Amihai Mazar on the Occasion of His Sixtieth Birthday.* Winona Lake, IN: 361–74.

Sherratt, S. and Crouwel, J. H. 1987. Mycenaean Pottery from Cilicia in Oxford. *OJA* 6: 235–52.

Shortland, A. 2004. Hopeful Monsters? Invention and Innovation in the Archaeological Record. In: Bourriau, J. and Phillips, J. (eds.) *Invention and Innovation: The Social Context of Technological Change 2: Egypt, the Aegean and the Near East, 1650–1150 BC.* Oxford: 1–11.

Singer, I. 1988. The Origin of the Sea People and Their Settlement on the Coast of Canaan. In: Heltzer, M. and Lipinski, E. (eds.) *Society and Economy in the Eastern Mediterranean (c. 1550–1000 B.C.).* Louvain: 239–50.

Singer, I. 1991. A Concise History of Amurru. In: Izre'el, S. *Amurru Akkadian: A Linguistic Study.* Vol. 2. Atlanta: 134–95.

Singer, I. 1992: Towards the Image of Dagon, the God of the Philistines. *Syria* 69: 431–50.

Singer, I. 1993. The Political Organization of Philistia in Iron Age I. In: Biran, A. and Aviram, J. (eds.) *Biblical Archaeology Today, 1990: Proceedings of the Second International Congress on Biblical Archaeology: Pre-Congress Symposium: Population, Production and Power. Jerusalem, June 1990.* Jerusalem: 132–41.

Singer, I. 1994. Egyptians, Canaanites, and Philistines in the Period of the Emergence of Israel. In: Finkelstein, I. and Na'aman, N. (eds.) *From Nomadism to Monarchy: Archaeological and Historical Aspects of Early Israel.* Jerusalem: 282–338.

Singer, I. 1999. A Political History of Ugarit. In: Watson, W. G. E. and Wyatt, N. (eds.) *Handbook of Ugaritic Studies.* Leiden: 603–733.

Singer, I. 2000. New Evidence on the End of the Hittite Empire. In: Oren, E. D. (ed.) *The Sea Peoples and Their World: A Reassessment* (University Museum Monograph 108). Philadelphia: 21–33.

Singer, I. 2006. Ships Bound for Lukka: A New Interpretation of the Companion Letters RS 94.2530 and RS 94.2523. *Altorientalische Forschungen* 33, no. 2: 242–62.

Singer, I. 2009. A Fragmentary Tablet from Tel Aphek with Unknown Script. In: Gadot, Y. and Yadin, E. (eds.) *Aphek II: The Remains on the Acropolis. The Moshe Kochavi and Pirhiya Beck Excavations.* Tel Aviv: 472–84.

Singer, I. forthcoming. "Old Country" Ethnonyms in "New Countries" of the "Sea Peoples" Diaspora. In: Koehl, R. B. (ed.) *Amilla: The Quest for Excellence: Studies in Honor of Günter Kopcke on the Occasion of His 75th Birthday.* Philadelphia.

Sjöberg, B. L. 2004. *Asine and the Argolid in the Late Helladic III Period: A Socio-Economic Study* (BAR International Series 1225). Oxford.

Sjöqvist, E. 1934. Enkomi: The Necropolis. In: Gjerstad, E., Lindros, J., Sjöqvist, W., and Westholm, A. *The Swedish Cyprus Expedition: Finds and Results of the Excavations in Cyprus 1927–1931.* Vol. 1: Text. Stockholm: 467–575.

Small, D. B. 1990. Handmade Burnished Ware and Prehistoric Aegean Economics: An Argument for Indigenous Appearance. *JMA* 3: 3–25.

Small, D. B. 1997. Can We Move Forward? Comments on the Current Debate over Handmade Burnished Ware. *JMA* 10: 223–8.

Small, D. B. 1998. Surviving the Collapse: The Oikos and Structural Continuity between Late Bronze Age and Later Greece. In: Gitin, S., Mazar, A., and Stern, E. (eds.) *Mediterranean Peoples in Transition: Thirteenth to Early Tenth Centuries BCE.* Jerusalem: 283–91.

Smith, J. S. 1994. "Seals for Sealing in the Late Cypriot Period." Ph.D. dissertation, Bryn Mawr College (UMI 9516578), Bryn Mawr, PA.

Smith, T. R. 1987. *Mycenaean Trade and Interaction in the West Central Mediterranean 1600–1000 B.C.* (BAR International Series 371). Oxford.

Spalinger, A. 2003. The Battle of Kadesh: The Chariot Frieze at Abydos. *Egypt and the Levant* 13: 163–99.

Sörensen, N. N. 1995. Roots, Routs and Transitional Attractions: Dominican Migration, Gender and Cultural Change. In: Wilson, F. and Frederiksen, B. F. (eds.) *Ethnicity, Gender and the Subversion of Nationalism.* London: 104–18.

South, A. K. and Russel, P. J. 1993. Mycenaean Pottery and Social Hierarchy at Kalavasos-Ayios Dhimitrios. In: Zerner, C., Zerner, P., and Winder, J. (eds.) *Proceedings of the International Conference "Wace and Blegen: Pottery As Evidence for Trade in the Aegean Bronze Age 1939–1989", Held at the American School of Classical Studies at Athens, December 2–3 1989.* Amsterdam: 303–10.

Stager, L. E. 1985. Merneptah, Israel and the Sea Peoples: New Light on and Old Relief. In: Mazar, B. and Yadin, Y. (eds.) *ErIsr* 18 (Avigad Volume): *56–*64.

Stager, L. E. 1991. *Ashkelon Discovered: From Canaanites and Philistines to Romans and Moslems.* Washington, D.C.

Stager, L. E. 1993. Ashkelon. In: Stern, E. (ed.) *The New Encyclopedia of Archaeological Excavations in the Holy Land.* Vol. 1. Jerusalem: 103–12.

Stager, L. E. 1995. The Impact of the Sea Peoples in Canaan (1185–1050 BCE). In: Levy, T. E. (ed.) *The Archaeology of Society in the Holy Land.* New York: 332–48.

Stager, L. E. 1998. Foraging and Identity: The Emergence of Ancient Israel. In: Coogan, M. D. (ed.) *The Oxford History of the Biblical World.* New York: 123–75.

Stager, L. E. 2006. Chariot Fittings from Philistine Ashkelon. In: *Confronting the Past: Archaeological and Historical Essays on Ancient Israel in Honor of William G. Dever.* Winona Lake, IN: 169–76.

Stager, L. E., Schloen, J. D., Master, D. M., and Press, M. D. 2008. Stratigraphic Overview. In: Stager, L. E., Schloen, J. D., and Master, D. M. (eds.) *Ashkelon 1: Introduction and Overview (1985–2006).* Winona Lake, IN: 213–323.

Starr, C. G. 1982. Economic and Social Conditions in the Greek World. In: Boardman, J. and Hammond, N. G. L. (eds.) *The Cambridge Ancient History*, 2nd ed., vol. 3, pt. 3. London: 417–44.

Steel, L. 1998. The Social Impact of Mycenaean Imported Pottery in Cyprus. *BSA* 93: 285–96.

Steel, L. 1999. Wine Kraters and Chariots: The Mycenaean Pictorial Style Reconsidered. In: Betancourt, P. P., Karageorghis, V., Laffineur, R., and Niemeier, W.-D. (eds.) *Meletemata: Studies in Aegean Archaeology Presented to Malcolm H. Wiener As He Enters His 65th Year* (Aegaeum 20). Liège: 803–11.

Steel, L. 2002. Consuming Passions: A Contextual Study of the Local Consumption of Mycenaean Pottery at *Tell el-ʿAjjul. JMA* 15, no. 1: 25–51.

Stein, G. J. 2005. The Comparative Archaeology of Colonial Encounters. In: Stein, G. J. (ed.) *The Archaeology of Colonial Encounters: Comparative Perspectives.* Santa Fe, NM: 2–31.

Steiner, G. 1989. "Schiffe von Aḫḫijawa" oder "Kriegsschiffe" von Amurru im Šauškamuwa-Vertrag? *Ugarit-Forschungen* 21: 393–411.

Stern, E. 1997. Discoveries at Tel Dor. In: Silberman, N. A. and Small, D. (eds.) *The Archaeology of Israel: Constructing the Past, Interpreting the Present* (JSOT Supplement 237). Sheffield: 128–43.

Stern, E. 1998. The Relations between the Sea Peoples and the Phoenicians in the 12th and 11th Centuries BCE. In: Gitin, S., Mazar, A., and Stern, E. (eds.) *Mediterranean Peoples in Transition: Thirteenth to Early Tenth Centuries BCE.* Jerusalem: 345–52.

Stern, E. 2000. The Settlement of Sea Peoples in Northern Israel. In: Oren, E. D. (ed.) *The Sea Peoples and Their World: A Reassessment* (University Museum Monograph 108). Philadelphia: 196–212.

Stoinas, H. 1999. Ikonisiki parastastiki se ostraka kratira apo tin ayia triada ilias. In: Froussou, E. (ed.) *I Perifereia tou Mykinaikou Kosmou: A' Diethnes Diepistimoniko Symposio, Lamia, 25–29 Septemvriou 1994.* Lamia: 257–62.

Stolcke, V. 1995. Invaded Women: Sex, Race and Class in the Formation of Colonial Society. In: Wilson, F. and Frederiksen, B. F. (eds.) *Ethnicity, Gender and the Subversion of Nationalism.* London: 7–21.

Stone, B. J. 1995. The Philistines and Acculturation: Culture Change and Ethnic Continuity in the Iron Age. *BASOR* 298: 7–32.

Strassler, R. B. (ed.) 1996. *The Landmark Thucydides: A Comparative Guide to the Peloponnesian War*. New York.

Sweeney, D. and Yasur-Landau, A. 1999. Following the Path of the Sea Persons: The Women in the Medinet Habu Reliefs. *Tel Aviv* 26: 116–45.

Tadmor, H. 1966. Philistia under Assyrian Rule. *BA* 29: 86–102.

Televantou, C. 2001. Ayios Andreas on Sifnos: A Late Cycladic III Fortified Acropolis. In: Karageorghis, V. and Morris, C. E. (eds.) *Defensive Settlements of the Aegean and the Eastern Mediterranean after c. 1200 B.C.* Nicosia: 191–213.

Thomas, C. G. 1995. The Components of Political Identity in Mycenaean Greece. In: Laffineur, R. and Niemeier, W.-D. (eds.) *Politeia: Society and State in the Aegean Bronze Age* (Aegaeum 12, 2). Liège: 349–54.

Thomas, C. G. and Conant, C. 1999. *Citadel to City-State: The Transformation of Greece, 1200–700 B.C.E.* Bloomington, IN.

Thomas, D. H. 1999. *Exploring Ancient Native America: An Archaeological Guide*. New York.

Tomasello, F. 1996. Fornaci a Festòs ed Haghia Triada dallíetà mediominoica alla geometrica. In: *Keramika Ergastiria stin Kriti apo tin archeotita os simera*. Rethymno: 27–37.

Thomatos, M. 2006. *The Final Revival of the Aegean Bronze Age: A Case Study of the Argolid, Corinthia, Attica, Euboea, the Cyclades and the Dodecanese during LHIIIC Middle* (BAR International Series 1498). Oxford.

Tournavitou, I. 1992. Practical Use and Social Function: A Neglected Aspect of Mycenaean Pottery. *BSA* 87: 181–210.

Tournavitou, I. 1995. *The "Ivory Houses" at Mycenae*. London.

Tournavitou, I. 1999. Oi toichografies san antikeimena kyrous stin YE III epochi: i periptosi tis Argolidas. In: *Eliten in der Bronzezeit. Ergebnisse zwier Kolloquien in Mainz und Athen*. Mainz: 199–28.

Triandis, H. 1997. Where Is Culture in the Acculturation Model? *Applied Psychology: An International Review* 46, no. 1: 55–8.

Trigger, B. G. 1968. *Beyond History: The Methods of Prehistory*. New York.

Tufnell, O., Inge, C. H., and Harding, L. 1940. *Lachish II (Tell ed Duweir): The Fosse Temple*. London.

Tzedakis, Y. and Martlew, H. 1999. *Minoans and Mycenaeans: Flavours of Their Time. National Archaeological Museum, 12 July–27 November 1999*. Athens.

Ussishkin, D. 1985. Levels VII and VI at Tel Lachish and the End of the Late Bonze Age in Canaan. In: Tubb, J. N. (ed.) *Palestine in the Bronze and Iron Ages: Papers in Honor of Olga Tufnell*. London: 213–30.

Ussishkin, D. 1998. The Destruction of Megiddo at the End of the Late Bronze Age and Its Historical Significance. In: Gitin, S., Mazar, A., and Stern, E. (eds.) *Mediterranean Peoples in Transition: Thirteenth to Early Tenth Centuries BCE*. Jerusalem: 197–219.

Vagnetti, L. 1999. Mycenaean Pottery in the Central Mediterranean. In: Crielaard, J. P., Stissi, V., and van Wijngaarden, G. (eds.) *The Complex Past of Pottery: Production, Circulation and Consumption of Mycenaean and Greek Pottery (Sixteenth to Early Fifth Centuries BC): Proceedings of the ARCHON International Conference, Held in Amsterdam, 8–9 November 1996*. Amsterdam: 137–61.

Vagnetti, L. and Jones, R. E. 1988. Towards the Identification of Local Mycenaean Pottery in Italy. In: French, E. B. and Wardle, K. A. (eds.) *Problems in Greek Prehistory*. Bristol: 335–48.

Vagnetti, L. and Jones, R. E. 1991. Traders and Craftsmen in the Central Mediterranean: Archaeological Evidence and Archaeometric Research. In: Gale, N. H. (ed.) *Bronze Age Trade in the Mediterranean: Papers Presented at the Conference Held at Rewley House, Oxford, in December 1989* (SIMA 90). Jonsered: 127–47.

Vandenabeele, F. 1988. Les Idéogrammes de vases du linéaire B et les peintures de la tombe de Ramsès III: une notice. In: Laffineur, R. (ed.) *Aegaeum* 2. Liège: 115–16.

Ventris, M. and Chadwick, J. 1973. *Documents in Mycenaean Greek*, 2nd ed. Cambridge, UK.

Venturi, F. 2000. Le premier age du Fer a Tell Afis et en Syrie septentrionale In: Bunnenes, G. (ed.) *Essays on Syria in the Iron Age* (Ancient Near Eastern Studies Supplement 7). Louvain: 505–36.

Vermeule, E. and Karageorghis, V. 1982. *Mycenaean Pictorial Vase Painting.* Cambridge, MA.

Vichos, Y. 1999. The Point Iria Wreck: The Nautical Dimension. In: Phelps, W., Lolos, Y., and Vichos, V. (eds.) *The Point Iria Wreck: Interconnections in the Mediterranean ca. 1200 B.C.: Proceedings of the International Conference, Island of Spetses, 19 September 1998.* Athens: 77–83.

Vichos, Y. and Lolos, Y. 1997. The Cypro-Mycenaean Wreck at Point Iria in the Argolic Gulf: First Thoughts on the Origin and the Nature of the Vessel. In: Swiny, S., Hohlfelder, R. L., and Wylde-Swiny, H. (eds.) *Res Maritimae: Cyprus and the Eastern Mediterranean from Prehistory to Late Antiquity.* Atlanta: 321–37.

Vlachopoulos, A. G. 1999. I Naxos kata tin YE IIIG periodo. I fysiognomia ke o charaktiras enos akmaiou nisiotikou kentrou. In: Froussou, E. (ed.) *I Perifereia tou Mykinaikou Kosmou. A' Diethnes Diepistimoniko Symposio, Lamia, 25–29 Septemvriou 1994.* Lamia: 303–14.

Vlachopoulos, A. 2003a. The Late Helladic III C "Grotta Phase" of Naxos. In: Deger-Jalkotzy, S. and Zavadil, M. (eds.) *LHIIIC Chronology and Synchronisms: Proceedings of the International Workshop Held at the Austrian Academy of Sciences at Vienna, May 7th and 8th, 2001.* Vienna: 217–34.

Vlachopoulos, A. G. 2003b. O Isteroeladios IIIC ikismos tis Grottas Naxou. Sto kentro I stin periferia tin mykenaikou Aigeou. In: Kyparissi-Apostolika, N. and Papakonstantinou, M. (eds.) *The 2nd International Interdisciplinary Colloquium: The Periphery of the Mycenaean World. 26–30 September, Lamia 1999.* Athens: 493–512.

Voskos, I. and Knapp, B. 2008. Cyprus at the End of the Late Bronze Age: Crisis and Colonization or Continuity and Hybridization? *AJA* 112: 659–84.

Voutsaki, S. 1995. Social and Political Processes in the Mycenaean Argolid: The Evidence from the Mortuary Practices. In: Laffineur, R. and Niemeier, W.-D. (eds.) *Politeia: Society and State in the Aegean Bronze Age* (Aegaeum 12, 1). Liège: 55–64.

Wachsmann, S. 1987. *Aegeans in the Theban Tombs.* Louvain.

Wachsmann, S. 1995. Paddled and Oared Ships before the Iron Age. In: Gardiner, R. and Morrison, J. (eds.) *The Age of the Galley: Mediterranean Oared Vessels since Pre-Classical Times.* London: 10–35.

Wachsmann, S. 1998. *Seagoing Ships and Seamanship in the Bronze Age Levant.* London.

Wachsmann, S. 2000. To the Sea of the Philistines. In: Oren, E. D. (ed.) *The Sea Peoples and Their World: A Reassessment* (University Museum Monograph 108). Philadelphia: 103–43.

Walberg, G. 1998. *Excavations on the Acropolis of Midea: Results of the Greek-Swedish Excavations.* Vol. 1, 2. *Plates: The Excavations on the Lower Terraces 1985–1991.* Stockholm.

Wallinga, H. T. 1995. The Ancestry of the Trireme 1200–525 BC. In: Gardiner, R. and Morrison, J. (eds.) *The Age of the Galley: Mediterranean Oared Vessels since Pre-Classical Times.* London: 36–48.

Walters, L. 1995. Ethnicity in Greek Dress. In: Eicher, J. B. (ed.) *Dress and Ethnicity: Changes across Space and Time.* Oxford: 53–77.

Wardle, K. A. and Wardle, D. 2003. Prehistoric Thermon: Pottery of the Late Bronze and Early Iron Age. In: Kyparissi-Apostolika, N. and Papakonstantinou, M. (eds.) *The 2nd International Interdisciplinary Colloquium: The Periphery of the Mycenaean World. 26–30 September, Lamia 1999.* Athens: 147–56.

Warren, P. and Hankey, V. 1989. *Aegean Bronze Age Chronology.* Bristol.

Washburn, D. K. 1994. The Property of Symmetry and the Concept of Ethnic Style. In: Shennan, S. J. (ed.) *Archaeological Approaches to Social Identity* (One World Archaeology 10). London: 157–73.

Wason, P. K. 1994. *The Archaeology of Rank.* Cambridge, UK.

Watrous, L. V. 1991. The Origin and Iconography of the Late Minoan Painted Larnax. *Hesperia* 60: 285–307.

Watrous, L. V. 1992. *Kommos III: The Late Bronze Age Pottery.* Princeton, NJ.

Webb, J. M. 1985. Appendix VI: The Incised Scapulae. In: Karageorghis, V. 1985. *Excavation at Kition V: The Pre Phoenician Levels*. Pt. 2. Nicosia: 317–28.

Webb, J. M. 1999. *Ritual Architecture, Iconography and Practice in the Late Cypriot Bronze Age*. Jonsered.

Webster, G. S. 1996. *A Prehistory of Sardinia 2300–500 BC* (Monographs in Mediterranean Archaeology 5). Sheffield.

Wedde, M. 1991. Aegean Bronze Age Ship Imagery: Regionalisms, a Minoan Bias and a "Thalassocracy." In: Laffineur, R. (ed.) *Thalassa: L'Égée prehistorique et la mer* (Aegaeum 7). Liège: 73–93.

Wedde, M. 1998. *Across the Bronze/Iron Divide: Thoughts on Continuity and Discontinuity: Ship Building As a Case Study*. An abstract of a lecture in the Trade and Production VIII: Crossing Borders. Swedish Institute, Athens, December 12–13, 1998.

Wedde, M. 1999. War at Sea: The Mycenaean and Early Iron Age Oared Galley. In: Laffineur, R. (ed.) *Polemos: Le contexte guerrier en Égée à l'âge du Bronze* (Aegaeum 19). Liège: 465–76.

Weickert, C. 1959–1960. Die Ausgrabung beim Athena-Tempel in Milet 1957. III: Der Westabschnitt. *IstMitt* 9–10: 63–6.

Weinstein, J. N. 1992. The Collapse of the Egyptian Empire in Canaan. In: Ward, W. A. and Joukowski, M. S. (eds.) *The Crisis Years: The 12th Century B.C. from beyond the Danube to the Tigris*. Dubuque, IA: 142–50.

Werner, K. 1993. *The Megaron during the Aegean and Anatolian Bronze Age* (SIMA 108). Jonsered.

Whitley, J. 1991a. *Style and Society in Dark Age Greece: The Changing Face of a Pre-Literate Society 1100–700 BC*. Cambridge, UK.

Whitley, J. 1991b. Social Diversity in Dark Age Greece. *BSA* 86: 341–65.

Whittaker, C. R. 1974. The Western Phoenicians: Colonization and Assimilation. *PCPS* 200: 58–79

Whittaker, H. 1997. *Mycenaean Cult Buildings: A Study in Their Architecture and Function in the Context of the Aegean and the Eastern Mediterranean* (Monographs from the Norwegian Institute at Athens, Vol. 1) Bergen.

Wiener, M. H. 1984. Crete and the Cyclades in LMI: The Tale of the Conical Cups. In: Hägg, R. and Marinatos, N. (eds.) *The Minoan Thalassocracy: Myth and Reality: Proceedings of the Third International Symposium at the Swedish Institute in Athens, 31 May–5 June, 1982*. Stockholm: 17–26.

Willey, G. and Latherap, D. 1956. An Archaeological Classification of Culture Contact Situations. In: Wauchope, R. (ed.) *Seminars in Archaeology: 1955* (Society for American Archaeology). Salt Lake City: 3–30.

Wilson, K. 1979. *A History of Textiles*. Boulder, CO.

Wiman, I. and Bruun-Lundgren, M. 2003. Industrial Activities and Personal Adornments. In: Hallager, E. and Hallager, B. P. (eds.) *The Greek-Swedish Excavations at the Agia Aikaterini Square Kastelli, Khania, 1970–1987 and 2001. Vol. 3:1. Text: The Late Minoan IIIB:2 Settlement*. Stockholm: 266–9.

Wimmer, S. and Maeir, A. 2007. The Prince of Safit: A Late Bronze Age Hieratic Inscription from Tell es-Ṣafi/Gath. *ZDPV* 123, no. 1: 37–48.

Wing, E. S. 1990. Evidence for the Impact of Traditional Spanish Animal Uses in Parts of the New World. In: Clutton-Brock, J. (ed.) *The Walking Larder: Patterns of Domestication, Pastoralism, and Predation*. London: 72–9.

Wood, B. G. 1990. *The Sociology of Pottery in Ancient Palestine* (JSOT/ASOR Monograph Series 4). Sheffield.

Wright, G. E. 1959. Philistine Coffins and Mercenaries. *BA* 22: 54–66.

Wright, J. C. 1995. From Chief to King in Mycenaean Society. In: Rehak, P. (ed.) *The Role of the Ruler in the Prehistoric Aegean* (Aegaeum 11). Liège: 63–80.

Wright, J. C. 1996. Empty Cups and Empty Jugs: The Social Role of Wine in Minoan and Mycenaean Societies. In: McGovern, P. E., Fleming, S. J., and Katz, S. H. (eds.) *The Origins and Ancient History of Wine*. Philadelphia: 287–309.

Yadin, Y. 1960. *Hazor II: An Account of the Second Season of Excavations, 1956*. Jerusalem.

Yadin, Y. 1963. *The Art of Warfare in Biblical Lands: In Light of Archaeological Study.* Jerusalem.

Yağci, R. 2003. The Stratigraphy of Cyprus WS II and Mycenaean Cups in Soli Höyük Excavations. In: Fischer, B., Genz, H., Jean, É., and Köroğlu, K. (eds.) *Identifying Changes: The Transition from Bronze to Iron Ages in Anatolia and Its Neighbouring Regions. Proceedings of the International Workshop Istanbul, November 8–9, 2002.* Istanbul: 93–106.

Yakar, J. 1993. Anatolian Civilization Following the Disintegration of the Hittite Empire: An Archaeological Appraisal. *Tel Aviv* 20, no. 1: 3–28.

Yasur-Landau, A. 1992. The Philistine Kitchen: Foodways as Ethnic Demarcators. *The Eighteenth Archaeological Conference in Israel, Abstracts.* Tel Aviv: 10 (in Hebrew).

Yasur-Landau, A. 2001. The Mother(s) of All Philistines: Aegean Enthroned Deities of the 12th–11th Century Philistia. In: Laffineur, R. and Hägg, R. (eds.) *Potnia: Deities and Religion in the Aegean Bronze Age* (Aegaeum 22). Liège: 329–43.

Yasur-Landau. A. 2003a. The Absolute Chronology of the LHIIIC Period: A View from the Levant. In: Deger-Jalkotzy, S. and Zavadil, M. (eds.) *LHIIIC Chronology and Synchronisms: Proceedings of the International Workshop Held at the Austrian Academy of Sciences at Vienna, May 7th and 8th, 2001.* Vienna: 235–44.

Yasur-Landau, A. 2003b. The Many Faces of Colonization: 12th Century Aegean Settlements in Cyprus and the Levant. *Mediterranean Archaeology and Archaeometry* 3, no. 1: 45–54.

Yasur-Landau, A. 2003c. Why Can't We Find the Origin of the Philistines? In Search of the Source of a Peripheral Aegean Culture. In: Kyparissi-Apostolika, N. and Papakonstantinou, M. (eds.) *The 2nd International Interdisciplinary Colloquium: The Periphery of the Mycenaean World. 26–30 September, Lamia 1999.* Athens: 578–98.

Yasur-Landau, A. 2003d. How did the Philistines Get to Canaan? Two: By Land. *BAR* 29, no. 2: 34–9, 66–7.

Yasur-Landau, A. 2003–4. The Last Glendi in Halasmenos: Social Aspects of Cooking in a Dark Age Cretan Village. *Aegean Archaeology* 7: 49–66.

Yasur-Landau, A. 2005a. The Chronological Use of Imported Mycenaean Pottery in the Levant: Towards a Methodological Common Ground. *Egypt and the Levant* 14: 339–46.

Yasur-Landau, A. 2005b. Old Wine in New Vessels: Intercultural Contact, Innovation and Aegean, Canaanite and Philistine Foodways. In: Cohen, Y. and Yasur-Landau, A. (eds.) *Between East and West: Eretz Israel and the Ancient Near East – Intercultural Ties and Innovations in the Second Millennium BCE. The Sonia and Marco Nadler Institute of Archaeology Annual Symposium,* April 29, 2004. *Tel Aviv* 32, no. 2: 168–91.

Yasur-Landau, A. 2006. A LHIIIC Stirrup Jar from Area K. In: Finkelstein, I., Ussishkin, D., and Halpern, B. *Megiddo IV: The 1998–2002 Seasons.* Tel Aviv: 299–302.

Yasur-Landau, A. 2007a. A Note on the Late Bronze Age Textile Industry. In: Mazar, A. and Mullins, R. (eds.) *Excavations at Beth Shean 1989–1996.* Vol. 2. *The Middle and Late Bronze Age Strata in Area R.* Jerusalem: 669–71.

Yasur-Landau, A. 2007b. Let's Do the Time Warp Again: Migration Processes and the Absolute Chronology of the Philistine Settlement. In: Bietak, M. and Czerny, E. (eds.) *The Synchronization of Civilisations in the Eastern Mediterranean in the Second Millennium B.C. III: Proceedings of the SCIEM 2000 – 2nd EuroConference Vienna, 28th of May – 1st of June 2003.* Vienna: 609–20.

Yasur-Landau, A. and Goren, Y. 2004. A Cypro-Minoan Potmark from Aphek. *Tel Aviv* 31: 22–31.

Yellin, J. and Gunneweg, J. 1985. Provenience of Pottery from Tell Qasile Strata VII, X, XI and XII. In: Mazar, A. *Excavations at Tell Qasile.* Pt. 2. *The Philistine Sanctuary: Various Finds, The Pottery, Conclusions, Appendixes* (Qedem 20). Jerusalem: 111–17.

Yener, K. H., Edens, C., Harrison, T. P., Verstraete, J., and Wilkinson, T. J. 2000. The Amuq Valley Regional Project, 1995–1998. *AJA* 104: 163–220.

Yon, M. 1992. The End of the Kingdom of Ugarit. In: Ward, W. A. and Joukowski, M. S. (eds.) *The Crisis Years: The 12th Century B.C. from beyond the Danube to the Tigris.* Dubuque, IA: 111–22.

Yon, M. 2000. Répartition et contextes. In: Yon, M., Karageorghis, V., and Hirschfeld, N. *Céramique mycénienne d'Ougarit* (Ras Shamra-Ougarit 13). Paris: 1–27.

Younger, J. G. 1995. The Iconography of Rulership: A Conspectus. In: Laffineur, R. and Niemeier, W.-D. (eds.) *Politeia: Society and State in the Aegean Bronze Age* (Aegaeum 12, 2). Liège: 151–211.

Zangger, E. 1994. Landscape Changes around Tiryns during the Bronze Age. *AJA* 98: 189–212.

Ziffer, I. 1999. "Metamorphosis of Ancient Near Eastern Metaphors of Rulership: The Towel, the Flower and the Cup." Ph.D. dissertation, Tel Aviv University (in Hebrew).

Zukerman, A. H., Lev-Tov, L. K. J., and Maeir, A. 2007. A Bone of Contention? Iron Age IIA Notched Scapulae from Tell es-Ṣafi/Gath, Israel. *BASOR* 347: 57–81.

INDEX

Abu Hawam, Tell, 195, 339
    bathtub, 206
    Cypriot influence, 205
    gateway community, 205
    Mycenaean imports, 205, 244, 250, 253
Acco, 164
    12th-century remains, 170
    LHIIIC-style pottery, 200, 203
    maritime activity, 121
    Persian Garden, 206
Agios Andreas, 71, 72, 76, 81
Agios Spyridon, 75, 81
Ahhiyawa, 38, 42, 55, 65, 83, 154, 155, 163
Aigeira, 71, 72, 82
Alashiyans, 42, 102, 140, 189
Albright, W. F., 2, 3, 320
Alt, A., 2, 3, 320
Amenhotep III, 38, 103
Amurru
    destruction, 166, 288, 339
    in the Medinet Habu inscriptions, 173
    ports, 43
    settlement of the Sea Peoples, 178, 319
Aphek
    cult, 305
    Cypro-Minoan signs, 195, 309, 312, 332
    foundation, 331
    Mycenaean imports, 196
    trade, 301
Argolid, 38, 65, 67, 72, 81, 82, 132, 335
Ashdod
    animal husbandry, 296, 297
    architecture, 271, 274
    biblical tradition, 312
    chipped-stone industry, 270
    chronology of the Philistine settlement,
        316, 317, 320, 322, 325
    cult, 302, 303, 304, 324

    Cypro-Minoan signs, 326
    destruction, 220, 226
    foodways, 228, 240
    foundation, 340
    hearths, 236, 314
    history of research, 3, 4, 6
    in the 13th century, 216
    Iron I settlement patterns, 283, 286, 287,
        288
    LHIIIC chronology, 328
    LHIIIC-style pottery, 243
    luxury items, 307
    Onomasticon of Amenope, 329
    population estimate, 295, 333
    pottery
        Canaanite pottery tradition, 255
        cooking jugs, 228, 235
        cylindrical bottle, 262
        deep bowls, 248
        dipper juglet, 260
        figurative decoration, 324
        hemispherical bowls, 256
        local shallow bowls, 256
        nature of LHIIIC assemblage, 262
        pilgrim flasks, 259
        ring-base kraters, 251
        shallow angular bowls, 250
        spouted and strainer jugs, 245
        stands, 260
        stirrup jars, 243
        storage jars and jugs, 259
        straight-sided alabastron, 244
        trays, 254
    publication of excavations, 220
    ruler's dwelling, 307, 331, 343
    rulership, 343
    seals, 4, 310, 311, 312
    *tabun*s, 237

Ashdod (*cont.*)
    textile production, 267, 268, 269, 333
    town plan, 290, 330, 341
    trade, 301, 302
"Ashdoda" figurines, 4, 305, 309, 314, 324
Ashkelon
    animal husbandry, 296, 297, 331
    architecture, 275
    Canaanite population, 289
    chronology of the Philistine settlement,
        316, 317, 320, 322, 325
    conquest by Merneptah, 216
    cult, 303, 305, 324
    Cypro-Minoan signs, 195, 309, 310, 312, 326
    destruction, 225, 226
    figurative decoration, 324
    foodways, 240
    foundation, 163, 340
    foundation deposit, 278
    hearths, 238
    history of research, 5, 6
    in the 13th century, 216
    Iron I settlement patterns, 283, 286, 287,
        288
    Lathyrus sativus, 300
    LHIIIC-style pottery, 243
    luxury items, 308
    Onomasticon of Amenope, 329
    population estimate, 295
    pottery
        cooking jugs, 228
        pictorial krater, 184, 338
    publication of excavations, 220
    ruler's dwelling, 331
    textile production, 132, 267
    town plan, 292, 294, 330, 341
    trade, 301, 302
Athens
    colonization in the Chersonese, 100
    continuity in the 12th century, 58, 82
    cooking pots, 124
    fleet, 111
    maritime evacuation, 108
    sea routes, 113
Athienou
    cooking jugs, 143

Bademgediği Tepe
    feathered hat, 184
    figurative pottery, 138
    nature of Aegean presence, 156, 157, 192
    ship imagery, 88, 105
basileus, 37, 59, 80, 112
Berry, J. W., 12, 15

Beth Shean
    Aegean cooking jug(?), 213
    Aegean material culture, 212
    Aegean torch, 212
    bimetallic knives, 208
    chronology of the Philistine settlement,
        316, 322, 337
    coffins, 208
    feathered hat, 209, 210
    history of research, 3
    LHIIIC chronology, 188
    LHIIIC-style pottery, 200, 203, 323
    mercenaries, 207
    Mycenaean imports, 196
    nature of Aegean presence, 215
    textile production, 133, 213, 268
Bliss, F., 2
Bourdieu, P., 15
Byblos, 40
    LHIIIC pottery, 168

Cape Gelidonya ship, 43, 44, 101, 104
Carthage, 28, 99
Chabas, F., 2, 180
Chadwick, J., 47
Chania
    continuity in the 12th century, 82
Chatal Hüyük
    LHIIIC pottery, 162
Chios. *See* Emporio
Cilicia. *See* Tarsus
Cilician Gates, 114, 116, 190
city-state system, 1
Corinth, 25
cultural transmission, 17, 18, 26, 195, 214, 280
Cumae, 28
Cypriots, 42, 43, 139, 145, 151, 195, 203, 312, 328,
        334, 339
Cypro-Minoan script, 4, 195, 301, 308, 309,
        310, 311, 326
Cyrene, 27, 98, 99, 110, 112, 289

Dan, Tel
    Mycenaean imports, 196
deep change, 14, 15, 17, 18, 19, 22, 24, 28, 29,
        30, 32, 51, 53, 122, 142, 149, 150, 156, 161,
        168, 190, 223, 227, 240, 270, 280
Deger-Jalkotzy, S., 59
Dor
    Early Iron Age, 171
    incised scapulae, 304
    large local population, 171
Dothan, M., 170
Dothan, T., 3, 4, 6

Ekron
    Achish inscription, 306
    animal husbandry, 296, 297, 331
    architecture, 276, 278
    biblical tradition, 312
    bimetallic knives, 208
    Canaanite population, 289
    chronology of the Philistine settlement,
        317, 322, 325
    cult, 302, 303, 304, 305, 306, 325
    destruction, 216, 223, 226
    foodways, 228, 240
    foundation, 340
    foundation deposit, 278
    hearths, 234, 236, 308
    history of research, 4, 6
    incised scapulae, 303, 326
    Iron I settlement patterns, 283, 286, 288
    kilns, 264, 338, 344
    Lathyrus sativus, 300
    LHIIIC chronology, 328
    LHIIIC-style pottery, 243
    luxury items, 308
    population estimate, 295
    pottery
        Canaanite cooking pots, 240
        Canaanite pottery tradition, 255
        cooking jugs, 228
        deep bowls, 250
        figurative decoration, 324
        hemispherical bowls, 256
        local shallow bowls, 256
        nature of LHIIIC-style assemblage,
          262
        oil lamps, 260
        pilgrim flasks, 259
        ring-base kraters, 251
        shallow angular bowls, 250
        spouted and strainer jugs, 245
        stirrup jars, 243
        straight-sided alabastron, 244
        trays, 254
    publication of excavations, 220
    ruler's dwelling, 331, 342
    rulership, 313, 343
    seals, 310
    *tabun*s, 236
    textile production, 267, 269, 333
    town plan, 289, 290, 292, 330, 341
    trade, 301, 302
Emporio
    defensible site, 190
    destruction, 157
    foundation, 337

    LHIIIC pottery, 242, 243, 253, 344
    nature of Aegean presence, 156, 158, 192
emporion, 48, 52, 195, 205
Enkomi
    bathtub, 206
    feathered hat, 151, 182, 209, 338
    hearths, 143, 145
    incised scapulae, 304
    LHIIIC chronology, 328
    LHIIIC-style pottery, 142, 253, 263
    Mycenaean imports, 49
    nature of Aegean presence, 151, 152, 190, 337
    ship imagery, 88

Finkelstein, I., 295, 312, 316
foodways, 5, 19, 20, 21, 22, 27, 29, 150, 214, 240,
    323, 343
French, E., 328

Gath
    biblical tradition, 312, 313
    Canaanite population, 289
    hearths, 238
    history of research, 2
    in the 13th century, 216
    incised scapulae, 304, 325
    Iron I settlement patterns, 283, 286, 288
    Late Bronze Age remains, 226
    population estimate, 295
    pottery
        cooking jugs, 228
Gaza, 113, 218
    biblical tradition, 282
    chronology of the Philistine settlement,
        320
    in the 13th century, 216
    Iron I settlement patterns, 283, 286
    land routes, 116
    Onomasticon of Amenope, 329
    population estimate, 295
    sea routes, 113
Gilboa, A., 171
Grotta, 71, 74, 77, 80, 86, 95
    a fortified site, 289, 290
    figurative pottery, 94, 138

habitus, 15, 18, 29, 32, 122, 270, 280, 314
Handmade Burnished Ware, 142, 147
Hatti, 38, 43, 98, 117, 165
    destruction, 319
    in the Medinet Habu inscription, 173
Hattusa, 43
Hellenization, 1
horned helmets, 182

Ialysos, 51, 118, 134, 155
    figurines, 303
innovation, 17, 19, 26, 149, 240

Karphi, 78, 82, 119
    cooking pots, 124
Kastrokephala, 71, 75, 95
    cooking pots, 124
Kavousi
    cooking pots, 124
    hearths, 123
    oven, 237
    ruler's dwelling, 80, 136
Kazel, Tell
    during the 13th century, 166
    Handmade Burnished Ware, 166, 192
    location of a Sea Peoples encampment,
        173
    nature of Aegean presence, 168
Keisan, Tel
    LHIIIC-style pottery, 200, 204
Kilian, K., 51
Killebrew, A., 5
Kition
    animal husbandry, 298, 299
    cooking jugs, 143
    hearths, 145
    incised scapulae, 304
    LHIIIC chronology, 328
    nature of Aegean presence, 190
    nature of Aegean settlement, 337
    textile production, 146, 153, 154
    Tomb 9 Upper Burial, 250, 256
Knossos
    animal husbandry, 298, 299
    continuity in the 12th century, 82
    in Kom el-Hetan list, 103
    Linear B evidence, 40, 46, 55
Kos. *See* Seraglio, Kos
Koukounaries, 65, 73, 81, 95, 336
    bathtubs, 276
    defensible site, 190
Kynos
    earthquake damage, 98
    feathered hats(?), 184
    figurative pottery, 86, 88, 91, 92
    ship imagery, 104, 106, 109
    similarity to the Medinet Habu ships,
        179
    textile production, 132
    unfortified center, 80

Lachish
    absence of LHIIIC pottery, 204

chronology of the Philistine settlement,
    316, 321, 322
    destruction, 216
    history of research, 3
    in the 13th century, 216
    textile production, 268
Langada, 80
lawagetas, 36
Lefkandi
    bathtubs, 276
    cooking pots, 124
    figurative pottery, 92
    figurines, 135
    hearths, 123, 235
    LHIIIC pottery, 157, 242, 243, 246, 253,
        344
    textile production, 132
    unfortified center, 77
Linear B, 34, 35, 36, 38, 39, 42, 43, 48, 50, 54,
    55, 56, 58, 59, 111, 119, 140, 154, 156, 159,
    195, 204, 298, 308, 313
Lukka, 42, 180

Maa-Palaeokastro
    animal husbandry, 298, 299
    architecture, 150
    bathtub, 206
    cooking jugs, 143
    Cypriot cooking pots, 143
    defensible settlement, 191
    hearths, 146
    Levantine imports, 300
    nature of Aegean presence, 151, 190
    nature of Aegean settlement, 337
    textile production, 146
Macalister, R. A. S., 2, 3, 312
Maeir, A., 220, 226
Malkin, I., 99, 314
Maspero, G., 2, 180
Massalia, 27, 314
Mazar, A., 3, 4
Medinet Habu
    depictions of women, 177
    feathered hats, 151, 180, 184, 208, 338
    history of research, 3
    land battle, 120, 288
    land-borne migration, 114, 118, 190
    ox carts, 118, 119
    Peleset, 163
    summary of different interactions, 174,
        340
    women, 313, 314, 333
    Year 8 inscription, 172
Megara Hyblaea, 23, 27, 289, 292

Megiddo
    Aegean-style dagger, 207
    Aegean-style double axe, 208
    chronology of the Philistine settlement,
        316, 322, 323
    derivative Aegean forms, 200
    ivories, 196
    LHIIIC-style pottery, 204
    textile production, 268
Melos, 75, 81
Merneptah
    conquest of Ashkelon, 216, 226
    history of research, 3
    Karnak inscription, 98
    Lybian campaign, 175, 180, 189
Metapontum, 23, 24, 52, 318
Midea
    continuity in the 12th century, 71
    earthquake damage, 98
    figurines, 135
    megaron, 81
    new ruler's dwelling, 95
    settlement hierarchy, 38
Miletus
    fortified site, 289
    continuity in the 12th century, 61, 64, 83,
        336
    continuity of rulership, 96
    Greek colonization, 27
    kilns, 265, 338
    LHIIIC pottery, 188
    LHIIIC remains, 154
    Linear B evidence, 40
    location of Ahhiyawa, 42
    Minoan colonization, 50
    Mycenaean cultural traits, 50
    origin of raiders, 192
    population estimate, 111
    routes, 117
Monochrome pottery, 4, 218, 242, 284
Mountjoy, P., 6, 187
multidimensional, 12
Mycenae
    fortified site, 289
    central hearth, 123
    continuity in the 12th century, 58, 66
    cooking amphora, 130
    demise of fresco art, 83
    destruction, 81
    earthquake damage, 98
    feathered hats, 184
    figurative pottery, 86, 92, 94, 138
    in Kom el-Hetan list, 103
    LHIIIC remains, 69, 70

Linear B evidence, 40, 41, 55, 138
location of Ahhiyawa, 42
population estimate, 111
residue analysis, 136
settlement hierarchy, 38
Mycenaean IIIC pottery, 3, 4, 6, 141, 142, 161,
    162, 166, 204, 220, 222, 241, 242, 322,
    326, 328
Mycenaean palaces, 1, 8, 34, 36, 44, 55, 58

Naxos, 66, 71, 74, 80, 81, 95, 294, 318

oikist, 27, 28, 100, 292
Onomasticon of Amenope, 283, 320,
    329

parameters of interaction, 12, 13
Paros, 65, 81, 95, 314
Peleset, 2, 151, 163, 171, 174, 180, 182, 208,
    283
Pentapolis
    biblical tradition, 218
    Canaanite population, 330, 334
    chronology of the Philistine settlement,
        316, 320
    circumstances of settlement, 324, 341
    cult, 303
    division of land, 294
    history of research, 3
    population estimate, 295
    reflecting an Iron I reality, 282
    rulership, 312, 313, 331, 343
    settlement patterns, 286, 330
    textile production, 314
penteconters, 46, 49, 106, 107, 108, 109, 110,
    111, 113
Perati, 80, 82, 134
    figurines, 303
Philistine Bichrome pottery, 3, 4, 169, 208,
    242, 262, 275, 284, 301, 309, 324
Phokaia, 27, 99, 107, 108, 112
Phylakopi
    fortified site, 289
    continuity in the 12th century, 61, 81, 336
    LHIIIC pottery, 242, 243, 246, 250, 253,
        344
    population estimate, 111
    ship imagery, 104
    shrines, 62, 134
Point Iria ship, 43, 44, 49, 109
political integration, 8, 36, 37, 38, 81, 82, 83,
    286, 297, 330
pull factors, 31
push factors, 31

Pylos
  animal husbandry, 299
  central hearth, 123
  cooking amphora, 130
  economic districts, 37
  functionaries, 37
  Linear B evidence, 36, 40, 41, 44, 45, 46, 47,
    48, 55, 156, 335
  palace pantries, 136
  settlement hierarchy, 37
  size of palatial sector, 101

Qasile, Tell
  Aegean-style adze, 208
  bimetallic knives, 208
  cult, 302, 305
  foundation, 331
  history of research, 3
  Iron I settlement patterns, 284, 287
  Lathyrus sativus, 300
  town plan, 292
  trade, 301, 302

Ramses III
  Beth Shean strata, 188
  chronology of the Philistine settlement,
    173, 219, 316, 319, 323, 333, 337, 339
  destruction of Arzawa, 117
  feathered-hatted mercenaries, 175
  history of research, 2, 3, 5, 320
  Papyrus Harris I, 172
  tomb, 200
Ramses IV, 316, 323
  end of Egyptian administration, 215
  in Beth Shean, 204
  scarabs in Lachish, 216
Ras Ibn Hani
  destruction, 191, 288
  history of research, 4
  nature of Aegean presence, 165, 179, 339
Rhegium, 98
Rhodes. *See* Ialysos
Rower Tablets, from Pylos, 40, 44, 45, 47, 48,
  55

Sandars, N., 4, 6
Sarepta
  LHIIIC pottery, 168
scapulae, incised, 301, 302, 303, 304, 306, 325,
  330, 334
Selinus, 23
Seraglio, Kos
  feathered hats, 182, 192
  figurative pottery, 80, 86

LHIIIC remains, 155
  ship imagery, 104
seranim, 282, 312, 313, 332
seren. *See seranim*
settlement hierarchy, 36, 37, 286, 330, 333
Shardana. *See* Sherden
Sherden, 39, 170, 172, 179, 180, 182, 207, 209,
  283, 320
Sherratt, S., 5, 6
Sikel, 110, 165, 170, 171, 172, 182, 208, 283,
  320
Sikila. *See* Sikel
Singer, I., 4, 313
Siphnos, 71, 72, 76, 81
Sparta, 99, 100, 112
Stager, L. E., 5, 184, 316
Stern, E., 171
Sybaris, 23
Syracuse, 28, 99, 292

Ta'yinat, Tell
  LHIIIC pottery, 162
*tabun*s, 236, 238
Taras, 26, 99, 112, 294, 318
Tarsus, 116
  cooking jugs, 161
  Cypriot imports, 158
  destruction, 118, 186, 191
  hearths, 234
  in the 12th century, 159
  in the 13th century, 158
  interaction patterns, 140
  land routes, 114, 116, 121
  LHIIIC pottery, 160, 246, 253, 263, 337
  nature of Aegean presence, 159, 160
Tel Miqne. *See* Ekron
Tell Afis
  LHIIIC pottery, 162
Tell el-ʿAjjul
  Mycenaean imports, 196
Tell el-Farʿah (S)
  chronology of the Philistine settlement,
    321
  coffin, 208
  Egyptian presence, 286
  feathered hats, 186, 209
  ivories, 196
  nature of Aegean presence, 215
Tell es-Ṣafi. *See* Gath
Thebes
  destruction, 78
  in Kom el-Hetan list, 103
  Linear B evidence, 39, 40, 41, 55
  location of Ahhiyawa, 42

residue analysis, 136
settlement hierarchy, 38
Tiryns
    fortified site, 289
    animal husbandry, 299
    Building T, 67
    Building W, 123
    central hearth, 123
    ceramic figures, 306
    continuity in the 12th century, 58, 66
    destruction, 81
    figurative pottery, 84, 85, 86, 91, 136
    flood, 98
    hearths, 235
    House W, 68
    Linear B evidence, 45
    oven, 237
    settlement hierarchy, 38
triaconter, 46, 48, 106, 110
Trianda, 51
trireme, 107, 108, 109, 113
Trojan War, 99
Tudhaliya IV, 42, 165

Tyre, 40, 116, 164
    continuity into the Iron Age, 169

Ugarit, 353
    bridgehead in Mukish, 173
    contacts with Alashia, 42
    destruction, 118, 164, 165, 178, 187, 288, 319,
        328, 337, 339
    history of research, 4
    LHIIIC pottery, 187, 337
    maritime activity, 110, 121, 159
    maritime raids, 156, 165, 179, 189, 339
    Sherden mercenaries, 182
    Sinaranu, 104
Uluburun ship, 43, 49, 55, 57, 103, 106, 109, 140
unidimensional, 12

Wachsmann, S., 46
wanax, 34, 36, 37, 45, 48, 59, 313
Welch, F. B., 2
Wen-Amon, 2

Zakynthos, 47, 48